GENEALOGICAL REGISTER OF PLYMOUTH FAMILIES

By William T. Davis

Originally Published
as Part II of
Ancient Landmarks of Plymouth
Second Edition
Boston, 1899

Reprinted
Geneological Publishing Co., Inc.
Baltimore, 1975, 1977, 1985, 1994

Library of Congress Cataloging in Publication Data
Davis, William Thomas, 1822-1907.
    Genealogical register of Plymouth families.

    Reprint of the 1899 ed. published by Damrell & Upham, Boston, as
pt. 2 of Ancient landmarks of Plymouth.
    1. Plymouth, Mass.—Genealogy. I. Title.
F74.P8D173   929'.1'0974482   74-18071
ISBN 0-8063-0655-6

Made in the United States of America

PUBLISHER'S PREFACE

Originally published as Part Two of *Ancient Landmarks of Plymouth*, second edition, 1899, Davis's "Genealogical Register of Plymouth Families" has established itself as one of a handful of standard genealogical dictionaries of New England and is quite possibly the most comprehensive register of Plymouth families ever assembled. Containing the names of thousands of individuals with *Mayflower* and sister-ship antecedents, there is little wonder why this work should claim the attention of persons of suspected Pilgrim descent. It contains a great quantity of material written in a style reminiscent of the older genealogical dictionaries, with families, in narrative form, worked through several generations, showing marriages, dates, children and children's marriages and offspring.

The method of arrangement consists of listing together everyone of the same surname and grouping them thereunder in alphabetical order, with their marriages, children, and children's children following. As each line is exhausted the text resumes with the person next in the alphabet. The genealogies are quite intricate and name many thousands of persons, though just how many is difficult to estimate.

The data is based largely on the records of the town of Plymouth, Massachusetts and draws on all marriage and birth records through the last quarter of the nineteenth century. To this basic collection has been added a large amount of material gathered from the records of other towns, from family bibles and private papers, and from probate records and deeds. As the work is supposed to contain nearly every name connected with Plymouth before the present century, it is every bit the equivalent of a directory of Pilgrim families and should certainly find a welcome place on the library reference shelf.

Michael Tepper
Editor
Genealogical Publishing Co., Inc.

GENEALOGICAL REGISTER.

[In most cases where the residence is not stated, it may be presumed to have been Plymouth.]

ABBOT, JOSEPH, m. Mary Kempton, 1740.

ADAMS, CHARLES, Kingston, son of Ebenezer, m. Mary C. Sampson, and had James, 1806, m. Martha A. Murray; William S., 1808, m. Lucy Eveline, d. of Joseph Holmes; Henry L., 1810, m. Elizabeth H. Fish; Nathaniel, 1812, m. Harriet M. Hendley of Boxboro'; Albert, 1815; Charles C., 1817; Edwin, 1819, m. Frances H. Frost of Charlestown. EBENEZER, Kingston, son of 3d John, m. Lydia Cook, and had George, 1766; Mary, 1769; Caleb, 1770; Nathaniel, 1773; Lydia, 1775, m. William Holmes of Peacham, Vt.; James, 1777; Charles, 1779; Lucy, 1784; Christiana, 1787; George, 1791, m. Hannah T. Brewer and Susan Brigham; Caleb, 1792, m. Pauline Butts and wid. Martha Harding. FRANCIS, son of Richard, came to America about 1692, at the age of fifteen, with a sister Jemima, who afterwards returned. (Their father had preceded them, and died before their arrival.) He settled in Plymouth about 1700, and m., about that time, Mary, d. of Thomas Buck of Scituate, by whom he had Mary, 1704, m. Nathaniel Atwood; Jemima, 1707, m. Barnabas Shurtleff; Thomas, 1709; Francis, 1711, m. Kesiah, d. of John Atwood; John, 1714; Richard, 1719, m. Mary Carver; and Sarah, 1721, m. Elisha Stetson. FRANCIS, son of above, m. Kesiah, d. of John Atwood, 1737, and had Francis, 1738; Samuel, 1740; Samuel, 1742; Lydia, 1744, m. Jonathan Crane of Bridgewater; Kesiah, 1746, m. Nathaniel Little; Francis, 1750, m. Mercy Adams. GEORGE, Kingston, son of Ebenezer, m. Hannah T. Brewster, and had George T., 1820, m. Lydia T. Bradford; Frederick C., 1821, m. Eveline, wid. of Horatio Adams; Horatio, 1823, m. Eveline Holmes; and Hannah T., m. Azel W. Washburn. GEORGE, son of 2d Thomas, m., 1829, Hannah Sturtevant, d. of Ephraim Harlow, and had George W., 1830, m. Mary Holland of Boston; Hannah, 1832, m. Dr. Edward A. Spooner of Philadelphia; Sarah S., 1840; and Theodore Parker, 1845, m. Nellie, d. of Joseph Cushman. GEORGE, m. Lucy Nye, 1811. JAMES, son of 1st John, removed to Marshfield and Scituate, and m., 1646, Frances, d. of Wm. Vassall, by whom he had William, 1647; Ann, 1649; Richard, 1651, Mary, 1653; and Margaret, 1654. JOHN, who came to Plymouth in the Fortune, 1621, m. Eleanor Newton, who came in the Ann, 1623. His children were James, John, and Susanna. JOHN, Marshfield, son of above, m. 1654, Jane James, and had Joseph, Martha, and perhaps others. JOHN, son of 1st Francis, m. Thankful Washburn, and had Joseph, 1740, m. Eleanor Carney; Francis, 1741, m. Rebecca Cook; John,

1743, m. Sarah Drew; Ebenezer, 1744; Jemima, 1746, m. Joseph Holmes; Melzar, 1750, m. Deborah Bradford of Duxbury; Sarah, 1752, m. Jedediah Holmes; Mercy, 1753, m. Francis Adams, Lydia, 1755, m. Robert Cook; Susanna, 1759, m. Eleazar Faunce. JOHN or WILLIAM (both names are in the records), a foreigner, m. Sophia Eddy, 1808. JOSHUA, son of 1st Thomas, m. Mary Godfrey, and had Sarah, 1760, m. John Perkins of Plympton; Saba, 1762, m. Zach. Cushman; Joshua, 1767, m. Nancy Gray of Barnstable; Thomas, 1770, m. Mercy, d. of Thomas Savery of Carver; Mary, 1772, m. Seth Perkins of Plympton; Bathsheba, 1775, m. Daniel Bradford of Plympton. LYMAN of Albany m. Elizabeth Goddard, 1805. RICHARD probably came from Chester, England, about 1680, and was afterward killed by the Indians. Mention is made of three children — Richard, Francis, and Jemima, of whom the first never came to America, and the last returned to England shortly after her arrival. SAMUEL, Kingston, born 1790, was son of Francis and Mercy Adams, and grandson of 2d Francis above mentioned. His brothers and sisters were Lydia H., born 1786, m. Luther Phillips; Jemima, 1788, m. Joshua Peterson; Eleanor, 1792, and Sarah, 1794. He m. Priscilla Ford of Marshfield, and Abigail Bruce of Kingston, and had no children. THOMAS, son of 1st Francis, m. Bathsheba, d. of Israel Bradford, and had Sarah, 1732, m. Caleb Cook and Gershom Cobb; Joshua, 1735; Bartlett, 1738; Nathaniel, 1740; Mary, 1744; Deborah, 1747. THOMAS, son of Joshua, m. Mercy, d. of Thomas Savery of Carver, and had Thomas, 1794; Thomas, 1795; John, 1797, m. Nancy Pratt of Carver; George, 1800; Thomas, 1802; Mary, 1805, m. John Bent of Middleboro' and Watson Goward of Croyden, N. H.; George, 1807; Ann Maria, 1809. THOMAS, son of above, m. Eunice H. Bugbee of Pomfret, Vt., and had Mary E., 1832, m. R. F. Briggs of Boston; Thomas H., 1834; Frederick E. and Frank W., twins, 1836; Luther B. and Ellen, twins, 1837; Miranda B., 1839; Harriet E., 1841; James O. and ——, twins, 1841; David B., 1845; Walter S. and ——, twins, 1848; and Adelaide V., 1849. (See Adams Genealogy.)

ALBERTSON, JACOB, of Swedish descent, probably grandson of John of Yarmouth, who was son of Nicholas of Scituate, 1636, m. Margaret Nicolson, 1750, and had Jacob, 1752; William, Elizabeth, and Rufus. JACOB, son of above, m., 1775, Lydia Rider, and had Martha, 1779, m. Amaziah Harlow; Joseph Rider, 1781; Lydia Gardner, 1783; Margaret, 1785. RUFUS, son of 1st Jacob, m. a wife Martha, and had Polly, 1787; Margaret, 1789; Sally, 1790; Betsey, 1794; Rufus, 1797; Martha, 1801; Sophronia, 1804; William, 1806.

ALDEN, FRANCIS L., from New Bedford, m., 1828, Eudora, d. of Zabdiel Sampson. GIDEON S., of New Bedford, m. Priscilla, d. of William Le Baron, 1803. JOHN, came in the Mayflower, 1620, and m., 1623, Priscilla, d. of William Mullins. His children were, John of Boston, m. Elizabeth, wid. of Abiel Ewrill and d. of William Phillips; Joseph, m. Mary, d. of Moses Simmons; David, m. Mary, d. of Constant Southworth; Jonathan, m. Abigail, d. of Andrew Hallet; Elizabeth, m. William Peabody; Sarah, m. Alexander Standish; Ruth, m. John Bass of Braintree; and Mary, m. Thomas Delano. JOHN, from Middleboro', pub., 1790, to Susanna Dunham.

ALEXANDER, BENJAMIN FRANKLIN, son of 2d James, died at Rose
Hill, Va., 1841. CHARLES EDWARD, son of Edward, place of residence un-
known to the writer, m. Lucia M. Hart, 1860, and had Mary Lilly, 1860; Nannie,
1863; and Frederick William, 1870. EDWARD, son of 1st James, m. Nancy
Young, 1832, and had Charles Edward, 1833; and Frederick William, 1835.
His place of residence is unknown to the writer. GILES, Boston, son of 1st
William, m. three wives, one of whom was Catherine Knapp of Vermont, by
whom he had Catherine, about 1813, m. in Vergennes, Vt. ISAAC BEMIS,
Provincetown, son of 1st James, m. Elizabeth Gillespie, 1831, and
had Elizabeth, m. in Ohio; Robert, m. in Provincetown; Mary; Martha.
JAMES, Boston, son of 2d William, m. Elizabeth Williston, 1803,
and had James, 1804; Edward, 1805; Isaac Bemis, 1810. JAMES,
son of above, Abingdon, Virginia, m., 1832, R. Ann Wills of Rose Hill,
Va., and had Lillie Helen, 1833, m. William M. Norris; James B. S.,
1836; William Wills, 1838; Benjamin Franklin, 1840; Nannie E., 1843, m.
Horace H. George of Charlotteville, Va.; and Nellie T., 1846. JAMES B. S.,
son of above, Charlotteville, graduated at West Point, 1856, a major-general
in the Confederate army, died at Alleghany Springs, 1861. SAMUEL,
Plymouth, son of 2d William, m. Deborah, d. of John Paty, 1804, and had
Maria Paty, 1805, m. Thomas Tribble; Mary Ann, 1806, m. Solomon Sylvester;
Samuel Lewis, 1808; John Thomas, 1810, m. Lavinia Harlow; Fanny, 1812;
Sylvanus, 1814; Sophronia, 1819, m. John Nickerson; Sylvia Cooper, 1821;
m. William T. Savery; George, 1823; Charles, 1825; William Bemis, 1828, m.
Mary, d. of Thomas Atwood. SAMUEL LEWIS, son of above, m., 1830,
Charlotte S. Faunce, and had Catherine Elizabeth, 1830; Samuel Thomas,
1833; John Knowles, 1837. WILLIAM of Sherburne, Mass., afterward
Boston, during the Revolution, had Giles, William, and others. WILLIAM,
son of above, Boston, m. Ann, d. of James McMillan, and had William, bap-
tized 1768; Giles, 1770; Ann, 1772; Polly, 1775; James, 1777; Samuel, 1780;
Benjamin, 1790.

ALLEN, ANTHONY SHERMAN, m. Marcia Finney, 1838. BENJAMIN, m.
Beza Delano, 1755, and had Benjamin, 1755. EZRA, m. Mary Durfey, 1745.
FRANCIS, m. Jane Kirk, 1725, and had Francis, 1728; Jenny, 1733. JAMES,
m. Elizabeth Cotton, 1690. JAMES of Boston, m. Priscilla Brown, 1804.
JOHN, who came from England about 1760, m. Esther, d. of Thomas Savery,
1768, and had Esther, 1769, m. Benjamin Robbins of Kingston; Elizabeth,
1772, m. Joseph Doten; John, 1774; William, 1779. JOHN, son of above, m.
Maria Smith, 1796, and had John, 1798; Maria, 1803, m. Timothy Berry;
George, 1806; Susan, 1808, m. Ezra Churchill; Louisa, 1813, m. Lewis G.
Bradford; Thomas, 1816. JOHN, from Middleboro', m. Susanna Dunham,
1790, and had Joseph, m. Mary Sherman, d. of Lewis Holmes; Timothy;
Samuel, m. Naomi Leach; Betsy B., m. Ezra Allen, and Jenette, m. Truman
Cook Holmes. JOHN of Salem, m. Mary Nicholson, 1801. THOMAS, son of
2d John, m. Betsy, d. of William Drew, and had Thomas Jefferson, 1839;
George, Maria, and Ella. TIMOTHY, son of 3d John, m., 1814. Thankful
Snow, and Rebecca Blackmer, 1836, and had Betsy, m. Calvin Ripley.
WILLIAM, son of 1st John, m. Betsy Holmes, 1798, and had Esther, m.

Southworth A. Howland of Brookfield; Eliza, m. Washington Heald; Caroline, m. Enos Dorr; Susan Holmes, m. James Harvey Drew; Betsey William m. John Gates; Jane B., m. Charles Whittemore; Winslow, m. Louisa Nash, William, m., 1st, Mary C. Gilmore; 2d, Emeline Huntington; 3d, Emeline Whittemore, and 4th, Rosamond (Washburn) Rider, wid. of Caleb Rider of Plymouth, and d. of Alden Washburn of Tamworth, N. H.

ALLERTON, ISAAC, of London, m. in Leyden, 1611, Mary Norris of Newbury, England, and came in the Mayflower with wife and three children —Bartholomew, Remember, m. Moses Maverick of Salem, and Mary, m. Thomas Cushman. He m. 2d, 1626, Fear, d. of William Brewster, and had Isaac, who moved to New Haven. He had a third wife, Joanna, and a child, Sarah, by one of the wives. ISAAC, New Haven, son of the above, had Elizabeth, m. Benjamin Starr and Simeon Eyre; and Isaac. JOHN came a sailor in the Mayflower, and died during the first winter.

ALLYN, JOSEPH, son of Samuel of Barnstable, m. Mary, d. of Edward Doty, and had Elizabeth, 1700; Mary, 1702, m. James Otis, father of the patriot. He removed to Wethersfield.

AMES, JONATHAN, m. Rebecca Stanford, 1713. OLIVER, born in Plymouth, was descended from Richard Ames of Bruten, Somersetshire, England, whose son William, born in 1605, came to Braintree about 1639. By wife Hannah, William had Hannah, 1641; Rebecca, 1642; Lydia, 1645; John, 1647; Sarah, 1651, and Deliverance, 1654. Of these, John, m. Sarah, d. of John Willis, and settled in West Bridgewater. His children were: John, 1672; William, 1673; Nathaniel, 1677, the ancestor of Fisher Ames; Elizabeth, 1680; Thomas, 1682; Sarah, 1685; David, 1688, and Hannah. Of these, Thomas, m. Mary, d. of Joseph Hayward, 1706, and had Thomas, 1707; Solomon, 1709; Joseph, 1711; Ebenezer, 1715; Mary, 1717; Susanna, 1720; Nathaniel, 1722; Sarah, 1724, and Betty, 1727. Of these, Thomas, m. Keziah, d. of Jonathan Hayward, 1731, and had Keziah, 1732; Susanna, 1734; Thomas, 1736; John, 1738; Mehitabel, 1740, and Sylvanus, 1744. Of these, John m. Susanna, d. of Ephraim Howard, 1759, and had David, 1760; Keziah, Susanna, Huldah, 1768; Abigail, 1769; Cynthia, 1772; John, 1775, and Oliver, 1777. OLIVER, m. Susanna, d. of Oakes Angier of West Bridgewater, and had Horatio, Oakes Angier, Angier, Oliver, Sarah, William, Harriet, and John. He carried on business for a time in Plymouth, where his son Oliver was born, and afterwards removed to Easton.

ANDERSON, ALEXANDER, m., 1755, Jean Seller. ANDREW, m., 1787, Elizabeth Raymond. JOHN m., 1795, Elizabeth Anderson. JOHN, m., 1804, wid. Sarah Fish. WILLIAM, m., 1778, Priscilla Tinkham.

ANDREWS, SAMUEL, m., 1819, Jerusha Bearse.

ANDROS, JOHN, by wife Mary, had Sarah, 1696; Joanna, 1697; John, 1699; Mary, 1701; Ebenezer, 1704.

ANGEL, THOMAS C., m., 1825, Julia Ann Robbins.

ANNABLE, ANTHONY, came in the Ann, 1623, with wife Jane and children, Sarah, m. Henry Ewell, and Hannah, m. Thomas Freeman. After arrival he had Susanna born in Barnstable. He m., 2d, 1645, Ann Clark,

and had Samuel, 1646, m. Mehitabel, d. of Thomas Allyn; Ezekiel, 1649. He
m., 3d, Ann Barker, and had Desire, 1653.

APPLING, WILLIAM THOMAS, from Carver, m. Deborah Barrows, 1813.

ARMITAGE, THOMAS, came in the James from Bristol, 1635, settled in
Lynn, but owned an estate in Plymouth, 1637.

ARMOR, GEORGE, m., 1804, Catherine Hubbard.

ARMSTRONG, GREGORY, m., 1638, Eleanor, wid. of John Billington.

ARNOLD, GAMALIEL, from Duxbury, m., 1766, Hannah Wait.

ASHLEY, JOSEPH, m. a wife Elizabeth, and had Thomas, 1704. JOSEPH
m. Elizabeth Swift, 1749.

ATKINS, HENRY, by wife Elizabeth had Mary, 1647; Samuel, 1651, born in
Plymouth; Isaac, 1657, in Eastham. He m., 2d, at Eastham, 1664, Bethiah
Linnell, and had Desire, 1655; John, 1666, Nathaniel, 1667; Joseph, 1669;
Thomas, 1671; John, 1674; Mercy, 1676; Samuel, 1679. JOSEPH m., 1822,
Sarah Cooper.

ATKINSON, THOMAS, at Plymouth, 1635.

ATTEQUIN, JEREMIAH, and Moll Simons, Indians, published 1736.

ATWOOD. The various branches of the Atwood family in Plymouth are
descended from John Wood of Plymouth, 1643. There was a John Atwood
in Plymouth, 1636, who died without children. BARNABAS, Plympton, son
of 2d Nathaniel, m. Lydia Shurtleff, 1723, and had Hannah, 1724, m. a
Barrows; Elizabeth, 1726, m. a Shaw; Isaac, 1728; Lydia, m. a Cobb; Mary,
m. a Shaw; Abigail, Lucy, Barnabas, and John. ELIJAH D., came to
Plymouth from Carver, and m., 1853, Catherine Robbins Cotton, d. of Josiah,
and had Catherine P., m. Elijah Dunham and Wilson Leroy. ISAAC, son of
2d John, m. Lydia Wait, 1740, and had Thomas, 1744; Isaac, 1747; Wait,
1749; Zacheus, 1752; Lydia, 1754; Hannah, 1756, m. Lemuel Taber. ISAAC,
son of above, by wife Hannah, had Isaac, 1772. JESSE, R. son of Thomas
of Wellfleet, m. Miriam, d. of Richard Atwood of same, and had
Anthony, m., 1868, Susan T. Holmes; Edward B., m., 1868. Deborah C., d.
of Lucius Pratt; Abby F., m. Henry H. Cole of Taunton, and Hettie S., m,
1880, Peleg S. B. Bartlett. JOHN, Plymouth, 1643, called Wood, alias
Atwood, m. Sarah, d. of Richard Masterson, and had John, 1650; Nathaniel,
1652; Isaac, 1654; Sarah, m. John Fallowell; Abigail, m. Samuel Leonard;
Mercy, Elizabeth, Hannah, m. Richard Cooper; Mary, m. Rev. John Holmes
of Duxbury, and Major William Bradford. JOHN, son of 2d Nathaniel,
assumed or received the name of Atwood, and is called sometimes in the
records John Wood, alias Atwood. He m. Sarah, d. of Josiah Leavitt of
Hingham, 1709, and had Sarah, 1709, m. Nehemiah Ripley; Mary, 1711, m.
Jacob Taylor; John, 1713; Lydia, 1715, m. James Hovey; Solomon, 1717;
Isaac, 1719; Keziah, 1721, m. Francis Adams; Hannah, 1723, and Experience,
1724. He married 2d, Experience Pierce, 1730, and had Experience, 1731;
Elizabeth, 1733, m. Samuel Pierce; Experience again, 1734, m. Samuel
Jackson; George, 1738; Priscilla, 1740, m. Ichabod Shaw; and Margaret, m.
Joshua Shaw. JOHN, son of above, m. Hannah Drew, 1735, and had Rebecca,
1737, m. Corban Barnes; John, 1739; George, 1741, m Joanna Bartlett;
Elijah, 1743; Abigail, 1745, m. Joseph Rider; Micah, 1747; William, 1749;

Saran, 1751; Elizabeth, m. David Drew, and Mary, m. Lemuel Robbins. JOHN, son of above, m. Deborah Doten, 1771, and had Deborah, m. Samuel Battles; Sarah, m. Experience Everson, and John, 1778. He probably had a 1st wife, Lydia Holmes, without children. JOHN, son of above, m. Nancy Churchill, 1799, and had John, William, Maria Shaw, m. Ignatius Pierce; Mary Ann, m. Ephraim Holmes, and Nancy. JOHN, son of above, m. Hannah Wiswell, 1828, and had Nancy Churchill, 1829, m. Lorenzo Tribble; John Murray, 1835, m. Aurina, d. of Aurin Bugbee; Miranda B., m. Christopher T. Harris; Paulina W., m. James H. Simmons; Adoniram J., 1837, m. Helen, d. of Ellis Barnes, and Hannah Tufts, 1839, m. Van Buren Holmes. JOHN, m. Hannah Richmond, 1806. JOHN B. came to Plymouth with wife Martha B., and had Rebecca W., m., 1851, Josiah A. Robbins; Martha B., m., 1856, Amory T. Skerry, and Alexander P., m., 1859, Mercy Ann, d. of Truman Bartlett. NATHANIEL, Plympton, m. Lydia Boult, 1776, and had Abner, Zenas, Levi, Nathaniel, Joshua, Mary, m. a Shurtleff; Joanna, m. Aaron Carey; Mercy, m. David Shurtleff, and Huldah, m. a Vaughn. NATHANIEL, son of 1st John, called Wood, by wife Mary had John, 1684; Elizabeth, 1687; Joanna, 1689; Mary, 1691; Nathaniel, 1693; Isaac, 1695; Barnabas, 1697; Joanna, 1700. NATHANIEL, Plympton, son of above, m. Mary, d. of Francis Adams, and had Mary, 1723, m. Benjamin Shaw; Nathaniel, 1725, m. Susanna, d. of Barnabas Shurtleff and Elizabeth Timberlake; Francis, 1728. By a second wife, Abigail, he had Sarah, m. Joseph Barrows; Mercy, m. Joseph Warren; Ebenezer, 1735; Keziah, 1737; William, 1740; Joseph, 1741, and Ichabod. SOLOMON, son of 2d John, m. Lydia, d. of Job Cushman, 1749, and had Solomon, who m. Hannah Rogers, 1773. THOMAS, son of 1st Wait, m. Mehitabel Shaw, 1799, and had Polly Shaw, 1800, m. Ezra Collier; Thomas, 1805; Darius, 1808, and Mehitabel Shaw. He m., 2d, Elizabeth Tufts, 1810, and had William Tufts. He m., 3d, Lydia (Savery) Holmes, wid. of Eleazer, 1814, and had George, Charles, and Elizabeth. THOMAS, son of above, m. Hannah R. Bartlett, 1827, and had Thomas B., 1829; Mary Frances, 1834, m. William B. Alexander; Timothy S., 1837; George H., m. Fanny H. Danforth, and Lydia, m. Martin F. Benson. THOMAS, brother of Jesse, came from Wellfleet and m., 1857, Lucy A., d. of Richard Pope. THOMAS B., son of 2d Thomas, m. Rebecca M. Holmes, and had Thomas H., 1849, m. Ada V. King, and Hettie S., m. Alvin S. Hallet. THOMAS C., son of 2d William, m. Betsey, d. of Samuel Lanman, 1840, and had William T., 1842; Charles H., 1844, m. Miranda Burgess; Mary E., 1848, m. Isaac T. Hall; Laura A., m. Samuel McHenry; Robert Winslow; Eldon Russell, 1855, m. Sarah J. Heath; Ella, and Martha. WAIT, son of 1st Isaac, by wife Susanna, had Thomas, 1769; Wait, and Phebe, m. Chandler Holmes. He m., 2d, Rebecca Bartlett, 1786. WAIT, son of above, m. Polly, d. of Joseph Tribble, 1802, and had Mary Wait, m. Sylvanus Bramhall. WILLIAM, son of 3d John, m. Lydia (Holmes) Savery, wid. of William, and d. of George Holmes, and had William. WILLIAM, son of above, m. Temperance, d. of Thomas Churchill, 1804, and had William, Nancy, m. Branch Johnson and Anthony Morse; Thomas C.; Henry; Isaac, m. Ann Brown; and Eunice, m. Charles Raymond. WILLIAM, son of above, m. Sarah Jane Brown, and

had Abby J., 1848; William B., 1850; George H., 1852; Joseph B., 1854.
WILLIAM, son of 5th John, m. Harriet, d. of Seth Morton, 1835, and had
Edward Winslow, 1835, m. Georgiana, d. of Elias Thomas; Harriet Elizabeth,
1837; and James M., 1841, m. Helen M., d. of Benjamin F. Field.

AUSTIN, ISAAC, m. Bethiah Johnson, d. of John Ridgebi, 1824, and had
Isaac L., 1824; Alva C., 1826; Elizabeth Owen, 1829; Selden, 1833; Henry
Carter, 1836. RICHARD, from Kingston, m. Rebecca Atwood, 1789.

AVERY, JOHN H., m. Harriet G. Whitmore, 1839. JOSEPH, from Holden,
m. Sarah Thaxter of Worcester, 1815.

BABB, RICHARD, m. Martha Bartlett, 1769, and had Betsey, m.
Samuel Rogers.

BACON, DAVID, son of Jacob, m., 1777, Abigail, d. of Stephen Sampson,
and had Lucy, 1778; David, 1779; Abigail, 1782; Elizabeth, 1784; Henry
Sampson, 1787; Jacob, 1788; Rufus, 1792; Mary, 1794; Charles Henry, 1797.
GEORGE, son of Nathan, m., 1798, Elizabeth, d. of Job Rider, and had
George Taylor, 1801; George Taylor, 1804; Betsey, 1808; Mary, 1810; Rebecca,
1812; Nathan, 1814; George Taylor, 1817; Lucretia Ann, 1819, m. Sylvanus
H. Churchill, and Leavitt Taylor, 1823. JACOB, probably great-grandson of
Jacob of Newton, 1677, born in Wrentham, m. Mary Wood of Boxford, 1749,
and had Mary, 1750, m. David Thurston of Rowley; Jacob, 1751, m. Mrs.
Mary Whitney of Dorchester; Thomas, 1753; David, 1754; Oliver, 1755,
Samuel, 1758; Charles, 1759. JOHN, Barnstable, son of Nathaniel, m., 1686,
Mary Howes, and had Hannah, 1687; Desire, 1689, m. William Green;
Nathaniel, 1692; Patience, 1694; John, 1697; Isaac, 1699; Solomon, 1701; Jude,
1703. JOHN, son of above, m., 1726, Sarah Warren of Plymouth, and had
Nathan, Jonathan, and Rebecca. JOHN of Barnstable m. Joanna Foster, 1754.
JOHN of Barnstable m. Priscilla Holmes, 1789. NATHAN, son of 2d John, m.
Mary Taylor of Plymouth, and had Nathan, 1767; Molly, 1771, m. Charles
Robbins, and George, 1773. NATHANIEL, Barnstable, m., 1642, Hannah, d.
of Rev. John Mayo, and had Hannah, 1643; Nathaniel, 1646; Mary, 1648;
Samuel, 1651; Elizabeth, 1654; Jeremiah, 1657; Mercy, 1660, m. John Otis,
and John.

BADGER, JOSIAH, m. Mary Raymond, 1782.

BAGNALL, BENJAMIN, son of 1st Richard, m. Hannah Jackson, 1751, and
had Richard, 1752; Benjamin, 1755. He m., 2d, Sarah, d. of Elkanah Totman,
1758, and had Lydia, m. Oliver Keyes; Hannah, 1761, m. James Harlow, and
Diman Bartlett; Benjamin, 1762; Elizabeth, 1766, m. John Douglass; Nich-
olas Spinks, 1767; and Nellie, m. Nathaniel Holmes. BENJAMIN, son of 2d
Richard, m. Lucy Churchill, 1821, and had Lucy Emily, 1822; Betsey Crocker,
1825, and Elizabeth. GEORGE, son of Joseph, m. Catherine, wid. of Lewis
Morton, and had Joseph W., m. Melinda Longfellow of Belfast, Maine.
JOSEPH, son of 2d Richard, m. Betsey Rickard, 1820, and had George.
NICHOLAS SPINKS, son of 1st Benjamin, m., 1st, Nancy Crocker, and 2d,
Mehitabel Finney, 1792, and had Frederick, m. Betsey Cushman, and removed
to Kingston; Oliver, m. wid. Phebe Jones; Ichabod P., m. Caroline Fisher,
Edna G. Burbank, and Ellen Devine; Sally, m. Josiah Holmes; Nancy, m.
Lemuel Rickard; Deborah, m. Jesse Lucas, and Susan, m. William Hall.

RICHARD appeared in Plymouth, 1723, in which year he m. Elizabeth Poland, and had Benjamin, 1724, and Hannah. RICHARD, son of 1st Benjamin, m. Bethiah West, and had Samuel West, 1787; Hannah Jackson, 1790, m. Jesse Dunham; Benjamin, 1792; Joseph, 1795; Nancy Ellis, 1799, m. Nathaniel Cobb Laman; Richard, 1802. RICHARD, son of above, m. Lydia, d. of Ebenezer Sampson, 1819, and had Susan Sampson, 1819, m. William Weston; Richard William, 1822, m. Harriet Allen, and Lydia, m. Horace A. Jenks. SAMUEL WEST, son of 2d Richard, m. Lois, d. of James Thomas of Middleboro', 1811, and had Benjamin, 1812, m. Sally Burgess, and Eleanor P. Kimball; Samuel West, 1815, m. Harriet N. Faunce; Bethiah, 1817, m. H. O. Steward. He m., 2d, Minerva Thomas, sister of his first wife, 1822, and had Lois Thomas, 1823, m. Ellis Barnes; Martha Jane, 1826, m. John Churchill; Ann Minerva, 1829, m. Stephen Cook of Mendon, and Sarah Frances, 1833.

BAILEY, CLIFT, m. Nancy Ellis, 1807. IRA, m. Phebe Bartlett, 1818. JOHN, m. Polly Wood, 1813. MELVIN, m. Maria Paty, 1820.

BAKER, ABNER, from Rochester, m., 1778, Hannah Morton. WILLIAM, Plymouth, 1643, and afterwards Portsmouth, R. I.

BALLARD, ROSWELL, from Plympton, m., 1816, Hannah Sampson.

BANDEN, STEPHEN, m., 1725, Deborah Pratt.

BANGS, EDWARD, came in the Ann, 1623, and prob. m. Lydia, d. of Robert Hicks, and had Rebecca, John, Sarah, m. Thomas Howes; Jonathan, 1640, m. Mary, d. of Samuel Mayo of Barnstable; Lydia, m. Benjamin Higgins; Hannah, m. John Doane; Joshua, m. Hannah, d. of John Scudder; Bethiah, 1650, m. Gersham Hall; Mercy, m. Stephen Herrick, and Apphia, m. John Knowles, and Joseph Atwood.

BANKS, ISAAC, m., 1798, Abigail Babb. LILLISTON had a wife Sarah, and the following children, prob. between 1820 and 1830: Sarah Cutton, Lilliston, and Clark Johnson.

BARKER, ISAAC, m., 1665, Judith, d. of Thomas Prence, and had Rebecca, Lydia, Judith, Martha, Francis, Thomas, Isaac, Jabez, Robert, and Samuel. THOMAS, son of above, m., 1712, Bethiah Little.

BARNABY, JAMES, m. Lydia, d. of Robert Bartlett, 1647, and had Stephen and James, 1670. JAMES, son of above, m. Joanna, d. of Wm. Harlow, and moved to Freetown. His children were James, 1628; Ambrose, 1706, m. Elizabeth, d. of Samuel Gardner of Swanzey. STEPHEN, son of 1st James, m., 1696, Ruth, d. of George Morton, and had Lydia, 1697, m. Thomas Faunce; Ruth, 1699; Elizabeth, 1701; Timothy, 1706; Hannah, 1709. He m., 2d, 1710, Judith, wid. of Joseph Church and d. of William Harlow, and had Joseph, 1712. TIMOTHY, son of above, m. a wife Martha, and had Stephen, 1728; Ruth, 1735, and so far as the writer knows this branch disappears.

BARNEL, STEPHEN, m. Judith Church, 1710.

BARNES, BENJAMIN, son of 1st William, m., 1742, Experience, d. of Josiah Rider, and had Alice, 1743, m. Samuel Battles; Mercy, 1745, m. Richard Holmes; Bradford, 1747; Benjamin, 1750; Josiah, 1752; Isaac, 1754; Experience, 1756, m. Elisha Corban of Dudley; Sarah, 1760. BENJAMIN, son of above, m., 1774, Deborah, d. of Ichabod Holmes, and had Benjamin; Bradford, 1777; Samuel; Deborah, m. John Gooding; Ellis. BENJAMIN, son

of above, m., 1800, Rebecca Shurtleff, and had Benjamin. He m. 2d, 1828,
Eliza Foster, wid. of John Lewis, and d. of William Dunham. BENJAMIN,
son of above, m. Deborah, d. of Robert Hutchinson, and had Robert
Hutchinson, 1834, m. Rebecca Holmes; Rebecca B., 1838, m. Lysander L.
Dunham; Laura E., m. Richard Holmes; Benjamin F. BENJAMIN, son of
Seth, m., 1762, Elizabeth Holmes, and had Elizabeth, 1762; Benjamin, 1764.
BENJAMIN, son of above, removed from Plymouth, and was the father of
Seth and Hilburn, twins, of Boston, and James H. of Springfield. BRAD-
FORD, son of 2d Benjamin, m., 1799, Jane Holmes, and had Bradford; Nancy,
m. John Washburn. BRADFORD, son of above, m., 1827, Mary Wood-
ward, and had Martha Jane, 1828, m. Samuel Talbot; Winslow Bradford,
1830, m. Emily P. Sweetser; Mary Woodward, 1833, m. A. W. B. Gooding of
Boston; Caroline Dorr, 1835, m. James W. Bicknell; Deborah Fanny, 1837;
Hannah Elizabeth, 1840, m. John McDonough; Nancy Agnes, 1840, m.
Pomroy Briggs; Ann Maynard, 1852. CORBAN, son of 3d John, m., 1755,
Rebecca Atwood. He m. 2d, 1765, Mary; d. of Jeremiah Finney of Bristol,
and had Mary, 1766, m. Eleazar Holmes; Rebecca, 1768; Betsey, 1771, m.
Thomas Davie; Levi Lucas, and a Mayhew; Charlotte, 1774, m. Stephen
Harlow; Corban, 1778; Patty, 1781, m. Ansel Holmes; Deborah, 1785, m.
Alden Lucas; Abigail, 1789, m. William Keen and Josiah Carver. CORBAN,
son of 1st Lemuel, m., 1783, Phebe Holmes, and had Lemuel, 1785, m. Lucy
Covington; Nathaniel; Elkanah; Betsey, m. Barnabas Dunham; Sarah Holmes,
m. John Parker Ellis; Joanna, m. Joseph Bradford and William Nickerson;
Phebe, m. Seth Paty and James G. Gleason; Corban. CORBAN, son of
above, m. Susan, d. of Hamblin Tilson, and had Susan, 1834, m. Charles
Hayden. He m. 2d, 1836, Mary Ann, d. of Ephraim Holmes, and wid. of
Sylvester Davie, and had Albert Corban, 1838; Corban, Lemuel, Mary; Mary
again, m. Amos Locke; Albert, George, and Frances, m. Daniel Critchenson.
ELLIS, son of 2d Benjamin, m., 1814, Mary Holmes, and had Eleazar H.,
1815, m., Deborah L., d. of Putnam Kimball; Ellis, 1817, m. Lois T. Bagnall;
Mary E., 1823, m. Daniel F. Goddard; Josiah W., 1826; John C., 1828, m ,
Elizabeth Saunders; Helen, 1836, m. Adoniram J. Atwood. ELKANAH, son of
1st Lemuel, m. Eliza Clark, and had Elkanah, John, Eliza, m. Bela Cushing;
Hannah, m. a Tirrell. ELKANAH, son of above, m., 1813, Cynthia Davis,
d. of Lemuel Simmons, and had Alexina Carlowitz, 1813, m. Sylvanus
Paulding; Lorenzo, 1816, m. Lucy Bonney and Betsey Brown; Catherine
Harriet, 1813, m. Stephen Faunce; Charles Elkanah, 1820, m. Betsey Ishmael,
George R. S., m. Sarah E. Meyer; Moses Simmons, m. Louisa W. Burgess;
Francilia A., m. Charles P. Leach. HENRY, son of 4th William, m., 1836,
Catherine W. Bradford, and had Charles Henry, 1837; Luther R. and Clara
E. ICHABOD, m., 1794, Jerusha Doten. ISAAC, son of 1st Benjamin, m.,
1780, Lucy Harlow, and had Lucy, 1784, m. Ivory Harlow; Polly, 1789, m.
George W. Virgin; Sally, 1793, m. James Collins; Isaac, 1796. ISAAC, son of
above, m., 1819, Betsey, d. of Thomas Davie, and had Isaac, 1820; Thomas
Davie, 1822; Samuel Davis, 1829; Winslow, and Betsey W. He m. 2d, 1830,
Lucy C., d. of Lewis Harlow, and had George Winslow, 1832; James Frank-
lin, 1834; Betsey Davie, 1836, m. William S. Kirk of Penn.; Mary Frances,

1839, m. Franklin B. Cobb; Harrison O., 1845, m. Mary A., d. of Andrew Blanchard. JAMES, son of Seth, m., 1750, Sarah Nash, and had James, 1755. JAMES, son of 4th William, m., 1827, Mary Weston. He m., 2d, Elizabeth Cobb, wid. of Isaac Swift, and d. of John Battles. JOHN appeared in Plymouth 1631. He m., 1633, Mary Plummer, and had Esther, m. John Rickard; John, 1639; Jonathan, 1643; Lydia, 1647; Hannah; Mary, m. Robert Marshall. He m., 2d, a wife Jane. JOHN, son of 1st Jonathan, m., 1693, Mary Bartlett, and had John, 1694; Hannah, 1696, m. Lemuel Drew; William, 1697; Seth, 1699; Mary, 1701; Jonathan, 1703; Thankful, 1705, m. Jonathan Bartlett; Elizabeth, 1707, m. Francis Curtis; Lydia, 1713, m. Lemuel Barnes. JOHN, son of above, m., 1725, Dorcas Corban of Haverhill, and had John, 1726; Lemuel, 1729; Corban, 1732; Mary, 1736, m. John Dyer; Hannah, 1740, m. Ezra Corban; Elkanah, 1742, m. Hannah Bartlett. JONA-THAN, son of 1st John, m., 1666, Elizabeth, d. of William Hedge of Yarmouth, and had Mary, 1667, m. John Carver; John, 1669; William, 1670; Hannah, 1672, m. Benjamin Rider; Lydia, 1674, m. Abiel Shurtleff; Elizabeth, 1677, m. Isaac Lathrop; Sarah, 1680, m. Benjamin Bartlett; Esther, 1682, m. Elkanah Cushman; Jonathan, 1684. JONATHAN, son of above, m. Sarah Bradford, and had Sarah, 1709; Rebecca, 1711; Lydia, 1715. He m., 2d, wid. Mercy Doten, and had Hannah, 1718, m. Stephen Churchill, and Jeremiah Howes; Lydia, m. Joseph Smith; Sarah, m. Thomas Doane. JONATHAN, son of 2d John, m., 1726, Phebe, d. of Josiah Finney, and had Mary, 1728; Margaret, 1732, m. Zacheus Bartlett; Jonathan, 1735; Nathaniel, 1740, m. Jerusha Blackmar; Zacheus, 1743. JONATHAN, son of 1st Zacheus, m. Lydia Curtis of Maine, and had Zacheus. JOSEPH, son of 1st Seth, m., 1760, Hannah Rider, and had Hannah, 1760, m. Isaac Thomas; Joseph, 1763; William, 1765; Nathaniel, 1771; Elizabeth, 1773, m. Thomas Rogers; Sarah, 1775, m. William Goddard; Thomas, 1779; Nancy, 1781. JOSEPH, son of above, m., 1787, Elizabeth, d. of Joseph Tribble, and had Joseph; Betsey, m. Bartlett Ellis. JOSEPH, son of above, m., 1808, Jane, d. of Job Brewster, and had Rosilla Lessington, 1809; William Brewster, 1811; Jane Emily, 1813, m. Simon R. Burgess; Hannah Ellis, 1817, m. Joseph W. Burgess; Betsey, 1819, m. William Nickerson; Ellis, 1823; Nancy Cotton, 1826, m. Charles H. Weston; Fanny, 1828, m. Augustus Norwood; Mary Ann Newman. LEMUEL, son of 3d John, m., 1751, Sarah, d. of Francis L. Baron, and had Sarah, 1751; John, 1752; Lemuel, 1754, m. Jedidah Harlow; Dorcas, 1756, m. Jonathan Farnum; Isaac, 1756; Corban, 1761; Betsey, m. Caleb Bryant; Elkanah. LEMUEL, m., 1802, Laura Stetson. LEMUEL, m., 1810, Susanna Marshall. LEMUEL, son of 1st William, m., 1735, Lydia, d. of John Barnes, and had Hannah, 1735, m. James Thomas; Lydia, 1737, m. Nathaniel Bartlett, William, 1740, m. Jane Fish; Alice, 1744, m. Josiah Finney; Lemuel, 1746; John, 1748, m. Margaret Rider; Isaac, 1750. LEVI, son of 4th William, m., 1827, Martha, d. of Ansel Holmes, and had George Orville; Albert, m. Sarah W., d. of Ebenezer Davie; Edward L., m. Agnes Gordon Chamberlin of Roxbury. NATHANIEL, son of 2d Corban, m., 1816, Hannah, d. of Benjamin Goddard, and had Betsey Goddard, 1821; John Ellis, 1826, m. Mary Antoinette, d. of Lemuel D. Holmes; Nathaniel, 1829. NATHANIEL CARVER, son of 5th William, m., 1832, Betsey W., d. of William Tribble, and had Betsey W., 1833; Nathaniel Franklin, 1835, m. Anna M. Churchill; Nancy Carver, 1837, m. Charles S. Robbins; George A., m. Katie C. Burgess. SAMUEL, son of 2d Benjamin, m. Lucy Perkins, and had Samuel, 1803. SAMUEL, son of above, m., 1833, Sarah Barrows of Middleboro', and had Sarah, m. Nathaniel B. Bradford; Lucy P., m. Charles Fuller. SETH, son of 2d John, m., 1722, Sarah Wooden, and had Elizabeth, 1722; Sarah, 1727, m. John Jones; Seth, 1726, m. Hannah Williams, and Elizabeth Rider, James, 1728; Mary, 1730; William, 1732; Joseph, 1737; Benjamin, 1737; Peter Wooden, 1742; Lucy, 1745, m. Ephraim Holmes. SETH, son of above, m., 1751, Hannah Williams. He m. 2d, 1754, Elizabeth Rider, and had Elizabeth, 1754. SOUTHWORTH, son of 5th William, m., 1833, Lucy, d. of John Burbank, and had Georgiana, 1834, m. Albert G. Hedge. WILLIAM, son of 1st Jonathan, m., 1704, Alice, d. of William Bradford. and had William, 1706; Lemuel, 1707; Mercy, 1708, m. Samuel Cole, and Barnabas Hedge; Benjamin, 1711; Benjamin again, 1717. WILLIAM, son of 3d Lemuel, m. 1764, Mary Rider, and had William, 1767. He m., 2d. Jane, d. of Lemuel Fish, and had Lemuel. WILLIAM, son of 1st Seth, m., 1755, Mercy, d. of Matthew Lemote, and had Abigail, 1755, m. Richard Pierce; Mercy, 1757, m. Levi Harlow; William, 1760. WILLIAM, son of 2d William, m., 1794, Sarah, d. of Joseph Tribble, and had William, m. a Hayden, and wid. Sarah Goddard; Levi, James, Henry; Lydia, m. Luther Ripley; Mary, m. Andrew Bartlett; Sarah, m. Joseph W. Hodgkins. WILLIAM, son of 3d William, m., 1790, Mercy, d. of Nathaniel Carver, and had William, Southworth; Ellen, m. John Sherman; Nathaniel Carver. WILLIAM, son of above, m. Phebe, d. of John Dickson, and had William M., 1822, m. Anna E. Holbrook; Winslow C., 1829, m. Eliza Diman; Ellis D., 1831; Caroline F., 1834, m. Thomas W. Hayden; Charles C., 1838, m. Alice G. Howland. WILLIAM BREWSTER, son of 3d Joseph, m. Harriet G., d. of Joshua Brewster, and had William E., m. Martha, d. of David Turner; Charles E., m. Eleanor N. Chase, and Hannah T. Chadwick; Joseph m. Ella R., d. of William Nightingale, and Harriet May. ZACHEUS, son of 3d Jonathan, m., 1765, Hannah Curtis, and had Phebe, 1766, m. a Morse of Portland; Hannah, 1768, m. Sylvanus Paty; Lydia, 1771, m. a Jordan of Portland; Jonathan; Jerusha, m. Thomas Paty. ZACHEUS, son of 4th Jonathan, m., 1821, Mary, d. of Lewis Churchill, and had Nancy Paty, m. Ozen Bates.

BARNEY, HOSEA, from Taunton, m., 1837, Hannah C. Nichols.

BARRETT, JOHN, m. Hannah Holmes, 1786, and had William. WILLIAM, son of above, m., 1812, Ruth, d. of Benjamin Westgate, and had William, m. Nancy Sherman of Rochester; John, m. Ann Gore, and a second wife now living; Clarissa, m. Edward Haley; Ruth, m. William Savery; Charles; Susan; Benjamin, m. Catherine A. Cosgrove.

BARROW (or BARROWS), ANDREW, Plympton, son of 1st James, m. Sarah Perkins, and had Joshua, 1772; James, 1773; Andrew, 1775; Ezra, 1777; Sarah, 1779, m. Jabez Sherman; Mary, 1781, m. Thomas Tilson; Hannah, 1784, m. Thomas Cobb; Elizabeth, 1785; Lothrop, 1788; George, 1790; Charles, 1793; John, 1796. ANSEL, Carver, son of 3d Moses, m. Hannah

Elliot of Sutton, and removed to Vermont. His children were Ansel, m. Lois Warren of Plymouth, now living in Cambridge; Asa, Harvey, m. Hannah Beckley of Maine; Moses, m. Mercy Maxim of Wareham; Betsey, m. Calvin Perkins; Sarah, m. Samuel Barnes of Plymouth; Esther, m. George Gibbs of Middleboro'; Thomas, and Deborah. ASA, son of Zadock, m. Deborah Dewey, 1789, and had Lydia, 1790; Wendell, 1791; Deborah, 1793; Betsey, 1795, m. Ezra Lucas; Asa, 1798; Mira, 1800; Lucy, 1802; Jane, 1804; Rebecca Drew, 1806; Anna, 1809; Sally, 1811; Isaac N., 1814. ASA, Carver, son of Ansel, m. Fanny Dunham, and had Simeon Harvey, 1829, m. Priscilla Ann, d. of William S. Burbank; Samuel; William; and Abigail, m. George Atwood. CHARLES, Carver, son of Andrew, m. Mary Cobb, and had Charles, 1815; James, 1821; Horatio, 1823; Mary Ann, 1830. ELISHA, son of 2d Robert by wife Thankful, had Zacheus, 1720; Lydia, 1723; Elisha, 1724; Patience, 1729. GEORGE, son of 1st Robert, m. Patience Simmons, 1695, and had Moses, 1697; George, 1698, m. Desire Doty, and Samuel. GEORGE, Carver, son of Peleg, m. Sophia Washburn, 1808, and had Sophia Washburn, 1809; Louisa, 1811; Lucy, 1813; Mary Ann, 1817; George D., 1820. JAMES, Plympton, m. Tabitha Rickard, and had Lydia, Kesiah, 1732; James, 1734; Ebenezer, 1736; Eleazar, 1738; Andrew, 1748; George, 1751. JAMES, Carver, son of Andrew, m. Agatha Cobb, and had Mary Cobb, 1795; Nancy, 1802. JAMES, Carver, by wife Elizabeth, had Mehitabel, 1785; Levina, 1789; Ruth, 1791; James, 1794; David, 1796; John, 1799; Elias Shaw, 1801; Elkanah Shaw, 1804; Moses Shaw, 1808; Alfred, 1810. JOHN, who died 1692, had by wife Deborah, Robert, Benajah, Joshua, Ebenezer, and perhaps Mary, Deborah and John. JOHN, perhaps son of above by wife Sarah, had Hannah, 1700; Samuel, 1703; Ruth, 1705. He m., 2d, Bethiah King, 1714. JOHN, by wife Sarah, had John, 1768; William, 1770; Thomas, 1772. JOHN, from Cambridge, m. Sarah Manning of Cambridge, at an unknown date. JOHN, Carver, m. Deborah C. Doten, and had Deborah, 1818; Mary, 1820; Edward D., 1822; George, 1824; Nathan Cobb, 1827; Sarah P., 1830, and Deborah. JONATHAN, Plympton, son of a Peleg, m. Lydia, d. of Nathan Perkins, and had Priscilla, 1772; Olive, 1774; Jonathan, 1777. JOSHUA, Carver, son of Andrew, m. Molly Sherman, and had Nathaniel Sherman, 1796; Sally Sherman, 1799, m. Larned Brown, Eliab Ward, and Noah Prince; Polly, 1802, m. Ebenezer Rogerson; Betsey, 1804; Joshua, and Maria, 1807. LOTHROP, Carver, son of Andrew, m. Sally Shaw, and had Andrew, 1813; Lothrop, 1815; Wilson, 1817; Sally, 1819; Mercy, 1821; Louisa, 1823; Winslow, 1827; Pelham Winslow, 1829, and others. He had a second wife, Margaret. LOTHROP, Carver, son of above, m. Lucinda Sherman, and had Sally Shaw, 1840. MOSES, Plympton, son of George by wife Mary, had Seth, 1719, and Moses. MOSES, Plympton, son of above, m. Deborah Totman, 1748, and had Moses. By a second wife, Mary, he had Carver, 1752, and Mary, 1755. MOSES, Plympton, son of above, had Ansel. NATHANIEL SHERMAN, son of Joshua, m. Abigail Newell, and had Nathaniel Sherman, 1818, m. Clyntha Cobb: Abigail Newell, 1821, m. George W. Nelson; Larned Swallow Brown, 1824, m. Marie E., d. of Timothy Barry; Oliver Newell, 1828, m. Eleanor Varnum, and Mary Jane, 1831. NELSON, Carver, son of

Peleg, m. Mary Bisbee, and had Arad, 1819; Jonathan, 1822; Olive, 1825; Nelson, 1828. PELEG, Carver, by wife Jemima, had Thomas, 1776; William, 1778; Mary, 1780; George, 1783; Stephen, 1785; Nelson, 1787; Abigail, 1789; Joseph, 1792. ROBERT, perhaps brother of 1st John, m. 1666, Ruth, d. of George Bonum, and had Eleazer, 1669; Samuel, John, Mehitable, m. Adam Wright, and probably George. ROBERT, son of 1st John, m. Lydia Dunham, and had Elisha, 1686; Robert, 1689; Thankful, 1692, m. Isaac King; Elisha, 1695; Thomas, 1697; Lydia, 1699, m. Thomas Branch. ROBERT, son of above, m. Bethiah Ford, 1711, and had Jabez, 1711; Samuel, 1714; Thomas, 1716; Lydia, 1718. ROBERT, by wife Rebecca, had Robert, 1765; Ebenezer, 1767, m. Clarissa Bartlett. SAMUEL, son of 3d Robert, m. Desire Rogers, 1744, and had Lucy, 1746; Willis, 1748; Isaac, 1750; Elizabeth, 1752; Lazarus, 1754; Samuel, 1762. SAMUEL, Plympton, m. Lydia Barrows, and had Samuel, 1724; John, 1727; Hannah, 1729; Abner, 1732; Zadock, 1734; Robert, 1738; Ebenezer, 1740; Lydia, 1745. SETH, Carver, by wife Abigail, had Ruth, 1771; Seth, 1773; Isaac, 1776. SETH, Carver, son of above, m. Ruth Atwood, and had Roxy, 1802; Isaac, 1804; Abigail Cobb, 1805; Seth, 1807; Enos, 1809; Mary, 1811; Ruth, 1813. THOMAS, Carver, by wife Mary, had Sarah, 1801; Thomas, 1804; John Jay, 1810; James Lloyd, 1816; Peleg, 1822. WILLIAM, Carver, m. Betsy Tillson, and had William DeLamater, 1832; Gustavus H., 1837; Andrew, 1839. He had a first wife, Mary. WILSON, Carver, son of 1st Lathrop, m. Elizabeth D. Sherman, and had Hannah S., 1841; Mercy F., 1843. ZADOCK, son of 2d Samuel, had Asa.

BARSTOW, ICHABOD WESTON, from Pembroke, m. Sarah Roberts, d. of John Clark, 1818.

BARTLETT, ABNER, son of 1st Sylvanus, m. Anna, d. of Ivory Hovey, 1774, and had Abner, 1776, m. Sarah Burgess; Anna, 1777, m. Ellis Bartlett; Betsey, 1779, m. Amasa Holmes; Martha, 1782, m. Meltiah Bartlett; Olive, 1783, m. Samuel Bartlett; Ellen, 1786, m. Thomas Clark; Fanny, 1790, m. Daniel Montague; Harriet, 1792, m. Isaac Manchester; Ivory Hovey, 1794; Eliza, 1801, m. Freeman P. Howland. AMASA, m. Hannah Morton, 1787. AMASA, son of 1st William, m. Sarah Taylor, 1788, and had Amasa; William Sampson, 1807; Hannah, 1792, m. Bourne Spooner; Sally T., 1794, m. William Bishop and Schuyler Sampson; and Mary Ann, m. Schuyler Sampson. AMASA, son of above, m. Esther, d. of Nathaniel Spooner, 1833, and had Amasa S.; Mary Ann, m. James D. Thurber, and Schuyler S. ANDREW, son of 1st Nathaniel, m. Lydia Churchill, 1764, and had Andrew, 1765; Caleb, 1767; Henry, 1768; Stephen, 1770; Hosea, 1772; Rebecca, m. Stephen Holmes; Lydia, 1779, m. Ezra Finney; Polly, m. Joseph Prior; Euphany, m. Nathan Holmes, and Lucy, m. Lemuel Bartlett. ANDREW, son of above, m. Sarah Holbrook, 1790, and had Sarah, m. David P. Reynolds; Andrew, and Orrin. ANDREW, son of above, m. Mary, d. of William Barnes, 1830, and had Victor A., 1841; Mary E., 1843; Andrew P. 1848. He m., 2d, Phebe J. Tenney, 1866. ANSEL, son of 2d Judah, m. Elizabeth Churchill, 1789, and had Ansel; Charles, m. Ellen Rider; Lewis, m. Mary Corbin Holmes, and Alexander Dewsbury; Harvey; Caroline, m. Marston Sampson, Betsey, m. Zacheus Parker; Elkanah, and Nancy, m. Zacheus

Sherman. ANSEL, son of 6th Benjamin, m. Polly Lanman, 1801, and had Polly, 1802, m. Joel Randall; Thomas Burgess, 1805, m. Bethiah, d. of John Churchill, and Rebecca W., d. of Avery Dean; Ansel, 1807; Jean, 1809, m. Alexander V. Harvey; Lucy E., 1813, m. William Packard, and Susan, 1816, m. William H. Inglis. ANSEL, son of 1st Ansel, m. Abigail Ripley, 1813, and had Kimball R.; Abigail W., m. Henry Burgess; Nancy, m. Samuel Savery; Rebecca; and Mary, m. Sylvester R. Swett. ARUNA, m. Remember Holmes, 1796, and had Temperance, 1797; Aruna, 1799; Rufus, 1802; Spencer, 1804; Remember, 1807; Sophia, 1809, and Hiram, 1811. BENJAMIN, son of 1st Robert, m. Sarah, d. of Love Brewster, 1656, and had Benjamin; Samuel; Ichabod, Ebenezer, who had a wife, Hannah; Rebecca, m. William Bradford; and Sarah, m. Robert Bartlett. He m. a second wife, Cicily, 1678. BENJAMIN, son of above, m. Ruth Pabodie, 1672, and had Robert, 1679; Benjamin; Mercy, m. John Turner; Priscilla, 1697, m. John Sampson; Deborah, m. Josiah Thomas; Ruth, m. John Murdock; Abigail, 1703, m. Gamaliel Bradford; Rebecca, m. John Bradford; Elizabeth, m. Ephraim Bradford; Sarah, m. Ismael Bradford, and William. BENJAMIN, son of 1st Joseph, m. Sarah, d. of Jonathan Barnes, 1702, and had Nathaniel, 1703, m. Abigail Clarke, Jonathan, 1705, m. Thankful Barnes; Benjamin, 1707; Joseph, 1709; Hannah, 1711; Sarah, 1713, m. John Cobb; and Elkanah. BENJAMIN, son of above, m. Hannah Stephens, 1737, and had Stephens. He probably m., 2d, Abigail Morton, 1741, and had William, 1742; Priscilla, 1744, m. Samuel Calderwood; Elizabeth, 1746, m. Nathaniel Ripley. BENJAMIN, son of 6th Joseph, m. Jemima Holmes, 1759, and had Jane, m. Nathaniel Ellis; Mary; Joanna, m. Ichabod Davie; Jemima; Nancy, m. Ichabod Davie; Benjamin; Elizabeth, m. William Rogers; Ansel; Sarah, m. Ansel Holmes; and Thomas. BENJAMIN, m. Jean Ellis, 1751, and had Benjamin, 1752. CALEB, m. Adrianna B. Holmes, 1837. CALEB, son of 3d Robert, m. Elizabeth Holmes, 1778; moved to Yarmouth, Me., and had Caleb; Betsey, Isaac; Rebecca, m. Isaac Bartlett; Robert; Susan; George; Charles; and Holmes. CALEB, son of above, m. Mary Small, and had Isaac; Elizabeth; Mary, m. Flavel Bartlett; and William, m. Jane Gardner, d. of Truman Bartlett. CHARLES, son of 11th Joseph, m. wid. Lucinda (Cornish) Bartlett, 1820; and had Charles, 1821; Hosea, 1826; Lucinda, 1829; Abigail, 1837. DAVID, son of 1st Elkanah, m. Mary Carver, 1796, and had Mary, 1796; Dolly, m. I. H. Lucas; and Abigail. DIMAN, son of 3d Ebenezer, m. Lydia Barrows, 1790, and 2d, 1802, Hannah, wid. of James Harlow, and d. of Benjamin Bagnall, and had Lewis and Ephraim. EBENEZER, Duxbury, son of 1st Benjamin by wife Hannah, had Lydia; Ebenezer, 1794. EBENEZER, son of above, m. Mary Rider, and had Rebecca, 1719; Lydia, 1721; and Nathaniel, 1723. He m., 2d, perhaps, Jerusha Sampson. EBENEZER, son of 2d Robert, m. Rebecca Diman, 1732, and had James, 1733; Chloe, 1735; Thomas, 1737; Phebe, 1740; Rebecca, 1745. He m., 2d, Abigail Finney, 1749, and had Ebenezer, 1754; Thomas, 1757; Diman, 1759; and Abigail, 1762, m. Consider Robbins. ELEAZER STEPHENS, son of Freeman, m. Betsey Cobb, and had William Stephens. He m., 2d, Eveline G., d. of Salisbury Jackson, and had Francis J., m. Henrietta C. Shipley; Mary L.; and Eveline Stephens.

ELLIS, son of 4th John, m. Anna Bartlett, 1796, and had John, m. a Dunbar; Mercy, m. Jonas Keith; Anna, m. Humphrey Manchester; Abner, m. Susan Case; Martha, m. Obadiah Burgess; Cyrus; Lewis, m. Sylvia Pierce; Ellis, 1817; and Freeman. ELLIS, son of above, m. Sophia Ashmead of Philadelphia, and had Ellis Lehman, 1844, and William Lehman Ashmead, 1846, m. Baroness Burdett Coutts. ELKANAH, son of 6th Joseph, m. Sarah Atwood, 1768, and had Elkanah, 1769, m. Rebecca Holmes; David, 1775; John, 1777; Jonathan, 1782; Sally, 1786; and Jennie and Joanna, twins, 1792. ELKANAH, son of 1st Ansel, m. Mary Morton, 1828, and had Mary E., m. Joseph Lasinby Brown; and Frank. ELKANAH, m. Sarah Code, 1802. ELNATHAN, son of 1st Joseph, m. Hannah Mansfield, 1712, and had Elnathan, 1713, moved to New York; and Hannah, 1714. EPHRAIM, son of 3d Robert, m. Mercy Churchill, 1759, and had James, 1760; Sylvanus, 1762; Susanna, 1764; and Rebecca, the last two of whom m. William Leonard. He m., 2d, Elizabeth Kempton, 1774, and had Elizabeth, 1775, m. Ephraim Whiting; Ephraim; Isaac; and Mercy, m. Finney Leach. EPHRAIM, son of Diman, m. Martha Cox, 1830, and had William Henry, 1832; Martha Ann, 1835, m. George E. Morton. EPHRAIM, son of 1st Ephraim, m. Abigail, d. of Richard Holmes, 1799. FRANCIS, son of Sylvanus, m. Anna Cornish, 1788, and had Annie, 1792; Cephas, 1794; Francis, 1797; Alfred, 1799; Anna Cornish, 1802; Marcia, 1805; Martha Waite, 1810. FREDERICK WILLIAM, Buffalo, son of 2d Uriah, m. Adelia, d. of Dr. James Hunter of Whitby, Canada, from Hull, England, and had George Frederick Hunter, 1856; Daisy Lillian, 1865. FREEMAN, son of Joshua, m. Sarah Stephens, 1797, and had Eleazer Stephens; Hannah, m. John Ransom; Sally, m. a Copeland; Mary; Elizabeth Thacher, m. William Reed; and William. GEORGE, son of 1st Zacheus, m. Sylvina Holmes, 1793, and had Phebe, m. Branch Blackmer; Margaret, m. Nathaniel Harlow; Triphosa, m. Robert Fitts; George W.; and Jerusha, m. Joseph Doten. GEORGE W., son of above, m. Sarah Bartlett, 1825, and had George W., m. Flora A. Holmes. He m., 2d, Melintha Harlow, and had Henry C., m. Emily F. Parker; Winslow, m. Emily, the wid. of his brother; William L., m. Mary E. Shaw; and Frank R., m. Anna Bates. GEORGE, m. Rebecca Lanman, 1798. HARVEY, son of 1st Ansel, m. Nancy Holmes, 1828, and had Nancy, 1830; Harvey, 1833; Ansel, 1835; Almira, 1837; and George. HENRY, m. Fanny Churchill, 1817. HENRY, m. Prudence Straffin, 1811. HOSEA, son of 1st Andrew, m. Mercy Bartlett, 1798; and had Abigail, 1799; Hosea, 1801; Maria, 1805; John, 1809; Abigail, 1810. HOSEA, son of above, m. Susan Cornish, and had Samuel. He m., 2d, Eliza, d. of Aaron Hovey, and 3d, Eleanor, d. of Benjamin Clark, 1840. ICHABOD, Marshfield, son of 1st Benjamin, m. Elizabeth Waterman of Marshfield, 1699, and had Ichabod; Josiah, 1701, m. Mary Chandler; Nathaniel, 1703, m. Abiah Delano; Joseph, 1706, m. Dorothy Wadsworth; Elizabeth, 1708; and Mercy. He m., 2d, Desire, d. of Seth Arnold, 1709, and had Sarah, 1710, m. Cornelius Drew; Josiah; and Seth. ICHABOD, son of above, m. Susanna Spooner, 1721, and had Ichabod; and Solomon, m., Joanna Holmes. ICHABOD, son of above, m. Hannah Rogers, 1753, and had Ichabod, 1754; Hannah; Jerusha; Mercy; and Peabody. ICHABOD, Honolulu, son of 2d Uriah, m.,

1855, Caroline Frances Gould, d. of James Stuart Gould of Maine, and had Carrie Adela, 1856, m. Thomas A. Mitchell of Oakland, Cal.; Laura Frances, 1857, m. Noah Helsey of Oakland; Lily, 1859; and George L., 1865. ISAAC, son of 1st Zacheus, m. Mary Bryant, and had Laura Ann; Mary; Elizabeth, m. Jason Winnett; Erastus H.; and Fayette. ISAAC, son of 1st Ephraim, m. Fear Cobb, 1801, and had Isaac, 1801; Eliza Ann, 1807, m. Stephen P. Brown; and Ephraim, 1809. He m., 2d, Rebecca, d. of Caleb Bartlett, and had Robert, 1817; and Rebecca, 1819. ISAAC, m. Sarah Cotton, 1825, and had Isaac T., 1826; Catherine C., 1832; Lilliston B., 1834; Henry I., 1836; Anna, 1838. IVORY HOVEY, son of Abner, m. Betsey Clark, 1814, and had Abner; Ivory; George; William; Robert; Catherine; and Dolor. JAMES, m. Emily Bradford, 1825. JAMES, m. Charlotte Covill of Sandwich, about 1832. JAMES, son of 1st Ephraim, m. Mary Taylor, 1783, and had Mary Taylor, 1784; James; Sylvanus; Mercy B., m. Leander Lovell; Rebecca A., 1798; Jane, 1800; and Susan, m. Abner S. Taylor. JAMES, son of above, m., 1807, Sarah Witherell, and had Sarah, m. Isaac Brewster; Margaret, m. Ethan Earle; Harriet; Jane Elizabeth, m. Thatcher R. Raymond; Sylvanus T., 1808; James T., 1818; Sylvanus Taylor, 1820; James Thomas; Charles T.; Mary A., 1825; and Rebecca T., 1828. JESSE, son of 1st Sylvanus, m. Polly Hovey, 1809, and had Sylvanus; William D.; and Catherine. John, son of 2d Robert, m. Sarah, d. of Ebenezer Cobb, 1723, and had Jerusha, 1724; Sarah, 1726, m. Thomas Faunce; and Hannah, 1727, m. Stephen Doten; Mary, 1731. He m., 2d, wid. Sarah Gray of Falmouth, 1734, and had Jerusha, 1735, m. George Peckham; John, 1738; Jennie, 1740; Lewis, 1743; Abigail, 1745, m. Eleazer Churchill; Maria, 1748, m. Richard Babb; Charles, m. Abigail Churchill; and George, m. Sarah Churchill. JOHN, son of 2d Samuel, m. Sarah Bartlett, 1756, and had Sarah, 1759, m. Thomas Morton; Eunice, 1761, m. William Morton; John, 1763; and Deborah. JOHN, son of 1st John, m. Dorothy Carver, 1768, and had Lewis, 1770, m. Hannah Paty; Dolly; John Lewis; John; and Henry. JOHN, son of 1st Nathaniel, m. Mercy Ellis, 1762, and had Abigail, 1763, m. Benjamin Washburn; John, 1766; Ellis, 1770; Ivory, 1772; and Samuel, m. Olive Bartlett. JOHN, son of 3d Joseph, m. Bathsheba Shurtleff, and had Rufus, 1771; Dorothy, 1774, m. Ellis Bradford; Sarah, 1776, m. Simeon Chandler; Betsey, 1779, m. Bradford Holmes; Olive, 1783, m. Thomas Bates; John, 1786; George, 1789; Bathsheba, 1793, m. Lazarus Drew; and Joseph. JOHN, m. Sophronia King, 1802, and had Alonzo Sydney, 1803; and Martha Adelaide, 1806. JOHN, son of 1st Elkanah, m. Rebecca Rider, 1799, and had John; Eliza, m. Brackly Cushing; Priscilla, m. a Wadleigh; and Joseph. He m. a 2d wife, Jerusha, wid. of Robert Davie, and d. of Joseph Trask. JOHN, son of 2d John, m. Polly Morton, 1795, and had John; Mary, m. Obadiah King; Rebecca, m. Peter Smith. JOHN, son of above, m. Caroline Lawrence, and had Polly Morton, 1823; Caroline Augusta, 1829; and John Edwards, 1836. JOHN, m. Cynthia Lucas, 1820. JOHN, son of 7th John, m. Eliza, d. of Ezra Finney, 1829, and had Caroline; John Bishop, m. Eliza, d. of Stephen Smith of Boston; Ezra Finney; Lydia; James Easdell, m. Adeline Mullikin of Philadelphia. He m., 2d. wid. (Austin) Robinson of Boston. JONATHAN, son of 3d Benjamin, m., 1731, Thankful, d. of John

Barnes, and had James, 1732, m. Elizabeth Bates; Sarah, 1734; Thankful, 1738; Jonathan, 1742; Lucy, 1744, m. Bartlett Holmes; William, 1747; and Thankful, 1750, m. Ansel Harlow. JONATHAN, son of 6th Joseph, m. Lydia Ellis, 1777, and had Mercy, 1782; Jonathan, 1787. JOSEPH, son of 1st Robert, m. Hannah, d. of Gabriel Fallowell, and had Joseph, 1665; Robert, 1663; Elnathan; Benjamin; Hannah, m. Joseph Sylvester; Mary, 1673, m. John Barnes; and Sarah, m. Elisha Holmes. JOSEPH, son of above, m. Lydia Griswold, 1692, and had Joseph, 1693; Samuel, 1696; Lydia, 1698, m. Lazarus LeBaron; Benjamin, 1699, m. Lydia Morton; and Sarah, 1703, m. Francis LeBaron and Joseph Swift. JOSEPH, son of 1st Ichabod, m. Dorothy Wadsworth, 1729, and had Mercy, 1733; Annie, 1735; Ichabod, 1736; Joseph, 1740; Dorothy, 1743, m. William Drew; Bathsheba; Uriah; Elizabeth, 1747, m. Robert Foster; and John. JOSEPH, son of 2d Joseph, m. Elizabeth Bartlett, 1717, and had William, 1718; Sylvanus, 1719; Jerusha, 1721, m. Joseph Croswell; Lydia, 1722, m. Jonathan Parker; Zacheus, 1725; Betty, 1727, m. Benjamin Rider; Joseph, 1729, m. Lydia Cobb. JOSEPH, son of 2d Robert, m. Sarah Morton, 1737 and had Sarah, 1737, m. John Bartlett; Joseph, 1738; Thomas, 1742; Josiah, 1744; Martha, 1747, m. a Jackson; Hannah, 1749, m. Daniel Hosea. JOSEPH, son of 3d Benjamin, m. Jean Swift, 1735, and had Benjamin, 1736; Mercy, 1738, m. Sylvanus Marshall; Jean, 1741, m. Matthew Claghorn; Joann, 1742, m. George Atwood; Joseph, 1745; Elkanah, 1747; and David and Jonathan, 1753. JOSEPH, son of 3d Joseph, m. Laurana Drew, and had Laurana, 1768; Joseph, 1770, m. Lucy Bradford; Seth, 1772, m. Mary Kimball; Ichabod, 1775; Lysander, 1777, m. Harriet Drew; Sarah D., 1780; Charles, 1786. JOSEPH, son of 5th Joseph, m. Mary Bartlett, 1770, and had Joseph; Frederick, m. Lydia Dunham; and Mary, m. Nathaniel Bartlett. JOSEPH, son of 6th Joseph, m. Lucy Holmes, 1770, and had Joseph, 1770; Zephaniah, 1772, m. Eliza, d. of Ebenezer Sampson; Lucy, 1775; Bradford, 1776. JOSEPH, son of 7th Joseph, m. Lucy Bradford, and had Betsey, 1799, m. Anthony E. Glynn; Lucy F.; Nancy, 1804, m. Nathaniel Drew; David B., 1806, m. Abigail Freeman; Ichabod, 1809; Cornelius A., 1811, m. Mabel Drew; Lucy F., 1814, m. Peter Pratt; Walter S., 1818, m. Susan A. Soule. JOSEPH, son of 1st Zacheus, m. Anna Clark, 1784, and had Charles, 1785; Joseph, 1786; Hannah, 1787, m. Thomas Mayo and Samuel Clark; Thomas, 1789, m. Lucinda Cornish; Zacheus, 1793, m. Sylvia Blackwell; Micah, 1793; Isaac, 1796; Abigail, 1798, m. Seth Clark; and Clark, 1800. JOSEPH, son of 3d Samuel, m. Rebecca Churchill, 1784, and had William, 1786; Rebecca; Susan, 1795; Joseph; Augustus; John; Samuel; Benjamin; and Eliza Ann, m. Albert Goodwin. He m., 2d, Lucy Dyer, 1821. JOSEPH, m. Grace Cornish, 1813. JOSEPH, Duxbury, son of 1st Samuel, m. Lydia Nelson, and had Isaiah, 1716; Patience, 1718; Hannah, 1721; Lydia, 1725. JOSHUA, son of 3d Robert, m. Mary Harlow, 1772, and had Freeman, m. Sarah Stephens; and Joshua, m. Elizabeth Goodwin. JUDAH, son of 1st William, m. Mercy Sylvester, 1788, and had William, m. Abiah Parsons. JUDAH, son of 2d Samuel, m. Love Sprague, 1763, and had Ansel; Mary, m. John Cronican; Nathaniel; Roxanna, m. Rufus Bartlett, and perhaps others. JUDAH, son of 5th Nathaniel, m. Jerusha Holmes, 1824, and had Eliza Ann, 1826. He m., 2d, wid. Eliza Jane

Lucas, 1831, and had Jerusha Holmes, 1832; John Franklin, 1835; Martha Washington, 1837; Amasa, 1839. LAZARUS, m. Thankful C. Bartlett, 1817. LEMUEL, son of 2d Robert, m. Mary Doty, 1742, and had Lemuel, 1744; William, 1746; Mary, 1749, m. a Sturtevant; Jean, 1754, m. a Doten; Stephen, 1756; Rebecca, 1760, m. a Holmes; Rufus, 1762, m. Mercy Churchill. LEMUEL, by wife Lucy, had Lucy, 1807. LEWIS, son of Diman, m. Mary C. Holmes, 1825, and had Charles Lewis, 1827; Martha Ann, 1830; William Marston, 1832; Mary Jane, 1834. LEMUEL, m. Lucy Bartlett, 1807. LEMUEL BRAD-FORD, m. Mary Holmes, 1785. NATHANIEL, son of 3d Benjamin, m. Abigail, d. of Thomas Clark, 1725, and had Thomas, 1725; Susanna, 1728, m. Elkanah Churchill; Mary, 1730, m. William Bartlett; Nathaniel, 1733, m. Lydia, d. of Lemuel Barnes; John, 1736; Andrew, 1738; Abigail, 1740, m. Solomon Holmes; Hannah, 1743, m. Elkanah Barnes. NATHANIEL, son of 3d Samuel, m. Mary Bartlett, 1793, and had Nathaniel; Harriet, m. Samuel M. Whitten; Mary, m. Henry Seymour; Almira, m. Nathaniel Churchill; Sophia, m. William Straffin; Betsey; Edward; Cornelius, m. wid. Marcia (Perkins) Sturtevant. NATHANIEL, son of above, m. Lucia, d. of Barnabas Holmes, 1821, and had Nathaniel, 1822, m. Sarah Soule; Frederick, 1824, m. Harriet Martin and Elizabeth G. Thrasher; David C., 1827; Lucia A., 1828;. Cornelius, 1831, m. Deborah A. Hoyt; and Mary J., 1837. NATHANIEL, m. Susan Diman, 1816. NATHANIEL, son of 2d Judah, m. Elizabeth Marshall, 1784, and had Susanna; Nathaniel, 1786; Ansel; Peabody; Samuel, m. Lydia Bartlett; Judah, and Amasa. NATHANIEL, son of above, m. Sarah Lucas, 1808, and had Susan and Sarah. NATHANIEL, son of 2d Solomon, m. Hannah Faunce, 1787, and had Nathaniel. NATHANIEL, son of the last, m. Priscilla, wid. of Thomas Pope, 1824. ORRIN, Brockton, son of 2d Andrew, m., 1841, Sarah Jane, d. of James C. Drake of Grafton, New Hampshire, and had Cordelia Frances, 1843; Henry Murray, 1847. PEABODY, son of 3d Ichabod, m. Lucy Turner, 1793, and had Deborah, 1794; Ichabod, 1797; Peabody, 1799; Turner Kimball, 1801; Coleman, 1803; Lucy, 1804; Hannah Rogers, 1806; Deborah, 1809; Jerusha, 1812. ROBERT came in the Ann, 1623, and m., 1628, Mary, d. of Richard Warren, by whom he had Benjamin, 1638; Joseph, 1639; Rebecca, m. William Harlow; Mary, m. Richard Foster and Jonathan Morey; Sarah, m. Samuel Rider; Elizabeth, m. Anthony Sprague; Lydia, 1647, m. James Barnaby and John Nelson; Mercy, 1651, m. John Ivey of Boston. ROBERT, son of 1st Joseph, m. Sarah, d. of Benjamin Bartlett, 1687, and Sarah, d. of Jacob Cooke, 1691, and had Hannah, 1691, m. Eleazer Churchill; Thomas, 1694, m., Abigail Finney; John, 1696; Sarah, 1699, m. John Finney; James, 1701; Joseph, 1704; Elizabeth, 1707, m. Thomas Sears; William, 1709, m. Sarah Foster; Ebenezer, 1710; Robert, 1713; Lemuel, 1715. ROBERT, son of above, m. Rebecca Wood, 1733, and had Robert, 1735; Ephraim, 1737; Rebecca, 1739, m. Ephraim Darling; Caleb, 1740; Isaac, 1742, m. Lois Harlow; Lazarus, 1744; Joshua, 1747; James, 1749; Susanna, 1750; Josiah, 1753, m. Martha Holmes. ROBERT, son of above, m. Jean Spooner, 1770. RUFUS, from N. H., m., about 1800, Roxanna, d. of Judah Bartlett, and had Rufus, Clark, Nancy C., and Thomas. SAMUEL, son of 1st Benjamin, m. Hannah, d. of William Peabodie, 1683, and had Benjamin, 1684; Samuel, 1688; Joseph, 1686,

m. Lydia Nelson; Ichabod; Lydia, m. Joseph Holmes; Sarah, m. Nathan
Thomas and Jedediah Bourne; Elizabeth, m.Ephraim Bradford. SAMUEL, son
of above, m. Hannah Churchill, 1725, and had Samuel, William, John, and
Judah. SAMUEL, son of above, m., in North Carolina, Betsey Moore, and
had Mary, m. Ephraim Finney; Betty, m. Amaziah Churchill; William; John,
and Joseph, 1762. He m. a 2d wife in Plymouth, Elizabeth Jackson, 1766,
and had Samuel, 1767; Nathaniel, 1769; Cornelius, 1771; Alexander; Truman,
and Stephen. SAMUEL, son of above, m. Zilpha Morton, 1794, and had Eliza,
m. Joseph Holmes. SAMUEL, son of 1st William, m. Joanna Taylor, 1783,
and had Samuel, Judah, and others, all of whom removed to Maine.
SAMUEL, son of 4th John, m. Olive Bartlett, 1801, and had Samuel, 1802;
Hiram, 1804, m. Euphany Holmes; Harvey Stetson, 1806; Fanny Hovey,
1809, m. Alfred Cole; Eliza Thomas, 1811, m. Alden S. Simmons; Bourne,
Frances, Ann, Harriet, and Abby. SAMUEL, m. Marcia Bartlett, 1825.
SAMUEL, m. Abigail Magoon, 1747. SAMUEL, son of 2d Joseph, m. Elizabeth,
d. of Isaac Lothrop, 1721, and had Lothrop, 1723; Elizabeth, 1725; Margaret,
1728; Hannah, 1731; Margaret, 1737. He m., 2d, Elizabeth (Lothrop), wid.
of Thomas Witherell, 1748, and had Samuel, 1749; Samuel, 1751; Elizabeth,
1753, m. Peleg Wadsworth; Lothrop, 1755; Hannah, 1757; Isaac, 1759.
SETH S., m. Ann C. Bartlett, 1836. SOLOMON, m. Clarissa Lindsey, 1817.
SOLOMON, m. Joanna Holmes, 1749, and had Solomon, 1751, m. Hannah
Rogers; James, 1751; Benjamin, 1755; Nathaniel, and Abigail. STEPHEN,
son of 1st Andrew, m. Polly Nye, 1799, and had Harriet, 1800; Stephen,
1801, m. Phebe Reed; Mary, 1804; Thomas Nye, 1806, m. Mercy Taylor
Wadsworth; Lorenzo, 1809; Lewis L.; Edward, m. Betsey Beal of Kingston;
and Harriet, m. Charles T. Holmes. STEPHEN, son of above, m. Phebe Reed,
and had Lorenzo; Elizabeth, m. Ezra Sampson Diman; and Mercy White,
m. James Macy. SYLVANUS, son of 4th Joseph, m. Martha Wait, 1743, and
had Wait, 1744; Elizabeth, 1749, m. Thomas Bartlett; Sylvanus, 1751; Mary,
1753, m. Joseph Bartlett; Abner, 1755, m. Anna Hovey; Martha, 1757;
Jerusha, 1759; Joseph, 1761, m. Anna Mary Witherell; Francis; Sophia, m.
Benjamin Drew; and Jesse, 1772, m. Betsey Drew and Mary Hovey. SYL-
VANUS, son of above, m. Sarah Loring, and had Bathsheba, Martha, Sylvanus,
Sarah, Isaac, Betsey, Alvin, Joseph, Loring, Ignatius; Jerusha, m. Nathaniel
Holmes; Isaiah, Lydia, Thomas, and Daniel. THOMAS, son of 3d Ebenezer,
m. Sarah Rider, 1778, and had Ebenezer, 1779; Thomas, 1781; Sarah,
1784; Ezra Rider, 1786; Seth, 1788; Sarah, 1791; Lemuel, 1794.
THOMAS, son of 1st William, m. Margaret James Drew, 1794, and had
Elizabeth, 1797; Thomas, 1799; William T., 1801; Margaret James, 1804, m.
George P. Fowler; Nathaniel, 1806; Mary, 1809, m. Nathaniel Brown; and
Sarah, 1812. THOMAS, son of 5th Joseph, m. Betty Bartlett, 1765, and had
Betsey, m. Solomon Churchill; Jerusha, Daniel, Thomas, and Deborah.
THOMAS, son of Rufus, m. Phebe Doten, 1823, and had Phebe T., 1835; and
Roxanna A., 1838. THOMAS BURGESS, son of 2d Ansel, m. Bethiah, d. of
John Churchill, and had Charles B., 1831; Mary A., 1836, m. Charles C.
Doten; Russell T., 1840, m. Emeline F., d. of William Savery; and Priscilla,
1845. He m. 2d, Rebecca W., d. of Avery Dean, 1850. THOMAS, son of 11th

Joseph, m. Lucinda Cornish, and had Thomas Mayo, who moved to Penn., and died, 1818. THOMAS, m. Ruth Rogers, 1798. TRUMAN, son of 3d Samuel, m. Experience Finney, 1798, and had William; Josiah, m. Fanny, d. of Ansel Robbins; Flavel, m. Mary Bartlett; Charles; Stephen; Truman, 1799; Azariah; Ann; Lucia, and Angeline. TRUMAN, son of above, m. Mercy Jennings, and had Charles T.; Mercy Ann, m. Alexander P. Atwood; Jane G., m. William Bartlett; Angeline, m. Isaac Dunham; and Caroline. URIAH, son of 3d Joseph, m., 1765, Lois (Doty) Washburn, and 2d, Susanna Cook, and had William, 1765; Lois, 1768, m. Samuel Spear; Peleg, 1771 m. Jane Adams and a Leach; Uriah, 1774; Frederick, 1779; Deborah, 1782, m. Elisha Barker; Clarissa, 1784, m. Aaron Nash and a Beckley; Nathaniel, 1786; Uriah, 1789, m. Olive Holmes; Susanna, m. a Clark and a Brigham; Isaac, and Polly. URIAH, son of above, m. Olive Holmes, 1823, and had Mahala, 1823, m. Stephen Holmes; Frederick William, 1826; George, 1827, m. Susanna H. Richardson; Ichabod, 1829; Thomas Holmes, 1831, m. Caroline E. Fuller; Robert Bruce, 1833, m. Elizabeth of San Francisco, where he lives; and Eugene, 1835. WILLIAM, son of 2d Samuel, m. Mary Bartlett, 1752, and had Hannah, 1752; William, 1754, moved to North Carolina; Samuel, 1757; Judah; Amasa, 1763; Mary; Sarah, 1768, m. Lemuel Drew; Thomas, 1770; Nathaniel, 1772. WILLIAM, son of 5th Benjamin, m. Rebecca Trask, 1761, and had William, 1761, m. Deborah Holmes; Zacheus, 1763, m. Hannah Thomas; Thomas, 1766; and Jabez, 1768. WILLIAM, son of 12th Joseph, m. Susan, d. of James Thacher, 1814, and had Susan Louisa, 1815, m. Charles O. Boutelle; Betsey Thacher, 1818; John, 1820, m. Hannah Willard of Cambridge; Eliza Ann, 1825; and Mary, 1827. WILLIAM, son of 1st Truman, m. Lucy Dyer Holmes, and had Lucia, Esther, and Mary. WILLIAM SAMPSON, son of 2d Amasa, m. Betsey, d. of Ezra Finney, and had Hannah Bourne, 1832, Elizabeth Holbrook, 1834; Abby James, 1835; Mary Eliza, 1838; Sarah Taylor, 1840; Leonice Sampson, 1842; William Bishop, 1845; and Charles Bourne, 1852. WILLIAM, son of 1st Judah, m. Abiah Parsons, 1809, and had William, m. Mary Phillips of Easton; Joann, m. Bartlett Holmes; Abby Washburn; Judah, m. Wealthy S., d. of Saml. Lewis; Rebecca, m. William Burgess; and Nathaniel Thomas, m. Hannah Billings of Boston. ZACHEUS, son of 4th Joseph, m. Margaret Barnes, 1753, and had George; Zacheus, 1765; Isaac; Maltiah, m. Patty Bartlett and a Cushman; Phebe, m. Daniel Perry of Sandwich; Betsey, m. Elias Nye; Joseph; and Mary, m. a Mayhew. ZACHEUS, son of above, m. Hannah, d. of Samuel Jackson, 1796, and had Sydney of Boston; Margaret, m. Winslow Warren; Dr. George of Boston; and Caroline, m. George Pratt of Boston. ZACHEUS, son of 11th Joseph, m. Sylvia Blackwell, and had Clark, 1825, m. Mary S. Knowles; Sarah, 1828, m. Paran Bartlett; Sylvia Ann, 1833; Zacheus, 1835; James, 1841, m. Sarah A. Briggs; and John F., m. Emma, d. of Hosea Bartlett. (See Bartlett Genealogy).

BARTON, JOHN, from Duxbury, m. Abigail Simmons, 1784.

BASSETT, JOHN, m. Hannah Holmes, 1787. THOMAS, m. Abby, d. of John Chase, and had, 1836, Angeline Stephens, m. George Bailey; Jesse Thomas, 1838; Avis, 1846; Samuel R., 1848; Edward E., 1852, m. Mary F. Swift; Harriet Elizabeth, 1854; George W., 1857; Albert, 1858. WILLIAM, m.

Abigail Lee, 1769. WILLIAM, m., in Leyden, 1611, Margaret Oldham, having previously m. Cecil Lecht, and came in the Fortune 1621, with wife, and had William; Nathaniel; Joseph, m. Martha, d. of Edmund Hobart of Hingham; Sarah, m. Peregrine White; Elizabeth, m. Thomas Burgess; and Jane, m. Thomas Gilbert of Taunton. In the division of cattle, 1627, his wife is called Elizabeth. He afterwards moved to Duxbury, and finally to Bridgewater.

BATES, BENJAMIN, Abington, son of 2d Edward, m. Betty, d. of Christopher Dyer of Weymouth not long after the year 1700, and had Christopher, and perhaps others. BENJAMIN, son of 4th Joseph, by wife Jemima, had William, 1813. BENJAMIN, son of 5th Joseph, m. Martha, d. of Ignatius Peirce, about 1830, and had Benjamin F., m. Adeline, d. of Nathan King; Ebenezer P., 1841; Maria, 1846; Betsey, m. Arvin M. Bancroft; Martha A., m. Thomas Collingwood and Thomas Everett Cornish; and Joseph N., 1856. BENJAMIN F., son of above, m. as above, 1857, and had Charles F., 1862. CHARLES, East Bridgewater, son of 1st Christopher, m. Huldah Noyes, and had Mary, Elizabeth, Abby, and another. CLEMENT came from Hertfordshire, England, 1635, according to the certificate of emigration, at the age of 40, a passenger in the Elizabeth, William Stagg, master, from London, with his wife Ann, and five children. James, 14 years of age; Clement, 12; Rachel, 8; Joseph, 5; and Benjamin, 2, and settled in Hingham. Family records and tradition state that he died Sept. 17, 1671, at the age of 81 years, and that Edward of Weymouth, George of Boston, and James of Dorchester were his brothers. CLEMENT, son of 2d Joseph, lived in that part of Scituate now Hanover, and m., 1730, Agatha Merritt, by whom he had Clement, 1730; James, 1732; Seth, 1735; Thomas; Joshua; Gamaliel, 1745; Paul, 1747; Nabby, 1750, m. John Chapman; Betsey, and Clement, baptized, 1755. CLEMENT, Hanover. son of above, m. Rebecca Stetson, 1785, and had Thomas M., 1787; Clement, Hira, Joshua; Lucy, m. Benjamin Stetson; Nabby, m. Thomas Damon, and Priscilla, m. Charles Leach. CLEMENT, son of above, moved to Plymouth in 1809, and in 1814, m. Irene Sanger, d. of Thomas Burgess, by whom he had Ruby, 1814, m. George A. Drew; Ozen, 1816, and Hira, 1819. He m., 2d, Betsey, sister of 1st wife, 1824, and had Elizabeth, 1826, m. Samuel R. Winslow; Augusta, 1831, m. Nathaniel Doten of Boston; Charles C., 1835; and Lucretia, 1837, m. Branch G. Blackmer. COMFORT, Pembroke, a descendant from 1st Clement, through his son Joseph and grandson Caleb, m. Millicent Carver of Marshfield, and had Comfort, and perhaps others. COMFORT, Pembroke, son of above, had Comfort, Caleb, and Spencer. COMFORT, Pembroke, son of above, had Joseph, m. Sarah, d. of John B. Barstow; Caleb; Edward, m. a Howland; Sylvanus, m. a Magoon; and a d. m. a Bishop. COMFORT, son of above, moved to Plymouth and m., 1814, Betsey, d. of Daniel Pierce of Pembroke, by whom he had Daniel Pierce, 1817, m. Lydia A., d. of Daniel Rider of Plymouth, and Elizabeth Mulligan of Blackstone; Elizabeth Ann, 1821, m. Samuel Harmon Davie; Gustavus Davie, 1823; George Henry, 1825, m. Hannah Fettyplace of Blackstone, and Mary A. Boyden of same; Abigail Whittemore, 1827, m. Edwin Lucas; Clarinda Maria, 1829, m. Benjamin Swift; Adoniram Judson, 1831; Francis, 1834, m. Nancy Pierce of Middleboro'; Andrew, 1837; Mary

Washington, 1853, m.W. W. Stockwell of Freetown. CHRISTOPHER, Bridgewater, son of 1st Benjamin, m. Mary, d. of John Brown, and had Christopher, Moses; Jacob, m. Lucy Dyer; Daniel, m. Jane Reed; Charles, m. Huldah Noyes; Mary, Anna; and Nahum, m. Julia A. Leavitt of East Bridgewater. CHRISTOPHER, Bridgewater, son of above, m. Polly Howland, and had James, George, Mary, Laurany, Harriet, William, Elbridge. DANIEL, son of 1st Christopher, m. Jane Reed, and had Daniel, Mary, and Eliza. DAVID, probably a descendant from 1st Clement, m. in Plymouth, about 1710, a wife Abigail, and had Remember, 1711; David, 1713; Joseph, 1715; Mary, 1717; Abigail, 1719; Lydia, 1722; and Ann, 1724. DAVID, son of 3d Joseph, m., 1774, Thankful (Cobb), wid. of John Savery of Middleboro', and had Hannah, m. Jonathan Harvey; Susan, m. Stephen Paine, and Joshua Torrey; and Mercy, m. George Simmons. DAVID, son of 4th Joseph, m. Lydia Atwood and Margaret Atwood, and had Sylvia E., m. Preston Manter. EDWARD, Weymouth, 1639, by wife Susan, had Prudence, 1639; Increase, 1641, and Edward. EDWARD, Weymouth, son of above, by wife Elizabeth had Susanna, 1680; Edward, 1683; John, 1687; Ebenezer, Benjamin, Eleazer, and Mary, 1697. EDWARD, Abington, son of above, m. Silence Richards about 1713, and had Edward, Silence, Daniel, Peter, and Samuel. GAMALIEL, Hanover, son of 2d Clement, m. Mary Carver of Pembroke, 1771, and had Lydia, 1772; Gamaliel, 1774; Mary P., 1776; Calvin, 1777; Hannah, 1779, m. Levi Fish; James, 1781; John Blaney, 1783; Rebecca, 1785; Deborah, 1787; Deborah again, 1789, m. Jacob Capron of Attleboro; Reuben, 1790; Betsey, 1792; Rufus, 1794; Ezekiel, 1795, and Abigail, 1797. GEORGE H. of Farmington, Me., m. Mary Holbrook, d. of Jacob Covington, 1844. GUSTAVUS DAVIS, son of 3d Comfort, m. Nancy D., d. of Josiah Finney, and had Josiah F., 1851; Lizzie Allen, 1853; Nancy D., 1865; Charles H., m. Clara P. King, and Angeline, 1868. HIRA, son of 4th Clement, m. Emily F., d. of Thomas Goodwin, 1847, and had Charles C., 1851, and Carrie Goodwin, 1856, m. Harvey Bartlett. HORACE W., son of 2d Moses, m. Fanny Gibbs, d. of Nathaniel Goodwin, 1862, and had Alice, 1865, and Sturgis, 1868. JACOB, East Bridgewater, son of 1st Christopher, m. Lucy Dyer, and had Jacob and Samuel. JAMES, son of 2d Christopher, m. Betsey J. Gurney of Boston, and had James C., m. Hattie, d. of Benjamin Gooding, and Clarissa, m. Alpheus K. Harmon. JOHN, m. Hannah S., d. of John Faunce, 1827, and was a descendant from 1st Clement, through three Josephs and two Benjamins. JOHN of Hanover, m. Hannah Sylvester, 1764. JOHN from Rochester, m. Marcia E. Southworth, 1844, and had Marcia S., m. Henry C. Rogers. JOHN BLANEY, son of Gamaliel, moved to Plymouth from Hanover, and m., 1807, Mary (Sylvester) Taylor, wid. of Edward Taylor, by whom he had Abby Washburn, 1808. JONATHAN, son of 4th Joseph, m. Fear Chubbuck, and had Joseph N., 1832; Harriet, 1838; Stephen, 1840. JOSEPH, Hingham, son of 1st Clement, m., 1659, Esther Hilliard, and had Joseph, Caleb, Hannah, Joshua, Bathsheba, Clement, Eleazer, and perhaps others. JOSEPH, Hingham, son of above, according to Savage, m., 1684, Mary, d. of Samuel Lincoln; according to Barry, by whom the wife was unknown, he had Ruth, 1695, m. Dea. Joseph Josslynn; Joseph, 1697; Mercy, 1699; Mary, 1701; Solomon,

1702; Amos, 1705; Clement, 1707; Rachel, 1710, m. Stephen Torrey. In this list all the children were born more than eleven years after marriage and after his removal to Scituate. It is probable therefore that he had other children in Hingham not recorded. JOSEPH, son of 1st David, m. Elizabeth Gibbs, 1741, and had Elizabeth, 1742; Joann, 1743; David, 1745; Samuel, 1749; Lydia, 1752, and Joseph. JOSEPH, son of above, m. Mehitabel Wright, 1776; and, 2d, Rebecca Harlow, 1783, by whom he had Joseph, Rebecca, Benjamin; Betsey, m. Tisdale Fuller; Patience, m. Abijah Lincoln; David; Jonathan, m. Fear Chubbuck, and Phebe, m. Wm. Dennis of Sandwich. JOSEPH, son of above, m. Lucy Douglass, 1807, and had Benjamin; Joseph; Lucy, m. Lewis King; Lydia, m. John Sturtevant, and Cynthia, m. George Phillips. MOSES, Bridgewater, son of 1st Christopher, m. Deborah Dyer, 1808, and had Mehitabel, 1809; Christopher, 1813; Moses, 1815; Deborah, 1819; Nahum, 1822; Samuel, 1826; Nahum again, 1828. MOSES, Plymouth and Bridgewater, son of above, m. Eliza Johnson, and had Horace W., m. Fanny Gibbs Goodwin; and Alice Gertrude, m. Frank Smith of East Bridgewater. NAHUM, son of 1st Christopher, m. Julia A. Leavitt of East Bridgewater, and had George G., 1858. OZEN, son of 4th Clement, m. Nancy Paty, d. of Zacheus Barnes, 1840, and had Ozen, 1841. He m., 2d, Abbie H., d. of Sylvanus Churchill, 1871. SAMUEL, brother of 1st David, m. Margaret Churchill, 1706, and had Thomas, 1709; Samuel, 1713; John, 1716; Barnabas, 1719; Job, 1721. STEPHEN, son of Jonathan, m. Lucinda Nye Burgess, 1864, and had Stephen H., 1864; Charles L., 1865; Lizzie E. F., 1867, and Edgar W., 1869. THOMAS, son of Samuel, m. Lydia, d. of Thomas Savery, 1737, and had Sarah, 1737, and probably Thomas, who m. Susanna, d. of Benjamin Cornish.

BATTLES, ASA, Bridgewater, son of 3d John, m., 1788, Mary, d. of John Pratt, and had Polly, 1788, m. Nathan Cleaveland; Asa, 1790, m. Polly Chesman, John, 1792, m. Millicent Porter; Betsey, 1794, m. Palmer Branch; William, 1796, Susanna, 1798, m. Thomas Reynolds; Amelia, 1800; Isabella, and Hannah. BENJAMIN, son of Joshua, m., 1800, Zilpha Wadsworth. BRADFORD LEWIS, son of 3d John, m., 1835, Nancy, d. of Ichabod Harlow, and had Jane White, 1836. CALEB, son of Joshua, m., 1797, Jane Rider, and had Caleb, 1798. He m., 2d, Lucy Rider, 1804, and had Winslow, 1808; Otis, 1810, m. Sally Burt; Ellis, 1812, m. Olive B. Lucas. CALEB, son of above, m., 1820, Rebecca Holmes Nickerson, and had Caleb, William L.; Lucy Jane, m. Lionel Churchill, and perhaps others. JOHN, Dedham, son of Thomas, m., 1678, Hannah Holbrook, and had Hannah, 1680; Mary, 1684; John, 1689; Ebenezer, 1692. JOHN, son of above, removed to Plymouth, and by wife Martha had Jonathan, 1718; Martha, 1720; John, 1721; Edward, 1723; Mary, 1726; Bathsheba, 1728; Timothy, 1730; Rebecca, 1732; Samuel, 1734; and Joshua. JOHN, Bridgewater, son of above, m. Hannah, d. of Edward Curtis, and had John; Jonathan, m. Hannah Porter; Samuel, Asa, Uriah, Edward, Curtis, Hannah, Rebecca, and Susanna. JOHN, son of 1st Samuel, m. Elizabeth, d. of Lemuel Cobb, and had John. He m., 2d, 1807, Lydia Rickard, and had Elizabeth, m. Isaac Swift and James Barnes; and Bradford Lewis. JOHN, son of above, m., 1828, Clarissa Spear, and had Harriet, m.

Timothy E. Gay. He m., 2d, Rebecca Fuller of Kingston, and had John and Angeline. JOSHUA, son of 2d John, m., 1758, Experience Cornish, and had Martha, 1758; Experience, 1760; Joshua, 1762; Timothy, 1764; Benjamin, and Caleb. SAMUEL, son of 2d John, m., 1762, Alice, d. of Benjamin Barnes, and had Elizabeth, 1763, m. John Stephens; Polly, 1765, m. Joseph Holmes; Samuel, m. Deborah Atwood; Sarah, m. John Gray of Kingston; Experience, m. George Perkins; and John. SAMUEL, m. 1819, Lydia Bennett Holmes. SAMUEL, Bridgewater, son of 3d John, m., 1786, Dorothy, d. of Christopher Dyer, and had Sybel, 1786, m. Ruel Fobes; Lucinda, 1788, m. Luke Packard; Daniel Dyer, 1790; David, 1792, m. Jerusha E., d. of Jedediah Adams of Quincy; Dorothy, 1796, m. Ansel Perkins; Samuel, 1798; Jason Dyer, 1800; Nahum, 1802, m. Polly, d. of Joseph Brett; Mary Dyer, 1806; Anson, 1810, m. Sophia, d. of Ephraim Littlefield of York, Maine; Mary Dyer, 1814. THOMAS Battele, Battle, or Battles, came, as is supposed, from France, and settled in Dedham, 1642. He m., 1648, Mary, d. of Joshua Fisher, and had Mary, 1650, m. John Bryant; John, 1653; Sarah, 1654, m. Silas Titus; Jonathan, 1658, and Martha. (See Kingman's History of North Bridgewater).

BAXTER, JAMES, from Boston, born 1791, m. Mary Dunham of Boston, and had James, 1815; Josiah Dunham, 1818; Mary S., 1825; Abner Morton, 1823; Ann Elizabeth, 1829; Lydia Keyes, 1832, m. William S. Scott, and Charles Homer, 1835. JOSIAH DUNHAM, son of above, m., 1840, Elizabeth B., d. of Sylvanus Rogers, and had J. Francis, m. Eliza C., d. of Barnabas H. Holmes.

BEALE, ASA, m., 1720, Rhoda Lathle, and had Susanna, 1723, m. Thomas Pattison; Margaret, 1725; Rhoda, 1727, m. Daniel Peake; Sarah, 1731, m. Martin Wright; Mary, 1733; John, 1735; Elizabeth, 1737, m. James Polden; Susanna, 1739; Margaret, 1740, m. Francis Crapo of Rochester. WILLIAM came in the Fortune, 1621, and died or removed before 1627.

BEARSE, CALVIN, by wife Maria had Calvin, 1830; Maria T., 1833; Margaret, 1837. ICHABOD, by wife Sally had Sarah Ann, 1833; Lucy James, 1836, m. Nathaniel Sydney Freeman; George Harlow, and Charlotte R., 1840. JOHN from Barnstable, son of a Joseph, and grandson of Austin, who came in the Confidence 1638, m., 1720, Sarah Holmes. THOMAS, brother of Ichabod, m. Pamelia, d. of Jacob Howland, and had Pamelia, 1826; Simeon, 1827; Lydia, 1830; Hannah, 1833; Thomas, 1835; Jacob, 1838.

BECK, WILLIAM, m., 1771, Mary Thomas.

BELCHER, JONATHAN, by wife Mary had Phebe, and Jonathan, 1773.

BELL, DANIEL, from Boston, m., 1779, Sarah Rider. GEORGE M., from Boston, m., 1835, Jane C. Dickson.

BEMIS, JOSIAH, m. a wife Joanna, and had Joanna, 1782.

BENIAS, FRANCIS, and Mary Thomas, Indians, published 1743.

BENSON, DAVID, Bridgewater, son of Jonathan m., 1780, Charity, d. of Seth Hayward, and had Tabitha, 1781, m. William Fuller of Bridgewater; Eunice, 1782, m. Abner Keith; Charity, 1784, m. Ebenezer Cushman of Kingston; Sarah, 1786, m. James Pool, Jr.; David, 1788, m. Maria Swift of Sandwich; Seth, 1790; Bethiah, 1793, m. Seth Thompson of Bridgewater; Kesiah, 1796, m. John Atwood Jackson of Middleboro' and Tobias Ricker;

Polly, 1798; Millicent, m. Ebenezer Chamberlin; and Martin. JOHN, Hingham, born 1608, came from Caversham, England, 1638, with wife Mary, and children John and Mary, both infants, and settled in Hingham. JOHN, Hull, son of above, had probably John, and Joseph, who m. 1st, a Prince, 2d, Mary Curtis of Scituate, 3d, Alice, d. of Nathan Pickels of Scituate. JOHN, Bridgewater, son of above, m., 1710, Elizabeth, d. of Jonathan Washburn, and had Susanna, m. Jonathan Cushman; Benjamin, m. Kesiah, d. of Amos Snell; Elizabeth, Mary; Hannah, m. James Dunbar, Jr.; and Jonathan. JOHN, Rochester, by wife Elizabeth, had Mary, 1689; Sarah, 1690; Ebenezer, 1693; John, 1696; Joseph and Benjamin, twins, 1697; Bennett, 1698; Martha, 1703; Joshua and Caleb, twins, 1705; Samuel, 1707. JOHN, Newport, perhaps son of above, thought by descendants to have been an immigrant, m., 1714, Anna, d. of William Collins, and had John, m., 1735, Ann Crocum or Slocum, and William, bap. 1718 (See published genealogy of his family). JONATHAN, Bridgewater, son of 3d John, m., 1740, Martha, d. of Amos Snell, and had John, 1742, m. Sarah Williams; Eunice, 1744, m. John Harden; Mary, 1745, m. Benjamin Hayward, Jr.; Martha, 1749, m. Elisha Waterman of Halifax; Lois, 1751, m. Cornelius Washburn, Jr.; Jonathan, 1752; Ebenezer, 1755, m. Silence, d. of Nehemiah Packard, and widow of Seth Leonard; David, 1756; Jonah, 1759, m. Martha Thompson of Halifax. JOSHUA, m., 1746, Sarah Shurtleff of Middleboro'. MARTIN, son of David, m., 1824, Phebe, d. of Nehemiah Leonard of Bridgewater, and had Phebe, 1825, m. Lemuel Bumpus; Maria, 1827, m. Solomon Sampson; Martin Francis, 1834, m. Lydia, d. of Thomas Atwood; Emily W., 1837, m. Martin Brewster; Nehemiah, 1842, m. Mary Ellen, d. of Eleazer H. Barnes. SETH, son of David, m., 1824, Bathsheba, d. of Elias Thomas, and had Seth, 1824, m. Mary Jane, d. of Nathaniel S. Barrows; Bathsheba Thomas, 1825, m. Lewis Tinkham of Middleboro'; George, 1828, m. Caroline Brown; Lydia West, 1829, m. Albert Benson; Elias Thomas, 1832, m. Helen Cole and Mary, d. of Levi Robbins; Ellis, 1833, m. Margaret, d. of Philip Williams; Lucinda Thomas, 1837, m. Stephen P. Brown.

BENT, EXPERIENCE, m. Abigail Sampson, 1703.

BERRY, or BARRY, TIMOTHY, came to Plymouth from Beverly and changed his name to Barry. He m. Maria Allen, and had Maria, 1826, m. Larned S. B. Barrows; Antoinette L., 1829, m. Franklin B. Holmes; William T., 1833, m. Fanny Federhen of Boston; Mary T., 1836, m. John M. Mayo of Lawrence; Timothy, 1836; and Harriet S., 1843.

BESSE, ANDREW, of Wareham, m. Eunice, d. of Barnaby Holmes of Plymouth, 1825. ANTHONY, came from England 1635, settled in Sandwich, 1637, and had by wife Jane, Ann; Mary, m. Benjamin Curtis; Elizabeth, Nehemiah, and David, 1649. BENJAMIN, m. Sarah Foster, 1823. BENJAMIN, by wife Martha, had Elizabeth, 1726. He was probably brother of David. DAVID, perhaps grandson of David, son of Anthony by wife Mary, had Samuel, 1726; Thankful, 1727; Nehemiah, 1729. EBENEZER of Wareham, m. Betsy Doty, 1776. JOSHUA, of Wareham, m. Mercy Morton, 1782.

BEST, JOSEPH, m. Elizabeth Waterman, 1759.

BICKNELL, ISAAC T., of New York, m. Abigail H. Bradford, 1824.

BILLINGTON, FRANCIS, son of John, came with his father in the Mayflower, 1620, and m. Christian (Penn) Eaton, widow of Francis Eaton, 1634, by whom he had Martha, m. Samuel Eaton; Elizabeth, m. a Patte of Providence; Rebecca, 1647; Mary, m. Samuel Sabin of Rehoboth; Isaac; Mercy, m. John Martin; Desire, Joseph, and Francis. FRANCIS, son of above, m. Abigail, d. of Eleazer Churchill, and had Sarah, 1702; Sukey, 1704; Francis, 1708; Jemima, 1710; Content, 1712, m. Francis Merrifield; Abigail, 1716; and Joseph, 1718. ICHABOD, with wife Polly, owned an estate in Plymouth, 1774. ISAAC, son of 1st Francis, m. Hannah, daughter of James Glass, and had a son Seth. JOHN, came in the Mayflower, 1620, with wife Eleanor and two children, Francis and John. The son of John died young, the father was hanged, 1630, for the murder of John Newcomen, and the widow married Gregory Armstrong, 1638.

BISBEE, GIDEON, m., 1808, Mary Williams Cuffs. JOSIAH, from Pembroke, m., 1769, Ruth Sherman. REUBEN, from Plympton, m., 1749, Lydia Faunce. SYLVANUS, from Rochester, m., 1800, Lydia Jackson. ZEBULON, from Kingston, m., 1827, Sally Nichols.

BISHOP, JAMES, Duxbury and Pembroke, by wife Mary had John, Hudson, James; Ebenezer, m. Amy Stetson, 1710; Abigail, m. James Bonney; Mary, m. a Lathley; Elizabeth, m. a Bonney; and Hannah m. a Simmons. JOHN, Pembroke, son of above, d. 1756, leaving John; Desire, m. a Witherell; Dorothy, m. a Ramsden; Josiah; a d. who m. a Weston, and a d. who m. a Rickard. JOHN, Middleboro', d. about 1817, leaving a widow, Hannah, and children, Kinney, Joshua, Alvin, John, Elizabeth, m. a Robertson, and Orpy, m. a Fuller. JOHN, Plymouth, came a young man from Bristol, England, and m., 1767, Abigail, d. of Ebenezer Holmes, by whom he had Susanna, 1768, m. Benjamin Crandon; Mary, 1772; Abigail, 1774; Mary again, twin, 1774; John, 1778; George, 1787; Henry, 1789; William, 1792. JOHN, son of above, m. 1799, Betsey, d. of Eliphalet Holbrook, and had Abby, 1801, m. James E. Leonard and Henry Mills. JONATHAN, m. Mary Woolston, or Woolson, and had Jonathan, 1745; Presbry, 1746; Dorcas, 1749; Ebenezer, 1754; Mary, 1757. JOSIAH, Pembroke, son of 1st John, died about 1749, leaving a wid. Sarah, and children, Joshua, Mary, Sarah, and Keturah, m. James Bonney. WILLIAM, son of 3d John, m. Sarah T., d. of Amasa Bartlett, 1821, and had William, 1822, m. Catherine B., d. of Seth Morton.

BLACK, JOHN, about 1825, by wife Sarah, had John.

BLACKMER, BRANCH, son of 2d John, m. Sarah Waite, 1756, and had Mary, 1758; William, 1760, m. Mary Bly; John, 1763; Sarah, 1764, m. James Harlow; Mary and Mercy, twins, 1767; Betty, 1769, m. Joseph Johnson; Richard, 1772; Jerusha, m. Seth Holmes; Branch and Ivory, twins, 1775. BRANCH, son of 4th John, m. Phebe Bartlett, and had Almira; Ivory, m. Maria F. Manter; Maltiah B., m. Zervia S. Manter; Branch Eliot, m. Lucretia Bates; Triphosa, m. Alonzo Warren; James W., m. Lydia Sherman; Alonzo L., m. Edith P. Sampson; and Betsey Nye, m. Benjamin F. Hodges. EZRA HOVEY, son of 4th John, m. Henrietta Bartlett, 1825, and had William B., 1827, m. Anna S. Hopkins; Sally C., 1831, m. Israel Clark; and Israel C.,

1840, m. Susan T. Bartlett and Marietta M. Griswold. JOHN, probably son of William, m. Anna, d. of John Branch, and had John, Stephen, and William. JOHN, son of above, m. Sarah Holmes, 1732, and had Branch, 1733; John, 1734; Sarah, 1736, m. John Dillingham; John, 1738; Susanna, 1740, m. Nathaniel Tupper; Mercy, 1742, Jerusha, 1745, m. Nathaniel Barnes; Betty, 1746, m. Jonathan Harlow; Experience, 1750, m. Joseph Bramhall. JOHN, son of above, m. Esther Bartlett, 1819, and had Laurette, 1821, m. Truman Holmes; Esther, 1823, m. Marston Holmes; Sarah H., 1827, m. Elias F. Fisher; John, 1829; Abigail S., 1831, m. Rev. D. H. Babcock; Sydney, 1841, m. Mercy A. Bartlett; and George A., 1839. He m. a second wife, Mary D. Main, 1867. JOHN, son of 1st Branch, m. Sarah Hovey, 1789, and had Ivory, 1790, m. Eliza Price of Baltimore; Ezra Hovey, 1793; John, 1797; Branch, 1799; Dominicus, 1802; Ruth Clark, 1806, m. Branch B. Holmes. PETER, of Rochester, son of William, had Joseph, Jane, and John. RICHARD, son of 1st Branch, m. Nancy Ellis, 1801, and had Sally, 1801, m. Ezra Clark; Nancy, 1804, m. Seth Holmes; and George Ellis, 1806, m. Rebecca Bartlett. WILLIAM, came from England to Scituate, 1665, m., 1666, Elizabeth Banks, and had Peter, 1667; John, 1669, both of whom moved to Rochester; Phebe, 1672, m. Ebenezer Holmes; and William, 1675.

BLANCH, John, m., 1778, Rebecca Morton.

BLISH, TIMOTHY, m., 1835, Lucia Ann Goodwin.

BLISS, ALEXANDER, from Boston, m. Elizabeth, d. of William Davis, 1825.

BLOSSOM, THOMAS, came over 1629, and died 1633, leaving children; Peter, m. Sarah Bodfish of Barnstable; Thomas, and others. THOMAS, son of above, m., 1645, Sarah, d. of Thomas Ewer of Charlestown, and had Sarah, and Thomas.

BOARDMAN, THOMAS, by wife Lucy had Thomas, and Elizabeth, born in London, and after arrival, about 1634, had Susanna, and Thankful. He m., 2d, Elizabeth, wid. of John Cole, and d. of Samuel Rider.

BONHAM or BONUM, GEORGE, appeared early in Plymouth, and m., 1644, Sarah, d. of George Morton. His children were Ruth, m. Robert Barrow; Patience, m. Richard Willis; Sarah, 1653; and George. GEORGE, son of above, m., 1683, Elizabeth, d. of Samuel Jenney, and had Samuel, 1686; Ruth, 1688; Elizabeth, 1689; Ann, 1690; Sarah, 1693; Lydia, 1696; Ebenezer, 1699; Susanna, 1700.

BONNEY, JOSEPH, m. Mercy Phillips, 1807.

BOSWORTH, BENJAMIN, came from England in 1634, and settled in Hingham, where he probably had Benjamin, and Nathaniel. BENJAMIN, Hull, son of above, m., 1666, Hannah, d. of Nathaniel Morton of Plymouth, and had Hannah, 1669, and probably Benjamin. He m., 2d, 1671, Beatrice, wid. of Abraham Josselynn, and probably had David, and Hezekiah. BENJAMIN, probably son of above, had by wife Joanna, Nathaniel, 1709; and Joanna, 1714. DAVID, probably brother of above, m. Mercy Sturtevant, 1698, and had David, 1699; Jonathan, 1701; Nehemiah, 1702; Hannah, 1705. HEZEKIAH, brother of above, m. Bethiah Bates, 1703, and had Hannah, 1703; Hezekiah, 1716. NATHANIEL, Hull, son of 1st Benjamin, m., 1670, Elizabeth,

d. of Nathaniel Morton of Plymouth, and had Nathaniel, 1673; Elizabeth, 1676; John, 1678; Samuel, 1680; Mary, 1682; Ephraim, 1684; Lemuel, 1686; Joseph, 1689; Bridget, 1691; Jeremiah, 1693. NATHANIEL, son of 3d Benjamin, m. Lydia Sampson, 1735. ORIN came from Halifax to Plymouth, and m., 1831, Jane Taylor Morton, and had Jane Taylor, 1831; and Orin Waterman, 1835. He m., 2d, Betsey B., d. of Alanson Hathaway, 1837, and had Hannah Elizabeth, 1838.

BOULT, CHARLES, m. Lydia Curtis, and had Lydia, 1757, m. Nathaniel Atwood of Plympton; Elizabeth, 1759. WILLIAM, m., 1768, Joanna Wood.

BOUTELLE, CALEB, from Lexington, m., 1809, Anna, d. of Nathaniel Goodwin.

BOURNE, JAMES, m., 1808, Cynthia Bartlett.

BOWDOIN, WILLIAM, from Boston, m., 1739, Phebe Murdock.

BOWEN, JOHN, at Plymouth, 1651.

BOWER or BOWERS, GEORGE, a purchaser of lands in Plymouth, 1639. He removed to Cambridge in the same year. By wife Barbara, he had John, and Matthew, born in England, and perhaps others. He m., 2d, 1649, Elizabeth Worthington, and had Jerathmael, 1650; Benanuel; Patience, and Silence. JOHN, son of above, was schoolmaster in Plymouth, 1650.

BOWLAND, MICHAEL, m., 1791, Mercy Lemote.

BOYLSTON, BENJAMIN, m., 1769, Mercy Bartlett, and had Mary, 1770, m. Lot Harlow; Joseph, 1772, m. Polly Doten; Nancy, 1775, m. William Bradford.

BRACE, THOMAS, m., 1741, Eliza Barnes.

BRADFORD, ABNER, Kingston, son of 1st Israel, m., 1733, Susanna Porter, and had Elijah, 1735, m. Sarah Jones; Lewis, 1737; Zenas, 1739; Mary, 1742; Abigail, 1744; Israel, 1748; Lydia, 1749; Hannah, 1751; Elisha, 1753; Lucy, 1755; Peggy, 1757, m. Calvin Ripley; Levi, 1759, m. Polly Ripley. ALDEN, Boston, son of 2d Gamaliel, m., 1795, Margaret, d. of Thomas Stephenson, and had Margaret Boice, 1796, m. William H. Eliot; William John Alden, 1797; Lucy Ann, 1800, m. Henry Dwight; Thomas Gamaliel, 1802; Duncan, 1804, m. Charlotte Jacques; Isabella Thomas, 1806; Sarah, 1808; John Robinson, 1813. ANDREW, Duxbury, son of 1st Gamaliel, m., 1775, Mary Turner of Scituate, and had James Harvey, 1778, m. Sally Roulston of Keene, N. H. BARTLETT, son of 1st James, m. Lucy, d. of Samuel Bradford, and had Lucy Bartlett, m. Caleb Rider; Lewis G., m. Louisa Allen; Bartlett; Eveline, m. Benjamin F. Field; and James. BENJAMIN, Kingston, son of 1st Israel, m. Zeresh, d. of Elisha Stetson, and had Thomas, 1733; Michael, 1735; Perez, 1736; Lydia, 1739; Benjamin, 1742; Mary, 1745; Lemuel, 1747; Lydia, 1749, m. Levi Holmes. BENJAMIN WILLIS, Salem, son of 2d Nathaniel, m., 1820, Hannah Cloutman, and had Benjamin Willis; Hannah E. CALVIN, Plympton, son of 1st Gideon, m., 1778, Lucy, d. of Nathaniel Pratt, and had Jane, 1779, m. Hezekiah Cole of Carver; Mary, 1781; Lucy, 1783, m. Josiah Fuller of Kingston; Calvin, 1785, m. Mary Hatch; Luther, 1787, m. Ruth Holmes and Mary Standish; Sarah, 1789, m. John Faunce; Phebe, 1792; Joseph Warren, 1795; Lydia, 1797. CARPENTER, Friendship, Maine, son of Elisha, m., 1761, Mary,

d. of David Gay of Stoughton, and had Chloe, 1762, Azubah, 1765, m. Enoch Wentworth; Hannah, 1767, m. Zenas Cook and William Jameson; William, 1770, m. Sarah Sweetland; Mary Gay, 1772, m. Levi Morse; Chloe, 1776, m. Thomas Knight and Thomas Palmer; Emily, 1781. CHANDLER, Turner, Maine, son of 1st Ezekiel, m., 1784, Sarah French, and had Benjamin, 1784, m. Patty Bisbee of East Bridgewater; Laurana, 1786; Seth, 1788, m. Lydia Rickard; Sarah, 1790, m. Justus Conant; Betsey, 1792; Celia, 1793; Olive, 1796, m. Luther Bailey; Laura, 1798, m. Elisha Stetson; Roxa, 1800; Chandler, 1806, m. Roxana Freeman; Laurana, 1810, m. Horace Carey. CHARLES, son of 1st Josiah, m., 1788, Priscilla Morton, and had Zephaniah; Charles; David; and Solomon. CONSIDER, Kingston, son of 1st James, m., 1807, Betsey Wilder of Middleboro', and had Alexander, 1808; Elizabeth Wilder, 1812, m. Thomas S. Cushman; Louisa, 1815, m. Cassander Williams. CORNELIUS, Friendship, son of Joshua, m., 1760, Prudence Davis, and had Hannah, 1761, m. Howland Rogers; Elsie, 1762, m. James Cook; Joshua, 1764, m. Polly Gray; Betsey, 1765, m. Hugh Spear; Josephus, 1768, m. Hannah Morton; Sarah, 1770, m. Jesse Thomas; Sylvia, 1772; Mehitabel, 1773; Prudence, 1776, m. Simeon DeMorse; Winslow, 1777, m. Mary Penny; Lydia, 1780, m. John DeMorse; Frederick, 1782, m. Mary Geyer; James, 1784, m. Lavina Hickman. DAVID, Kingston, son of 4th William, m., 1714, Elizabeth, d. of John Finney, and had Nathaniel, 1715; Jonathan, 1717; Lydia, 1719, m. Elkanah Cushman and Lazarus LeBaron; Nathan, 1722; Lemuel, 1727. DAVID, son of 2d Lemuel, m., 1819, Betsey Briggs, and had David Lewis, 1821; Betsey, 1822; Cornelius, 1825, m. Hannah J. Ripley, and Mary P. Delano; Desire Harlow, 1826, m. Frederick Leland; Lemuel, 1828, m. Elizabeth B. Whiting; Nathaniel, 1830; Andrew Jackson, 1832; Lydia Holmes; Allen, 1837, m. Lydia G. Nye, Harriet, 1841; Mary Briggs, 1842, m. W. W. Waterman. He m., 2d, Louisa F. Bartlett, 1845. DAVID, Bristol, son of 2d Gershom, m. Mary Church and Susan Jarvis, and had Priscilla, 1752, m. Sylvester Child; Elizabeth, m. Nathaniel Fales; Daniel, 1778, m. Sarah Reynolds; Leonard Jarvis, 1779, m. Sarah Turner; and Samuel, m. Elizabeth Reynolds. EDWARD WINSLOW, son of 2d Joseph, m., 1827, Mary Dillard, and had Nathaniel, 1831; Mary Winslow, 1832; Catherine E., 1834, m. Charles Thomas; Nathaniel B., 1837, Josephine, 1839; Anna E., 1841; Hannah B., 1843; Emma F., 1846; Alice M., 1848; Edward Winslow, 1850. He m., 2d, Betsey Courtney (Dillard) Kempton. ELIPHALET, Duxbury, son of 7th William, m., 1751, Hannah Prince, and had Hannah, 1752, m. Benjamin Freeman; Lydia, 1754, m. Samuel Bradford; Eunice, m. Uriah Wadsworth. He m., 2d, 1758, Hannah Oldham, and had Lucy, 1758, m. Zachariah Sylvester; Abigail, 1759, m. Bisbee Chandler; William, 1761, m. Lucy Sampson; Zadock, 1765, m. Lucy Gray; Deborah, 1767, m. Freeman Loring; Mary, 1773. ELISHA, Duxbury, son of 1st Joseph, m. Hannah, d. of James Cole. He m., 2d, 1718, Bathsheba Le Brock and had Hannah, 1719, m. Joshua Bradford; Joseph, 1721; Sylvanus, 1723; Nehemiah, 1724; Laurana, 1726, m. Elijah McFarland; Mary, 1727; Elisha, 1729; Lois, 1731; Deborah, 1732, m. Jonathan Sampson; Alice, 1734, m. a Waters of Sharon; Asenath, 1736; Carpenter, 1739; Abigail, 1741; Chloe, 1743; Content, 1745. ELLIS, Kingston, son of 1st James, m., 1796,

Dorothy Bartlett, and had Rufus Bartlett, 1797; Ellis, 1799, m. Leonice Brewster; Dorothy Bartlett, 1802, m. Peleg Bryant; George Bartlett, 1805, m. Martha Drew Perly; Rufus Bartlett, 1807; William, 1810; Sarah Ellis, 1813, m. Thomas Russell; Ann Gurley, 1815, m. Horace Holmes. EPHRAIM, Duxbury, son of 4th William, m., 1710, Elizabeth Brewster, and had Deborah, 1712; Anna, 1715; Elizabeth, 1717, m. Azariah Whiting; Ephraim, 1719; Abigail, 1720; Susanna, 1721, m. Seth Everson; Elijah, 1723; Ezekiel, 1728; Simeon, 1729; Wait, m. Wealthy Bassett. EPHRAIM, Duxbury, son of 2d Nathaniel, m., 1806, Hannah, d. of Ezekiel Morton, and had Eleanor; Ephraim, m. Lucia Keen; Sally, 1810, m. Briggs B. Delano; Hannah; Morton, m. Catherine E. Burt of Plymouth. He m., 2d, 1823, Lucy, d. of Reuben Peterson, and had John, 1823, m. Jane W. McLaughlin; Lucy, 1825; George, 1828; Lucy, 1831, m. George J. Nickerson; Ellen, 1837. EPHRAIM, New Gloucester, Maine, son of 1st Ezekiel, m. Judith Morton, and had Betsey, 1779; Stephen, 1800, m. Mercy Chandler; Rebecca, 1782, m. Robert Low; Isaac, 1784, m. Shuah Jordan; Reuben, 1789; Judith, 1804; Charles, 1806. EPHRAIM, Turner, son of Wait, m., 1807, Louisa, d. of Ebenezer Dawes of Duxbury, and had Lucia, 1808, m. Levi Glass; Maria, m. Peter W. Maglathlin; Seth D., 1815, m. Zilpha Lewis; Philemon, 1816, m. Lydia Noyes. EZEKIEL, Kingston, son of 1st Ephraim, m. Betsey, d. of Philip Chandler, and removed to Turner. He had Ephraim, 1750; Deborah, 1752, m. Barnabas Winslow; William, 1754, m. Asenath Mason; Rebecca, 1756, m. William True; Jesse, 1758, m. Judith Weston; Ezekiel, 1759, m. Mary House; Chandler, 1761, m. Sarah French; Martin, 1763, m. Prudence Dillingham; Philip, 1765, m. Polly Bonney; Betsey, 1767, m. Darius Briggs. EZEKIEL, Turner, son of above, m., 1786, Mary House, and had Betsey, 1789, m. Charles H. Richardson; Mary, 1794; Sarah, 1794, m. Royal Whitman; Cyrus, 1798; Nancy, 1804, m. William B. Bray. GAMALIEL, Duxbury, son of 1st Samuel, m., 1728, Abigail, d. of Benjamin Bartlett, and had Abigail, 1728, m. Wait Wadsworth; Samuel, 1730; Gamaliel, 1731; Seth, 1733; Peabody, 1735; Deborah, 1738, m. Melzar Adams; Hannah, 1740, m. Joshua Standford; Ruth, 1743, m. Elijah Sampson; Peter, 1745; Andrew, 1745. GAMALIEL, Duxbury, son of above, m., 1757, Sarah, d. of Samuel Alden, and had Perez, 1758, m. Lucy C. Rand; Sophia, 1761; Gamaliel, 1763; Alden, 1765; Sarah, 1768, m. William Hickling of Boston; Jerusha, 1770, m. Ezra Weston; Daniel, 1771, m. Sarah Drew and Nancy Blanchard; Gershom, 1774. GAMALIEL, Boston, son of above, m., 1792, Elizabeth, d. of William Hickling, and had Sarah Alden, 1793, m. Samuel Ripley of Waltham; Elizabeth Hickling, 1794; Gamaliel, 1795; Daniel Neal, 1797; Martha Tilden, 1799, m. Josiah Bartlett of Concord; John Brooks, 1803; Margaret Stephenson, 1804, m. Seth Ames of Lowell; George Partridge, 1807; Hannah Rogers, 1810, m. Augustus Henry Fisk of Boston. GAMALIEL, Boston, son of above, m., 1821, Sophia B., d. of Nathan Rice of Hingham, and had Harriet Mills; Frances; Gamaliel; and Sarah Hickling. GEORGE, Attleboro', son of 2d Perez, m. Sarah Carpenter, and had George, 1757; Perez; Carpenter; Betsey; Sally; Ereck; Matilda; Hannah; and Sylvester. GERSHOM, Duxbury, son of 2d Gamaliel, m. Sarah B. Hickling of Boston, and had Maria W., m. Claudius Bradford; Lucia A.; Elizabeth H.; and Charlotte.

GERSHOM, Bristol, son of 1st Samuel, m., 1716, Priscilla Wiswell, and had Alexander; David, 1720, m. Mary Church and Susan Jarvis; Noah, m. Hannah Clark; Job; Jeremiah, m. Rebecca Dart; Priscilla, m. Moses Norman; Hopestill, m. Joseph Nash; Rachel; Solomon, m. Elizabeth Greenwood. GIDEON, Plympton, son of 4th Samuel, m., 1741, Jane, d. of Ichabod Paddock, and had Levi, 1743; Joseph, 1745, m. Susanna Weeks; Sarah, 1748, m. Freeman Ellis; Samuel, 1750; Gideon, 1752; Calvin, 1754; Jenny, 1756, m. Noah Bisbee. GIDEON, Plympton, son of above, m. Abigail, d. of Zabdiel Sampson, and had Zabdiel, 1779, m. Mary Standish; Gideon, 1781, m. Grace Holmes; Abram, 1784, m. Deborah Randall; Isaac, 1784, m. Sarah Holmes; Abigail, 1786, m. Thomas Ellis; Elizabeth, 1789; Cynthia, 1791; Sampson, 1793; William, 1797, m. Fanny Standish. HEZEKIAH, Duxbury, son of 4th William, m. Mary Chandler, and had Mary. ICHABOD, Kingston, son of 1st Israel, m., 1743, Mary Johnson, and had Ichabod, 1744, m. Rachel Wright and Ruth Fuller; Elizabeth, 1747; Rhoda, 1751; Lemuel, 1755; Anne, 1758. He m., 2d, 1763, Mary Cook, and had Israel, 1765. ISRAEL, Duxbury, son of 4th William, m., 1701, Sarah, d. of Benjamin Bartlett, and had Ruth, 1702; Bathsheba, 1703, m. Thomas Adams; Benjamin, 1705; Abner, 1707; Joshua, 1710; Ichabod, 1713; Elisha, 1718, m. Mary Sturtevant. ISRAEL, Kingston, son of Ichabod, m., 1785, Hannah Everson, and had Lemuel, 1788; Polly, 1786, m. Charles Cobb and Clark Winsor; Sally, m. Richard Cowen of Rochester; Hannah, m. John Pharo; Lucy, m. John Coad; Nancy, m. Ezra Finney of Plymouth; Betsey, m. Otis Finney, and William Putnam. He m., 2d., wid. Olive (Luce) Jeffries. JAMES, Kingston, son of 1st Peleg, m., 1773, Sarah Ellis, and had Ellis, 1773, m. Dorothy Bartlett and Priscilla Tupper; Nathaniel, 1776; Lydia, 1778, m. Samuel Soule; Consider, 1781, m. Betsey Wilder; Bartlett, 1784; James, 1786; Thomas, 1790, m. Lydia Cook. JAMES, son of above, m., 1819, Eleanor Huston, and had Eleanor, 1821; James, 1823; Nathaniel, 1832; and William. JAMES MADISON, son of 2d Joseph, m. Betsey, d. of Samuel Doten Holmes, and had Elizabeth M., 1833; James M., 1835; Branch Johnson, 1838; Samuel H., 1846; Louisa D., 1850. JAMES, Canterbury, Conn., son of 2d Thomas, had two wives, Edith and Susannah, and had Thomas, 1712, m. Eunice Adams; John, 1715; Jerusha, 1716, m. Jonathan Pellett; William, 1718; Sarah, 1720; Anna, m. Eleazer Cleveland; Mary, m. Joseph Woodward. JAMES, Plainfield, son of 7th William, m. Zerviah, d. of John Thomas of Marshfield, and had Samuel; Joseph; Anthony, m. Olive Douglass; James; Priscilla, m. Lemuel Dorrance; Desire, m. Waterman Clift; Hannah. JESSE, Turner, son of 1st Ezekiel, m., 1781, Judith Weston, and had Hara, 1783, m. Rebecca Dillingham; Dura, 1785, m. Sally Dillingham; Charles, 1787; Philip, 1789, m. Lucy Greenwood; Alfred, 1791; Eliphalet, 1791, m. Abigail Tirrell; Judith, 1793, m. Joel Fairbanks; Jeanette, 1797, m. Isaac Allen; Salome, 1799, m. Amos Shaw. JOB, Boston, son of 2d Gershom, m., 1758, Elizabeth Parkman, and had Elizabeth, 1760, m. Benjamin Reynolds; Dorcas, 1762, m. Silas Noyes; William Bowes, 1763, m. Mary Tufts; Abigail, 1765, m. John Allyne of Duxbury; Rufus, 1767; Joseph N., 1769, m. Ann Tufts. JOHN, son of 2d William, m. Martha, d. of Thomas Bourne of Marshfield, and removed to

Norwich, where he died, 1678, childless. JOHN, Kingston, son of 4th William, m., 1674, Mercy, d. of Joseph Warren, and had John, 1675; Alice, 1677, m. Edward Mitchell and Joshua Hervey; Abigail, 1679, m. Gideon Sampson; Mercy, 1681, m. Jonathan Freeman of Harwich, and Isaac Cushman of Plympton; Samuel, 1683, m. Sarah Gray; Priscilla, 1686, m. Seth Chipman of Kingston; William, 1688; James, Zadock, Eliphalet. JOHN, Kingston, son of above, m., 1701, Rebecca, d. of Benjamin Bartlett, and had Robert, 1706; Rebecca, 1710. JOHN, Plympton, son of 4th Samuel, m., 1743, Elizabeth Holmes, and had Elizabeth, 1744, m. James Magoon; Molly, 1746, m. John Churchill; John, 1748; Priscilla, 1750, m. Nathaniel Rider; Perez, 1752; Hannah, 1755, m. Jabez Waterman; Lydia, 1757, m. Levi Bryant; Oliver, 1759; Mercy, 1761, m. Holmes Sears; William, 1766; Sarah, 1769, m. Jabez Bosworth. JOHN, Kingston, son of 1st Robert, m., 1754, Ruth Cobb, and had Sylvanus, 1755; Exuma, 1757; Priscilla, 1760; Noah, 1761. He m., 2d, wid. Hannah Eddy of Middleboro', and had Stephen, 1771; Pelham, 1776; Daniel, 1780, and Hannah. JOHN, Conn., son of 3d Joseph, m., 1736, Esther Sherwood, and had Samuel, 1738, m. Bridget Comstock; John, 1739, m. Mary Fitch; Joseph, 1742, m. Eunice Maples; Sarah, 1744, m. Nathaniel Comstock; Perez, 1746, m. Betsey Rogers; Benjamin, 1748, m. Parthena Rogers; Eleanor; Rebecca, 1754; Mary, 1756. JOHN, Plympton, son of 4th John, m., 1776, Eunice, d. of Ignatius Loring, and had Polly, 1777, m. Ellis Standish; Eunice, 1779, m. Asa Washburn; Olive, 1781; Olive, 1782, m. Asaph Soule; John, 1785; Susanna, 1786; Nancy, 1789, m. Joseph Sherman; Mercy, 1791; Sophia, 1793, m. William Perkins; Susanna, 1795, m. Thomas Ellis; Jane, 1797, m. Zacheus Sherman. JOHN, Plympton, son of above, m., 1807, Patience, d. of Zephaniah Perkins, and had Eunice, 1808, m. Philemon Fuller of Fairhaven; John, 1809; Daniel Perkins, 1811, m. Harriet Newell Rice; Maria, 1813, m. Erastus Leach of Kingston; Patience Perkins, 1815, m. Jesse Briggs; Thomas Gray, 1816; William Loring, 1819; Hannah, 1823, m. David Cannon. He m., 2d, a d. of Billya Wright. JOHN, Illinois, son of above, m. Sarah Fuller, d. of Nathaniel Bradford of Plympton, and had John, 1833; Frederick Milton, 1834; Arabella, 1837, m. Frederick A. Knickerbocker; Mary Winslow, 1841, m. Gerard C. Kneeland; Sarah Maria, 1842; Luella, 1847, m. John W. Saucerman; Thomas Gray, 1852, m. Lizzie Chase. JONATHAN, Minot, son of Nathan, m. Mary, d. of John Southworth of North Yarmouth, Maine, and had Elizabeth, m. Samuel Freeman; David; Mary, m. Jonathan S. Ellis; Jonathan, 1796; Lucy, William, and John Southworth. JOSEPH, son of 3d William, m., 1664, Jael, d. of Peter Hobart, and had Elisha; Joseph, 1665. JOSEPH, son of 2d Nathaniel, m., 1800, Nancy, d. of Joseph Barnes, and had Nathaniel Bemis, 1803; Joseph, 1805, m. Joanna Barnes; Edward Winslow, 1807; James Madison, 1810. JOSEPH, Norwich, son of 4th William, m. Anna, d. of Daniel Fitch, and had Joseph and nine daughters, of whom three pairs were twins. He m., 2d, Mary, wid. of Daniel Fitch, and had John, 1717. JOSEPH, Norwich, son of above, m. Henrietta Swift of New London, 1730, and had Elizabeth, 1731; Ann, 1732; William, 1734; Henry Swift, 1736; Hannah, 1740. JOSEPH M., from Falmouth, m. Anna R., d. of George Raymond, and had Cornelius F., 1845. JOSEPH N., Boston, son of Job, m. Ann

Tufts, and had Claudius, 1801, m. Maria W. Bradford; Eleanor, 1802, m. Benjamin Kent; Lawrence, 1803; Lewis H., 1804; Louisa, 1806, m. Charles Henry Thomas; Charles F., 1806, m. Eliza E. Hickling. JOSIAH, son of 6th William m., 1746, Hannah Rider, and had William, 1749; Hannah, 1751; Josiah, 1754; Samuel, Charles, Zephaniah, Betsey, Lois, and Mercy. JOSIAH, son of above, m., 1781, Elizabeth Holmes, and had Betsey, m. William Tribble. JOSHUA, Friendship, Maine, son of 1st Israel, m., 1737, Hannah, d. of Elisha Bradford, and had Cornelius, 1737; Sarah, 1739, m. John Davis; Rachel, 1741, m. Ebenezer Morton; Mary, 1744; Melatiah, 1744, m. Isaac Churchill of Plympton; Joshua, 1746; Hannah, 1748; Joseph, 1751, m. Abigail Starling; Benjamin, 1753; Elisha, 1755; Winslow, 1757. JOSHUA, Friendship, son of above, m., 1773, Martha Jameson, and had Rachel, 1774; Paul, 1776; Isaiah, 1778; Nancy, 1780; Robert, 1784; Ann, 1785; Cornelius, 1788; Joshua, 1791. LEBARON, Bristol, son of 8th William, m. Sarah, d. of Thomas Davis of Plymouth, and had LeBaron, 1780. LEMUEL, son of 2d Israel, m., 1812, Bathsheba Nelson, and had Lemuel, 1813, m. Jerusha C. Holmes; Ebenezer Nelson, 1818; Charles, 1821; Lydia Nelson, 1824; Bathsheba, 1825; Winslow, 1826, m. Almira, d. of Samuel Lanman; Lydia Nelson, 1830; Hannah Everson, 1833; Ebenezer Nelson, 1836. LEMUEL, son of 1st Nathaniel, m. Mary, d. of Ebenezer Sampson, and had Lemuel, 1775; Thomas, 1778, m. Polly Holmes, and removed to Ohio; Mary, 1780, m. Ephraim Holmes and John Tribble; George, 1783, m. Harriet Churchill; Eleanor, 1785, m. Solomon Faunce. He m., 2d, Lydia Holmes, and had Cornelius, 1793; Lydia, 1795; David, 1796; William Holmes, 1798; Lewis, 1801; Lewis, 1802. LEMUEL, son of above, m. Mehitabel Hinckley of Barnstable, and had George, Abigail, Charles A., and Mehitabel, m. Andrew Mackie. LEVI, Kingston, son of Abner, m., 1782, Polly Ripley, and had Polly and Pamelia, 1786; Sophia, 1794; Lucy, 1797. LEVI, Plympton, son of 1st Gideon, m., 1764, Elizabeth, d. of Daniel Lewis of Pembroke, and had Lewis, 1768; Joseph, 1770; Levi, 1772, m. Mercy Sampson; Daniel, 1774, m. Bathsheba Adams; Ezra, 1776, m. Mary Tobey; Elizabeth, 1778; Sarah, 1782, m. Isaiah Tilson. LEVI, Homer, N.Y., son of above, m. Mercy, d. of Simeon Sampson, and had Marcia Sampson, 1801; Simeon Sampson, 1804; William Lewis, 1807; Thomas Thaxter, 1809; Levi Gray, 1811. MARTIN, Turner, son of 1st Ezekiel, m., 1790, Prudence Dillingham, and had Martin, 1791, m. Polly Howard; Calvin, 1793, m. Kesiah Keen; Freeman, 1797, m. Virah Niles; Ezekiel, 1795; Richmond, 1800, m. Amy Carey. NATHAN, Kingston, son of 1st David, by wife Elizabeth, had Lydia, 1750; Jonathan, 1752, m. Mary Southworth; Elizabeth, 1754; Thomas, 1755; David, 1757, m. wid. Betsey (Robinson) Thomas of Duxbury. NATHANIEL, son of 1st David, m., 1746, Sarah Spooner, and had Nathaniel, 1748; Lemuel, 1751. NATHANIEL, son of above, m. Rebecca, d. of Ichabod Holmes, and had Nathaniel, 1775; Joseph, 1778; John Howland, 1780; Sarah, 1783; Ephraim, 1785; Rebecca, 1788, m. Samuel Doten; Benjamin Willis, 1791; Elizabeth. NATHANIEL, Kingston, son of 1st James, m., 1800, Sarah Cook, and had Deborah, 1800; Levi, 1802; Charles, 1804, m. Mary Bradford; Nathaniel, 1807; Bartlett, 1809; Caleb Cook, 1811, m. Betsey T. Goodwin; Julia,

1816, m. Peleg Simmons; George Anson, 1818, m. Ruth Ann, d. of James T. Ford of Duxbury. NATHANIEL, New York, son of 2d Nathaniel, m., 1799, Deborah, wid. of Benjamin Wright and d. of George Sampson, and had Nathaniel, 1801; Deborah, 1802; Nathaniel Governeur, 1804; Elizabeth Holmes, m. Martin Willard, and Rebecca. NATHANIEL GOVERNEUR, New York, son of above, m., 1830, Rachel Miller, and had Nathaniel Governeur, 1831; Rachel Louisa, 1836; Benjamin Wright, 1839, m. Catherine Allen. OLIVER, Fairhaven, son of 4th John, m., 1782, Sarah Chipman, and had Abigail, 1782; Seth Chipman, 1783; Valentine, 1785; Matilda, 1787, m. Warren Norton, Marlboro, 1789; Melvin, 1791; George, 1793; Priscilla, and Aaron Wing. PEABODY, Duxbury, son of 1st Gamaliel, m. Lydia Freeman, and had Peabody, 1757. He m., 2d, 1760, Wealthy, d. of Joshua Delano, and had Lewis, 1761, m. Priscilla Tupper of Kingston; Ira, 1763; Pamelia, 1764, m. Nathaniel Little; Charles, 1767; Cynthia, 1770, m. Rufus Washburn; Joah, 1772;- Sylvia, 1774, m. Ichabod Washburn; Wealthy, 1776; Lucy, 1778; Joseph Bartlett, Ira, Delano, 1783. PELEG, Kingston, son of 1st Robert, m., 1746, Lydia Sturtevant, and had Elizabeth, 1747; James, 1749; Bartlett, 1751; Consider, 1755; Rebecca, 1757; Lydia, 1762; Susan, and Sarah. PELEG, Kingston, son of Stetson, m., 1813, Deborah, d. of Jeremiah Sampson, and had Charles, 1814, m. Clarissa Graves of Maine; Peleg Sampson, 1817, m. Lydia H., d. of Jacob Robinson. He m., 2d, 1820, Sally Johnson, and had William Stetson, 1825. He m., 3d, Sally (Johnson) Holmes, wid. of Asaph Holmes. PELHAM, Kingston, son of 5th John, by wife Selah, had Selah, 1799, m. Osborn Morton; John, 1803; Jason, m. Phebe Crocker of Carver; Pelham. PEREZ, Plympton, son of 4th John, m. Sarah, d. of Kimball Prince, and had Christopher Prince, 1777; Louisa, 1779; Elizabeth, 1782; Deborah, 1783, m. Samuel Bryant; Sarah, 1785; Ruth, 1787, m. Jonathan Ripley; Lucy Prince, 1789, m. Frederick Cobb of Carver, and Hezekiah Cole. He m., 2d, wid. Lydia Cushman of Kingston, and had Sarah, 1799, m. Oliver Churchill; Joanna, 1800; Salome, 1802, m. William Bradford. PEREZ, Attleboro', son of 1st Samuel, m. Abigail Belch, and had Perez, Joel; George, m. Sarah Carpenter; John; Joseph, m. Beulah Morse; Abigail, m. Samuel Lee; Hannah, Mary, and Elizabeth. ROBERT, Kingston, son of 3d John, m., 1726, Zeresh Stetson, and had Peleg, 1727; Zilpha, 1728, m. Thomas Loring; Rebecca, 1730, m. Micah Holmes; John, 1732; Elethea, 1734; Orpha, 1736; Stetson, 1739; Robert, 1741; Sarah, 1742; Consider, 1745; Sarah, 1748; Robert, 1750, m. Kesiah Little. ROBERT, Austerfield, England, son of 1st William, m. 1585, Alice Waingate, and had William, 1587; Robert, 1591, m. Elizabeth Satwood (or perhaps Southworth); Maria, 1593; Alice; Elizabeth, 1597; Margaret, 1600. ROBERT, Austerfield, son of above, m., 1615, Elizabeth Satwood, and had Judith, 1617; Elizabeth, 1621; Mary, 1626; Mary, 1618; Jane, 1623; and Thomas. RUFUS BARTLETT, Boston, son of Ellis, m., 1830, Elizabeth Ann, daughter of Henry Jackson, and had Henry Jackson, 1832; Ellis, 1833; Elizabeth Ann, 1834; Mary Finney, Charles H., Frank Thornton, Anna Gurley, John Russell, Alice Southworth, and Willie Bartlett. He m., 2d, Rebecca S., wid. of Edwin Parker of Boston, and d. of Samuel Butler of Martha's Vineyard. SAMUEL, Duxbury, son of 4th William, m. Hannah

Rogers, 1687, and had Hannah, 1689, m. Nathaniel Gilbert of Taunton; Gershom, 1691; Perez, 1694, m. Abigail Belch; Elizabeth, 1696, m. William Whiting; Jerusha, 1699, m. Ebenezer Gay of Hingham; Wealthy, 1702, m. Peter Lane of Hingham; Gamaliel, 1704. SAMUEL, son of 1st Josiah, m., 1785, Lucy Churchill, and had Samuel; Stephen, m. Hannah Wadsworth; Hannah, m. Stevens Mason Burbank; Lucy, m. Bartlett Bradford; Ellen, m. Charles Brewster; Harvey, m. Wealthy Hathaway of Rochester. SAMUEL, son of above, m. Lucy Gibbs, and had Lucy Gibbs, m. Timothy Holmes; and Samuel. He m., 2d, Eunice Rider, and had Mary Ann, m. Charles H. Drew of Brookline. SAMUEL, Plympton, son of 2d John, m., 1714, Sarah, d. of Edward Gray of Tiverton, and had John, 1717; Gideon, 1718; William, 1720; Mary, 1722, m. Abiel Cook; Sarah, 1725, m. Ephraim Paddock; William, 1729; Mercy, 1731; Abigail, 1732, m. Caleb Stetson; Phebe, 1735; Samuel, 1740. SAMUEL, Duxbury, son of 1st Gamaliel, m., 1749, Grace, d. of Samuel Ring of Kingston, and had Deborah, 1750, m. Melzar Adams; Samuel, 1752, m. Lydia Bradford; Lydia, 1754; William, 1755, m. Hannah Parker; Wealthy, 1757, m. Isaac Drew; Lyman, 1760; Grace, 1763; Eli, 1765; George, 1767; Isaiah, 1769, m. Elizabeth Dingley. SAMUEL, Martha's Vineyard, son of 4th Samuel, m. Lydia Pease, and had Shubael, Sarah, Samuel, Edward Gray, Pardon, and Lydia. SAMUEL, Conn., son of 6th John, m. Bridget Comstock, and had Eleanor, m. Mulford Raymond; Samuel, m. Abby Dolbeare; Nathaniel, m. Lucy Raymond; Bridget, m. Ephraim Wells; Sarah, m. George Dolbeare; William, m. Parthena Bradford and Hannah Dolbeare; Margaret, m. Daniel Prentiss; Esther, m. Reynolds Johnson. SAMUEL, Plympton, son of 1st Gideon, m., 1779, Susanna, d. of Daniel Vaughan, and had Susanna, 1780, m. Hamblin Tilson; Abigail, 1781; Samuel, 1783, m. Susanna Cole; Winslow, 1785, m. Zillah Lucas of Plymouth. He m., 2d, Sarah, d. of Amos Fuller, and had Nathaniel, 1788, m. Abigail Cobb; Nelson, 1791. SAMUEL, Canterbury, son of 3d Thomas, m. Lydia Dean, and had Sarah, 1778; Annis, 1780; Samuel, 1783; Sarah, 1784; Parmelia, 1788; Simeon, 1794. SETH, Duxbury, son of 1st Gamaliel, m., 1760, Lydia, d. of Jedediah Southworth, and had Joel, 1761; Isaac, 1763, m. Hannah Trask of Gloucester; Lydia, 1765, m. Dura Wadsworth; Abigail, 1768; Hannah, 1768; Seth, 1779, m. Abigail Bailey and Betsey Sables; Sarah, 1773, m. Ezra Cushman. SIMEON, Kingston, son of 1st Ephraim, removed to New Hampshire. By wife Phebe he had Asa, 1758; Simeon, 1760; Lucy, 1761; Joel, Hosea, Elizabeth, and Rebecca. SIMEON, Turner, son of Wait, m. Martha True, and had Lydia, Wealthea, True, Almira, Charles W., Jabez, Ephraim, and James. He m. a 2d wife. SOLOMON, Providence, son of 2d Gershom, m. Elizabeth Greenwood, and had Elizabeth; Huldah, m. James Morse; and one son. SPENCER, Kingston, son of Stetson, m., 1814, Lydia Faunce, and had Alden Spencer, 1815; Lydia Smith, 1817; Lucy Holmes, 1820; Frances Alden, 1824, m. Simeon McLaughlin. STEPHEN, Duxbury, son of 2d Samuel, m. Hannah, d. of Dura Wadsworth, and had Stephen, 1815, m. Mary E. Coverly; Otis, 1817; Otis, 1819, m. Jane Collins; Hannah, 1821, m. James Mulligan; Lucy Bartlett, 1824; Erastus, 1827; Alexander W., 1830; Julius, 1832; Alexander, 1838. STEPHEN, Turner, son of 3d Ephraim, m., 1805, Mercy

Chandler, and had Nancy, 1806; Judith, 1808; Lucius, 1811; Alanson, 1814; Jane, 1817; Jonathan, 1824. STETSON, Kingston, son of 1st Robert, m., 1771, Lurana Holmes, and had Elizabeth, 1772; Zilpha, 1773, m. Levi Waterman; William, 1776; Charles, 1777; Spencer, 1781; Peleg, 1787. SYLVANUS, Kingston, son of 5th John, m., 1779, Irena Briggs of Halifax, and had Ruth, 1781; Remember, 1784; Deborah, 1786; Jane, 1789; Sylvanus, 1792; Robert, 1795; Noah, 1798. THOMAS, son of 2d Lemuel, m., 1800, Mary Holmes, and had Mary Sampson, 1800; Thomas, 1803; Abigail Holmes, 1804; Thomas Lewis, 1806; Amos Sturtevant, 1808; Sarah Spooner, 1810; David, 1813; Lewis, 1816. THOMAS, Norwich, son of 4th William, m. Anna, d. of James Fitch. He m., 2d, Priscilla, d. of John Mason, and had Joshua, 1682; and James. THOMAS, Canterbury, son of 4th James, m. Eunice Adams, and had Thomas, 1734; John, 1735; Susanna, 1737, m. Ebenezer Brown; Eunice, 1739; Edith, 1741, m. Asa Bacon; Lydia, 1744; James, 1746; Samuel, 1748, m. Lydia Dean; Submit, 1750, m. Joseph Pellett; Thomas, 1751, m. Philenas Davidson; John, 1754. WAIT, Turner, son of 1st Ephraim, m., 1763, Wealthea, d. of Moses Bassett of Kingston, and had Sarah, 1768, m. Snow Keen; Simeon, 1770, m. Martha True; Deborah, 1777, m. William Putnam; Ephraim, 1783, m. Louisa Dawes. WILLIAM, Austerfield, England, had William, Thomas; Robert, bap., 1561; Elizabeth, bap., 1570, m. James Hill. WILLIAM, Austerfield, son of above, m., 1584, Alice, d. of John Hanson, and had Margaret, bap. 1585; Alice, bap. 1587; William, bap. 1589. WILLIAM, son of above, came in the Mayflower, 1620, with wife Dorothy May, and son John. He m., 1623, Alice, wid. of Edward Southworth, and d. of Alexander Carpenter, and had William, 1624; Mercy, 1627, m. Benjamin Vermayes; Joseph, 1630. WILLIAM, son of above, m. Alice, d. of Thomas Richards of Weymouth, and had John, 1652; William, 1655; Thomas, m. Anna Fitch; Samuel, 1668; Alice, m. William Adams of Dedham, and James Fitch of Norwich; Hannah, m. Joshua Ripley of Hingham; Mercy, m. Samuel Steele of Hartford; Meletiah, m. John Steele of Norwich; Mary, m. William Hunt of Weymouth; Sarah, m. Kenelm Baker of Marshfield. He m., 2d, a wid. Wiswall, perhaps d. of Thomas Fitch of Norwalk, Conn., and had Joseph, 1674. He m., 3d, Mary, wid. of John Holmes, and d. of John Atwood, and had Israel, 1679; Ephraim, 1690; David, and Hezekiah. WILLIAM, son of above, m., 1679, Rebecca, d. of Joseph Bartlett, and had Alice, 1680, m. William Barnes; William; Sarah, m. Jonathan Barnes. WILLIAM, son of above, m., 1713, Elizabeth, d. of Josiah Finney, and had Elizabeth, 1714; Charles, 1716; Sarah, 1718, m. Zephaniah Holmes; Josiah; Jerusha, 1722, m. Edward Sparrow; William, 1726; Mercy, 1729; Elizabeth, 1730. WILLIAM, son of 2d John, m. Hannah, d. of John Foster, and had James, 1717, m. Zeruiah, d. of John Thomas; Zadock, 1719; Samuel, 1721; Eliphalet, 1723, m. Hannah Prince; Hannah, 1724, m. a Spaulding; William, 1728. WILLIAM, Bristol, son of 4th Samuel, m., 1750, Mary, d. of William LeBaron, and had William, 1752, m. Betsey B. James; LeBaron, 1754, m. Sarah, d. of Thomas Davis of Plymouth; John, m. Jemima Wardwell; Ezekiel, m. Abby DeWolf, and Abby Atwood; Lydia, m. Charles Collins; Nancy, m. James DeWolf; Mary, m. Henry Goodwin; and Hannah, m. G. Baylies. WILLIAM, son of

1st Josiah, m., 1773, Ruth, d. of Amos Dunham, and had Josiah, m. Mary Robbins; Jesse, Deborah, William, Amos; Mary, m. Abner Holmes; Isaac; and Elizabeth, m. Benjamin Howland. WILLIAM, son of above, m. Nancy Balston, and had William; Mercy B., m. Ebenezer Davie; Anna, m. Solomon Richmond; and Emily, m. Micah Richmond. WILLIAM, son of above, m. Alice Sylvester, and had Mary Ann, 1822, m. William Holmes; Alice S., 1823; Nancy, 1827, m. Francis H. Robbins, and Amasa Holmes; William, 1829; Eudora, 1831, m. Frederick L. Holmes. WILLIAM HOLMES, son of 2d Lemuel, m., 1827, Mary Holmes, and had George F., Lydia, William H.; Mary H., m. Samuel Harlow. WILLIAM BOWES, Boston, son of Job, m. Mary Tufts, and had Mary, 1786, m. George Joy Homer; William Bowes, 1787; Elizabeth, 1789, m. T. Bedlington; John, 1790, m. Phebe Harrington; Rufus, 1792; Samuel, 1795; Joseph, 1796. WILLIAM BOWES, Boston, son of above, m. Nancy Child, and had Julia Child, 1817; William Bowes, 1819; Martin Luther, 1821. WILLIAM, Plympton, son of 4th John, m., 1791, Polly, d. of Asaph Soule, and had Saba Soule, 1792, m. Asa Sherman; William, 1795; Polly Soule, 1798; Mercy, 1800. WILLIAM, Friendship, son of Carpenter, m. Sarah Sweetland, and had Lydia, 1790, m. Zenas Cook; Elisha, 1794; Charles, 1795; Mary, 1797; William, 1799; Enoch, 1802; Nehemiah, 1806. WILLIAM, Canterbury, son of 4th James, m. Zerviah Lothrop, and had Zerviah, 1740. He m., 2d, 1743, Mary Cleveland, and had Mary, 1744, m. William Pellett; William, 1745, m. Anna Spaulding; Ebenezer, 1746, m. Elizabeth Green; David, 1748, m. Rhoda Palmer; John, 1750, m. Elizabeth Bond, and Hannah Lyon; Joshua, 1751, m. Anna Cleveland; Abigail, 1753, m. Lewis Barton; James, 1755; Olive, 1756, m. Hezekiah Barstow; Josiah, 1757, m. Elizabeth Merritt; Lydia, 1760, m. Rufus Hibbard; Beulah, 1763, m. Moses Butterfield; Moses, 1765, m. Charlotte Bradstreet and Sarah Eaton. He m., 3d, Martha Warren, and had Joseph, 1767; Benjamin, 1768, m. Ruby Allen; Kesiah, 1770; Zerviah, 1770; Samuel, 1772. He m., 4th, a wid. Stedman. WILLIAM, Turner, son of 1st Ezekiel, m., 1776, Asenath Mason, and had William, 1778, m. Chloe Phillips; Asa, 1780, m. Betsey Bray. ZADOCK, Duxbury, son of Eliphalet, m., 1795, Lucy Gray, and had Zadock, 1798, m. Lydia, d. of Frederick Peterson; Nancy, 1800, m. Seth Bartlett; George, 1801; Lucy, 1803, m. Bradford Chandler; Caroline, 1805, m. Joshua Cushing, Charles, 1806; Lewis Eldridge, 1809, m. Olive Furber; James, 1812, m. Zerviah Holmes. ZEPHANIAH, son of Charles, m., 1822, Sally, d. of Philip Richardson of Boston, and had Priscilla Morton, 1823; Charles Coburn, 1824, m. Eliza N. Coburn; Priscilla Morton, 1826, m. Thomas F. Sherman; Zephaniah, 1827, m. Susan Kendrick of Bridgeport; Elizabeth Richardson, 1829, m. Solomon Kenyon; William, 1830; David, 1831; Sarah E., 1832; James Bugbee, 1833; Rebecca Holmes, 1835, m. Alexander Christian of Boston; Sarah James, 1839, m. Thomas Merritt; Adaline Augusta, 1843; and James B.

BRAMHALL, BENJAMIN, son of 1st Sylvanus, m. Priscilla Burbank, 1786, and had Benjamin, 1787; Priscilla, 1789, m. John Sampson; Mercy W., 1793; Charles, 1795; William, 1797, m. Betsey, d. of Southworth Shaw; Sylvanus, 1799, m. Mary Wait Atwood; Joshua, 1802; Mary, 1804; Sarah, 1807; Thomas

Murdock, 1809; Cornelius, 1811. BENJAMIN, son of the above, m. Phebe, a Virginian, and moved to Quincy, and had Benjamin. CHARLES, son of 1st Benjamin, m. Nancy E. Brewster, and had Ellis Brewster, 1819, m. Martha Fuller, wid. of Alexander Chute of Newburyport, and d. of Jesse Gould of Malden; and Charles W., 1824. GEORGE, at Dover, 1670, Casco, 1678, killed by the Indians, 1689, m. Martha, and had Joseph, m. Grace, moved to Falmouth, and died in Boston; George at Hingham in 1733; Hannah, m. Jonathan Hall of Harwich; and Joshua, m. Sarah Rider of Plymouth. GEORGE, son of 1st Sylvanus, m. Zilpha Richmond, 1766, and had Zilpha, 1772, m. William Clark; George, 1774, m. Lucy and Sarah Morton, sisters; Sylvanus, 1776, m. Ruth Marshall; Sally, 1779; Martha, 1783; Lydia, 1786. GEORGE, son of above, m. Lucy Morton, 1801, and had Lucy, 1803; George, 1806, m. Eleanor Leonard. He m., 2d, Sarah Morton, 1810, and had Sarah, 1811; Otis, 1813, m. Mary Clark; William, 1815; Ezra, 1817. GEORGE, son of above, m. Eleanor Leonard, 1831, and had George W., 1832, m. Naomi A. Swift; Mary W., 1835; Charles, 1843. JOSEPH, son of Joshua, m. Sarah Tilson, 1747, and had Edmund, 1749; Joseph, 1750; William, 1752. JOSHUA, son of 1st George, m. Sarah Rider, 1707, and had Cornelius, 1708; Sylvanus, 1712; Joseph, 1714; Martha, 1718, m. Jonathan Darling, and perhaps Joshua, who m., 1747, Katherine Hall of Marshfield. SYLVANUS, son of Joshua, m. Mercy Bennett, 1735, and had Joshua, 1736, m. Rebecca Sears; Sarah, 1737, m. Jonathan Elwell; Sylvanus, 1739; Nehemiah, 1741; Joseph, 1742, m. Kesiah Thomas; George, 1745; Lydia, 1748; Cornelius, 1749, m. Mercy Torrey; Mary, 1751, m. Robert Brown. He m., 2d, Mercy Warren, 1762, and had Benjamin. SYLVANUS, son of 2d George, m. Ruth Marshall, 1799, and had Bartlett, 1799; Ruth, 1801; Sylvanus, 1803; Bathsheba, 1806; Samuel, 1809; George Henry, 1813; Martha, 1817. WILLIAM, son of 3d George, m. Laura A. Bickford, and had Otis, William, and Sarah.

BRANCH, EXPERIENCE, Marshfield, son of John by wife Lydia, had Thomas and others. JOHN, Scituate, son of Peter, came with his father, who died on the passage, about 1638, and m. Mary Speed, 1652, and had John, killed in King Philip's war; Elizabeth, 1656; Peter, 1659; Thomas; Mercy, 1664, m. Ebenezer Spooner; Experience. THOMAS, son of Experience, m., 1720, Lydia Barrows, and had Lydia, 1721, m. Nathaniel Shurtleff; Mercy, 1723, m. Ebenezer Churchill; John, 1725; Thankful, 1727, m. a Howard; Thomas, 1729; Experience, 1732, m. Samuel Sherman.

BRAND, JAMES, m., 1785, Betty Scipio, Indians.

BRECK, MOSES, born 1767, by wife Mary had Sarah Tyler, 1800, and perhaps others.

BRETT, NATHANIEL, m., 1774, Mary Dyer.

BREWER, THOMAS, and Elizabeth Barnes, pub. 1741.

BREWSTER, AMERICA, son of 1st Job, m. Sally Cobb, d. of Nathaniel. BENJAMIN, Duxbury, son of 2d William, removed to Conn., and had a d. Lois, m. Zadock Brewster. BENJAMIN, Camden, Maine, son of Zadock, m., 1807, Betsey Tolman, and had Eliza, 1807, m. Thomas Gardner; William, 1809, m. Eliza Acorn; Esther, 1811, m. Joseph Wentworth; Mary, 1813; Eunice, 1815, m. Robert Gregory; Clarissa, 1817, m. John Ross; Sarah, 1820,

m. Joseph Packard; Hannah, 1823, m. William Gregory; Lois, 1825. BEN-
JAMIN, Thomaston, son of Darius, m., 1821, Hannah, d. of Daniel Kiff, and
had Asa; Sarah; Washington. BENJAMIN, Montreal, son of last William,
m. Sarah French, and had Henry; Benjamin, m. Anna W., d. of Nathaniel
H. Emmons of Boston; Fanny Maria, m. George S. Brush; Ann Matilda;
George Perkins; Sarah Amelia, m. John W. Warner; and Edward Emmons,
m. Sarah Orr. CHARLES, son of 1st Martin, m., 1817, Ellen Bradford,
and had Eleanor, 1818, m. Daniel L. Jackson; Caroline, 1820; Deborah
Nye, 1824; Eveline Bradford, 1825, m. Richard Holmes; and Martin.
CHARLES, Orland, son of 4th Joseph, m. Polly Loring of Plympton, and had
Charles; Joseph; Joshua; Melzar, m. Charlotte Town; and Mary, m. Samuel
Peakes. CYRUS, Duxbury, son of Zadock, m., 1798, Ruth, d. of Elijah
Sampson and her sister Deborah, and had Zadock, 1799; Dorcas, 1801, m.
George Barstow and William Bradford; Sally, 1803, m. Augustus Sampson.
DANIEL WHITE, Camden, son of Zadock, m. Bethiah Packard of Thomaston
and Mathilda Paul of Camden, and had Samuel; Daniel, 1828; William W.,
1829; Lucy Ann; and Daniel. DANIEL, Camden, son of 1st Ira, m. Lucy
Tolman, and had Samuel; Clarissa A.; and Arisa. DANIEL W., Duxbury,
son of 1st Joshua, m., 1807, Polly Hall, and had Lydia W., 1807, Julia Ann
T., 1811, m. Lewis Peterson; Mary W., 1821, m. John Alden; Lydia W.,
1829, m. Peleg Chandler. He m., 2d, Mrs. Elizabeth Swett, 1854. DARIUS,
son of Zadock, removed to Maine. He m. Esther, d. of Micah Soule of Duxbury, 1791, and had Martin, 1792; Asa, 1793; Benjamin, 1796. He m., 2d,
1823, Sally Fales. ELISHA, Kingston, son of Thomas, m., 1833, Elizabeth B.
Bates, and had Mary Thomas, 1834; Elizabeth Emeline, 1834; Emma Frances,
1835; Eudora Frances, 1840; Ada Augusta, 1842; Emma Eudora, 1846; Flora
Louisa, 1849; Eva Octavia, 1853; Earnest; Wrestling; and Elisha. ELISHA,
Middlebury, Vt., son of Seabury, m., 1811, Rebecca Fish of Hartford, and had
Elisha; Wrestling, 1814; Martha Leffingwell, 1816, m. Henry Nichols of
Haverhill; Edward Seabury, 1818; William Arthur, 1820; Robert Raikes,
1822; George Fish, 1824; John Howard, 1826; Henry Whitman, 1828; and
Sarah Huntington, m. Charles Wheaton of Aurora, Ill. ELLIS, son of 1st
Job, m., 1791, Nancy Holmes, and had Nancy E., m. Charles Bramhall.
GEORGE BRADLEY, from Pembroke, m., 1853, Nancy Paulding Westgate,
and had Lydia Morton, 1855, m. Lewis Gould; Georgiana, 1856; Charles,
1859; Carrie E., 1862; William E., 1865; Mary A., 1872. HENRY WHITMAN,
Middlebury, 1st son of 2d Elisha, m. Charlotte B. Stowell, 1859, and had
William Henry, 1861; Susan Stowell, 1874. HIRAM, Rockland, Maine, son
of 1st Ira, m. Charlotte Ames, and had Melvina, m. Robert Dyer; and John
Jarvis. He m., 2d, Mrs. Sarah Sleeper. HOSEA, Kingston, son of 3d Wrestling,
m., 1792, Rebecca Bryant, and had Hosea, m. Hannah Bryant. ICHABOD,
Duxbury, son of 3d William, m., 1725, Lydia Barstow of Pembroke, and
removed to Conn. He had Ichabod, the father of Lot E. of Cincinnati. IRA,
Thomaston, son of Zadock, m. Patience Crooker of Bristol, Maine, 1796, and
had Elijah, 1797; Joseph, 1800, m. Abigail Tilden; Sally, 1803, m. John Brown;
Ira, 1805, m. Mary Thorndike; Hiram, 1808, m. Charlotte Ames and Mrs.
Sarah Sleeper; Daniel, 1811; Lorenzo, 1816, m. Susan Tolman. IRA, Cam-

den, son of above, m., 1830, Mary Thorndike, and had Lovina, 1831, m. Shephard H. Tolman; Harriet F., 1833, m. George Storer; Mary F., 1836, m. Charles B. Watts; Edward B., 1838, m. Lucy R. Watts; Charles W., 1853. ISAAC, Duxbury, son of 2d Wrestling, m. Leonice, d. of Aaron Soule of Halifax, and had Pelham, 1773; Spencer, 1778. ISAAC, son of 1st Spencer, m. Sarah J., d. of James Bartlett of Plymouth, and had Sarah A., 1839, m. Henry R. Reed of Boston; James Bartlett, 1842; and William W., and Isaac S., twins, 1849. JAMES BARTLETT, son of above, m., 1870, Martha, d. of Isaac N. Stoddard, and had Laura S., 1872; William, 1878. JOB, Duxbury, son of 2d Joshua, m., 1754, Elizabeth Ellis of Plymouth, and had Joshua, 1755; Job; America; Ellis, 1768; William, 1770; Joshua, 1763; Jane, m. Asa Weston; and Deborah, 1761, m. Charles Thomas. JOB, Duxbury, son of above, m., 1785, Betsey Paulding, and had Deborah, m. Robert Hutchinson; Jane, m. Joseph Barnes; Job, m. Mary Oldham; and Betsey, m. Thomas Oldham. JOB E., Duxbury, son of 1st Joshua, m. Lydia (Dunham) Doten, and had Lydia E., 1821, m. Henry Delano; Caroline D., 1824, m. Abner G. Wood of Woburn; Jane T., 1831, m. Albert Weston; and Harriet, m. Albert Wood of Woburn. JOHN, Duxbury, son of 2d Wrestling, m., 1795, Deliverance Catta, and had Joseph, and Job. JOHN, Kingston, son of 1st Wrestling by wife Rebecca, had Rebecca, m. John Sampson; Abigail, m. Lemuel Brewster; Sarah; and others. JONATHAN, Duxbury and Norwich, son of 1st William, born in England, came in the Fortune 1621, and, by wife Lucretia, had William; Mary, m. John Turner of Scituate; Jonathan, 1627; and Benjamin. JONATHAN, Duxbury, son of 1st Wrestling, m., 1709, Mary, d. of John Partridge, and removed to Windham, Conn. JOSEPH, Duxbury, son of 2d William, by wife Elizabeth, had Lemuel, m. Abigail Brewster; Eunice, m. Timothy Walker; and Truelove. JOSEPH, Duxbury, son of Nathaniel, m. Jedidah, d. of Benjamin White of Marshfield, and had Zadock, 1742; Mary, m. Silas Freeman; Joseph, 1747, m. Deborah Hunt; Nathaniel, 1755, m. a Dimmock; Ruth, m. Samuel Sampson; Truelove, m. Lydia Brewster. JOSEPH, Duxbury, son of Lemuel, m., 1796, Susanna, d. of Seth Bradford, and had Lydia, 1797, m. Otis Weston. JOSEPH, Duxbury, son of 2d Joseph, m., 1773, Deborah Hunt, and had Aruna, 1774; Wealthy, 1776; Asenath, 1778, m. Simeon Soule; Charles, m. Polly Loring; Stephen, 1783, m. Philip Simmons; Irena, 1780; Olive, 1789; Asa, 1787; Melzar, 1792, m. Betsey R. Watson; Lois, 1795; and Aruna. JOSEPH, Duxbury, son of Zadock, m., 1802, Sally, d. of Lot Hunt, and had Eunice, 1804; Joseph, 1805, m. Almira Baker; Samuel, 1807; Emerson, 1809; Sarah, 1810, m. Nathaniel Delano; Nancy, 1810, m. James Ellis of Plympton; William, 1812; Asa, 1815; m. Lydia Drew; Jane, 1817; Eunice, 1818, m. Nathaniel Ellis of Plympton. JOSEPH, Duxbury, son of above, m., 1828, Almira, d. of Edward D. Barker, and had Henry O., 1828, m. Mary S. Sampson; Joseph B., 1830, m. Ellen M. Sampson; Wilbur F., 1834, m. Elizabeth Sampson. JOSEPH, Belmont, Maine, son of 1st Ira, m. Abigail Tilden, and had Joseph, m. Priscilla Pottle; Eunice; Ira; Hiram; Patience, m. Martin B. Hunt; Abigail; and Warren. JOSHUA, Duxbury, son of 1st Job, m., 1785, Lydia, d. of Warren Weston, and had Daniel W., 1788; Job E., 1791;

Mary B., 1793, m. John Mackenzie; William N., 1796, m. Sarah, d. of David
Warren; Betsey E., 1799; Sarah C., 1801, m. David Warren; Warren W.,
1803; Priscilla W., 1806, m. Nathaniel Delano; and Harriet G., 1808, m.
William Brewster Barnes of Plymouth. JOSHUA, Duxbury, son of 2d
William, by wife Deborah, had Job; Nathan, 1723; Rachel, 1727; and Sarah,
m. Joshua Wright. JOSHUA, Duxbury, son of Nathan, m. Ruth, d. of
Nathan Chandler, and had Deborah, 1787; Rachel, 1790; Selah, 1792, m.
Baker Weston; Nathan C., 1796; Hannah, 1798, m. Hosea Delano; Joshua,
1801; Ruth, 1810. JOSHUA, Duxbury, son of above, m., 1823, Deborah S.,
d. of Jesse Chandler, and had Joshua T., 1824, m. Maria Hunt; Deborah W.,
1826, m. Henry Peterson; Henry L., 1829; Selah B., 1831; Roxelana W.,
1835; Annis M., 1837, m. E. R. Litchfield; Mary Otis, 1845. LEMUEL, Kingston, son of 1st Joseph, m., 1756, Abigail, d. of John Brewster, and had
Elizabeth, 1759, m. Samuel Walker; Rial, 1761; Rebecca; Joseph, m. Susanna
Bradford; and John. LORENZO, Camden, son of 1st Ira, m. Susan
Tolman, and had George; Jarvis; Hiram; Lorenzo. LOVE, Duxbury, son of
1st William, m., 1634, Sarah, d. of William Collier, and had Nathaniel;
William, m. Lydia Partridge; Wrestling; and Sarah, m. Benjamin Bartlett.
MARTIN, Kingston, son of 3d Wrestling, m., 1786, Sarah, d. of James Drew,
and had George, m. Christiana, d. of Samuel Stetson; Martin; Henry;
Clement; Charles; Deborah; and Sally, m. Peleg Tupper and Timothy
French. MARTIN, Kingston, son of above, m., 1823, Betsey, d. of George
Russell, and had James, m. in New York; and Elizabeth, m. Horace Stevens.
MARTIN, son of 1st Charles, m., 1865, Emily W. Benson, and had Edwin L.,
1873, and others. MELZAR, Duxbury, son of 4th Joseph, m. Betsey R., d.
of John Watson, and had Elizabeth, 1816; Deborah, 1818; Lucia W., 1820, m.
Joseph Hunt; Melzar, 1822, m. Angeline Oregon; Jane Maria, 1824; Maria
W., 1826; Janette T., 1829, m. Hiram Lucas; John W., 1832, m. Margaret
Noyce; Charles, m. Mary H. Alexander. NATHAN, Duxbury, son of 2d
Joshua, m. Keziah Barden Kent; 2d, 1760, Hannah Hunt; 3d, Diadema
Dawes, 1784, and had Anne; Keziah; Joshua, m. Ruth Chandler; William, m.
Ada Chandler; Benjamin, 1768; Francis; and Samuel. NATHAN C., Duxbury,
son of 3d Joshua, m. Abigail, d, of Isaac Sampson, and had Nathan, 1823, m.
Julia, d. of Samuel Loring. NATHANIEL, Duxbury, son of 2d William, m.,
1705, Mary Dwelley, and had Samuel, 1708; Ruth, 1711, m. Joseph Morgan;
William, 1715; Joseph, 1718; and Mary, m. a Woodcock. PELHAM, Kingston,
son of 1st Isaac, m. Sarah Symmes, and had Leonice, m. Ellis Bradford;
Lucy, m. Azel Sampson; Hannah, m. Rev. Mr. Carl; Pelham, m. Ann Mc-
Laughlin; Frances Augusta, m, John Locke; and Sally, m. Augustus Thomas.
SEABURY, Norwich, son of 3d Wrestling, m. Sally Bradford, and had William.
He m., 2d, 1789, Lucy Leffingwell, and had Elisha, 1790. He m., 3d, 1798,
Fanny Starr, and had Christopher Starr; Lucy Leffingwell; and Seabury.
SPENCER, Kingston, son of 1st Isaac, m. Clynthia Drew, and had Aaron,
1804; Spencer; Sylvina, m. William Morton Jackson of Plymouth. He m.,
2d, Experience Holmes, and had Isaac. He m., 3d, Persis Cobb. SPENCER,
Kingston, son of above, m. Hannah Simmons, and had Clynthia, m. Frank
H. Holmes. STEPHEN, Duxbury, son of 4th Joseph, m. Phillippe Simmons

of Marshfield, and had Stephen; Phillippe, 1824. THOMAS, Duxbury, son of
2d Wrestling, m., 1794, Molly, d. of Simon Hall, and had Mary, 1795; Elisha,
1801; Hannah T., 1796, m. George Adams; Sophia, m. Rufus Prince of
Bangor; Judith, 1806. TRUELOVE, Duxbury, son of 2d Joseph, removed to
Conn., where he m. Lydia, d. of William Brewster of Groton. WILLIAM,
the Elder, came in the Mayflower 1620, with two younger sons, Love and
Wrestling, and Lucretia, wife of son Jonathan, and her son William. Mary,
the wife of William, came in the Ann, 1623, with d. Fear, m. Isaac Allerton;
and Patience, m. Thomas Prence. WILLIAM, Duxbury, son of Love, m.,
1672, Lydia, d. of George Partridge, and had Sarah, 1674, m. Caleb Stetson;
Nathaniel, 1676; Lydia, 1680; William, 1681; Benjamin, 1688; Joseph, 1694.
Joshua, 1698. WILLIAM, Duxbury, son of above, m. Hopestill, d. of John
Wadsworth, and removed to Lebanon, Conn., and had Oliver, 1708; Ichabod,
1710; Elisha, 1715; Seth, 1720; Lot, 1723; Huldah, 1726, m. George Gould of
Hull. WILLIAM, son of 1st Job, m., 1795, Betsey Taylor, and had Betsey
Taylor, 1796; William, 1799; Betsey Taylor, again, 1801; and William, 1803.
WILLIAM W., son of 2d Isaac, m., 1878, Annie L., d. of Ellis Barnes, and
had Sarah, 1880. WILLIAM, Duxbury, son of Nathaniel, m., 1747, Pris-
cilla, d. of John Sampson, and had Timothy; Lydia; Daniel; Nathaniel; and
Stephen. WILLIAM, Camden, son of Zadock, m. Martha Jameson, and had
Deborah, m. John Manning; Isaac; William, m. Eliza Smith; Robert, m.
Susan May; Martha, m. William Morton. He m., 2d, Nancy Nutt, and had
Zadock, m. Sarah Brown; Jerry T., m. Belinda Plaisdell; John M.; Nancy,
m. John Cleveland; and Hiram C. WILLIAM N., Boston, son of 1st Joshua, m.
Sarah Warren of Plymouth, and had Sarah, 1821; William, 1823; Daniel,
1825; Catherine, 1828; Lucy A., 1830; Catherine, 1832, m. Peter Read of
Kingston; Isabella, 1834, m. Nathaniel Ellis of Abington; Ellen, 1837; Sarah,
1839; Edward, 1843. WILLIAM, Hanson, son of Nathan, m. Ada, d. of Philip
Chandler of Duxbury, and had Philip; and William. WILLIAM, Norwich,
probably son of Seabury, m. Amelia DeWitt of Windham, and had Benjamin;
Cyrus, m. a Tappan; William, m. Laura Mills of Albany; Nancy; and Maria,
m. Henry Benson of Montreal. WRESTLING, Duxbury, son of Love, by wife
Mary, had Jonathan; Wrestling; John; Mary; Sarah; Abigail, 1683, m. Elisha
Stetson; Elizabeth; and Hannah. WRESTLING, son of above, m. Hannah,
d. of John Thomas, and had Wrestling, 1724; Isaac, 1727; Thomas, 1729;
Elijah, 1732; Elisha, 1734; Hannah, 1737; Mary, 1740. WRESTLING, Kingston,
son of above, m., 1750, Deborah, d. of Samuel Seabury of Duxbury, and had
Hannah, 1752, m. Seth Drew; Huldah, 1756, m. Samuel Stetson; Seabury,
1754; Martin, 1758; Hosea, 1762, m. Rebecca Bryant; Deborah, 1764, m.
Elnathan Holmes; Violet, 1766, m. Peleg Tupper; Olive, 1768, m. Elisha
Stetson; Wrestling, 1770, m. Martha Symmes. ZADOCK, Duxbury, son of
2d Joseph, removed to Preston, Conn., where he m. Lois, d. of Benjamin
Brewster, and had Darius, 1764, m. Esther Soule; Eunice, 1766, m. James
Jones; Sarah, 1768; Cyrus, 1772, m. Ruth Sampson; Ira, 1775, m. Patience
Crooker; Benjamin, 1777, m. Betsey Tolman; Joseph, 1777, m. Sally
Hunt; Daniel W., 1780; Lois, 1782, m. Reuben Keen; Ruth, 1784, m. John
May; and, 2d, an Arey; Samuel, 1786; William, 1789, m. Martha Jameson;

Lucy, 1795, m. John Elms of Camden. He m., 2d, Lucy Knight of Canterbury the mother of the last six children.

BRIGGS, CLEMENT, came in the Fortune, 1621, m., in Dorchester 1631, Joan Allen, and had Thomas, 1633; Jonathan, 1635; John; David, 1640, and Clement, 1643. He finally settled in Weymouth. ISAAC, who died about 1802, had Samuel, Isaac, Israel, Lewis, and Ruth. ISRAEL, Wareham, son of above, m., 1816, Nancy Clark. JOHN, m. Ruth Barrow, 1701. SAMUEL, son of Isaac by wife Sarah, had Samuel, 1805; Harvey, 1808; Lois, 1810; Jerusha, 1813; Cornelius, 1816; Isaac, 1819; Henry, 1822; Sarah, 1825. SAMUEL, son of above, by wife Amelia Ann, had Samuel, 1834; Sarah M., 1836; Amelia Ann, 1838; Harvey, 1839; John B., 1841; Sabin, 1842. SETH, from Rochester, m. Lucy Bartlett, 1783.

BRIGHAM, ANTIPAS, Sudbury, son of Samuel, had wife and children unknown. ANTIPAS, from Sudbury, probably descendant from above, m. Mercy S., d. of Seth Morton of Plymouth, and had Antipas, 1828; Mary Ann, 1830. SAMUEL, Sudbury, son of Thomas, m. Elizabeth, d. of Abraham Howe of Marlboro', and had Elizabeth, 1685; Hepsibah, 1687; Samuel, 1689; Lydia, 1691; Jedediah, 1693; Jotham, 1695; Timothy, 1698; Charles, 1700; Persis, 1703; Antipas, 1706. THOMAS, Cambridge, 1636, m. Mercy Hurd, and had Thomas, 1642; John, 1645; Mary; Hannah, 1650; Samuel, 1653.

BRIMMER, MARTIN, from Boston, m., 1779, Sally, d. of George Watson.

BRITTERIGE, RICHARD, came in the Mayflower, and was the first to die after landing.

BROOK, SAMUEL, m., 1786, Elizabeth Jackson.

BROOKS, WILLIAM P., from Boston, m., 1835, Mary Clark.

BROWN, CHARLES, m. Lucy Cotton, d. of Charles Jackson, 1820, and had Sophia and Frank. GEORGE W., m. Susan M. Polden, 1838. Job, of Sandwich, m. Mrs. Lydia Swift, 1738. JOHN, probably came before 1636 with his wife Dorothy and three children; James, m. Lydia, d. of John Howland, Mary, m. Thomas Willet, and John, and lived in Plymouth, Duxbury, and Swansea, at which last place he died 1662. JOHN, Duxbury, possibly grandson of above, and son of his son John who died before his father, by wife Ann, had Ann, 1673, and John, 1675. JOHN, m. Harriet Chummuck, 1839. JOHNSTON, son of 2d William, m. Mary B. Brewster, 1847, and had Alonzo F., 1850; Mary S., 1852, m. Joseph S. Buckingham of New York; Charles Foster, 1854, m. Sarah J. McLean; Osceola W., 1859, and Irving W. JOSEPH LASINBY of Boston, m. Mary E., d. of Elkanah Bartlett, 1856, and had Alice H., 1857, and Arthur, 1859. JOSEPH P., son of Lemuel, m. Margaret, d. of George Washburn, 1837, and had Joseph A., and George W., 1848, m. Hannah M., d. of Lyman Shaw. LEMUEL, born 1772, came from Sudbury with wife Sarah Palmer of Cambridge, and had Anne Rice, 1798; Lemuel, 1800; Sarah Palmer, 1804; Catherine B., 1806, m. Seth Morton; Mary B., 1808; Stephen P., 1809; and Joseph P., 1812. He m., 2d, Nancy, wid. of Job Cobb and d. of Jabez Doten, 1829. LEWIS, from Roxbury, m. Caroline Matilda, d. of Nathaniel Wood, 1836, and had Lewis Henry, m. Susan B. Howland. NATHANIEL, son of 1st Robert, m. Rebecca Doten, 1779. NATHANIEL, son of Samuel of Boston, m. Mary, d. of Thomas Bartlett, 1834, and had Mary

Jane, 1835. PETER, supposed to have been brother of 1st John, came in the Mayflower, 1620, probably m. wid. Martha Ford, who came in the Fortune, 1621, and had Peter, Mary, and perhaps others. PETER, son of the above, was one of the Dartmouth purchasers in 1652. There was a Peter m. in Windsor, 1658, Mary, d. of Jonathan Gillett, who may have been his son. PRINCE, m. Martha Harvey, 1792. ROBERT, possibly son of 2d John, or perhaps a son of Robert of Cambridge, was born 1682, and m. Priscilla Johnson of Boston, 1724, by whom he had Priscilla, 1725, m. John Greenleaf of Boston; Mercy, 1728, m. William Greenleaf of Boston; Martha, 1730; Rebecca, and Robert, 1739. He m., 2d, Elizabeth Murdoch, 1752. ROBERT, son of above, m. Mary Bramhall, 1777, and had Robert, 1779; William, 1781; William, 1784; and Mary, 1789. ROBERT, son of 2d William, m. Eunice, d. of Lemuel Simmons, and had Robert S., 1849; Jane B., 1853, and Robert Allen, 1856. STEPHEN P., son of Lemuel, m. Eliza Ann, d. of Isaac Bartlett, 1832, and had Stephen P., 1836, m. Lucinda T., d. of Seth Benson; Annie E., m. Charles Anderson and Simeon Perkins; Caroline E., m. George Benson, and Alice W., m. Charles A. Raymond. WILLIAM, m., 1649, Mary Murcock or Murdock, and had Mary, 1650; George, 1652; William, 1654; Samuel, 1656; John, James, and Mercy. WILLIAM, son of 2d Robert, m. Abigail Allen of Boston, 1808, and had Lydia Allen, 1809; William, 1810; Abigail Allen, 1813; Lydia Allen, 1814; William, 1815; Robert, 1817; Charles, m. Charlotte Ann Pratt of Kingston; and Johnston, m. Mary B. Brewster. WILLIAM, son of above, m. Ruth T. Holmes, 1852, and had Charles T. WILLIAM of Middleboro', m. Sally Barrows, 1831. WILLIAM, m. Sally Thomas, 1810.

BRYANT, CALEB, m. Betsey Barnes, 1795. ICHABOD, Bridgewater, son of 2d Stephen, m. Ruth Staples, and had Philip, m. Silena Howard; Nathan, Seth, Job, Gamaliel of New Bedford, Phebe, Ruth, Sarah, Anna, Prudence. JOHN, Scituate, m. Mary, d. of George Lewis of Barnstable, 1644, and had John, 1644; Hannah, 1645, m. John Stodder of Hingham; Joseph, 1646; Sarah, 1648; Mary, 1650; Martha, 1652; Samuel, 1654. He m., 2d, 1657, Elizabeth, d. of William Witherell, and 3d, 1665, Mary, d. of Thomas Hiland, by whom he had Elizabeth, 1666; Benjamin, 1669; Joseph, 1671; Jabez, 1672; Ruth, 1673; Thomas, 1675; Deborah, 1677; Agatha, 1678; Ann, 1680; Elisha, 1682. Prudence. JOHN, son of above, m. Abigail Bryant, 1665, and had Mary, 1666; Hannah, 1668; Bethiah, 1670; Samuel, 1673; Jonathan, 1677, m. Margaret West and probably Mary Little; Abigail, 1682, m. John Faunce; Benjamin, 1688. JOHN, son of 1st Stephen by wife Sarah, had John, 1678; James, 1682; Ruth, 1685; Sarah, 1688; Joanna, 1690; George, 1693. JOHN, son of above, m., 1700, Mary West, and had James, 1702; Ebenezer, 1705. JONATHAN, son of 2d John, m., 1700, Margaret West, and had Rebecca, 1702; Priscilla, 1703; Mary, 1705. SAMUEL, son of 2d John by wife Joanna, had Samuel, 1699; Josiah, 1702, m. Josiah Waterman; Abigail, 1703, m. a Finney; Sylvanus; Lydia, m. Thomas Sampson; Elizabeth, m. a Waterman; and Nathaniel. SAMUEL, probably grandson of above, m. Eleanor Tinkham, and had Sarah, 1758; Samuel, and Lydia. STEPHEN, Duxbury, 1643, moved to Plymouth, 1650, m. Abigail, d. of John Shaw, and had John, 1650; Mary,

1654; Stephen, 1658; Sarah, 1659; Lydia, 1662, m. William Churchill; Elizabeth, 1667, m. Joseph King. STEPHEN, Middleboro', son of above, by wife Mehitabel had Stephen, 1684; David, 1687; William, 1692; Hannah; Ichabod, 1699; Timothy, 1702. TIMOTHY, perhaps brother of above, m. Margery West, and had Rebecca, 1702; Priscilla, 1705, and Mercy. (See Kingman's History of North Bridgewater.)

BUCKLEY, JOHN, m. Rebecca Loring, 1820.

BUDGE, JOSIAH, m., 1782, Mary Raymond.

BUGBEE, AURIN, m. Deborah Barnes, d. of John Gooding, perhaps about 1838, and had Aurina, m. John M. Atwood; James Henry; John, now of Quincy, Ill., and George, living in Texas. The name was formerly spelled Bugby, and an Edward and a Richard came over in 1634 and 1630, respectively, and settled in Roxbury.

BUMPASS, OR BUMPUS, or BOMPASSE, EDWARD, came in the Fortune, 1621, and finally removed to Duxbury and Marshfield. His children were Faith, 1631; Sarah; John, 1636; Edward, 1638; Joseph, 1639; Jacob, 1644; Hannah, 1646; and perhaps Thomas. JOSEPH, son of above, had Lydia, 1669; Wybra, 1672; Joseph, 1674; Rebecca, 1677; James, 1679; Penelope, 1681; Mary, 1684; Mehitabel, 1692. JOSEPH, m. Lydia Wingfield, 1801. WARREN of Wareham m. Sarah Valler, 1816.

BUMPO, MICHAEL, m. Nabby Stevens, 1804.

BUNDY, JOHN, by wife Martha, had Martha, 1649; Mary, 1653; Patience; James, 1664; and Sarah, 1669. The two last were probably born in Taunton.

BUNKER, JAMES, m. Hannah Shurtleff, 1757.

BURBANK, DAVID, son of Timothy, m. Polly Bryant, 1806, and had David. DAVID, son of above, m. Olive Soule, 1829, and had Susan Soule, 1830, m. Henry L. Chubbuck; David Winslow, 1835, m. Sarah H. Lakin; Mary Thomas, 1837, m. Hiram Kendricks; Asaph S., m. Lucretia W. Bumpus; and George, m. in Virginia. EZRA, son of Timothy, m. Priscilla, d. of Thomas Savery, 1762, and had Ezra, 1764; Priscilla, 1766, m. Benjamin Bramhall; Thomas, 1768; John, 1770; Mary, 1772; Samuel, 1774; Nehemiah, 1777; and Joanna, m. Thomas Savery. EZRA, son of above, m. Lydia Drew, 1792, and had Lydia, m. Thomas Marsh and James Doten; Priscilla, m. Samuel W. Gleason; and William S. He m., 2d, Polly, wid. of David Burbank, 1819. JOHN, son of 1st Ezra, m. Lydia Mason, 1794, and had John, 1795; Stevens Mason, 1798; Henry, 1802, m. a Horton of New Bedford; Lydia, 1804, m. Winslow Holmes; Betsey, 1806; Lucy, 1807, m. Southworth Barnes; Nehemiah, 1811. JOHN, son of above, m. Lucy Ann Joyce, and had Betsey, 1829; and Amy Allen, 1831. JOSEPH, son of Timothy, m. Joanna, d. of William Holmes, 1766. JOSIAH, son of Thomas, m. Polly, d. of Richard Durfey, and had Josiah Durfey, now living in Charlestown. NEHEMIAH, son of 1st Ezra, m. Hannah, d. of David Torrey of Weymouth, and had Hannah Torrey, 1803; Daniel Torrey, 1804; and Priscilla Lovell, 1806, m. Israel W. Munroe of Boston. He m., 2d, Rebecca, d. of Daniel Soule of Plympton, and had Rebecca, 1813, m. Barnabas H. Holmes. SAMUEL, son of 1st Ezra, m. Sally Coye, 1798, and had Samuel, m. Louisa Crocker; Sally, m.

John Sylvester; William; Mary Ann, m. Henry Flanders; Walter, m. Thirza (Fearing) Tobey, wid. of Curtis Tobey; David; Catherine, m. Nathaniel C. Covington. STEVENS MASON, son of 1st John, m. Hannah, d. of Samuel Bradford, 1823, and had Stevens Mason; Caroline A., m. William R. Clark, 1848; Charles, m. in Texas; and Nehemiah. STEVENS MASON, son of above, m. Cornelia, d. of Samuel Doten, 1851, and had Hannah, Alfred S., Nellie D., and Stevens M. THOMAS, son of 1st Ezra, m. Mary Clark of Middleboro', and had Josiah and Ezra. TIMOTHY of Boston, originally from Rowley, born 1703, came to Plymouth and m., 1728, Mercy Kempton, and had Mary, 1730; Timothy, 1732; Isaac, 1733, m. Mary Marble of Swansea; Rebecca, 1736, m. Snow Keen of Pembroke; Ezra, 1738; Hannah, 1740, m. Theodosius Ford; Joseph, 1743, m. Joanna Holmes; Lucy, 1745, m. Stephen Churchill; Mary, 1748, m. James Savery; David, 1750. WILLIAM S., son of 2d Ezra, m. Abigail S., d. of Luke Perkins, 1821, and had William, Abigail; William, 1824, m. Steven Turner; Ezra Lewis, 1828, m. Sally Wood; Priscilla Ann, 1830, m. Simeon H. Barrows; William Sherman, 1832, m. Phebe T. Bartlett; Calvin Perkins, 1834; Elijah Walker, 1837, m. Corinna Wilder of Weymouth; George; Georgiana, m. George Shaw of East Bridgewater; and Luke Perkins, m. Addie Curtis of Scituate.

BURCHARD, or BURCHER, EDWARD, came in the Ann, 1623, with probably a wife, but died or removed before 1627.

BURGESS, ABNER, son of 1st William, m., 1807, Deborah, d. of Joshua Wright, and had Abner, m. Hannah Whiting; Nathaniel, m. Emily Knapp; Sydney, m. Abby Knapp and Harriet Whiting; Spencer; Deborah, m. Gideon Perkins; Lucy, m. Lemuel R. Wood; William, m. Lucy Dunham. BANGS, Sandwich, son of Simeon, m., about 1780, Eunice Russell, and had Charity, Abigail, Jonathan, and James. BENJAMIN, son of 1st Nathan, m., 1823, Deborah Burgess, and had Deborah, m. Jason Smith; and Maria. CHANDLER, son of 2d John, m. Jane Manter, and had Chandler, 1806, m. Catherine, d. of John Burgess; Lewis, 1808, m. Sarah Churchill and Catherine, d. of John and wid. of Chandler Burgess; Jane, 1810, m. Freeman Morton; Ruth W., 1812; Hannah, 1815, m. Samuel Cole; Winslow, 1817, m. Elizabeth C. Thomas; Jabez, Cordelia, Lucy M., and Experience. CHARLES, Kingston, son of Stephen, m., 1811, Anna Prince, and had Charles C., Elsie, Mary S., Deborah Z., Lucy T.; Noah P., m. Lydia J., d. of Leavitt T. Robbins of Plymouth, and now lives in Portland; Rebecca C., Betsey P., Thomas H., George C., Hannah H., Marian H. DANIEL, son of 1st Nathan, m. Deborah Brewster of Duxbury, and had Betsey, Judith, Samuel, Daniel, Deborah. EBENEZER, Sandwich, son of Jacob by wife Mercy, had Elizabeth, 1702; Samuel, 1703; Thankful, 1704; Nathaniel, 1706; Ebenezer, 1707; Benjamin, 1709; Mary, 1712; Jabez, 1717; and Thomas. GEORGE, m., 1796, Deborah McLaughlin. GEORGE, m., 1833, Caroline Maxim. JABEZ, son of 2d John, m., 1814, Sally Manter. JACOB, Sandwich, son of 1st Thomas, m., 1660, Mary Nye, and had Samuel, 1671; Ebenezer, 1673; Jacob, 1676. JAMES, Sandwich, son of Bangs, m. Lydia Bates, and had James of Plymouth, and others. JAMES, son of above, m. Betsey Otis, d. of Jesse Robbins, and had Elizabeth James, 1838. JOHN, Yarmouth, son of 1st Thomas, m., 1657, Mary Wooden, and had John, Thomas, Joseph, Samuel, Jacob, Martha, and perhaps others. JOHN, son of 1st Nathaniel, m. Annie, d. of Joseph Tribble, and had John, Chandler; Annie, m. John Harlow; Nathan; Lucy, m. Josiah Manter; Serviah; Hannah, m. Joseph Sampson; Jabez, m. Sally Manter; Sarah, m. Chandler Robbins; Rebecca, m. Joseph Robbins; Nathaniel. He m., 2d, Ruth, d. of Phineas Sprague of Duxbury, and had Phineas Sprague. JOHN, son of above, m., 1805, Susan, d. of Sylvanus Sampson, and had Susan, 1808; Anna T., 1810, m. David Drew; Catherine, 1815, m. Chandler Burgess and Lewis Burgess; Mary Ann, 1817, m. Pelham Finney; John, 1819, m. Eliza Chitman of New London. He m., 2d, Sophia Sampson, sister of his 1st wife, 1822, and had Albert Thomas, 1825, m. Cynthia Chitman; Sophia, 1828, m. Benjamin Nye Adams. JOHN ALLYNE, son of 2d Joseph, m. Hannah, d. of Cyrus Shaw, and had Sally, Joseph, John F., 1861; John A., 1866. JOSEPH, Sandwich, son of 1st John, m. Thomasine Bangs, and had Joseph, Lydia, John, Jonathan, Mercy, Remember, Simeon. JOSEPH, son of 4th Thomas, m., 1812, Sally, d. of Simon Richmond, and had Joseph William Simon R., John Allyne; Eunice Thomas, m. a Delano; Fenelon Thaxter, 1822. He m., 2d, Hannah, wid. of John Atwood, and d. of Simon Richmond, and had Lydia A. JOSEPH WILLIAM, son of above, m., 1835, Hannah E., d. of Joseph Barnes, and had Thaxter Fenelon, 1837, m. Delia, d. of Stephen D. Drew; Joseph William, 1838; James Kendall, 1844, m. Betsey, d. of Daniel Burgess; Erford A., 1847, m. Martha, d. of William Shurtleff. He m., 2d, Sarah Elizabeth, d. of Joseph Davis, and had George Boutwell, 1852; Hannah Ellis, 1854, m. William Green of Stoneham; Charles Davis, 1856; Mary Clark, 1860, m. John Frank Lovell; Lucy Ella Haskel, 1865; Susie Mary, 1870. NATHAN, son of 1st Nathaniel, m. Deborah Hunt, and had Caroline, Samuel, Benjamin; Nathan, m. Maria Burgess; Betsey, m. an Oldham; Ruth, m. Trueman Sampson; Judith, m. Aaron Sampson; Deborah, m. John Pierce; Abigail, m. Albert Mortimer Watson; Sally, m. Benjamin Bagnall; Daniel. NATHAN, son of 2d John, m., 1813, Susanna, d. of Joshua Wright, and had Augustus, m. Mary O. Finney; Betsey Ann, m. J. A. Perkins and William Parsons; Serviah, m. Elkanah C. Finney; Henry, m. Abby Bartlett; Ezra, m. Almira Pratt; Ivory, m. Mary Pratt; Francis, m. Mary Ann Meagher; Susan W., m. Josiah P. Robbins; Isabelle, m. Andrew Shannesy; Eveline, m. James F. Robinson. NATHANIEL, son of 3d Thomas, m. Ruth Chandler, and had Jacob, m. Sarah Glass of Duxbury; Nathaniel; Patience, m. Malachi Delano; Thomas; Ruth, m. Abner Sampson; Lucy, m. Benjamin Pierce of Duxbury; William, John; Mercy, m. John Taylor; Nathan; Rebecca, m. Jesse Ballou; Zerviah, m. Joseph Sampson. NATHANIEL, son of 2d John, m. Jane Bisbee, and had Georgiana and Austin. PHINEAS SPRAGUE, son of 2d John, m. Charlotte, d. of Ezra Thomas, and had Phineas Frank, 1833, m. Harriet Francis; Isaac S., 1835, m. Ruth Burgess; Ezra Thomas, 1837, m. Ellen Bumstead; Peleg S., 1840, m. Jane A. Nicol; Charlotte Thomas; Ruth A., m. Benjamin B. Manter. SAMUEL, son of Ebenezer, m., 1732, Jedidah Gibbs, and had Jabez, 1733; Nathaniel, 1735. SAMUEL, Sandwich, son of 1st John, by wife Elizabeth, had Samuel,

Patience, Elizabeth, Abigail, Jacob, Remember, Thomas, Martha, Kesiah.
SIMEON, Sandwich, son of 1st Joseph, m. Deborah Edwards, and had Abigail,
Lucy, Ruth, Thankful, Hannah, Bangs, Dorothy, and Dolly. SIMON RICH-
MOND, son of 2d Joseph, m., 1837, Jane E., d. of Joseph Barnes, and had
William Wallace, m. Mercy T., d. of Henry Weston; George Augustus, 1842;
Rosilla Barnes, 1847. STEPHEN, son of 5th Thomas, m. Temperance Wing,
removed to Middleboro', and had Launcelot, Charles C., Thomas, Phebe,
Stephen, Temperance, James, John. THOMAS, called Burge, Lynn, removed
to Sandwich, 1637, and had Joseph, 1639; Jacob, John, Thomas; Elizabeth,
m. Ezra Perry, and others. THOMAS, Sandwich, son of above, m., 1648,
Elizabeth Bassett; and, 2d, Lydia Gaunt, and had Thomas. THOMAS,
Little Compton, son of above by wife Esther, had Edward, m. Elizabeth Coe;
Deborah, m. Jeremiah Brownell; Esther, m. William Wilbur; Lydia, m. a
Collins. He m., 2d, Martha Clossen, and had Joseph, m. Anna Tew; John,
m. Hannah James; Mary, m. John Wood; Thomas, m. Hannah Taylor;
Jacob, m. Susanna Williston. By a 3d wife, Patience, he had Mercy, m.
Joseph Thurston; Rebecca, Martha, Nathaniel. THOMAS, son of 1st Na-
thaniel, m., 1781, Lydia, d. of Joseph Tribble, and had William, 1782; Polly
and Lydia, twins, 1784, who m., respectively, James Woodward and George
Delano; Ruby, Esther, Eunice, Sarah Howard, Thomas, Joseph, Edward
Wilbur, Irene Sanger, and Betsey; the last two of whom m. Clement Bates.
THOMAS, Yarmouth, son of 2d Samuel, m. Mary Covill, and had Nathaniel,
Thomas, Jonathan, Covill, Stephen, Philip, Mary. THOMAS, son of above,
m., 1804, Lucy, d. of Samuel Lanman. THOMAS, son of Ebenezer, m., 1745,
Patience Doty, and had Elizabeth, 1745; Thomas, 1748. THOMAS, son of
above, by wife Mary, had Joseph, 1779; Thomas, 1782; Josiah, 1786; Elizabeth, 1789, m. Eber Hall; Sarah, 1791, m. Nathan Hall. VINAL, son of 1st
William, m., 1819, Esther Clark, and had Asenath, 1821, m. Solomon Holmes
and Aaron Sampson; Lydia C., 1825, m. Sylvanus Sampson; Experience,
1827; Seth, 1830; Frederick, 1832, m. Harriet Leland; Sylvanus William,
1834; Esther C., 1837, m. Gustavus G. Sampson; Sarah T., 1837; Ruth, 1841,
m. Isaac J. Burgess; Lucy S., m. Joseph P. Thurston. WILLIAM, son of
4th Thomas, m. Ruth Sampson, and had Ruth, m. Sylvanus Sampson;
Abner; Lucy, m. Joseph Wright; William; Mercy, m. Thomas Sampson;
Vinal; Wealthea, m. Prince Manter; Deborah, and Maria. WILLIAM, son
of above, m., 1816, Polly Bartlett, and had Nancy C., m. Henry Whiting;
William C., m. Rebecca Bartlett, and R. C. Atwood; Mary B., m. Edmund
Tallman; Otis, m. Mary S., d. of Franklin B. Cobb; Hannah; Jeanette D.,
m. John D. Manter; Lucy S.; Margaret B., m. Ebenezer Nickerson; Lemuel
B., m. Ruth Cobb; and Ruth.   (See Burgess' Genealogy.)
     BURK, JOHN, m., 1693, Sarah Doty.
     BURN, JOHN, in Plymouth, 1641. MICHAEL, by wife Elizabeth, had Mar-
garet, 1737; Elizabeth, 1738; Samuel, 1740; Tomasin, 1741; Michael, 1744;
George, 1746.
     BURT, EDWARD, from Boston, who had two brothers, William and John,
and a sister, Tamson, m. Betsey Dunham, 1817, and had Tamson Clark,
1817, m. Elial Benson; Silas Hathaway, 1820, m. Almira Hathaway; Benja-

min Thomas, 1822, m. Sarah White; John E., 1823; Charity S., 1826, m. Lewis Perry and Stephen Drew; Charlotte K., 1828; Elizabeth C., 1830, m. William Staples; William B., 1832, m. Priscilla E. Holmes; Phineas, 1833, m. Cynthia T., d. of George W. Burgess; Adoniram, 1836; Eunice D., 1837; Thomas B., 1839. JOHN E., son of above, m. Eliza J., d. of Adoniram Thomas, and had Edward T., 1848; Addie Eliza F., 1856; and Eldora Jane. LABAN, m. Hannah, d. of William Holmes, 1807, and had Hannah, 1807; Amelia Ann, 1811; Sally, 1813; Susan Lincoln, 1815; Laban, 1817; Mary Winslow, 1819, m. Richard Pierce; Janette Allen, 1821; John, 1823; Catherine Elizabeth, 1824; and Harriet Holmes, 1827, m. Henry Briggs.

BUTTERWORTH, JOHN, m., 1777, Elizabeth Bott.

CÆSAR, CÆSAR, and Hester, negroes, had Eunice, 1768; Philip, 1774, made free by their master, Edward Winslow; and Esther, 1775, given to her parents by Edward Winslow.

CAHOON, FREEMAN, by wife Rebecca, had Phebe B., 1822; Deborah Y. 1825; Andrew J. S., 1834. MARK, by wife Marietta, had Ebenezer Y., 1821; William S., 1825; Mark, 1827; Nathan S., 1829; Jay, 1831; Ann S., 1834; James F., 1837; Lafayette, 1840; Marietta N., 1843. SAMUEL, m., 1806, Mary Swift.

CALDERWOOD, JOHN, m., 1792, Patience, d. of Isaac Churchill. SAMUEL, m. Priscilla Bartlett, and had Samuel, 1761.

CALLEY, STEPHEN, pub. to Catherine Flaney of Chatham, 1747.

CALWELL, THOMAS, from Middleboro', m., 1817, Mercy D. Valler.

CAMPBELL, ANDREW, m., 1775, Bathsheba Rickard, and had Susanna 1775; Mary, 1777; Andrew, 1779. DUNCAN, m., 1779, Susanna McKeel. JOHN m., 1837, Sarah Holmes, d. of Samuel Lanman, and had Sarah E., 1837, m. Andrew J. Bradford; Frances M., 1841, m. Seth W. Eddy and Joseph T. Robbins.

CANNON, JOHN, came in the Fortune 1621, and disappeared before 1627.

CAPEN, HENRY G., from Boston, m., 1838, Charlotte A. Marcy.

CAPET, JOHN, pub. to Desire Wood, 1733, Indians. JOSLIN, m. Hannah Capet, 1744, Indians.

CARTER, BENJAMIN, m. Elizabeth Marshall, and had Benjamin, 1740. HENRY, m., 1833, Maria Bartlett Banks. ROBERT came in the Mayflower, servant of William Mullins, and died soon.

CARVER, CALEB, Marshfield, son of 7th John, by wife Abigail, had Caleb, 1734; Ruth, 1736; John, 1738; Israel, 1740, m. Margaret Sherman; Stephen, 1743; Joseph, 1745; Charles, 1746; Amos, 1748; Abigail, 1751. CALEB, Marshfield, son of above, m. Abigail Damon, 1756, and had Melzar, 1756; Ruth, 1758; Abigail, 1764. CHANDLER, by wife Catherine, had Lucy, 1837; James M., 1839. He m., 2d, 1842, Harriet Totman. DAVID, Marshfield, son of Joshua, m., 1775, Sarah Holmes, and had David, 1776; Rebecca, 1779. JAMES, son of 1st Josiah, m., 1756, Hope, d. of Isaac Doten, and had James, 1757. JAMES, son of above, m., 1779, Mary Harlow, and had James, 1782. JOHN came in the Mayflower 1620, with wife Catherine, and both died early, leaving no children. JOHN, Duxbury, son of 1st Robert, m., 1658, Millicent, d. of William Ford, and had William, 1659; John; Elizabeth, 1663; Robert; Eleazer; David; Mercy, 1672; Anna; Mehitabel; and Rebecca. JOHN, son of above, m., 1689, Mary, d. of Jonathan Barnes, and had Josiah, 1690; John, 1692; Robert, 1694; Mary, 1696; Hannah, 1700. JOHN, son or grandson of above, m., 1748, Grace, d. of John Crandon, and had Sarah, 1749; Lemuel, 1751. JOHN, son of 1st Nathaniel, m., 1797, Elizabeth, d. of Richard Holmes, and had John, 1800; and Betsey, m. Sylvanus Churchill. JOHN, son of above, m., 1822, Sarah Perkins, and had John, 1824, m. Sarah Ann Hiscox of New Bedford; Sarah Jane, 1827; Nathaniel, 1835, m. Mary Jane, d. of Benjamin H. Crandon; Ichabod, m. Esther Ellis; and Josiah, m. Betsey M. Taylor. JOHN, Marshfield, son of 1st William, m., 1709, Mary Rogers, and had Mary, 1713; Caleb, 1715; Jemima, 1716. JOSIAH, son of 3d John, m., 1718, Dorothy, d. of Ephraim Cole, and had Josiah, 1724; Dorothy, 1727; James, 1729. He m., 2d, Bethiah (Spooner) Churchill, wid. of John, 1732. He m., 3d, 1735, Mercy Faunce, and had Dorothy, 1736, m, John Bartlett; Mercy, 1738; Nathaniel, 1740; Mercy, 1743; John, 1747. JOSIAH, son of above, m., 1747, Jerusha (Bradford) Sparrow, wid. of Edward. JOSIAH, son of 1st Nathaniel, m., 1797, Elizabeth, d. of Robert Davie, and had Eliza, m. Calvin Fuller; Sarah, m. William Nelson; Josiah; and Ichabod. He m., 2d, Abigail, d. of Corban Barnes, and wid. of William Keen, 1816, and had William, 1817, Abigail, 1818, m. Obed Kempton and Nahum Thomas; Theodore S., 1820; Emeline, 1822, m. Kenny H. Barnes; Theodore, 1824; Nathaniel, 1825. JOSHUA, Marshfield, son of 1st William, m., 1728, Martha Ford, and had Isaac, 1729; Joshua, 1732; a son, 1736; David, 1738; Sarah,'1739. NATHANIEL, son of 1st Josiah, m., 1764, Sarah Churchill, and had Nathaniel, 1766; John; Josiah; Mercy, 1770, m. William Barnes; Lucy, m. Rufus Sherman of Carver; Sally, m. Barnabas Faunce; Betsey, 1774, m. Barnabas Faunce; Polly, m. David Bartlett. NATHANIEL, son of above, m., 1789, Joanna, d. of Benjamin Churchill, and had Stephen; Nathaniel, 1791; Sally, m. Seth F. Nye of Sandwich; Nancy; and Mary. NATHANIEL, son of above, m., 1812, Betsey Woodward, and had Elizabeth, m. Jeremiah Farris. He m,, 2d, Nancy Luce, and had Nancy, 1823. REUBEN, from Marshfield, m., 1747, Phebe Holmes. ROBERT, Marshfield, 1638, had John; William, and others. ROBERT, son of 3d John, m. Mary, d. of Caleb Cook, and had Elizabeth, 1718; Mary, 1721, m. Richard Adams; Robert, 1723. WILLIAM, Marshfield, son of 2d John, m., 1682, Elizabeth, d. of John Foster, and had John, 1683; William, 1685; Josiah, 1688; Caleb, 1690; Mary, 1695, m. a Standish; Joshua, 1698; Millicent; Elizabeth, m. a Taylor; Sarah, m. a Taylor. WILLIAM, Marshfield, son of above, m., 1712, Abigail Branch, and had Elizabeth, 1715; Reuben, 1718; Amos, 1720; Deborah, 1722; Abigail, 1724; William, 1727; Huldah, 1730; Keziah, 1738. He, perhaps, m., 2d, Elizabeth Rouse. WILLIAM, from Marshfield, son of above, m., 1755, Margaret, d. of Thomas Kempton, and had Thomas, 1755; William, 1757; Branch, 1759.

CASE, JOHN, m., 1732, Rebecca Pierce, and had John, 1736; and John again, 1737.

CASSIDY, HENRY, m., 1810, Betsey Lewis Holmes. JOHN, m., in Ireland, Nancy McGoigen. His children have been Elizabeth, m. Gridley T. Poole; Andrew; Owen; Ellen, m. a Southmayd of Compton, N. H.; and John. JOHN, son of above, m., 1845, Mary McClinchy, and had Margaret Ann, m. Edward Wright of Plympton; John Thomas; Elizabeth, m. John Burt of Abington; Ellen; Andrew, m. Katie Frawley; and Katie. WILLIAM, m., 1784, Lydia Finney, and had Sally, m. Job Rider.

CASWELL, JAMES, m., 1794, Dorcas Brooks of Sandwich. THOMAS, from Carver, m., 1793, Susanna Wing. THOMAS, m. 1835, Deborah Brailey. WILLIAM, m., 1807, Nancy, wid. of Lewis Churchill.

CATO, CATO, pub. to Jesse, slave of John Foster, 1731.

CATTO, JOHN MACK, m. Mary Sampson, 1777.

CHALKER, RICHARD, from Saybrook, m., 1825, Mary Ann Cornish.

CHAMBERS, WILLIAM, m., 1756, Susanna Lemote.

CHANDLER, EDMUND, Duxbury, 1633, had Sarah; Anna; Mary; Ruth; Benjamin, m. Elizabeth, d. of John Buck; Samuel; and Joseph. IRA, Duxbury, son of Nathan, had four wives, one of whom was a Phillips; and had Joseph, and perhaps others. JOHN B., grandson of 3d Samuel, m. Hannah Sturtevant, and had Nancy B., m. Edmund Robbins; Samuel B., m. Jerusha, d. of Peabody Bartlett; Phineas; William; John T., Lucy S.; Lydia, m. Josiah Sylvester and Benjamin Pierce; Thankful S., m. Winslow M. Tribble; Hannah S., m. Richard B. Dunham. JOSEPH, son of Edmund, Duxbury, had John, m. Sarah Weston; Joseph; Edmund; and Benjamin. JOSEPH, son of above, Duxbury, m. Martha Hunt, 1701, and had Philip, 1702; Mary, 1704; Joshua, 1706; Zachariah, 1708; Edmund, 1710; Ebenezer, 1712; Sarah, 1714; Martha, 1716; Jonathan, 1718; and Judah, 1720. JOSEPH, Duxbury, son of Ira, m. Eliza, d. of Peleg Churchill of Plymouth, and had Peleg Churchill, m. Lydia Weston; Albert C.; Ezra C., and others. NATHAN, Duxbury, son of Philip, by wife Ruth, had Ephraim; Lucy; Celah; Hannah; Ruth; and Deborah. He m., 2d, Esther Glass, 1770, and had Joseph, and Ira. PHILIP, Duxbury, son of 2d Joseph, m. Rebecca, d. of Thomas Phillips, 1725, and had Nathan, 1726; Betty, 1728; Perez, 1730; Esther and Maria, twins, 1732; Peleg, 1735; Philip, 1738, m. Christian, d. of Blaney Phillips; Mary, 1744; Elijah, 1747. SAMUEL, Duxbury, son of Edmund, had probably Samuel. SAMUEL, son of above, by wife Margaret, had Martha, 1719; Abigail, 1721; Samuel, 1723; Thomas, 1725. SAMUEL, son of above, had a son Samuel who m. Nancy Brown, and was the father of John B., above mentioned. SAMUEL B., son of John B., m. Jerusha, d. of Peabody Bartlett, and had Samuel Bartlett, 1832; David Lothrop, 1834; Eveline Coleman, 1835; John Brown, 1837.

CHAPMAN, SAMUEL, pub. to Nancy Churchill, 1815.

CHASE, JOHN, appeared in Plymouth in 1778, and m. in that year Rebecca Dunham, and had Rebecca, who went to England; and John, 1781. Rebecca, his wid., m. Noah Gale. JOHN, son of above, m. Abigail Rogers, 1802, and had John; William, 1807; George E., 1809; Henry, 1811; Lorenzo, m. Rachel Lothrop; Abby, m. Thomas Bassett; Caroline, m. Charles Burgess; Henry again, 1817; and Samuel R., 1829. JOHN, son of above, m. Lydia (Simmons)

Ripley, wid. of Zenas, and had Zenas, 1833, m. Elizabeth Lovell; Lydia, 1836, m. George H. Chase; William; John; and Elizabeth. SYLVANUS D., son of Consider of Carver, m. Hannah S. Holmes, 1826, and had George H., m. Lydia, d. of John Chase; Henry W.; Ambros; and Hannah T., m. George F. Weston.

CHAUNCY, CHARLES, came from England, 1637, with wife Catherine, d. of Robert Eyre, and children Sarah, 1631, m. Gershom Bulkley; Isaac, 1632; Ichabod, 1635. After arrival he had Barnabas; Nathaniel; and Elnathan, the two last twins; Israel; and Hannah. In 1641, he removed to Scituate, and in 1654 to Cambridge.

CHILDS, THOMAS, m. Anna, and had Mary Knowles, 1815.

CHILTON, JAMES, came in the Mayflower with wife and child Mary, who m. John Winslow. He died at Provincetown, and his wife in Plymouth, soon after landing. Another daughter m. in England, and following her parents was living in Plymouth in 1650.

CHIPMAN, JOHN, m. Hope, d. of John Howland, and had Elizabeth, 1647; and John born in Plymouth; and Hope, 1652; Lydia, 1654; John, 1657; Hannah, 1658; Samuel, 1662; Ruth, 1663; Bethiah, 1666; Mercy, 1668; John, 1670; Desire, 1673, born in Barnstable. SAMUEL, m., 1814, Nancy Churchill. SETH, m. Priscilla Bradford, 1721. He had a second wife Sarah, and had Seth, 1724.

CHUBBUCK, NATHANIEL, by wife Mary, had Benjamin, 1716; Ellis, 1715; Jonathan, 1717; Mary, 1719; Susanna, 1726. The following children were previously born in Hingham: Nathaniel, 1707; Martha, 1708; and Sarah, 1711.

CHUMMUCK, JESSE, m. Hannah Reed, 1814.

CHURCH, BENJAMIN, son of 1st Richard, m., 1667, Alice, d. of. Constant Southworth, and had Thomas, 1674; Constant, 1676; Benjamin; Edward; Charles; Elizabeth, 1684; and Nathaniel, 1686. CHARLES, son of above by wife Mary, had Benjamin, 1706; Deborah, 1707; Charles, 1710; Rebecca, 1713; Joseph, 1715; Sarah, 1718. JOSEPH, perhaps son of Nathaniel, m. Judith Harlow, 1705, and had Sarah, 1706. NATHANIEL, Scituate, son of 1st Richard, had Abigail, 1666; Richard, 1668, Nathaniel, 1670, m. Mary Curtis; Alice, 1679; Joseph, 1681; Charles, 1683; Sarah, 1686. RICHARD, Plymouth, 1633, m. Elizabeth Warren, and had Joseph; Benjamin, 1639; Richard; Caleb; Nathaniel; Hannah; Abigail, 1647, m. Samuel Thaxter; Charles, Deborah, 1657, m. John Irish; and Mary. RICHARD, m. Anna Sturtevant, 1720.

CHURCHILL, AMAZIAH, son of 2d Elkanah, m. Elizabeth, d. of Solomon Sylvester, and had Caleb, 1747, m. Patience Nelson; Elizabeth, 1749; Amaziah, 1750; Faith, 1753, m. Ezekiel Morton; Elizabeth, 1755, m. Samuel Churchill; Lucy, 1757, m. Lewis Weston; Mary, 1758, m. William Weston; Mendall, 1760; Solomon, 1762, m. Betsey Bartlett. AMAZIAH, son of above, m. Betty Bartlett, 1776, and had Edward; Ellen; Betsey, m. George Robbins; Harriet, m. George Bradford; and Amaziah. AMAZIAH, son of above, m. Martha Doten, 1799, and had Martha, 1800; and Betsey B., m. Henry Rob_bins. He m., 2d, Polly Harlow, 1808, and had Louisa H., m. Thomas B.

Sears; Amasa, m. Leonice M. Harlow; and Lionel, 1817, m. Lucy Jane, d. of Caleb Battles. ANSEL, son of 1st Ephraim, m. Bethiah Holmes, 1765, and had Ansel, who removed to Rhode Island; Priscilla, m. Benjamin Sampson; Patience, m. John Calderwood; John, m. Nancy, d. of Isaac Jackson; Bethiah, m. Zephaniah Holmes. ANSEL, son of 4th Ebenezer, m. Lois Caswell of New Bedford, and had Ansel, m. Sarah Delano and a Morse; Eliza, m. Smith Fuller; Henry James; George, m. Louisa Bonney; Maria, m. Samuel Fuller; and Mercy, m. Robert Weston. ASAPH, Milton, son of Zebidee, m., 1810, Mary, d. of Edward Gardner of Charlestown, and had Mary, 1811; Juliet, 1812; Asaph, 1814, m. Mary, d. of Darius Brewer of Framingham, and Mary Anne, d. of Jonathan Ware of Milton; Charles Marshal Spring, 1819; Joseph McKean, 1821, m. Augusta Phillips Gardner; Charles Marshal Spring, 1825, m. Susan, d. of John Phillips Spooner of Dorchester. BARNABAS, son of 1st Joseph, m. Lydia Harlow, and had Barnabas, 1714; William, 1716, m. Susanna Clark; Ichabod, 1719; Joseph, 1721; Lemuel, 1723; Isaac, 1726, m. Sarah Cobb; Thomas, 1730, m. Mary Ewer; Ebenezer, 1732, Lydia, 1735, m. Nathaniel Holmes; John, 1739. BARNABAS, son of above, m. Lydia, d. of Eleazer Holmes, 1744, and had Elizabeth, 1746, m. Robert Davie; Barnabas, 1747; Job, 1751; Samuel, 1753; Seth, 1754, m. Elizabeth Sylvester; Job, 1756; Lydia, 1758, m. William Rider. BARNABAS, son of above, m. Sarah Faunce, 1780, and had Barnabas, 1784; Job, 1787; Barnabas, 1789. He perhaps m., 2d, Lydia Cole, 1803. BARNABAS, son of Job, m. Eliza, d. of John Eddy, 1833, and had Barnabas Lothrop, 1834; Elizabeth E., 1837, m. Lothrop T. Kimball; Robert Roberts; Frances Maria; Emma Frances, m. Henry L. Larned of Buffalo; Robert Bruce; Mary Louise, 1847, m. Charles Cobb; and Ann Lothrop, 1861, m. Arthur E. Lewis. BENJAMIN, son of 1st Stephen, m. Ruth Delano, and had Wilson, 1746; Benjamin, 1748; Abner, 1750. BENJAMIN, son of above, m. Phebe (Tinkham) Randall, wid. of Enoch, 1782, and had Nathan and Benjamin, 1785. BENJAMIN, Plympton, son of 1st William, m., 1717, Mary Shaw, and had Mary, 1720; Perez, 1722; Elizabeth, 1725; James, 1726; Benjamin, 1728; Susanna, 1733. BRANCH, m. wid. Sarah Holmes, 1809. CHARLES, son of 1st Ephraim, m. Sarah, wid. of Isaac Churchill, 1765, and had Charles, Joseph, Rufus, 1771; Samuel, m. Bathsheba Collins; Elkanah, m. Eunice Finney; Sarah, m. Seth Finney; and Ephraim, m. Sally Finney. CHARLES, son of above, m. Hannah Bates, and had Charles, 1797; Betsey, 1799, Joseph, and Elkanah. CHARLES, son of 2d Thomas, m. Abigail, d. of Jonathan Russell of Barnstable, 1818, and had Charles Otis, m. Annie C., d. of Asa Whiting; Betsey R., m. Nathaniel Wood; Mary Elizabeth, 1819; Rebecca T., 1833; Catherine Bridgham, 1839. DANIEL, son of 3d Stephen, m. Sarah, d. of James Collins, 1797, and had Daniel; Lois, m. William F. Soule of Kingston; Sally, m. Harvey Weston; Jane, m. George Rider; Heman, m. Almira Holmes; and Eleanor, m. Albert Leach. DANIEL, son of above, m. Mary B. Brown, 1826, and had Daniel O., m. Eliza M. Hudson of Wareham; and Sarah Palmer, m. James Stone of Carver. DAVID, Plympton, son of 2d William, m., 1729, Mary Magoon, and had David, 1729; Hannah, 1733; William, 1739; Elias, 1742; James, 1746. EBENEZER, son of 3d John, m. Mercy, d. of Thomas Branch of Marshfield,

1747, and had Ebenezer, 1749, m. Jane Bartlett; Branch, 1751, m. Mary
Churchill; Bethiah, 1753; Bethiah, 1754; Rebecca, 1756; Mercy, 1759; George,
1761; Mercy, 1763. EBENEZER, son of 1st Barnabas, m. Jean Fisher, 1755,
and had Ebenezer, 1755; Timothy, 1757; John, 1759; Jean, 1761; John, 1763;
Martha, 1767. EBENEZER, m. Patience Faunce, 1775, and had Ebenezer,
Branch, Bethiah, George, and Mercy. EBENEZER, son of above, m.
a Palmer, and had Ansel, Alfred, Cornelius, and Rebecca. EBENEZER,
Plympton, son of 2d William, had Hannah, Ruth, Leah, Joshua, Rebecca,
Isaac, John. EDMUND, m. Mary Hueston, 1801. ELEAZER, son of 1st John,
by wife Mary, had Hannah, 1676; Joanna, 1678; Abigail, m. Francis Billing-
ton; Eleazer; Stephen, 1685, m. Experience Ellis; Jedidah, m. Thomas
Harlow; Mary, m. Edward Stephens; Elkanah, Nathaniel, and Josiah.
ELEAZER, son of above, m. Hannah, d. of Robert Bartlett, and had Eleazer,
1714; Josiah, 1716; Jonathan, 1720. ELEAZER, son of above, m. Sarah
Harlow, 1738, and had Hannah, 1739; Hannah, 1740; Sarah, 1741; Mercy,
1743; Eleazer, 1744, m. Jane Rider; James, 1747; Asa, 1748; Sylvanus, 1750;
Sarah, 1755; Joseph, 1757; Phebe, 1759. ELEAZER, m. Abigail Bartlett,
1776, and had Charles. ELKANAH, son of 2d Charles, m. Lydia, d. of John
Sherman of Carver, and had Charles Henry and Ellen Barnes. ELKANAH,
son of 1st Eleazer, m. Susanna Manchester, and had Amaziah; Meriah, m.
Jabez Mendall of Plympton; and Elkanah, 1726. ELKANAH, son of above,
m. Susanna Bartlett and had Susanna, 1749; Meriah, 1751; Elkanah, 1754;
Jabez, 1756; Andrew, 1758; Abigail, 1760; Andrew, 1763. ELLIS, son of
1st Ephraim, m. Patience, d. of Josiah Churchill, 1764, and had Ellis, 1765;
and Lewis. EPHRAIM, son of 1st Stephen, m. Priscilla Manchester, 1730,
and had Mary, 1730, m. James Drew; Charles, 1733; Zacheus, 1734, m. Mary
Trask; Ephraim, 1738; Priscilla, 1739, m. John Rider; Ellis, 1742; Ansel,
1745; John, 1748, m. Olive Cobb. EPHRAIM, son of 1st Charles, m. Sally,
d. of William Finney, 1804, and had Ephraim Finney, and perhaps others.
EPHRAIM FINNEY, son of above, m. Martha H. Whiting, 1827, and had
Winslow W., m. Mary A. Burgess; Ephraim F., 1829, m. Hannah T. Atwood; Martha Ann, 1833; Almira C., 1839. GEORGE, son of 1st Ebenezer,
m. Elizabeth Harlow, 1786, and had Ebenezer, 1787; Elizabeth, 1789; Branch,
1792; Sarah Warren, 1795. GEORGE, son of 5th John, m. Martha T., d. of
Joseph Holmes, 1826, and had John, m. Martha, d. of Samuel West Bagnall;
and Martha, m. George Sampson and William McAdams. HEMAN, son of
3d Stephen, m. Jane Churchill, 1795, and had Patience, m. William Randall;
and Mary Ann. HOSEA, m. Eunice Morey, 1811, and had Hosea, 1813; Betsey
W., 1815; Silas M., 1817; Bartlett and Henry, twins, 1822; John Clark, 1827.
ICHABOD, Plympton, son of 2d William, by wife Rebecca, had Ebenezer,
1744; Joanna, 1747; Deborah, 1749; Ichabod, 1751; Rebecca, 1753, m. Ebenezer Cushman. By a 2d wife, Susanna, he had Thomas, 1756; Sarah, 1758;
William, 1761; Eunice, 1765. ISAAC, m. Sarah Morton, 1780, and had Isaac,
1781; Sally, 1783. ISAAC, son of 5th Ebenezer, had Seth and Isaac. ISAAC,
Plympton, who died 1778, by wife Susanna, had Isaac; Susanna, m. a Weston,
and a d., m. a Standish. JABEZ, son of 3d Elkanah, m. Nancy Bartlett,
and had Jabez; Mercy, m. William Sears; and others. JABEZ, son of above,

m. Charlotte W., d. of William Keen, and had Jabez, Sylvester, Charlotte, and William Keen, m. Sarah A. E., d. of William Nelson. JAMES, Plympton, son of David, m., 1765, Priscilla Soule, and had Oliver, 1766; Priscilla, 1768, m. Joseph Wright; James, 1771; Isaiah, 1773; Jane, 1776; Christian, 1778; James, 1782, m. Jael Ellis; Harriet, 1785; Sophia, 1787; Hannah, 1791. JAMES, m. Rebecca, d. of Heman Crocker, and had Edwin, and Alice, m. Luther W. Savery. JESSE, son of 1st Jonathan, m. Abigail, and had Jesse, 1772; Jesse, 1773; Lemuel, 1775; Abigail, 1778; Joseph, 1779; Abigail, 1782; David, 1784; Simeon, 1786; Hannah, 1789; David, 1795. JOB, son of 3d Barnabas, m. Hannah T. Harlow, 1808, and had Barnabas, 1810; Job, 1812, m. Jane D. Reed, Susan (Hutchinson) Rogers, and Nancy (Stetson) Mann; Sylvanus H., 1815; Hannah T., 1817, m. Allen Holmes; Sally, 1819; and Cornelius Bradford, 1824, m. Sarah F., d. of Ezra Cushing. JOHN, came to Plymouth 1643, and m., 1644, Hannah, d. of William Pontus, by whom he had Joseph, Hannah, Eleazer, 1652; Mary, 1654; William, John, and Henry, 1658, m. Mary, wid. of Thomas Doty. JOHN, son of above, m. Rebecca, d. of Philip Delano, and had Elizabeth, 1687, m. Joel Ellis; Rebecca, 1689, m. George Morton; John, 1691; Sarah, 1695; Hannah, 1697, m. Samuel Bartlett. He m., 2d, 1715, Hannah (Mansfield) Bartlett, wid. of Elnathan. JOHN, son of above, m. Bethiah, d. of Ebenezer Spooner, and had Ebenezer, 1721; John, 1723; John, 1727. JOHN, son of above, m. Sarah Cole, 1750, and had Sarah, 1750. JOHN, son of 1st Ansel, m. Nancy, d. of Isaac Jackson of Carver, and had George, John, Hannah, m. Bartlett Ellis; Bethiah, m. Thomas Burgess Bartlett; Nancy; Sally Ann, m. Alden Winsor of Duxbury; and Lillis, m. Joshua B. Loud of Abington. JOHN, son of 1st Joseph, m. Desire Holmes, and had Priscilla, 1701, m. Thomas Rogers; Samuel, 1704; Sarah, 1706, m. Elkanah Totman; Phebe, 1708, m. Joseph Holmes; Rebecca, 1713, m. Azariah Whiting. JOHN, m. Elizabeth Eames, 1771. JOHN DARLING, son of 1st Sylvanus, m., 1840, Marcia James, d. of Thomas Holmes, and had John Franklin, 1840, m. Clara B., d. of Elkanah C. Finney; Josiah D., 1843, m. Martha E. Tillson; Frederick Lee, 1846, m. Mary Nelson, d. of Ezra Diman. JONATHAN, son of 2d Eleazer, by wife Hannah, had Jonathan, 1745; Jesse, 1746; Samuel, 1750; Hannah, 1760; Francis, 1761; Hannah, 1763; Reuben, 1765, m. Hannah Sampson. JONATHAN, son of above, by wife Lydia, had Olive, 1768; Mercy, 1770. JOSEPH, son of 1st John, m. Sarah Hicks, 1672, and had John, 1678; Margaret, 1684, m. Samuel Bates; Barnabas, 1686; Joseph, 1692. JOSEPH, son of above, m. Abiah Blackwell of Sandwich, 1716, and had Abiah, 1717; Margaret, 1719; Joseph, 1722; Samuel, 1724, m. Mercy Ellis; Joshua, 1726; Sarah, 1728; Mercy, 1733. JOSEPH, son of above m. Meriah Rider, 1745, and had Ichabod, 1746; Joseph, 1748; Lucy, 1750. JOSEPH, son of 1st Charles, m. Betsey, d. of William Ellis, and had Reenet E., m. Charles F. Harlow; Frederick, m. a Leach; Joseph Lothrop, 1842; Ann Maria, m. Nathaniel Barnes; Hannah; and Betsey, m. Benjamin Weston. JOSEPH, son of Thaddeus, m. Mercy Goodwin, 1804, and had Joseph Lewis, 1805; Amelia, 1807; Edward, 1808; George, 1811; Gustavus, 1814; Marcia Goodwin, 1817; and Charles Thomas. He m., 2d, Lydia LeBaron, d. of Thomas Goodwin, 1823. JOSEPH, Plympton, son of 4th Nathaniel, had

Joseph, Hosea, and Hiram. JOSEPH, son of above, m. Rebecca Morey, and
had Rebecca, Ann, Eunice, and George H., m. Mary Ness. JOSIAH, son of
2d Eleazer, m. Patience, d. of Eleazer Harlow, 1741, and had Josiah, 1742;
Josiah, 1743; Thaddeus, 1745, m. Asenath Delano, Patience, 1747, m. Ellis
Churchill; Samuel, 1754; Enos, 1759, m. Mary Paine; Sylvanus, 1765.
LEMUEL, son of 1st Barnabas, m. Lydia Sylvester, and had Nathaniel, 1743.
He m., 2d, Abigail Rider, and had Lemuel, 1754; Abigail, 1756; Ezra, 1758.
LEWIS, son of Ellis, m. Nancy Mitchell, 1791, and had Lewis, 1794, m.
Hannah Covington; Sylvanus, 1796, m. Elizabeth Carver; Mary, 1798, m.
Zacheus Barnes; Joseph, 1804. NATHAN, son of 2d Benjamin, m. Elizabeth
Sylvester, 1804, and had Mary Sylvester, m. John Parsons; Solomon S., m.
Ruth Nelson, d. of John Kempton Cobb; Nathan; Charlotte Sylvester, m.
James A. Sylvester; and Betsey, m. Abbot Drew. NATHANIEL, son of 1st
Stephen, m. Mary Curtis, and had Experience, 1735. NATHANIEL, m.
Susanna Harlow, 1798. NATHANIEL, Plympton, son of 2d William, had
Levi, Stephen, Joseph, and Nathaniel, and died 1794. NATHANIEL, Plymp-
ton, son of above, by wife Lydia, had Abigail, m. a Bisbee; Lydia, m. a Ham-
mond; Levi, Joseph, and Nathaniel. He mentions in his will, probated 1803,
grandchildren Lewis, Hosea, and Stephen. OLIVER, Plympton, son of
James, m., 1793, Saba Soule, and had Oliver, 1794, m. Sally Bradford and
Mary Ann Loring; Frances, 1797, m. Stephen Bonney; Saba Soule, 1800, m.
Samuel Churchill of Halifax; Isaiah, 1805, m. Polly Stevens Parker, Jane
Bradford, d. of Martin Hayward, and Angeline, wid. of John Standish;
Mary Magoon, 1811, m. Martin Bosworth; Jane Hudson, 1817, m. Charles W.
Englested. PELEG, son of 3d Stephen, m. Hannah Hosea, and lived in Dux-
bury. He had Peleg; Harriet, m. Prince Bradford; William; Otis, m. Esther,
d. of Nathaniel Ellis; Albert; Ezra; and Eliza, m. Joseph Chandler, father
of Albert C. and others, in Plymouth. PEREZ, Middleboro', son of 3d Ben-
jamin, m. Deborah Thayer of Carver, and had Deliverance, 1742; Zebedee,
1745; Deborah, 1747; Perez, 1753; Lydia, 1756; Isaac, 1758; Joseph, 1761.
He m., 2d, Persis, wid. of Lemuel Rickard of Plympton, and d. of James
Harlow. RUFUS, son of 1st Charles, m. Eunice Covington, 1797, and had
Rufus, m. Lucy W., d. of William Nye; Eunice, m. Richard Pope; and
William, m. Emily Tribble. SAMUEL, son of Josiah, m. Elizabeth, d. of
Amaziah Churchill, 1776, and had Samuel; Caleb, m. Lydia Greenold; Mendell, Lucy, and Henry. SAMUEL, son of above, m. Mercy Covington, and
had Samuel, Ezra, Francis, Polly, Nancy, Jacob, and John E., m. Eleanor,
d. of Samuel Sherman. SAMUEL, son of 1st Charles, m. Bathsheba Collins,
and had Samuel. SAMUEL, son of above, m. Calista, d. of Perez Pool, and
had Calista, m. Micah Nash of Abington. SAMUEL, m. Sarah Thomas,
1784. SAMUEL, m. Elizabeth Totman, 1788. SAMUEL, son of 6th John, by
wife Mary, had Mercy, m. a Darling; Mehitabel, m. James Harlow; Jesse,
and Elizabeth. SETH, m. Sally Seabury Simmons, 1810. STEPHEN, son of
1st Eleazer, m. Experience Ellis of Sandwich, 1708, and had Ephraim, 1709;
Nathaniel, 1712, m. Mary Curtis; Mary, 1716; Stephen, 1717; Zacheus, 1719;
Benjamin, 1725. STEPHEN, son of above, m. Hannah Barnes, 1738, and had
Sarah, 1739, Mercy, 1739; Stephen, 1743; Hannah, 1745, m. John Otis of

Barnstable; Zadock, 1747, m. Bathsheba Rider; Peleg, 1749. STEPHEN, son of above, m. Lucy, d. of Timothy Burbank, 1766, and had Heman, Daniel; Stephen, m. Nancy, wid. of John Churchill; Peleg; Maria, m. Southworth Shaw; Nancy, m. John Atwood; Polly, m. Samuel Dickson; Lucy, m. Samuel Bradford; Sally m. David Drew; and Hannah, m. Lewis Harlow. SYLVA-NUS, son of Josiah, m. Lydia, d. of Wilson Churchill, 1798, and had Sylvanus; Hiram, m. Eliza Ashley of New Bedford; Sylvanus again, m. Lydia, d. of Elihu Russell of New Bedford; Thomas, m. Mary Jane Wells of Wells, Maine, and wid. Margaret (Gilchrist) Greenwood; Benjamin, Josiah, and John Darling, m. Marcia James, d. of Thomas Holmes. SYLVANUS, son of Lewis, m. Elizabeth Carver, and had Abigail Holmes, 1827; Nancy Lewis, 1831; Sylvanus; Joanna Mitchell, 1834; Elizabeth Carver, 1839. SYLVANUS, m. Betsey Holmes, 1821. SYLVANUS H., son of Job, m. Lucretia Ann, d. of George Bacon, 1837, and had Lucretia L., 1839, m. Isaac W. Jackson; George Bacon, 1841, m. Mary Ramsey of Nevada; Job, 1843; Timothy G., 1846; Alice G., 1848; Jennie E., 1851; Rebecca J., 1856, m. Lucian P. Nelson. THADDEUS, son of Josiah, m. Asenath Delano, and had Thaddeus, m. Mercy Fuller; Joseph; William, m. Martha Alderson, and Asenath, m. John Paty. THOMAS, son of 1st Barnabas, m. Mary Ewer, had Gamaliel, 1759. THOMAS, Plympton, son of Ichabod, m. Mary, d. of Zacheus Holmes of Plymouth, 1778, and had Zacheus, 1779; Nancy, 1781; Temperance, 1783; Polly, 1786; Charles, 1792; Thomas, 1789; Thomas, 1796. WILLIAM, Plympton, son of 1st John, m. Lydia, d. of Stephen Bryant, 1683, and had William, 1685; Samuel, 1688, m. Joanna Bryant and wid. Meribah Gibbs; James, 1690, m. Mary McFarlin; Lydia, 1699, m. John Lovell; Josiah, 1702, m. Jemima Hamblin; Isaac, m. Susanna Leach; Benjamin, m. Mary Shaw; and Mehitabel m. Elkanah Shaw. WILLIAM, Plympton, son of above, m. Ruth Bryant, 1704, and had Ebenezer, 1705; Hannah, 1707, m. a Bisbee; David, 1709; Rebecca, 1711, m. a Ford; William, 1714; Ruth, 1716, m. a Cole; Nathaniel, 1718; Abigail, 1721, m. a Bryant; Ichabod, 1722; Sarah, 1724, m. a Marshall; Joanna, 1727. WILLIAM, son of 1st Barnabas, m. Susanna Clark, 1746, and had Rebecca, 1747; Mordecai, 1749; William, 1751. WILLIAM, m. Mary Holmes, 1823. WILLIAM, m. Patty Harlow, 1807. WILSON, son of 1st Benjamin, m. Lydia, d. of Jonathan Darling, and had Lydia, m. Sylvanus Churchill; Wilson, 1780; Hannah, m. James Howard. WILSON, son of above, m. Ruth, d. of Jabez Hinckley of Barnstable, 1804, and had Ruth Hinckley, 1812, m. William L. Finney; and Deborah Hinckley, m. Ephraim Finney. He m., 2d, Susan Lucas, 1816, and had Ansel; Wilson; Susan, 1820, m. Ephraim Finney; and Deborah Weston, m. Ephraim Finney. ZACHEUS, son of 1st Ephraim, m. Mary Trask, 1754, and had Elizabeth, 1755; Zacheus, 1757; Mary, 1758; and Ephraim. ZEBEDEE, Middleboro', son of Perez, m., 1764, Sarah, d. of Caleb Cushman, and had Asaph, 1765, and Zebedee.

CLAGHORN, MATTHEW, of Chilmark, m. Jean Bartlett, 1759.

CLARK, AMASA, m. Polly Morton, 1812. ANDREW, Boston and Harwich, son of 1st Thomas, m., 1671, Mehitabel, d. of Thomas Scottow of Boston, and had Thomas, 1672; Susanna, 1674; Mehitabel, 1676;

Andrew, 1678; Scottow, 1680, m. Elizabeth, d. of Kenelm Winslow of Harwich; and Nathaniel, 1682. BENJAMIN, m., 1791, Lydia Atwood, the double widow of William Savery and William Atwood, and d. of George Holmes. BENJAMIN, son of Lothrop, m. Jerusha Morey, 1814, and had Benjamin F., 1823, m. Mercy A. Courtney; Lothrop, 1832, m. Marcia B. Clark; Betsey, m. Nathaniel Fessenden of Sandwich; Eleanor, m. Hosea Bartlett; and Eliza F., 1835, m. Stephen Holmes; Jerusha C., 1830; Rebecca B., 1825; Josiah M., 1828. CONSIDER, son of 9th Thomas, m. Sally Sampson, 1803, and had Thomas, 1803, m. Abigail Bartlett; Consider, 1805, m., in Middleboro'; Henry Pelham, 1808; Abby, m. a Thomas; and Sarah, m. in Middleboro'. CORNELIUS of Rochester, m. Susanna Dunham, 1731. DANIEL, m. Martha Bramhall, 1805. DAVID, son of Ezra, m. Sophia Harlow, 1848; Lucretia W. Holbrook, 1853; and Sarah J. E. Thurston, 1865. By the last he had Ella S., m. Laban B. Briggs; Herbert; and Gideon Holbrook. He m., 4th, Ann M. Bartlett, 1879. EDWARD of Boston, m. Elizabeth Watson, 1769, and had Edward. EZRA, son of 6th James, m. Sarah Blackmer, 1819, and had David; Lucy, m. Charles H. Peterson; Sarah, m. James Ellis; and Lewis. He m., 2d, Mary, wid. of Joseph Davis, and d. of William Rogers, 1859. ISRAEL, son of 1st Josiah, m. Deborah Pope of Sandwich, 1741, and had Josiah, 1744; Jerusha, 1745, m. Thomas Ellis; Thomas, 1747, m. Ruth Hovey and Lydia Ellis; Thankful, 1750, m. Miles Long and Ezra Holmes; Lurania, 1752, m. Elisha Perry; Betty, 1754, m. John Cornish; Abigail, 1756, m. Josiah Cornish; Olive, 1759; Grace, 1761, m. Sylvester Holmes and John Clark; Seth, 1766, m. Eunice Ellis. ISRAEL, son of 5th Thomas, m. Phebe Cornish, and had Betsey, 1802; Thomas, 1803; Israel, m. Lucia Bartlett and Sally Curtis Blackmer; and John, m. a wid. Thurston. JAMES, son of 1st Thomas, m., 1657, Abigail, d. of Rev. John Lothrop, and had John; James; Susanna; Abigail; Joanna; Thomas and Bathsheba. JAMES, son of above, m. Ann Rider, 1722, and had James, 1723; Ann, 1724; Abigail, 1727. JAMES, son of above, m. Susanna Haskell, 1750, and had Abigail, 1752; John, 1754. JAMES, son of 1st John, m. Meriba Tupper, 1722, and had Rebecca, 1725; James, 1727. JAMES, son of above, m. Hannah Swift, 1747, and Meriah, 1748, m. Nathaniel Sherman; Lothrop, 1749; Mary, 1753; Mary again, 1756; Hannah, 1758, m. Jonathan Gibbs; Anna, 1760, m. Joseph Bartlett; James, 1762, m. Lucy Bartlett; Sarah, 1765, m. Gideon Holbrook; Seth, 1767, m. Mary Tupper; John, 1771. JAMES, son of above, m. Lucy Bartlett, 1784, and had Jonathan, 1785; Bartlett, 1786; James, 1787; Lucy, 1788; Thankful, 1791; Sarah, 1794, m. Otis Nichols; Rebecca, 1796, m. Ellis Morey; Ezra, 1798; David, 1800; Lewis, 1802. JAMES EASDELL, son of John Howard, m. Avis F. Thresher, 1856, and had James H., and Daniel. JOHN, son of 1st James, by wife Rebecca, had James, 1696; Abigail, 1698; John, 1701; Joseph, 1704; Mary, 1712. JOHN, son of above, m. Rebecca Hathaway of Dighton, 1725, and had John, 1728; Rebecca, 1734. JOHN, son of 5th James, m., 1791, Betsey, d. of Miles Long, and had Thankful, m. Charles Peterson. He m., 2d, Grace, wid. of Sylvester Holmes, and d. of Israel Clark, 1796, and had Betsey, 1796, m. Ivory H. Bartlett; Deborah, 1798, m. Nathaniel Nye of Sandwich, and John, 1800. JOHN, son of 7th William, m. Eleanor Shurtleff, and had John Howard, 1794; Eleanor Washburn, 1797, m. Joseph Chamberlin; David, 1800, m. Mary J. Lucas; Amasa S., 1803; Edward Doten, 1800. JOHN, Hanover, son of 7th Thomas, m. Abigail Tolman of Scituate, and had Hannah, 1722; Ruth, m. James Blackenship of Rochester; Nathaniel, 1731; Eleanor, 1732; John; Benjamin; Lydia, m. Joshua Barker; Belcher; Abigail, m. a Bolles of Rochester; and Sage, m. Josiah Mann of Scituate. JOHN, son of 3d Nathaniel, m. Mary, d. of Robert Roberts, 1796, and had Eliza Healey; Sarah Roberts, 1796, m. Ichabod Weston Barstow; and Robert, m. Deborah Douglass. JOHN, son of 4th Nathaniel, m. Sarah Rider, 1808, and had Abigail Dunham, 1809; Sarah, 1810; John William, 1811. JOHN, son of Zoeth, m. Abigail T. Holmes, 1821, and had John T., 1821; Zoeth, 1823; Elizabeth Brown, 1825, m. Otis Wright; and Abigail Thomas, 1827, m. Asa Green. JONAS of Boston, m. Martha Rickard, 1765. JOSIAH, son of 2d Thomas, m. Thankful Tupper; and had Elizabeth, 1719; Israel, 1720; Elizabeth, 1725. JOSIAH, son of 1st Israel, m. Hannah Harlow; and had Josiah, 1767; Deborah; and Polly. JOSIAH, son of 5th Thomas, m. Elizabeth Gifford, 1806, and had Josiah Franklin, 1808. JOSIAH, son of 4th William, m. Elizabeth Cornish, and had Elizabeth, 1778; Josiah, 1780; Thomas, 1782; William, 1785; Anna, 1788; Experience, 1791; Lydia, 1793; Abigail, 1795, m, Temple H. Holmes; and Lydia again, 1801. LEMUEL, m. Lydia Bartlett Finney, 1817. LOTHROP, son of 5th James, m. Mary Rider, 1772, and had Mary, 1775; Lothrop, 1778, m. Polly Bartlett; Betsey, 1781; Hannah, 1784, m. Obadiah King; Sarah, 1787; Eleanor, 1790; Benjamin, 1792, m. Jerusha Morey; and Stephen, 1797, m. Cynthia Harlow. NATHANIEL, son of 1st Thomas, one of the council of Andros, and secretary of Plymouth Colony, m. Dorothy, wid. of Edward Gray, and d. of Thomas Lettice, and left no children. NATHANIEL, son of 4th William, m. Lydia Sampson, 1796, and had Lydia, 1798, m. a Hoxie; Esther, 1801, m. Vinal Burgess; Naomi, 1804, m. Thomas Manter; Experience, 1806, m. Hiram Sampson; Mary, 1809, m. George Finney and William Cox; and Nathaniel, 1811, m. Rebecca Finney. NATHANIEL, Hanover, son of 5th John, m. Alice Healey, and had John; Nathaniel; Benjamin, m. Mary Gill of Hingham, and settled in Marshfield; Chloe M., m. John Studley of Hanover, and Alice, m. Levi Caswell of Maine. NATHANIEL, son of above, m. Abigail Dunham, 1786, and had Lydia, 1787, m. Daniel Rider; John, 1789, m. Sally Rider; Nancy, 1791, m. Elijah Edson; Nathaniel, 1796, m. Deborah Mead and a second wife; Amos, 1799; Amos Dunham, 1801; and Harvey, m. a Whitmarsh of Bridgewater. PELEG W. of Middleboro', m. Sarah S. Clark, 1837. RICHARD came in the Mayflower, and soon died, leaving no family. SAMUEL, son of 2d William, m. Mary Finney, 1716, and had Sarah, 1717; Lucie, 1719, m. Abiel Shurtleff; Hannah, 1721; Lurany, 1726; Samuel, 1729. SETH, son of 5th James, m. Mary Tupper, 1780, and had Seth, 1780; Nathaniel, 1792, m. Harriet Washburn; Israel, 1794, m. Catherine Dunbar and Laura Perkins; Nancy, 1796, m. Israel Briggs; Susanna, 1799, m. Howard Nichols of New Bedford; Joseph S., 1801, m. Harriet B., d. of Joseph Bourne of New Bedford. SETH, son of 1st Israel, m. Eunice Ellis, 1789, and had Samuel, m. Hannah (Bartlett) Mayo, 1821; Seth, m. Abigail Bartlett; Deborah, m. Reuben Peterson of Duxbury; and

Lydia, m. Clark Peterson of Duxbury. SETH, son of above, m. Abigail Bartlett, 1820, and had Seth Pope, 1821, m. Mary S. Weeks and Sarah S. Bartlett; Abba A., 1823; Adaline, 1828, m. Benjamin Finney; and Abby N. B., m. Nathaniel Cornish. THOMAS came in the Ann 1623, and m. before 1634, Susanna, d. of wid. Mary Ring, by whom he had Andrew, 1639; James, 1636; Susanna, m. Barnabas Lothrop; William, 1656; John; and Nathaniel. He m., 2d, 1664, wid. Alice Nichols, d. of Richard Hallet. Savage says he m. for a third wife, Elizabeth Crow, but falls into the error of confounding him with Thomas, the son of 1st James. THOMAS, son of 1st James, m. Rebecca Miller, 1682, and had Susanna, 1684, m. Elisha Holmes; Thomas, 1685. He m., 2d, Elizabeth Crow, 1690, and had Josiah, 1690; Elizabeth, 1692, m. Josiah Morton; Rebecca, 1694, m. Nathaniel Morton. He m., 3d, 1697, Susanna Miller, and had Annah, 1700, m. Gideon Ellis; Abigail, 1701, m. Nathaniel Bartlett; and Sarah, 1704. THOMAS, son of above, by wife Mary, had Meriah, 1714; Sarah, 1716; Thomas, 1718, m. Ruth Morton; Rebecca, 1720, m. Thomas Swift; Susanna, 1723, m. Joseph Fulgham; and Mary. THOMAS, son of 2d William, m. Joanna Colman, 1717, and had William, 1718; Abigail, 1720, m. John Thomas; and Lydia, 1725. THOMAS, son of 1st Israel, m. Lydia Ellis, and had Patience, 1776; Israel, 1779; Thomas, 1782; and Josiah, 1784. THOMAS, Scituate, 1676, said to have gone from Plymouth, but probably not connected with Thomas, the passenger in the Ann, m. Martha, d. of Richard Curtis, and had Thomas; Joseph; Daniel; Samuel; Nathaniel; Mercy; Deborah; Rachel; Ann: Charity; and Mary. THOMAS, Scituate, son of above, m. Alice Rogers, 1705, and had John, and perhaps others. THOMAS, Norwich, Conn., m. Elizabeth, d. of Samuel Leonard, 1703, and had Mary, 1705; Thomas, 1709; Elizabeth, 1711; Joseph, 1714; Ruth, 1722. THOMAS, son of 4th Josiah, m. Ellen Bartlett, and had Thomas Edward, 1809, m. Abby Bartlett; and Ivory Hovey, 1812, m. Maria E., d. of Levi Robbins. THOMAS, son of 4th William, m. Abigail Morton, and had Consider, and others. TRISTRAM came to Plymouth from Ipswich, in England, in the Francis, 1634, at the age of 44, with perhaps a wife Faith, and certainly a daughter Faith, who m. Edward Dotey and John Phillips. He had also two sons, Tristram or Thurston, and Henry, both probably without issue. WILLIAM, Duxbury, is erroneously stated by Savage to have been son of 1st Thomas. He m. Martha, d. of Samuel Nash, and probably died without issue. WILLIAM, son of 1st Thomas, m., 1678, Hannah, d. of Francis Griswold of Saybrook, and had Sarah, 1678, m. Ephraim Little; William, 1682; Nathaniel, 1684; Samuel, 1687; and Thomas. He m., 2d, Abiah Wilder, 1692, and had Hannah, 1697, m. Joseph Cobb. Savage calls this William of Saybrook, but the births of his children are recorded in Plymouth, and the writer has, in the course of his investigations, discovered a deed from the 1st Thomas to William and Abiah, called his children, dated January 30, 1695, of lands conveyed to them in consideration of his support by them in his old age. Thomas died in 1697, at the age of 98. WILLIAM, son of above, m. Bethiah Mayhew, 1707, and had Nathaniel, 1709; Sarah, 1712, m. Jabez Holmes; and Matthew, 1714. WILLIAM, son of 4th Thomas,

m. Experience Dotey, 1738, and had Nathaniel, 1738; William, 1741; Josiah, 1743; Lydia, 1744; Nathaniel, 1747, m. Lydia Sampson; Josiah, 1750, m. Elizabeth Cornish; Thomas, 1753, m. Abigail Morton; Experience, 1755; Abigail, 1758, m. Josiah Cornish. WILLIAM, son of 4th Josiah, m. Nancy Bartlett, 1808. He m., 2d, Betsey, wid. of Joseph Whiting, and d. of Ichabod Morton, 1831, and had Elizabeth H., m. Sydney T. Holmes. WILLIAM, m. Zilpah Bramhall, 1790. WILLIAM, son of 4th William, m. Sarah Howard, and had John, born 1765, and others. ZOETH, Carver and Plymouth, born 1766, m. Rebecca Thomas of Middleboro', and had John, m. Abigail T. Holmes; Patience, m. Abraham Dunham; Hannah, m. Thomas F. White; and Rebecca. ZOETH, son of 7th John, m. Rebecca M. Wright, 1848, and had Ella Maria, 1851; John Thomas, m. Mary Fernside; Zoeth; and Horatio Cushman. (See Clark Genealogy).

CLOUGH, or CLUFF, RICHARD, Plymouth, 1634.

COADE, JAMES, m. Hannah Ward, and had Sarah, 1764; Mary, 1765. JOSEPH, m., 1794, Sally Atwood.

COBB, ANSEL, son of last William, m. Sarah Howard of Bridgewater, and had Howard; and Lucinda, 1805, m. Oliver H. Alden. BARTLETT, son of 2d Lemuel, m., 1818, Betsey Douglass. BENJAMIN, Plympton, son of Nathan, m. Sally Ransom, and had Olive, 1775, m. Arthur Bennett; Ebenezer, 1781, m. Polly Sherman and Mrs. Lucy (Fuller) Shaw; Benjamin, 1788; Ransom, 1792; Sally, 1779; Charles, 1780, m. Sylvia Rickard; Martha, 1785; Otis, 1795. CHARLES, Kingston, son of 2d Seth, m., 1805, Polly Bradford, and had Stephen; Charles; Almira, m. Peter Holmes; Seth, m. Harriet Gerrish of Taunton; Philander, m. Marcia Otis; and Martin, m. Elizabeth, d. of Clark Winsor. CHARLES, Kingston, son of above, m. Rebecca S. Wadsworth, and had Charles S., m. Julia E. W., d. of Samuel Briggs; Wealthea E., m. Nehemiah S. Savery; Almira, m. Winsor T. Savery. CORNELIUS, son of 1st Job, m., 1774, Grace Eames, and had Cornelius, 1775; Betsey, 1777; Grace, 1781; Isaac Eames, 1789. CORNELIUS, Hanson, son of above, m. Betsey, d. of Nathaniel Thomas, and had Eliza, m. Elijah Cushing; Theodore, m. Sarah Harlow Perkins of Minot, Maine; Grace; Jane, m. Elmer Hewett of South Weymouth; Cornelius; Betsey, m. Philemon Harlow Perkins of Minot; Helen Maria, m. Thomas S. Mitchell of Freeport. EBENEZER, son of 1st John, m., 1693, Mercy Holmes, and had Ebenezer, 1694; Mercy, 1696; Nathaniel, 1698; Hannah, 1699, m. Jacob Tinkham; Sarah, 1702; Mercy, 1705, m. Samuel Doten and Cornelius Holmes; Nathan, 1707; John, 1709; Mary, 1711; Elizabeth, 1714, m. Thomas Holmes; Job, 1717; Roland, 1719. EBENEZER, son of above, died in Kingston, 1801, at the age of 107, having lived in three centuries. He m. Ruth, d. of Hilkiah Tinkham, 1722, and had Ebenezer, 1724; He m., 2d, Lydia, d. of William Stephens of Marshfield, 1727, and had Ruth, 1728; Lydia, 1730, m. Daniel Pratt, of Plympton; John, 1732; Sarah, 1735, m. a Lucas; William, 1738; Meltiah; Seth, 1740; Hannah, 1742; Ruth, 1744. EBENEZER, Kingston, son of above, m. Jerusha, d. of Robert Cushman, 1747, and had Ruth, 1747, m. Job Cobb; Sylvanus, 1748, m. a Chandler, and moved to Maine; Eleanor, 1750, m. John Howard; Mary, 1751, m. Gershom Drew; Francis, 1753, m. Phebe Hob; Meltiah, 1755, m. Rebecca Brewster;

Elisha, 1756; Jerusha, m. Barnabas Cobb of Carver; Joseph, 1759, m. Jerusha Loring; Ebenezer, 1760, m. Mercy Porter; Mercy, 1762, m. Paul Tinkham; Fear, 1766, m. Abiel Brewster of Carver; William, 1764, m. Charlotte Coffin of Nantucket. He m., 2d, Martha, wid. of Isaac Cole, and d. of John Harlow, and had Zenas, 1772, m., 1st, Dorcas Rowe; 2d. wid. Sarah Wood; 3d, a wid. Talbot of Maine. EBENEZER, son of Ebenezer and Phebe (Sherman) Cobb of Carver, came to Plymouth from Carver, and m. Lizzie C., wid. of Lemuel Morton, 1867. ELIJAH W. of Barnstable, m. Mercy Ruggles, d. of Daniel Jackson, 1854. ELISHA, son of 1st John, m., 1703, Lydia Rider, and had Elisha, 1704; Lemuel, 1706; Sylvanus, 1709; Hurst, 1711; Lydia, 1713, m. Jonathan Darling; Hannah, 1716, m. James Cushman; John, 1719; Jabez, 1721. ELISHA, son of above, m. Priscilla Merrick of Harwich, 1735, and had Lemuel, 1736. EPHRAIM, perhaps son of 2d John, by wife Margaret, had Susanna, 1731, m. Joseph Sylvester and Eleazer Stephens; Hannah, m. Isaac Symmes; Abigail, 1732, m. a Tupper; John; Olive; Rebecca, m. James Seller and Lazarus; and Lucy, m. Ralph Merry. FRANKLIN B. came to Plymouth from Vermont with his brother George W. m. Judith, d. of Benjamin Eaton, and had Franklin B., m. Mary F., d. of Isaac Barnes and Mary Chamberlain of Worcester; Abbie E., m. James Millar; Caroline E., m. Francis Howland; Mary S., m. Otis W. Burgess; and Charles H., 1850, m. Mary L., d. of Barnabas Churchill. FREEMAN, m. Rachel Holbrook, 1789. GEORGE W., brother of Franklin, m. Catherine, d. of Isaac Perkins, and had Kate Helen, m.Ichabod Morton; Celia A., m. Eugene H. Glassure; William P., 1849. GEORGE, son of 3d Job, removed to Baltimore, m., 1829, Eliza Smith of Baltimore, wid. of Lieut. Gilchrist of English navy; George F., m. Mary A., d. of Alexander W. Poulson; and Helen F., m. Thomas W. Ball of Virginia. GEORGE F., Baltimore, son of above, m. Mary A. Poulson, and had George; Bessie; Helen; and Walker Ball. HENRY appeared in Plymouth in 1629, in Scituate, 1633, and afterwards in Barnstable. He m., 1631. Patience, d. of James Hurst of Plymouth, and had born in Plymouth, John, 1632; Edward, m.Mary Hoskins; and James, 1635; born in Scituate, Mary, 1637, m. Jonathan Dunham; Hannah, 1639, m. Edward Lewis; and born in Barnstable, Patience, 1642, m. Robert Parker; Gershom, 1645, m. Hannah Davis; Eleazer, 1648. He m., 2d, Sarah, d. of Samuel Hinckley, 1649, and had Mehitabel, 1651; Samuel, 1654; Sarah, 1658; Jonathan, 1660, m. Hope Huckins; Sarah, 1663, m. Samuel Chipman; Henry, 1665; Mehitabel, 1667; Experience, 1671. HENRY, Barnstable, son of above, m. Lois Hallet, 1690, and had Gideon, 1691; Eunice, 1693; Lois, 1696; Nathan. HEMAN, m. Betsey Whitmarsh, 1803, and had Sarah F., m. Jesse Harlow. ISAAC EAMES, son of 1st Cornelius, m. Elizabeth, d. of Thomas Bartlett, 1816, and had Elizabeth, m. Joseph Holmes. JABEZ, son of 1st Elisha, m. Sarah Bartlett, 1750, and had John, 1751; Sylvanus, 1754; Sarah, 1757, m. Samuel Lanman; Jabez, 1759. JAMES, son of 1st John, m. Patience Holmes, 1705, and had Meltiah, 1706; James, 1708; Gershom, 1711; Joanna, 1715; Gershom, 1717, m. Sarah, wid. of Caleb Cook; Martha, 1719, m. Ebenezer Drew of Kingston. JAMES, Barnstable, son of 1st Henry, m. Sarah, d. of George Lewis, 1663, and had Mary, 1664; Sarah, 1666; Patience, 1668; Hannah, 1671; James, 1673, m.

Elizabeth Hallet; Gershom, 1675; John, 1677; Elizabeth, 1680; Martha, 1683; Mercy, 1685; Thankful, 1687. JAMES of Kingston, m. Ruth, d. of Nathaniel Fuller, and had Joshua, 1733; Ruth, 1735, m. John Bradford; Joanna, 1737; Patience, 1739; James, 1740; Martha, 1743; James, 1744; and James and Joshua, twins, 1745. He m., 2d, 1766, Meltiah Holmes of Plymouth. JAMES, m. Lydia Robbins, 1705. JOB, son of 1st Ebenezer, m. Patience, d. of Cornelius Holmes, 1743, and had Lydia, 1744; Job, 1745; Cornelius, 1747; Rowland, 1748, m. Jerusha Bartlett; Lydia, 1750; Nehemiah, 1754; David, 1756; Patience, 1759, m. Osborn Morton. JOB, son of above, m. Ruth, d. of Ebenezer Cobb, 1773, and had Job; Elisha; Patience, m. John Kempton Cobb; and Ruth, m. Nathan Holmes. JOB, son of above, m. Nancy, d. of Jabez Doten, 1803, and had George, who moved to Bateman; and Henry, who moved to Alleghany City, Penn. JOB, m. Mary Barnes, 1747. ∤JOHN, son of 1st Henry, m. Martha, d. of William Nelson, 1658, and had John, 1662; Samuel; Elizabeth; Israel; Patience, 1668; Ebenezer, 1671; Elisha, 1678; James, 1682. JOHN, son of above, m. Rachel Soule, 1688, and had probably Ephraim. JOHN, son of 1st Ebenezer, m. Sarah Bartlett, and had John, 1736; Josiah, 1738; Mary, 1741; Sarah, 1745. JOHN, Kingston, son of 2d Ebenezer, m. Hannah, d. of Robert Cushman, 1756, and had Hannah, 1756; Patience, 1758, m. Samuel Atwood; Joanna, 1759, m. Thomas Morton; Lydia, 1761, m. William Pettingil; Sarah, 1762; Abigail, 1765, m. Joseph Rickard. He m., 2d, Persis Lucas, 1766, and had William, 1767; Elizabeth, 1769, m. Stephens Cobb; Eleanor, 1770; John, 1773; Ruth, 1775; Josiah, 1780, m. Mary, d. of Abijah Lucas; Persis, 1783, m. Spencer Brewster. JOHN KEMPTON, son of 2d Lemuel, m. Sukey Edwards, 1807. He m., 2d, Polly, d. of Samuel Nelson, 1810, and had Mary, 1813, m. Ezra S. Diman; Susan Edwards, 1816, m. James P. Baxter; John Kempton, 1818, m. Harriet, d. of Caleb Rider; Ruth Nelson, 1820, m. Solomon S. Churchill; Jerusha Bartlett, 1821, m. Joab Thomas; Clyntha Holmes, 1823, m., 1st, Nathaniel Barrows; 2d, Charles Parsons; and Hezekiah Nelson, 1825. He m., 3d, Patience, d. of Job Cobb, 1829, and Mrs. Mary Brown, 1870. JOHN KEMPTON, son of above, m. Harriet, d. of Caleb Rider, 1841, and had Harriet, m. Martin Keith; Lemuel C., 1847; Eugene; Alice; Sarah F., 1851, m. Edward Winslow King; Laura; and John Kempton, m. Victorine A. Holbrook. JONATHAN, Barnstable, son of 1st Henry, m. Hope Huckins, 1683, and had Samuel, 1684; Jonathan, 1686; Ebenezer, 1688; Joseph, 1690, m. Hannah Clark; Lydia, 1693. JOSEPH, Plympton, son of Nathan, m. Rebecca Crocker, and had Joseph, 1775; Crocker, and Heman. He m., 2d, Susanna Dunham, and had Arthur. JOSEPH, Carver, son of above, m. Susanna, d. of Jabez Weston, and had Joseph, 1805. LEMUEL, son of 1st Elisha, m. Fear, d. of Joseph Holmes, 1738, and had Lydia, 1741, m. Joseph Bartlett; Lemuel, 1743. LEMUEL, son of above, m. Hannah Kempton, 1771, and had Fear, m. Isaac Bartlett; Hannah, m. Ansel Robbins; Jerusha, m. John Cooper; Bartlett; Lemuel, m. Clarissa Sampson; Elizabeth, m. John Battles; William, m. Cynthia, wid. of Lemuel Nelson; and John Kempton. NATHAN, son of 1st Ebenezer, m. Joanna Bennett, and had William, 1735, m. Mary Pynchon; Elizabeth, 1736, m. John Sampson; Deborah, 1738; Timothy, 1742; Nathan,

1743, m. Jerusha Harlow; Joseph, 1748, m. Rebecca Crocker and Susanna Dunham; Benjamin, 1750, m. Sally Ransom; Nehemiah, m. Mehitabel Rickard. NATHANIEL, son of 1st Ebenezer, m., 1720, Mary Waterman, and had Mary, 1722; Nathaniel, 1724; Hannah, 1728; Lucy, 1730; Rowland, 1732; Samuel, 1736. NATHANIEL, Plympton, son of above, by wife Rebecca, had Nathaniel, 1747; Jonathan, 1749; Hannah, 1752, m. Joseph Vaughan; Lydia, 1755; Rowland, 1757, m. Jerusha Bartlett; Rebecca, 1759, m. Stoddard Totman. NATHANIEL, son of above, m., 1772, Sarah Holmes, and had Sarah, m. America Brewster. NEHEMIAH, Carver, son of Nathan, m. Mehitabel Rickard, and had Lemuel, 1774, m. Polly Whitmore; Nathan, 1778, m. Betsey Whitmore; Persis, 1780, m. Thomas Hammond; Nehemiah, 1783, m. Lois Vaughan; Bennett, 1785, m. Mercy Doten; Mehitabel, 1788, m. Ezra Cobb; Melissa, 1789; Frederick, 1792, m. Lucy P. Bradford. OTIS, son of Benjamin, m. Mercy Morse, and had Benjamin R., 1824; Otis, 1827; Mercy B., 1837. ROWLAND, Carver, son of 2d Nathaniel, m., 1783, Jerusha Bartlett of Plymouth, and had Jerusha, 1786; Nathaniel, 1788; Rebecca, 1790; Mercy, 1793; Rowland, 1796; Jonathan, 1798. SAMUEL, son of 1st Henry, m., 1680, Elizabeth, d. of Richard Taylor, and had Sarah, 1681; Thomas, 1683; Elizabeth, 1685; Henry, 1687; Samuel and Mehitabel, twins, 1691; Experience, 1693; Jonathan, 1694; Eleazer, 1696; Lydia, 1699. SETH, perhaps son of 1st Ebenezer, though not recorded among his children, m., 1736, Sarah Nelson, and had Sarah, 1739, m. Isaac Churchill. SETH, Kingston, son of 2d Ebenezer, m. Margaret, d. of John Cook, and had Stevens, 1766; Olive, 1767; Olive, 1768; Oliver, 1770; Charles, 1771; Nathaniel, 1773; Desire, 1775; Cynthia, 1777; Charles, 1781; Anna, 1783. STEVENS, Kingston, son of above, by wife Elizabeth, had Henry, 1795; Fanny, 1797; Lucy, 1799; Anna Stevens, 1802. SYLVANUS, son of 1st Elisha, m., 1734, Elizabeth Rider, and had Elizabeth, 1736. TIMOTHY, son of Nathan, m. Deborah Churchill, and had Deliverance, 1766; Timothy, 1769, m. Rebecca Fuller; Zabdiel, 1771; Deborah, 1774; Elizabeth, 1776; Mary, 1778; Nathaniel, 1780; Thomas, 1782; Elizabeth, 1785; Alvan, 1787. WILLIAM, from Portland, perhaps son of 4th John, m. 1797, Elizabeth Ripley. WILLIAM, son of 2d Lemuel, m., 1816, Cynthia, wid. of Lemuel Nelson, and had Harvey R., m. Jane D. Luce of Rochester. WILLIAM, Plympton, son of Nathan, m., 1761, Mary Pynchon; and had Agatha, 1762, m. James Barrows; William, 1764; Joanna, 1766, m. Calvin Tilson; George, 1771; Ansel, 1773, m. Sarah Howard.

CODING, GEORGE, from Taunton, m., 1757, Mary Faunce.

COFFIN, GARDNER, from Nantucket, m., 1794, Mary Jackson Goodwin.

COLBURN, LEMUEL, pub. to Susan Moore, 1819.

COLE, ASAHEL, m. Jane Barrows, 1823. BENJAMIN, m. Rebecca Harlow, 1732. DAVID, m. Thankful Covill, and had Thankful, m. James Young; Isaac, David, Charles, and Sally. EPHRAIM, son of either 1st or 2d James, m. Rebecca, d. of Edward Gray, 1687, and had Ephraim, 1691; Samuel, 1694; Rebecca, 1696; Mary, 1698, m. Peleg Durfey; Dorothy, 1701, m. Josiah Carver; James, 1705; Samuel, 1709. EPHRAIM, son of above, by wife Sarah, had Ephraim, 1718; Rebecca, 1727, m. Richard Durfey, and

Sarah, 1730, m. John Churchill. HUGH, son of 1st James, m., 1654, Mary, d. of Richard Foxwell of Scituate, and had James, 1655; Hugh, 1658; John, 1660; Martha, 1662; Ann, 1664, m. William Salisbury; Ruth, 1666; Joseph, 1668. HUGH, son of above, m. Elizabeth Cook, 1689. ISAAC, m. Martha, d. of John Harlow, 1761, and had Martha, m. Coomer Weston. ISAAC, son of David, m. Sarah, d. of Richard Holmes, 1807, and had Isaac; Winslow, m. Lydia, d. of Samuel Sampson; and Sarah, m. Benjamin Jenkins. JAMES, Plymouth, 1633, by wife Mary, had James, 1626; Mary, m. John Almy of Portsmouth, R. I., and a Mr. Poeveke; John, m. Elizabeth Rider; Hugh; and perhaps Ephraim. JAMES, son of above, m., 1652, Mary Tilson, and had Mary, 1653, m. John Lothrop. He m., 2d, Abigail Davenport, and had Elizabeth, m. Elkanah Cushman; John; Martha, m. Nathaniel Howland; Joanna, m. Thomas Howland. JOB, Carver, son of 1st Joseph, m. Mary, d. of Thomas Savery, and had Samuel, 1780; Zilpha, m. Barnabas Shurtleff; Ruth, m. Zebedee Chandler of Carver; Hannah, m. Ezra Thomas of Middleboro'; Mary, m. John Freeman; Mercy, m. Micah Leonard; and Job. JOB T., son of 2d Samuel, m. Hannah Fry of Andover, and had Thomas Morton, m. Sarah Abby Harrub of Plympton; Albert Fry, m. Josephine Osborne of Boston; George Samuel, m. Fanny Peabody; Charles Henry, m. Minnie Ball of Boston; and Sarah Elizabeth. He m., 2d, Lucy, sister of 1st wife. JOHN, son of Hugh, m. Susanna, d. of Edward Gray, and had John; Edward; Thomas, m. Mary Ripley; Joseph, 1706; Benjamin, 1708; Elizabeth, 1710; Samuel; Mary, m. Isaac Wright; and Susanna, m. Robert Harlow. JOHN, Plympton, perhaps son of above, by wife Elizabeth, had John, Lemuel, Joshua, Caleb, Asahel, Ebenezer; Mary, m. Noah Pratt; Hannah, m. John Gammons; and Ephraim. JOHN, m. Elizabeth Rider, 1667. JOHN, son of 2d James, by wife Patience, had Patience, 1700; Ebenezer, 1711; John, 1713; and Joseph. JOSEPH, Plympton, son of above, m. Ruth, d. of Gershom Sampson, and had Joseph, Gershom, Betsey; Job, 1775; Levi, 1761, m. Susanna, d. of Daniel Crocker; Ruth; Hannah, m. Joseph Barrows; Bethiah, m. Adam Turner; Phebe, m. Joshua Raymond; and Consider, m. Abigail Vaughan. JOSEPH, Plympton, son of 1st John, by wife Sarah, had Gershom, Lemuel, Ruth, Hannah, Bethiah, Phebe, Job, and Consider. JOSEPH, probably Bridgewater, m. Mary Stephens of Plymouth, 1729, and had Samuel, Ephraim, Joseph, Molly, Susanna, Catherine, Eliza; Eleazer, 1747; Sarah, 1749; Silence, 1755. NATHANIEL, m. Elizabeth Coite, 1742. PETER, m. Mary Marshall, 1726. SAMUEL, son of 1st Ephraim, m. Mercy, d. of William Barnes, 1728, and had James, 1729; Ephraim, 1730; and Samuel, 1731. SAMUEL, son of 1st Job, m. Sally Morton, 1803, and had Mary, 1803, m. Winslow Wright of Plympton; Sarah, 1806, m. Ephraim Paty; Samuel, 1808; Job T., 1811; Esther S., 1813, m. William Beckman; Martha M., 1816, m. Charles T. Holmes; Deborah B., 1819; Caroline E., 1822; Jane R., 1825. SAMUEL, son of above, m. Hannah Burgess, 1833, and had Samuel H., 1834; Jabez Burgess, 1839, m. Lucy Holmes; and Alfred Winslow, 1841, m. Mary Bird of Boston. He m., 2d, Jane Morton. SAMUEL HARMON, from Kingston, m. Lydia Sylvester, 1785.

COLEWAY, GEORGE, m., 1828, Mary Ann Thomas.

COLLIER, EZRA, m., 1823, Mary Shaw Atwood, and had Mary Atwood, 1825; Ezra Warren, 1826; Frances Mehitabel, 1834.

COLLINGWOOD, GEORGE, son of William, born in North Shields, England, 1818, m. Mary Chandler, d. of James Fuller of Kingston, 1857, and had Mary Ella, Beulah Jane, William C., and Laura. JAMES B., son of William, m. Marian W., d. of Jonathan Thrasher, 1852, and had Lucy J., 1853, m. William H. Clark; Marian F., 1855, m. Henry Harlow; Ella M., 1857, m. William C. Chandler; James A., 1860; William, 1862, m. Lottie May Johnson; Joseph T., 1867; and Helen L., 1869. JOHN B., brother of James, m. wid. Susan Weston, d. of Ebenezer Sampson of North Carolina, 1852, and had Olive M., 1853, m. John T. Holmes of Kingston; Augusta B., 1856, m. Admiral J. Bailey of Marshfield; Susan F., 1860. JOSEPH W., brother of above, m. Rebecca Richardson, and had Eleanor W., 1849; Mary Jane, 1851; George W., 1854; Herbert W., 1857; and Charles Barnard, 1860. THOMAS, son of William, m. Martha, d. of Benjamin Bates, 1852, and had Martha T., 1852; William Lewis, 1854; William B., 1856; Charles S., m. Angie S., d. of Jirah Tripp of Middleboro'; and Nellie F., 1861. WILLIAM, m. Eleanor Harrow in Sunderland, England, 1817, and had George and William, twins, 1818. He came to Nantucket 1819, and there had Joseph W., 1821, and Mary. He afterwards came to Plymouth, and had Mary Surfield, 1825, m. Calvin Raymond; Eleanor Harrow, 1827, m. Charles S. Peterson; John B.; James Bartlett, 1830; Thomas, 1831; Jane Brown, 1834; and Robert Surfield, 1836.

COLLINS, GAMALIEL, son of John, had a d. m. a Lewis, and sons Gamaliel, 1742; James, 1749; Benjamin, and Jesse. GAMALIEL, son of 1st James, m. Eliza Clark, d. of Josiah Finney, 1819, and had James, George M., Rebecca; Mary E., m. Sargent S. Swett; Gamaliel, and Sarah. GEORGE M., son of above, m. Lydia, d. of John Nickerson, 1846, and had George M., Alice M., and Maria E., m. George Wilbur Lewis of Westfield. He m., 2d, Henrietta E. Chesnut, 1859, and had James and George A.; and m., 3d, Sarah, d. of Burgess P. Terry, 1877. JAMES, son of 1st Gamaliel, m. Lois, d. of Rufus Robbins, 1775, and had Sarah, 1775, m. Daniel Churchill; and Bathsheba, m. Samuel Churchill. He m., 2d, Mary (Wesson) Avery, wid. of Samuel Avery of Truro, and had Mary, 1785; Lois, 1787; Nancy, 1789, m. Samuel Jackson; James, 1791; Samuel Avery, 1794, m. Esther Churchill, and moved to Taunton; and Gamaliel, 1798. JAMES, son of above, m. Sally, d. of Isaac Barnes, 1839, without issue. JOHN, the first comer in Plymouth, possibly son of Joseph of Eastham, m. Bathsheba Dunham, 1719, and had Gamaliel, and perhaps others. JOHN, a native of London, m. Mercy Harris, 1797.

COMSTOCK, WILLIAM, of Lyme, Conn., m. Hannah Faunce, 1808.

CONANT, CHRISTOPHER, came in the Ann 1623, but disappeared before 1627. JOHN, by wife Phebe, had Cynthia, 1814; Marcia, 1818; William R., 1829. LOTHROP, m. Sarah Albertson, 1812, and had Lothrop, 1814; Albert Augustus, 1816. ROGER was in Plymouth 1623, but removed to Nantasket and Salem. His children were Exercise, Lot, Elizabeth; Mary, m. William Dodge; Sarah, and perhaps others. LOT, one of the children of Roger, had a d. Martha, who m. Luke Perkins of Plympton.

CONGDON, WILLIAM, from New Bedford, m. Eleanor, d. of James
Howard, 1831.

CONKLIN, SAMUEL, m. Deborah Barrows, 1786.

CONNELL, JEREMIAH, pub. to Elizabeth Engles, 1775.

CONNER, WILLIAM, came in the Fortune 1621, but disappeared before
1627.

CONNETT, GEORGE, m. Mary Howland, 1718, and had Charles, 1720;
George, 1723; Elizabeth, 1726. JOHN, m. Bathsheba Valentine, 1811. WIL-
LIAM, pub. to Martha Wicket of Sandwich, 1740. WILLIAM, pub. to Harrison
Joseph, 1817.

COOK, CALEB, son of 1st Jacob, by wife Jane, had John, 1682; Mary,
1684; Ann, 1686, m. a Johnson; Jane, 1689, m. a Harris; Elizabeth, 1691, m.
Robert Johnson; Mary, 1694, m. a Carver; Caleb, 1697; James, 1700; Joseph,
1703. FRANCIS came in the Mayflower, 1620, with child John. Wife Esther
came in the Ann in 1623, with children Jacob, Jane, Esther. In 1626, child
Mary was born; Jane m., about 1628, Experience Mitchell; Esther, m.
Richard Wright, 1644; Mary, m. John Thompson, 1645. JACOB, son of
above, born in Holland, m. Damaris, d. of Stephen Hopkins, 1646, and had
Elizabeth, 1648, m. John Dotey; Caleb, 1651; Jacob, 1653; Mary, 1658;
Martha, 1660, m. Elkanah Cushman; Francis, 1663, m. Elizabeth Latham;
Ruth, 1666. He m., 2d, Elizabeth, wid. of William Shurtleff, 1669. JACOB,
son of above, m. Lydia Miller, 1681, and had William, 1683; Lydia, 1685;
Rebecca, 1688, m. Benjamin Sampson; Jacob, 1691; Margaret, 1695; Josiah,
1699; John, 1703, m. Hannah Morton; and Damaris. JACOB, son of
above, by wife Phebe, had Jane, 1717; Asa, 1720; Phebe, 1722; Jacob, 1725.
He had a 2d, Mary; and had Stephen, 1729. JOHN, son of 1st Francis, m.
Sarah, d. of Richard Warren, 1634, and had Sarah, m. Arthur Hathaway;
Elizabeth, m. Daniel Wilcox; Esther, 1650; Mercy, 1654; and Mary, 1657.
JOHN, son of Caleb, by wife Elizabeth, had Silas, 1708; Paul, 1711, m. Joanna
Holmes; Robert, 1714; Mercy, 1718. JOHN, m. Lydia Raymond, 1807.
JOSIAH, perhaps son of 1st Francis, m. Elizabeth, wid. of Stephen Deane,
1635, moved to Eastham, had Josiah; Ann, m. Mark Snow; Bethiah, m.
Joseph Harding. JOSIAH, son of above, m. Deborah Hopkins, 1668, and had
Elizabeth, 1669; Josiah, 1670; Richard, 1672; Elizabeth, 1674; Caleb, 1676;
Deborah, 1679; Joshua, 1683; Benjamin, 1687. ROBERT, by wife Abigail,
had Charles, 1717; Nathaniel, 1719; Robert, 1721; Sarah, 1724. WILLIAM,
son of 2d Jacob, m. Tabitha Hall, 1707, and had Hannah, 1707; Lydia,
1710; Huldah, 1712; William, 1715; Elisha, 1717; Tabitha, 1719; Priscilla,
1722.

COOMBS, JOHN, Plymouth, 1633, by wife Sarah, d. of Cuthbert Cuthbertson, had Francis, and others.

COOMER, WILLIAM, Plymouth and Plympton, by wife Joanna, had
Hannah, m. Benjamin Weston; Sarah, m. Nathaniel Cushman; Priscilla,
1726; Rebecca, 1728; Ruth; Lois; Joanna; Susanna; William; Elizabeth;
Mary; and Eunice. WILLIAM, Duxbury, son of above, m. Mabel Kempton,
1753, and had William. WILLIAM, Duxbury, son of above, m. Priscila
Anderson, 1780.

COOPER, BENJAMIN, son of 3d John, m. Susanna King, 1794, and had Sarah, m. Daniel Finney, and perhaps others. He moved away from Plymouth. EDWARD TAYLOR, son of 1st Joseph, m. Caroline, d. of John Paty, 1823, and had Caroline A., 1825, m. Edwin Morey; Edward Taylor, 1827, m. Lucretia O. Pratt. GEORGE, son of 1st Joseph, m. Mary, d. of Isaac Covington, 1825, and had Sylvia; James, 1825; Isaac Covington, 1828; George William and Jacob Taylor, twins, 1830; Mary Emeline, 1833; and Lucy Taylor, 1843. HUMILITIE came in the Mayflower, but returned to England. JOHN, Scituate, 1634, m., in that year, Priscilla, wid. of William Wright, and d. of Alexander Carpenter of England, and sister of Alice, the 2d wife of Governor Bradford. He removed in 1639 to Barnstable, and is said by Savage to have there died without children. His wid. died in Plymouth in 1689, at the age of 92, and there is reason to suspect that Richard, married in Plymouth in 1693, was her son, or grandson. JOHN, son of 1st Richard, m. Hannah, d. of John Rider, 1737, and had Samuel, m. Mary Smith, 1774; Nathaniel, m. Margaret Glover, 1788; John, m. Sarah Sampson, 1769; Thomas, m. Experience, d. of George Holmes, 1772; and Richard, m. Hannah Sampson; and Joseph. JOHN, son of above, m. Sarah, d. of Ebenezer Sampson, 1769, and had Benjamin, m. Susanna King. His wid. m. Bennet Simmons. JOHN, son of 2d Richard, m. Jerusha, d. of Lemuel Cobb, 1801, and had Ellen, 1801; John; Southworth; and William Henry of Brockton, m. Harriet Augusta, d. of Ziba Babbitt. The last removed to North Bridgewater, and it is believed that his brothers also left Plymouth. JOHN, m. Remembrance Walker, 1783. JOSEPH, son of 2d Richard, m. Lucy, d. of Jacob Taylor, 1791, and had Joseph, 1791; George, 1797; Edward Taylor, 1800; Lucy Taylor, 1805; William B., 1807; Mary, 1810; James, 1812. JOSEPH, son of above, m. Sylvia, d. of John Paty, 1814, and had Joseph Calvin; Hannah; and Sylvia. RICHARD, son or grandson, probably of 1st John, m. Hannah Wood, 1693, and had Sarah, 1693; Isaac, 1695; John, 1697; Elizabeth, 1700, m. Edward Tillson. RICHARD, son of 2d John, m. Hannah, d. of Ebenezer Sampson, 1761, and had Hannah, 1761, m. George Sampson; Richard, 1763; Elizabeth, 1764, m. Nymphas Marston; Joseph; John; Priscilla, m. John Virgin and Ezra Weston; Esther, m. Samuel Virgin. RICHARD, Plympton, son of above, m. Hannah, d. of Zabdiel Sampson, and had Richard, 1784; Hannah, 1786, m. John Fuller of Halifax; Eleanor, 1788, m. Ezra Rider of Halifax; Polly, 1791; Betsey, 1793; Priscilla Virgin, 1797; Eliza, 1799; John Dexter, 1802, m. Sarah B. Newton. RICHARD, called of Plympton, son of above, m., in Plymouth, Mercy Wright of Plympton, 1814, and 2d, Deborah Sampson. THOMAS, son of 2d John, m. Experience, d. of George Holmes, 1772. His wid., by her will, mentions brothers, sisters, and nieces, and it is probable that she had no children.

CORBAN, EZRA, from Killingley, m., 1765, Hannah Barnes, and had Dorcas, 1768. ELISHA, from Dudley, m., 1772, Experience Barnes.

CORNISH, ALLEN, son of Josiah, m., 1809, Clarissa, d. of George Cornish, and had Temperance, 1809; Allen Wendall, 1810; Clarissa, 1812. AARON HOVEY, son of Spooner, m. Mary A., d. of Amasa Holmes, and had Aaron Spooner, m. Ariadne Bearse; and Mary A. BENJAMIN, son of 1st Samuel, m., 1725, Experience Gibbs, and had Benjamin, 1727; Susanna, 1729; Mercy, 1732; John, 1734; Experience, 1740, m. Samuel Battles; Nathaniel, 1743, m. Abigail Swift; Thomas, m. Elizabeth Burton. BENJAMIN, son of above, m., 1750, Rhoda Swift, and had Deborah, 1753, m. Benjamin Gammons; Susanna, 1755, m. Thomas Bates; William, 1757, m. Mercy Swift; Rhoda, 1759; Stephen, 1760; Nancy, 1762, m. Joshua Swift; Benjamin, 1765; Sarah, m. Nehemiah Savery; George, 1767; Lemuel. BENJAMIN, son of above, m., 1789, Experience, d. of Nathaniel Cornish, and had Nathaniel, 1791, m. Abby N. B., d. of Seth Clark; Benjamin, 1797; Experience, 1800, m. a Harlow; Joshua; Isaiah, m. Marcia W. Swift. DAVID, son of 1st Thomas, m., 1793, Mercy, d. of Barnabas Holmes, and had Mercy, 1794, m. Joseph Sturtevant; Ann, 1796; James, m. Margaret, d. of Lemuel Morton; Thomas Everett, 1810; Polly, m. David Robertson. EDWARD, a passenger in the William and John, Samuel Legg, master, from Barbadoes to Boston, 1679. It is quite possible that he was the son of Richard Cornish who was in Plymouth 1637. In the early days of Plymouth Colony communications with Barbadoes were frequent, and Edward may have gone with his father, and returned. ELLIS, son of 2d Thomas, m. Sally Holmes, and removed to Halifax, in Plymouth Co. FREEMAN, son of 1st John, m. Sally Reed, and had Bailey, 1807, m. Sarah Harlow; Betsey, 1810, m. Thomas Cornish; Sarah, m. Gorham Crosby; Mary, m. Cromwell W. Holmes; and John, m. a Stephens. GEORGE, son of 2d Benjamin, m. Joanna Reed, and had Temperance, 1790, m. Isaac Savery; Clarissa, 1792, m. Allen Cornish; Hannah, 1794, m. Phineas Savery; Grace, 1796; Lucinda, 1798, m. Thomas Mayo Bartlett and Charles Bartlett; Eveline, 1800; George, 1802; Hosea, 1804; Sarah, 1806; Rhoda, 1808; Bernard, 1810. JOHN, son of 1st Benjamin, m., 1756, Lydia Shurtleff, and had Hannah, 1758, m. Benjamin Swift; Mary, 1761, m. James Perry of Rochester; Lydia, 1763, m. Elnathan Lucas. He m., 2d, 1769, Sarah Bartlett, and had John, 1771. He m., 3d, Phebe (Spooner) Pope, and had John, 1772; Freeman, 1774; Sarah, 1776; Spooner, 1779. He m., 4th, 1782, Elizabeth, d. of Israel Clark, and had Freeman and Clark, twins; and Phebe, m. Israel Clark. JOHN, son of above, m., 1803, Polly Nichols, and had Harrison, 1804; Mary Ann, 1806, m. Richard Chalker of Saybrook; Edward N., 1808, m. Martha Battles; Susan Andrews, 1811, m. Hosea Bartlett. He m., 2d, Maria Dunbar. JOSIAH, son of 1st Thomas, m. Abigail, d. of Israel Clark, 1782, and had Grace, 1787, m. Elijah Morey; Allen, 1789; Josiah, 1791, m. Charlotte Wadsworth; Aaron, 1793; Abigail Clark, m. Abraham Williams Nye. RICHARD, Plymouth, 1637, may have had Edward. SAMUEL, perhaps son of Edward, as a tradition exists in the family that their ancestor came from Barbadoes. There was, however, a Samuel in Salem, 1637, who had a son Samuel, born 1641, and the Plymouth Samuel may have been his son, or grandson. He m., 1693, Susanna, d. of James Clark, and had Samuel, 1694; Abigail, 1696; Josiah, 1698; Joseph, 1702, m. Patience Pratt; Benjamin, 1704; Thomas, 1706; Naomi, 1710; James, 1711, m. Abiah Churchill. SAMUEL, son of above, m., 1731, Meribah Clark, and had Samuel, 1732; Annaniah, 1734; Abigail, 1741. SAMUEL, son of 1st Thomas, m. Lucy, d. of Barnabas Holmes, and had Samuel, 1799, m. Esther Holmes and Betsey Cornish; Lucy, 1802; Eliza,

1804; Hiram, 1807; Hannah, 1810. SPOONER, son of 1st John, m., 1817,
Ruth, d. of Aaron Hovey, and had Aaron Hovey, 1818; Ivory Spooner, 1820,
m. Frances S. Perkins; Theodore O., 1824, m. Louisa Rois; Francis, 1827;
Sarah S., 1829; Susan B., 1834. THOMAS, son of 1st Samuel, m., 1752,
Elizabeth Bunten. He m., 2d, Anne Bates, and had Elizabeth, 1757, m.
Josiah Clark; Thomas, 1758, m. Jerusha Holmes and Deborah Leach; Josiah,
1760; Anne, 1763, m. Francis Bartlett; Abigail, 1764; Samuel, 1767; David.
THOMAS, son of above, m., 1798, Jerusha Holmes, and 2d, Deborah Leach,
and had Thomas, m. Betsey Cornish; Ellis, m. Sally Holmes; Giles, m.
Zerviah T. Bosworth; Jerusha, m. Charles G. Mann; Content, m. George
Thresher; Betsey, m. Samuel Cornish. THOMAS, son of above, m. Betsey,
d. of Freeman Cornish, and had Thomas, 1830, m. Emily C. Sturtevant of
New Bedford; Freeman, 1834; Celia, 1841, m. Nathaniel Swift. THOMAS
EVERETT, son of David, m., 1834, Zoraida Thompson, and had Abbie Howard,
1836, m. Joseph L. Weston; Thomas Everett of Philadelphia, 1838, m. Mary
Frances Phelps of Brooklyn, N. Y.; Louisa T , 1840, m. Benjamin W. Sears;
Annette, m. Harvey Briggs; and Mary. He m., 2d, 1870, Martha A., d. of
Benjamin Bates, and wid. of Thomas Collingwood.

CORPSE, ABNER, m., 1734, Hannah Ransom.

COTTON, FREDERICK AUGUSTUS, son of 3d Josiah, m., 1819, Elizabeth
Foster, and had Elizabeth, 1822; Sarah O., 1826. JOHN, son of Rowland of
Derby, England, born 1585, came to Boston, 1633. By 1st wife, Elizabeth
Horrocks, he had no issue. He m., 2d, Sarah Story, and had Seaborn, 1633,
born on the passage, m. Dorothy Bradstreet; Sarah, 1635; Elizabeth, 1637,
m. Jeremiah Eggington; John, 1640; Mary, 1642, m. Increase Mather; Rowland, 1643. JOHN, Weathersfield and Plymouth, son of above, m., 1660,
Joanna, d. of Bray Rossiter of Weathersfield, and had John, 1661; Elizabeth,
m. James Alling and Caleb Cushing; Rowland, 1667; Maria, 1672, m. a Brad-
bury; Josiah, 1675; Samuel, 1678; Josiah, 1680; Theophilus, 1682; Ann, and
Lydia. Of these, John, m. Sarah Hubbard of Ipswich, and perhaps Bath-
sheba Dunbar of Plymouth; Rowland, m. wid. Elizabeth Denison, d. of
Nathaniel Saltonstall. JOHN, son of 1st Josiah, m. Hannah Sturtevant of
Plymouth, and had Josiah, 1747; Hannah, 1748, m. Ebenezer Nye; Mary, 1750,
John, 1753; Sophia, 1755, m. Seth Parker of Falmouth; Rossiter, 1758;
Joanna, 1760; Sophia, 1762, m. Seth Parker; Sarah, 1763, m. Jesse Harlow;
Elizabeth, 1765; Lucy, 1768, m. Charles Jackson; Ward, 1770, m. Rebecca
Jackson. JOHN, son of above, m.; 1781, Experience, d. of Samuel Jackson.
JOHN WINSLOW, son of Rossiter, by wife Mary B., had John Rossiter, 1826.
JOHN, m. Lucy Little, 1780, and had Lucy, m. George Goodwin. JOSIAH,
son of 2d John, m., 1708, Hannah Sturtevant, and had Hannah, 1709, m.
Thomas Phillips and William Dyer; Mary, 1710, m. John Cushing; John,
1712; Bethiah, 1714, m. Abiel Pulsifer; Theophilus, 1716; Lucy, 1718, m.
Charles Dyer; Josiah, 1720; Edward, 1722; Josiah, 1723; Josiah, 1724;
Edward, 1726; Rowland, 1727; Margaret, 1730, m. Thomas Sawyer. JOSIAH,
son of 3d John, m. Lydia Parker, and had Josiah; and Lydia, m. Elisha Pope.
He m., 2d, Rachel, d. of David Barnes of Scituate, and had John, 1791, m.
Susan Buckmenston of Framingham, and settled in Marietta; David Barnes,

1794; Mary Ann, 1798, m. Isaac L. Hedge. He m., 3d, 1808, Priscilla, d. of Elkanah Watson. JOSIAH, son of Theophilus, m. Temperance Robbins, and had Josiah, m. Lydia, wid. of Sylvanus Bisbee, and d. of Isaac Jackson; Eliza, m. William Duparr; Frederick Augustus, m. Betsey Foster; Abigail S., m. Charles Hathaway; Catherine, m., 1st, a Robbins; 2d, Elijah D. Atwood; and 3d, Elijah Dunham. ROSSITER, son of 3d John, m., 1783, Priscilla, d. of Thomas Jackson, and had Thomas Jackson, 1785, m. Phebe Stephens; Charles, 1788, m. a Northam of Newport; Polly, 1792; Rossiter, 1794; Sophia, 1796, m. William L. Gordon; Rossiter Mather, 1798; John Winslow, 1800; Rowland Edwin, 1802; William Cushing, 1804. ROWLAND EDWIN, son of above, m. Susan Augusta, d. of Daniel Watson, and had Rowland Edwin; Louisa; and Sudlar. He m., 2d, Hannah Hammond, and had Sophia; Sarah Delfthaven; and Augusta. He m., 3d, wid. Lovell of Leominster. THEOPHILUS, son of 1st Josiah, m., 1742, Martha Sanders, and had Bethiah, m. Charles Dyer; Polly, m. Joseph Jennings; Eliza, m. Lot Haskell; Theophilus; William Crow; Josiah; and Edward.

COVELL, DAVID, m., 1803, Cynthia Bassett. DAVID, m., 1802, Susanna Myrick. EBENEZER, m., 1801, Mary Carter of Kingston. ENOS, pub., 1791, to Mary Besse. LOT, pub., 1804, to Mehitabel Weeks. NATHANIEL, from Sandwich, m., 1816, Sarah Holmes. OBADIAH, m., 1808, Mary Collings.

COVINGTON, ISAAC, son of 1st Thomas, m. Mary, d. of Ebenezer Sampson, 1794, and had Mary, 1797, m. George Cooper. JACOB, son of 1st Thomas, m. Patty, d. of Gideon Holbrook, and had Elam, 1817, removed to California, and there married; Mary Holbrook, 1820, m. George H. Bates of Farmington, Maine; Martha Ann, 1822; Edwin, 1825, m. Maria, d. of Isaiah Rich of Boston; Harriet, 1827; Helen, 1830; Jacob, 1832, m. Laura Montague of Vermont; Leonard, 1834, m. Catherine B., d. of Ichabod Shaw and Augusta Brown. NATHANIEL C., son of 2d Thomas, m. Catherine D., d. of Samuel Burbank, 1833, and had Catherine, 1836, m. Ezra Harlow; Nathaniel and William, 1839, twins. THOMAS, came to Plymouth probably from the South, and m. Sarah, d. of Joseph Tribble, 1771, and had Jacob; Isaac; Thomas; Sally, m. John Edwards and Daniel Doty; Triphena, m. Barnabas Hedge; Betsey, m. Fisher Ames of West Bridgewater; Eleanor, m. Samuel Sherman; Mary, m. Benjamin Dillard; Lucy, m., 1st, Lemuel Barnes, and 2d, James Howard; Eunice, m. Rufus Churchill; Nancy, m. Samuel Churchill and Benjamin Dillard; Lydia, m. Caleb Finney; and Hannah, m. Lewis Churchill. THOMAS, son of above, m. Elizabeth Hueston, 1797, and had Elizabeth Hueston, 1798; Nathaniel C.; Beza; Arad, and Thomas.

COWEN, ISRAEL, Scituate, died 1720, leaving children Rachel, Job, Josiah, Gathelus, Israel, Joseph. JOSEPH, Bridgewater, son of above, died 1791, leaving wid. Anne, and children Joseph and Ward, and a d. who m. a Hooper. ROBERT, Scituate, d. 1720. ROBERT, m. Ann T., d. of Samuel Robbins of Plymouth, and had Mary Ann, 1831; Robert, 1833.

COX, ELIAS, Pembroke and Plymouth, son of 1st James, m., about 1790, Abigail Witherell of Pembroke, and had Abigail, m. Zacheus Kempton; Elias, m. Eliza O. Kempton; John; and James, now living, who m. Nancy Holmes. He m., 2d, 1807, Patience, d. of Isaac Churchill, and wid. of John

Calderwood. JAMES, Pembroke, m., about 1760, Ruth Magoon, and had James, Elias, Isaac; Ruth, m. Isaac Chandler of Duxbury; Mary; Abigail, m. a Keen of Pembroke; and Lucy, m. a Crooker of New Hampshire. JAMES, son of above, removed to Nova Scotia, where he m. Elizabeth Rowland about 1800, and had William Rowland of Plymouth; Martha Taylor, m. Ephraim Bartlett of Plymouth; Elizabeth, James, and others, of Nova Scotia. JOHN, son of Elias, m. Eliza, wid. of David Richards of Nova Scotia, and lived in Pembroke, where he had Abigail; Eliza; Mary A., m. William Rowland Cox, Jr.; and Isaac M. WILLIAM ROWLAND, son of 2d James, came from Nova Scotia to Plymouth, and m., 1836, Mary Ann, d, of Ansel Holmes, and had William Rowland, and Mary A. He m., 2d, Abigail Pierce, d. of Daniel Goddard, and wid. of Nathan G. Cushing, and had Winslow Warren, 1844, m. Fannie S. Holmes; and Lemuel. He m., 3d, Mary C. Finney, 1847, and had Mary C., 1848, and Sylvanus Clark, 1854, m. Hattie J., d. of Richard W. Harlow. He m., 4th, Maria E. Vaughn, 1869.

COYE, WILLIAM, m. Ruth Savery, 1772. WILLIAM, m. Mary Carver, 1790. WILLIAM, m. Rebecca Brown, 1799. WILLIAM, m. Elizabeth Shurtleff, 1814.

CRACKSTONE, JOHN, came in the Mayflower 1620, with son John. He died 1621, and his son 1628. His wife was probably a Smith.

CRANDON, BENJAMIN, son of Thomas, m., 1790, Susanna, d. of John Bishop, and had Susan, m. Alvin Sampson; Nancy B., 1792, m. Cornelius Sampson Jackson; Abby, m. Joseph N. Leonard; Sally, 1797; Mary B.; Ruth, 1794; Jane, Emily, and Benjamin H. BENJAMIN H., son of above, m., 1836, Mary Ann, d. of Daniel Goddard, and had John H.; Mary Jane, m. Nathaniel Carver; Sanford; Daniel G. CONSIDER HOWLAND, Lewiston, New York, son of Philip, m., 1828, Ann Corbin, and had Esther D., Ann, Sarah, Thomas F., Jane C., Charles H., Ruth J., and Harriet S. DANIEL G., Chelsea, son of 2d Benjamin, m. Florence J. Pillsbury of Chelsea, and had Leroy G., Mary Howland, Florence E., and Laura Bishop. JAMES, son of John, m. Sarah Delano, and had John, 1751. JOHN, born in England, first settled in Dartmouth, and m. Jean Bess, born in Scotland. He had Jean, 1722; Grace, 1724, m. John Carver; John, 1726, died in the West Indies; James, 1728; Sarah, m. John Witherell; Thomas, 1729. JOHN H., Chelsea, son of 2d Benjamin, m. Emily S., d. of Abijah Drew of Plymouth, and had Edwin S., Emma Agnes, and Helen. JOSEPH, Columbia Falls, Maine, son of Philip, m., 1829, Ruth C., d. of Thomas Ruggles, and had Emily, James, George R., Lorenzo, John H., Sophia R., and Augustus. He m., 2d, 1842, Alice B., wid. of Levi Small, and d. of William Frankland of Grand Menan, and had Alice B., Ruth A., and Joseph. PHILIP, Rochester, son of Thomas, m., 1793, Esther, d. of Benjamin Dillingham, and had John, Consider Howland, Ruth, m. Lewis Shaw; and Joseph. He m., 2d, 1806, Rebecca Hathaway, and had Philip. He m., 3d, 1812, Bathsheba Bartlett, and had Rebecca. SANFORD, son of 2d Benjamin, m. Olivia B. Bangs of Chelsea, and had Sanford, Charles F., Frank S., and Edward. THOMAS, son of 1st John, m., 1751, Ruth, d. of Consider Howland, and had Thomas, 1752; Jean, 1753;

James, 1755; Thomas, 1757; Ruth, 1760; John, 1763; Benjamin, 1764; Consider, 1767; Philip, 1769; and Joseph, 1771.

CRAPO, FRANCIS, from Rochester, m., 1760, Margaret Beale.

CROADE, NATHANIEL, m., 1742, Elizabeth Coite, and had Elizabeth, 1743; Nathaniel, 1745. THOMAS, by wife Rachel, had Priscilla, 1725. Nathaniel was perhaps son of Thomas, and Thomas son of John of Marshfield, who m., 1692, Deborah Thomas, and grandson of John of Salem, who m., 1659, Elizabeth Price.

CROMBIE, Calvin, son of 1st William, m., 1797, Naomi, d. of Samuel Jackson, and had Naomi; Fanny, 1796; Mercy; James, 1802; Catherine, m. William Thomas of Boston. WILLIAM, born in Andover, 1731, came to Plymouth about 1762. He m. Zeruiah Kimball of Andover, and had Williar 1763; Kimball, 1767, m. Deborah Davie; Annie, 1771, m. Nathaniel Bra.. street of Newburyport; Calvin, 1773; and Nancy, m. John D. Dunbar. WILLIAM, son of above, m., 1794, Deborah, d. of Samuel Jackson, and had Nancy, Deborah, Kimball, and William.

CROSBY, GORHAM, m., 1833, Sarah F. Cornish.

CROSSMAN, NATHANIEL, from Taunton, m., 1751, Esther Hatch.

CROSWELL, ANDREW, m., 1736, Rebecca Harlow, and had Andrew, 1737, and Joseph. ANDREW, son of above, m., 1763, Mary Clark. He m., 2d, 1775, Sarah Palmer of Falmouth, and had Andrew, 1776; Rebecca; Sarah, 1781. ANDREW, son of above, graduated at Harvard, 1798, removed from Plymouth, and had a d. Susan C., m., 1831, Admiral Henry Knox Thatcher. JOSEPH, from Groton, m., 1743, Jerusha Bartlett. JOSEPH, son of 1st Andrew, by wife Lucy, had David, 1782; Rebecca, 1783.

CROW, SAMUEL, from Providence, m., 1755, Hannah Rider. WILLIAM, born 1629, m., 1664, Hannah, d. of Josiah Winslow. YELVERTON had Thomas and Elizabeth, twins, 1649, born in Yarmouth.

CROWLEY, EDWARD, m., 1722, Jane Rich.

CRYMBLE, QUENTON, m. Elizabeth Holmes, and had Holmes, 1720; Charles, 1722; Elizabeth, 1725; Phebe, 1727; Mercy Holmes, 1729; Phebe, 1732, m. Jeremiah Holmes; Abigail, 1735.

CUFF, WILLIAM, m., 1775, Hannah Dunham, and had William, 1776; Hannah, 1780; Mary William, 1784.

CUFFEE, CUFFEE, slave of Isaac Lothrop, pub. to Nanny, slave of Samuel Bartlett, 1734. CUFFEE, slave of George Watson, m. Nannie, slave of Samuel Bartlett, 1768.

CUNNINGHAM, GUILFORD E., son of Jesse, m. Mary Ann, d. of John Hall, 1844. JESSE of Marion, m. Sarah, d. of Guilford Evans of Freetown, about 1817, and had John C.; Mary Ann, m. Lewis Hall; Guilford E., 1822; Stephen; Joseph; Rebecca; and Sarah E., 1834, m. Lemuel S. Bumpus. JOHN C., son of Jesse, m. Catherine W. Luce of Maine, and had Sarah A., 1843, m. Hezekiah C. Mendall of Rochester; Stephen G., 1845; Catherine W., 1848, m. Barnabas L. Harlow; and Stephen G. again, 1850.

CURTIS, BENJAMIN, son of 1st Francis, m., 1700, Mary, d. of Nehemiah Besse of Sandwich, and had Mary, 1701; Benjamin, 1704. DAVID, prob. from Hanover, m., 1743, Hannah Ward, and had Elizabeth, 1744; David, 1746.

DAVID, m. Sally Clark, 1810. EBENEZER, son of 1st Francis, m., 1710,
Mary, d. of Hilkiah Tinkham, and had Jacob, 1710; Caleb, 1712; Mary, 1714,
m. Nathaniel Churchill; Sarah, 1717. He m., 2d, 1718, Martha Doty, and
had Eunice, 1723, m. John Howard; Martha, 1725; Seth, 1727; Ebenezer,
1731. EDWARD, m. Sarah Freeman, 1750. FRANCIS appeared in Plymouth
1671, and m. in that year Hannah Smith, and had John, 1673; Benjamin,
1675; Francis, 1679; Elizabeth, 1681; Elisha, 1683, m. Amy West; and Ebenezer. FRANCIS, son of above, m., 1700, Hannah Bosworth, and had James,
1701; Elkanah, 1703; Francis, 1705; Nathaniel, 1707; Sylvanus, 1710, m.
Dorothy Delano of Duxbury; Hannah, 1712, m. Joshua Finney; Lydia, 1718,
Zacheus, 1720. FRANCIS, son of above, m., 1731, Elizabeth, d. of John
Barnes, and had Lydia, 1732, m. Charles Boult; James, 1735; Elizabeth,
1739. JACOB, son of Ebenezer, m., 1731, Fear, d. of Eleazer Dunham, and
had Elizabeth, 1732, m. Joseph Totman; Sarah, 1734; Caleb, 1737; Fear, 1740;
Jacob, 1742; Mary, 1745, m. Thomas Faunce; Hannah, 1747, m. Zacheus
Barnes. JOHN, son of 1st Francis, had Francis, 1696; Hannah, 1698; John,
1702; Elizabeth, 1704. NOAH, from Pembroke, m., 1781, Deborah Lucas.
WILLIAM, Pembroke, m. Hannah Tinkham, 1768, and had William, 1769;
Hannah, 1771; James, 1773, m. Sally Churchill of Plymouth. ZACHEUS, son
of 2d Francis, m. Lydia Thomas, and had Zacheus, 1743; Lydia, 1745, m.
Ezra Holmes; Hannah, 1748, m. Timothy Swinerton; Zacheus, 1753; Nathan-
iel, 1756; Mary, 1764. ZACHEUS, son of above, m., 1777, Deborah Turner,
and had Sarah, m. Jesse Robbins; Lydia, m. Ebenezer Davie; Mary, m.
Anthony Dike.

CUSHING, BENJAMIN, Hingham, son of Solomon, m., 1753, Ruth, d. of
Thomas Croade of Halifax, and had William, 1754; Rachel, 1755, m. Ezra Lin-
coln; Benjamin, 1758; Solomon, 1760; Thomas Croade of Salem, 1764; Matthew,
1768; Charlotte, 1771; Caleb, 1773, of Charleston, S. C.; Joshua, 1775, of Lynn;
Henry, 1777; Jerome, 1780. BENJAMIN, son of 3d Matthew, m. wid.
Blanchard of Harwich, and had Reuben; James; Caleb; Joseph; John, and
Mary. BRACKLEY, m. Eliza, d. of John Bartlett, about 1828. DANIEL,
Hingham, son of 1st Matthew, m. Lydia, d. of Edward Gilman, 1645,
and had Peter, 1646; Daniel, 1648; Deborah, 1651; Jeremiah, 1654; Theophilus, 1657; Matthew, 1660. EZRA, m. Betsey B., d. of John Allen, 1825.
FRANCIS of Scituate, m. Lucy Dyer, 1786. IGNATIUS, son of Jeremiah,
m. Mary Rickard, and had Hannah 1710; Ignatius 1711; Hannah, 1714.
JEREMIAH, Scituate, son of Daniel, m., 1685, Hannah, d. of Thomas Lo-
ring, and had Hannah, 1687, m. Samuel Barker; Ignatius, 1689, Jeremiah,
1695; Ezekiel, 1698. MATTHEW, Hingham, came over 1638, with wife Naza-
reth, d. of Henry Pitcher, and children Daniel, 1619; Jeremiah, 1621;
Matthew, 1623; Deborah, 1625, m. Matthias Briggs; John, 1627. MATTHEW,
Hingham, son of Daniel, m., 1684, Jael, d. of John Jacob, and had David,
1685; David, 1687; Solomon, 1692; Job, 1694; Moses, 1696; Samuel, 1699;
Isaac, 1701; Obadiah, 1703; Jael, 1706, m. John Lasell. MATTHEW,
Plymouth and Middleboro', son of 1st Benjamin, m., 1794, Lydia, d. of James
Drew of Plymouth, and had Lydia, 1795; Lydia, 1797; Caleb, 1799, m. Pris-
cilla Gorham; Charles, 1800; Mary, 1802, m. Joshua Deane of Wareham;

Matthew, 1804; Hannah, 1806, m. Joshua LeBaron; and Benjamin, 1809.
MATTHEW, Middleboro', son of above, m. Elizabeth S. Shurtleff, and had
Nathaniel Shurtleff, 1830; Matthew Henry, 1832; Gamaliel, 1838. NATHAN
G., m. Abby P., d. of Daniel Goddard, 1829. SOLOMON, Hingham, son of
2d Matthew, m. Sarah, d. of Thomas Loring, 1716, and had Mary, 1717;
Matthew, 1720; Solomon, 1722; Benjamin; and Joseph, 1724; Benjamin,
1725; Sarah, 1727; Joseph, 1728; Isaiah, 1730; Caleb, 1732.

CUSHMAN, EBENEZER, Kingston, son of Jonathan, m., 1775, Susanna, d.
of Josiah Holmes, and had Lydia, 1775; Sylvester, 1777, m. Hannah Brown;
Joseph, 1780; Ebenezer, 1782, m. Charity Benson and Celia Sampson;
Susanna, m. Levi Morton; Ruth, m. Barsillai Holmes; Elizabeth, 1786; Rob-
ert, 1788; Harvey, 1791. ELEAZER, son of 1st Thomas, m., 1687, Elizabeth
Combes, and had Lydia, 1687, m. John Waterman; John, 1690; Moses, 1693;
James; and William, 1710. ELKANAH, son of 1st Thomas, m., 1677,
Elizabeth Cole, and had Elkanah, 1678; James, 1679; Jabez, 1681. He m.,
2d, Martha, d. of Jacob Cooke, 1683, and had Allerton, 1683, m. Mary Buck,
and Elizabeth, d. of George Sampson; Elizabeth, 1685, m. Robert Waterman;
Josiah, 1688; Mehitabel, 1693; and Martha, m. Nathaniel Holmes. ELKANAH,
son of above, m., 1703, Hester, d. of Jonathan Barnes, and had Elizabeth,
1703; Elkanah, 1706; James, 1709, m. Hannah Cobb. ELKANAH, son of
above, m. Lydia Bradford, 1740, afterwards the 2d wife of Lazarus LeBaron,
and had Elkanah, and perhaps others. ELKANAH, son of above, m. Mary,
d. of Ansel Lothrop, and had Elkanah. ELKANAH, Plympton, son of Josiah,
m., 1743, Hannah, d. of Zachariah Standish, and had Ezra, 1744; Susanna,
1746; Elkanah, 1748, m. Hannah Churchill; Ebenezer, 1750, m. Rebecca, d.
of Ichabod Churchill, and Lucy, d. of Abner Bisbee; Zachariah, 1753; Levi,
1755. He m., 2d, Patience, wid. of John Perkins, and d. of Ichabod Paddock,
and had Hannah, 1759, m. Elias Churchill; James, 1761; Rebecca, 1764, m.
Robert Waterman; Joanna, 1767, m. Isaac Bosworth. ELKANAH, son of
above, born in the house on the southerly corner of Court Square, m., 1790,
Susanna Wendell Lothrop, and had Ansel Lothrop; Eleanor Wendell; Cordelia Howard; Alexander; Mary Ann; and Isabella. He m., 2d, Mary Eliza
Babbit of Boston, and had Charlotte Saunders, the distinguished actress,
Charles Augustus; Fitz Henry, Augustus Babbit; and Susan Webb, who m.,
1st, Nelson M. Merriman of Boston; and, 2d, Prof. James Sheridan Muspratt
of Liverpool, England, the founder of the Royal College of Chemistry.
GEORGE, Duxbury, son of 4th Joseph, m. Anna Perry of Hanover, and had
Anna, 1788, m. Joseph Weston; Nabby, 1790; George, 1791, m. Judith
Weston; Nabby, 1793, m. Dura Wadsworth; Hannah, 1796; Betsey, 1798;
Joseph, 1801, m. Saba Ripley; Sylvia, 1802; Briggs, 1807, m. Lucy Keen; Lucy,
1805. ICHABOD, son of 1st Isaac, m. Patience, d. of John Holmes, and had
Joanna; William; Sarah; Experience; Patience; Mary; Ichabod; Rebecca; and
Isaac. IGNATIUS, Plympton, m. Ruth Washburn, 1793. ISAAC, son of 1st
Thomas, m. Rebecca, d. of Giles Rickard, 1675, and had Isaac, 1676; Rebecca,
1678; Mary, 1682, m. Robert Waterman; Sarah, 1684, m. James Bryant; Icha-
bod, 1686; Fear, 1689, m. William Sturtevant. ISAAC, son of above, m.
Sarah Gibbs, 1701, and had Phebe, 1703; Alice, 1705. He m., 2d, wid.

Mercy Freeman, d. of Jonathan Bradford. JAMES, son of 1st Elkanah, m. Sarah Hatch, 1722, and had Lydia, 1723; James, 1725. JAMES, Kingston, son of 3d Thomas, m. Mercy, d. of Nathaniel Morton of Plymouth, 1780, and had Nathaniel, m. Rebecca Stetson; James; Mary; Zenas, m. Deborah Johnson; Sarah; Job; Martin; Spencer; and Samuel Ellis. JOB, son of 2d Thomas, by wife Lydia, had Meriah, 1707; Job, 1711; Lydia, 1718. JONATHAN, Kingston, son of 2d Robert, m., 1736, Susanna, d. of John Benson, and had Ebenezer, 1748; Jonathan; Mary; Benson; Artemas. JOSEPH, Middleboro', son of William, m., 1768, Deborah Barrows, and had Susanna; Mary; Isaac; and Joseph. JOSEPH, Middleboro', son of above, m., 1804, Sally, d. of Nathaniel Thompson, and had Isaac Newton; Mary; Deborah; Sarah; Thomas; Nathaniel; Hannah; Leonidas; Joseph; and Ann Leonard. JOSEPH, son of above, removed to Plymouth, and m. Sarah Thomas, d. of Barnabas Hedge, 1835, by whom he had Elizabeth H., 1836; Mary A., 1841, m. Alfred E. Walker of New Haven; Ellen Blanche, 1844, m. Theodore Parker Adams of Boston; William H., 1846; Annie L., 1849, m. John W. Page of New Bedford. JOSEPH, Middleboro', son of Joshua, m. Elizabeth, d. of George Sampson of Plympton, and had George, 1759; Hannah, 1761, m. Anna Perry of Hanover; Joseph; David; Abigail, m. Lewis Cobb; Lydia, 1772, m. Asa Delano; Sarah, m. John Vaughn; Betsey, m. Elisha Thomas. JOSHUA, Duxbury, son of 2d Robert, m., 1733, Mary, d. of Josiah Soule, and had Joseph, 1733; Joshua, 1735; Cephas; Mary; Soule; Paul; Appollos; Ezra. He m., 2d, Deborah Ford of Marshfield, and had Mial, 1753; Consider, 1755; Robert, 1758; Deborah, 1762. JOSIAH, son of 1st Elkanah, m., 1709, Susanna, d. of William Shurtleff, and had Susanna, 1710; Martha, 1713; m. Robert Waterman; Susanna, 1715, m. Benjamin Shurtleff; Ann, 1717, m. Robert Avery; Josiah, 1719; Elkanah, 1721; William, 1723; Elizabeth, 1728; Isaiah, 1731. ROBERT, came in the Fortune 1621, with son Thomas, 14 years of age, child of a 1st wife Sarah. He m., in Leyden, 1617, Mary Chingelton, or Singleton, of Sandwich, England. He returned to England in the Fortune, and left his son in the care of Gov. Bradford. ROBERT, son of 2d Thomas, by a 1st wife Persis, m. about 1697, had Robert, 1698; Ruth, 1700, m. Luke Perkins; Abigail, 1701; Hannah, 1705, m. Moses Washburn; Thomas, 1706; Joshua, 1707, m. Mary, d. of Josiah Soule; Jonathan, 1712. He m., 2d, at the age of 80, Prudence Sherman of Marshfield. ROBERT, Kingston, son of above, m., 1725, Mary Washburn, and had Lydia, 1726, m. Josiah Fuller; Jerusha, 1728, m. Ebenezer Cobb; Rebecca, 1730, m. Barnabas Fuller of Plympton; Mercy, 1731, m. James Harlow of Plympton; Hannah, 1732, m. John Cobb; Thankful, 1734; Ruth, 1735, m. Samuel Rickard; Abigail, 1737, m. Benjamin Robbins of Plymouth; Robert, 1738, m. Martha Delano; Eleanor, 1740; Martha, 1742; Isaac, 1745; Jabez, 1750. ROBERT, Maine, son of above, m., 1759, Martha Delano, and had Robert, 1761; Mary, 1762; Hopestill, 1764; Joshua, 1766; Martha, 1769; Beza, 1771. THOMAS, son of 1st Robert, m., 1636, Mary, d. of Isaac Allerton, and had Thomas, 1637; Sarah, m. John Hawks of Lynn; Lydia, m. William Harlow; Isaac, 1648; Elkanah, 1651; Fear, 1653; Eleazer, 1657; and Mary. THOMAS, son of above, m., 1664, Ruth, d. of John Howland, and had Robert, 1664. He m., 2d, 1679, Abigail Fuller of Rehoboth, and had Job; Bartholomew; Samuel, 1687; and Benjamin. THOMAS, son of 2d Robert, m. Alice Hayward, and had Thomas, 1736, m. Bethiah Thomas of Bridgewater. He m., 2d, Mehitabel, d. of John Faunce, and had Lydia, 1739; Job and Elkanah, twins, 1742; Bartholomew, 1744; Mary, 1746; Desire, 1748, m. John Gray; Sarah, 1750, m. Josiah Ripley; Amaziah, 1752; Elisha, 1755; James, 1756; John, 1759, m. Betsey Barrows of Carver and Betsey Pierce; Samuel, 1761. THOMAS, Kingston, grandson of above, and son of his son Elisha, who m. Lydia, d. of Josiah Fuller, m. Sylvia, d. of Seth Drew, and had Asa; Thomas S.; and Edwin. WILLIAM, Middleboro', son of Ichabod, m., 1735, Susanna Sampson, and had Joseph; Joanna; William; Zenas; and Noah. He m., 2d, 1751, Priscilla Cobb, and had Priscilla; Isaac; Susanna; Andrew; Perez; Patience; and Wealthea. ZACHARIAH, Needham, son of 5th Elkanah, m. Saba, d. of Joshua Adams, and had Sally, 1783; Levi, m. Elizabeth Gray of Williamston, N. C.; and Mercy, m. Josiah Robbins of Plymouth. (See "Cushman Genealogy" for further details.)

CUTHBERTSON, CUTHBERT, came in the Ann 1623. He m. at Leyden, 1621, Sarah, double wid. of John Vincent and Degory Priest, and sister of Isaac Allerton, and had Samuel; Sarah, m. John Coombs; and others. SAMUEL, son of above, was one of the original purchasers of Dartmouth.

CUTLER, ROBERT, m., 1689, Sarah Dunham.

CUTTNETT, JOSIAH, pub. to Hannah Quoy, 1742, Indians.

DAMON, or DAMAN, or DAMMAN, DANIEL, Scituate, son of Zachary, had two wives, the first unknown, by whom he had Daniel, 1716. He m., 2d, 1721, Jemima Stetson, and probably had by her Joseph, Amos, Bathsheba, Jemima, Robert, David, Isaac, and Abiel. DANIEL, Scituate, son of above, by wife Juda, had Daniel, John, Simeon, Samuel, Joshua, and Bathsheba. DANIEL, Scituate, son of above, m. Lydia, d. of Josiah Witherell, and had Daniel Edwin, 1829; Simeon, 1831, m. Zoa Clapp; Lydia James, m. Charles H. Wilder; Albion, m. Abby Clapp; Alpheus, m. Abby Jones; Josiah m. a Gardner; and Harriet. DANIEL EDWIN of Plymouth, son of above, m., 1860, Ruth W., d. of Martin W. Stetson of Hanover, and had Edwin Stetson, 1862; and Ruth Stockbridge, 1866. JOSHUA, Scituate, son of 2d Daniel, m. Judith Litchfield, and had Wealthea, Joshua, Daniel, Judith, and Mahala. JOHN, Scituate, m. 1644, Katharine, d. of Henry Merritt, and had Deborah, 1645; John, 1647; Zachary, 1649; Mary, 1651; Daniel, 1652; Zachary again, 1654. He m., 2d, 1659, Martha, d. of Arthur Howland of Marshfield, and had Experience, a son, 1662; Silence, 1663; Ebenezer, 1665; Ichabod, 1668; Margaret, 1670; Hannah, 1672. ZACHARY, Scituate, son of above, m., 1679, Martha, d. of Walter Woodworth, and had Zachary, m. Mehitabel Chittenden; and Daniel, and others.

DANFORTH, ALLEN, son of Asa of Taunton, m., 1818, Lydia Presbry, d. of William Seaver of Taunton, and had James Allen, 1819; Nathaniel Seaver, 1821. He removed to Plymouth, 1822, and had Lydia Ann, 1825; Mary Adeline, 1828, m. John J. Russell; William Seaver, 1832. ASA, Taunton, m., 1788, Deborah Thayer of Taunton. He was the father of Allen, and son of James, who m. Mehitabel Baker. James was the son of James who m.,

1720, Sarah Dean, and grandson of Samuel, who m., 1688, Hannah, d. of
James Allen of Boston. Samuel was the son of Samuel, who m., 1651, Mary,
d. of John Wilson, and grandson of Nicholas, who came from Framling-
ham, England, and settled in Cambridge, 1634. ELKANAH, belonging
to a family distinct from that of the above, had Ira; Benjamin; Mary,
m. William Gifford, and Henry. HENRY, son of above, m. Martha Raymond, and had Charles Henry, 1827, m. Phebe Reynolds, and Adrianna,
d. of Stephen Faunce; Otis, 1829; Allen, 1833; Martha J., 1834, m. Caleb F.
Wright; Fanny H., m. George H. Atwood; Aurelia, m. Alexander Wood.
JAMES ALLEN, son of Allen, m., 1842, Sarah T., d. of Daniel Jackson, and
had Sarah; Allen, 1846; and Allen again, 1848. WILLIAM SEAVER, son of
Allen, m., 1858, Abby D. P., d. of J. M. Mace of Colbrook, Conn., and had
William Henry, 1860. (See "Danforth Genealogy.")
   DANIEL, PETER, m., 1743, Sarah Waterman.
   DARLING, EPHRAIM, m., 1768, Rebecca Bartlett. JONATHAN, m., 1735,
Lydia Cobb. JONATHAN, m., 1749, Martha, d. of Joshua Bramhall, and had
Lydia, 1750, m. Wilson Churchill; Benjamin, 1752; Sarah, 1754, m. Lazarus
Harlow; Mary, 1756; John, 1758.
   DAVIE, CURTIS, son of 2d Ebenezer, m., 1859, Lucy T., d. of Charles
Nelson, and had Nelson, 1860; Nathaniel and Martha, twins, 1863. He m.,
2d, 1874, Annie Greenwood of Hyde Park. EBENEZER, son of 1st William,
m., 1798, Lydia Curtis, and had Ebenezer; Lydia, m. Thomas Torrey; Wil-
liam; Susan, m. Oliver Edes; Jane, m. Frederick Robbins; Curtis; Patience
C., m. George A. Hathaway; Nathaniel Curtis; Deborah Curtis; George, and
John, m. Priscilla H. Snow. EBENEZER, son of above, m. Mercy Bartlett,
d. of William Bradford, and had Curtis, 1827; Mercy Ann, 1829; Sarah W.,
1833, m. Albert Barnes; Emeline, 1835. ICHABOD, son of 2d Robert, m.,
1797, Joanna Bartlett, and had Sarah, 1798; Joanna, 1799; Elizabeth, 1801.
He m., 2d, 1807, Nancy Bartlett. ISAAC, son of 1st William, m., 1816, Rhoda,
d. of John Perry, and had Isaac Lewis, and Mary B. C., m. James Morton.
ISAAC LEWIS, son of above, m. Lydia A., d. of Thomas Torrey, and had
Thomas Torrey, 1847, and removed to Springfield. JOHN, son of 1st Ebenezer,
m., 1837, Priscilla H. Snow, and removed from Plymouth. JOHNSON, son
of 1st Solomon, m., 1823, Phebe, d. of Ephraim Finney, and had Ezra John-
son, 1824, moved to Smyrna, and m. there Betsey Ghout and Amelia Marian
Garaphelia Ghout; Betsey Thomas, 1826; Harriet E., 1828, m. Charles T.
May; Susan Augusta, 1830, m. James S. Parker; Mary S., 1834, m. William
Davis Simmons; Sylvester, 1837; Thomas, 1842. JOSEPH, son of 1st William,
m., 1803, Hannah, d. of Peleg Faunce, and had Lydia W., m. Hiram B.
Sears; Mary F., m. George K. Wood; Amanda, m. James Waterman; Han-
nah, m. William Sargent Holmes; Matilda, m. Leonidas Jewett and William
Sargent Holmes; Betsey F., m. Nathaniel Holmes. JOSEPH, son of above,
m., 1839, Deborah W. Manter, and had George Francis, 1844; Charlotte M.,
1846; Joseph L., 1849; Joseph F., 1851. ROBERT, perhaps grandson of
Humphrey, who came from London to Boston 1662, m., 1716, Deborah
Howes, and had Thomas, 1718. ROBERT, son of 1st Thomas, m., 1766,
Elizabeth, d. of Barnabas Churchill, and had Samuel, 1766; Robert, 1768;

Ichabod, 1771; Elizabeth, m. Josiah Carver; Lydia, 1775, m. Ezra Harlow.
ROBERT, son of above, m., 1796, Jerusha Trask, and had Robert, 1797; Elizabeth, 1798; Priscilla, 1800; and Jerusha, m. Samuel Talbot. ROBERT, son
of above, m., 1821, Harriet, d. of Gideon Holbrook, and had Harriet E.,
1823; and Jerusha Trask, m. Nathaniel M. Hobart. He m., 2d, 1827, Fanny,
d. of John Eddy, and had Harriet Frances. SAMUEL COLE, Kingston, son of
1st Solomon, m. Mercy, d. of William Douglass, and had Samuel Harmon.
SAMUEL HARMON, son of above, m., 1840, Eliza Ann, d. of Comfort Bates.
He m., 2d, Isabella, d. of George Simmons, and had Samuel Cole, 1845; Elizabeth A., 1847, m. Frank H. Pratt of Winchester; Mary, 1849; John W.,
1859. SOLOMON, son of 1st Thomas, m., 1786, Jedidah Sylvester, and had
Betsey, 1786; Solomon, 1789, m. Esther, d. of Marcus LeBaron and Sarah D.,
d. of Seth Washburn; Abigail, m. John Virgin; Samuel Cole; Thomas,
1797, moved to Maine; Johnson; Edward Taylor, 1801; Sylvester, 1806, m.
Mary Ann Holmes; Sarah Jane, 1809. SOLOMON, son of above, m., 1821,
Sally Washburn, and had Sarah Ann, and Solomon, 1836. He had as
either 1st or 2d wife, Esther, d. of Marcus LeBaron. SOLOMON, Kingston, son of above, m. Eliza Wood, d. of Francis Washburn, and had Ella.
SYLVESTER, son of Johnson, m., 1864, Eveline C., d. of Lucius Pratt, and
had Ida H., 1864; Alice P., 1865; Ezra J., 1867; Lucius Pratt, 1869; Charles
W., 1871; William H., 1872; Edward P., 1874; George, 1876; Amelia M.,
1880. THOMAS, son of 1st Robert, m. Sarah Johnson, and had Robert, 1741;
Thomas, 1743; William, 1746; Deborah, 1749; Betty, 1752; Joseph, 1756;
Solomon, 1759; John, 1761. He m., 2d, 1761, Hannah Rogers, and had
Johnson, 1762; George, 1764, m. Susanna Furn of Boston; and Deborah.
THOMAS, son of above, m., 1768, Jennie Holmes, and had Thomas, 1771;
and Deborah, m. Kimball Crombie. THOMAS, son of above, m., 1794, Bet-
sey, d. of Corban Barnes, and had Betsey Thomas, m. Isaac Barnes; and
Deborah, m. in New Bedford. WILLIAM, son of 1st Thomas, m., 1768,
Lydia Harlow, and had William, m. Experience Stetson; Ebenezer, Isaac,
Lydia, and Joseph. WILLIAM, son of 1st Ebenezer, m., 1830, Marcia, d. of
Lewis Weston, and had George, 1832; Marcia Torrey, 1834, m. Charles A.
Hammond of Fairhaven. He m., 2d, Lydia Ann Baker of Maine, and had
George, 1853; William, 1856; and Emma Woodward.

DAVIS, CHARLES GIDEON, son of 2d William, m. Hannah Stevenson, d.
of John B. Thomas, 1845, and had Charles Howland, 1853; Joanna, 1856;
Charles S., 1858; and Edward, 1860. DAVID, son of 1st Thomas, born in
Albany, 1724, came to Kingston, from North Carolina, 1733, and was educated under the care of Silas Cook. He m., 1751, Sarah Cozzens of Edgartown, and removed to that place, dying, 1765, leaving children, Catherine,
born 1752; Mary, 1754, m. Meletiah Davis; David, 1759; Wendell, 1761; Sanford, 1763; William, 1765; Rufus, 1767; and Sarah, m. John Davis. DAVID,
Industry, son of above, m. Olive Mayhew, and had John, William, Nathaniel, Olive, Betsey, Susan, and Almira. FRANCIS BASSETT, son of John Watson, m., 1858, Susan Elizabeth, d. of Isaac L. Hedge, and had John Cotton,
1863. GEORGE THOMAS, Greenfield, son of 1st Wendell, m., 1834, Harriet,
d. of Nathaniel Pope Russell of Boston, and had Wendell, 1836; James C.

1838; Ellen Harriet, 1853. He m., 2d, 1865, Abba Isabella, wid. of Josiah S. Little of Portland, and d. of Daniel Chamberlain of Boston. GEORGE THORNTON, Greenfield, son of Wendell Thornton, m., 1879, Ellen Southgate Keith of Greenfield, and had Sarah Russell, 1880. ISAAC P., Boston, son of 2d Thomas, m., 1807, Susan, d. of David Jackson of Philadelphia, and had Thomas Kemper, 1808; George Cabot, 1812. JAMES, Plymouth, 1639, of whom nothing is known. JAMES, Scituate, m., 1673, Elizabeth, d. of William Randall, and removed to Boston. JAMES C., Boston, son of 1st George, m., 1873, Alice Worthington, d. of Charles Paine of Worcester, and had Ellen Harriet, 1876; and Alice Paine, 1882. JOHN, son of 1st Thomas, removed from North Carolina to Tennessee, and had Thomas, John, Enoch, Benjamin, Anna, Rosa, Rebecca, Nesmy, and Zilpha. JOHN, Boston, son of 2d Thomas, m., 1786, Ellen, d. of William Watson of Plymouth, and had Ellen Watson, 1787, m. Ezra Shaw Goodwin; Elizabeth Marston, 1789, m., William Sturgis; Marcia, 1790, m. Miles Whitworth White; John Watson, 1792; Sarah, 1793, m. Ashel Plympton. JOHN WATSON, Boston, son of above, m., 1820, Susan Hayden, d. of Elkanah Tallman of New Bedford, and had John, 1822; Henry Tallman, 1823; William Watson, 1826; John Watson, 1828; Robert Smith, 1829; William Nye, 1830, m. Mary, d. of William H. Gardner of Boston; Francis Bassett, 1832. JOSEPH, from Newburyport, a descendant from John, a resident of Newbury, 1641, m., 1811, Eliza, d. of Joshua Colby of Newburyport, and had John Roberts, 1812; Mary Ann, 1814, m. Adoniram Holmes; Eliza C., m. Asa Pierce; Charles William, m. Mary Harvey; and William Charles of Wareham, m. a Sampson. He m., 2d, Mary, wid. of Edward Nichols, and d. of William Rogers, and had Sarah Elizabeth, 1829, m. Joseph W. Burgess; Nancy Rogers, 1830; Hannah Ackus, 1834; Francis Edward, 1836; Susan Nichols, 1838. NATHANIEL MORTON, son of 1st William, m., 1817, Harriet Lazell, d. of Nahum Mitchell of East Bridgewater, and had William, 1818; Abby Morton, m. Robert B. Hall; Elizabeth Bliss, m. Henry G. Andrew of Boston. NICHOLAS, Kingston, m., 1751, Lydia Washburn, and had Nicholas, and Lydia, 1760. He m., 2d, 1764, Lois Fuller. NICHOLAS, Kingston, son of above, m., 1775, Martha Morton, and had Zenas, 1776; Timothy, 1777; Henry, 1779; John, 1785; Martha, 1794. PHILIP, Plymouth, 1638, removed to Duxbury, and no more is known of him. RUFUS, Edgartown, son of 1st David, m. Rebecca Mayhew, and had Mary Dennis, 1800. SANFORD, Farmington, son of 1st David, m. Deborah Coffin of Edgartown, and had Daniel, Henry, David, Sarah, Deborah, and Rebecca. THOMAS, Albany, came from England and m. Catherine Wendell, by whom he had Robert, 1708; John; Catherine, 1714, m. John Creecy of North Carolina; Thomas, 1722; David, 1724; Benjamin, and Miles. He removed from Albany to North Carolina. THOMAS, son of above, came to Plymouth 1737, to be educated under the care of Elkanah Morton, and m., 1753, Mercy, d. of Barnabas Hedge, by whom he had Sarah, 1754, m. LeBaron Bradford of Bristol, R. I.; Thomas, 1756; William, 1758; John, 1761; Samuel, 1765; Isaac P., 1771; Wendell, 1776. THOMAS, Boston, son of above, m., 1797, Elizabeth (Knight) Hinckley, wid. of Isaac, and had George, 1800. WENDELL, son of 2d Thomas, m. Caroline Willmans, d. of Dr. Thomas Smith, 1810, and had George Thomas, 1810; Wendell Thornton, 1818. WENDELL, Industry, son of 1st David, m. Polly Smith of Edgartown, and had Polly and Sally. WENDELL THORNTON, Greenfield, son of 1st Wendell, m., 1841, Maria Louisa, d. of Nathaniel Pope Russell of Boston, and had Nathaniel Russell, 1842, m. Lucy Alice, d. of Paschal Matthews of Chicago; George Thornton, 1844; Caroline Williams, 1845; Mary Russell, 1846, m. John Conness of California; Maria Louisa, 1848, m. Charles Edgar Clark; Charles Devens, 1850. WILLIAM, son of 2d Thomas, m., 1781, Rebecca, d. of Nathaniel Morton, and had William, 1783; Nathaniel Morton, 1785; Thomas, 1791; Elizabeth, 1803, m. Alexander Bliss and George Bancroft. WILLIAM, son of above, m., 1807, Joanna, d. of Captain Gideon White of Shelburne, Nova Scotia, an officer in the English army, and had William Whitworth, 1808; Rebecca, 1810, m. Ebenezer Grosvenor Parker and George S. Tolman; Hannah White, 1812, m. Andrew L. Russell; Sarah Bradford, 1814; Charles Gideon, 1820; William Thomas, 1822; and Sarah Elizabeth, 1824. WILLIAM THOMAS, son of above, m., 1849, Abby Burr, d. of Thomas Hedge, and had Abby Warren, 1854, m. Alexander Jackson of Boston; Howland, 1855; Catherine Wendell, 1859; Alice Whitworth, 1864. WILLIAM, son of Nathaniel Morton, m., 1850, Helen, d. of John Russell, and had Harriet M., 1851; William, 1853, m. Sally, d. of Charles Otis Holyoke of Medford. WILLIAM, m., 1734, Elizabeth Bagnell. WILLIAM, m., 1750, Sarah Doggett.

DEACON, DANIEL, m. Mary Torrence about 1830, and had Mary and James. JOHN, died in Plymouth 1636.

DEAN, STEPHEN, came in the Fortune 1621, m., 1627, Elizabeth, d. of Wid. Ring, and had Elizabeth, m. William Twining; Miriam; and Susanna, m. Joseph Rogers and Stephen Snow.

DEBURROUGHS, ANDREW, pub. to Sarah Ross, 1780.

DECOSTA, ANTHONY, had a wife Joanna, and owned an estate in Plymouth which he bought in 1723. His children were Robert; Jacob; and Margaret, m. Robert Roberts. JACOB, son of above, m. Elizabeth, d. of John Cole, 1745. ROBERT, son of Anthony, by wife Joanna, had Elizabeth, 1757.

DECRO, ANTHONY, m. Elizabeth Bacon, 172—.

DEERSKINS, JOHN, m. Kate Shanks, 1737.

DELANO, AVERY, m., 1792, Betsey Faunce, and had Lucy, m. Merrick Rider; and perhaps others. BENJAMIN, Duxbury, m., 1745, Lydia Jackson, and had Benjamin, 1746, and Lydia, twins. BENJAMIN, Pembroke, son of above, m., 1774, Mary, d. of William Brooks of Scituate, and had William, 1775; Mary, 1776, m. Elijah Leonard of Marshfield; Sarah, 1782, m. Samuel Foster of Scituate. BENJAMIN, Kingston, son of 2d Joshua, m., 1803, Susanna, d. of Melatiah Holmes, and had Eliza, 1803, m. Ebenezer Farrington of Boston; Augusta, 1806; Susan, 1808, m. Melzar Whitten and Thomas E. Keely; Joshua, 1809; Angeline, 1812, m. John D. Sweet; Lucy, 1817, m. a Waterman; Catherine, 1820, m. Oliver Ditson of Boston. BENJAMIN FRANKLIN, Brooklyn, son of 1st William, m. Jane, d. of Seth Foster of Scituate, and had Alfred Otis, 1839; and Charlotte. BERIAH, Duxbury, by wife Naomi, had Ichabod, 1735; William, 1737; Sylvanus, 1739; Lemuel, 1741; Elizabeth, 1743; Benjamin, 1745. EBENEZER, Duxbury, son of 2d

Jonathan, m., 1745, Lydia Wormall, and had Nathaniel, m. Deborah Sprague; Luther, m. Irene Sampson; Bernice, m. John Glass. EBENEZER, Duxbury, prob. son of 2d Philip, m., 1699, Martha Simmons, and had Joshua, 1700; Thankful, 1702; Abiah, 1704, m. Nathaniel Bartlett. EDWARD HARTT, son of 1st William, m. Mary, d. of William James of Scituate, and had Edward Franklin about 1854. He had a 2d wife. ELKANAH, m., 1728, Mary Sanders, and had Elkanah, 1730; Hannah, 1732; Mary, 1735; Barsillai, 1737; Eunice, 1741, m. Samuel Gray; Deborah, 1743, m. Gershom Holmes; Sarah, 1746. HOPESTILL, Duxbury, son of 1st Joshua, m., 1758, Abigail Everson, and had Ephraim, 1760; Ebenezer, 1761; Abigail, 1763; Hopestill, 1765; Aaron, 1767; Richard, 1769; Thankful, 1771; Peleg, 1773; Beza, 1776. ICHABOD, m., 1725, Elizabeth Cushman, and had Lemuel. JONATHAN, Duxbury, son of 1st Philip, m., 1678, Mercy, d. of Nathaniel Warren, and had Jabez, m. Mercy Delano; Jonathan, 1676; Sarah; Mercy; Nathan; Bethiah; Susanna; Nathaniel; Esther; Jethro; Thomas; and prob. Ebenezer. JONATHAN, Duxbury, son of above, m., 1699, Hannah Doten, and had John, 1699, m. Sarah Cole; Jonathan, 1701; Nathan, 1703; Amasa, 1705; Ruth, 1707; Amasa, 1709; m. Ruth Sampson; Hannah, 1711; Dorothy, 1714; Dorothy, 1715, m. Sylvanus Curtis of Plymouth; Ebenezer, 1717; David, 1720, m. Abigail Chandler. JOSHUA, Duxbury, son of 2d Ebenezer, m. Hopestill Peterson, and had Lydia, 1723, m. Thomas Prince; Rhoda, 1731, m. Samuel Winsor; Sylvia, 1733, m. Charles Foster; Hopestill, 1735, m. Abigail Everson; Beza, 1737, m. Benjamin Allen; Martha, 1739, m. Asa Chandler; Wealthea, 1741, m. Peabody Bradford; Joshua, 1744; Thankful, 1749. JOSHUA, Kingston, son of above, m., 1766, Mary Chandler, and had Charlotte, 1767, m. Peter Winsor; Joshua, 1769, m. Abigail Ripley; William, 1771; Lucy, 1772; Polly, 1773, m. James Fuller; Lucy, 1776, m. Thomas Washburn; Benjamin, 1778; Rebecca, 1782, m. Zebulon Bisbee; Wealthea, 1785, m. Melzar Whitten. JOSHUA, Kingston, son of 3d Benjamin, m., 1842, Marcia, d. of William Simmons, and had Augusta, 1843; Marcia, 1845; Joshua, 1848. JUDAH, Duxbury, son of 3d Philip, by wife Lydia, had Alpheus, 1744, m. Margaret Sides; Salome, 1746; Malachi, 1748, m. Patience Burgess; Judah, 1752; Naomi; Jepthah, 1754. JUDAH, Duxbury, son of above, m., 1781, Penelope Sampson, and had Salome, 1782; Penelope; Elizabeth, 1786; Henry, 1788; Judah, 1792; Priscilla, 1793. LEMUEL, Marshfield, son of Ichabod, m. Mary Eames, 1762, and had Mary, 1763; Thomas, 1767; William, 1770; Elizabeth, 1772. NATHAN, son of 2d Jonathan, m., 1726, Bathsheba, d. of Nathaniel Holmes, and had Ruth, 1726, m. Benjamin Churchill; Sarah, 1729, m. James Crandon; Bathsheba, 1731, m. James Doten; Joanna, 1733, m. Nathaniel Morton; Hannah, 1735; Nathan, 1737, m. Sarah Cobb; Amasa, 1739; Ichabod, 1742; Abigail, 1746. PHILIP came in the Fortune 1621, probably a Walloon, who joined the Pilgrims in Leyden. He was prob. son of Jean and Marie de Launey, and was baptized in the Walloon Church in Leyden in 1603. He settled in Duxbury, and m., 1634, Esther Dewsbury, and had Thomas, m. Mary, d. of John Alden, and wid. Hannah Bartlett; Mary, m. Jonathan Dunham; Philip; John; Jane; Rebecca; Jonathan; and Esther. He m., 2d, 1657, Mary, wid. of James Glass, and d. of William Pontus, and had Samuel,

m. Elizabeth, d. of Alexander Standish. PHILIP, Duxbury, son of above, died, 1708, leaving Samuel; Martha, m. John Harlow; Jane; and Ebenezer; and Philip, born 1678. PHILIP, Duxbury, son of above, m., 1717, Elizabeth Dingley of Marshfield, and had May, 1717, m. John Hanks; Elizabeth, 1719; Malachi, 1721; Judah, 1724; Abigail, 1725, m. Abisha Soule. THOMAS, Duxbury, son of 1st Philip, m. Mary, d. of John Alden, and had Benoni; Thomas; David; Mary; Sarah, m. John Drew of Halifax; Ruth, m. Samuel Drew of Kingston; Josiah; and Jonathan. He m., 2d, wid. Hannah Bartlett, 1699. WILLIAM, Scituate, son of 2d Benjamin, m., 1802, 'Sarah, d. of Edmond Hartt of Boston, and had Mary Elizabeth, 1803; William Hartt, 1804; Prudence Clark, 1807; Benjamin Franklin, 1809; Edward Hartt, 1811; Sarah, 1813; Lucy Snow, 1814. WILLIAM HARTT, son of above, m. Sarah Farrar, and had Mary Frances; Hannah Maria; and Emma.

DENNIS, WILLIAM, owner of an estate in Plymouth 1640.

DERBY, JOHN, son of a Christopher, Plymouth, 1637, had Matthew, 1650. RICHARD, brother of John, also owner of an estate in Plymouth 1637.

DEXTER, CHARLES, by wife Hannah, had John, 1810; James Wilson, 1814. EPHRAIM of Rochester, m. Martha, wid. of Return Wait, 1754.

DEWET, CHRISTOPHER, pub. to Susanna Beale, 1746.

DICK, DICK, slave of Nathaniel Thomas, pub. to Phebe, slave of Haviland Torry, 1731.

DICKSON, DAVID, son of 1st Samuel, m. Hannah, d. of Elias Thomas, and had Mary, m. Joseph B. Shaw. JOHN, m. Phebe Childs, and had Phebe, m. William Barnes; Sarah Palmer, m. Ellis Drew; and John. SAMUEL, brother of above, m. Polly Churchill, 1803, and had Samuel; David; Mary, m. Benjamin Bullard; and James. SAMUEL, son of above, m. Ruth F. Lucas, and had Samuel Russell, 1834; Calvin Luther, 1835; Jacob Washburn, 1839; and Jane B., m. John M. Cobb.

DIKE, ANTHONY, Bridgewater, son of 1st Samuel, m., 1775, Mary Pool of Abington, and had Anthony, 1779, m. Mary Curtis; Asa, 1789, m. Rosanna Pearsons; Samuel, 1783, m. Diana Clark Gibbs; Simeon, 1781; Thomas, 1785; John, 1787, m. Bathsheba Washburn, and removed to Baltimore; Mary, 1791, m. Clemons Jones; Rebecca, 1795, m. Ezra Harlow; Sybil, 1796, m. Charles Knapp; Susan, 1798; Sarah, 1793, m. Libian Packard. ANTHONY, Bridgewater, son of above, m., 1800, Polly Curtis, and had Anthony, m. Christiana Soule of Kingston; Jonathan Russell, m. Phebe S., d. of George Raymond; Curtis; Mary, m. a Randall; Susan, m. a Lincoln; Betsey Allen, m. Harvey Raymond. JOHN, Beverly, son of 1st Samuel, m., 1777, Abigail Stephens, and had Abigail, 1780, m. William H. Lovett; John, 1783, m. Mercy Wood and Priscilla Manning; Nancy, 1785, m. John W. Ellingwood; Thomas, 1786; Samuel, 1788; Nathaniel, 1792, m. Anna Wood; Thomas, 1793; Samuel, 1794. He m., 2d, 1798, Anna Chipman. He m., 3d, 1807, Elizabeth Thorndike, and had Samuel, 1808, m. Mary Morgan; Isaac T., 1809. He m., 4th, 1823, Lydia Thorndike. SAMUEL, Ipswich and N. Bridgewater, born in Scotland, 1722, m. Mary Perkins, and had Samuel, 1748; Anthony, 1751; John, 1753; Nathaniel, 1766; Veren, 1769, of Southbury, Conn.; Mary, 1755, m. Job Ames;

Sarah, 1758, m. Ephraim Noyes; Anna, 1760, m. James Loud; Abigail, 1762.
SAMUEL, Bridgewater, son of above, m., 1772, Lois, d. of Isaac Fuller, and
had Lucinda, 1773; Salmon, 1775; Fuller, 1778, m. Jerusha Harlow; Olive, 1780,
m. Joseph Shaw; Rebecca, 1782, m. Ira Bisbee; Oliver, 1785, m. Sybil, d. of
Bela Howard; Nathaniel, 1787, m. Nancy Jackson; Samuel, 1790. He m.,
2d, Mehitabel, wid. of Bela Howard, and d. of Simon Cary, 1793, and had
Bela Cary, 1798. SAMUEL, Bridgewater, son of above, m., 1812, Betsey, d.
of John Burrill, and had Samuel Fuller, 1815; Mary Perkins, 1819; Olive
Shaw, 1824; Experience Phillips; and John Burrill. SIMEON, son of 1st
Anthony, m., 1803, Mary Gibbs of Wareham, and had William Prince, 1805;
Mary Gibbs, 1810, m. Samuel Shaw; Parna Young, 1812; Simeon, 1815, m.
Isabella F., d. of Lewis Goodwin; Rebecca, 1826.

DILLARD, BENJAMIN, came to Plymouth from Virginia, and m., 1804,
Mary, d. of Thomas Covington; 2d, 1808, Mercy, wid. of George Ellis; 3d,
Nancy, d. of Thomas Covington, and wid. of Samuel Churchill; and 4th,
wid. Betsey Fisher, 1850. His children were Mary, m. Edward Winslow
Bradford; Nancy, m. Sylvanus Holmes; Betsey, m. Isaac Kempton; Benja-
min, m. Lucy Stetson; and George, m. Lucy Ann, d. of Lemuel Reed.
BENJAMIN, son of above, m. Lucy, d. of Lot Stetson, 1844, and had
Adriana, m. a Burt; George; and Charles. He now lives at Glencove,
Long Island.

DILLINGHAM, JOHN, of Sandwich, m. Sarah Blackmer, 1758.

DIMAN, BENJAMIN, son of Josiah, m. Judith, d. of Lewis Gray of Kings-
ton, and had Maria Sampson, 1836; Elizabeth Gray, 1838; Harriet A., 1842;
Henry H., 1844; Merriam, 1846; Franklin, 1848. DANIEL, son of 3d Thomas,
m. Elizabeth, d. of Josiah Morton, and had Rebecca W., 1752, m. Job Rider;
Daniel, 1756; David, 1758; Elizabeth, 1760; Josiah, 1766; and Jeremiah.
He m., 2d, Susanna Southworth of Middleboro', and had Susanna, 1770. He
m., 3d, wid. Mary Smith of Bristol, 1787; and 4th, Patience Holmes, 1792.
DAVID, son of above, m. Lois Grover, and had Daniel, 1782; David, 1785;
Lois, 1787; Elizabeth, 1791, m. Cyrus Hayward; David again, 1794; Jona-
than, 1797; Patience, 1798; and Abigail Grover, 1801, m. John Kempton.
DAVID, son of above, m. Abigail Bartlett Nelson, 1818, and had Abigail
Nelson, 1819; David, 1821, m. Mary, d. of James Baxter; Sophia, 1825;
Erastus William, 1827; Elizabeth, 1830, m. Winslow C. Barnes; Polly Nelson,
1833; Sarah Nelson, 1836; and Ann Eliza, 1839. EZRA SAMPSON, son of
Josiah, m. Mary Cobb, 1833, and had Ezra Sampson, 1834; William Alfred,
1837, m. Mary W., d. of Edward Winslow Bradford; Josiah Morton, 1838,
m. Maria Boardman of Erie, Penn.; and Mary N., 1849. He m., 2d, Eliza-
beth R., d. of Stephen Bartlett, 1857. EZRA SAMPSON, son of above, m.
Joanna, d. of Sylvanus Churchill, 1856, and had Frederick Lee; Laura, 1859,
m. Edward W. Whitten; Katie E., 1861; Susie; Clara; and Ezra, 1872.
JAMES, son of Josiah, m. Rebecca H., d. of Lot Harlow, 1833, and had
Rebecca Harlow, 1834, m. Charles H. Finney; Mary Boylston, 1837, m. James
H. Chapman, and Eliza A., m. Stephen T. Atwood of Carver. JEREMIAH, son
of Daniel, had Jonathan and Thomas. JONATHAN, son of 3d Thomas, m.
Hannah, d. of Joseph Morton, 1736, and wid. Rebecca Brown, 1779. JOSIAH,

son of Daniel, m. Susan Gray of Barnstable, 1791, and had Daniel, m.
Rebecca Moncreife. He m., 2d, Sophia Sampson of Plympton, 1799, and
had Thomas, 1803; James, 1805; Ezra Sampson, 1808; Benjamin, 1810. He
m., 3d, Polly Holmes, 1814, and had Samuel Newell, 1815. SAMUEL
NEWELL, son of above, m. Margaret H. Holmes, 1844; and, 2d, Sarah A.
Norwood, and had by latter Margaret Newell, 1856; and Charles A., 1858.
THOMAS, Fairfield, 1656, had Thomas, Moses, and John. THOMAS, New
London, son of above, m. Elizabeth, d. of Peter Bradley, and had Elizabeth,
Ruth, Thomas, Moses, and John. THOMAS, Bristol, son of above, m. a
Finney, and had Rev. James of Salem, who had a d. and a son James;
Jeremiah of Bristol, who had eight sons and two daughters; Thomas, m.
Salome Foster; Lucinda, m. a Smith, and settled in Bristol; Phebe, a daughter,
m. a Bartlett of Plympton; and Jonathan, and Daniel. THOMAS, son of
Josiah, m. Polly Sylvester, 1830, and had Sophia Sampson, 1832, m. William
D. Sherman; Abby Phillips, 1833, m. William G. S. Wells; Polly, 1835; Mary
Harlow, 1837, m. John E. Luscomb; Eugene F., m. Amasa C. Sears; Thomas,
1844, m. Elizabeth Ann Pile of England; and Margaret H., 1847.

DIX, ANTHONY, came in the Ann 1623. He had a wife Tabitha, and
removed to Charlestown.

DOANE, ISAIAH, m. Hannah Bartlett, 1775. JOHN, Plymouth, 1630,
Eastham, 1644, had by wife Abigail, Daniel, m. Hepsibah Cole; John, m.
Hannah, d. of Edward Bangs; Ephraim, m. Mercy Knowles; Lydia, m.,
1645, Samuel Hicks; Abigail, 1632, m. Samuel Lothrop. THOMAS, from
Chatham, m. Sarah Barnes, 1729.

DOGGETT, EBENEZER, son of Samuel of Marshfield, m. Elizabeth Rickard,
and had Ebenezer, 1722; John, 1724; Ebenezer, 1726; Samuel, 1729. EBENE-
ZER, son of above, m., 1749, Elizabeth Brace, and had Elizabeth, 1749;
Bathsheba, 1751; Ebenezer, 1754, m. Lydia Holmes. JABEZ, from Middleboro' m. Rebecca Rich, 1760. JOHN, came over 1630 with Winthrop, and m.,
1667, at Plymouth, Bathsheba Pratt. SAMUEL, Marshfield, m., 1682, Mary
Rogers, and had Samuel, Mary, and Sarah. He m., 2d, 1691, Bathsheba, d.
of Abraham Holmes, and had Elizabeth, Ebenezer, Bathsheba, John, Isaac;
Lydia, m. Nicholas Drew; Persis; Seth, m. Elizabeth Delano; and Abigail.
SAMUEL, son of 1st Ebenezer, m., 1756, Deborah, d. of Thomas Foster, and
had Deborah, 1758. SETH, m. Jenna Harlow, 1792.

DOLPHIN, DOLPHIN, slave of Nathaniel Thomas, pub. to Flora, slave of
Mrs. Priscilla Watson, 1731.

DOTY, or DOTEN, CHANDLER W., son of 4th Stephen, m. Mary Holmes,
1840, and had Marcia W., 1849, m. Alvin Finney; Charles S., m. Clara M.
Morton; Jennie S., 1856, m. Elkanah Finney; Caroline W., m. Nathaniel C.
Hoxie; and Hannah. CHARLES C., son of 4th Samuel, m. Mary A. Bartlett,
1860, and had Charles M., 1861; Mary C.; Lizzie F., 1868; Alfred R., and
Mabel W., 1873. EBENEZER of Plympton, m. Mary Whitton, 1749. EBE-
NEZER, m. Rebecca Rickard, 1785. EDWARD, a passenger in the Mayflower,
m. Faith Clark, 1635, and had Edward; John; Desire, m. William Sherman,
Israel Holmes, and Alexander Standish.; Thomas, m. a wife Mary (probably
Churchill); Samuel moved to New Jersey, and there m. Jane Harmon, Isaac,

1648, moved to Long Island; Joseph, 1651; Elizabeth, m. John Rouse of Marshfield; and Mary. He probably had a wife before Faith. EDWARD, son of above, m. Sarah Faunce, 1663, and had Edward, 1664; Sarah, 1666, m. James Warren; John, 1668; Martha and Mary, twins, 1671, the first m. Joseph Allyn, and the second Thomas Morton; Elizabeth, 1673, m. Tobias Oakman; Patience, 1676; Mercy, 1678; Samuel, 1681; Mercy, 1684. m. Daniel Pratt; Benjamin, 1689, m. Hester Bemen. EDWARD, son of 1st Elisha, m. Phebe Finney, 1738, and had Elisha, 1743, m. Mercy Harlow; Edward, 1745; Thomas, 1748, m. Lois Bartlett; John, 1750; Lemuel, 1753; James, 1757; Lois, m. William Robbins. EDWARD, son of above, m. Esther Hollis, 1801, and had Edward, 1801; Samuel, 1803, m. a Wade; Esther, 1806, m. David Holmes; Lewis, 1813; Lemuel, 1816; Phebe, 1815; Hannah, 1819, m. Joshua Thrasher; and John, 1823, m. Betsey Hughes, and moved to Hanover. EDWARD, son of above, m. Salina Pratt, and had Charles S., m. Rebecca S. Pierce; Salina F., 1824, m. William S. Faunce; Fidelia T., 1835, m. Charles E. Tilson; Edward L., 1827, m. Mary W. Hall; Elisha S., 1830; Betsey P., 1833; Louisa, 1844; and Charles A., 1849. ELISHA, son of 1st John, by wife Hannah, had Elisha, 1709, m. Deborah Tubs of Duxbury; Samuel, 1712; Hannah, 1714; Edward, 1716; Hannah, 1718; Paul, 1721; Lois, 1724, m. Amaziah Harlow; Stephen, 1726; James, 1728, m. Bathsheba Delano. ELISHA, son of 1st Lemuel, m. Jane Warren, and had Lemuel, m. Nancy Sears. ELLIS of Rochester, son of 1st Joseph, by wife Eleanor, had Joseph, m. Susanna Smith. ETHAN ALLEN of Albany, son of 9th Samuel, m. Keturah Tompkins, and had Warren Samuel. ETHAN ALLEN, now living in Brooklyn, son of Warren Samuel, m. Elizabeth E. McFarlan of Brooklyn. ISAAC, son of 1st John, m. Martha Faunce, 1703, and had Elizabeth, 1704, m. John Studley; Jane, 1706, m. John Palmer of Scituate; Isaac, 1709; Rebecca, 1710, m. Benjamin Warren; Neviah, 1712; Jabez, 1716, moved to New York; Hope, 1718; Ichabod, 1721; and Mary, m. Lemuel Bartlett. ISAAC, son of above, m. Mary Lanman, 1734, and had Isaac, 1735; James, 1737; Hope, 1739; Mary, 1740; Jean, 1741; Ichabod, 1742; Thomas, 1744; Mary, 1747, m.Daniel Whitman; Jean, 1749; William, 1751, m., 1st, Abigail Sylvester, and 2d, Jane (Bartlett) Churchill; Rebecca, 1754; Jabez, 1755; John Palmer, 1758; Rebecca, 1762, m. Nathaniel Whiting. JABEZ, son of 2d Isaac, m. Hannah Sylvester, and had Hannah, m. Coomer Weston; and Nancy, m. Job Cobb. JAMES, m. Ruth Finney, 1749. JAMES, son of 1st Lemuel, m. Mary (Bartlett) Clark, and had James, Peter, Lemuel; Betsey, m. George Stone of Brookfield; and Catherine, m. Nathan Holmes, of Brockton. He m., 2d, Lydia (Burbank) Marsh, wid. of Thomas, 1841. JAMES, son of 2d Isaac, m. Elizabeth Kempton, 1764, and had Hope, 1765, m. Samuel Smith; James, 1766, m. Martha Torrey of New Hampshire; Isaac, 1768; John, 1769, m. Sarah Morton, and moved to Vermont; Elizabeth, 1770; Daniel, 1772, m. Sarah (Covington) Edwards, wid. of John Edwards; Mary, 1774; Thomas, 1776, moved to Bangor; Elizabeth, 1778, m. Barnaby Morton; Lucy, 1780, m. Levi Reed; Lois, 1782, m. Joab Thomas; and Eleanor, 1784, m. John Porter. JOHN, son of 1st Edward, m. Elizabeth Cook, and had John, 1668; Edward, 1671; Jacob, 1673; Elizabeth, 1676, m. Joshua Morse; Isaac, 1678; Samuel,

1682; Elisha, 1686; Josiah, 1689; Martha, 1692, m. Ebenezer Curtis. He m. a 2d wife, Sarah, and had Sarah, 1696, m. Joseph Paterson; Patience, 1697; and Desire, 1699, m. George Barrows. JOHN, son of above, m. Mehitabel Nelson, 1693, and Hannah Sherman, and had Mehitabel, 1694, m. William Lucas; Edward, 1697; John, 1700, moved to Plympton; Jacob, 1704; Sarah, 1707; Susanna, 1710, m. Elkanah Pratt and John Finney; Lydia, 1713, m. John Lucas. JOHN, son of 3d James, m. Sarah Morton, and had Sarah, 1696; Patience, 1697; Desire, 1699. JOHN, perhaps son of 1st Stephen, m. Mary Wright, and had James, 1797; Molly, 1799; Faith Chandler, 1802; John, 1804 ; Bartlett, 1807; Caleb, 1809. JOSEPH, son of 1st Edward, moved to Rochester, m. a Hatch, and had Joseph, 1683; Deborah, 1685; John, 1688; Mercy, 1692; Fish, 1697; Mary, 1699, and Ellis. JOSEPH, grandson of Ellis, Rochester, m. Susanna Smith, and had Annis, Nathaniel, James, Richard, Joseph, Albert, Jeduthun, Hannah, Smith, Susanna, Clark, Agatha. JOSEPH, son of 1st Stephen, m. Elizabeth Allen, 1794, and had Bathsheba, 1795; Elizabeth, 1797; Joseph, 1802. JOSEPH, son of above, m. Jerusha Bartlett, and had Lucius H., m. Mary A. Holmes; Joseph M., m. Mary J, Dixon; William W., m. Betsey L. Harlow; Frank, Andrew, and Abby. JOSIAH, son of 1st John, by wife Abigail, had Josiah, 1715, m. Deborah Rider; Abigail, 1716; Experience, 1719, m. William Clark; Patience, 1721, m. Thomas Burgess; Sarah, 1723. LEMUEL, son of 3d Edward, m. Phebe Pearson, 1778, and had Betsey Warren, 1780, m. John Pierce; James, 1782; Elisha; Thirza, m. Sylvanus Sampson. LEMUEL, m. Jean Fish, 1748, and had Jean, 1749. LEMUEL, son of 4th Edward, m. Pamelia J. Bearse, 1843, and had Lemuel T., 1845; Lewis Drew, 1848. LEMUEL, son of 2d Elisha, m. Nancy Sears, and had Lemuel W., m. Hannah E. Atwood; and Charles H., 1844. NATHANIEL, son of 6th Samuel, m. Mercy Rider, 1765, and had Nathaniel and Prince. NATHANIEL, son of above, m. Mary Farmer, 1802, and had Nathaniel, 1803, m. Caroline Goddard; Mary Farmer, 1806, m. Eliab Wood; Marcia Rider, 1808, m. Barnabas Ellis; Nancy Farmer, 1811, m. John Morse; Jane, 1814, m. William Stevens; and Eliza Ann. NATHANIEL, son of 2d Joseph, m. Olive Sampson of Wareham, and had Olive Sampson, m. Jacob Cushman; Rosena, m. Jacob Holmes; Nathaniel, Cyrus, Richmond, Calvin Bradford; Bethiah Sampson, m. Edward Warren of Taunton; and Parnel, m. William Butts of Fall River. NATHANIEL, son of above, m. Joanna Bailey, 1843, and had Nathaniel T., 1845; Nathaniel, 1847; Nathaniel, 1849; Olive S., 1854; Cyrus R., 1859; and Ezra J., 1862. PAUL, son of 1st Elisha, m. Ruth Rider, 1749, and had Paul, 1750; Ruth, 1752, m. Bartlett Marshal; Bathsheba, 1756, m. Bartlett Marshal; Lydia, m. Samuel Sherman; and Susanna, born at Liverpool, Nova Scotia. PRINCE, son of 1st Nathaniel, m. Susan Price, 1808, and had Susan, 1809; Phebe, 1811; Hannah, 1814; Prince, 1816; Sarah Ann, 1818, m. Thomas Bartlett; Naomi, 1821; George Henry, 1830, m. Sarah A. S. Weston. PRINCE, son of above, m. Ann Eaton, and had Annette, 1843, m. John Washburn; George H., 1850; William C., 1858; Charles C., 1861. SAMUEL, son of 1st John, m. Mary Cobb, 1727, and had Samuel, 1729; Mercy, 1733; Hannah, 1735, m. Joshua Holmes; Sarah, 1736, m. Benjamin Smith. SAMUEL, son of above, m. Mary Cook, 1753, and had Rebecca, 1753; Samuel, 1758; Mary, 1762; Hannah, m. William Holmes; and Rebecca, m. John Tuell. SAMUEL, son of above, m. Eunice Robbins, and had Samuel, 1783; Ebenezer, 1785; James Robbins, 1787, m. Betsey Robbins; Ansel, 1789; an infant, 1791; Eunice Robbins, 1793; Thaddeus Robbins, 1796; Ammi Ruhama, 1798, now living at Marion, Maine; Thaddeus Robbins, 1800; and Ebenezer, 1803. He m., 2d, wid. Deborah Bucknum Johnson Hurley, and had an infant, 1808; another, 1809; John Hurley, 1810; William Holmes, 1812; Deborah Bucknum, 1813; an infant, 1816; Joseph Johnson, 1817; Benjamin, 1819. He m., 3d, Lydia Hardy, and had Alvah, 1821; Mary Ann, 1823; William, 1825; Louisa, 1827; James, 1829. SAMUEL, son of above, m. Rebecca Bradford, 1807, and had Samuel H., 1812; Rebecca II., m. Nathaniel Brown Faunce and Samuel Talbot; Laura Ann m. Eleazer Stevens Turner; Euphelia F., m. Theodore Drew; Cornelia N., m. Stevens M. Burbank; Eunice, m. Seth Morton; Alfred R.; Lizzie; and Charles C. SAMUEL H., son of above, m. Abby D. Virgin, 1836, and had Priscilla Abby Virgin, 1839; Elizabeth M., 1841; and Samuel H., 1843. He m., 2d, Laura M. Lane, 1848. SAMUEL, son of 1st Elisha, m. Joanna Bosworth, 1733, and had Hannah, 1733, m. Joshua Holmes; Joanna, 1737, m. Lemuel Fish; Samuel, 1739; Nathaniel, 1740; Elizabeth, 1744. SAMUEL, Saybrook, son of 2d Edward, m. Ann Buckingham, and had Samuel. SAMUEL, son of above, Saybrook, m. Mageria Parker, and had Samuel. SAMUEL, Stephentown, N. Y., son of above, m. Mercy Doty, and had Ethan Allen. STEPHEN, m. Jane Dunham, 1784. STEPHEN, son of 1st Elisha, m. Hannah Bartlett, 1746, and had Mary, 1746, m. Jonathan Bartlett; Stephen, 1748; Sarah, 1751, m. Isaac Howland; Mercy, 1753, m. Charles Renoff; Hannah, m. Samuel Horton; Esther, Joseph, and John. STEPHEN, son of above, m. Betsey Holmes, 1773, and had Stephen, 1774; Paul, 1776; Betsey, 1779; Bartlett, 1782; Mercy, 1785; Hannah, 1788; Deborah, 1791, m. John Howard Clark; Mary, 1793; Esther, 1796. He m., 2d, Abigail Clark, 1798, and had Betsey, Joseph, and Elizabeth. STEPHEN, son of above, m. Hannah Wright, and had Nancy, m. Josiah Finney; Hannah, m. Ezra Leach; Chandler W.; Stephen; Caroline Winslow; Betsey Bartlett, m. Josiah Finney; Jane Southworth, m. Ezra Leach; Eliza, m. David Leach; Elbridge Gerry, m. Jerusha H. Thrasher; Everett W., m. Caroline Holmes; and George W., m. Caroline M. Thrasher. STEPHEN, son of above, m. Betsey Leach and Hannah Leonard Morton, and had Stephen, m. Sarah I. Cushman. THOMAS, son of 2d Isaac, m. Jerusha Howes, 1768, and had Jerusha, 1770, m. Ephraim Harlow; and Meriah. THOMAS, afterwards of Truro, son of 1st Edward, m. Mary, and had Hannah, 1675; Thomas, 1679. THOMAS, son of above, m. Elizabeth Harlow, 1703, and had Thomas, who moved to Middleboro', Boston, and Stoughton. THOMAS, of Plympton, m. Joanna Waterman, 1784. WARREN SAMUEL, son of 1st Ethan Allen, Brooklyn, m. Sarah M. Child, and had Ethan Allen. WILLIAM, son of 2d Isaac, m. Abigail Sylvester, and had Abigail; Martha, m. Amaziah Churchill. He m., 2d, Jane (Bartlett) Churchill, wid. of Ebenezer, 1784, and had Cynthia, m. Elijah Sherman; Polly; William, m. Lydia Dunham; Hope, m. Isaac M. Sherman; and Isaac, who moved to Kingston and m. Saba Bryant. WILLIAM W., son of 4th Joseph, m. Betsey L. Harlow, and had Albert L., 1853, m. Roxana C. Thrasher.

DOUGLASS, GEORGE, son of 2d John, by wife Eliza, had Abiah, 1822; George, 1823; Eliza Ann, 1825; John, 1826; Martha, 1828; Maria, 1834; Andrew, 1836; Cynthia, 1839; Noah, 1841. JOHN, by wife Mercy, had John, 1761; Jean, 1763. JOHN, son of above, m. a Southworth of Carver, and had John, m. Elizabeth Haskins; Warren, m. Rhoda Thrasher; George; Joshua; Ephraim; and Earl. JOSHUA, son of above, m. Mary Pierce, 1813, and had Jeremiah, 1815; Elisha, 1817; William, 1819; Mary, 1822; Nathan, 1824; Warren, 1827; Martin, 1828; Alonzo, 1841. WILLIAM, m. Mary Polden, 1828. WILLIAM, m. Nancy Nichols, 1831.

DOW, ALEXANDER, m. Sarah Dunham, 1739, and had Alexander, 1741, m. Lydia Eames, 1766.

DONNLEY, JOHN, m. Joann B. Morton, 1835.

DRAKE, ISAAC, pub. to Elizabeth Morton, 1801.

DREW, ABBET, afterwards called Abbot, son of the last Nicholas, m., 1823, Elizabeth Churchill, and had Mary Churchill, 1827, m. Benjamin F. Pierce; Ann Russell, 1830, m. Robert D. Fuller; Frances Abbet, 1832, m. Margaret Coates of Morristown, Penn.; George Franklin, 1835, m. Lucy Pettingell of Lynn; Charlotte Augusta, 1837; Josiah Russell, 1839, m. Hatty, d. of Samuel Whitten; Adaline, 1841; Helen Augusta, 1844, m. Gideon F. Holmes. He m., 2d, 1852, Sarah, d. of Cornelius Drew of Kingston. ABIJAH, Kingston, son of 1st Cornelius, m. Betsey Stetson, and had Deborah, 1777; Nancy, 1779, m. Cornelius Drew; Harriet, 1781, m. Lysander Bartlett; Nathaniel, 1784; Lazarus, 1787, m. Bathsheba Bartlett; John, 1789; Betsey, 1794; James Harvey, 1796; Lucretia, 1791, m. Spencer Chandler; Abijah, 1803. He m., 2d, Sylvia Washburn. ABIJAH, son of above, m. Sally Faunce Chubbuck, and had Hiram; Edwin; Sarah Frances, 1832, m. Hosea C. Bartlett; Emily Stevens, 1835, m. John H. Crandon of Chelsea; Charles H., 1838, m. Mary A., d. of Samuel Bradford; and Stephen Curtis, m. Martha Glover. He m., 2d, 1845, Lucy Fisher, and had Mary L., 1848; Lucy Evangeline, 1854. ATWOOD, son of 1st David, m., 1802, Lydia, d. of William Rider, and had Lydia, 1802; Eliza Atwood, 1804; Lydia Williams, 1805; Atwood Lewis, 1807; George Henry, 1808; Lydia Rider, 1811, m. Gorham H. Nye; Josiah, 1812, m. Sarah W. Hodgkins; William Rider, 1814; Eliza, 1816; William Rider, 1818; Eliza Ann, 1820, m. Ziba B. C. Dunham. ATWOOD LEWIS, son of above, m., 1830, Jane, d. of Ephraim Harlow, and had Jane Sturtevant, 1831, m. Ira D. Vandusee of Boston; Atwood H., 1833; and Charles C., m. Mary Haywood Ellis. ATWOOD, Carver, son of last Nicholas, m. Eliza Rickard, and had Edwin Ora, 1835; Atwood Russell, 1837; Eliza Ellis, 1839; William H., 1841; and Atwood. BENJAMIN, son of 1st Seth, m. Elizabeth Doggett, and had Elizabeth, 1765, m. William Sherman; Benjamin, 1767; Bathsheba, 1768; Margaret, 1771, m. Ansel Rickard and Barnabas Holmes; Ebenezer, 1773, m. Deborah Ransom of Carver; Desire, 1776; Simeon, 1780; and Malachi. BENJAMIN, son of above, m., 1797, Sophia, d. of Sylvanus Bartlett, and had Martha Bartlett, 1798, m. Lewis Weston; Elizabeth, 1799, m. Nathaniel Freeman; Benjamin, 1800; Sophia, 1802; Sophia, 1803; Fanny,

1805; Sophia, 1807; Mary, 1810, m. Sylvanus Harvey; Benjamin, 1812. BEN-
jamin, Washington, D. C., son of above, m. Caroline Bangs of Brewster, and
had Edward Bangs, m. Annie Abby Davis of Medfield; Helen; Eudora, m.
Abbot Bassett of Chelsea; Charles Acton, m. wid. Harriet Clark of Chelsea;
Caroline Bangs, m. Herbert Nickerson of Orleans. CHARLES H., son of 2d
Abijah, m., 1867, Mary A., d. of Samuel Bradford, and had Ethel, 1874. CON-
SIDER, from Duxbury, son of 3d Samuel, m., 1768, Jennie Ellis, and had
Ellis, 1769; Lucia, 1771. CORNELIUS, Kingston, son of 2d Samuel, m., 1729,
Sarah, d. of Ichabod Bartlett, and had Ichabod, 1730; William, 1731, m.
Dorothy Bartlett; James, 1733, m. Deborah Nye of Dartmouth; Zenas, 1735,
m. Saba Gray and Polly Ripley; Luranna, 1738, m. Joseph Bartlett; Sarah,
1740, m. John Adams; Seth, 1747, m. Hannah Brewster; Cornelius, m.
Sarah Stetson; Abijah, m. Betsey Stetson and Sylvia Washburn. COR-
NELIUS, Kingston, son of above, m. Sarah, d. of Elisha Stetson, and had
Edward, 1783, m. Eunice Drew; Luranna, 1784; Cornelius, 1787, m. Nancy
Drew; Robert Adams, 1790. CORNELIUS, Kingston, son of above, m.
Nancy, d. of Abijah Drew, and had Sarah, m. Abbot Drew; Thomas
Cornelius, and Robert. DAVID, son of 2d Nicholas, m., 1774, Elizabeth
Atwood, and had David; Atwood; William; and Joanna. DAVID,
son of above, m., 1803, Sally, d. of Stephen Churchill, and had Ellis,
m. Sarah, d. of John Dickson; David; Lucinda, m. William T. Drew;
and Sarah, m. Lewis Perry. DAVID, son of above, m. Ann D., d. of John
Burgess, and had David Lewis, 1834; Harrison Warren, 1836; Sally Ann,
1838, m. Lucian Wilbur of Middleboro'; Austin, 1841; Charles H., 1844;
Florence, 1847. He m., 2d, 1853, Caroline, d. of William Tribble. EBEN-
EZER, Kingston, son of 2d Samuel, m., 1738, Martha Cobb, and had Samuel,
1739; Nehemiah, 1742, m. Ruth Putnam; Job, 1744, m. Thankful Delano
Prince; Martha, 1745, m. Thadeus Ransom; Ebenezer, 1748; Gershom, 1750,
m. Molly Cobb; and Lebbeus. EDWARD, Kingston, son of 2d Cornelius, m.
Eunice Drew of Duxbury, and had George, 1806; Betsey Prior, 1809; James
Edward, 1810; Spencer, 1813, m. Catherine Sampson of Duxbury; Lydia
Bradford, 1817; Julia, 1819, m. Lyman L. Drew and Thomas Delano;
Wealthea Bradford, 1822, m. Hiram Sampson; Charles Lyman, 1825;
Laurana Ellis, 1827; Miranda Wadsworth, 1829. FRANCIS, Kingston, son of
2d Seth, m., 1816, Joanna Bradford, and had Mary Bradford, 1816; Joanna
Bradford, 1819. He m., 2d, 1827, Lucy Sampson; and 3d, 1834, Betsey
Southworth of Duxbury, and by the last had Elizabeth Frances, 1835, m.
Cornelius A. Faunce. GAMALIEL, son of 3d William, m. Abigail Elwell of
Honolulu, and had Joanna, m. Newton Ladd. He m., 2d, 1854, Nancy
Holmes of Plymouth. GEORGE, son of 2d Lemuel, m., 1805, Fanny Glover,
and had Charles Lee, 1805; Fanny Lee, 1807, m. Solomon Townsend;
Augusta Elizabeth, 1810; George Augustus, 1811; Charles Thadeus, 1818;
John Glover, 1821. GEORGE AUGUSTUS, son of above, m., 1834, Ruby, d. of
Clement Bates, and had Georgiana, 1836, m. Joseph Merrill of Boston;
Charles Lee, 1839; Edward A., 1845; Laurelia, 1850. GEORGE PRINCE,
Sandwich, son of 1st William, m. Martha Southworth, and had Sarah Clark;
and Ida Washburn. ISAAC, Duxbury, son of 4th Samuel, m., 1781, Wealthea

Bradford, and had Timothy; Lazarus; Wealthea; and John. JAMES, son of 3d William, m. Elizabeth K. Raymond, and had Celia J., and Ella W. JAMES, son of 1st Lemuel, m. Mary Churchill, and had Hannah, 1751; James, 1754; William, 1755; Mary, 1757; William, 1760; Sarah, 1762; Priscilla, 1765; Lydia, 1767, m. Matthew Cushing; Betsey, 1769. JAMES, Kingston, son of 1st Cornelius, m., 1760, Deborah Nye of Dartmouth, and had Stephen, 1761, m. Sylvia Prince; Clement, 1763, m. Judith Briggs of Pembroke; James, 1765; Sarah, 1766, m. Martin Brewster; Judith, 1768, m. Joseph Sampson and John Thomas; James, 1771. JAMES HARVEY, son of 1st Abijah, m., 1836, Susan H. Allen, and had Caroline W., 1838; Bathsheba J., 1837; Augustus Allen, 1839; Caroline Winslow, 1841. JOB WASHBURN, Kingston, son of 3d Seth, m,, 1833, Mary Ann, d. of Ward Bailey, and had Thomas Bradford of Plymouth, 1834, m. Mary Holbrook, d. of Henry Mills; Allen Judson, 1836; Martha Elizabeth, 1839, m. Walter E. Waterman; Juliet Maria, 1843, m. Martin Parris Washburn. JOB, Kingston, son of Ebenezer, m. Thankful Delano, d. of Thomas Prince, and had Prince, 1768; Fanny, 1770; Job, 1773; Keziah, 1775, m. Ezra D. Morton; Lebbeus, 1777; Nehemiah, 1778; Charles, 1781; Sophia, 1782; Thomas Prince, 1784; Ira, 1786; Ezra, 1788; Sukey, 1791, m. Elisha Ford; Harvey, 1793. JOHN appeared in Plymouth about 1660. He is supposed to have been the son of William Drew, and grandson of Sir Edward Drew, knighted by Queen Elizabeth, 1589. He was born in England 1642, and m., in Plymouth, about 1673, Hannah, d. of John Churchill, and had Elizabeth, 1673; John, 1676, m. Sarah, d. of Thomas Delano of Duxbury, and settled in Middleboro'; Samuel, 1678; Thomas, 1681; Nicholas, 1684; Lemuel, 1684, m. Hannah Barnes. JOSEPH P., son of 1st Samuel, m., 1818, Ruth Rogers Bartlett. JOSHUA, son of 1st Nicholas, m., 1733, Joanna Kempton, and had Levi, 1734; Isaac, 1736; Josiah, 1738, m. Sarah Sherman; Joshua, 1740; William, 1741; Ephraim, 1743; Patience, 1746. JOSIAH, son of 2d Nicholas, m. a wife Bathsheba, and had Josiah, 1774; Bathsheba, 1778; Caleb, 1779; Nicholas, 1780; Nicholas, 1783. JOSIAH, son of 2d Lemuel, m., 1806, Desire Goodwin, and had Desire, 1806; Charles Thomas, 1808. JOSIAH, son of 1st Atwood, m. Sarah W. Hodgkins, and had Sarah D., 1838, m. Joseph N. Morton; Anna G., 1850. LEMUEL, son of John, m., 1715, Hannah Barnes, and had Mary, 1716; Seth, 1718; Hannah, 1722; Lemuel, 1725, m. Priscilla Warren; Sarah, 1726; James, 1728, m. Mary Churchill; William, 1731. LEMUEL, son of 1st Seth, m., 1768, Elizabeth Rider, and had Lemuel, 1769, m. Sally Bartlett, and removed to Lynn; Seth, 1771, m. Temperance Pixby; Elizabeth, 1773, m. Nathaniel Holmes; Margaret James, 1775, m. Thomas Bartlett; George, 1777; William, 1779; Sarah, 1781; Thomas, 1785; Josiah, 1787, m. Desire Goodwin; Isaac, 1790. LEVI, son of Joshua, m., 1756, Mary Milk of Boston, and had Mary, 1756; Joanna, 1759; Levi, 1761; Lydia, 1764; Levi, 1766; John Milk, 1769. LEWIS, from Duxbury, son of 3d Samuel, m., 1809, Mira LeBaron. NATHANIEL, Kingston, son of 1st Abijah, m., 1809, Dorcas Delano, and had Nathaniel Delano, 1809, m. Nancy Bartlett; Mary, 1813, m. Seth J. Winsor; John Newton, 1821, m. Caroline Beytes; Albert, 1825; Albert, 1829, m. Mary S. Swift; Horace Judson, 1822, m. Miranda Bugbee Holmes of Plymouth. NEHEMIAH, Kingston, son of Ebenezer, m., 1767, Ruth Putnam, and had Pamelia, 1768, m. Timothy Davis; Martha, 1769, m. Micah Louden of Duxbury; Elizabeth, 1771; Lucy, 1774, m. Levi Simmons; Clarissa, 1780, m. Ansel Holmes; Polly, 1785, m. Henry Davis and Abner Holmes. NICHOLAS, son of John, by wife Abigail, had Joshua, 1709; Josiah, 1711; Nicholas, 1713; Lemuel, 1715, m. Hannah Dunham. He m., 2d, 1716, Rebecca Morton, and had Joanna, 1717; Lucy, 1719; James, 1721; Abigail, 1723. He m., 3d, Lydia Doggett, 1730, and had Rebecca, 1731; and John Hicks. NICHOLAS, son of above, m., 1736, Bathsheba Kempton, and had Abigail, 1737; Abigail, 1739; Lois, 1741; Nicholas, 1743, m. Mercy Holmes; Josiah, 1745; Abbet, 1747; Samuel, 1749, m. Elizabeth Pierce; David, 1752; Stephen, 1754, m. Jerusha Bryant. NICHOLAS, son of 1st Samuel, m. Asula, d. of David Wood, and had David, m. Rachel Dancer of New Jersey; Betsey, m. George Sherman; Nicholas Henry, m. Ruth Freeman; Joseph Russell; Atwood, and Abbott. PEREZ, Kingston, son of 2d Samuel, m., 1730, Abigail Soule, and had Lemuel, and John. SAMUEL, son of 2d Nicholas, m. Elizabeth Pierce, and had Abbet, 1773; Rebecca, 1775; Nicholas, 1776, m. Asula, d. of David Wood; Elizabeth, 1784; Samuel, 1787; Rebecca, 1790; Joseph P., 1795. SAMUEL, son of John, m. Lydia ———, and had Cornelius, 1702; Perez, 1704, m. Abigail Soule of Duxbury; Zebulon; Lydia, m. Isaac Peterson; Samuel, 1713; Ebenezer, m. Martha Cobb; Deborah, m. Joseph Chandler; Hannah. He m., 2d, Ruth Delano, and had Abijah; Nahum; and Ruth. SAMUEL, son of Ebenezer, by wife Beza, had Beza. He m., 2d, 1774, wid. Hannah Cook, and had Beza, 1777; Cynthia, 1776, m. Spencer Brewster; Samuel, 1778; Beza, 1781; Hannah, 1783; Sally, 1786, m. Eleazer Fuller; Ebenezer, 1788. SAMUEL, Duxbury, son of 2d Samuel, m., 1736, Anna, d. of Richard White, and had Joseph; Sylvanus; Perez; Isaac; Consider; Lewis; Sarah, m. James Southworth; Abigail, m. Samuel Delano; Lucy; Eunice; Lydia; Ann, m. Joseph Wadsworth. He m., 2d, Faith Peterson, 1746. SETH, son of 1st Lemuel, m. Margaret James of Scituate, and had Seth; Lemuel; and Benjamin. SETH, Kingston, son of 1st Cornelius, m., 1772, Hannah, d. of Wrestling Brewster, and had Nathaniel, 1773; Hannah, 1776, m. Eli Cook; Christiana, 1783; Sylvia, 1785, m. Thomas Cushman; Seth, 1778; Francis, 1788, m. Joanna Bradford, Lucy Sampson, and Betsey Southworth. SETH, Kingston, son of above, m., 1803, Mary, d. of Elisha Washburn, and had Thomas Bradford, 1804; Clement, 1806, m. Elizabeth Teal of Boston; Christiana, 1809, m. Levi S. Prince; Job Washburn, 1811, m. Mary Ann Bailey; Christopher Prince, 1815, m. Rebecca Simmons and Lucy Foster; Eliza, 1817, m. Lysander Bartlett; Hannah Cook, 1819, m. John Keely of Haverhill; Seth, 1822, m. Emily F., d. of Charles Robbins; Eli Cook, 1825, m. Harriet K. Eaton of Middleboro'. SETH, son of 2d Lemuel, m., 1795, Temperance Pixby, and had Harriet, 1796; James, 1797; Nancy, 1799; Lemuel, 1801; Joshua, 1805. STEPHEN D., son of 3d William, m. Lydia Rider, and had Stephen D., 1844, m. Fanny Tribon of Middleboro; Adelia, m. Thaxton F. Burgess; Leman Louvelle, 1852; and John. He m., 2d, 1854, Charity Perry, and had Elizabeth R., m. Charles Lucas of Carver and George Lewis. He m., 3d, 1858, Hannah E. Burgess. STEPHEN CURTIS, Boston, son of 2d Abijah, m., 1867, Martha Glover of

Boston, and had Lillian Curtis, 1867; Thomas Livermore, 1871; Alden Glover, 1879. SYLVANUS, Duxbury, son of 4th Samuel, m. Mercy Clark, and had Charles, 1765; Reuben, 1766; Clark, 1769; Sally; Hannah; Wealthea; Lucy; Zilpha. THEODORE, son of 1st William, m., 1842, Euphelia F., d. of Samuel Doten, and had Theodore F.; Francis; Laura S.; and Abby. He m., 2d, 1851, Olive Crowell, and had Lucinda Thomas, and Augusta Winslow. THOMAS, son of 2d Lemuel, m., 1816, Lucia Watson, and had Frances Elizabeth, 1817, m. Lucian Ayer; Thomas, 1819, m. Mary Chauncy Cushing Shute of Hingham; Lucia Watson, 1821; Charles Elkanah, 1823; Cornelia, 1826, m. Hervey G. Upham of Worcester; Arthur Lee, 1828; Herbert Marston, 1830; Martha Fisk, 1835, m. Charles Chauncy Cushing Thompson of Haverhill. THOMAS B., son of Job Washburn, m., 1863, Mary Holbrook, d. of Henry Mills, and had James, 1864; Mary Coville, 1866; Henry J. W., 1870. WILLIAM, son of 2d Lemuel, m. Priscilla Washburn, and had Priscilla W., 1803, m. George Washburn; William T., 1806, m. Lucinda, d. of David Drew; Winslow, 1809; Betsey, 1815, m. Thomas Allen; Matilda, 1818, m. George Frederick Weed; and Barnabas F. Perkins; Theodore, 1820; Rufus W., 1822; Marcia C., 1825, m. Loton Jennings; George Prince, 1827. WILLIAM RIDER, son of 1st Atwood, m., 1848, Susan, d. of Peter Holmes, and had Mary, 1852; William Holmes, 1856, m. Mary Caroline Hathaway; and Annie, 1856, twin to William H. He m., 2d, 1873, Emeline, sister of his 1st wife. WILLIAM, son of 1st David, m., 1804, Sarah Holmes, and had William, 1805; Lucy, 1807, m. Charles Robertson of N. H.; Gamaliel, 1808; Elizabeth, 1810, m. Isaac W. Proctor of N. H.; Stephen D., 1812; Sarah Woodward, 1814, m. Elisha A. Bradeen of Waterbury, Maine; Joanna, 1817, m. Joseph Rider; Reuben, 1819, m. Elizabeth Lanton of New Bedford; Charles, 1821; Sophronia, 1822; Charles, 1824; James, 1826. WILLIAM, son of above, m. Anne, d. of Elijah Macomber, and had William Warren, 1831, m. Susan Babbitt of Fairhaven; Frederick Augustus, 1833, m. Emily Gardner of Woodshole; Augusta Ann, 1837; Helen, 1847; and Charles Russell. WILLIAM, son of 2d James, m., 1780, Eunice Howard, and had Betsey Lewis, 1780. WILLIAM, Kingston, son of 1st Cornelius, m., 1759, Dorothy Bartlett, and had Catherine, 1761; Dorothy, 1763, m. Charles Thomas and Levi Whitman; Jenny, 1765, m. John Washburn; William, 1767, m. Charity Allen; Julia, 1770, m. Martin Parris; Frederick, 1773; Marcia, 1774, m. Jedediah Holmes; Clarence, 1777; Betsey Foster, 1779, m. George Russell; Amelia, 1785, m. George Russell. WILLIAM, Kingston, son of above, m. Charity Allen, and had Lucia, 1794; William, 1798; Allen, 1808. WINSLOW, son of 1st William, m. Abigail Winslow, d. of Hamlin Tilson, and had Augusta Winslow, 1833, m. William F. Spinney of Lynn; Edward Winslow, 1835, m. Lizzie C. Holmes of Cambridge, 1870; Emma Frances, 1848. ZENAS, Kingston, son of 1st Cornelius, m. Saba, wid. of Wait Gray, and had Abigail, 1765; Saba, 1767; Abigail, 1769; Zenas, 1772, m. Lucy Smith of Duxbury; Lydia, 1777; Asa, 1774; and Sally. He m., 2d, wid. Polly Ripley.

DUCY, WILLIAM, m., 1816, Rebecca Cole.

DUGLE, JAMES, m., 1816, Elizabeth Sarah Beaumart.

DUNBAR, JESSE, from Scituate, m., 1785, Sally Witherell. JOHN DAN-

FORTH, born 1771, came to Plymouth, and m., 1794, Nancy, d. of William
Crombie, and had William Crombie, 1795; John, 1797; Elijah, 1799;
Zerviah, 1801; Thomas, 1804. WILLIAM, from Halifax, m., 1805, Jerusha
Holmes, and had James Henry, 1805; William, 1807; George, 1809; Hosea,
1811.
    DUNHAM, ABRAHAM, son of Elijah, m. Patience Clark, 1813, and had
Patience Clark, 1820; Hannah Williams, 1822, m. William H. McLaughlin of
Boston; Joseph Avery, 1824, m. Nancy Everson, d. of Stephen Thomas;
Rebecca Bartlett, 1827; Samuel Newell, 1831, m. Betsey Foster, d. of John
Dunham; Isaac Thomas, 1838, m. Angie Bartlett. AMOS, son of 1st Josiah,
m. Abigail Hill, 1741, and had Amos, 1741, m. Abigail Faunce. He m., 2d,
Ann McLeroy, 1744, and had Robert, 1744; Mary, 1746; Ann, 1748, m. George
Dunham; Amos, 1751; Ruth, 1753, m. William Bradford; Mary, 1755; Josiah,
1757; Catherine, 1759; Abigail, 1763. BARNABAS, son of 1st Ebenezer, m.
Lydia Cole, 1766, and had Barnabas and Benjamin. BARNABAS, son of
above, m. Phebe Fobes, 1794, and had Phebe, m. Caleb Bryant of Portland;
and Barnabas. BARNABAS, son of above, m. Betsey King, 1827, and had
Barnabas, 1827; Benjamin F., 1829; Barnabas again, 1834, m. Harriet Nickerson; Betsey, 1837, m. Richard Arthur; and Benjamin F. again, 1841, m. Mary
F. Clark and Mary B. Thomas. He m., 2d, Betsey, d. of Corban Barnes,
1846; 3d, Nancy, wid. of Sylvanus Holmes, 1863; and 4th, Betsey, wid. of
Edward Winslow Bradford, and sister of 3d wife, 1876. BENAIAH, Eastham,
son of 1st John, m., 1660, Elizabeth Tilson, and had Edward, 1661; John, 1663;
Elizabeth, 1664; Hannah, 1666; Benjamin, 1667. BENJAMIN, Eastham, son
of 1st John, m., 1660, Mary Tilson. CORNELIUS, Plympton, son of Israel,
had probably Cornelius and George. CORNELIUS, son of above, m. Lydia
Atwood, 1774, and had Cornelius, 1780; Henry, 1782; Ezra, 1785; Isaac, 1787;
Thomas, twin, 1787; Lydia Atwood, 1790. DANIEL, son of 1st John, had Me-
hitabel, m. Joseph Hayward of Bridgewater. EARL, m. Jerusha Lynch, 1807.
EBENEZER, son of 2d Samuel, by wife Abigail, had Abigail, m. James Weston;
Samuel; Ebenezer; John, m. Mary Thomas; Moses, Mary, Barnabas, and
William. EBENEZER, son of above, m. Hannah Morton, 1756, and had Abigail,
1757; Ebenezer, 1759. EBENEZER, son of 3d John, m. Ann Ford, 1707, and had
Seth, 1708; Patience, 1717. EBENEZER, Plympton, son of Israel by a second
wife, Lydia (Perry) Fuller, wid. of Nathaniel, had Joanna, 1750; Abigail,
1763, m. Ebenezer Wright; Sylvanus, Jesse, Nathaniel, Ebenezer, Phebe,
Hannah, and Eunice. ELEAZER, son of Joseph, m. Bathsheba, and had
Eleazer, 1682; Nathaniel, 1685; Mercy, 1686, m. Samuel Ransom; Israel,
1689; Elisha, 1692; Josiah, 1694; Bathsheba, 1696; Susanna, 1698; Joshua,
1701. ELEAZER, son of above, by wife Meriam, had Rebecca, 1706; Fear,
1708, m. Jacob Curtis; Nathaniel, 1711; Ezekiel, 1717, m. Patience Holmes;
Elizabeth, 1724; Jerusha, 1726. ELIJAH, son of 1st Nathaniel, m. Eunice
Thomas, and had Isaac, 1779; Jacob, 1782; Deborah, 1784; Abraham, 1787;
Eunice Thomas, 1791; Bartlett, 1794; Elizabeth, 1798; Benjamin, 1801, m.
Alice Finney. GEORGE, m. Patience Churchill, 1789. GEORGE, son of 1st
Cornelius, m. Phebe, d. of Joseph Lucas, and had Patience, 1780; Phebe,
1782, m. Levi Vaughn; George, 1785, m. Polly Albertson; Mary, 1787, m.

Daniel Vaughn; Lucas, 1790; Harvey, 1792; Jesse, 1794; Cornelius, 1797.
GEORGE, came from England, and m. Ann, d. of Amos Dunham, 1771, and
had Josiah. ICHABOD, son of 3d Samuel, m. Sarah Wood of Woodstock, Vt.,
and had Ephraim, m. Rebecca Barrows; Betsey, m. George Barrows; Nathan,
1805, m. Anna H. Vaughn of Middleboro'; Nancy, m. Alden Bisbee of Mid-
dleboro'; and Mary H., m. Benjamin Dunham of Carver. ISAAC, son of
Elijah, m. Elizabeth Savery, 1806, and had Elizabeth; William, 1808; Susan
Marston, 1809; Isaac, 1813; Elijah, 1815. ISRAEL, Plympton, son of 1st
Eleazer, m. Joanna Rickard, and had Sylvanus, 1714; Cornelius, 1716;
Ebenezer, 1718; Susanna, 1721, m. Daniel Crocker; and James, 1723. JACOB,
son of Elijah, by wife Susanna, had Jacob Bartlett, 1810; Eleazer, 1812.
JAMES, son of Joshua, m. Elizabeth Wood, 1748, and had Sarah, 1750.
JESSE, son of 4th Samuel, m. Hannah Jackson, d. of Richard Bagnall, 1808,
and had Richard Bagnall; Lucy Wright, m. Benjamin Harvey; William Jack-
son, m. Ann H., wid. of his brother Chandler; Samuel West; Joseph Bag-
nall; Chandler Davis, m. Ann Hinckley; Eliza Rich, Nancy, Sarah, and
Hannah. JOHN, Plymouth, 1633, by wife Abigail, had probably John;
Benaiah; Jonathan; Daniel; Abigail, m. Stephen Wood; Persis, m. Benaiah
Pratt; Samuel, Thomas, Benjamin, Joseph, and probably Hannah, m. Giles
Rickard. JOHN, son of above, by wife Mary, had John; Jonathan, 1650;
Samuel, 1652; Mercy; Susanna, m. Bartholomew Hamblin; Mary, m. James
Hamblin; and Lydia, m. Robert Barrow. JOHN, son of above, m. Mary Smith,
1680, lived in Barnstable, and had Thomas, 1680; John, 1682; Ebenezer, 1684;
Desire, 1685; Elisha, 1687; Mercy, 1689; Benjamin, 1691. JOHN FOSTER, son
of 3d William, m. Lydia Tufts Wiswell, 1819, and had John; Thomas;
Hannah Nickerson, 1823, m. Eleazer Shaw; Saloam Nickerson, 1827, m.
Joshua L. Edes; George Foster, 1831; Elizabeth Foster, 1833, m. Samuel
Newell Dunham; Lydia Ann, 1837, m. Daniel H. Paulding; and William
Thomas. JOHN, son of 1st Ebenezer, m. Mary Thomas, 1755, and had Moses,
1757, m. Margaret Morton; Mary, 1758; Saloam, 1762; John, 1764. JONA-
THAN, Barnstable, probably son of 1st John, m. Mary, d. of Philip Delano,
1655. He m., 2d, 1657, Mary, d. of Henry Cobb. JOSEPH, son of 1st John,
m., 1657, Mercy, d. of Nathaniel Morton, and had Eleazer; Nathaniel, m.
Mary Tilson; Micajah, Joseph, Benaiah, Daniel, and Mercy. He m., 2d,
1669, Esther Wormall, and some of the above children were by her. JOSIAH,
son of 1st Eleazer, m. Ruth Kempton, 1716, and had Amos, 1716; Hannah,
1720; Charles, 1721; Ruth, 1722; Lydia, 1725; Mary, 1727; Josiah, 1730.
JOSIAH, son of 3d George, m. Betsey, d. of Robert Dunham, 1806, and had
Betsey Ann, m. John Eddy. JOSHUA, son of Micajah, by wife Sarah, had
James, 1723; Sarah, 1726; Joshua, 1727; Mary, 1729; Bathsheba, 1732; Elizabeth, 1733; Joshua, 1736; Lucy, 1738; Levi, 1743; Elisha, 1744. LUCAS, son of
1st George, m. Matilda Elbridge, and had George, 1816; Lysander, 1818; Alfred,
1819; Henry, 1822; Patience, 1824; Ruth; Matilda E., m. Henry H. Packard;
and Elbridge Gerry, m. Harriet Shaw of Randolph. LYSANDER, son of
above, m. Sarah H., d. of William Simmons, and had Lysander L., m. Rebecca B., d. of Benjamin Barnes, and Salissa P. Melvin of Providence; and
Abbie P., m. Lewis H. Shaw of Brockton, MICAJAH, son of Joseph, m.

Elizabeth Lazell, 1701, and had Joshua, 1701; Joseph, 1705; Abigail, 1707.
NATHAN, son of Ichabod, m. Anna H. Vaughn of Middleboro', and had
Benjamin F., m. Anna C. Rand of California; and Rhoda. NATHANIEL,
son of 2d Eleazer, by wife Ann, had Elijah, 1736; Hannah, 1739; Susanna,
1741; Rebecca, 1743; Abner, 1746. NATHANIEL, son of 2d Samuel, m. Re-
becca King, 1725, and had Nathaniel, m. Hannah King; Silas, m. Bethiah
Bartlett; Rebecca, Hannah, Elizabeth, and Martha. RICHARD BAGNALL,
son of Jesse, m. Hannah J., d. of John B. Chandler, 1838, and had George
H., 1842, m. Eliza S. Cole; William C., 1849, m. Elizabeth Lewis; and
Samuel West. ROBERT, son of Amos, m. Ruth, d. of Nathaniel Hatch, 1767,
and had Nancy, 1768; Ruth, 1770; Sarah, 1775; Robert, 1778; Josiah, 1781;
Betsey, 1785; Eleanor, 1789; Lydia, 1791. ROBERT, son of above, m. Sarah
(Barnes) Goddard, wid. of William, 1801, and had Mary Ann, 1802, m.
Thomas Long; Caroline, 1803, m. John D. Gardner; William Goddard, 1805,
m. Nancy, wid. of John Taylor, and d. of Edward Southworth; and Sally
Barnes, 1807, m. Phineas Leach. SAMUEL, son of 1st John, m. Martha, wid.
of William Falloway, 1649, and had Sarah, 1650. SAMUEL, son of 2d John,
m. Mary Harlow, 1680, and had Samuel, 1681; William, 1684; Mary, 1687;
Ebenezer, 1692. He probably m., 2d, wid. Sarah Watson, 1693, and had
Nathaniel, 1698. SAMUEL, son of 1st Ebenezer, m. Susanna, d. of John
Thomas, 1755, and had Samuel, 1758; Elizabeth, 1761; Susanna, 1763;
Deborah, 1765, m. Gideon Southworth; Ichabod, 1768; Elijah, 1770; Nathaniel Thomas, 1772; Nancy, 1774, m. Abraham Thomas; Ephraim, 1777; Andrew, 1779; Lewis, 1785. SAMUEL, son of above, m. Elizabeth Morton, and
had Samuel, Jesse Davis, Chandler, Mary, Eliza, and Sally. SILAS, m.
Lydia Polden, 1792. SYLVANUS, m. Mary Tribble, 1778, and had Sylvanus,
1780, who died at Martinique. SYLVANUS, Plympton, son of Israel, m.
Rebecca, d. of Abel Crocker, and had Patience, 1740, m. Perez Shaw; Israel,
1741; Sylvanus, 1744; Rebecca, 1745; Simeon, 1747; Silas, 1749; Susanna,
1751; Elijah, 1753; Isaac, 1755; Molly, 1757; Asa, 1759; Eleazer, 1761. WIL-
LIAM, son of 2d Samuel, m. Anna, d. of William Norcutt of Marshfield, and
had William, 1710; Martha, 1713, m. Nathaniel Freeman. WILLIAM, son of
1st Ebenezer, m. Abigail Thomas, 1764, and had William, 1765; Josiah,
1770. WILLIAM, son of above, m. Elizabeth Foster, 1788, and had John
Foster, and Betsey, who m. John Lewis and Benjamin Barnes. WILLIAM
GODDARD, son of 2d Robert, m. Nancy, wid. of John Taylor, and d. of
Edward Southworth, 1835, and had Sally, 1836; Robert, 1837; and William,
1838. WILLIAM, m. Nancy Raymond, 1770.

DUPARR, WILLIAM, m. Eliza Cotton, 1816.

DURFEY, PELEG, m., 1721, Mary, d. of Ephraim Cole, and had Mary, 1722,
m. Ezra Allen; Peleg, 1724; Peleg, 1726. RICHARD, m., 1749, Rebecca, d.
of Ephraim Cole. RICHARD, m., 1758, Sarah Bayley, and had Sarah, 1763;
Thomas, 1764; Hannah, 1767; Mary, 1769. He m., 2d, 1770, Elizabeth West,
and had Richard, 1771. RICHARD, son of above, m., 1792, Mary Holmes, and
had Richard, 1793; Susan, m. Thomas Branch Sherman; Polly, m. Josiah
Burbank; and Thomas. RICHARD, son of above, m. in New Bedford, and
had Susan T., 1822; Abby H., 1824; Richard T., 1826; Benjamin B., 1828.

DURKIN, JABEZ, by wife Bethiah, had Samuel, 1705.

DUTCH, SAMUEL, m., 1777, Susanna Straffin.

DYER, CHARLES, probably son of 1st John, m. Lucy, d. of Josiah Cotton, 1736, and had Charles, 1738; and Lucy, 1741. CHARLES, son of above, m. Bethiah, d. of Theophilus Cotton, 1772, and had Charles; Mary; Lucy, m. Joseph Bartlett; Martha Cotton, m. Joseph Holmes; and Margaret, and Bethiah, both of whom m. Jeremiah Holbrook, GEORGE GUSTAVUS, son of Christopher of Abington, removed to Plymouth, and m., 1852, Mary Ann Bartlett, d. of Schuyler Sampson, and had George S., 1854; Horace W., 1858; and Mary S., 1864. Christopher, the father of George G., m. Betsey Porter, and was the son of Christopher, who m. Deborah, d. of Samuel Reed. The last Christopher was the son of Christopher who m. Hannah, d. of Ensign Nash, and grandson of William of Weymouth, before 1699. JOHN, perhaps son of a John of Weymouth, was born, 1671, and taught school in Plymouth about 1700. His children were probably William; John; and Charles. JOHN, son of above, m. Hannah Morton, 1734, and had John, 1735. JOHN, son of above, m., 1757, Mary, d. of John Barnes, and had John, 1758. WILLIAM, son of 1st John, m. Hannah (Cotton) Phillips, wid. of Tomson, 1730, and had William, 1731. He m., 2d, Hannah, d. of Thomas Howland, 1734, and had Hannah, 1736, and Hannah again, 1737, m. Stephen Miller of Milton.

EAMES, ANTHONY, Marshfield, m., 1686, Mercy Sampson, and had Mercy, m. Joseph Phillips; Mary, m. Thomas Phillips; Jerusha, m. Thomas Sayer. JONATHAN, by wife Rebecca, had Jonathan, 1715; Isaac, 1717; Lydia, 1721; Rebecca, 1727.

EASTLAND, JOHN, m. Mary Finney, and had Zeruiah, 1703; Joseph, 1705; Ebenezer, 1708; Mercy, 1710; Hannah, 1713; Joan, 1715; Joshua, 1718; Mary, 1720.

EATON, APOLLOS, son of Joel, m. Parna Leach, and had Charles, m. a Leonard; Calvin; Henry; Adam, m. a King of Taunton; Diana, m. Oliver Eaton; Lucy, m. a Richmond and a Bailey; Caroline, m. Cyrus King of Providence; Alice, m. Abiathar Leonard; and Parna. BARNABAS, Middleboro', son of 2d Samuel, by 1st wife, Mehitabel, had Hannah, 1732; Samuel; Mary, 1735; Sarah, 1737; Seth, 1739. He m., 2d, 1743, Elizabeth Clemens, and had Lot, 1744, m. Martha Cobb; Mehitabel, 1747; Elizabeth, 1749; Ziba, 1750; Nathan, 1753; Wealthy, 1755; Keziah, 1757; Meribah, 1760. BENJAMIN, son of 1st Francis, m., 1660, Sarah Hoskins, and had William; Benjamin, 1664; Rebecca, m. Josiah Rickard; and Ebenezer. BENJAMIN, son of above, m. Mary Coombs, and had William, 1691; Hannah, 1692; Francis, 1693; Sarah, 1695, m. Benjamin Cushman; John, 1697, m. Elizabeth Fuller, and probably Mary; Elizabeth; Benjamin, 1698; Elisha; and David. He had a 2d wife, Susanna. BENJAMIN, Kingston, son of above, by wife Mercy, had Mary, 1726; Jabesh, 1728; Noah, 1734; Mary, 1735; Seth, 1738; James; and Benjamin. He m., 2d, 1746, Mary Tinkham, and had Benjamin, m. Hannah Holmes, 1771. DAVID, Kingston, son of 2d Benjamin, m. Deborah Fuller, and had Jabez, 1746; Job, 1749; Consider, 1752; Joshua, 1755; Eunice, 1759; Lot; and Abner. EBENEZER, son of 1st Benjamin, m., 1701, Hannah Rickard, and had Ebenezer, 1702; Benjamin, 1704; Mercy, 1706; Elisha, 1708; Gideon, 1712; Joanna, 1716. FRANCIS came in the Mayflower 1620, with wife Sarah, and son Samuel. He had a 2d wife by whom he had Rachel, m. Joseph Ramsden; and a 3d, Christian Penn, before 1627, by whom he had Benjamin, 1627. FRANCIS, Middleboro' who died about 1749, had Susanna; Benjamin; Mary; Elijah; and John. FRANCIS, Kingston, son of 2d Benjamin, m., 1727, Thankful Alden, and had Joseph, 1728; Jabez, 1731. He m., 2d, Lydia, d. of John Fuller, 1733, and had Sylvanus, 1734, m. Deborah Caswell; Thankful, 1735; John, 1737; Mary, 1739; Elijah, 1740, m. Sarah Shaw; Benjamin, 1742; Susanna, 1743. ISRAEL, Middleboro', son of 4th Samuel, m., 1781, Eunice Rickard, and had Zenas, 1782; Lindall, 1785; Eunice, 1787; Israel, 1790; Andrew, 1795; Oliver, 1799. By a 2d wife, Keziah, he had Daniel. JOEL, son of Joseph, m., 1774, Lucy Leonard, and had Apollos, 1775; Polycarpus, 1777; Alfred, 1779; Cynthia, 1782; Caroline, 1787, m. Josiah Robinson. JOSEPH, Middleboro', son of 3d Francis, m., 1750, Hannah Crossman, and had Joel, 1751; Abigail, 1754; Francis, 1756; Mary, 1760. NATHAN, Middleboro', son of Barnabas, by wife Margaret, had Hannah; Martha, 1777; Barnabas, 1782; Ziba, 1784; Sarah, 1786; Mehitabel, 1789; Nancy, 1791; Luther, 1793; Elizabeth, 1796. SAMUEL, Duxbury and Middleboro', son of 1st Francis, m., 1661, Martha Billington, and had probably Mercy, m. Samuel Fuller; and Samuel. SAMUEL, Middleboro', son of above, m. Elizabeth, d. of Samuel Fuller, and had Mercy, 1695; Keziah, 1700; Elizabeth, 1701; Barnabas, 1703. SAMUEL, Middleboro', who died about 1820, had Israel; Enos; Daniel; Darius; Samuel; Mehitabel; and Eunice. SAMUEL, Middleboro', son of Barnabas, m., 1753, Patience Tinkham, and had Samuel, 1754; Barnabas, 1757; Israel, 1760; Mehitabel, 1763; Daniel, 1767; Darius, 1770; Eunice, m. a Bryant; Enos, 1773. TIMOTHY, Boston, m. Eliza Kinsbury of Canton, and had Timothy T. TIMOTHY T., son of above, m., 1844, Salina, d. of Samuel Eliot of Plymouth, and had Timothy, 1846; Timothy E., 1847; Charles A., 1848. m. Addie E. Wrightington; Helen S., m. John Dunn; and Salina H. ZIBA, Middleboro', son of Barnabas, m., 1773, Ruth Leonard, and had Solomon, 1774; Betty, 1777; Clemmons, 1780; Ruth, 1783.

EBED, EBED, slave of Madam Thatcher of Middleboro', pub. to Betty Cunnett, 1764.

EDDY, BENJAMIN, Boston and West Cambridge, son of 2d Caleb, m., 1763, Martha Bronsden, and had Martha, 1764, m. Z. Jennings of Cherry Valley, N.Y.; Mary, 1766, m. Eleakim Morse; Hannah, 1768, m. Luke Bemis of Watertown; Sarah, 1770; Charlotte, 1773; Robert Rand, 1774; Eunice, 1776; Sarah, 1779, m. William Cotting; Robert Rand, 1781; Caleb, 1784. CALEB, son of 1st Samuel, by wife Elizabeth, had Caleb, 1672; Samuel, 1675; and Zachariah. He removed to Swansea. CALEB, Boston, son of above, m., 1711, Hannah Brown, and had Samuel, 1716, m. Mary Grover, Joanna Savage, and 3d, Lucy Clark; Hannah, 1718, m. John Simpson; Caleb, 1721. CALEB, Boston, son of above, m., 1740, Martha Parks, and had Hannah, 1741, m. Robert Gardner and Robert Currie; Benjamin, 1743; Martha, 1745, m. Matthew Grice. CALEB, Boston, son of Benjamin, m., 1810, Caroline, d. of

Timothy Gay of Boston, and had Robert Henry, 1812, m. Annie Goddard, d. of John Knight Pickering of Portsmouth, N. H.; Mary Caroline, 1817; Benjamin, 1820; Thomas Melville, 1822; Benjamin, 1829, m. Nellie M., d. of George Weld of Jamaica Plain; Albert Melville, 1832. DARIUS, Dorchester, son of 3d John, m., 1835, Lydia Otis Hersey of Hingham, and had Darius Francis, 1837, m. Jerusha, d. of Samuel Talbot of Plymouth; Lydia A., 1839; Lydia H., 1841; Otis, 1843, m. Mary Willard; Lewis, 1846, m. Mary P., d. of Samuel Talbot; Isaac H., 1849, m. Rebecca, d. of Benjamin Hathaway of Plymouth; George, 1852, m. Helen D. Tilden; and John Lodge. HENRY HOLMES, son of 2d Seth, m., 1831, Abigail, d. of Alpheus Richmond, and had Seth W., 1837, m. Frances M., d. of John Campbell; Henry F., 1839; George T., 1841; James T., 1846; Abby J., 1849, m. Henry Telling; and Harriet F., m. Heman Robbins. JAMES T., son of above, m., 1863, Mary A. Whall, and had Eliza R., 1874; Mary A., 1875; Sarah T., 1877; James T., 1879. JOHN came to Plymouth from Cranbrook, England, in the Handmaid 1630, with his brother Samuel, and settled, 1633, in Watertown. He was a son of William, and by wife Amie had Pilgrim, 1634, m. William Baker; John, 1637; Benjamin, 1639; Samuel, 1640; Abigail, 1643; Sarah, m. John Marion; Mary, m. Thomas Orton; and Ruth. JOHN, son of 1st Samuel, m., 1665, Susanna, d. of Robert Paddock, and had Mary, 1667; John, 1670; Eleazer, 1671. He m., 2d, 1672, Deliverance Owen, and had Mercy, 1673; Hannah, 1676; Ebenezer, 1679; Eleazer, 1681; Joseph, 1683; Benjamin, 1685; Abigail; Jonathan, 1689; Susanna, 1692; Patience, 1696. He had a 3d wife, Hepzibah. JOHN, son of 1st Seth, m. Abiah Sturtevant of Halifax, and had Fanny, 1804, m. Robert Davie; Sally Sturtevant, 1806, m. Coomer Weston; John, 1807; Darius, 1809; Mercy Morton, 1811, m. Henry Howard Robbins; Eliza, m. Barnabas Churchill; and Lewis. JOHN, son of above, m, Betsey Ann, d. of Josiah Dunham, 1831, and had Ann Elizabeth, 1832; George, 1835; Curtis, 1837, m. Mary Ann, d. of Samuel Rider of West Bridgewater; John, 1841; Ann Elizabeth, 1847; George; and Ann Eliza. JOSHUA, Middleboro', son of 3d Zechariah, m. Lydia, d. of Zechariah Paddock, and had Joshua, 1779; Zechariah, 1780; Ebenezer, 1783; Nathaniel, 1785; Lydia, 1787; William S., 1789; Jane, 1792; Morton, 1797, m. Irene, d. of Isaac Lazell of Bridgewater; and John Milton, 1800. LEWIS, son of 3d John, m. Sarah Hersey of Hingham, and had Frank Lewis, 1854. OBADIAH, son of 1st Samuel, m. a Bennett, and had John, 1670; Hasadiah, 1672; Samuel, 1675: Jabez; Benjamin; Elizabeth; Mary; Mercy; and Joel. SAMUEL, son of William of Cranbrook, England, came, as above, with his brother John, and by wife Elizabeth, had John, 1637; Zechariah, 1639; Caleb, 1643; Obadiah, 1645; Hannah, 1647. SAMUEL, Watertown, son of 1st John, m., 1664, Sarah, d. of Gabriel Meade, and had Samuel, 1668; Sarah, 1670; Benjamin, 1673; Deliverance, 1676; Elizabeth, 1679; Ruth, 1681; Joanna, 1685. SAMUEL, Middleboro', son of Obadiah, m. Meletiah Pratt, and had Samuel, 1696; Zechariah, 1701; Bennett; Fear; and Meletiah. SAMUEL, son of 3d Zechariah, m. Jerusha Barden, and had John, 1780; Mary, 1782; Thomas, 1789; Seth, 1786; Sally, 1788, m. Crocker Cobb of Plymouth and Caleb Lapham of Pembroke; Joseph, 1790; Apollos, 1792; Lucy, 1794, m. Lemuel Cole of

Plympton; and Ezra Holmes, m. Nancy Churchill of Plympton. SETH, son of above, m., 1803, Sophia Holmes, and had Henry Holmes, and Harriet. His wid. m. John Morehead. SETH W., son of above, m., 1858, Francis M., d. of John Campbell, and had William F., 1858. WILLIAM, Vicar of St. Dunstan, in Cranbrook, England, m., 1587, Mary, d. of John Foster, and had Mary, 1591; Phineas, 1593; John, 1597; Ellen, 1599; Abigail, 1601, m. John Benjamin; Anna, 1603; Elizabeth, 1606; Samuel, 1608; Zechariah, 1610; Nathaniel, 1612. He m., 2d, 1614, wid. Elizabeth Taylor, and had Priscilla, 1614. ZECHARIAH, son of 1st Samuel, removed to Middleboro' and Swansea. He m., 1663, Alice, d. of Robert Paddock, and had Zechariah, 1664; John, 1666; Elizabeth, 1670, m. Samuel Whipple of Providence; Samuel, 1673; Ebenezer, 1676; Caleb, 1678; Joshua, 1681; Obadiah, 1683. ZECHARIAH, son of above, m., 1683, Mercy Baker of Swansea, and had Alice, 1684; Eleanor, 1686. ZECHARIAH, Middleboro', son of 3d Samuel, m., 1737, Mercy, d. of Ebenezer Morton, and had John, 1738; Mercy, 1740; Ebenezer, 1742; Nathaniel, 1744; Joshua, 1748; Hannah, 1749; Zechariah, 1752; Seth, 1754; Thomas, 1756; Lucy, 1758; Samuel, 1760.

EDES, JOSHUA L., m. Salome N., d. of John Foster Dunham, 1847, and had Abby L. OLIVER, brother of above, from Braintree, m. Susan Davie, 1836, and had William W., 1847, m. Ellen M., d. of Calvin H. Eaton of Carver; Lydia C., 1851, m. Jason W. Mixter; Edwin L., 1853, m. Mary E., d. of Edgar C. Raymond. WILLIAM, brother of above, born in East Needham, 1828, died in the war.

EDSON, ELIJAH, from Bridgewater, m., 1818, Nancy Clark.

EDWARDS, JOHN, m., 1771, Lydia Sampson. JOHN, m., 1775, Sarah Covington.

ELDRIDGE, JOSHUA, from Truro, m. Elizabeth Dammon, 1775.

ELLENWOOD, THEODORE, m., 1806, Grace Robbins.

ELLIOTT, DANIEL ROBERT, of Savannah, Georgia, m. Betsey H., d. of James Thacher, 1804, and had Jane A., m. Charles Sever; Catherine, m. Nathaniel Russell; and Susan Louisa, 1811. SAMUEL, born in N. H., son of a Benjamin, m. Clarissa, d. of Elkanah Danforth, and had Samuel, m. Louisa Bonney of Rochester; Daniel; Salina, m. Timothy T. Eaton; Harriet; Clarissa, m. Plina Belcher of South Weymouth; and Eliza, m. Thomas G. Hunt of Maine. He m., 2d, Mercy, d. of Jacob Vail of Carver, and had Susan; Mercy, m. John Morrison; Nancy, m. Simeon Morrison; Fanny; and Harriet.

ELLIS, ABNER, came from Middleboro', and m., about 1818, Sophia Peterson of Duxbury, by whom he had Mary, m. Phineas Leach; Anna W., m. Francis Henri Weston; and Abner. ABNER, son of above, m. Maria Sharp of East Bridgewater, and had Abner, 1857. BARNABAS, son of 1st Eleazer, m. Ruth Swift, and had Eleazer, 1771; Reuben, 1772, m. Patience Blackwell of Sandwich; Lewis, 1774; Francis, 1776; William, 1779; Lewis again, 1781; Jane, 1784, m. Uriah Savery. BARNABAS, son of 3d William, m. Marcia A., d. of Nathaniel Doten, 1832, and had Marcia Ann, 1833, m. Benjamin D. Freeman; Mary, 1835; Betsey W., 1838, m. Charles Hathaway; Isabella, 1840, m. Sumner Leonard; William, m. Delia Hewitt of Raynham;

Thomas H., 1845, m. Mary R. Jenkins; and Clark, 1849. BARTLETT, son
of 1st Nathaniel, m. Elizabeth, d. of Joseph Barnes, 1817, and had Charles,
1818. He m., 2d, Hannah J., d. of John Churchill, 1821, and had Nancy C.,
1822, m. Willard Wood; Nathaniel B., 1830; George Francis, 1832; and
Hannah Elizabeth, 1842, m. Charles E. Ryder of West Bridgewater. BENJA-
MIN, probably son of Matthias, m. Harriet Gibbs, and had Benjamin, 1724;
Hannah, 1726; Sarah, 1728; Benjamin, 1732; Joseph, 1734; Susanna, 1736;
Freeman, 1738; Nathaniel, 1742; Betty, 1746. ELEAZER, son of 1st William,
by wife Deborah, had Zilpha, 1747; Barnabas, 1749; Jesse, 1751; Abigail,
1753, m. Thomas Gibbs; Deborah, 1756; Molly, 1758; Pelham, 1761; Wil-
liam, 1764. ELEAZER, son of 1st Barnabas, by wife Deborah, had Betsey,
1790; Stephen, 1793; Deborah, 1796. ELISHA, son of 2d Thomas, m. Priscilla Crowell, and had Elisha W., 1837; Priscilla, 1845; Nathaniel, 1847; and
E. Winslow, m. Gertrude Nichols. FRANCIS, son of 1st Barnabas, m.
Joanna Briggs, and had Alonzo, 1800; Patty, 1801, m. Barsillai Sears of Sandwich; Rufus, 1803, m. Lydia Sears; Ruth, 1805, m. Ezra Swift; Eleazer, m.
Lydia Cahoon; Isaac Briggs, 1806; Martin, 1807; Watson; 1810; Israel
Briggs, 1812, m. Mary Ann Cahoon; Joanna B., m. Thomas Ellis; Deborah,
m. Jacob Swift; and Ziba. FREEMAN, Rochester, probably son of 1st John,
by wife Mercy, had Joel, Ebenezer, Mordecai, and Gideon. GIDEON, son of
above, m. Ann Clark, and had Abigail, 1720; Gideon, 1722; Thomas, 1724;
Eleazer, 1725; Elijah, 1727; Ebenezer, 1729. GEORGE FRANCIS, son of
Bartlett, m. Anna M., d. of Grenville Gardner, 1852, and had Harriet Maria,
1855; Louisa, m. Edward G. Ditman; Hannah B., 1860; Jennie P., 1866;
and George F., 1871. HARRISON GRAY OTIS, Wareham, son of Josiah
Thompson, m. Margaret D., d. of Jeremiah Holbrook of Plymouth, 1832,
and had Sydney, J. S., Margaret H., Lucy, Emma G., and Margaret E.
HIRAM, m. Mercy Shaw, 1844. JOEL, Plympton, son of 1st Samuel, m.
Elizabeth Churchill, 1710, and had Joel, 1712; John, 1714; Matthias; Samuel;
John, m. Elizabeth Coomer; Elizabeth, m. Gideon Southworth; Rebecca, m.
Samuel Lanman; Charles, m. Bathsheba Fuller; and Thomas, m. Ruth
Thomas. JOHN, Sandwich, m., 1645, Elizabeth, d. of Edmund Freeman,
and had Bennet, 1649; Mordecai, 1651; Joel, 1655; Nathaniel, 1657; Mat-
thias; and probably John, Samuel, and Freeman. JOHN, son of above, m.
Sarah Holmes, 1700, and had perhaps John and Jonathan. JOHN, son of
above, by wife Rose, had Jabez, 1732; Mary, 1733; John, 1735. JONATHAN,
brother of above, by wife Patience, had Deborah, 1740; Lucy, 1742; Mary,
1744. JOSIAH THOMPSON, Plympton, son of 1st Stephen, m. Sophia, d. of
Isaac Wright, and had Harrison Gray Otis, 1810; Mary Thompson, 1812, m.
Charles L. Babbit of Taunton; Mercy, 1814; Sophia, 1817; Selah, 1819, m.
Samuel M. Tinkham; Emeline, 1821, m. Edward S. Wright; Josiah Thomp-
son, 1824, m. a Leach, and a 2d and 3d wife; Stephen, 1826, m. Louisa How-
ard of Wareham; William Irving, 1829, m. Hattie Griffin of Winchester;
Charles Leonard, 1833. MATTHIAS, son of 1st John, had Matthias, 1681;
Freeman, 1683; Mary, 1685; Experience, 1687, m. Stephen Churchill; Mala-
chi, 1689; Remember, 1691; Benjamin; Samuel, 1699; and perhaps William.
MORDECAI, son of Freeman, m. Rebecca Clark, 1715, and had Mordecai,

1718, who moved to Hanover; and perhaps others. MORDECAI, Hanover, son of above, m. Sarah Otis, 1739, and had Ruth, m. John Bailey; Rebecca, 1741, m. George Bailey; Sarah, 1742; David, 1744, m., 1st, a wife Ruth, and 2d, Ann Jenkins; Mordecai, 1746; Lucy, 1748, m. Charles Otis; Priscilla, 1750, m. John Little of Marshfield; Elizabeth, 1752, m. Joseph Ramsdell; Clark, 1754, m. Ruth Spooner of Abington; Nathaniel, 1756; Otis, 1762. MORDECAI, Hanover, son of above, m. Priscilla Rogers of Marshfield, 1777, and had Huldah, 1779, m. Nathan Studley; Rebecca, 1781, m. William Gifford of Falmouth; Abigail, 1782, m. John Sherman of New York; Mordecai, 1785; Priscilla, 1787, m. Theophilus Gifford of Falmouth; David, 1789, m. Maria Loud; Sarah, 1791, m. Simeon Hoxie of Sandwich; Otis, 1795, m. Ruth Barker of Dartmouth; Elizabeth, 1797, m. Jonathan Pratt of Lynn. NATHAN, from Sandwich, m. Betsey G. Barnes, 1844. NATHANIEL, son of 3d Samuel, m. Jane, d. of Benjamin Bartlett, 1784, and had Lydia, 1789, m. George Harlow; Nathaniel, 1791; Samuel, 1793, m. Lydia, d. of Coomer Weston; Bartlett, 1795; Jane, 1797, m. William Paty; Esther, 1799, m. Otis Churchill; Rebecca, 1808. NATHANIEL, son of 1st Thomas, m. Remember Swift, 1810, and had William, 1811; Curtis, 1814, m. a Nightingale; Nathaniel, 1818; Betsey H., 1820; Lucy H., 1823, m. Theodore F. Bassett; James W., 1833, m. Sarah Clark. NATHANIEL, son of above, m. Nancy W., d. of William Swift, 1845, and had Walter H., 1846. NATHANIEL B., son of Bartlett, m. Lucy Emeline Whitman, and had Charles, 1856; Emma F., 1859. SAMUEL, son of 1st John, had Joel and perhaps others. SAMUEL, son of Matthias, by wife Mercy, had Mary, 1718; Esther, 1721; Samuel, 1722; Remember, 1725; Jane, Rebecca, and Mercy. SAMUEL, son of above, by wife Lydia, had Sarah, 1755; Nathaniel, 1757; Esther, and Jane. SAMUEL, Plympton, son of Joel, m. Mary, d. of Allerton Cushman, 1741. He m., 2d, 1744, Mercy Merrick of Taunton, and had Stephen, 1748. He m., 3d, 1761, Lydia, d. of Zebedee Chandler, and had Lydia, 1761. He m., 4th, Catherine, d. of Othniel Campbell, and had Willard, 1767; Molly, 1769. STEPHEN, Plympton, son of above, m. Susanna, d. of Ebenezer Thompson, and had Mercy, 1773; Susanna, 1774; Stephen, 1776; Molly, 1778; Ebenezer, 1785; Maverick, 1787; Josiah Thompson, 1789; Lydia, 1793. STEPHEN, Wareham, son of Josiah Thompson, m. Louisa Howard of Wareham, and had Stephen I., Mary L., and Hattie H. THOMAS, son of 2d William, m. Jerusha, d. of Israel Clark, 1767, and had Betsey, 1770, m. a Swift; William, 1771; Lydia, m. a Morey; Jerusha, Polly, Lucy, Nathaniel, and Thomas. THOMAS, son of above, m. Rebecca Burgess, and had Hannah, 1803, m. Joseph Harlow; Elisha, 1805, m. Priscilla Crowell; Betsey, 1807; Lydia, 1808, m. Paul Crowell; Thomas, 1811, m. Joanna B., d. of Francis Ellis; Anson B., m. Harriet N. Howes of Dennis; Hiram; and Clark S., m. Eliza A. Swift. THOMAS, son of above, m. Joanna B. Ellis, 1838, and had Anna Augusta, 1846; Thomas A., 1848, m. Delia, d. of Henry T. Lanman; Martha and Mary, twins, 1854; and Charles F., m. Hannah J. Burgess. WILLIAM, perhaps son of Matthias, by wife Jane, had William, 1719; Experience, 1722; Eleazer, 1724; Thomas, 1726. WILLIAM, son of above, by wife Patience, had Thomas, 1744; Betty, 1748, m. Ezra Harlow; Lydia, 1750, m. Thomas Clark; and Mary, 1753.

WILLIAM, son of 1st Barnabas, m. Betsey, d. of Ezra Harlow, and had Freeman, 1804, m. Mary Lothrop, d. of Lothrop Clark; Betsey, 1805, m. Joseph Churchill; Hannah, m. Silas Rickard, and removed to Iowa; Barnabas; and William. WILLIAM, son of 1st Thomas, by wife Hepzibah, had Russell. 1794; Micah, 1796; William, 1798; Cynthia, 1800; Lucy, 1802; Thomas, 1804; and Seneca. WILLIAM, son of above, by wife Martha, had William E., m. Lucy E. Gibbs. ZIBA, son of Francis, m. Mary Burgess, and had Eliza Burgess, 1843. He m., 2d, Deborah E. Gibbs of Wareham, 1848, and had Ziba, 1853; Ruel G., 1859. He m., 3d, Anna B., sister of 2d wife, 1873.

ELLISON, GEORGE, m. Lydia, d. of Nathaniel Morton, about 1670.

ELY. A hired man bearing this name came in the Mayflower, and after serving out his time returned to England.

EMERSON, RALPH WALDO, from Concord, m., 1835, Lydia, d. of Charles Jackson.

ENGLISH, PETER, m., 1732, Alice Randall. THOMAS came in the Mayflower, and died the first winter, leaving no wife nor child.

EPHRAIMS, WILLIAM, pub. to Elizabeth Nero, 1770.

ERECK, ERECK, slave of George Watson, pub. to Rose, slave of William Clark, 1757.

ERLAND, EDWIN FRANCIS, son of Henry, m., 1858, Martha A., d. of Ansel Holmes, and had Martha F., 1859. HENRY, m. Sally C., d. of Daniel Finney, and had Henry Thomas, 1828, m. Lydia K., d. of Micah Sherman of Carver; and Edwin Francis, 1833. JOHN, m., 1700, Elizabeth, d. of Samuel Jenney.

EVANS, THOMAS, died, 1635.

EVERSON, JOHN, had James, 1703; Mercy, 1705. RICHARD, by wife Elizabeth, had Richard, 1700; Ephraim, 1702; Ebenezer, 1705.

EWER, SETH, from Barnstable, m., 1762, Lydia Holmes. THOMAS, m. Lydia Harlow, and had Thomas, 1750; Eleazer, 1751.

FALES, TIMOTHY, of Bristol, m. Elizabeth Thomas, 1748.

FALLOWELL, GABRIEL, an early comer, by wife Catherine, had William, and died, 1667. JOHN, son of William, m. Sarah Wood, 1669, and had Wiiliam, and a d. m. a Tobey. WILLIAM, son of Gabriel, m., 1640, Martha Beal, and had John.

FARMER, THOMAS, m., 1768, Susanna, d. of Ebenezer Tinkham, and had Susanna, m. George Price; Thomas, 1770; Mary, 1776, m. Nathaniel Doten. THOMAS, son of above, m., 1791, Margaret, d. of John Paty, and had Nancy, m. Enoch Randall; and Thomas, m. Phebe, d. of Jeremiah Holmes.

FARNAM, JONATHAN, m., 1780, Dorcas Barnes, and had Sarah, 1785; Dorcas, 1786.

FARRIS, JEREMIAH, Barnstable, m. Abigail Eldridge, and had Betsey, 1794, m. Bridgham Russell of Plymouth; Washington, 1796, m. Olive Allen; Jeremiah, 1798; Abby, 1800; Abby, 1802; Jeremiah, 1804. He m., 2d, Lydia Eldridge, and had Lydia E., 1806, m. Henry Crocker of Boston; Alice, 1808; Jeremiah, 1810; and Abby, 1814, m. James W. Davis. His wid. m. Sylvanus Bourne,

and had Sarah, m. John Wilson; Russell; and Louisa, m. Nelson Chipman.
JEREMIAH, son of above, m., 1832, Mary, d. of Nathaniel Carver of Plymouth,
and had Mary Joanna, 1834; Elizabeth, 1836, m. John T. Stoddard; Henry
Crocker, 1841; Annie Carver, 1846, m. William P. Stoddard; and James Herbert, m., 1850, Emma N., d. of Benjamin Norwood of Bucksport, Maine, and
adopted d. of Nathaniel E. Harlow of Plymouth.
    FAUNCE, ANSEL, son of 3d Thomas, m. Hope Besse of Middleboro', 1779,
and had Barnaby probably. BARNABY, probably grandson of 2d Thomas, often
called incorrectly, Barnabas, m. Sally Carver, 1793. He m., 2d, Abigail, d.
of William Sturtevant of Carver, 1804; 3d, Zilpha, sister of Abigail, 1807; and
4th, Betsey Carver, 1838. BARNABY, son of Ansel, by a 1st wife, had Ansel,
and Eunice. He m., 2d, wid. Reed, and had Alvin, Leonard, Enos, Adoniram, Hiram, and Almira. BARTLETT, son of 1st Thadeus, m. Lydia H., d. of
Thomas Savery, 1811, and had Bartlett, 1811; Charles L., 1814; George Henry,
1817. BENJAMIN, Kingston, son of 3d John, m. Lydia Trouant of Marshfield, and had Benjamin, 1764; Lydia, 1765; Lucy, 1767; John, 1770; Tilden,
1772, m. Lydia, d. of Josiah Cook; Stephen, 1774, m. Mary Sampson; and
Molly. CALEB, son of 1st Thadeus, m. Rebecca Brown, 1800, and had Caleb,
Rebecca; Dorcas M., m. Phineas Pierce; Jane, m. Peter W. Smith, and Nathaniel Brown. CHARLES L., son of Bartlett, by wife Jerusha, had Abigail
Thomas, 1839. CHARLES COOK, Kingston, son of Elijah, m., 1831, Amelia,
d. of Seth Washburn, and had Walter Hamlett, 1832; Amelia Washburn,
1834, m. George McLaughlin; Charles Thomas, 1835; Sewall Allen, 1841.
CHARLES THOMAS, Kingston, son of above, m. Nancy Inglee, d. of Thomas
Adams, 1859, and had Emily, 1861; Amelia, 1864; Carl Clayton, 1872.
ELEAZER, son of 1st Joseph, m. Hannah, d. of Benjamin Warren, 1724, and
had Hannah, 1725, m. Benjamin Morton; Elizabeth, 1727; Patience, 1730;
Mary, 1731, m. Peleg Faunce; Abigail, 1735, m. Amos Dunham; Priscilla,
1739. ELEAZER, Kingston, son of 5th John, m. Susanna, d. of John Adams,
and had Eleazer, 1780; John, 1782, m. Sarah, d. of Calvin Bradford; Zenas,
1784, m. Jerusha Wadsworth of Duxbury; Lucy, 1788, m. Zenas Cook; Eli,
1793; Hannah, 1795, m. Martin Cook. ELIJAH, Kingston, son of 5th John,
m. Lydia, d. of Ichabod Waterman, 1785, and had Elijah, 1787; Kilborn,
1789; Nathaniel, 1791; Lydia, 1793, m. Spencer Bradford; Sally, twin of
Lydia, and Charles Cook, 1801. GEORGE, Kingston, son of Kilborn, m.
Adeline, d. of William Winslow of Marshfield, and had Elmer, 1846; Ellen,
1848; Winslow, 1850, m. Nellie, d. of Joseph Stranger; Myron, 1852; Linus,
1854; Alton, 1856; George, 1858; Bertha, 1859; Sarah Cushing, 1864.
ICHABOD, Kingston, son of Nathaniel, m. Ann Lincoln, d. of William Bennett of Abington, and had Anna Washburn, 1858; Alma Lincoln, 1861.
JAMES, son of 2d Thomas, by wife Sarah, had Nathaniel, 1743; James, 1745;
John, 1747; Seth, 1749. / JOHN came in the Ann 1623, and m., 1634, Patience,
d. of George Morton, and had Priscilla, m. Joseph Warren; Mary, m. William
Harlow; Patience, m. John Holmes; Sarah, m. Edward Doty and John Buck;
Thomas, the Elder, born 1647; Elizabeth, 1648, m. Isaac Robinson; Mercy,
1651, m. Nathaniel Holmes; John, 1654; and Joseph, 1653. JOHN, son of
1st Joseph, m. Abigail, d. of John Bryant, 1705, and had Nathaniel, 1706;

John, 1709; Mercy, 1711, m. Josiah Carver; Abigail, 1715, m. Jabez Hammond; Jane, 1717, m. Ichabod Swift; Patience, 1721. JOHN, son of 1st Thomas, m. Lydia, d. of Jacob Cook, 1710, and had Judith, 1711, m. Jabez Washburn; Lydia, 1714, m. Ebenezer Washburn and Thomas Waterman; John, 1716; Hannah, 1718, m. Charles Cook; Mary, 1720; Mehitabel, 1722, m. Thomas Cushman; Rebecca, 1724, m. Tilson Ripley of Plympton. He m., 2d, Ruth Sampson, 1733, and had Mary, 1734, m. Amos Curtis of Scituate. He m., 3d, Lydia (Tilden) Cook, wid. of Simeon, and had Benjamin, 1742. JOHN, son of 1st Thadeus, m. Hannah Sampson, 1805, and had John, now in the Revenue Service; and Hannah S., m. John Bates. JOHN, Kingston, son of 3d John, m. Hannah, wid. of Robert Cook, and d. of Elijah Bisbee, and had Lydia, 1746, m. Josiah Cook; John, 1747; Hannah, 1749; Eleazer, 1751; Eleanor, 1753; Molly, 1755, m. John Cook; Joanna, 1757, m. Zenas Cook; Elijah, 1759; Sarah, 1760; and Sarah again, 1764. JOSEPH, son of 1st John, m., 1678, Judith Rickard, and had Hannah, 1679; Mary, 1681, m. Nathaniel Morton; John, 1683; Mercy, 1686; Mehitabel, 1689, m. Judah Hall; Joseph, 1693; Eleazer, 1696; Thomas, 1698, m. Hannah Damon; Benjamin, 1703. JOSEPH, son of 1st Peleg, m. Mercy Bartlett, 1785, and had Eleazer, 1786; Joseph, 1787. KILBORN, Kingston, son of Elijah, m. Nancy, d. of Josiah Cook, and had George, 1816; Joanna Cook, 1818; Sarah, 1827. LEMUEL BRADFORD, son of 1st Solomon, m. Lydia B., d. of Eliab Wood, and had Lemuel B., 1834; George F., 1837; Lydia Emily, 1844, m. James Tinkham; and Caleb W. He m., 2d, Elizabeth A., d. of Ephraim Morton, 1846, and had Cassandra M., 1849, m. George Lewis of Lynn; Joshua B., 1852, m. Eldora Drew of Kingston; Content, m. Silas Dean of Middleboro; Lizzie E., 1857; George W., 1859; Mary E., 1863; Nellie B., 1866; Etta C., 1869; Rebecca J., 1872. NATHANIEL, Kingston, son of Elijah, m. Marcia, d. of Seth Washburn, and had Seth, 1819, m. Hannah, d. of Thomas Cushman; Elijah, 1820, m. Ellen Partridge of Randolph; Quincy Adams, 1824; Arthur, 1822, m. Harriet A. Blake and Georgianna Lane of Abington; Marcia Washburn, 1826, m. Joseph Addison Stranger; Ichabod Washburn, 1828; Albert, 1830, m. Isabella Simmons; Lucia Drew, 1831, m. Davis W. Bowker of Scituate; Cornelius Adams, 1833, m. Elizabeth Frances, d. of Francis Drew; Mary Howard, 1836, m. Thomas Whittemore Mitchell of Maine; Jane, 1840. NATHANIEL BROWN, son of Caleb, m. Rebecca H., d. of Samuel Doten, 1833, and had Rebecca Jane, 1835; Martha Ellen, 1836; and Nathaniel Brown, 1838. PELEG, son of 2d Thomas, m. Mary, d. of Eleazer Faunce, 1756, and had Eleazer, 1757; Peleg, 1759; Joseph, 1763; Benjamin, 1765. PELEG, son of above, m. Hannah Churchill, 1781, and had Hannah, m. Joseph Davie; and Peleg. PELEG, son of above, m. Olive, d. of Daniel Finney, 1823, and had Daniel Wooster, 1829; Caroline Augusta, 1833, m. Henry H. Perry. QUINCY ADAMS, Kingston, son of Nathaniel, m. Mary Louisa, d. of Seth Waterman, 1850, and had Quincy Ray, 1854; Lucy Winsor, 1860. SEWALL ALLEN, Kingston, son of Charles Cook, m., 1868, Ann Eliza, d. of Edward Holmes, and had Sewall Edward, 1871. SOLOMON, son of 1st Thadeus, m. Eleanor, d. of Lemuel Bradford, 1806, and had Solomon; William, m. Matilda, d. of Josiah Bradford; and Lemuel Bradford. SOLOMON, son of above, m. Mary

Olive, d. of Nathaniel Harlow, and had Solomon E., 1841, m. Annie C. d. of William D. Winsor of Kingston. STEPHEN, son of 1st Thadeus, m. Betsey Shurtleff, 1803, and had Jane, 1803; Charlotte Sylvester, 1806, m. Samuel L. Alexander; Thadeus, 1809; Elizabeth T., 1811, m. Henry W. Green; Harriet Newell, 1815; Stephen, 1818; William Shurtleff, 1824. STEPHEN, son of above, m. Catherine Harriet, d. of Elkanah Barnes, 1838, and had Adrianna, m. Charles H. Danforth; Stephen H., 1846; Kate Herbert, 1852; Arthur Elbert, 1854. THADEUS, son of 3d Thomas, m. Elizabeth Sylvester, 1772, and had Stephen; Caleb; John; Solomon; Thomas; Thadeus; Bartlett; and Betsey, m. Avery Delano. THADEUS, son of 1st Stephen, m. Mary Ann Warner, and had Elizabeth Davis, 1834, m. George S. Peterson; Mary Ann, 1836; Thadeus, 1838, m. Julia F., d. of Daniel Sears; William H., 1841; and William H. again, 1845. THOMAS, the Elder, son of 1st John, m. Jean, d. of William Nelson, 1672, and had Patience, 1673, m. Ephraim Kempton; John, 1678; Martha, 1680, m. Isaac Doten; Priscilla, 1684; Thomas, 1687; Joanna, 1689, m. Ichabod Paddock of Middleboro'; Jean, 1692, m. Ebenezer Finney of Bristol. THOMAS, son of above, m. Sarah Ford, 1711, and had Hannah, 1713; Sarah, 1716. He m., 2d, Lydia, d. of Stephen Barnaby, 1718, and had James, 1719; Thomas, 1721; Ruth, 1723, m. Paul Doty; Barnaby, 1726; Seth, 1729; Peleg, 1730; Sarah; and Lydia, m. Reuben Besse. THOMAS, son of above, m. Sarah, d. of John Bartlett, 1743, and had John, 1743; Thomas, 1745, m. Mary, d. of Jacob Curtis; Thadeus; Lydia; Sarah, m. Barnabas Churchill; Ansel; Priscilla, 1758; Stephen, 1760; Jerusha, 1763; George, 1765. THOMAS, son of 1st Thadeus, m. Sally Everson, d. of Thomas Savery, and had Thomas. THOMAS, son of 1st Joseph, m. Hannah Dammon, 1732, and had Bathsheba, 1734; Hannah, 1736; Daniel, 1738; and Sarah. WALTER HAMLETT, Kingston, son of Charles Cook, m., 1863, Arabella, d. of Merrick Rider of Plymouth, and had Lucy Delano, 1865; Charles Merrick, 1868. He m., 2d, 1874, Elizabeth, d. of Waterman Brown of Smithfield, R. I. WILLIAM SHURTLEFF, son of 1st Stephen, m. Salina F., d. of Edward Doten, 1845, and had Mary S., 1846; William A., 1847, m. Maggie C. McCartey; Betsey T., 1849; George A., 1856, m. Mercy J. Sharp; David Millard, 1853; Elizabeth Green, 1854; John H., 1856; Arthur N., 1864. WILLIAM, son of 1st Solomon, m. Matilda, d. of Josiah Bradford, and had Matilda B., 1835, m. Weston C. Vaughn; William, 1837; Ellen, 1840. Burke's Landed Gentry states that " Bonham Faunce of Cliffe, Co. Kent, died 1552, and his son, Thomas Faunce, also of Cliffe, died there 1609, at the age of 84, leaving, by his wife Alice, a son Thomas, who entered young into the naval service, and was present at the attack on the Spanish Armada in 1588. This son married Martha, d. of J. Baynard of Shorne, and was Mayor of Rochester in 1609. He had two sons, Robert and Thomas. Thomas joined the Pilgrim Fathers in America in 1640." The error in this statement is in making Thomas, the Pilgrim, the son of Thomas, and making him join the Pilgrims in 1640, when he was born in Plymouth in 1647, and was the son of John who came over in the Ann in 1623. It is possible that John was the son of the Thomas who is said above to have joined the Pilgrims in 1640.

FEAREN, or FEARING, ISRAEL, m., 1722, Martha Gibbs, and had Israel,

1723; John, 1725; Benjamin, 1726; Ann, 1729; Noah, 1732; David, 1733; Elizabeth, 1736. JOHN, an owner of an estate in Plymouth, 1680.

FESSENDEN, NATHANIEL F., m. Betsey H. Clarke, 1835.

FIELD, BENJAMIN F., m., 1833, Eveline, d. of Bartlett Bradford, and had Helen M., m. James M. Atwood; and Bartlett B. JAMES, m., 1779, Mary Drew.

FINN, DANIEL, m., 1760, Mary Sampson.

FINNEY, ALBERT, son of 2d William, m., 1833, Lucinda Thomas, and had Albert Thomas, 1834, m. Carrie C. Paty; Charles Harlow, 1835, m. Rebecca Diman; Costello, 1837, m. Nellie Nelus; Thomas Weston, 1838, m. Isabella Griffith; Rufus, 1841, m. Maria Nelus; Emeline, 1843; Frederick, 1846; Lucinda, 1848; Clara V., 1852. BENJAMIN COOPER, son of Daniel, m., 1833, Elizabeth D. Wood, and had Elizabeth D., m. Joshua Savage and George H. Green. CALEB, son of 2d Ephraim, m., 1799, Lydia Covington, and had Ephraim, 1810, m. Deborah and Susan Churchill; Benjamin D., m. Mary Ann Churchill and Adeline Clark; Caleb; and Mary, m. Reuben Leach. He m., 2d, 1817, Phebe Leonard. CLARK, son of 3d Robert, m., 1797, Polly Wethered, and had Mary, m. William Swift; Experience, m. Nathan Whiting; Everett, m. Susan (Leach) Howland, wid. of Henry; Susan, m. James Finney; John, m. Marcia W. Doten and Deborah Swift; Clark, and George. CLARK, son of 1st Elkanah, m., 1837, Jeanette R. Burt, and had Jeanette, Lucy, Clark, and Elkanah. DANIEL, son of 4th Josiah, m., 1795, Sarah Cooper, and had Benjamin Cooper; Sally C., m. Henry Erland; Polly, and Lydia, both m. Daniel Goddard; Harriet C., 1808; Alice, m. Benjamin Dunham; Olive, m. Peleg Faunce. EBENEZER, from Bristol, m., 1726, Jane Faunce. EBENEZER, from Barnstable, m., 1730, Rebecca Barnes. ELKANAH, son of 3d Robert, m., 1798, Lucy Morton, and had Josiah; Elkanah; Lucy, m. Lemuel Leach; Henry; William; Clark; Betsey, m. David Manter; Marcia, m. Anthony S. Allen. ELKANAH, son of above, m., 1827, Sorena Finney, and had Angeline, m. Augustus Hadaway. ELKANAH C., son of 1st Seth, m., 1829, Hannah Howland. He m., 2d, Serviah Burgess, and had Elkanah and Clarinda. EPHRAIM, son of 1st Ezra, m., 1804, Phebe Wright, and had Phebe, 1804, m. Johnson Davie; Harriet, m. Granville Gardner; Ephraim, m. Salome B. Newell; Susan, 1819, m. James R. Shaw. EPHRAIM, son of 3d John, m., 1776, Mary Bartlett, and had Caleb, Solomon and Sylvanus. EZRA. son of 3d John, m. Hannah, d. of Seth Luce, 1769, and had Hannah, 1769; Ezra, 1776; Seth, Lydia, Ephraim, and Elizabeth. EZRA, son of above, m. Lydia, d. of Andrew Bartlett, 1797, and had Lydia Bartlett, 1799, m. Lemuel Clark; Ezra, 1804; and Eliza, 1804, m. John Bartlett. He m., 2d, Betsey, wid. of John Bishop, and d. of Eliphalet Holbrook, 1808, and had Betsey Bishop, 1809, m. William Sampson Bartlett; Mary Coville, 1811; Caroline, 1814; Ezra, 1817; Mary Coville, 1819, m. Henry Mills; and Caroline, 1822. GEORGE, son of 3d Robert, m. Abigail Finney, 1797, and had Sorena, m. Elkanah Finney; Eunice, m. Nathaniel W. Leonard; Rebecca, m. Nathaniel Clark; David, m. Abigail Warner and Julia A. Morton; James, m. a Wright and Susan Clark; Ezra m. Lydia Benson. GEORGE, son of 1st Clark, m. Mary Clark, 1829, and had George, 1830, m. Abby Warren Morton;

Adaline, 1832, m. Ebenezer Cobb; Alvin, m. Hannah Vaughn and Marcia
W. Doten; Nancy, 1836, m. Augustus Hadaway. GERSHOM of Sandwich, m.
Martha Swift, 1821. HENRY, son of 1st Elkanah, m. Betsey Langford, 1828;
Adaline Howland, 1837; Lucy Manter; Eliza Benson and Abby (Clark)
Thomas; having by his 4th wife Henry Allerton. JOHN, an early settler in
Plymouth, who came from England with his brother Robert and mother, by
wife Christian, had John, 1638. He m., 2d, Abigail Coggin, wid. of Henry,
1650; and, 3d, Elizabeth Bayley, 1654, and had Jonathan, 1655; Robert, 1656;
Hannah, 1657, m. Ephraim Morton; Elizabeth, 1659; Josiah, 1661, Jeremiah,
1662; Joshua, 1665. JOHN, son of above, m. Mary Rogers, 1664, and had
John, 1665; Maltiah, 1666; Joseph, 1668; Thomas, 1672; Ebenezer, 1674;
Samuel, 1676; Mary, 1678, m. John Erland; Mercy, 1679; Rebecca, 1681; Benjamin, 1682; Jonathan, 1684; Hannah, 1687; Elizabeth, 1691, m. David
Bradford. JOHN, son of 1st Josiah, m. Sarah Bartlett, 1721, and had Sarah,
1722, m. Ephraim Holmes; Phebe, 1725, m. Edward Doty; Josiah, 1727;
Ruth, 1728, m. James Doten; John, 1730. He m., 2d, Susanna (Doten)
Pratt, wid. of Elkanah, and had Josiah, 1740; Robert, 1741; Ezra, 1743; Sylvanus, 1746, m. Mary Morton; Ephraim, 1748; and William, 1750. JOHN,
son of above, m. Rebecca Holmes, 1757, and had Ruth, 1757; Sarah, 1758;
Elizabeth, 1761, m. Levi Paty; James, 1764; John, 1766. JOSEPH, son of
2d John, m. Mercy Bryant, 1693, and had Alice, 1694; John, 1696, m. Rebecca
Bryant of Kingston; and Mary, m. Samuel Clark. JOSEPH, m. Esther West,
1706. JOSIAH, son of 1st Robert, m. Elizabeth Warren, 1688, and had Josiah,
1688; Elizabeth, 1690, m. William Bradford; Robert, 1693, m. Ann Morton;
Priscilla, 1694, m. Samuel Marshall; Josiah, 1698, m. Abigail Bryant; John,
1701; Phebe, 1705, m. Jonathan Barnes; and Joshua, m. Elizabeth Pope.
JOSIAH, son of 3d John, m. Alice Barnes, 1763, and had Alice B., 1764, m.
Nathaniel Sylvester; Susanna, m. Ebenezer Sampson; Mary, m. Joseph
Holmes; and Daniel. JOSIAH, son of 3d Robert, m. Rebecca Warren, 1791,
and had Nancy, 1792; Nancy, 1793; Sally, 1795; Betsey, 1797; George, 1800.
He m., 2d, Sally Sylvester, 1806, and had Josiah Morton; Joseph Sylvester;
Josiah Thomas, 1810; Nathaniel Sylvester, 1813. JOSIAH, son of 1st Elka-
nah, m. Nancy Doten, 1821, and had Nancy, m. Gustavus D. Bates; and
Josiah. He m., 2d, Betsey B. Doten, 1832. JOSIAH, m. Mary Thomas, 1726.
JOSHUA, m. Hannah Curtis, 1727. LEAVITT, son of 2d William, m. Mary
Weston, 1834, and had Leavitt Weston, 1837; Lydia W., 1840; and Mary E.,
1850. LEWIS, son of 1st William, m. Betsey Weston, 1804, and had Eliza
Sherman, m. David Harlow; Lewis, m. Rhoda Ann Wood; Pelham, m. Mary
Ann Burgess; Angeline, m. Nathaniel Wood; and Harrison. ROBERT, prob-
ably brother of 1st John, came with his mother from England, m. Phebe
Ripley, 1641, and had Josiah. ROBERT, son of 1st Josiah, m. Ann Morton,
1716, and had Lydia, 1718; Rebecca, m. David Morton, Josiah; Elizabeth, m.
William Wood; and Jerusha, m. Isaac Harlow. ROBERT, son of 3d John,
m. Lydia Clark, 1765, and had Lydia, m. Henry Cassady; Robert, 1768;
Clark, George, Josiah, Elkanah; and Experience, m. Truman Bartlett.
ROBERT, son of above, m. Sarah Leach, 1793, and had Sarah, 1794, m.
Thomas Smith; Lydia, 1797; Christiana, 1799; Susan L., 1802, m. Benjamin

Whiting; Robert, 1804, m. Susan Holmes. ROBERT, son of above, m. Susan Holmes, 1827, and had Robert, m. Isabella Holmes; Susan Holmes, 1844, m. George Pierce; and Lydia, m. John T. Morton. SETH, son of 1st Ezra, m. Sally Churchill, 1798, and had Seth; Elkanah C.; Hannah, m. Ephraim Howard; and Mary Otis, m. Augustus Burgess. SETH, son of above, m. Betsey D. Whiting, 1821, and had Seth, m. Sarah Finney. He m., 2d, Ruth (Nickerson) Howland, wid. of Isaac, and had Sarah C., 1844. SETH of Boston, m. Lydia Eames, 1742. SOLOMON, son of 2d Ephraim, m. Patience Churchill, 1797, and had Solomon, 1798; Sylvanus, 1800; Harvey, 1803; Alvin, 1807; John, 1811. He moved to Ohio with his family and with his nephew Caleb, son of Caleb. THOMAS of Bristol, m. Elizabeth Clark, 1760. WILLIAM, son of 3d John, m. Elizabeth Sherman, 1773, and had Elizabeth, m. Abraham Howland and Nathan Whiting; Sally, m. Ephraim Churchill and Barsillai Holmes; Lewis; and William. WILLIAM, son of above, m. Patty Harlow, 1806, and had William, m. Betsey Hackett; Albert; Leavitt; Cordana, m. Nathaniel Smith of New Hampshire; and Laura, m. Justus Harlow and Benjamin Ransom. WILLIAM L., son of Elkanah, m. Ruth H. Churchill, 1834, and had William; and Ruth H., m. Marsina F. Holmes. There is a will in the probate office of wid. Elizabeth Finney of Plymouth, in which her children are named Mary Holmes, Josiah, Ruth, Thomas.

FISH, CALEB, son of 2d Lemuel, m., 1788, Sarah Paine, and had Caleb, 1790; Polly, 1792, m. Elisha Lapham; Samuel, 1796; Sarah, 1798, m. Nathaniel Holmes. ISAIAH, m., 1745, Hannah Finney. JOHN, from Sandwich, m., 1779, Lydia Pratt. LEMUEL, from Rochester, m., 1731, Deborah Barden. LEMUEL, perhaps son of above, m., 1754, Joanna Doten, and had Jane, 1754, m. William Barnes; Lemuel, 1758; Deborah; Joanna; Samuel, 1762; Lucy, Caleb, Elizabeth, Mary, and Lemuel. NATHAN, m., 1687, Deborah Barnes. NATHAN, m., 1808, Hannah Robinson. SAMUEL, son of Caleb, m., 1818, Ruth Rogers Goddard. THOMAS, from Pembroke, m., 1805, Cynthia Doten. WILLIAM, m., 1746, Mercy Morey.

FISHER, ARCHIBALD, m., 1733, Elizabeth Dean.

FITTS, ALBERT, by wife Triphosa, had Phebe Ann, 1823; George B., 1825; Albert, 1826; Louisa A., 1830; William D., 1834; Charlotte D., 1836; Mary C., 1837; Edwin F., 1839.

FITZGERALD, JOHN, m., 1798, Anna Raymond.

FLANDERS, HENRY, m., 1824, Mary Ann Burbank.

FLAVELL, THOMAS, came in the Fortune 1621, and his wife in the Ann, 1623, but both disappeared before 1627.

FLEMMONS, ROBERT, published to Emily Sturtevant, 1830.

FLETCHER, MOSES, came in the Mayflower, and died the first winter. He m. in Leyden, 1613, Sarah, wid. of William Dingby, having previously m. Maria Evans. THOMAS JEFFRIES, m., 1834, Maria Lindsey.

FLOOD, EDMUND, came in the Ann 1623, and disappeared before 1627.

FOGG, RALPH, by wife Susanna, had Ezekiel, about 1638, and David, 1640, and John. He removed to Salem.

FORD, JOHN, came with his mother Martha, brother William, and sister Martha in the Fortune 1621. MARTIN, from Pembroke, m., 1824, Phebe

Saunders. THEODOSIUS, m., 1758, Hannah Burbank. WILLIAM, brother of John, after going back to England with his mother, returned and settled in Duxbury. By wife Ann he had William; Michael; Melicent, m. John Carver; and Margaret.

FOSTER, CHARLES, Kingston, son of Samuel, m., 1752, Sylvia Delano, and had Lucy, 1753, Lucy, 1756; James, 1758, m. Fear Washburn. DANIEL, m., 1819, Lucy Carver Faunce. JAMES, Kingston, son of Charles, m. Fear Washburn, and had James, 1793, m. Sarah, d. of Daniel Ripley. JOHN, Marshfield, son of 1st Thomas, m. Mary, d. of Thomas Chillingworth, and had Elizabeth, 1664, m. William Carver; John, 1666; Josiah, 1669, m. Sarah Sherman, and removed to Pembroke; Mary, 1671, m. John Hatch of Scituate; Joseph, removed to Sandwich; Sarah; Chillingworth; James, 1683; Thomas, 1686, m. wid. Faith (Oakman) White. He m., 2d, 1702, wid. Sarah Thomas. JOHN, son of above, m. Hannah Studson or Stetson, 1692, and had Hannah, 1694, m. William Bradford and William Partridge; Sarah, 1696, m. William Bartlett; Mercy, m. Ebenezer Morton of Middleboro'; Samuel; John, 1699; Thomas, 1705; Ichabod, 1707; Gershom, 1709; Nathaniel, 1711; Seth, 1713. JOHN, son of Nathaniel, m., 1767, Elizabeth Rider, and had John, 1768; Elizabeth, 1770, m. William Dunham; William; and Peter Thacher. JOSEPH, Kingston, m. Lydia Cook, and had Amelia, 1806, m. Cephas Bumpas; Joseph, 1809; Lydia Cook, 1811, m. Asa Cushman; Sally Cook, 1814, m. Joseph Lovering; Caroline, 1815; Betsey, 1817; Mary Ann, 1819; Lucia Merton, 1821. NATHANIEL, son of 2d John, m., 1735, Mercy, d. of Peter Thacher of Middleboro', and had Mary, 1736, m. Thomas Foster of Marshfield; Mercy, 1737, m. John Russell and William Sever; Nathaniel, 1740; Hannah, 1743; Peter, 1745; and John. He m., 2d, Abigail Billings of Little Compton, 1748, and had Hannah, 1749; Sarah, 1750; Nathaniel, 1751; Abigail, 1753; Gershom, 1754; Hannah, 1755; Betty, 1757. NATHANIEL, Kingston, son of Robert, m. Abigail Adams, and had Nathaniel, 1799, m. Betsey Filkins; Abigail Adams, 1801, m. Jonah Willis; Lucy, 1804, m. Thomas Howard of West Bridgewater. RICHARD, m., 1651, Mary, d. of Robert Bartlett, and had Mary, 1653. ROBERT, Kingston, son of Samuel, by wife Elizabeth, had Robert, 1767; Nathaniel, 1774, m. Abigail Adams; Charles, 1769, m. Sarah Cook; Joseph, m. Lydia Cook; John, and Samuel. SAMUEL, son of 2d John, m., 1722, Margaret, d. of Nathaniel Tilden, and had John, 1724; Samuel, 1726; Margaret, 1728; Charles, 1730, m. Sylvia Delano; Hannah, 1732; Sarah, 1735, m. Joseph Tilden; Robert, 1737; Lydia, 1739. He m., 2d, Margaret Wadsworth. THOMAS, Weymouth, had Thomas, 1640; John, 1642; Increase; Hopestill, 1648; Joseph, 1650. THOMAS, son of 2d John, m., 1725, Lois, d. of Jabez Fuller of Barnstable, and had Thomas, 1727; Elisha, 1730; Gershom, 1733; Lois, 1735, m. Josiah Sturtevant and Samuel Savery; Deborah, 1737, m. Samuel Doggett; John, 1739; Gershom, 1740; Hannah, 1742. He m., 2d, 1744, Mary Morton of Plymouth, and had Mary, 1745; Elizabeth, 1747, m. Nathaniel Jackson; Salome, 1749, m. Thomas Diman; Mary, 1751; Seth, 1753; Job, 1755; Eunice, 1757; Seth, 1758; Philemon, 1760; Susanna, 1762; Eunice, 1764, m. Thomas Prince. THOMAS, son of above, m. 1747, Mercy, d. of Thomas Witherell, and had Hannah, 1748; Lucy, 1750; Thomas,

1751; Priscilla, 1753; George, 1755; Mercy, 1758, m. John May. THOMAS, Marshfield, m., 1757, Mary Foster. WILLIAM, m., 1749, Joanna, d. of James Lanman, and had William, 1749. WILLIAM, from Sandwich, m., 1726, Hannah Rider, and had William, Joseph, and Mary.

FOTTEARS, GEORGE, pub. to Violet Saunders, 1806.

FOUNTAIN, BARNABAS, pub. to Elizabeth Joyce of Marshfield, 1755.

FOWLER, GEORGE P., from Lynn, m. Margaret James, d. of Thomas Bartlett, 1830.

FREEMAN, EDMUND, from Sandwich, m., 1804, Lucy Churchill. JAMES, m., 1808, Abigail Sewell. JONATHAN, m., 1728, Sarah Rider. JONATHAN, m., 1708, Mercy Bradford. JOSHUA, m., 1728, Mrs. Patience Rogers of Ipswich. NATHANIEL, m., 1738, Martha Dunham. NATHANIEL, from New Bedford, m., 1826, Betsey, d. of Benjamin Drew, and had Weston Gales, 1827; Benjamin D., 1829, m. Marcia, d. of Barnabas Ellis; Nathaniel Sydney, 1831, m. Lucy James, d. of Ichabod Bearse; George, 1833, m. Frances O., d. of Alfred Cole; and Abner, 1835.

FRENCH, JOHN, from Hampton, m., 1757, Rhoda Peck.

FRINK, CHARLES H., m. Emma Louise, d. of Samuel Shaw, 1864. THOMAS, by wife Isabella, had Peter, 1746.

FULGHAM, JOSEPH, from England, m. Rebecca Young, 1745, and had Charles, 1749. He m., 2d, Laurana, and had Joseph, 1756; Mercy, 1760; Hannah, 1764.

FULLER, ABIEL, m. Anna Parker and had John, 1704. AMASA, from Attleboro', m., 1817, Nancy Finney. ALDEN, from Sandwich, m., 1784, Mary Ellis. AUGUSTUS H., son of Calvin, m. Bathsheba J., d. of Winslow Holmes, 1854, and had Lydia, 1856. BARNABAS, son of Nathaniel, m., 1748, Rebecca Cushman, and had Jesse, 1748, m. Ruth Prince; Barsillai, 1751; Robert, 1752; Martha, 1754; Azubah, 1756; Joshua, 1758; Rebecca, 1761; Ruth, 1764; Barnabas, 1768. BARNABAS, Barnstable, son of 3d Samuel, m., 1680, Elizabeth Young, and had Samuel, 1681; Isaac, 1684; Hannah, 1688; Ebenezer, 1699; Josiah, 1709. CALVIN, probably from Needham, m. Eliza, d. of Josiah Carver, and had Josiah C.; Theodore S., 1838; Charles; Augustus H.; Ichabod C.; and Robert D., m. Ann R. Drew. CHARLES, son of above, m., 1857, Lucy P., d. of Samuel Barnes, and had Emma Lee, 1861, m. Herbert C. Churchill. CHIPMAN, Halifax, son of Nathan, by wife Thankful, had Ebenezer; Nathan; Ruth; Priscilla; and Nancy. CONSIDER, Kingston, son of 2d Ezra, by wife Sarah, had Ezra, 1791; Elizabeth, 1792; Joann Tilden, 1794; Sarah, 1799; John, 1801; Caleb Tilden, 1802. By a second wife, Hannah, he had Nathan Thompson, 1807, m. Cornelia, d. of Robert Cook; Smith, 1809, m. Eliza Churchill; Daniel W., 1812; Samuel, 1814, m. Maria Churchill; Hannah, 1819; Waldo Ames, 1821, m. Sarah A. Stetson. EBENEZER, son of 5th Samuel, m. Joanna, d. of John Gray, and had Josiah, 1722, m. Lydia, d. of Robert Cushman; Samuel, 1723; Rebecca, 1725; Hannah, 1727; Mercy, 1730; Lois, 1733; Eunice, 1736; Ebenezer, 1738. EBENEZER, son of above, m. Hannah Rider, 1761, and had Ebenezer. EBENEZER, Halifax, son of 4th Jabez, had Ebenezer; Nathan; and Elizabeth. EBENEZER, Halifax, son of above, by wife Deborah, had Priscilla; Lydia; Eunice; Chipman; and Ruth,

m. Elijah Leach. EDWARD came in the Mayflower with his brother Samuel, wife Ann, and son Samuel. His son Matthew followed later. ELEAZER, Kingston, son of 4th John, m. Sally Drew, and had Alexander, m. Rebecca Strong of Sandwich; George; Samuel, m. Catherine Bachelder of N. H.; Hiram; Eleazer; Rebecca, m. John Battles; Hannah Drew, m. Philip Washburn; and Sarah, m. Thomas Staples. ELEAZER, Kingston, son of 2d John, by wife Margaret, had Abigail, 1764; Daniel, 1765; Jenny, 1769; Sally, 1771. EPHRAIM, Kingston, son of 2d Josiah, m. Lydia Johnson, 1812, and had Lydia, 1812, m. Leavitt T. Robbins of Plymouth; Lemuel, 1814; Deborah C., 1816, m. Elbridge Winsor; Content, 1818. EZRA, Kingston, son of Consider, had Sarah Tilden, 1822; Elisha Baker, 1823; Ezra Tilden, 1825; Betsey, 1827. EZRA, Kingston, son of 2d John, by wife Elizabeth, had Samuel, 1759; Susanna, 1761, m. Thomas Hunt; Molly, 1763; Consider, 1765; James, 1768. GEORGE, son of 1st Eleazer, m., 1845, Mary, d. of Joab Thomas of Plymouth, and had Mary, m. Cornelius F. Bradford; and Alice Drew, 1854. ICHABOD C., son of Calvin, m., 1863, Anna E., d. of Edward Winslow Bradford, and had William, 1863; Frank T., 1866; Lothrop, and Alton. ISAAC, Middleboro', son of 2d Samuel, had Micah; Samuel; Jabez, 1723; Isaiah; Isaac, and perhaps others. ISAAC, probably Middleboro', son of above, m., 1737, Sarah Packard, and had Isaac, 1738, m. an Alden; Olive, 1740, m. an Edson; Lemuel, 1742; Isaiah, 1744, m. a Kesan; Sarah, 1746, m. a Truelove; Susannah, 1748, m. a Curtis; Lois, 1751, m. Samuel Dike; Benjamin, 1754, m. an Ames; Rebecca, 1756, m. Josiah Edson. ISSACHER, Kingston, son of 2d John, m., 1748, Elizabeth Doten, and had Lydia, 1749; Isaac, 1751; John, 1753; Deborah, 1756; Noah, 1758; Sylvia, 1760; Issacher, 1762; Elizabeth, 1764. He m., 2d, a Tinkham. JABEZ, Medfield, son of 1st Isaac, m. Elizabeth Hilliard, and had Jonathan; Thomas; and Jabez, 1754, m. Lucy Loring of Duxbury. JABEZ, Kingston, son of above, m., 1781, Lucy Loring of Duxbury, and had Seth, 1784; Nancy, 1784, m. Jesse Inglee; Lucy, 1786, m. Timothy Davis; Betsey, 1789, m. Silas Tobey and Phineas Sprague; Polly, 1791; Sophia, 1798; and Sally, 1801, m. Ebenezer Parker of Charlestown. JABEZ, son of 5th Samuel, m., 1724, Deborah, d. of Ebenezer Soule of Plympton, and had John. He m., 2d, Mercy Gray, and had Thomas, 1734; Joanna, 1736; James, 1737; Jabez, 1739; John, 1741; Mercy, 1747. JABEZ, Middleboro', son of 4th Samuel, had Samuel, 1687; Jonathan, 1692; Mercy, 1696; Lois, 1704; Ebenezer, 1709; and Mary. JAMES, Kingston, son of 4th John, m. Polly, d. of Joshua Delano, and had Emily, m. Charles Robbins; James; and Mary Chandler, m. William Churchill. JOHN, from Kingston, m. Hannah Macomber, 1792. JOHN, son of 5th Samuel, m. 1723, Deborah, d. of Eleazer Ring, and had Eleazer, 1723; Issacher, 1725; John, 1727; Deborah, 1729, m. Kimball Prince; Susanna, 1733, m. Jacob Dingley; Noah, 1734; Ezra, 1736; Consider, 1738, m. Lydia, d. of Samuel Bryant; Eleazer, 1740; Hannah, 1743, m. a Bisbee. He m., 2d, 1764, Mercy Cushman. JOHN, Kingston, son of Consider, m., 1829, Caroline, d. of Daniel Bisbee, and had John Andre, 1830; Caroline Elizabeth, 1833, m. Thomas H. Bartlett; Emily Jane, 1841. He m., 2d, Elizabeth, wid. of Henry Bartlett. JOHN, Kingston, son of 3d Jabez, m. Rebecca Robbins of Carver, and had James, John, and Eleazer.

JOHN, Barnstable, son of Matthew, had, by a 1st wife, Lydia, 1675. By a 2d wife, Hannah, he had Bethiah, 1687; John, 1689; Reliance, 1691. JOHN, Barnstable, son of above, m., 1710, Thankful Gorham, and had Hannah, 1711; John, 1712; Mary, 1713; Bethiah, 1715; Nathaniel, 1716; Thankful, 1718. JOHN, Barnstable, son of 3d Samuel, by wife Mehitabel, had Samuel; Thomas; Shubael; Tnankful; John, 1697; Joseph, 1700; Benjamin, 1701; Mehitabel, 1706. JOHN, Barnstable, son of 1st Thomas, m., 1709, Joanna Crocker, and had Rebecca, ₁709; Bethiah, 1712. JOHN, m. Hannah Morton, 1687. JOSIAH, Kingston, son of 1st Ebenezer, m., 1746, Lydia, d. of Robert Cushman, and had Hannah, 1747; Josiah, 1748, m. Elizabeth Holmes; Zephaniah, 1750, m. Polly Loring; Thankful, 1751, m. Sylvanus Everson; Malachi, 1753; Lemuel, 1755; Lina, 1757; Lydia, 1759, m. Elisha Cushman and Perez Bradford; Joanna, 1761; Joanna, 1763, m. a Sumner of Taunton; James, 1768; and Eleazer. JOSIAH, Kingston, son of above, m. Elizabeth Holmes, 1772, and had John Holmes, 1774; Content, 1777; Josiah, 1783, m. Lucy Bradford of Plympton; Ephraim, 1786, m. Lydia Johnson. JOSIAH, Kingston, son of above, m. Lucy Bradford of Plympton, 1807, and had Josiah, 1808; Charles Warren, 1810; Elizabeth Holmes, 1812, m. Thomas Howe of Boston. JOSIAH C., son of Calvin, m. Elizabeth A., d. of Oliver T. Wood of Plymouth, 1851. He m., 2d, Nancy C., d. of Joseph Bradford, 1854, and had Lizzie May, 1855; Annie B., 1856; Russell B., 1859; Joseph C., 1860; Sarah H., 1866; Joanna B., 1871. MATTHEW, son of Edward, by wife Frances, had Mary, m. Ralph Jones; Elizabeth, m. Moses Rowley; Samuel; Matthew; and John. By a 2d wife, Hannah, he had Ann, m. Samuel Fuller. MATTHEW, Barnstable, son of above, m., 1692, Patience Young, and had Anna, 1693; Jonathan, 1696; Content, 1699; Jean, 1704; David, 1707; Young, 1708; Cornelius, 1710. NATHAN, Halifax, son of 3d Ebenezer, by wife Mary, had Noah, Chipman, Hannah, Asenath, Thomas; and Susanna, m. a Wood. NATHANIEL, son of 5th Samuel, m., 1712, Martha Sampson, and had Sarah, 1712, m. Isaac Sturtevant of Halifax, and perhaps, 2d, Austin Bearce; Ruth, 1714, m. James Cobb; Amos, 1719, m. Abigail Harlow, and a 2d wife, Rachel; Nathaniel, 1721, m. Lydia Perry; Barnabas, 1723, m. Rebecca Cushman; Jesse, 1726, and Samuel, 1729. ROBERT D., son of Calvin, m. Ann R. Drew, 1851, and had Elizabeth, 1852; and George F., 1864. SAMUEL, who came in the Mayflower 1620, had three wives — Elsie Glascock, probably m. in England; Agnes, d. of Alexander Carpenter, m. in Leyden, 1613; and Bridget Lee in Leyden, 1617. Bridget came in the Ann in 1623, with a child, which soon died, and afterwards had Samuel; and Mercy, m. Ralph James. SAMUEL, son of above, Middleboro, by wife Elizabeth, had Mercy, m. Daniel Cole; Samuel, 1659; Experience, m. James Wood; John; Elizabeth, m. Samuel Eaton; Hannah, m. Eleazer Lewis; and Isaac. SAMUEL, son of Edward, m., 1635, Jane, d. of Rev. John Lothrop, and had Hannah, m., 1659, Nicholas Bonham; Samuel; Sarah; Mary, m. Joseph Williams; Thomas; Sarah; Barnabas; and John. He settled in Barnstable about 1641. SAMUEL, Barnstable, son of 1st Matthew, by wife Mary, had Thomas; Jabez; Timothy; Matthias; Abigail; Ann; and Samuel. SAMUEL, Plympton, son of 2d Samuel, m. Mercy Eaton, and had Nathaniel, 1687; Samuel, 1689; William, 1691;

Seth, 1692, m. Sarah, d. of Adam Wright, and wid. Deborah Cole; Ebenezer, 1695, m. Joanna Gray; Benjamin, 1696; Elizabeth, 1697; John, 1698; Jabez, 1701; Mercy, 1702, m. Ebenezer Raymond; James, 1704, m. Judith, d. of Henry Rickard. SAMUEL, Barnstable, son of 3d Samuel, m. Ann, d. of Matthew Fuller, and had Matthew, Barnabas, Joseph, Benjamin, Desire, and Sarah. THOMAS, Halifax, son of Nathan, by wife Hannah, had Thomas, Cyrus, Hannah, Wheelock, Sylvanus, and Joanna, m. Abiel White. THOMAS, Barnstable, son of 3d Samuel, m., 1680, Elizabeth Lothrop, and had Hannah, 1681; Joseph, 1683; Mary, 1685; Benjamin, 1690; Elizabeth, 1692; Samuel, 1694; Abigail, 1696.

GALE, DANIEL, son of Noah, m. Elizabeth, d. of Edward Winslow of Duxbury, and had Betsey Winslow, 1817. He m., 2d, 1819, Harriet Sampson, and had Daniel W., 1822; Stephen, 1827. NOAH, m., 1787, wid. Rebecca Chase, and had Daniel, and Stephen.

GAMBLE, ROBERT, m. Rebecca Polden, and had George, 1759; Mary, 1762.

GAMMON, or GAMMONS, WILLIAM, m., 1736, Hannah Hubbard. WILLIAM, m., 1753, Fear Curtis, and had Rebecca, 1753; and Benjamin.

GARDINE, JACQUES, m., 1778, Rachel Finly.

GARDNER, JOHN, by wife Ann, had William; Susan Gear, 1824; Ann Maria, 1830; John, 1832; Andrew Gear, 1834; Mary Clark, 1837. RICHARD came in the Mayflower 1620, became a seaman, and died abroad. SAMUEL, m., 1682, Susanna Shelley, and had Samuel, 1683; Nathaniel, 1685, m. Sarah Turner; Susanna, 1687; and Thomas. THOMAS, son of above, m., 1737, wid. Hannah Baker of Boston, and had Mary, 1738.

GARLIC, DANIEL, pub. to Amsten Allen, 1788.

GERMAN, WILLIAM, m. Eleanor Thomas, and had William, 1747; Mary, 1748.

GIBBS, ANSELM, from Wareham, m., 1800, Lucy LeBaron. BENJAMIN, from Sandwich, m., 1787, Deborah Pope. BARTLETT, from Wareham, m., 1816, Jerusha Harlow. JABEZ, from Sandwich, m., 1750, Susanna Cornish. JONATHAN, from Wareham, m., 1776, Hannah Clark. JOB, by wife Judith, had Elizabeth, 1706. JOHN, by wife Hesther, had Joshua, 1690; Nancy, 1695; Jane, 1697; John, 1699; Hannah, 1701; Experience, 1703, m. Benjamin Cornish. JOSHUA, son of above, by wife Mercy, had Temperance, 1712; Ruth, 1715; Mercy, 1717; Betsey, 1720; Joshua, 1724; John, 1725; Phebe, 1727. JOSIAH, m., 1752, Mercy Cornish. JOSIAH, from Sandwich, m., 1814, Jane Swift. MICAH, by wife Sarah, had Thankful, 1733. RUFUS, from Sandwich, m., 1815, Abigail Whiting. STEPHEN, m., 1808, Deborah Swift. THOMAS, from Sandwich, m., 1773, Abigail Ellis.

GIFFORD, ABRAHAM, m., 1807, Delia Norris, and had Delia, 1810. DANIEL, from Sandwich, m., 1768, Sarah Valler. GIDEON, from Rochester, m., 1743, Lois Jackson.

GILBERT, DAVID, of Marshfield, a graduate of Harvard, 1797, and a descendant from John of Dorchester, who came over, 1630, in the Mary and John, with sons Thomas, and John, m. Deborah, d. of Rowland Green, and

had Henry Hamilton; Gustavus of Plymouth, m. Caroline Eliza, d. of Isaac
LeBaron; Hannah Green, m. Joseph Warren; David Humphreys of
Plymouth; William Augustus, m. Mary Ann Southers; Deborah Maria;
Sophia Maria, m. Alson Briggs. DAVID HUMPHREYS, son of above, m.
Mary Wales, and had Annie Maria; Mary Jane; Walter L., m. Josephine J.
Peckham; and Elizabeth Arria, m. Andrew T. Holmes. PETER, pub. to
Mary Gamble, 1779.

GILMAN, BENJAMIN J., of Marietta, m., 1790, Hannah Robbins.

GILMORE, SYDNEY, from Taunton, m., 1821, Nancy Thresher.

GINNEY, GINNEY, slave of Joshua Drew, m. Hager, slave of Rev. Nathaniel Leonard, 1747.

GLASSE, GLASE, or GLASS, JAMES, m., 1645, Mary, d. of William
Pontus, and had Hannah, 1647; Wybra, 1649; Hannah, 1651; Mary,
1652.

GLEASON, JAMES G., came to Plymouth, and m. Lucy T., d. of
Joshua Bartlett, 1816. He m., 2d, Asenath, d. of John Paty, 1820, by
whom he had Lucy G., 1821; James H., 1825, m. Catherine Watson; Frances
A., 1826, m. Augustus Tribble; John G., 1827, m. Ellen F. Odell; and Her
bert, 1828, m. Elizabeth Upton. He m., 3d, Phebe, d. of Corban Barnes, and
wid. of Seth Paty, 1835. SAMUEL W., brother of above, came to Plymouth
from Middleboro', and m. Priscilla, d. of Ezra Burbank, 1823. He afterwards
moved with his family to Boston.

GLOVER, GEORGE, m. Mary Fisher, and had Mary, 1758; George, 1761;
Margaret, 1763; Samuel, 1764.

GODDARD, BENJAMIN, son of 1st William, had Nathaniel, 1698; Benja-
min, 1705; Martha; John, 1709; Thomas, 1720. BENJAMIN, son of 1st John,
m. Mary Morton, 1766, and had Daniel; Benjamin; William, m. Sarah
Barnes; Elizabeth, m. John Douglass; and Rufus, m. Elizabeth Bartlett.
BENJAMIN, son of above, m. Hannah Luce, 1792, and had Hannah, m.
Nathaniel Barnes; Betsey; Polly, m. Frank Southworth; Ruth Rogers, m.
Samuel Fish and Oliver Harris; Nancy, m. James Thomas of Taunton; Caro-
line, m. Nathaniel Doten; Emily W., m. Jason Hart; William, m. Lucy
Tripp of New Bedford. DANIEL, son of 2d Benjamin, m. Beulah Simmons,
1794, and had Mary Simmons, 1795; Daniel, 1797, m. Polly and Lydia,
daughters of Daniel Finney; William, 1799; Mary, 1801; Beulah, 1802;
Lemuel Simmons, 1804; Lucia, 1806; Lucia William, 1808, m. William Tribble
and Charles Cushing; Abigail Pierce, 1809, m. Nathan Cushing and William
R. Cox; Mary Ann, 1811; Benjamin, m. Lucy Harlow; and Francis J.
DANIEL, son of above, m. Polly Finney, 1817, and had Mary Ann, m. Ben-
jamin Crandon; Catherine L., m. Henry C. Bisbee; Daniel F., m. Mary E.
Barnes; Harriet; and Charles. He m., 2d, Lydia Finney, 1849. EDWARD,
Cambridge, son of 1st William, m. Susanna Stow, and had Edward, 1698;
Susanna, 1700; Simon, 1702; Benjamin, 1704; David of Leicester, 1700;
William, 1709; Mary, 1711; Ebenezer, 1714. FRANCIS J., son of 1st Daniel,
m. Caroline, d. of Ichabod Harlow, 1833, and had Caroline F., m. Isaac B.
Cummings; Sarah E., m. George A. Whiting; Mary T., m. Walter K. F.
Vila; William, m. Susan H. Bryant; Alice, m. Charles S. Morton; Ella Sophia;

Lucy H., m. Arthur Tribble; and Frank. JOHN, son of 1st Benjamin, m.
Lydia Polden, and had John, 1736; Sarah, 1738, m. Nicholas Spinks; Lemuel,
1739; Benjamin, 1745. JOHN, son of above, m. Mary Polden, 1757, and had
Mercy, Lydia, Mary; John, 1769. JOHN, son of above, m. Grace Hay-
man, d. of John Otis, 1796, and had Harriet Otis, m. Abraham Jackson; and
Mary, m. Arthur French of Boston. JOSEPH, son of 1st William, Cambridge,
m. Deborah Treadway, and had Elizabeth, 1681; Joseph, 1682; James, 1693,
m. Mary Woodward; Robert, 1694, m. Mehitabel Spring; John, 1699, m.
Lucy Seaver and Hannah, wid. of Jonathan Stone and d. of Samuel
Jameson. JOSIAH, Cambridge, son of 1st William, m. Rachel Davis, and
had Ebenezer, 1696; Rachel, 1699; Josiah, 1701; Jane, 1706; Samuel, 1709;
Jane, 1710; Samuel, 1712; Elizabeth, 1714; and William. LEMUEL, son of
1st John, m. Nancy Kinstown, 1762, and had Sarah, 1762; Lemuel, 1764.
ROBERT, Cambridge, son of 1st William, m. Elizabeth Shattuck, and had
Elizabeth, 1714. RUFUS, son of 2d Benjamin, m. Elizabeth Bartlett, 1800.
WILLIAM, Watertown, came from London, 1665, with wife Elizabeth, and
had William, 1653; Joseph, 1655; Robert; Thomas, 1667; Benjamin, 1668;
Elizabeth, 1671; Josiah; and Edward. WILLIAM, son of above, m. Leah
Fisher, and had Elizabeth, 1687; William, 1689; Sarah, 1693; Abigail, 1697.
WILLIAM, son of 3d Benjamin, m. Lucy Tripp, and had Celia. WILLIAM,
son of 2d Benjamin, m, Sarah Barnes and had William.

GOODING, BENJAMIN BARNES, son of 1st John, m. Harriet, d. of Charles
Goodwin, 1841, and had Charles Walter, 1844, m. Mary Ann Twitchell; Benjamin W., 1846, m. Lydia S., d. of Weston Freeman; George, 1850, m. Carrie
F., d. of Darius A. Weston of Taunton; Harriet E., 1848, m. James C. Bates;
Flora Leslie, 1854, m. William G. Josslyn; and John T., 1859. GEORGE
came from England at a date unknown, perhaps about 1720, with wife, whose
maiden name was Deborah Walker, and settled in Dighton. His children
were Mathew, and Deborah. JAMES BUGBEE, Waltham, son of 1st John,
m. Almira T., d. of Henry Morton of Plymouth, 1851. He m., 2d, Rhoda
Ann White of Worcester, and had Frederick Morton, 1859. JOHN, son of
Joseph, m. Deborah, d. of Benjamin Barnes, 1805, and had Deborah Barnes,
1805, m. Aurin Bugbee; John, 1808; William, 1810; Benjamin Barnes, 1813;
Eliza Ann, 1818, m. Orin Alderman; George Barnes, 1822, m. Eliza Merrill
of Concord, N. H.; James Bugbee, 1826. JOHN, son of above, m. Betsey H.,
d. of Ephraim Morton, and had John, 1837; Caroline, 1839. JOSEPH, Taunton, son of Matthew, m. Rebecca Macomber of Taunton, about 1775, and
had Deborah, m. Daniel Standish of Dighton; Joseph, m. Betsey Austin of
Dighton; Elizabeth, m. Luther Perry of Hanover; Josiah, m. Ann Smith of
Dighton; John; Henry, m. Betsey Brown and Rhoda Brown, both of Duxbury; and Alanson, m. Rebecca Kempton and Sophia Hammond. MATHEW,
Dighton, son of George, m. Abigail Richmond of Dighton, probably about
1725, and had George, m. Sarah Reed of Dighton; Joseph; Mathew, m.
Marcia Crane of Berkley; William, m. Bathsheba Walker of Dighton; Job,
m. Polly Clacket of Newport; and Deborah, who m. Jacob Packard of Bridgewater. WILLIAM, son of 1st John, m. Lydia Ann, d. of Putnam Kimball,
1836, and had William Putnam, 1838, m. Nannie E., d. of Edward Stephens;

Edward F., 1840, m. Abby Johnson; Orin L., 1842, m. Jennie Watts, of Waltham; Eugene Russell, 1845; and Mary Emma, 1847, m. Elijah Baker of Wellfleet.

GOODMAN, JOHN, came, unmarried, in the Mayflower, and probably died the first winter.

GOODWIN, ALBERT GARDNER, son of 3d Nathaniel, m. Eliza Huzzey of Nantucket, 1831, and had Nathaniel. He m., 2d., Eliza Ann, d. of Joseph Bartlett, 1840, and had Eliza Huzzey, m. Charles H. Frothingham of Boston. CHARLES, son of 1st Thomas, m., 1815, Hannah, d. of Lewis Harlow, and had Hannah Lewis, 1816, m. Benjamin Bramhall; Hannah, 1819, m. Benjamin Barnes Gooding. CHRISTOPHER, Charlestown, by wife Mary, had Nathaniel, 1643; Christopher, 1645; John, 1647; Timothy, 1649. HENRY, son of 1st William, m. Juliet Almy, d. of Asher Robbins of Rhode Island, and had William LeBaron; Maria Ellery, m. James MacKaye; Juliet Hunter; and Isaac Bradford. HERSEY BRADFORD, son of 1st William, m., 1830, Lucretia Ann, d. of Benjamin Marston Watson, and had William Watson, 1831. He m., 2d., Amelia Mackey of Boston, and had Amelia; and Hersey Bradford, m. Ellen Hopkinson of Cambridge. ISAAC, son of 1st William, m., 1810, Eliza, d. of Abraham Hammatt, and had Lucy Lothrop, 1811, m. Thomas Aurelio of Fayal; Elizabeth Mason, 1813, m. Frantz Graeter; William Hammatt, 1817, m. Nancy Seavey; John Emery, 1820; John Abbot, 1824; and Mary Jane, 1834, m. Loring Henry Austin of Boston. JACOB, Wethersfield, son of last Thomas, m., 1764, Sarah, d. of George Starr, and had Abigail, 1765; Lucy, 1767; Jacob, 1769; Sarah, 1774, m. Robert Hathaway; Maria, 1776; Fanny, 1778, m. Justin Lyman of Hartford; Thomas, 1780; Comfort, 1782, m. Betsey Pinto; Jabez, 1784, m. Sarah Magill. JOHN, Charlestown, son of Christopher, m., 1669, Martha, d. of Benjamin Lothrop, and had Nathaniel, 1672; Martha, 1674, m. Ebenezer Clough of Boston; John, 1677; Mary, 1679, m. Francis Hudson; Benjamin, 1683, m. Frances, d. of John White; Samuel, 1686; Hannah, 1687, m. William Parkman of Boston; Elizabeth, 1694, m. Joseph White of Boston; Mercy, 1689. JOHN, son of 6th Nathaniel, m., 1722, Mercy, d. of William Robie, and had John, 1724; Nathaniel, 1726; William, 1728; Joseph, 1730; Benjamin, 1732, m. Hannah, d. of Lazarus LeBaron. JOHN, Boston, son of 1st John, m., 1700, Mary, d. of Charles Hopkins of Boston, and had John, 1701; Mary, 1702; Martha, 1703; Margaret, 1705; Abiel, 1707. JOHN, son of 1st Nathaniel, m., 1774, Hannah, d. of Thomas Jackson, and had Hannah Jackson; and Sally, 1776, m. Salisbury Jackson. He m., 2d., Fear, d. of John Thacher, 1777, and had Nancy B., m. Thomas Clark; Eliza, m. William Williams; Lydia, m. Dr. Revere; Emily, m. Daniel Poor; Lucy, m. Thomas Gurley. JOHN, m. Dorothy Gibbs of Sandwich, 1817. JOHN MARSTON, son of Lazarus, m., 1832, Emeline Connor Phillio of Amenia, N. Y., d. of Calvin, and had John Marston, 1833; Elizabeth Wheeler, 1835, m. Frank C. Brown; LeBaron, 1838, m. Mary Elizabeth Pierce; Frank, 1845, m. Laura A. Hastings of Brandon, Vt. JOHN ABBOT, Lowell, son of Isaac, m. Martha M. Fisher, and had William Bradford, 1858. JOHN MARSTON, son of John Marston, m., 1862, Helen Louisa, d. of John Van Pelt of Springville, N. Y., and had John Marston, 1863.

LAZARUS, Boston, son of 1st Nathaniel, m., 1779, Eunice, d. of John Marston, and had John Marston, 1780; and Harriet L., m. Winslow Watson. LE-BARON, son of 1st William, m., 1811, Sarah Thomas of Plympton. LEWIS, son of 1st Thomas, m., 1804, Anne Lucas, and had Anna Lewis, 1808; Lewis, 1809; Lucia Ann, 1811, m. Timothy Blish; Horatio, 1813; Isabella Frances, 1816, m. Simeon Dike; Lorenzo, 1818. NATHANIEL, son of 2d John, m. Lydia, d. of Lazarus LeBaron, 1746, and had Nathaniel, 1748; Lydia, 1750, m. Thomas Lothrop and Thomas Page; John, 1751; Lazarus, 1753; William, 1756; Thomas, 1757; Mercy, 1759, m. John Read of Boston; Robie, 1761; Francis LeBaron, 1762, m. Jane Prince, d. of Chandler Robbins; Anna, 1765; George, 1767, m. Lucy Cotton, and removed to Maine. NATHANIEL, son of above, m. Molly, d. of Thomas Jackson, 1769, and had Nathaniel, 1770; Hannah, 1772; Mary Jackson, 1773, m. Gardner Coffin; Thomas, 1775, m. Abigail Croswell; Hannah, 1776, m. John Locke; Lazarus, 1778; Lydia, 1779, m. Joseph Locke. He m., 2d., Ruth, d. of John Shaw of Bridgewater, 1782, and had Ann, 1785, m. Caleb Boutelle; and Ezra Shaw, 1787, m. Ellen Watson, d. of John Davis of Boston. NATHANIEL, son of above, m. Lydia, d. of Nathaniel Gardner of Nantucket, 1794, and had Nathaniel, 1797; Nathaniel Gardner, 1799; Lydia Coffin, 1800, m. Thomas Hedge; Albert Gardner, 1802; Edward Jackson, 1803; Mary Ann, 1805; Nathaniel, 1809. NATHANIEL, son of above, m. Arabella, d. of William White of New Bedford, 1833, and had Ezra Shaw, 1834, m. Susan S. Palmer of New Bedford; Fanny Gibbs, 1836, m. Horace W. Bates; Mary Ann, 1838; and William White, 1840. NATHANIEL, son of 1st William, m. Deborah Cushing, 1852, and had Hersey Bradford, 1853; Thomas Russell, 1854. He m., 2d., Mrs. H. Weaver. NATHANIEL, Middletown, Conn., son of 1st John, m., 1696, Elizabeth Eames, and had Nathaniel, 1696; John, 1699; Elizabeth, 1700; Thomas, 1705. He m., 2d., 1709, Bridget, wid. of John Salisbury. NATHANIEL, Middletown, son of above, m., 1724, Rebecca, d. of Samuel Eaton of Boston, and had Elizabeth, 1726; Rebecca, 1730; Bridget, 1732; Nathaniel, 1736. THOMAS, son of 1st Nathaniel, m. Desire, d. of Joseph Rider, 1779, and had Elizabeth, m. Joshua Bartlett; Mercy, m. Joseph Churchill; Lewis, 1783; Thomas, 1786; Desire Rider, m. Joseph Drew and Samuel Hollis; Charles; Lydia Le-Baron, 1794, m. Joseph Churchill; and Joseph. THOMAS, son of above, m. Abigail Thomas, d. of Thomas Torrey, 1809, and had Betsey Thomas, 1810, m. Caleb Cook Bradford; Abby, 1811, m. Nathan Soule; Lydia, 1813, m. Willard Clark; George Torrey, 1815; Charles T.; Desire, 1820; Haviland Thomas, 1822; Desire, 1824, m. William B. Tribble; Emily F., 1825, m. Ahira Bates. THOMAS, Wethersfield, son of 6th Nathaniel, m. Abigail, d. of Jacob Gale, 1731, and had Abigail, 1732; Jacob, 1733; Gale, 1735; John, 1737; Elizabeth, 1739; Thomas, 1741. TIMOTHY, born 1747, from Charlestown, m, Lucy, d. of Abiel Shurtleff, and had Timothy, 1779; Lucy, 1781, m. Caleb Holmes of Dennis; Nabby, 1785; John, 1788, m. Deborah Barnes; Sally, 1791, m. Joseph S. Read. WILLIAM, son of 1st Nathaniel, m. Lydia Cushing, d. of Simeon Sampson, and had Simeon Sampson, 1782, m. Hannah DeWolf; William, 1783; Isaac, 1785; Charles, 1790; Isaac again; Frederick Henry; Le-Baron; Hersey Bradford; Jane Frances; Mary Ann, m. Thomas Russell; and

Nathaniel, though not in the order named. WILLIAM WATSON, Cambridge, son of Hersey Bradford, m. Emily Jenks, 1835, and had Charles.

GORDON, WILLIAM L., m. Sophia Cotton, 1816.

GORHAM, DAVID, m. Abigail Jackson, and had Mary, 1752; Penelope, 1757. EBENEZER, of Barnstable, m. Hope Carver, 1764. JABEZ, m. Mary Burbank, and had James, 1751; Jabez, 1753. JOHN, son of Ralph, m., 1643, Desire, d. of John Howland, and had Desire, 1644, m. John Hawes; Temperance, 1646; Elizabeth, 1648; James, 1650, m. Hannah, d. of Thomas Huckins; John, 1652, m. Mary, d. of John Otis; Joseph, 1654; Jabez, 1656; Mary, 1659, m. George Denison; Lydia, 1661, m. John Thacher; Hannah, 1663; and Shubael, 1667, m. Priscilla Hussey. Desire was born in Plymouth; Temperance, Elizabeth, James, and John, were born in Marshfield; Joseph was born in Yarmouth; and Jabez, May, Lydia, Hannah, and Shubael were born in Barnstable.

GOULD, JOHN, m. Mary Coombs, 1720. JOHN, m. Sarah Clark, 1731. MARTIN, m. wid. Ruth Barrett, 1836.

GRAY, DAVID, m., 1809, Rebecca Snow. EDWARD, Plymouth, 1643, m., 1651, Mary, d. of John Winslow, and had Desire, 1651, m. Nathaniel Southworth; Mary, 1653; Elizabeth, 1658; Sarah, 1659; John, 1661. He m., 2d., 1665, Dorothy, d. of Thomas Lettice, and had Edward, 1667; Susanna, 1668, m. John Cole; Rebecca, m. Ephram Cole; and Lydia m. Caleb Loring. JOHN, Kingston, son of 2d Samuel, m., 1775, Desire Cushman, and had Molly; John, 1777; Thomas; Betsey, m. Joseph P. Cushman; Lewis, m. Judith Holmes. JOHN, son of Edward, m. Joanna Morton, and had Edward, 1687; Mary, 1688; Ann, 1691, m. Edward Tinkham; Desire, 1693; Joanna, 1696, m. Ebenezer Fuller; Samuel, 1702, m. Patience Wadsworth; Mercy, 1704, m. Jabez Fuller. JOHN, Kingston, son of 1st John, m. 1805, Sarah, d. of Samuel Battles, and had William; John, m. Mary Ann Winsor; Edward, m. Sarah Brown; Sarah Winslow, m. T. C. Holmes and Thomas Newcomb. JOHN, Kingston, son of above, m. Mary Ann Winsor, and had Samuel Winsor, and John Chilton. LEWIS, Kingston, son of 1st John, m., 1812, Judith Holmes. SAMUEL, Kingston, son of 2d John, m. Patience Wadsworth, and had Elizabeth; John, 1729; Mary, m. Benjamin Cook; Samuel; and Wait. SAMUEL, Kingston, son of above, m., 1761, Eunice Delano, and had Mary, 1763; Abigail, 1765; Sally, m. James Winsor; Lucy, m. Zadock Bradford; Elizabeth, m. Stephen Churchill; Hannah, m. Samuel Hunt; Sophia, m. Snow Magoon; and Eunice, m. Ephraim Everson. THOMAS, bro. of Edward, was in Plymouth, 1643, and died, 1654. THORNTON, m., 1728, Katharine White, and had Thornton, 1729. WAIT, Kingston, son of 1st Samuel, by wife Saba, had Waity, m. John Thomas.

GRAYTON, AYLWIN M., from Sandwich, m., 1822, Mary, d. of Joseph Holmes, and had Charles.

GREEN, ASA, son of 2d Richard, m., 1847, Abby T., d. of John Clark, and had Mary J., 1848; George W., 1851; Asa Thomas, 1852; John A., 1856; Franklin A., 1858. HENRY W., m. Elizabeth T., d. of Stephen Faunce, and had Henry T., 1833; Harriet Elizabeth, 1838; Madalena, 1841, m. James M. Beytes; Sarah J., 1847, m. William F. Munroe; Emma, 1848. JOHN, son of

2d Richard, m. Olive, d. of Thomas Holmes, and had Olive Frances, 1845.
JOHN, pub. to Lucy Ripley, 1798. JOSEPH, a holder of real estate in
Plymouth, 1654. RICHARD, in Weymouth, 1622, and afterwards in Plymouth,
where he died. RICHARD, Portland, had by 2d wife, Judith, Amos; Asa;
John; Albert; Mary Jane; and Eunice, m. Thomas Sampson of Plymouth.
By a first wife, Sarah, he had William C.; Richard; and Sarah, m. Thomas
Carter of Virginia.   He moved to Plymouth with 2d wife and family.
RICHARD, son of above, m. Mary T. Green of Portland, and had Rachel,
1828, m. Royal T. Currier of Portland; Mary Jane, 1832, m. Joshua B. Noyes;
Richard F., 1834, m. Mary Kingsbury; Charles G., 1833; George F., 1836;
Albert; Edward E., 1837, m. Betsey A., d. of Thomas Jackson; Caleb B.,
1846, m. the wid. of Edward E.; Gustavus C., 1844, m. Emma F., d. of William
Churchill; William Harrison, 1841, m. Emma F., d. of Levi Robbins; Ervin
M., 1850; and Thomas C., 1852. THOMAS of Wareham, m. Abigail
Holmes, 1817. WILLIAM, m. Desire Bacon, and had Mary, 1710.
WILLIAM C., came from Portland to Plymouth with his father, Rich-
ard, and m., 1829, Marcia C., d. of Nathaniel Holmes, and had William
Henry, 1830, m. Fannie A. Swift; Nathaniel Holmes, 1832, m., in New Bed-
ford, and Marcia Ann, 1835. WILLIAM, from Vermont, m. Phebe, d. of
Nicholas Barker of N. Y., and had George H., 1830, m. Eliza A., d. of
Benjamin Sawyer.

GREENLEAF, JOHN, of Boston, m. Priscilla, d. of Robert Brown, 1743.
WILLIAM of Boston, m. Mary, or Mercy, d. of Robert Brown, about
1750.

GRIFFIN, EBENEZER S., son of Perry, m. Rebeeca, d. of William Rogers,
1841, and had Rebecca Frances, 1845; Francis S., 1848; Frank S., 1849, m.
Ella, d. of Charles Elkanah Barnes; George W., 1851; George Ware, 1853, m.
Exie R. Benson. GEORGE W., from Norfolk, Va., m. Marcia T., d. of Jonathan Harvey, 1832, and had George Henry, 1833, m. Lucia S., d. of Thomas
Jackson; Hannah Elizabeth, 1835; Sarah Williams, 1837; Marcia Ann, 1845,
m. Thomas B. Whiting of Hanover. GRENVILLE, son of Perry, m. Rebecca,
d. of Benjamin Holmes, 1831, and had Grenville, 1833; Benjamin H., 1835,
m. Betsey L. Leach; Edward, 1837; Emeline, 1844, m. Edward F. Phinney;
Rebecca J., 1850. PERRY came from Virginia, and m., 1807, Olive, d. of
Ebenezer Sampson, by whom he had Grenville, and Ebenezer S.

GRIMES, SAMUEL, Boston and Plymouth, by wife Frances, had Mary,
1639; by 2d wife, Ann, he had Susanna, 1657, m. Daniel Vaughn of Newport.

GUNDERSON, CHRISTOPHER, m. Sarah Wright, 1775.

GURNET, JOHN, m. Bathsheba Valentine, 1814.

HACKET, CALVIN, m., 1827, Mary Caswell. JOSEPH, from Taunton, m.,
1815, Deborah Doty.

HACKMAN, THOMAS, m., 1771, Lydia Sutton.

HADAWAY, THOMAS, from Chatham, England, m. Frances, d. of Benjamin Seymour, and had John B. S., 1825, m. Sarah H., d. of Ephraim Morton;
Augustus S., 1833, m. Angeline, d. of Elkanah Finney, and Nancy L., d.
of George Finney; William S., 1848, m. Lucy, d. of Clark Finney;

Susan S., 1854, m. Henry J. Seymour. The two first were born in England.

HADEWAY, JOHN, Barnstable, m., 1656, Hannah Hallet, and had a son, 1657; John, 1658; Hannah, 1662; Edward, 1663.

HALL, EBER, son of 4th William, m. Elizabeth, d. of Thomas Burgess, 1812, and had Mary; Belinda, m., 1st, a Hamilton; and 2d, Daniel Sears; Eber W.; William; and John T. EBER W., son of above, m. Deborah Ann Potter of Needham, 1845, and had Helen M., m. Sylvanus F. Swift; Edwin F., 1848; William H., m. Catherine M. Rogan; Ann Elizabeth, 1854, m. Nathaniel B. Pratt and Samuel Nutter; Almira D., 1857, m. Otis H. Raymond; Walter D., 1859, m. Emma F., d. of Benjamin Holmes; and John T., 1862. ICHABOD, m. Priscilla Cowit, 1804. ISAAC T., son of James, m. Nancy Rickard, and had James M., 1859; and Nancy E., 1861. He m., 2d, Mary E., d. of Thomas C. Atwood, 1866, and had Mary T., 1866; and Herman W., 1868. He m., 3d, Eliza, d. of William Cripps, 1872, and had Mary E., 1872; Eldora M., 1874; Emma F., 1876; and Carrie A., 1880. JAMES, son of 2d John, m. Mary, d. of Samuel N. Holmes, and had Isaac Thomas; James M., 1841; and Mary E., 1846, m. Charles N. Bourne. JASPER, m. Violet Otis, 1782. JOHN, Yarmouth, from Coventry, England, had two wives, Bethiah and Elizabeth; and had Joseph, 1642; John, 1645; Elizabeth, 1648; William, 1651; Samuel; Benjamin; Nathaniel; Elisha; and Gershom. JOHN, son of 1st Luke, m. Mary Pixley, 1805, and had Wendell, 1806; James, 1808; Eliza, 1809, m. Robert King; William, 1810; Hannah, 1812; Reuben, 1814; John, 1815; Lewis, 1817; and Mary Ann, 1819, m. Guilford E. Cunningham. He m., 2d, 1822, Hannah, d. of Cornelius Holmes. JOHN T., son of 1st Eber, m. Betsey, d. of Joab Thomas, 1843, and had Laura, 1844, m. Joseph B. Whiting; and Emma S., 1850. JOHN F., son of 6th William, m. Abby T. Dunning, 1865, and had Herbert D., 1870. He m., 2d, Addie E., d. of Charles Nelson, 1875. JOHN, m. Mary Leach, 1761. JOSEPH, son of a John of Rochester, and grandson of 1st John, m. Mary Morton, 1711. JUDAH, son of an Elisha of Yarmouth, and grandson of 1st John, m. Mehitabel Faunce, 1714, and had Judah, 1714. LEWIS, son of 2d John, m. Mary Ann Cunningham, 1840, and, 2d, Mehitabel P., d. of Oliver Holmes, 1860, by whom he had Lucy K., 1861; Mariana T., 1863; and Addie. LUKE, Rochester, son of 3d William, m. Elizabeth Westgate, and had William; Luke; Seth; Hannah, m. a Westgate; Lucy, m. a Blake; Wealthea, m. a Pixley; Huldah, m. a Crossman of Taunton; and Rhoda, m. John Johnson of Charlestown. LUKE, of Duxbury, or Marshfield, m. Lucy Ann (Joyce) Burbank, wid. of John, 1844. NATHAN, from Cape Cod, m. Sally, d. of Thomas Burgess, 1827, and had Nathan Thomas, 1828. PRINCE of Bridgewater, m. Alice Crook, 1785. REUBEN, son of 2d John, m. Joanna King, 1836, and had Joanna, 1837; Hannah H., 1839; and James K., 1850. ROBERT B., son of Charles of Boston, and wife Catherine, d. of Robert and Sally (Cunningham) McNeil, m. Abby Morton, d. of Nathaniel Morton Davis, 1841, and had Alice B., 1842, m. Dwight Faulkner. The grandfather of Robert B., was Stephen, m. Margaret Cunningham, who was the son of Pelatiah, who m. Sarah, d. of Samuel and Mary (Breck) Paul of Dorchester; the father of Pelatiah was Stephen, the son of Stephen of Concord, who m., 1663, Ruth, d. of Dolor Davis. SYLVANUS, brother of Judah, m. Elizabeth Doggett, 1725. WENDALL, son of 2d John, m. Mary Ann Gray, 1829, and had Mary W., 1830, m. Edward L. Doten. He m., 2d, Betsey D. Mayo, 1835, and had John Atwood, 1838; Harriet C., 1840, m. Shepard B. Wilbur of Brockton; and Seth M., 1847. WILLIAM, Rochester, son of 1st John, by wife Rebecca, had William, and probably others. WILLIAM, son of above, lived in Rochester, and had a son William. WILLIAM, Rochester, son of above, m. Betsey Haskins, and had William, and Luke. WILLIAM, son of above, m. Temperance Saunders, and had William; Eber; Temperance, m. Levi Haskins of Marion; Orpha, m. John Haskins and John Hammond; Ruby, m. Levi Maxim and a Sears; and Cynthia. WILLIAM, son of 1st Luke, m. Lucinda Maxim, 1808, and had Eunice R., m. Elijah Caswell of Middleboro. WILLIAM, son of 2d John, m. Susan, d. of Nicholas Spinks Bagnall; and had Susan Williams, 1834, m. Robert B. Leach; John Frederick, 1837; William, 1839; Lucy Ann, 1840; Georgiana, 1842; William C., 1844; Edward W., 1845; Leonice A., 1848; Alvira, 1851; Charles H., 1852; Edna Bagnall, 1854; Emily Judson, 1856; and Henry W., 1860.

HALLET, ANDREW, came to Plymouth from Lynn, 1637, and afterwards removed to Sandwich and Yarmouth. His children were Dorcas, 1646; Jonathan, 1647; John, 1650; Mehitabel; Abigail, m. Jonathan Alden; and Ruhamah, m. Job Bourne, all probably by wife Ann, and born in Yarmouth.

HAMBLETON, SAMUEL, m., 1730, Elizabeth Jones.

HAMBLIN, ELKANAH, from Pembroke, m., 1734, Margaret Bates.

HAMILTON, BENJAMIN, m., 1833, Belinda Hall.

HAMMATT, ABRAHAM, m., 1748, Lucy, d. of Consider Howland, and had Abraham, 1750; William; Lucy, m. Nathaniel Lothrop. ABRAHAM, son of above, m., 1774, Priscilla, d. of Lazarus LeBaron, and had Abraham; William; Howland; Sophia; George; Lucia, m. William Simmons; Eliza, m. Isaac Goodwin. WILLIAM, son of 1st Abraham, m. Ann Sigourney of Boston, and had Ann Sigourney, m. George Bond of Boston. WILLIAM, son of 2d Abraham, m. Esther Parsons, and had Hannah Phillips; William; Esther Parsons; Ann Parsons, m. Edward F. Hodges of Boston.

HAMMOND, FAUNCE, from Rochester son of Jabez, m., 1761, Mary Holmes. JABEZ, m., 1736, Abiah Faunce, and had Faunce. JOB, m., 1743, Hannah Quoy.

HANBURY, WILLIAM, Plymouth, Duxbury, and Boston, m., 1641, Hannah Souther, and had William and two others.

HANCKFORD, RICHARD, died 1633, without family.

HANKS, BENJAMIN, by wife Mary, had Isaac, 1725; Abigail, 1726; William, 1728; John, 1730; Richard White, 1734; Uriah, 1736; Benjamin, 1738; Mary, 1741; Silas, 1744. JOHN, in Plymouth, 1633.

HARDING, CALEB, m., 1825, Jane F. Saunders.

HARLOW, AMAZIAH, son of 1st John, m., 1746, Lois Doten, and had Amaziah, 1747; Lois, 1749. AMAZIAH. son of above, m., 1786, Lucy Torrey, and had Amaziah. He m., 2d, 1796, Martha Albertson. AMAZIAH, son of above, m., 1823, Ruth R. Drew, and had Martha D. W., m. John Boutell.

ANSEL, son of 1st Jonathan, m., 1770, Hannah Barnes, and had Rebecca, 1770; Sarah, 1773, m. Oliver Kempton; Hannah, 1775, m. Luke Perkins; Jedidah, 1778, m., Hosea Vaughn; Ansel, 1780; Stephen, 1783; Mary, 1785. He probably m., 2d, 1791, Thankful Bartlett. BENJAMIN, Middleboro', son of 3d William, m. Elizabeth, d. of Edward Stephens, and had Kesiah, m. John Atwood of Plympton; Stephen, and Elizabeth. BRADFORD, East Bridgewater son of 2d Isaac, m., 1807, Betsey, d. of Solomon Leonard, and had Solomon Leonard, 1808; Isaac, 1810; Louisa, 1812; Joanna W., 1815; Huldah L., 1817; Isam B., 1819; Benjamin F., 1823; Lavina W., 1824; Elizabeth B., 1829; Joseph S., 1837. BRANCH, son of 3d James, m. Rebecca H., d. of Sylvanus Jones of Sandwich, and had Richard W., 1829; Lydia T., 1831; Rebecca C., 1833; Susan W., 1835; Minerva E., 1837; Sarah W., 1838; William G., 1840; Hannah J., 1842. DAVID, son of 1st Jesse, m., 1823, Eliza S. Finney, and had David L., m. Lucy Cook of Kingston; Isaac Newton, m. Catherine Weston; Ezra, m. Catherine Covington; Henry M., m. Sarah F. Cowen; Ann Eliza; Hannah; Pelham W., m. Etta H. Mayo; Edward P., m. Nancy Sanford of Taunton; William H., m. Annie Gibbs of Providence. EBENEZER, son of 2d John, m., 1758, Rebecca Bartlett and had Rebecca, 1759, m. Ichabod Holmes; Mary, 1761; Ebenezer, 1765. He m., 2d, 1766, Lydia Doten, and had Zebulon, 1768; Andrew, 1770; Ebenezer, 1772; Zebulon, 1772; Philemon, 1774; George, 1778; James, 1781; Asa, 1784; and Hosea. ELEAZER, son of 1st Samuel, m. Hannah, d. of Benoni Delano of Duxbury, and had Eliphas, 1716; Lemuel, 1717, m. Joanna, d. of Ichabod Paddock; Eleazer, 1719, m. Abigail Thomas of Marshfield, Abigail Clark of Plympton, and Mrs. Dabney of Boston. He m., 2d, 1720, Hannah Pratt of Plympton, and had Elizabeth, 1721; Patience, 1722, m. Josiah Churchill. ELLIS, son of 3d Ezra, m., 1785, Sarah Harlow, and had Bradford, 1785; Sally, 1787, m. Cornelius Morey; Ellis, 1790; Jabez, 1793, m. Hannah Harlow; Lucia, 1795. ELLIS J., son of Reuben, m., 1822, Jerusha, d. of Thomas Paty, and had Thomas Paty. EPHRAIM, son of 1st Sylvanus, m., 1794, Jerusha, d. of Thomas Doten, and had Jerusha Howes, Ephraim, Thomas Doten, and Jabez. He m., 2d, Ruth, d. of William Sturtevant of Carver, and had Jane, 1808, m. Atwood L. Drew; Hannah Shaw, 1810, m. George Adams; Ruth Sturtevant, 1815; Zilpha Washburn, 1818, m. Nathaniel Bourne Spooner; Desire Sampson, 1821. EZRA, son of 2d John, m., 1767, Susanna, d. of Nathaniel Warren, and had Susanna, m. Lemuel Leach; Ezra; Martha, m. Benjamin Whiting; and John. EZRA, son of above, m., 1797, Lydia Davie, and, 1818, Rebecca Dike, without issue. EZRA, son of 7th William, m., 1768, Elizabeth, d. of Benjamin Ellis, and had Joseph, Ellis, Thomas, Lydia, Betsey, William, Otis, Samuel, Hannah, Josiah, Patience, Sally, and Ezra. GEORGE, son of 3d Samuel, m., 1813, Lydia, d. of Nathaniel Ellis, and had Nathaniel Ellis, 1813, m. Julia A. Whiting of Bangor; Lydia, 1819, m. Albert Tribble; Esther, 1821, m. John Henry Hollis; George Henry, 1823, m. Sarah E. Morton; Samuel, m. Mary H. Bradford. ICHABOD, son of 3d Samuel, m., 1803, Patience, d. of Abner Holmes, and had Jane D., 1803, m. John K. Wight; Ansel H., 1804, m. Bathsheba James, d. of William Holmes, and Mary Otis, d. of Joseph White; Albert, 1807; Ichabod, 1809; Abner H.,

1813, m. Mary A. Snow and Jane Randall; Caroline, 1817, m. Francis J. Goddard; Mary, 1812, m. Bradford L. Battles; Huldah H., 1821, m. Simeon Richardson of Medford; George H., 1823. ISAAC, son of 1st Robert, m. Jerusha Finney, and had Isaac, Betsey, Jerusha, William, Rebecca; Deborah, m. Caleb Raymond; and Lemuel. ISAAC, son of 5th William, m., 1770, Martha Swinerton, and had Isaac, 1771; Stephen, 1775; Joseph, 1776; Bradford, 1778; Sylvanus, 1780; Lewis, 1783; Timothy, 1786; Bradford, 1788. ISAAC, East Bridgewater, son of 1st Joseph, m., 1831, Mary Ann, d. of Nathaniel Adams of Barnstead, N.H., and had Joseph Henry, 1833; Mary Ellen, 1837. IVORY, son of 2d Jonathan, m., 1807, Lucy, d. of Isaac Barnes, and had Ivory L., m. Rebecca B. Holmes; Justus, m. Laura Finney; Lucy, m. Benjamin Goddard. JABEZ, son of 2d John, m., 1752, Experience Churchill, and had Jabez, 1754; Experience, 1756; Nathaniel, 1758, m. Mary Shaw; Rebecca, 1760; John, 1762. JAMES, son of 1st Robert, m., 1759, Jerusha Holmes, and had Nathaniel, 1759; Susanna, 1761, m. Nathaniel Churchill; James, 1763, m. Sarah Blackmer; Reuben, 1766, m. Hannah Johnson. He m., 2d, 1770, Hannah Delano. JAMES, son of 5th William, m., 1780, Hannah, d. of Benjamin Bagnall, and had James, 1781; Hannah, 1782, m. Job Churchill; Clarissa, 1785, m. Thomas Spear; Benjamin, 1788; Simeon, 1791; Harriet, 1794, m. Joshua Kneeland. JAMES, son of 1st James, m., 1784, Sarah, d. of Branch Blackmer, and had James, 1785; Sarah, 1790; James, 1795; Nathaniel, 1798, m. Margaret Bartlett; Branch, 1801, m. Rebecca H. Jones. JAMES, son of 1st Nathaniel, m. Hannah Shaw, and had Mary, 1720, m. Lemuel Vaughn and Jacob Staples; Abigail, 1722, m. Amos Fuller; Hannah, 1723, m. Theophilus Rickard; James, 1725; Jonathan, 1726; Persis, 1728, m. Isaac Shaw, Lemuel Rickard and Perez Churchill; James, 1730, m. Mercy Cushman and wid. Sarah Bryant, d. of Edward Sears of Halifax; Abner, 1733, m. Rachel, d. of Samuel Rickard; William, 1734; Sarah, 1736, m. Benjamin Bryant. He m., 2d, Mehitabel Finney, and had Barnabas, 1750, m. Mary West of Kingston. JESSE, son of 1st Sylvanus, m., 1784, Hannah Turner, and had Sylvanus, 1786; Hannah Turner, 1789; Elizabeth, 1791, m. John Holmes; Jesse, 1793; Lucy, 1795; Desire, 1797; David, 1799; Barnabas, 1801; Isaac Newton, 1805; John, 1807. JESSE, son of above, m., 1819, Mary Lothrop, d. of William Nelson, and had Jesse, m. Sarah F. Cobb; William Nelson; Edward, m. Laura Ann. d. of Coomer Weston; Mary Lothrop, and Lothrop. JESSE, son of 2d John, m., 1762, Elizabeth Sampson, and had Elizabeth, 1762, m. John Torrey. He m., 2d, Sarah, d. of John Cotton. JOHN, son of 1st Samuel, m., 1706, Martha Delano, and had John, 1707; Elizabeth, 1709; Rebecca, 1711; Martha, 1715; Mary, 1717; Amaziah, 1721; Thankful, 1724. JOHN, son of above, m., 1731, Mary, d. of Joseph Rider, and had Jabez, 1732; John, 1734, m. Rebecca Howes; Ebenezer, 1735; Sylvanus, 1738; Jesse, 1739; Ezra, 1741; Martha, 1744, m. Isaac Cole and Ebenezer Cobb; Mary, 1747; Lydia, 1748, m. William Davie; Mary, 1750, m. Joshua Bartlett; Zacheus, 1753, m. Hannah, d. of Joseph Barnes; Lazarus, 1755, m. Sarah, d. of Jonathan Darling and wid. Lucy Bradford. JOHN, son of 1st Ezra, m., 1810, Anna, d. of John Burgess, and had Susan Leach, 1814, m. Allen Crocker Spooner; John, 1812, m. Paulina Nickerson. JOHN, son of

2d Jonathan, m., 1805, Betsey Harlow, d. of John Torrey, and had William, 1805, m. Caroline Porter of Wrentham. He m., 2d, Elizabeth, d. of Jesse Harlow, 1809, and had Betsey Torrey, m. Edwin Morton; Marcia Ann, m. Asaph Gray of Brewster; Leonice, m. Amasa Churchill; John H., 1821, m. Mary, d. of James Morton; Lucy, 1823; Mary L., 1825; Samuel H., 1827. JOHN, m., 1749, Lydia Holmes. JONATHAN, son of 1st Thomas, m., 1742, Sarah, d. of Elisha Holmes, and had Ansel, 1743; Jonathan, 1746; Sarah, 1751, m. Solomon Thomas; Jedidah, 1755, m. Lemuel Barnes; Clarissa, 1755, Lucy, 1758, m. William Holmes; Mary, 1761, m. James Carver. JONATHAN, son of above, m., 1770, Betty, d. of John Blackmer, and had Mercy, 1770; Lewis, 1772; Eleazer, 1774; Jonathan, 1776; John, 1778; Lewis, 1780; Ivory, 1783. JOSEPH, East Bridgewater, son of 2d Isaac, m., 1803, Sarah Herrick of Beverly, and had Isaac, 1804; Joseph Swineton, 1810. JOSEPH, son of 3d Ezra, by wife Susanna, had Joseph, 1796; Thomas, 1798, m. Lucy, wid. of Hiram Harlow; Cynthia, 1801; Hiram, 1803; Harriet, 1805; Susanna, 1808; Caroline and Dennis, twins, 1811. JOSEPH, son of above, m. Hannah Ellis, and had Charles F., 1829 m. Reenet E., d. of Joseph Churchill; Thomas C., 1830, m. Sarah D. Swift. LAZARUS, son of 2d John, m., 1779, Sarah, d. of Jonathan Darling, and had Grace; Lazarus, m. Lucy Bradford; Lot; Sarah, m. Peter Holmes; Martha, m. William Finney. LEMUEL, from Plympton, m., 1768, Joanna Holmes. LEVI, m., 1774, Mary Barnes. LEWIS, son of 2d Jonathan, m., 1796, Hannah, d. of Stephen Churchill, and had Lewis; Lucy C., m. Isaac Barnes; Hannah, m. Charles Goodwin; Betsey, m. Jabez Harlow; John, m. Jane C. Bradford. LEWIS, son of above, m., 1821, Betsey, d. of Barnabas Holmes, and had Elizabeth Frances, 1822; Lewis Otis, 1824; Lucy James, 1827, m. Chauncey M. Howard; Charles Goodwin, 1830, m. Elizabeth, d. of Seth Mehuren; and Barnabas L., m. Catherine W. Cunningham. LEWIS, Bridgewater, son of 2d Isaac, m. Lydia, d. of Francis Bent, and had Thomas Paty, 1809; Lewis, 1811; and William. LOT, son of Lazarus, m., 1803, Polly Boylston, and had Rebecca M., m. James Diman; Mary B., m. William Sylvester; Nancy, m. David Leach. NATHANIEL, son of 1st William, m. Abigail Burt, and had Abigail, 1693, m. Robert Cook; Nathaniel, 1696; James, 1698. NATHANIEL, son of above, m. 1717, Patience Lucas, and had Nathaniel, 1726, m. Sarah, d. of Isaac Binney; Ephraim, and Susanna. NATHANIEL, son of Seth, m., 1796, Sarah, d. of Elnathan Holmes, and had Rebecca; Nathaniel, m., 1st Sylvia Lincoln of New Bedford, 2d, Hannah Stanton of Stonington, and 3d, a wife Melinda of Stonington; Benjamin, m. Sarah Potter of Stonington; Abner, m., 1st, Julia Wood of Middleboro', 2d, Sylvia (Doty) Freeman of Mattapoisett; Mary Olive, m. Solomon Faunce; Eliza Warren, m. Hallett Cannon of Mattapoisett; Caleb Boutelle, and Sally. He m., 2d, Betsey (Vaughn) Harlow, wid. of his brother Benjamin, and had William, m. Adeline Pulsifer of Stonington; Sarah V., m. Asa Kendrick; and Catherine and Samuel, twins. NATHANIEL, son of Jabez, m., 1782, Mary Shaw, and had Mary, 1783; Nathaniel, 1785. NATHANIEL, son of 3d James, m., 1819, Margaret Bartlett, and had Betsey Morton, 1820; James Morton, 1825; Margaret, 1835. REUBEN, son of 1st James, m., 1790, Hannah Johnson, and had Nancy, m. Nathaniel Hueston; Kimball, m. Nancy

C., d. of Rufus Bartlett; Hannah, m. a Cushing; Jerusha, m. a Gibbs; and Ellis J. ROBERT, son of 2d William, m. Susanna, d. of John Cole of Plympton, and had Ebenezer, 1719, m. Maria Morey; Benjamin, 1723; Isaac, 1725; Robert, 1728; Reuben, 1730; James, 1732; Susanna, 1736; Mary, 1739, m. James Hovey; Elizabeth, 1743; Submit, 1745. He m., 2d, Remembrance Wethered, and had Susanna, 1750, m. William King; Lydia, 1752. ROBERT, son of above, m. Jean West, and had Sarah, 1751; Robert, 1755; Sarah, 1757. SAMUEL, son of 1st William, by wife Priscilla, had Rebecca, 1678, m. Thomas Taber. By a 2d wife, Hannah, he had John, 1685; Hannah, 1689; Samuel, 1690, m. Mary Barstow; William, 1692; Eleazer, 1694; Priscilla, 1695. SAMUEL, son of 3d William, m. Mercy, d. of William Bradford, and had Samuel, 1747; Mercy, 1749; Mercy, 1752; Jerusha, 1754; Josiah, 1756; James, 1757; George, 1759. He m., 2d, 1763, Mary Morton. SAMUEL, son of above, m., 1768, Remembrance, d. of Ichabod Holmes, and had Jane, 1768, m. Seth Doggett; Samuel, 1776, Ichabod, 1779; Henry, 1782; Nancy, 1785; George, 1789; and Remembrance, 1775. SETH, son of 3d William, m., 1763, Sarah, d. of Nathaniel Warren, and had Benjamin, 1764; Seth, 1766, m. Priscilla Nelson; Elizabeth, m. George Churchill and Ephraim Leonard; Sarah, m. Oliver Kempton; Nathaniel; Mercy; Benjamin, 1782. SIMEON, m., 1775, Susanna Churchill. SYLVANUS, son of 2d John, m., 1758, Desire, d. of Noah Sampson, and had Jesse, 1761; Sylvanus, 1764, m. Catherine Manter; Desire, 1767, m. Lemuel Stephens; Ephraim, 1770. SYLVANUS, son of 1st Jesse, m., 1809, Hannah Weston, and afterwards Elizabeth A. Lucas, and had a son Sylvanus, now living in Elgin, Illinois. SYLVANUS, East Bridgewater, son of 2d Isaac, m. Polly, d. of Francis Bent, and had Sylvanus, 1805, m. Hope Shaw; Lewis, 1806; Stephen, 1808; Francis, 1810; Columbus, 1814; Mary, 1816; Sylvia, 1818; Sally, 1820; Southworth, 1824. THOMAS, son of 2d William, m. Jedidah, d. of Eleazer Churchill, and had Thomas, 1712; Elizabeth, 1715; Jonathan, 1718, m. Sarah Holmes; Lydia, 1721; Eleazer, 1723; Jedidah, 1726, m. Abner Sylvester; Nathaniel, 1729. THOMAS, son of above, m. Patience Tilson of Plympton, and had Elizabeth, 1738, m. John Totman; Patience, 1741; Elijah, 1743, m. Patience Drew; Mary, 1746; Thomas, 1751; Abigail, 1753. THOMAS, son of 3d Ezra, by wife Joanna, had Betsey, 1799. TIMOTHY, East Bridgewater, son of 2d Isaac, m. Huldah, d. of Ziba Howard, and had Calvin Howard, 1806; Martha Swinerton; Lucy Conant, 1811; Huldah Howard, 1813; Harrison Gray; Jonathan Bosworth; Harriet Newell, 1827; Almira Niles. WILLIAM, appeared a young man in Lynn in 1637. He removed to Sandwich, and then to Plymouth, where he m., 1649, Rebecca, d. of Robert Bartlett. His children were William, 1650; Samuel, 1652; Rebecca, 1655; William again, 1657. He m., 2d, Mary, d. of John Faunce, 1658, and had Mary, 1659, m. Samuel Durham; Repentance, 1660; John, 1662; Benjamin; Nathaniel, 1664. He m., 3d, 1665, Mary, d. of Robert Shelley of Scituate, and had Hannah, 1666; Bathsheba, 1667, m. Richard Sears of Yarmouth, 1696; Joanna, 1669; Mehitabel, 1672; Judith, 1676, m. Joseph Church. WILLIAM, son of above, m. Lydia, d. of Thomas Cushman, and had Elizabeth, 1683, m. Thomas Doty; Thomas, 1686, m. Jedidah Churchill; Robert; Isaac; Lydia, m. Barnabas Churchill; Mary; Rebecca, m. Jabez

Holmes; and William. WILLIAM, son of 1st Samuel, m. Mercy, d. of John
Rider, and had Sarah, 1715, m. Eleazer Churchill; Benjamin, 1716; William,
1718; Hannah, 1720, m. Ebenezer Sampson; Mercy, 1722, m. Sylvanus
Holmes; Kesiah, 1723; Samuel, 1726; Phebe, 1728, m. Edward Stephens;
Rebecca, 1732; Seth, 1736. WILLIAM, son of 2d William, m. Joanna Jack-
son, and had Joanna, 1714, m. Daniel Snell; William, 1715; Mary, 1717, m.
Sylvanus Holmes; Hannah, 1721, m. Stoughton Willis and John Snow, both
of Bridgewater; Lydia, 1724; Isaac, 1726; Sarah, 1728. WILLIAM, son of
above, m., 1742, Hannah, d. of Henry Littlejohn, and had Sarah, 1743, m.
Isaac Mackie; William, 1744; Isaac, 1746, m. Martha Swinerton; Zephaniah,
1748, m. Patience, d. of Josiah Johnson; Hannah, 1751; Simon, 1754, m.
Susanna Churchill; Mercy, 1756; James, 1760, m. Hannah Bagnall. WIL-
LIAM, son of above, m., 1764, Sarah Holmes, and had Sarah, 1765; Deborah,
1768; William, 1771; Deborah, 1778; Southworth, 1781. WILLIAM, Middleboro', son of 3d William, m. Hannah Bartlett, and had Joseph, Ezra, Hannah, Mary, William, Joshua, and Ephraim, WILLIAM, Middleboro', son of
above, m. Olive Jackson, 1810, and had William J., m. Susan A. Sampson;
Olive J., m. Obadiah King. WILLIAM, son of 1st Isaac, m., 1780, Susanna,
d. of Thomas Harlow, and had William. WILLIAM, son of above, m., 1816,
Sophia Holmes, and had Melintha; William, 1817; William, 1820; Sarah W.,
1823, m. Cornelius Briggs; Sophia, 1828, m. David Clark; Betsey L., 1835, m.
William W. Doten. ZEPHANIAH, son of 5th William, m., 1772, Patience, d.
of Josiah Johnson, and had Zephaniah, 1773; Patience, 1775, m. Lemuel
Holmes; Freeman, 1776; Josiah, 1780; Betsey, 1782, m. William Tribble;
Elizabeth, 1787.

HARMON, JOHN, Plymouth, 1643; Duxbury, 1657, perhaps son of a James
who came from London, 1635, with a son John, twelve years of age, and a d.
Sarah, ten years of age, m. a d. of Henry Sampson of Duxbury, and removed
to Saco.

HARRINGTON, JOSEPH, from Douglass, m., 1804, Sally Raymond.

HARRIS, JOSEPH, m., 1810, Desire Harlow. OLIVER, from New Bedford,
m., 1835, Ruth Rogers (Goddard) Fish, wid. of Samuel, and d. of Benjamin
Goddard, and had William O., m. Hannah H., d. of Henry Weston; Christopher T., m. Miranda B., d. of John Atwood. OWEN, m., 1791, Mercy
Holmes.

HART, JASON, m., 1833, Emily W. Goddard, and had Orin B., Emily,
Martha Washington, Mary Jason, 1847, Anna B., 1850.

HARVEY, BENJAMIN, came to Plymouth from Orange, New Jersey, and
m., 1833, Lucy Wright, d. of Jesse Dunham, by whom he had Hannah C.,
1837, m. Charles L. Jones, from Pembroke; Benjamin B., 1840; Joseph B.,
1842. DAVID O., son of Sylvanus, m., 1863, Hannah S. Barrows of Carver,
and had Lizzie S., 1864. FREDERICK T., came to Plymouth from Alton,
Illinois, and m. Mary J. Archer, 1872, and Henrietta Pugh, 1879. JONA-
THAN, m., 1799, Hannah, d. of David Bates, and had Jonathan, 1800; David
Bates, 1802; Hannah, 1805, m. George W. Griffin; Marcia Turner, 1808;
Sylvanus, 1812; James A., 1817; John W., 1820; Algernon F., 1824. SYLVA-
NUS, son of above, m., 1833, Elizabeth Vaughn, and had David O., 1841; Sarah

E., m. George F. Wood; Maria E., m. Ivory W. Harlow; Eliza S. N., m.
Erastus Harlow. He m., 2d, 1845, Mary, d. of Benjamin Drew.

HASKELL, ABRAHAM, from Rochester, m., 1804, Experience Cotton.
HUNNEWELL, from Rochester, m., 1802, Lucy Ellis. LOT, from Rochester,
m., 1792, Eliza Cotton.

HASKINS, DAVID, m. Rhoda, d. of Benjamin Westgate, and had Eliza
Thomas, 1814. JAMES, brother of David, m. Lucy, d. of Benjamin West-
gate, and had Eliza T., m. Isaac Marshall Robbins; David; and James. JERE-
MIAH, m., 1796, Lucy Cowit. JOHN, m., 1817, Orpha Hall. LEVI, m.,
1818, Temperance Hall. NATHAN H., brother of David and James, m.
Keziah Davis, d. of David Wade, and had Sarah Royal, 1826, m. Joseph F.
Towns; Nathan Thomas, 1828, m. Elizabeth Torrence; George Henry, 1831,
m. Hannah Barnes, d. of Edward Winslow Bradford; Keziah Davis, 1834, m.
Horatio Cameron. THOMAS, m., 1815, Deborah Chamberlin. WILLIAM,
Scituate and Plymouth, had Mary, m. Edward Cobb; William; a son, 1647;
Samuel, 1654; prob. Sarah, m. Benjamin Eaton; Elizabeth, m. Ephraim Til-
son. WILLIAM, son of above, had William, 1681.

HATCH, ASA, son of Rodolphus, m., 1740, Mary Wait, and had Asa, and
Richard. NATHANIEL, son of Rodolphus, m., 1746, Ruth Rider, and had
Mary, 1746, m. John Kempton; Ruth, 1749, m. Robert Dunham. His wid.
m. Thomas Robinson. RODOLPHUS, son of 2d Thomas, m., 1729, Elizabeth
Holmes, and had Nathaniel. John, Joseph, Asa; Sarah, m. Joshua Atwood;
Mary, m. Thomas Mayo; Noah; and Thomas. He had a 2d wife, Hester.
THOMAS, Dorchester and Scituate, 1634, had Jonathan, William, Thomas;
Alice, m. John Pickels; and Hannah, born after 1646. THOMAS, Scituate,
son of above, m., 1662, Sarah, d. of Rodolphus Elms, and had Thomas,
Sarah, Lydia, Keturah, Rodolphus, 1674; Hannah, Mary, Joseph, Margaret,
Abigail, and Jeremiah, 1684. THOMAS, son of above, m., 1714, Sarah
Jackson.

HATHAWAY, ABRAHAM, Freetown, probably son of Arthur, m. a Wilbur,
and had Ebenezer, 1689, and perhaps others. ALANSON, son of 1st Silas,
m. Rebecca Battles, 1789, and had Benjamin, Joshua, Allen, Edward, Betsey
E., m. Orin Bosworth; Joseph; Deborah, m. Thomas Cushing; Gardner; and
Rebecca, m. Reuben Tower. ALLEN, son of Alanson, m., 1838, Betsey Ellis,
and had Elizabeth A., 1841, m. Charles M. Ford; Thomas A., 1842; Ann H.,
1844; Fanny E., 1849, m. Charles F. Washburn; Emma F., 1852; Clara W.,
1855; David S. E., 1857. He m., 2d, 1860, wid. Betsey Nutter of Kingston.
ARTHUR, Marshfield, 1643, m., 1653, Sarah Cook, and had John, 1653; prob-
ably Abraham, and Sarah, 1656. BENJAMIN, son of Alanson, m. Hannah,
d. of William Nye, 1828, and had Benjamin Allen, 1834; George Chandler,
1836; William Nye, 1840; Ann E., 1845; and Rebecca, 1847, m. Samuel H.
Eddy; Albert F., 1850; besides Hannah E., Rebecca, and two children, named
William Nye, who died before 1840. He m., 2d, Sally Barnes, d. of George
W. Virgin, 1857. BENJAMIN ALLEN, son of above, m. Maria Elizabeth
Brooks of Scituate, and had Emma Dana, 1868; and Helen B., 1876. BEN-
JAMIN F., a stranger in Plymouth, m. Fanny Shaw, 1838, and had Benjamin
F., 1838; Fanny E., 1846; and perhaps others. CHARLES, son of 3d Silas, m.

Abigail G. Cotton, 1832, and had Charles, m. Betsey W. Ellis. DAVID of Wareham, m. Sarah King, 1825. EBENEZER, Freetown, son of Abraham, m. Hannah Shaw, and had Silas, 1721, and perhaps others. EDWARD, son of Alanson, m., 1836, Priscilla Whiting of Frankfort, Maine, and had Edward Whiting, 1839. He m., 2d, 1843, Lucy N., wid. of Charles Gibbs Morton, and d. of Ebenezer Sherman of Carver, and had Charles Gibbs, 1845, m. Mary, d. of Isaac Nelson Stoddard. GEORGE A., son of Joshua, m. Patience C. Davie, 1836, and had Abby Seaver, 1838. He m., 2d, Eliza H., d. of Ebenezer Nelson, 1844, and had Abby S., 1846; Charles L., 1848; George P., 1851, m. Ella J. Smart; Emory Clifford, 1853, m. Agnes C., d. of Henry M. Morton; and Elmer W., 1856. JOSEPH of Dartmouth, m. Lucy Raymond, 1832. JOSHUA, son of 2d Silas, m. Rebecca Foster, 1813, and had George A., 1814; Charles F., 1816, m. Temperance Blackwell of Waterville, Maine; Betsey W., 1819, m. James King of New Bedford; Joshua T., 1821, m. Lucinda —— of Boonsboro', Md.; Frederick C., 1823; John A., 1825, m. Charlotte —— of Cincinnati; Sarah Carver, 1827; Samuel G., 1829; Sarah Ann, 1832, m. Harrison Gibbs and Harvey Pratt; and Edward Emerson, 1835. LEANDER of Wareham, m. Phebe Pierce, 1836, and had Betsey W., m. Samuel W. Gould. SILAS, Freetown, son of Ebenezer, m. Deborah Carlisle, and had Benjamin; Abigail, m., 1st, a Pierce, and 2d, Joshua Howland; Lydia, Phylena, Joseph, Eleazer, Samuel, Silas, Nathaniel, Deborah, Esther, Polly, and Alanson. SILAS, son of above, m. Charles Read of Freetown, and had Silas, m. Deborah Dunham; Sally, m. James Read; and Joshua. SILAS, son of above, m. Deborah, d. of Elijah Dunham, and had Charles; and Charlotte, m. a Lucas.

HATHERLY, TIMOTHY, came in the Ann, 1623; went back to England, returned, and settled in Scituate. He m. a 2d wife, Lydia, wid. of Nathaniel Tilden, 1642, and had no children. He may have had by 1st wife, a son, Arthur, who was in Plymouth, 1660, and a son, Thomas, of Boston.

HAYES, JOHN, m. Bethiah Churchill, 1726.

HAYNES, GILBERT, of Lowell, m. Lydia Churchill, 1831.

HAYWARD, ANSEL, son of 4th Thomas, m., 1807, Huldah, d. of Thomas Johnson, and had Ansel Lorenzo, 1808; Harriet Ann, 1810; Lorenzo Thomas, 1812; John Elbridge, 1814; Lucy Maria, 1815; Daniel Johnson, 1819; Marshall Francis, 1823, m. Orpha Bliss of Longmeadow. He wrote his name "Howard." BEZA, son of 1st Nathan, m. Abigail, d. of Briggs Alden of Duxbury, and had John Alden; Beza, 1792. He m., 2d, Experience, d. of Ichabod Shaw, and wid. of James Russell, 1801, and had John S. of Hillsboro', Ill., m. Harriet Comstock of Hartford; and Susan S. CYRUS, m., 1807, Betsey Diman. JAMES THACHER, Boston, son of 2d Nathan, m., 1828, Sarah Appleton Dawes, and had Nathan, 1830; Mary Chilton, m. Henry Mitchell; James W., m. Sarah Howard of Springfield; Margaret Greenleaf, 1838, m. Henry Mitchell, as his 1st wife. JOSIAH, Bridgewater, son of 2d Nathaniel, m., 1715, Sarah, d. of Samuel Kingsley, and had Josiah, 1717; Nathan, 1720; Abraham, 1722; Sarah, 1724, m. Silas Willis; Martha, 1727. He m., 2d, Sarah, wid. of Theodosius Moore, and had John Prior, 1738; and Hannah, m. Eliphas Prior. NATHAN, Bridgewater, son of above, m., 1748,

Susanna, d. of Charles Latham, and had Adam, 1749; Beza, 1752; Cephas 1754; Susanna, 1757, m. James Thacher of Plymouth; Sarah, 1759; Eunice, 1761; Nathan, 1763; Betsey, 1767. NATHAN, son of above, m., 1795, Anna d. of Pelham Winslow, and removed to Plymouth. His children were Mary Winslow, 1798, m. William S. Russell; Penelope Pelham, 1801; James Thacher, 1802; Elizabeth Ann, 1805; Edward Winslow, 1808; George W., and J. A., 1806, died in infancy; Pelham Winslow, 1810; Charles Latham, 1812, m. Emmeline Greenwood of Boston; George Partridge, 1815, m. Elizabeth Winslow, d. of Samuel K. Williams of Boston. NATHANIEL, Bridgewater, son of 1st Thomas, m. Hannah, d. of John Willis, and had Nathaniel, 1664; John, Thomas, Samuel, Benjamin, 1677; Elisha; Patience, m. Israel Alger. NATHANIEL, East Bridgewater, son of above, by wife Elizabeth, had Josiah, 1688; Nathaniel, 1690; Isaac, 1691; Hannah, 1694; Sarah, 1696, m. Joseph Latham; Elizabeth, 1698, m. Samuel Reed; Timothy, 1700, m. David Whitman; Bethiah, 1711, m. Jonathan Perkins. THOMAS, with wife Susanna, came from Aylesford, England, in the William and Francis, 1632, returned, came back in 1635 in the Hercules, settled in Duxbury 1638, and was one of the original proprietors of Bridgewater. He had Thomas; Nathaniel; John, m. Sarah Mitchell; Joseph, m. Alice Brett and Hannah Mitchell; Elisha; Mary, m. Edward Mitchell; Martha, m. John Howard. He had a brother John who settled, 1st in Plymouth, and afterwards in Dartmouth. THOMAS, Bridgewater, son of 1st Nathaniel, m., 1772, Susanna, d. of John Hayward, and had Elizabeth, 1706; Thomas, 1708; Susanna, 1711, m. David Dunbar; John, 1713; Jacob, 1717; Jemima, 1721. THOMAS, Bridgewater, son of above, m., 1746, Elizabeth, wid. of Nicholas Byram, and d. of Matthew Gannett, and had Susanna, 1747, m. Jesse Edson; Mary, 1749, m. Benjamin Marshall; Betty; and Thomas, 1753. THOMAS, Bridgewater, son of above, m., 1781, Hannah, d. of Jacob Hayward, and had Ansel, 1782; Betsey, 1784, m. Nathaniel Edson; Hannah, 1793, m. Thomas Johnson; Harriet, 1795, m. Francis Cary; Thomas, 1798, m. Lucy Foster.

HEARD, WILLIAM, came in the Ann, 1623, and disappeared before 1627.

HEDGE, ALBERT GOODWIN, son of Thomas, m., 1851, Georgianna, d. of Southworth Barnes, and had Lucy S., 1852; Edward G., 1854, m. Olive S., d. of Nathaniel Doty; Georgianna, m. John Newcomb; Mabel Lothrop, 1867; Albertha; and Ethel. BARNABAS, son of 1st John, m. Mercy, wid. of Samuel Cole, and d. of William Barnes, 1734, and had Mercy, 1734, m. Thomas Davis; Samuel, 1736; Abigail, 1737; Barnabas, 1740; Lemuel, 1742; Lothrop, 1744; Sarah, 1746; John; and William. BARNABAS, son of above, m., 1761, Hannah Hedge of Yarmouth, and had Barnabas, 1764. BARNABAS, son of above, m., 1791, Eunice Dennie, d. of Thaddeus Burr of Fairfield, Conn., and had Barnabas, 1791; Hannah, 1793; Eunice Dennie, 1794; Eunice Dennie, 1795; Isaac Lothrop, 1797; Isaac Lothrop, 1798; Thomas, 1800; Abigail, 1802, m. Charles H. Warren; Hannah, 1804, m. John Thomas; Eunice Dennie, 1806, m. Chandler Robbins; Ellen Hobart, 1808, m. William P. Lunt; John Sloss Hobart, 1810; Priscilla Lothrop, 1811; Elizabeth, 1813, m. George Warren; Priscilla Lothrop, 1816. BARNABAS, son of above, m., 1812, Tri-

phena, d. of Thomas Covington, and had James Gorham, 1812; Sarah
Thomas, 1814, m. Joseph Cushman; William, 1815; Nathaniel Lothrop,
1817. BARNABAS, son of Isaac Lothrop, m., 1845, Priscilla, d. of Reuben
Sherman of Carver, and had Emma Hobart, 1846, m. George L. Churchill;
Eunice Dennie, 1847, m. Frank Eugene Damon; Lizzie Sherman, 1849, m.
Edward N. Stranger of Kingston; Ellen Frances, 1850, m. William M. Til-
son of Halifax; Barnabas, 1852, m. Helena A. Blanchard of Plympton; Pris-
cilla Sherman, 1854; Mary Anna, 1857, m. Robert A. Brown of Kingston;
Isaac Lothrop, 1859, m. Eudora M. Pierce of Kingston. EDWARD GOOD-
WIN, son of Thomas, m., 1866, Helen F., d. of Leavitt T. Robbins, and had
Mary Gardner, 1869. ELISHA, Yarmouth, son of 1st William, by wife Mary,
had John, 1773. ISAAC LOTHROP, son of 3d Barnabas, m., 1821, Mary Ann,
d. of Josiah Cotton, and had Priscilla Lothrop, 1822; Barnabas, 1824; Isaac
Lothrop, 1826; Mary Anna, 1830, m. Dwight Faulkner; Susan Elizabeth,
1835, m. Francis Bassett Davis. JAMES GORHAM, son of 4th Barnabas, m.,
1836, Sarah B., d. of Ansel Holmes, and had Alice Bradford, m. Edward B.
Whiting of New Bedford. JOHN, Yarmouth, son of Elisha, m., 1699, Thankful, d. of Barnabas Lothrop of Barnstable, and had Abigail, 1700, m. Nathaniel Clark; John, 1702; Barnabas, 1704; Susan, 1706; Elisha, 1707; Sarah,
1709, m. Ebenezer Hawes; Thankful, 1712, m. Edward Sturgis; Mercy,
1714; Anna, 1716, m. a Hawes. JOHN, Yarmouth, son of above, m., 1724,
Desire Hawes, and had, with others, a d. who m. Silas Lee of Wiscasset.
JUBA, m., 1794, Judith Turner. NATHANIEL LOTHROP, son of 4th Barnabas, m., 1844, Sarah, d. of John Sylvester, and had Ellen, 1850; Charles,
1852; Nathaniel Lothrop, 1861. THOMAS, son of 3d Barnabas, m., 1824,
Lydia Coffin, d. of Nathaniel Goodwin, and had Mary Ellen, 1825, m. William
G. Russell; Abby Burr, 1826, m. William T. Davis; Nathaniel Gardner, 1827;
Edward Goodwin, 1828; Thomas B., 1830; Albert Goodwin, 1832; Lydia
Goodwin, 1834, m. Joshua R. Lothrop; Thomas B., 1838, m. Helen Angier,
d. of James H. Mitchell of East Bridgewater; William, 1840. WILLIAM, Lynn,
1634, and afterwards Sandwich and Yarmouth, m. wid. Blanche Hull; and
had Elizabeth, 1647, m. Jonathan Barnes of Plymouth; Mary, 1648, m. a son
of Edward Sturgis; Sarah, m. a Matthews; Abraham, Elisha, William, John,
Lemuel, and Mercy. WILLIAM, son of Thomas, m., 1871, Catherine Elliott,
d. of Nathaniel Russell, and had Lucia Russell, 1872; William, and Henry,
twins, 1876.

HELY, TIMOTHY, m. Alice Chubbuck, and had Benjamin, 1738; Timothy,
1741; Alice, 1743.

HERSEY, GIDEON, from Abington, m., 1758, Elizabeth Atwood.

HEWARD, JOHN, had Sarah, 1647.

HEWES, or HUGHES, JOHN, Scituate, 1639, Plymouth, 1643, had Mary,
m., 1657, Jeremiah Hatch; and John, who died 1661. THOMAS, died
1697, leaving a wife, Abigail, and three children, Edward, Ann, and
Elizabeth.

HICKS, ABRAHAM, prob. a descendant from Robert, m., 1751, Rebecca
Dunham, and had John, 1756. ROBERT came in the Fortune, 1621, and his
wife, Margaret, in the Ann, 1623, with the following children: Elizabeth, m.

John Dickarson; Ephraim, who m., 1649, Elizabeth, d. of John Howland; Samuel; Lydia, m. Edward Bangs; Daniel, m. Elizabeth Hanmore; and Phebe, m., 1635, George Watson. SAMUEL, Eastham, son of above, m. Lydia, d. of John Doane of Eastham, and had Samuel, 1651; Margaret, 1654.

HIGGINS, RICHARD, Plymouth, 1633, m., 1634, Lydeon Chandler, and had Jonathan, 1637; Benjamin, 1640. He removed to Eastham, 1644, and m., 2d, 1651, Mary Yates, by whom he had Mary, 1652; Eliakim, 1654; William, 1655; Judah, 1657; Zeruiah, 1658; Thomas, 1661; Lydia, 1664.

HIGHTON, HENRY, m. Elizabeth Polding, and had Henry, 1769; Margaret, 1771.

HILL, ANDREW, m., 1766, Elizabeth Burgess. DANIEL, m., 1764, Elizabeth Holmes. JOHN, Plymouth, 1630, and removed to Boston. JONATHAN, m., 1784, Mary Sargent. JONATHAN, m. 1800, Mary Hines. RALPH, Plymouth, 1638, m. Margaret Toothaker, and had born at Woburn, Jonathan, Nathaniel, Ralph, Martha, and Rebecca. THOMAS, Plymouth, 1637, removed to Newport.

HILTON, WILLIAM, came in the Fortune 1621, followed by his wife in the Ann, 1623, with two children, one of whom was William. He removed to York, and m., prob. a 2d wife, Frances, wid. of Richard White of Dover. WILLIAM, son of above, settled in Newbury, and had Sarah, 1641; Charles, 1643; Ann, 1649; Elizabeth, 1650; William, 1653. He m., 2d, in Charlestown, where he removed, Mehitabel, d. of Increase Nowell, 1659, and had Nowell, 1663; Edward, 1666; John, 1668; Richard; and a 2d Charles. Mr. J. T. Hassam thinks it possible that he had two sons, William, and that one was living in York, 1683. Was he not his grandson?

HINCKLEY, SAMUEL, came over, 1635, with wife Sarah, and four children, Thomas, born 1613; Susanna; Mary; Sarah, m. Henry Cobb. After arrival he had Elizabeth, 1635, m. Elisha Parker; Samuel, 1638; Samuel, 1639. In 1640 he removed to Barnstable, and had Samuel, 1642, John, 1644. He m., 2d, 1657, Bridget, perhaps wid. of Robert Bodfish. THOMAS, m., 1748, Elizabeth Decosta. THOMAS, from Barnstable, m., 1752, Phebe Holmes.

HINES, JOHN, m., 1806, Lucy Dunham.

HIX, HUBBARD, from Troy, m., 1835, Caroline Luce.

HOBART, NOAH, from Fairfield, Conn., m. Priscilla (Thomas) Lothrop, wid. of Isaac, 1758.

HODGE, JAMES THACHER, son of Michael, m., 1846, Mary Spooner, d. of John Russell, and had Elizabeth Thacher, 1846, m. George Gibbs of Riverton, Ky.; John Russell, 1847, m. Harriet, d. of Seth Evans of Cincinnati; James Michael, 1850. MICHAEL, from Newburyport, born 1780, m., 1814, Betsey Hayward, d. of James Thacher, and wid. of Daniel Robert Elliott of Savannah, Georgia, and had James Thacher, 1816.

HODGES, NATHANIEL, from Duxbury, m., 1819, Rebecca Holmes.

HODGKINS, JOSEPH W., m. 1828, Sarah, d. of William Barnes, and had William E. of Boston; and Adelaide. WILLIAM, m., 1636, Sarah Cushman, perhaps d. of Robert, and 1638, Ann Haynes. He prob. had a sister, Elizabeth, who m., 1633, William Palmer of Scituate, and John Willis of Bridgewater.

HOGE, BENJAMIN, m., 1775, Elizabeth Sturney.

HOLBECK, WILLIAM, came in the Mayflower 1620, and died soon.

HOLBROOK, ELIPHALET, son of Peter, had Naaman, Elisha, Ezekiel, David, Gideon, Jonathan, Eliphalet, and Mary. ELIPHALET, son of Elisha, m. Mary Coville, and had Huldah, m. Henry Jackson; Jeremiah; Gideon; Betsey, 1781, m. John Bishop and Ezra Finney; Sarah, m. Joseph Jennings; Mary, m. William Holmes. ELISHA, son of 1st Eliphalet, had Gideon, Eliphalet, and Jonathan. GIDEON, son of 2d Eliphalet, m., 1808, Elizabeth Howland, and had Gideon, m. Victorine Annette, d. of George Simmons; Eliphalet, m. Amelia, d. of Frederick Zahn; Anna E., m. William M. Barnes; and Sarah. GIDEON, son of Elisha, m., 1788, Sarah Clark, and had Lois, 1788, m. Isaac Tribble; Sally, 1791; Patty, 1793, m. Jacob Covington; Betsey, 1795, m. Ichabod Morton; Hannah, 1797; Harriet, 1799, m. Robert Davie; Polly, 1801. He m., 2d, 1818, Nancy (Ellis) Blackmer, and had Gideon, m. Lucretia W. Bartlett; Richard B.; Elisha; Mary; Eliphalet. JEREMIAH, son of 2d Eliphalet, m., 1810, Margaret Dyer, and had Margaret Dyer, 1811, m. Harrison Gray Otis Ellis. He m., 2d, 1812, Bethiah Dyer. NAAMAN, son of 1st Eliphalet, m., 1793, Hannah, d. of Seth Luce, and wid. of Ezra Finney, and had Betsey, m. Jonathan Arey; Rachel, m. Freeman Cobb; Sarah; Lois; Ruth, m. Branch Dillingham; Polly; Naaman; and Samuel. PETER, Braintree, son of 2d Thomas, by wife Alice, and a 2d, Elizabeth Pool, had John, 1679; Peter, Joanna, Joseph, Sylvanus, Mary, Richard, Eliphalet, William, Samuel. THOMAS, Weymouth, 1643, came from England with wife Experience, d. of Hopestill Leland; and John, 1617; Thomas; William; Elizabeth, m. Walter Hatch of Scituate; and two other daughters. He m. a 2d wife, Jane. THOMAS, Braintree, son of above, by wife Joanna, had Thomas; John, 1653; Peter, 1655; Joanna, 1656; Joseph, 1660; Mary; and Susanna. He m. a 2d wife, Jane.

HOLLAND, WILLIAM, m. 1774, Joanna Atwood, and had William.

HOLLIS, ABEL, m., 1820, Betsey Pratt of Hanover, and had Abigail, 1826, m. Zenas Sturtevant; Joshua, 1828; Betsey S., 1833; Betsey S., 1836; Samuel, 1841; Lorenzo, 1844. BENJAMIN, Weymouth, son of 1st Samuel, by wife Ruth, had Ebenezer, 1838. EBENEZER, Weymouth, son of above, by wife Mary, had Mary, 1763; Rachel, 1765; Chloe, 1767; Taber, 1769; Ruel, 1772; Nehemiah, 1772; Phebe, 1776; Ebenezer, 1778; Samuel, 1780. HENRY, son of 2d Silas, m., 1819, Deborah, d. of Thomas Leonard, and had John Henry, 1820; Elizabeth Owen, 1821; William T., 1826. JOHN, Weymouth, m. Elizabeth, d. of James Rust, and had John, 1664; Thomas, 1667; Elizabeth, 1669; Mercy, 1675; and Samuel. JOHN, Weymouth, son of above, m. Mary Yardley, and had John, m. Hannah Ruggles, Mary, 1696, m. John Wild; Dorothy, 1700; Elizabeth, 1703; Hannah, 1705, m. Gideon Thayer; Thomas, 1710; James, 1712, m. Elizabeth Thayer; Sarah, 1715, m. Joseph Lovell. JOHN HENRY, New York, son of Henry, m., 1846, Esther, d. of George Harlow of Plymouth, and had William and Henry. SAMUEL, Weymouth, son of 1st John, by wife

Abigail, had Samuel, 1711; Abigail, 1712; Deborah, 1713; Thomas, 1715; Benjamin, 1716; John, 1718; Stephen, 1721; Jael, 1722; Lydia, 1723; Stephen, 1725. SAMUEL, Weymouth, son of above, m., 1735, Deborah Tower of Scituate, and had Bethiah, 1736; Samuel, 1738; Joshua, 1742; Bethiah, 1744. SAMUEL, son of above, m., 1768, Abigail Drew. SAMUEL, m., 1826, Desire R., wid. of Joseph Drew and d. of Thomas Goodwin. SILAS, Weymouth, son of 1st Thomas, m., 1768, Sarah Owen, and had Sarah, 1769, m. Ambrose Thayer; Silas, 1770; Joseph, 1772; Daniel, 1774, m. Nabby Lambert of Scituate; Barnabas, 1776; Charles, 1778, m. Lydia Copeland; John, 1779, m. Lydia Hobart. SILAS, Weymouth, son of above, had Henry, Mary, Ruth, Zebediah, Joseph, John, and Lydia. SILAS, Hanover, grandson of above, through his son John, m. Hannah B. Dwelley, and had Mary D., 1833, m. Charles E. Thayer; Lydia A. S., 1836, m. Owen Stiles of Grafton, Vt.; Hannah J., 1838; Elizabeth A., 1844. THOMAS, Weymouth, son of 2d John, m. Rachel Wachusett, and had Deborah, 1738, m. Micah Wild; Rachel, 1739, m. Howland Cowen; Thomas, 1741, and Silas. THOMAS, Weymouth, son of 1st Samuel, m. Lydia Holbrook, and had Jonathan, 1735; Thomas, 1737; Esther, 1739; Susanna, 1741. THOMAS, Weymouth, son of above, by wife Elizabeth, had Betty, 1758.

HOLMAN, EDWARD, came in the Ann, 1623; went back to England; returned, 1632; and, in 1652, was one of the purchasers of Dartmouth.

HOLMES, ABNER, son of 1st Thomas, m., 1737, Bathsheba, d. of Samuel Nelson, and had Abner, 1739; Bathsheba, 1741, m. Elnathan Holmes. ABNER, son of above, m., 1775, Sarah Kent, and had Ansel, m. Clarissa, d. of Nehemiah Drew; Peleg; George of Kingston, m. Marcia D., d. of Jedediah Holmes; Abner, m. Polly Davis; Lydia, m. Ezekiel Bonney; Bathsheba Nelson, m. Ellis Wright; Sarah; Huldah; and Patience, 1779, m. Ichabod Harlow. ABNER, m., 1801, Polly Bradford. ALBERT, son of Micah, m. Jerusha Tilson, and had Carrie Clifton, Charles Edward, Albert, and Hattie. AMASA, son of 1st Seth, m., 1798, Elizabeth, d. of Abner Bartlett, and had Tristram, 1799; Amasa, 1801; Temple, 1804; Caleb Bartlett, 1806, m. Lucy L. Bartlett, Susan Prior, and Lucy B. Prior; Ellen, 1808; Meletiah, 1811; Isaac B., m. Lucy, d. of Dura Wadsworth; George; Charles T., m. Martha M., d. of Samuel Cole, Harriett, d. of Stephen Bartlett, and Martha C., d. of Henry Robbins. AMASA, son of above, m. Mary N. Bartlett, and had Mary Ann, 1826; Frederick L., 1836; Harriet C., 1838; Esther F., 1841. He m., 2d, Nancy, d. of William Bradford, and wid. of Francis H. Robbins. ANDREW, son of 1st Jeremiah, m. Sarah Conant of Wareham, 1793; and had Peter; Sally, m. Samuel Long; Nabby, m. Thomas Green; and Andrew. He m. a 2d wife, who may have been mother of one or more of the above children. ANSEL, son of Sylvanus, m., 1770, Martha Howard, and had Martha, m. Samuel Watson; and Ansel. ANSEL, son of above, m., 1801, Sarah Bartlett, and had Sylvanus, m. Nancy, d. of Benjamin Dillard; Robert: Mary, m. William R. Cox; Martha, m. Levi Barnes; and Sarah, m. James G. Hedge. ANSEL, m., 1801, Patty Barnes. BARNABAS, m., 1784, Mercy Bates, and had Joseph, 1786; Abner, 1789; Barnabas, 1791; David, 1793; Ebenezer, 1795. BARNABAS, son of 1st James, m., 1768, Mercy, d. of John Wethered, and had Bar-

nabas, 1769; Mercy, m. David Cornish; and Lucy, m. Samuel Cornish. He
m., 2d, 1778, Priscilla, d. of Samuel Marshall, and had John; Nehemiah, m.
Eunice Morton; James; Joseph; Lucia, m. Nathaniel Bartlett; Content, m.
Daniel Soule of Plympton; Betsey, m. Lewis Harlow; Bartlett; and Priscilla,
m. Amos Whitten. BARNABAS, son of 2d Nathaniel, m., 1732, Abigail
Shepard, and had Rebecca, and Abigail. BARNABAS, son of 2d George, m.,
1787, Anna Damon of Pembroke, and had Lydia West; Nancy; Judith, m.
Lewis Gray. He m., 2d, 1812, Margaret, wid. of Anselm Rickard, and d. of
Benjamin Drew. BARNABAS, son of 2d Barnabas, m., 1797, Thankful Gam-
mons, and had Mercy, 1798, m. John Fogg; Thankful, 1800, m. Thomas
Peckham; Lemuel; Mercy, 1804, m. James Peckham and Benjamin Good-
win; Barnabas G., 1806, m. Betsey Phillips; Elizabeth, 1809, m. James Dean
of Easton; Bethiah S., 1812, m. John F. Hoyt; Benjamin also 1812, twin, m.
Nancy Hoyt and Penelope Swift. BARNABAS HINCKLEY, son of 3d Thomas,
m., 1836, Rebecca, d. of Nehemiah Burbank, and had Helen Rebecca; Eliza
Crocker, 1839, m. J. Francis Baxter; Sarah Sturgis, 1842, m. James Ellis
Sherman; Barnabas Hinckley, 1845. BARTLETT, son of 2d Elisha, m., 1765,
Lucy Bartlett, and had Bartlett, 1768. BARTLETT, son of 2d Barnabas, m.,
1807, Betsey, d. of Levi Paty, and had Nancy, 1807, m. Harvey Bartlett;
Bartlett, 1810; Almira, 1813; Betsey Paty, 1818; Abigail, 1822; Eunice Fin-
ney, 1824. BARSILLAI, son of 2d Josiah, m., 1805, Ruth, d. of Ebenezer
Cushman of Kingston, and had Richard, 1816, m. Almira, d. of Robert
Cushman of Kingston; Solomon Maynard, 1814, m. Asenath, d. of Vinal
Burgess; Josiah, 1811, m. Betsey, d. of Lewis Morton; George H., 1819, m.
Pamelia, d. of Lewis Morton; Hasadiah Sturtevant, 1809, m. Josiah Morton;
Susan, 1807, m. Robert Finney; Sally Ann, 1824; Ruth, 1826. He m., 2d,
1829, Sally, wid. of Ephraim Churchill, and d. of William Finney. BENJA-
MIN, son of 2d Cornelius, m., 1797, Meriah, d. of Ichabod Thomas, and had
Meriah, 1798, m. Leonard Snow; Ichabod, 1802; Benjamin, 1800; Hannah
Morton, 1806, m. Sylvanus D. Chase; Rebecca, 1809, m. Grenville Griffin;
Oliver, 1811, m. Pamelia Smith; Ichabod Thomas, 1813, m. Susan C., d. of
Joshua Standish, and Ruth, d. of Jonathan Thrasher; Priscilla, 1815, m.
Grenville Griffin. BENJAMIN, son of 1st Cornelius, m., 1766, Rebecca Drew.
CALEB, m., 1807, Mrs. Lucy Goodwin. CALVIN, m., 1812, Thankful Clark.
CHANDLER, son of Ichabod, m. Phebe Atwood, 1796, and had Chandler;
Atwood, m. Almira Ward; Ichabod S., m. Tabitha Kingman; Allen, m.
Hannah, d. of Job Churchill; Susan, and Mehitabel. CHARLES, m., 1789,
Sarah Raymond. CORNELIUS, son of 12th John, by wife Lydia, had Patience,
1722, m. Job Cobb; Cornelius, 1723; Ebenezer, 1725; Benjamin, 1731; Eph-
raim, 1734; Lydia, 1735, m. Nathan Simmons of Kingston; Priscilla, 1738.
CORNELIUS, son of above, m., 1753, Lydia Drew, and had Cornelius, 1754,
m. Elizabeth Lanman; Samuel N., 1756; Benjamin, 1759; Oliver Thomas;
Ebenezer; Priscilla, m. Samuel Rickard; and Roland. CORNELIUS, son of
above, m., 1780, Elizabeth, d. of Samuel Lanman, and settled in Bridgewater,
and had Cornelius, 1781; Ellis, 1783; Benjamin, 1784; Thomas, 1788, m.
Phebe Douglass; Betsey, 1791; Charles and Henry, twins, 1793; William, 1794.
CORNELIUS, Bridgewater, son of above, m. Mehitabel, d. of Ezra Conant,

and had Cornelius, 1807; George W., 1811; Gaius, 1816. CORNELIUS, m.,
1743, Mary Doten. CORNELIUS, m., 1791, Rhoda Richmond. CORNELIUS,
m., 1815, Lucy Morton. DAVID, son of Jabez, m., 1772, Rebecca Morton,
and had David. DAVID, son of above, m., 1798, Polly Holmes, and had
David, m. Persis, d. of Eliab Wood, and Hannah, d. of Prince Doten;
Rebecca, m. Stephen Lucas; Mary, m. William Holmes Bradford. DAVID
COBB, son of 1st Nathan, m., 1830, Louisa, d. of Nehemiah Savery, and had
David W., 1832; Andrew and Albert, twins, 1833; Louisa, 1835; Mary S.,
1837; Nehemiah S., 1839; Cephas S., 1840; Edward W., 1842. EBENEZER,
son of 2d John, m., 1695, Phebe, d. of William Blackmer, and had Ebenezer,
1696; Elizabeth, 1699, m. Quentin Crymble. EBENEZER, son of above, m.,
1719, Patience Finney, and had William, 1720, m. Ruth Morton; Ebenezer,
1722; Patience, 1724; Phebe, 1726, m. Quentin Crymble; Jeremiah, 1728, m.,
Phebe Crymble; Peter, 1729; John, 1733; Elizabeth, 1735; Nathaniel, 1737;
Joseph, 1739, m. Phebe Bartlett; Abigail, 1742; Gilbert, 1745, m. Mercy
Holmes; Esther, 1747, m. Ichabod Bearse. EBENEZER, son of above, m.,
1745, Susanna, d. of Elisha Holmes, and had Ebenezer, 1745. EBENEZER,
son of 4th Nathaniel, m., 1799, Sally Sturtevant of Kingston, and had Maria,
m. Calvin Bearse; Rebecca, m. Benjamin Hodges; Mary Bartlett, m. James
Tribble; Sally, m. Job Rider; Jerusha; Nathaniel; David, m. Esther Doten;
and Ezra. EBENEZER, m., 1766, Hannah Nelson. EBENEZER, m., 1797,
Margaret Howard. EBENEZER, m., 1807, Susanna Frize. ELEAZER, son
of 1st Nathaniel, m., 1711, Hannah, d. of Joseph Sylvester, and had Hannah,
1712; Eleazer, 1714; Lydia, 1716, m. Barnabas Churchill; Lemuel, 1719, m.
Abigail Rider; Elizabeth, 1723, m. John Bradford of Plympton; Ichabod,
1726, m. Rebecca Ellis; Job, 1728; Jonathan, 1731; Joshua, 1735. ELEAZER,
son of above, m., 1743, Esther, d. of Samuel Ellis, and had Hannah, 1744;
Jane, 1747, m. Thomas Davie; Eleazer, 1749; Betty, 1754, m. Stephen Doten;
Mercy, 1756, m. William Bartlett; Eleazer, 1761. ELEAZER, son of above,
m., 1785, Polly Barnes, and had Esther, 1786; Eleazer, m. Betsey Rogers;
Mary, and Elizabeth. He m., 2d, Elizabeth, d. of Samuel Avery, 1798, and
had Jane Avery. ELISHA, son of 1st Nathaniel, m., 1695, Sarah, d. of
Joseph Bartlett, and had Mercy, 1696, m. Edward Stephens; Elisha, 1698;
Joseph, 1700; Elizabeth, 1702, m. Elkanah Morton; Jabez, 1704; Mercy, 1705;
Elnathan, 1706; John, 1708; Sarah, 1709, m. John Blackmer. He m., 2d,
1719, Susanna Clark, and had Rebecca, 1720, m. Andrew Croswell; Nathaniel,
1722. ELISHA, son of above, m., 1721, Sarah Bartlett, and had Samuel,
1722; Sarah, 1724, m. Jonathan Harlow; Susanna, 1726, m. Ebenezer Holmes;
Nathaniel, 1730; Elisha, 1732, m. Sarah Ewer; Betty, 1735. He probably
m., 2d, 1739, Mary Ellis, and had Jerusha, 1740; Mary, 1742; Bartlett, 1744;
Ellis, 1747. ELLIS, son of Ichabod, m., 1791, Grace, d. of Isaac Symmes,
and had Polly; Ellis; Grace, m. Henry Whiting; Kendall; Hannah; Rebecca,
m. Obadiah Burgess; Deborah, and Davis. ELLIS, son of above, m. Catherine Gibbs, 1819, and had Hannah Gibbs, 1821; Alvin Ellis, 1825; Catherine,
1828, m. Alvin G. Morton; Grace, 1829. ELLIS, Halifax and Bridgewater,
son of 2d Elisha, m., 1768, Content, d. of Abraham Howland, and had Jerusha, 1769; Lydia, 1771; Content, 1774; Samuel, 1777; Ellis, 1779, m. Patty

Conant and Lucy Copeland; Howland, 1780; Susanna, Luther, and Calvin.
He m., 2d, 1788, Betsey, d. of John Leach, and had Betsey, 1789, m. Alpheus
Brett; Mary, 1790, m. Caleb Bassett; Samuel, 1793, m. Deborah Pack-
ard; John, 1795. He m., 3d, Sarah, d. of Jacob Chipman of Halifax.
ELLIS, Bridgewater, son of 3d Cornelius, m. Lois Holbrook Bartlett of
Plymouth, and had Louisa Bartlett, 1813; Ellis Winslow, 1816. He
m., 2d, Mehitabel, d. of Stephen Hearsey. ELNATHAN, son of 1st Elisha,
m., 1731, Rebecca, d. of John Churchill, and had Sarah, 1732; Rebecca,
1734; Elnathan, 1735. ELNATHAN, son of above, m., 1761, Bathsheba, d. of
Abner Holmes, and had Elnathan; Thomas; Sarah, m. Nathaniel Harlow;
Olive, Abner, and Nelson. ELNATHAN, son of above, m., 1784, Deborah
Brewster of Kingston, and had Deborah, m. John Sampson Paine; Bathsheba, m. John Tribble; Samuel; and Leonice, m. Marston Sampson.
EPHRAIM, son of 2d Nathaniel, m., 1742, Sarah, d. of John Finney, and had
Elizabeth, 1743; Ephraim, 1745; Joanna, 1748; Nathaniel, 1751; Sarah, 1756;
Bathsheba, 1763. EPHRAIM, m., 1692, wid. Mary Harlow. EPHRAIM, son
of 1st Ephraim, m., 1767, Lucy, d. of Seth Barnes, and had Ephraim; Nathan-
iel; Mary, m. Joseph Tribble; Sally, m. William Drew and Isaac M. Sher-
man; Lucy, m. John Harden of Bridgewater; and Joanna. EPHRAIM, son
of above, m., 1800, Polly, d. of Lemuel Bradford, and had Joanna, m. Jacob
Jackson; Mary Ann, m. Sylvester Davie and Corban Barnes; and Ephraim.
EPHRAIM, son of above, m. Mary Ann, d. of John Atwood, and had William
Wallace; Ann Maria, m. Frank Lewis; Mary Bradford, m. Charles Lanman;
and Ephraim. EZRA, son of 1st James, m., 1772, Lydia, d. of Zacheus
Curtis, and 2d, 1780, Thankful, wid. of Miles Long and d. of Israel Clark,
and had Miles. GEORGE, son of 2d John, m., 1720, Lydia Wood, and had
George, 1721; Richard, 1724. GEORGE, son of above, m., 1741, Lydia, d. of
George West, and had Lydia, m. William Savery and William Atwood and
Benjamin Clark; George, 1742, m. Ann Rich, Experience, m. Thomas Cooper;
Joshua; Richard, 1745; Barnabas, 1756; Mary, m. Peter Lanman; Sarah,
m. Nathaniel Cobb and Samuel Lanman; Bethiah, m. Ansel Homes; Eliz-
abeth, m. a Bartlett. GEORGE, Kingston, son of 2d Abner, m., 1819, Marcia
D., d. of Jedediah Holmes, and had Marcia, m. a Shaw, of Bridgewater;
Eveline, m. Frederick C. Adams; Helen, m. Charles H. Richardson; Eliz-
abeth Cole, m. George Bryant of Brockton. GERSHOM, son of 1st Richard, m., 1736, Lydia, d. of Isaac King, and had Gershom, 1739, m. Deborah
Delano; Lydia, 1742; Richard, 1743; Isaac, 1745; Lydia, 1747, m. John
Atwood; Thankful, 1749, m. Thomas Hatch Whittemore; Joseph, 1751.
GERSHOM, from Taunton, m., 1787, Mercy King. GERSHOM, Kingston, son
of 2d Josiah, m. Lucy Fuller, and had Gershom, John, Almira, Elizabeth,
and Micah. HOWLAND, Bridgewater, son of 3d Ellis, m., 1804, Huldah, d.
of Joseph Copeland, and had Rebecca Hooper, 1808; Lydia, 1810; Huldah,
1812; Howland, 1815; Susanna, 1817; Joseph, 1819; Wealthy, 1822. He m.,
2d, 1823, Hannah Oldham of Duxbury, and had John, 1824; Joseph and
Hannah O., twins, 1826; Calvin, 1828, Minerva A., 1830. HOWLAND, Lexington, son of above, m., 1849, Maria Wellington, d. of William Cotting of
West Cambridge; and had Mary Eddy, 1850, Carrie Marie, 1852; Francis

Howland, 1853; Sarah Eddy, 1855; Charlotte Bronte, 1857. ICHABOD, son of 1st Eleazer, m., 1748, Rebecca, d. of Samuel Ellis, and had Remembrance, 1750, m. Samuel Harlow; Rebecca, 1753, m. Nathaniel Bradford, Deborah, 1755, m. Benjamin Barnes; Ichabod, 1757, m. Rebecca Harlow; Samuel, 1761, m. Mary Finney; Mary, 1763, m. Nathaniel Spooner; Ellis, 1767; Esther, 1769, m. Ichabod Shaw; Chandler, 1771; Elizabeth, 1774, m. Ichabod Shaw. ISAAC, m., 1705, Mary Nye of Sandwich, and had Hannah, 1706; Mary, 1709; Zerviah, 1714; Susanna, 1716; Isaac, 1722. ISAAC, m. 1767, Ruth Ransom. ISAAC, m., 1783, Margaret Eames. ISAAC, m., 1790, Mary Poor. JABEZ, son of 1st Elisha, m., 1730, Rebecca, d. of William Harlow. He m., 2d, 1734, Sarah Clark, and had Rebecca, 1736; Jabez, 1738; Mary, 1740; Sarah, 1742; Stephen, 1744; Meriah, 1746, m. Reuben Washburn; and David. JAMES, son of 2d Nathaniel, m., 1729, Content, d. of Joseph Sylvester, and had Zacheus, 1729; Solomon, 1731; James, 1733; Seth, 1735; Nathaniel, 1738; Lothrop, 1740, m. Mary Bartlett; Barnabas, 1743; Caleb, 1745; Ezra, 1748, m. Lydia Curtis. JAMES, son of above, m., 1763, Remember, d. of John Wethered, and had James, 1763; Zephaniah, 1766; Rufus, 1769; Remember and Robert, twins, 1772. He m., 2d, Anna Fish, 1773, and had Sarah, Ann, Lucy, and Zacheus. JAMES HINCKLEY, son of 3d Thomas, removed to North Carolina where he m., 1822, Rebecca Wilson, and had Leander, Louisa, and Mary, both of whom m. James T. Wilson. JAMES S., son of 5th Joseph, m. Priscilla Savery of Carver, and had James A., Thomas S., and Olivia. JEREMIAH, son of 2d Ebenezer, m., 1749, Phebe, d. of Quentin Crymble, and had Joanna, 1750; Jeremiah, 1752; Peter, 1756; Betsey; Abigail; Phebe, m. Corban Barnes; Charles; Andrew, 1768; and William. JEREMIAH, son of above, m., 1782, Nancy, d. of Thomas Robertson, and had Nancy, Thomas, Jeremiah, and William. JEREMIAH, m., 1796, Polly Lucas, and had Rufus, 1797; Phebe, 1799, m. Thomas Farmer; Benjamin, 1800; Ansel, 1801; Polly, 1803; Joanna Lucas, 1804; Jeremiah, 1806; Ruth, 1807; Seth Lucas, 1810. JOB, son of 1st Eleazer, m., 1752, Mehitabel Stewart, and had Lydia, 1753; Jonathan, 1755. JOHN, Plymouth, 1632, had John, 1636; Josiah, Nathaniel, and Sarah. JOHN, son of above, m., 1661, Patience, d. of John Faunce, and had John, 1663; Richard; Patience, m. James Cobb; Mehitabel, m. Manasseh Kempton; Sarah, m. John Ellis; George; Nathaniel, m. Eleanor Racer; Ebenezer, m. Phebe Blackmer; Thomas, m. Joanna Morton; Joseph; Desire, m. John Churchill. JOHN, perhaps, son of 1st Nathaniel, m., 1709, Sarah, d. of Nathaniel Church. He m., 2d, 1711, Mercy Ford, and had Desire, 1712; John Ring; Mary Ann, 1713; Peleg, 1715; Josiah, 1716; Deborah, 1717; Jonathan, 1719; Mercy, 1725; and John. JOHN, m., 1661, Mary Atwood. JOHN, m., 1730, Rebecca Harlow. JOHN, from Duxbury, m. Polly Holmes, 1804. JOHN, m., 1775, Priscilla Marshal. JOHN, m., 1802, Polly Finney. JOHN, son of 1st Elisha, m., 1733, Lois Kempton, and had Lois, 1735; Mercy, 1736; John, 1738; Nehemiah, 1740; Lois, 1744; Margaret, 1746, m. James Howard; Ruth, 1749, m. Thomas Howard. JOHN, son of above, m., 1761, Abigail Finney, and had Abigail, 1766. JOHN, son of 1st Peter, m. Polly Cooper, and had John B., m. Amy H. Randall; and Mary G., m.

Jabez Pierce of New Bedford. JOHN, Middleboro', son of 2d John, by wife Sarah, had Patience, 1690, m. Ichabod Cushman and Elnathan Wood; Nathaniel, 1692, m. Martha Cushman of Plympton; John, 1694; Cornelius, 1697; Sarah, 1699. By a 2d wife, Experience, he had Samuel, 1704; Benjamin, 1706; Thomas, 1709; Susanna, 1711. JOHN FLAVEL, son of Micah, m., 1855, Laura A., d. of Abner H. Harlow, and had Mary S., m. James Paine; Annie L., Mira C., Flavella E., and Albert Frederick. JOSEPH, son of 2d John, by wife Mary, had Joseph, 1697; Ephraim, 1699; Mary, 1701; Sarah, 1703; Abigail, 1705; Jonathan, 1709; Micah, 1714; Keziah, 1719. JOSEPH, m., 1705, Lydia Griswold, wid. of Joseph Bartlett, and had Fear, 1706, m. Lemuel Cobb; Joseph, 1714. JOSEPH, son of 1st Joseph, m., 1726, Phebe, d. of John Churchill, and had Jonathan, 1726; Phebe, 1729, m. William Bendick Pearson; Desire, 1731, m. John Swift; Samuel, 1733; Hannah, 1735; Meriah, 1737; Jane, 1738; Joseph, 1741; Micah, 1743; Elkanah, 1745; Susanna, 1747. JOSEPH, son of above, m., 1763, Phebe Bartlett, and had Joseph; Phebe, m. Thomas Holmes; Lewis, and James. JOSEPH, son of above, m., 1788, Polly Finney, and had Polly, m. George Weston. He m., 2d, 1797, Lydia Lucas, and had Phebe, m. Ira Bailey; Lewis, and James S. JOSEPH, m., 1768, Rebecca Eames, and had Joseph, 1770; Rebecca, 1772; Cornelius, 1774; Ansel, 1777; Barten, 1779. JOSEPH, son of 1st Gershom, m., 1774, Lydia, d. of William Sargent, and had Joseph. JOSEPH, son of above, m., 1797, Martha Cotton, d. of Charles Dyer, and had Martha Cotton, m. George Churchill; William Sargent; Mary D., m. Aylwin M. Grayton; Joseph; and Lucy Dyer, m. William Bartlett. JOSEPH, son of 2d Barnabas, m. Eliza Bartlett, 1822, and had Elizabeth, m. William Perkins; Pella, Samuel B., Priscilla, Sylvanus, Priscilla, Joseph, Rebecca, Joseph. JOSEPH, m. Polly, d. of Samuel Battles, 1796. JOSEPH, son of 8th Joseph, m., 1838, Elizabeth, d. of Isaac Eames Cobb. JOSEPH, son of 6th Nathaniel, m., 1812, Esther, d. of Seth Rider, and had Joseph, 1813; Adoniram, 1815; Angelina, 1817; Cornelius, 1820; Esther, 1821; Nathaniel, 1825; Mercy J., 1827; Bartlett Rogers, 1829; Bathsheba, 1831; Caroline, 1833; Van Buren, 1835. JOSEPH THOMAS, son of 3d Thomas, m. Eliza, d. of Ezekiel Crocker of Barnstable, and had Henry Hersey, and Eliza Crocker. He m., 2d, Lucy, d. of Samuel Crocker of Barnstable, and had Lucy. JOSIAH, Duxbury, probably son of 1st John, m., 1666, Hannah, d. of Henry Sampson, and had Hannah, 1667; Deborah, 1669; Josiah, 1672; Mary, 1674; John, 1678; William, 1680. JOSIAH, Kingston, son of 3d John, by wife Ruth, had Simeon, 1741; Frances, 1744; Josiah, 1745; Jonathan, 1748; Gershom, 1752; John, 1754; Sylvester, 1756; Ruth, 1748; Grace, 1760; Eleazer, 1763; Susanna, 1750, m. Ebenezer Cushman; Elizabeth, 1764. JOSIAH, Kingston, son of above, had Barsillai, 1777; and Sarah, m. John Adams. JOSHUA, son of 1st Eleazer, m., 1755, Hannah, d. of Samuel Doten, and had Elizabeth, 1756, m. Joseph Bradford; Joshua, 1759, and Nathaniel. JOSHUA, son of above, m., 1782, Abigail, d. of John McKeel, and had Polly, 1782; Levi, 1785; Sukey, 1787; Joshua, 1789; Sally, and Abigail. KENDALL, son of 1st Ellis, m., 1824, Betsey, d. of Ephraim Paty, and had Elizabeth, 1825; Mary F., 1830; Lucy M., 1833; Rebecca, 1835, m. Robert Barnes; James Kendall, 1838;

Alfred, m. Hannah J. Holmes; and Anna. LEMUEL, m., 1746, Abigail
Rider. LEMUEL, m., 1781, Rebecca Bartlett. LEMUEL, from Kingston, m.,
1794, Patience Harlow. LEMUEL DREW, son of 5th Nathaniel, m. Polly, d.
of Joseph Freeman of Duxbury, and had Mary E., and Mary Antoinette,
1837, m. John Ellis Barnes. LEWIS, son of 4th Joseph, m., 1790, Betsey
Sherman, and had Betsey Lewis, m. Henry Cassidy; and Mary Sherman, m.
Joseph Allen. LEWIS, Bridgewater, son of 5th Joseph, m. Ruth S. Morse of
Middleboro', and had Lewis James. He m., 2d, Rebecca Conant of Bridge-
water, and, 3d, Mary A. Besford of Nova Scotia, by the last of whom he had
Belle, Albert, Annie, Hattie and Amanda, twins, and Emerson. LOTHROP,
m., 1769, Mary Bartlett. MICAH, son of 3d Gershom, m. Nancy, d. of Silas
Morey, and had Albert, 1822; Almira, m. Heman Churchill; Elizabeth, m.
Peter B. Grimes; Truman; Edward Payson; and John Flavel. NATHAN,
son of 6th Nathaniel, m., 1799, Ruth, d. of John Cobb, and had David Cobb;
Nathan, 1802; Nathan Henry, 1804; Nathaniel, 1806; Ruth Cobb, m. George
Nelson and Samuel Hopkins; Mary Rickard, 1811, m. Charles Whitten;
Jerusha Cushman, 1814, m. Lemuel Bradford; Margaret Howard, 1817, m.
Samuel Newell Diman; and Patience. NATHAN HENRY, son of above, m.
Polly Wright, and had Mary, 1827; Elizabeth, 1828; Nathan, 1831; Frederick,
1835. He m., 2d, Lucinda Wright, 1865. NATHAN, son of 1st Seth, m.,
1805, Euphaney, d. of Andrew Bartlett, and had Nathan; Euphaney, m.
Hiram Bartlett; Jason, Wealthy, Henry B., Elisha, Ellis H., Stillman,
Harriet, and Ahira. NATHANIEL, son of 1st John, m., 1667, Mercy, d. of
John Faunce, and had Elisha, 1670; Mercy, 1673, m. Ebenezer Cobb; Na-
thaniel, 1676; Sarah, 1680, m. an Ellis; John, 1682; Elizabeth, 1686, Eleazer,
1688. NATHANIEL, son of above, m., 1698, Joanna Clark, and had Nathaniel, 1699, m. Priscilla Pratt; James, 1700; Bathsheba, 1703, m. Nathan
Delano; Sarah, 1707; Barnabas, 1710, m. Abigail Shepard; Zephaniah, 1714,
m. Sarah Bradford; Joanna, 1715, m. Paul Cook; Ephraim, 1719. NATHAN-
IEL, son of 2d John, m., 1700, Eleanor Racer, and had Mercy, 1701, m. Caleb
Tinkham; Nathaniel, 1702; Joshua, 1705; Patience, 1707; Eleanor, 1709;
Joseph, 1712; Benjamin, 1715; Richard, 1718; Meltiah, 1720. NATHANIEL,
son of 2d Ebenezer, m., 1760, Chloe Sears, and had Ebenezer; Elizabeth,
m. Eleazer Nichols; Rebecca, m. Ezra Howard; and Patience. NATHANIEL,
son of 6th Nathaniel, m., 1797, Elizabeth, d. of Lemuel Drew, and had Lemuel
Drew, 1798; Elizabeth Crossman, 1800; Mary, and Lucy. NATHANIEL, son
of 1st Ephraim, m. Mary Rickard, and had Nathaniel, 1775; Henry, Nathan,
Thomas, Joseph, Cornelius; Jane, m. Bradford Barnes; Betsey, m. William
Allen; Polly, m. David Holmes; Sophia, m. Seth Eddy and a Morehead;
Bathsheba, m. an Everson; and Marcia C., m. William C. Green. NA-
THANIEL, son of 2d Elisha, m., 1754, Lydia Churchill, and had Nathaniel,
1755. NATHANIEL, son of 2d Nathaniel, m., 1721, Priscilla Pratt, and had
Priscilla and Joanna. NATHANIEL, from Wareham, m., 1828, Betsey T.
Davie. NATHANIEL, son of 1st Joshua, m., 1793, Sally, d. of Benjamin Bag-
nall, and had Nathaniel, m. Sally Fish; Elizabeth Davis, m. Simeon Dunham
of West Bridgewater; Sally; Oliver; and Andrew, m. Beulah Sherman of
Marshfield. NATHANIEL, son of above, m. Sally, d. of Caleb Fish, and had

Susan W., m. James, Simmons. NEHEMIAH, m. Fear Reading of Middle-
boro', 1791. NELSON, son of 3d Thomas, m., 1836, Lois, d. of Joab Thomas,
and had Henrietta F., 1838, m. Job N. Sherman of Rochester; Elizabeth, m.
Daniel D. Howard; Arabella N., 1842, m. Sylvanus L. Churchill; Barnabas
H., 1853, m. Alice J., d. of William H. Shaw. OLIVER, son of 1st Benjamin,
m. Pamelia Smith, and had Pamelia Ann, 1831, m. John Smith; Mártha
Thomas, 1833; Fanny Winsor, 1839, m. James Frothingham; Mehitabel
Paine, 1839, m. Lewis Hall; Henry F., m. Elizabeth Barnes; Charles H., m.
Lydia Noyes; and Oliver S. PETER, son of 1st Jeremiah, m., 1777, Mary
Brooks, and had Peter; Eleanor, m. Chandler Robbins; John; and Polly, m.
Ezekiel Rider. PETER, son of above, m., 1801, Sally, d. of Lazarus Harlow,
and had Sally, 1802, m. Samuel Nelson; Peter, 1804; Lucia H., 1807, m.
Abraham Whitten; Charles, 1809; Eliza, 1811, m. a Delano of Marshfield;
Lewis, 1813, m. Lydia K., d. of Pickels Cushing of South Scituate; Polly D.,
1815, and Susan, 1818, both m. William R. Drew; Franklin B., m. Antoinette,
d. of Timothy Berry, and Catherine Murray; and Leander, m. Jane Tarr of
Portland. PETER, son of Andrew, m., 1819, Mary Richmond Flemmons, and
had Galen R., 1820, m. Juline E. Valler; Peter Augustus, 1822, m. Matilda
Benson; Robert R., 1831, m. Lydia Valler; Eliza Ann, 1834, m. Thomas A.
Burgess of Wareham; Bethiah, 1836, m. Joseph Williams of Taunton; Lydia
A., 1838, m. Ira Debolton of Troy and Abel Harris of Sandwich; Mary Ann,
m. Lucius Doten. RICHARD, son of 2d John, m., 1711, Hester Wormwell,
and had Mary, 1713, m. Thomas Kempton; Gershom, 1714; Sylvanus, 1716.
RICHARD, son of 1st Gershom, m., 1764, Mercy Barnes, and had Elizabeth,
1764; Richard, 1766, m. Sarah Howard; William, 1768; Lydia, 1770; Samuel
W.; Polly, 1779, m. Thomas Bradford; Sarah, m. Isaac Cole. RICHARD, son of
2d George, m., 1771, Abigail Dammon, and had Abigail, m. Ephraim Bartlett and William Leonard; Richard; Thomas Cooper, m. Jerusha Harlow,
and removed to Kingston; Experience, m. Spencer Brewster; Nancy, m.
Isaac Louden; Elizabeth, m. John Carver; Jane, m. Isaac Lanman;
and Sarah. RICHARD, son of above, m., 1806, Mary, d. of William
Rider, and had Richard William, 1807, m. Caroline, d. of Seth
Morton; Ephraim Bartlett, 1809, m. Lydia, d. of Thomas Sampson;
Mary D., 1812, m. Alonzo Scudder, RICHARD, m., 1806, Hannah Sampson.
RUFUS, m., 1793, Patience Clark. SAMUEL, Amherst, son of 1st Zacheus,
m. Mary Bryant of Cummington, and had Eliza, m. Christie Dickinson;
Mary, m. Ebenezer Nelson. He m., 2d, Polly Orcutt of Bridgewater, and
had Salome; and Samuel, 1797, m. Clara, d. of David Marston of Monmouth,
Me. He m., 3d, Esther, d. of Moses Bissell of East Windsor, Conn., and had
Orpheus, m., 1st, Sarah Prentiss; 2d, Sally Gray; 3d, Martha Ann Dodge;
and Olive. He m., 4th, wid. Abigail (Gorham) Davis of Barnstable, wid. of
James, and had Zacheus, 1811, m. Emily Dawes. SAMUEL N., son of 2d
Cornelius, m., 1796, Mary, d. of Ichabod Thomas, and had Lydia, m. Samuel
Battles; Abigail Thomas, m., John Clark; Benjamin; Mary, m. James Hall;
Isaac S., m. Deborah, d. of Lemuel Rickard; Catherine B., m. Francis Pauld-
ing; Samuel; Cornelius, m. Sophronia Sullivan; and Abner. SAMUEL W., son
of 2d Richard, m., 1802, Sally, d. of Seth Luce, and had Seth Luce; and Eliza,

m. John Williams. SAMUEL, m., 1784, Mary Finney. SAMUEL DOTEN, son of 2d William, m., 1812, Betsey, d. of Joseph Johnson, and had Elizabeth Mason, 1812, m. James Madison Bradford; Harriet, 1815, m. William Davis Simmons; Rebecca, 1819; Mercy Johnson, 1822; Emeline Frances, 1825; Samuel Doten, 1827; Joseph Johnson, 1830. SETH, son of 1st James, m., 1762, Mary Holmes, and had Deborah, 1763; Mary, 1765; Rebecca, 1767; Seth, 1768; Sylvanus, 1770; Stephen, 1771; Jerusha, 1773; Amasa, 1775; Caleb, 1777; Nathan, 1779; Jesse, 1781; Jerusha, 1783. SETH, son of above, m., 1795, Jerusha, d. of Branch Blackmer, and had Stephen, 1796; Seth, 1798; Branch Blackmer, 1801; Jesse, 1802; Jerusha, 1805; Hiram, 1807; Jerusha Blackmer, 1809; Esther, 1811. SETH LUCE, son of 3d Samuel, m. Salome, d. of George R. Wiswall, and had Sarah Elizabeth, 1827, m. Samuel T. Spear; Rebecca W., 1830, m. Thomas B. Atwood; Salome N., 1834, m. Henry R. Raymond and Stephen Glass; Lydia Ann, 1836; Seth Luce, 1838, m. Lydia Ann Chubbuck; Lydia Morton, m. Edward Doten; Samuel W., 1846. SIMEON, Kingston, son of 2d Josiah, by wife Mercy, had Mercy, 1763; Esther, 1766; Simeon, 1767; Esther, 1768; William, 1770; Ruth, 1772; Elizabeth, 1774; Olive, 1777; Susanna, 1779. SOLOMON, son of 1st James, m., 1760, Abigail Bartlett, and had Nathaniel, 1760, m. Jerusha Bartlett; Abigail, 1762; Solomon, 1764; Mary, m. Josiah Diman; Clyntha; and Thomas. SOLOMON, son of above, m., 1808, Mercy Crocker of Carver, and had Jane B., m. William Paulding; and Daniel Crocker, m. Caroline Lamson of Columbus, Ohio. SOLOMON, m., 1768, Mary Delano. STEPHEN, son of 1st Seth, m., 1798, Rebecca Bartlett, and had Wealthy, 1799; Stephen, 1800; Clark, 1804; Cromwell W., 1806; Ezra, 1808; Truman, 1811. SYLVANUS, son of 1st Richard, m., 1741, Mercy, d. of William Harlow, and had Mary, 1743; Sylvanus, 1744, m. Rebecca Churchill; Rebecca, 1747; Ansel, 1749, m. Martha Howard. SYLVESTER, son of 1st Zacheus, m., 1787, Grace, d. of Israel Clark, and had Sylvester. SYLVESTER, son of above, m., 1810, Esther Holmes, and had Mary, m. Charles B. Adams; Elizabeth, Esther, John Sylvester, and Alexander. He m., 2d, Fanny Kingman of Bridgewater, and had Fanny Kingman. SYLVESTER, Kingston, son of 2d Josiah, m. Molly Washburn, 1789, and had Josiah, 1790, m. Sally, d. of Nicholas Spinks Bagnall and Ruth Shurtleff; Lois, 1800, m. Josiah Everson; Mary, 1798, m. Seneca Briggs. THOMAS, son of 2d John, m., 1697, Joanna Morton, and had Joanna, 1697; Jemima, 1705, m. Lazarus Sampson; Thomas, 1710; Abner, 1712. THOMAS, son of above, m., 1736, Elizabeth, d. of Ebenezer Cobb, and had Thomas, 1739, m. Mercy Bartlett; Jemima, 1741, m. Benjamin Bartlett; Sarah, 1744, m. William Harlow; Elizabeth, m. Benjamin Barnes; Mercy, 1746, m. Nicholas Drew. THOMAS, son of 2d Elnathan, m., 1794, Annah, d. of Jabez Hinckley of Barnstable, and had Thomas; James Hinckley, 1795; Joseph, 1797; Deborah K., 1804. He m., 2d, wid. Mercy (Mayo) Snow, 1805, and had Joseph Thomas, 1806; Nelson, 1807; Barnabas Hinckley, 1809; Olive, 1812, m. John Green; Henrietta H., 1815, m. Henry Weston; Marcia James, 1818, m. John Darling Churchill. THOMAS, son of above, m. Polly Phinney of Barnstable, and had Anna Hinckley, m. Washington Warren of Boston; Marietta, m. a Knowles; William, James, and Joseph. THOMAS, m.,

1804, Eunice Morton. THOMAS, m., 1772, Sarah Tinkham. TRUMAN
COOK, son of 2d William, m., 1815, Jeanette, d. of John Allen, and had
Truman Cook, 1816; Timothy A., 1818; William, 1821; Mary S., 1826; Rich-
ard, 1828; Mary S., 1830; Joseph S., 1833; and Curtis. WILLIAM, son of 2d
Ebenezer, m., 1741, Ruth, d. of Thomas Morton, and had William, 1744;
Joanna, 1750, m. Joseph Burbank; Lucy, 1753. WILLIAM, son of 2d Rich-
ard, m., 1787, Hannah Doten, and had Hannah, 1788, m. Laban Burt; Wil-
liam, 1790; Samuel Doten, 1792; Truman Cook, 1795; Harriet, 1797, m.
Caleb Rider; Richard, 1799; Winslow, 1801. WILLIAM, m., 1783, Margaret
Morton. WILLIAM, m., 1810, Mary Holbrook. WILLIAM, son of 2d Wil-
liam, m., 1812, Bathsheba Doten, and had Betsey Doten; and Bathsheba
James, m. Ansel H. Harlow. WILLIAM, m., 1791, Lucy Harlow. WILLIAM,
m., 1784, Meriah Churchill. WINSLOW, son of 2d William, m. Lydia, d. of
John Burbank, and had Betsey, 1825; Winslow S., 1827; Lydia, 1828; Lydia
Mason, 1829; Henry B., 1831; Bathsheba J., 1833; Emeline Frances, 1836.
ZACHEUS, son of 1st James, m., 1754, Ruth Bryant, and had Content, 1755,
m., 1st, a Packard, and, 2d, Japhet Beal; Sylvester, 1757; Sarah, m. Samuel
Robbins; Mercy, m. Thomas Churchill; Zacheus, 1762, m. Meriam Churchill;
Ruth, m. Simeon Valler; Hannah, m., 1st, a Robinson, and, 2d, a Fish; and
Samuel. ZACHEUS, m., 1802, Charlotte Wingboth. ZEPHANIAH, son of 2d
Nathaniel, m., 1739, Sarah, d. of William Bradford, and had Bradford, 1739;
Zephaniah, 1741, m. Mercy Bradford; Sarah, 1743; Lucy, 1747; Deborah, 1750.
ZEPHANIAH, son of 2d James, m., 1796, Bethiah Churchill, and had John
Calderwood, 1797. For other branches of the Holmes family, including that
of Kingston, see "The Holmes Genealogy," in Giles' Memorial.

HOLT, DANIEL, m., 1836, Sarah A. Sanborn.

HOOK, JOHN, came in the Mayflower 1620, and died the first
winter.

HOOKER, SAMUEL, m. Mary, d. of Thomas Willet, 1658, and had
Thomas, 1659; Samuel, 1661; William, 1663; John, 1665; James, 1666;
Roger, 1668; Nathaniel, 1671; Mary, 1673, m. James Pierpont of New
Haven; Hezekiah, 1675; Daniel, 1679; Sarah, m. Stephen Buckingham of
Norwalk, Conn.

HOPKINS, BARNABAS, by wife Henrietta, had Clement, 1804; Eusebius,
1806; Zervia, 1808. CALEB, son of Stephen, died, unmarried, at Barbadoes,
after 1644. GILES, Yarmouth, son of Stephen, came in the Mayflower with
his father. He m., 1639, Catherine Wheldon, and had Mary, 1640; Stephen,
1642, m. Mary, d. of William Merrick; John, 1643; Abigail, 1644, m. William
Merrick; Deborah, 1648; Caleb, 1651; Ruth, 1653; Joshua, 1657, m. Mary, d.
of Daniel Cole; William, 1661; Elizabeth, 1664. STEPHEN, came in the Mayflower 1621, with 2d wife, Elizabeth, and two children of 1st wife, Giles, and
Constance, the latter of whom m. Nicholas Snow. He had, on the passage,
Oceanus, and after arrival, Damaris, m. Jacob Cooke; Deborah, m. Andrew
Ring; Caleb, Ruth, and Elizabeth. THOMAS went from Plymouth, 1636, to
Providence, and m. Elizabeth, d. of William Arnold, and had William,
Thomas, and perhaps Joseph.

HORTON, SAMUEL, m., 1767, Hannah Doty.

HOSEA, DANIEL, m., 1768, Hannah Bartlett. ROBERT, m., 1758, Mercy Churchill.

HOSMER, GEORGE WASHINGTON, from Northfield, m., 1831, Hannah Poor, d. of James Kendall.

HOVEY, AARON, son of 1st Dominicus, had Joseph; Ruth, m. Spooner Cornish; Frances; Sarah C.; Eliza, m. Hosea Bartlett; Aaron; and Samuel Temple. DANIEL, Ipswich, 1637, m. Rebecca, d. of Robert Andrews, and had Daniel, 1642; John; Thomas, 1648; James; Joseph; Nathaniel, 1657; Abigail; and Priscilla, m. John Ayers. He afterwards lived in Brookfield and Hadley. DOMINICUS, son of 2d Ivory, by wife Mehitabel, had Dominicus, Aaron, and Gideon. DOMINICUS, son of above, by wife Elizabeth, had Dominicus, 1800; Elizabeth, 1802, m. James Picket, of Freetown; and Josiah C., 1806. EBENEZER, son of 1st Ivory, had a son Thomas. IVORY, Ipswich, son of John, had prob. a d. m. an Adams; James, 1709; Ebenezer, John, and Ivory. IVORY, son of above, m. Olivia Jordan, and had Dominicus, Ivory, Samuel; Olive, m. a Pope; Ruth, m. a Clark and James Winslow; Anna, m. Abner Bartlett. JAMES, son of 1st Ivory, m., 1735, Lydia, d. of John Atwood, and prob. had Abiah, m. Thomas Southworth Howland. He m., 2d, 1771, Mary Harlow, and 3d, 1774, Margaret Connell. JOHN, Ipswich, son of Daniel, m., 1665, Dorcas Ivory of Topsfield, and had John, 1666; Dorcas, 1668, Elizabeth, 1672; Susanna; Luke, 1676; Ivory; Abigail, 1680. JOSIAH C., son of 2d Dominicus, m., 1830, Judith Witherill, and had Dominicus, 1831; Frances E., 1833; Adelaide A., 1836, m. Austin Morton; Josiah C., 1842; and Freelove Scott Barden, 1844. SAMUEL, son of 2d Ivory, by wife Catherine, had Olive, 1779; Mary, 1780; June, 1782; Catherine, 1785; Samuel, 1787; Sylvanus Jourdaine, 1791.

HOWARD, EBENEZER, son of 2d John, m., 1777, Bethiah Rogers, and had William, Ebenezer, Samuel Thomas, Mary, Bethiah, and Eunice. EBENEZER, son of 3d John, m., 1804, Thankful Lemote. FRANCIS, son of 2d James, m., 1751, Elizabeth Curtis, and had Francis, 1753, m. Mary Dunham. JAMES, Bridgewater, son of 1st John, m. Elizabeth, d. of John Washburn, and had Elizabeth, 1686, m. Thomas Buck; Mercy, 1688; James, 1690. JAMES, Bridgewater, son of above, m., 1710, Elizabeth Wallis, and had Mercy, 1714; Huldah, 1716. He removed to Plymouth, and m., 2d, 1723, Sarah Billington, and had John, 1724; Mary, 1726, m. Thomas Pitts; James, 1728; Francis, 1731; Sarah, 1734, m. Joseph Tribble; William, 1742. He prob. m., 3d, 1747, Thankful Branch, and had Thomas, 1747, m. Ruth, d. of John Holmes. JAMES, son of above, m., 1752, Mercy Warren of Middleboro'. JAMES, m., 1772, Margaret Holmes. JAMES, son of 3d John, m., 1800, Hannah, d. of Wilson Churchill, and had Hannah, m. William D. Winsor of Kingston; James Henry; Cordelia, m. Thomas May; Ellen, m. William Congdon; John W.; Curtis Cushman, m. Roxanna Hatch. JAMES, son of 4th John, m. Angelius M. Wells, and had Jane A., Chester J., Caroline M., Charles W. JOHN came from England before 1643, with a brother, James, and settled in Duxbury. James went to Bermuda, and John remained in the family of Miles Standish. He was one of the original proprietors of Bridgewater, where he m. Martha, d. of Thomas Hayward. He and his descendants wrote their name Hayward until 1700, when it was changed to Howard, to conform to the pronounciation in use. It is possible that the original name was Hayward, and that the first step in the change was the omission of the third letter. His children were John, m. Sarah, d. of Robert Latham; James; Jonathan, m. Sarah Dean; Elizabeth, m. Edward Fobes; Sarah, m. Zacheus Packard; Bethiah, m. Henry Kingman; Ephraim, m. Mary, d. of James Keith. JOHN, son of 2d James, m., 1746, Eunice Curtis, and had John, 1748; James, 1750, m. Margaret Holmes; Martha, 1753, m. Ansel Holmes; Ebenezer, 1755, m. Bethiah Rogers; Mary, 1757; Eunice, 1759, m. William Drew; Sarah, 1765, m. Richard Holmes. JOHN, son of above, m., 1770, Eleanor Cobb, and had John; Meltiah, m. Lydia, d. of Ebenezer Luce; James; Eleanor, m. Charles Howard of Bridgewater; Ebenezer; Margaret, m. Rufus Robbins. JOHN, son of above, went to Cornish, N. H., and there m., 1803, Margaret Ray. He then removed to Morristown, Vt., and finally to Rochester, Vt. His children were Meltiah Cobb, m. Charity Trask; James, m. Angelius M. Wells; Louisa, unmarried. MELTIAH, son of 2d John, m., 1803, Lydia, d. of Ebenezer Luce, and had Meltiah. MELTIAH, son of above, m., 1833, Ruth Ann Bradford, and had Daniel Dillaway, 1834, m. Elizabeth, d. of Nelson Holmes; Margare Robbins, 1837, m. William K. Blake; Alice B., m. Martin F. Benson; Lydia A., 1848; Meltiah, 1851; Josiah B., 1855. MELTIAH COBB, son of 3d John, m. Charity Trask, and had Horace H., and Cynthia. THOMAS, Bridgewater, son of 2d James, m. Ruth, d. of John Holmes of Plymouth, and had Thomas, m. Sarah, wid. of Miles Standish.

HOWE, THOMAS, from Boston, m., 1832, Elizabeth H. Fuller of Kingston.

HOWES, JEREMIAH, son of Joseph, m., 1734, Meriah Morton, and had Sylvanus, 1735, m. Thankful Rider; Rebecca, 1738; Ebenezer, 1740; Meriah, 1743; Jerusha, 1746; Sarah, 1751. He m., 2d, Hannah Churchill, and had Meriah, 1762. JOSEPH, m., 1714, Hannah Rider.

HOWLAND, ABRAHAM, Pembroke, son of 1st Samuel, m., about 1700, Ann, d. of Nathaniel Colson of Newport, and had Rouse, 1706; Abraham; Samuel, 1717; Joseph, 1722; Benjamin, 1724, m. Experience Edgarton of Halifax; Sarah, 1707, m. a Dawes; Elizabeth, 1706, m. a Bonney; Mary, 1704, m. Jacob Mitchell, and a d. m. Jedediah Beals. ABRAHAM, Pembroke, son of above, m., 1731, Sarah Simmons, and had Ann, 1732; Hannah, 1734, m. Isaac Delano; Sylvesta, 1736; Rachel, 1738, m. Stephen Stockbridge; Sarah, 1740, m. a Haynes; Betty, 1743; Lydia, 1745, m. Noah Simmons; Rebecca, m. a Martin; Abraham; Isaac, m. Sarah Doten; Joanna, m. a Harlow; Jacob, m. Sarah Holmes; Naomi; Ruth, m. Luke Stetson; Content, m. Ellis Holmes. ABRAHAM, son of above, m., 1793, Elizabeth Finney, and had William, 1794, m. Polly Bramhall Clark; Betsey, 1797, m. John Swift. ABRAHAM, son of 8th John, m. Caroline Vaughn, and had Walter, Clarence, Edwin D., and Emma. ABNER, Freetown, son of 11th John, m. Ruth Gould, and had Otis. ANSEL, Sandwich, son of 3d Jabez, m. Elizabeth Bodfish, and had Jason, James, Shadrach Nye, Ansel, Betsey, Sally, Sophronia. ALLEN, Pembroke, son of 2d Robert, m. Sally Oldham, 1796, and had James, 1797:

Allen, 1799; Michael, 1800; Mahala, 1803; Lucy O., 1805; Candace, 1807; Sally, 1809. ARTHUR, Marshfield, brother of 1st John and 1st Henry, m. wid. Margaret Read and had Arthur; Mary, m. Timothy Williamson; Deborah, m. John Smith of Plymouth; Martha, m. John Damon of Scituate; Elizabeth, m. John Low. His will mentions a grandson, John Walker. ARTHUR, Marshfield, son of above, m., 1667, Elizabeth, d. of Thomas Prence, and had Ebenezer, 1671; Prince, 1672; Thomas, Arthur, Abraham. ARTHUR, Marshfield, son of above, by wife Deborah, had Thomas, Arthur, Prince; Mary, m. a Goddard; Elizabeth, m. a Saunders; Hannah, m. a Smith. ARTHUR, Marshfield, son of above, m. Abigail Eames, 1721, and had Abigail, 1722; Elizabeth, 1723, m. a Whitmore; Arthur, 1728. ARTHUR, Marshfield, son of above, m., 1750, Jerusha Ford, and had Susanna, 1751; Jane, 1753; Elizabeth, 1755, m. Gershom Sherman; Arthur, 1758; Consider, 1760, m. Ruth Church; Lucy, m. Benjamin White. ARTHUR, Marshfield, son of above, m., 1786, Beulah Wadsworth, and had Sophronia, m. William Weston; and Arthur, m. Sarah Porter. BENJAMIN, Dartmouth, son of Zoeth, m., 1684, Judith Sampson, and had Isaac, 1684, m. Hannah Allen; Abigail, 1686, m. Jonathan Ricketson; Benjamin, 1688; Desire, 1696, m. John Lapham; Barnabas, 1699, m. Rebecca Lapham; Lydia, 1701, m. George Soule. BENJAMIN, Pembroke, son of 1st Abraham, m., 1743, Experience Edgarton of Halifax, and had Colson, 1744; Priscilla, 1746. BENJAMIN, son of 3d Job, m., 1794, Hepsibah Hastings, and had Benjamin Jenkins, 1795; Mary, 1796; George, 1798; William, 1800; Warren, 1803; Mary Ann, 1805; John Adams, 1808; Hepsibah Dana, 1809. BENJAMIN JENKINS, son of above, m. Hannah Slade, and had Emily, 1822; Matilda, 1824; William, 1826; Louisa, 1827; Frances, 1830; Edward, 1832; Cornelia, 1834; Horace, 1836; Horace, 1839; Helen, 1842. BENJAMIN, Providence, son of 5th Joseph, m. Susanna Andrews, and had Charles Andrews, 1795; George, 1797; Susan Andrews, 1799; Juliette, 1800; Edward, 1802; John, 1803; Henry Augustus, 1806; Cyrus, 1807; John Andrews, 1809; Elizabeth Eddy, 1812; Thomas Grinnell, 1815. CALEB, m., 1784, Mary Sylvester of Hanover. CALVIN, son of 2d Isaac, m., 1816, Lydia Nickerson, and had Calvin, 1819; William N., 1822, m. Mary B. Soule; Lydia N., 1825, m. Benjamin Whitmore; Samuel, 1827, m. Martha A. Bartlett; Frederick, 1829, m. Mary Jane Bartlett; Isaac, 1833; Francis, 1837, m. Caroline E., d. of Franklin B. Cobb; Charles H., 1839, m. Nancy L. G. Raymond. CALVIN, son of above, m., 1842, Susan T. Wood, and had Calvin T., 1846; Emeline, 1849; Susan A., 1852. He m., 2d, Harriet A. Savery of Middleboro', and had Harriet, 1859; Angeline T., 1871. CALVIN, Carver, by wife Abigail, had Polly, 1792; John Calvin, 1799. CHARLES, son of 2d Isaac, m., 1806, Deborah Clark, and had Charles; Sally, 1807, m. Ira Litchfield; Adeline, 1809, m. Henry Finney; Deborah, m. John Harlow. CHARLES ALLEN, Quincy, son of Southworth Allen, m. Abbie F., d. of I. W. Munroe of Quincy. He m., 2d, 1871, Helen M., d. of Josiah Moore of Duxbury, and had Mabel, 1872; Charles Allen, 1877. CONSIDER, son of 1st Thomas, m., 1725, Ruth Bryant, and had Lucy, 1726, m. Abraham Hammatt; Elizabeth, 1728; Ruth, 1730, m. Thomas Crandon; Mary, 1732, m. William Thomas; Thomas Southworth, 1734, m. Abiah Hovey; Consider, 1736;

Joanna, 1738; Martha, 1739, m. Isaac LeBaron; Joseph, 1742; Bethiah, 1743, m. a Delano; Consider, 1745; Experience, 1748, m. Samuel West of Tiverton; John and Joseph, 1751, twins; Hannah, 1753. DANIEL, son of 4th John, m. Thankful Morse of Falmouth, and had John, 1780, m. Nancy Winsor; Daniel; Joseph, m. Eunice Salmon; Lucia, m. a Cushman of Plympton; Betsey, m. a Folger of Nantucket; Cynthia, m. a Chaddock of Nantucket; Susan, m. a Bartlett of Bridgewater. DANIEL, Dartmouth, son of Zoeth, m. Mary Sampson, and had Daniel, 1691; John, 1696, m. Bathsheba Barker; Isaac, 1698; Mercy; Thomas, 1701, m. Sarah Wanton; Benjamin, 1703; William, 1705; Joseph, 1708. EBENEZER, son of 2d Thomas, m., 1723, Sarah Green, and had Prince, 1725; Sarah, 1727; Susanna, 1729; Thomas, 1732; Mary, 1735; Ruth, 1738; and Lemuel. EBENEZER, Freetown, son of 1st Malachi, m., 1786, Hope Allen, and had Jedediah, Elizabeth, Hope, Caroline, Sarah. EBENEZER, Barnstable, son of 6th Isaac, m. probably Elizabeth Justice or Justus, and had Justus. ELLIS, Sandwich, son of 3d Lemuel, m. Fear Crowell, and had Solomon C., m. Adeline F. Hatch; Edward B., m. Abby S. Percival; Thomas T., m. Emeline C. Crocker; Gustavus, m. Clarissa Hatch; Eliza C. m. Lemuel Nye; Emily C. EZRECK, Freetown, son of 10th John, m., 1778, Phebe Sears of Middleboro', and had John, Ezreck, Elkanah, Polly, Abigail, Lucinda. FRANCIS, son of 1st Calvin, m. Caroline E., d. of Franklin B. Cobb, and had Judith E., 1856; Edgar T., 1859; Flora, 1865; Arthur, 1867; Carrie, 1869. FREDERICK, son of 1st Calvin, m., 1854, Mary Jane Bartlett, and had Mary Jane, 1854; Charlotte E., 1856, m. Charles O. Tribou of Brockton; Jennie A., 1857; Lewis W., 1859. FREEMAN PARKER, Abington, son of 3d William, m., 1826, Eliza, d. of Abner Bartlett of Plymouth. He m., 2d, Deborah, d. of Edward Cushing of Hanson and wid. of Daniel Sawin, and had Eliza Bartlett, 1830; Deborah Cushing, 1831; Freeman Parker, 1833; Edward Cushing, 1836; Charles William, 1838, m. Mariesta Dodge; Caroline Frances, 1840; Isaac Cushing, 1843; John Sawin, 1845. FRIEND WHITE, Hanson, son of Jonathan, m. Lucy Osborne, and had George B., m. Nancy Tilson of East Bridgewater; Friend White, m. Naomi T., d. of Alden Beal; Davis Williamson, m. Harriet Burnham; Lucy O., m. George C. Hobart; Calvin L., m. Mira Reed of Pembroke and Ada Crapo of East Bridgewater. GARDNER GREENE, New York, son of 3d Joseph, m., 1812, Louisa, d. of William Edgar, and had William Edgar, 1813; Ann Annabella Edgar, 1815, m. Rufus W. Leavitt; Abby Woolsey, 1817, m. Frederick H. Woolcott; Robert Shaw, 1820, m. Mary Woolsey; Maria Louisa, 1825, m. James Brown and James Clendennin. He m., 2d, Louisa, d. of Jonathan Meredith of Baltimore, 1829, and had Rebecca Brien, 1831, m. James Roosevelt; Meredith, 1833, m. Adelaide, d. of Daniel Torrence; Gardner Greene, 1835, m. Mary Grafton, d. of Grafton L. Dulaney of Baltimore; Joanna Howe, 1842, m. Irving Grinnell; Emma Meredith, 1847; Samuel Shaw, 1849, m. Frederika, d. of August Belmont. GEORGE, Freetown, son of 1st Isaac, m. Deborah Shaw of Middleboro', and had Elizabeth, 1776; Jacob, 1778; Deborah, 1782; Ruth, 1783; Malachi, 1787; Catherine, 1790; Joanna, 1791; Hannah, 1793; Pamelia. He m., 2d, Betsey (Barden) Chase, wid. of Otis of Freetown. GEORGE GILL, son of 3d John, m. Abigail Crocker, and had

John, Seth, and George. HARRISON OTIS, son of Southworth, m., 1845, Hannah O. Bailey of Amesbury, and had William Bailey, 1849, m. Ella May Jacobs; Mary Louisa, 1851; Abby Bailey, 1853; Ellen Maria, 1854. HENRY, Duxbury, brother of 1st John and 1st Arthur, appeared as early as 1633, and m. Mary Newland, and had Joseph, m. Rebecca, d. of John Huzzey of Hampton; Zoeth; John, m. Mary Walker; Samuel removed to Freetown; Sarah, m. Robert Dennis of Newport; Elizabeth; Mary, m. James Cudworth; Abigail, m. John Young, HENRY, Dartmouth, son of Zoeth, m., 1698, Deborah Briggs, and had Edward, 1698; Zoeth, 1701; Henry, 1703, m. Hannah Smith; Mary, 1706, m. James Russell; Abigail, 1708; Thomas, 1709, m. Content Briggs; Hannah, 1711, m. Edward Briggs. He m., 2d, 1713, Elizabeth Northrop, and had Stephen, 1716, m. Mary Briggs; Deborah, 1717; William, 1720, m. Joanna Ricketson. HENRY, son of 5th Joseph, m. Susan Baker, and had Benjamin Baker. HENRY, son of 2d Isaac, m., 1813, Susanna Leach, and had Susan W., m. Everett Finney. HENRY JENKINS, son of Southworth, m., 1832, Ellen Maria Smith, d. of Phineas Dow of Boston, and had Harriet Louisa, 1833, m. David Whitney of Auburn; Caroline Dow, 1836; Frances Ellen, 1838; Henrietta, 1840, m. Henry D. Ward of Worcester; Sarah Wyman, 1843, m. Henry Gould of Worcester; Mary Carver, 1846, m. Cyrus Henry Lang of Springfield; Horace Henry, 1850. ICHABOD, son of 2d Isaac, m., 1803, Deborah Crocker of Carver, and had Lemuel Crocker, 1808; Isaac, m. Ruth Nickerson; Susan B.; Hannah, 1805, m. Elkanah C. Finney; Maria, m. Samuel Vaughn. ISAAC, son of 1st Joshua, m., 1749, Catherine Howard of Freetown, and had George, 1752; Samuel, William, Rachel, Roba, and Hannah. He m., 2d, Ruth Mitchell. ISAAC, son of 2d Abraham, m., 1768, Sarah Doten, and had Jacob, m. Jane Hovey; Ichabod, 1781, m. Deborah Crocker; John, 1784, m. Nancy Lucas; Henry, 1786; Charles, 1788; Samuel, 1792, m. Mary Corban Holmes; Calvin, 1797; Isaac, m. Phebe Saunders; Pamelia, m. William Morton; and Joseph. ISAAC, son of 1st John, m. Elizabeth, d. of George Vaughn of Middleboro', and had Isaac, 1679; Seth, 1677, m. Elizabeth Delano; Nathan, 1687, m. Frances Coombs; Priscilla, 1681, m. Peter Bennett; Susanna, 1690, m. Ephraim Wood; Jael, 1688, m. Nathaniel Southworth; Elizabeth, 1682; Hannah, 1694, m. John Tinkham. ISAAC, Middleboro', son of above, m. Sarah, d. of Jeremiah Thomas, and had Isaac, 1714; Jeremiah, 1715, m. Betty Vaughn; Charles, 1722; and Joseph. ISAAC, Dartmouth, son of 1st Benjamin, m. Hannah Allen, and had Abraham, 1726, m. Ruth Hicks. ISAAC, Barnstable, son of 2d John, m., 1686, Ann Taylor, and had Ebenezer, 1687; Isaac, 1689, m. Elizabeth Jennings; Hannah; Mary, 1691; Ann, 1694; John, 1696; Noah, 1699; Joseph, 1702. ISAAC, Barnstable, son of above, m. Elizabeth Jennings, and had Anne, 1721; Sarah, 1722; Joseph, 1726; Benjamin, 1729; Rachel, 1734; Lemuel, 1741. JABEZ, son of 1st John, m. Bethiah Thatcher of Yarmouth, and settled in Bristol. His children were Jabez, 1669, m. Patience Stafford; John, 1673; Bethiah, 1674; Josiah, 1676, m. Yetmercy Shove; John, 1679, m. Martha Wardell; Judah, 1683; Seth, 1685; Samuel, 1686, m. Abigail Carey; Experience, 1687; Joseph, 1692, m. Bathsheba Carey of Swansea; Elizabeth, m. Nathan Townsend of Newport. JABEZ, Bristol, son of above, m. Patience Stafford and had

Bethiah, 1702; Mercy, 1704; Elizabeth, 1707, m. Samuel Little; Sarah, 1711, m. Isaac Lawton; Jabez, 1713; Bethiah, 1717, m. Samuel Barker; Thomas, 1719. JABEZ, Sandwich, son of Shubael, m., 1727, Elizabeth Percival, and had James, 1729; Jabez, 1730; Nathaniel, 1736; Elizabeth, m. Francis Wood; Ansel, 1738; Zacheus, 1747; Mary, m. John Bursley. JACOB, son of 2d Abraham, m., 1777, Sarah Holmes, and had Jacob; Sally, m. Ephraim Morton; Betsey, m. Gideon Holbrook; Lydia, m. John Nickerson. JACOB, son of above, m. Bethiah W. Curlew of Scituate, 1821, and had Jacob. He m., 2d, Sally Curlew, and had Samuel S.; Sally Ann, m. Nathaniel Jones. JACOB, son of above, m. Betsey Page of Maine, and had Lizzie Page, Arthur; and Arthur L., 1857, m. Aurilla L., d. of Alpheus K. Harmon. JACOB, son of 2d Isaac, m., 1798, Jane Hovey, and had Catherine, m. Isaac J. Lucas; and Pamelia, m. Thomas Bearse. JAMES, son of 2d Joseph, m., 1697, Mary Lothrop, and had Hannah, 1699, m. James Rickard; Abigail, 1702, m. Caleb Cook; Elizabeth, 1704, m. Thomas Washburn; Thankful, 1709; John, 1711, m. Mary Walker and Patience Spooner; James, 1713. JEDEDIAH, Freetown, son of 2d Ebenezer, by wife Susan, had James; Irene, 1829; Benjamin, Shubael, and John. JEPTHAH A., Freetown, son of Seth, m. Ruth Pearce of Freetown, and had Harrison, 1843; Amelia F., 1845; Irene B., 1848; Alfred and Anginette, twins, 1852. JEREMIAH, son of 4th Isaac, m., 1745, Betty Vaughn, and had Thankful, 1748, m. George Simmons; Betty, 1750, m., Jedediah Miller; Sarah, 1752, m. Nehemiah Burnett; Hope, 1757; Charles, 1759; Susanna, 1764. JOB, Freetown, son of 1st Joshua, m., 1750, Jemima Booth of Middleboro', and had Judith, m. Joseph Richmond; and Job. JOB P., Barnstable, son of Zacheus, m. Anna Lovell, and had Amanda Ann, 1814, m. Owen Bearse; John Fish, 1816; George Lovell, 1818. JOB, son of 3d John, m. Hannah Jenkins, and had Mary, 1755; John, 1757; Shove, 1759; Hannah, 1762; Job, 1764; Joanna, 1766; Benjamin, 1770; Mehitabel, 1773, m. Heman Nye of Sandwich; Southworth, 1775; Timothy, 1777. JOB, Conway, son of above, m., 1792, Mary Fisher, and had Catherine, 1794; Otis, 1796; Warren Shove, 1798; Fisher, 1800; Mary, 1803; Catherine, 1805; Job Fisher, 1808; Jonathan Otis, 1810; Charles Jenkins, 1814; William Milton, 1817. JOB FISHER, son of above, m., 1834, Emily Alvord of Greenfield, and had Mary Catherine, 1836; Catherine Elizabeth, 1837; Elijah Alvord, 1839, m. Susan A. Williams; Henry Raymond, 1844, m. Rebecca Letchworth of Mt. Holly, N. J. JOHN came in the Mayflower 1620, and m. Elizabeth, d. of John Tilley, and had Desire, m. John Gorham; John, 1626; Jabez; Hope, 1629, m. John Chipman; Joseph, m. Elizabeth Southworth; Isaac, 1649, m. Elizabeth Vaughn; Elizabeth, m. Ephraim Hicks and John Dickerson of Barnstable; Lydia, m. James Brown of Swansea; Ruth, m. Thomas Cushman. JOHN, Barnstable, son of above, m., 1651, Mary, d. of Robert Lee of Barnstable, and had Mary, m. John Allen; Elizabeth, 1655, m. John Bursley; Isaac, 1659; Hannah, 1661, m. Jonathan Crocker; Mercy, 1663, m. Joseph Hamblin; Lydia, 1665, m. Joseph Jenkins; Experience, 1668; Ann, 1670, m. Joseph Crocker; Shubael, 1672, m. Mercy, d. of Peter Blossom; John, 1674. JOHN, Barnstable, son of above, by a 1st wife, had George Gill, 1705, m. Abigail Crocker; Hannah, 1708; Mary, 1711; Joanna, 1715. He m., 2d, 1719, Mary

Crocker, and had John, 1721, m. a d. of Daniel Lewis of Pembroke; and
Job, 1726   JOHN, son of above, m. a d. of Daniel Lewis of Pembroke, and
had John, died in the West Indies; Anna, m. Rev.
Ezra Weld of Braintree;
Daniel, m. Thankful Morse of Falmouth; William, m. Elizabeth Lewis Ripley;
James, m. Sarah Thomas; and Charles, m. Sophia Thompson; and Calvin,
m. Abigail, d. of Lemuel Church of Rochester. JOHN, Duxbury, son of
Daniel, m. Nancy Winsor, and had Ann Thomas, 1809, m. Nathaniel Winsor;
John, 1812; Cordelia Maria, 1813; Lucian Lorenzo, 1819, m. Elizabeth Newell
Smith of Barre; and Jerome F., 1827, m. Harriet, d. of James Fowle of Bos-
ton. JOHN, son of James, m., 1st, Mary Walker, and 2d, Patience, d. of
Thomas Spooner, 1742, and had Patience, 1746; Patience, 1749, m. Ben-
jamin Rider. JOHN, son of 5th Joseph, m. Mary, d. of John Carlisle, 1788,
and had Alfred, 1790; Penelope, 1792, m. Amherst Everett of Attleboro';
Benjamin Russell, 1793, moved to Nashville; Janetta, 1801; Mary, 1805, m.
Roland Lyman of Easthampton. JOHN, son of 2d Isaac, m. Nancy Saunders,
1816, and Nancy Lucas, 1819, and had Charles H., m. Betsey L. Morton and
Eunice B. Finney; John, m. Mercy Jane Tinkham of Middleboro; Abraham,
m. Caroline Vaughn; Sarah, m. John Whiting; and Allen. JOHN, Freetown,
son of 1st Samuel, had a wife, Rebecca, and the following children: a son,
born 1717; Rebecca, 1718; Sarah, 1720; Penelope, 1722; Susanna, 1723.
JOHN, Freetown, son of 1st Joshua, m. Abigail, d. of Isaac Peirce of Middleboro', 1736, and had Judah, 1738; Elizabeth, m. Job Simmons of Freetown;
John, m. Lydia, d. of Shadrach Peirce of Middleboro, 2d, Beulah Bemis,
and 3d, Rachel, d. of Hilkiah Peirce and wid. of John Perkins; Abigail,
m. Lot Hathaway of New Bedford; Mercy, m. John Edminster of Freetown;
Rufus, m. Bathsheba Cannedy; Lavina, m. Noah Ashley of Freetown; Judith,
1775, m. Earl Sears of Middleboro'; and Ezreck, m. Phebe Sears of Middleboro'. JOHN, Freetown, son of above, m. Lydia Peirce, 1763, and had Eber,
1763, m. Lucretia Lamb; Abiah, 1765; Abner, 1767; Abner, 1769, m. Ruth
Gould of Sutton; Lydia, m. Welcome Jenks of Brookfield; and Judith,
m. Leonard Watson of Spencer. JOHN, Conway, son of 3d Job, m., 1786,
Grace, d. of William Avery of Dedham, and had Asa, 1787, m. Phebe Thompson of Heath and Mrs. Nancy Tilton; Joseph, 1789; Grace, 1791; William
Avery, 1794; Timothy Metcalf, 1796; Allen, 1799. JOHN, son of 2d Nathaniel, m. Jane King, and had John; Nathaniel, 1775. JONATHAN, Hanson, son
of 4th Samuel, m. Lucy White, and had Samuel, 1802; Sapphira, 1804; Alvan,
1808; Friend White, 1811. He m., 2d, 1812, Lydia Jennings, and had Isaac
Jennings, 1813; Lucinda White, 1815; Lydia Jennings, 1817; Betsey, 1820;
John, Martin, and Sarah. JOSEPH, Duxbury, son of 1st Henry, m. Rebecca,
d. of John Huzzey of Hampton, N. H., and had Jedediah, 1685; Patience,
1687; Lydia, 1689. JOSEPH, son of 1st John, m., 1664, Elizabeth, d. of
Thomas Southworth, and had Lydia, 1665, m. Jeremiah Thomas; Elizabeth;
Mary, m. George Connett; Thomas, James; Nathaniel, 1671; Benjamin, 1680;
Sarah, 1697; and Joseph. JOSEPH, Norwich, son of 2d Nathaniel, m., 1772,
Lydia, d. of Ephraim Bill of Norwich, and had Lydia, 1773, m. Levi Coit;
Abigail, 1776, m. George Muirson Woolsey; Susan, 1779, m. John Aspinwall
of New York; Joseph, 1780; Elizabeth Burt, 1782, m. George Brinckerhoff;

Harriet, 1784, m. James Roosevelt; William Bill, 1786; Gardner Greene, 1787; Nathaniel, 1789; Samuel Shaw, 1790, m. Joanna Hone; Mary Ann, 1792, m. Ezra C. Woodhull; Edward, 1794; Francis, 1796. JOSEPH, Swansea, son of 1st Jabez, m. Bathsheba Carey, and had Lydia, 1715; Joseph, 1717; Elizabeth, 1719. JOSEPH, Newport, son of above; m. Sarah, d. of Jeremiah Barker, and had Henry, 1751, m. Susan Baker; Penelope, 1755, m. John Taber; John, 1757, m. Mary, d. of John Carlisle of Providence; Benjamin, 1768; Samuel, Edward, and Josiah. JOSEPH, Pembroke, son of Rouse, m., 1768, Lydia Bearse, and had Perez; Sylvia, 1772; Joseph, 1776; Peddy, 1778. JOSEPH AVERY, Worcester, son of Southworth, m. Adeline, d. of Josiah Henshaw of West Brookfield, and had Abby Caroline, 1848; Arthur Henshaw, 1852. JOSHUA, Freetown, son of 1st Samuel, m., 1709, Elizabeth Holloway of Taunton, and had John, 1710, m. Abigail Pierce of Middleboro'; Malachi, m. Hopestill Dwelley; Job, Gershom, Joshua; and Elizabeth, m. William Nelson of Middleboro'. He m., 2d, Dorothy Lee, and had Samuel, 1726; Isaac, 1727; Philip, 1730; George, 1733; Phebe, 1736; Lydia, 1739; Betsey, 1741, m. Levi Rounseville of Freetown. JOSHUA, Freetown, son of above, m. Mary Allen, and had Joshua, m. Phebe Chase, and wid. Abigail Pierce, d. of Silas Hathaway of Freetown; Seth, m. Mary Russell of Nantucket; Keturah; and Wealthea, m., 1771, Seth Hathaway. JOSHUA, Freetown, son of above, m. Phebe Chase, and had Mary, 1778, m. William Rounseville of Carlisle, N.Y.; Wealthea, 1780, m. Edmund Peirce of Freetown; Phebe, 1783, m. Joseph Evans of Freetown; Katurah, 1785, m. Malachi Howland. He m., 2d, 1789, Abigail (Hathaway) Peirce, and had Seth, 1789, m. Abigail Ashley and Philena Hoskins. JOSIAH, Bristol, son of 1st Jabez, m. Yetmercy Shove, and had Yetmercy, 1713, m. Isaac Palmer and Nathaniel Howland; Elizabeth, John, Samuel, Patience; Josiah, 1717. JUSTUS, Barnstable, son of 3d Ebenezer, by wife Abigail, had Benjamin, 1737; Elizabeth, 1739; Lemuel, 1742; Nathaniel, 1745; Ellis, 1747. LEMUEL CROCKER, son of Ichabod, m., 1828, Hannah Jane Burt, and had Lemuel Crocker, 1828, m. Charlotte B. Swift; William H., 1830, m. Charlotte G. Courtney and Lucy Baker; Hannah, 1833, m. Philip W. Loud; Susan B., 1837, m. Lewis Henry Brown; and Isaac, 1840, m. Sarah Nash. He m., 2d, Ann M. Rich of Falmouth. LEMUEL CROCKER, son of above, m. Charlotte B. Swift, and had Herbert L., 1856; Richard W., 1859; and Edgar W., 1863. LEMUEL, Sandwich, son of Justus, m. Abigail Hamlin, and had Ellis, 1779, m. Fear Crowell; Nathaniel, m. Mercy Fish; Benjamin; Betsey, m. Chipman Fish; Abigail, m. Seth Hamblin; Sarah, m. Calvin Goodspeed; Diadema, m. Charles Goodspeed; and Bethany, m Ansel Fish. LUCIEN LORENZO, son of 5th John, had Lucien Herbert LUTHER, Pembroke, son of 2d Robert, m. Hannah Oldham, and had Luther, 1798, m. Peggy Bonney; Hannah O., 1801; Deborah, 1804; Sarah C., 1810; Mehitabel N., 1811; James H., 1812; Ebenezer B., 1815; Jairus, 1817. MALACHI, Freetown, son of 1st Joshua, m., 1744, Hopestill Dwelley, and had Consider, m. Betsey Hall; Mary, 1744, m. Peregrine White; Samuel, 1746, m. Hope Clark of Middleboro' and Lucy (Pearce) Babcock; Ebenezer, m. Hope Allen; Abraham, and Elizabeth. MALACHI, son of 1st George, m., 1809, Katurah, d. of Joshua Howland, and had James, 1809; Ruth, 1812, m. John Calvin Haskins of Freetown; Mary, 1815, m. Daniel Macomber of Taunton; Harriet, 1817, m. William H. Haskins and Russell Haskins, both of Taunton; Phebe, 1819; Charles, 1821, m. Lydia Dean of Taunton; Abigail, 1824, m. William King Richmond of Freetown; Edmund P., 1827; Roba, 1830. MICHAEL, from East Bridgewater, m., 1827, Elizabeth Bartlett. NATHAN, Middleboro', son of 3d Isaac, m. Frances Coombs, and had Desire, 1712; Seth, 1715; Caleb, 1717; Priscilla, 1720; George, 1723; Ruth, 1727. NATHANIEL, son of 2d Joseph, m., 1697, Martha, d. of James Cole, and had Joseph, 1699; Mary, 1702, m. Thomas Watson; Nathaniel, 1705; Joseph, 1708; Southworth, John, and Consider. He m., 2d, 1725, Abigail, d. of Eleazer Churchill, and wid. of Francis Billington. NATHANIEL, son of above, m., 1733, Yetmercy, wid. of Isaac Palmer of Bristol, and d. of Josiah Howland, and had Nathaniel, 1735. He m., 2d, 1739, Abigail, d. of John Burt of Boston, and wid. of Richard Lane, and had Abigail, 1740, m. Joshua Pico; Nathaniel, 1742, m. Sarah Atkins; John, 1744, m. Jane King of New York; Joseph, 1750; Martha, m. Silas Atkins of Boston; Susanna, 1752. NATHANIEL, son of above, m., 1767, Sarah, d. of Silas Atkins of Boston, and had Sarah, 1768, m. Asa Whittaker. NATHAN-IEL, Dartmouth, son of Zoeth, m. Rose, d. of Joseph Allen, and had Re-becca, 1685, m. James Russell; John, 1687, m. Mary, d. of John Cooke; James, 1689, m. Deborah Cooke; Sarah, 1690, m. Timothy Aiken; George, 1693, m. Hannah Aiken; Mary, 1699, m. Peleg Smith; Content, 1702, m. a Briggs. NATHANIEL, son of last John, m., 1798, Elizabeth Coit, and had Jane King, Abbie Woolsey, George Snowden, Elizabeth Coit, and Lucy Per-kins. He m., 2d, Elizabeth Sheldon, and had Alice Goddard, Charles Shel-don, and Francis Noyes. NICHOLAS, Dartmouth, son of Zoeth, m. Hannah, d. of John Woodman, and had Abigail, 1698, m. Benjamin Russell; Mary, 1700, m. Joseph Tucker; Rebecca, 1702, m. William Sandford; Samuel, 1704, m. Sarah Soule; and Ruth. NOBLE, Freetown, son of Rufus, m. Betsey Peirce, of Middleboro' and had Pardon, Benjamin, and seven others un-known. PEREZ, Pembroke, m. Bathsheba Foster, 1804, and had Perez, 1805; Luranna C., 1807, Asa, 1811, Andrew Bearse, 1813, Daniel Foster, 1816. PRINCE, son of 2d Arthur, by wife Deborah, had Prince, 1710; Alice; and Robert, m. Margaret Sprague. PRINCE, son of 1st Robert, m., 1779, Abigail Wadsworth, and had Eden, Peleg B., and Alice. ROBERT, son of 1st Prince, m., 1733, Margaret Sprague, and had Prince, m. Abigail Wadsworth; and Robert. ROBERT, Pembroke, son of above, by wife Ruth, had Ruth, 1770; Allen, 1771; Luther, 1774; Robert, m. Mary Boylston. ROUSE, Pembroke, son of 1st Abraham, m., 1729, Anna Bonney, and had Perez; Beulah, m. Charles Bisbee; Joseph, m. Lydia Bearse, Zeruiah, 1743. He m., 2d, 1744, Lydia, d. of Samuel Bowles of Rochester, and had Diana, m. Lot Phillips. RUFUS, Middleboro', son of 10th John, m. Bathsheba Kennedy, and had Betsey, m. Elkany Peirce of Middleboro'; Mercy, m. Benjamin Reed of Free-town and John Peirce of Middleboro'; Noble, m. Betsey Peirce; Bathsheba, m. Martin Peirce; Pardon, 1793; Lucy, m. William Howland. SAMUEL, Freetown, son of 1st Henry, by wife Mary, had Content, m. a Sanford; Samuel; Isaac; Abraham, 1675; John; Joshua, m. Elizabeth Holloway and

Dorothy Lee; Gershom; and Mary, m. Philip Rounseville. SAMUEL, Pembroke, son of above, by wife Sarah, had Zebulon, m. Lydia Cushing; Caleb, m. Deborah Oldham; Ruth; Samuel, m. Sarah Joy; Ichabod, and Abigail. SAMUEL, son of 1st Calvin, m., 1850, Martha Ann Bartlett, and had Adeline, 1851; William N., 1854; Samuel H., 1862; Emma C., m. John P. Romaine of Albany. SAMUEL, Pembroke, probably son of 1st Abraham, m., 1770, Lydia Robinson, and had Lucy, 1771; Sarah, 1773; Warren, 1775; Jonathan, 1778. SAMUEL S., son of 2d Jacob, m., 1851, Rebecca M. Bartlett of New Bedford, and had Emma M., 1852. SAMUEL, Middleboro', probably son of 1st Isaac, m. Ruth Thomas, and had six children, names unknown. SAMUEL, son of Josiah, had Tabithy, m. John Peckham of Newport; and others. SAMUEL, son of 2d Isaac, m. Mary Corban Holmes, and had Calvin, and Charles. SETH, Freetown, son of 3d Joshua, m., 1808, Abigail Ashley of Middleboro', and had Joshua, 1809; Almira, 1811, m. Noah H. Evans of Freetown; Adeline, 1813; Jeptha A., 1814, m. Ruth Pearce of Freetown; William A., 1817, m. Frances A. Hundley of North Carolina; Harrison, 1820; Frank, 1822, m. Harriet Montague. He m., 2d, 1824, Phylena Hoskins, and had Maria J., 1825, m. D. H. Wilbur; Angeline, 1828; Sumner M., 1829; Caroline C., 1830, m. Levi S. Cook of Milton; Melicca D., 1833; Amanda M. F., 1835, m. Jacob C. Haskins of Lakeville; Orleans Jackson, 1837; Seth A., 1840. SHUBAEL, Sandwich, son of 2d John, m., 1700, Mercy, d. of Peter Blossom, and had Jabez, 1701; Mercy, 1710, m. Joseph Jenkins; and Zacheus. SOUTHWORTH, son of 3d Job, m., 1799, Esther Allen of Brookfield, and had Southworth Allen, 1800; Maria, 1802, m. William Avery; Harriet, 1804; Louisa, 1808, m. Galen Carpenter of Worcester; Henry Jenkins, 1810; Harrison Otis, 1813. He m., 2d, 1816, Polly, d. of Samuel Ware of Conway, and had William Ware, 1817, m. Susan Reed of Heath; Samuel, 1819; Joseph Avery, 1821; Elizabeth Sherwood, 1826, m. Hezekiah D. Perry of Monson. SOUTHWORTH ALLEN, Worcester, son of above, m., 1823, Esther Allen of Plymouth, and had Southworth Allen, 1826; Esther Allen, 1828; Charles Allen, 1829; Edward Payson, 1834, m. Elizabeth Holden of Quincy; William Otis, 1838, m. Ella F. G., d. of Isaac F. Shepard of Boston. THOMAS, son of 2d Joseph, m., 1699, Joanna, d. of James Cole, and had Consider, 1700; Joanna, 1702; Experience, 1705, m. Benjamin Lothrop; Thomas, 1707; Elizabeth, 1710; Hannah, 1712, m. William Dyer and Edward Winslow; Joanna, 1716, m. Gideon White; Joseph, 1718. THOMAS, Marshfield, son of 2d Arthur, by wife Mary, had Mercy, 1698; Rebecca, 1699; Ebenezer, 1700; John, 1702; Rebecca, 1704; William, 1708; Thomas, 1708; Samuel, 1711; Hannah, 1713. WARREN, Pembroke, son of 4th Samuel, m. Peddy Howland, 1805, and had Lewis, 1806; Ethan, 1807; Charles, 1809; Lydia, 1810; Warren, 1813; Wealthea, 1815; James Hervey, 1818. WILLIAM, son of 3d Abraham, m., 1816, Polly Bramhall Clark, and had Mary. WILLIAM EDGAR, New York, son of Gardner Greene, m., 1747, Annie, d. of Dr. Cogswell of Hartford. He m., 2d, 1854, Hortense Marie de la Roche de la Pereire, d. of Edward, of Paris, France, and had Louis Meredith, 1855; Reine Marie Antoinette, 1857. WILLIAM, son of Zacheus, m., 1796, Aurelia Yost, and had Freeman Parker, 1797; Charles, 1799; Charles,

1801; Aurelia Yost, 1806, m. Thomas Shiverick; William Henry, 1816, m. Martha Poor and Helena M. Eels. WILLIAM HENRY, Falmouth, son of above, m. as above, and had, by 1st wife, Mary Lee and Walter Channing, and by 2d, Alice and Elizabeth. WILLIAM, Freetown, son of 1st Isaac, m. Elizabeth Bryant of Freetown, 1790, and had William, m. Lucy, d. of Rufus Howland. WILLIAM A., son of Seth, m. Frances A. Hundley of North Carolina, and had James, Caroline, Henry, Alonzo, John, and Ellen. WILLIAM, Marshfield, son of 2d Thomas, by wife Mercy, had Rebecca, 1737. WILLIAM AVERY, Conway, son of 12th John, m., 1819, Hannah, d. of Consider Morton of Whately, and had Edward, 1821; William, 1822; George, 1824; Henry, 1827; Allen, 1832; Eliza Sophia, 1833; Francis, 1836; Francis, 1838; Walter Morton, 1840. WILLIAM, Lynn, son of above, m., 1860, Caroline G., d. of William L. Russell of Barre, and had William Russell, 1863; Bertha Morton, 1867. WILLIAM OTIS, Worcester, son of Southworth Allen, m., 1870, Ella F. G., d. of Isaac F. Shepard of Boston, and had Shepard, 1871; Allen Shepard, and Gerald Shepard. WILLIAM WARE, Ceylon, son of Southworth, m., 1845, Susan Reed of Heath, and had William Southworth, 1846, m. Mary L. Carpenter; Samuel Whittlesey, 1848, m. Mary E. R. Richardson; Susan Reed, 1849; Edward Hitchcock, 1851; John, 1854; Daniel Poor, 1856; Henry Martyn, 1858; David Brainard, 1861. ZACHEUS, son of 3d Jabez, m. Mary, d. of Samuel Palmer of Falmouth, and had William, 1773; Samuel Palmer, 1776; Thomas Palmer, 1778; Sarah, 1779, m. William Scudder; Susanna; Freeman and Parker, twins, 1780; Henry, Allen; Mary Palmer, m. Zenas D. Bassett of Barnstable; Job Palmer, m. Anna Lovell of Barnstable; and Allen again. ZOETH, Dartmouth, son of 1st Henry, m. a wife, Abigail, 1656, and had Nathaniel, 1657; Benjamin, 1659; Daniel, 1661; Lydia, 1663; Mary, 1666; Sarah, 1668; Henry and Abigail, twins, 1672; and Nicholas.

HOXIE, ABIATHAR, m. Lydia Clark, and had Abiathar, 1823, m. Lucy L., wid. of Alonzo Bartlett, and d. of Josiah Morton; Nathaniel C., 1828, m. Elizabeth Sampson and Caroline W. Doten; William, 1831; Edward W., 1833, m. Ruth C. Morton and Mary C. Holmes; Lydia S., 1837, m. Thomas C. Smith.

HOYE, BENJAMIN, m. Elizabeth Steiney, 1775.

HOYT, CURTIS, son of 1st Moses, m. Hannah Rider, and had Curtis, Nancy, Harriet; Bessie L., m. Elnathan Holmes. ISRAEL, son of Jonathan, m. Susanna Perkins, and had Sarah, Moses; Rachel, m. James Smith; Jonathan; Lydia, m. an Underwood. By a 2d wife he had Israel; and Susan, m. Lathly Haskins. ISRAEL, son of above, m. Ruth Allen, and had Harriet, m. Isaac B. King; Betsey, and Susan, both of whom m. Loyd Keith; and Caroline. JOHN, Salisbury, 1639, by wife Frances, had Frances, m. John Colby and John Bernard; John; Thomas, m. Mary Brown; Gregory, and Elizabeth. By a 2d wife, Frances, he had Sarah; Mary, m. Christopher Bartlett; Joseph, Marah; Naomi, m. John Lovejoy; and Dorothy. JOHN, Salisbury, son of above, m. Mary Barnes, and had William, 1660, m. Dorothy Colby; Elizabeth, 1662, m. Joseph Lanckester; John, 1663; Mary, 1664, m. John Whittier; Joseph, 1666, m. Dorothy Worthen; Sarah, m. Faun Clements; Rachel, 1670, m. Joseph Weed; Dorothy , 1674, m. perhaps Nathaniel Lovejoy; Grace, 1676; and Robert, m. Martha Stevens and Mary Currier. JOHN, Salisbury, son of Joseph, m. Mary Eastman, and had Joseph, 1727, m. Sarah Collins and wid. Meriam (Brown) Hobbs; Jonathan, 1731, m. Sarah Shepard and wid. Elizabeth (Eastman) Currier; David, 1734, m. Joanna Smith; Benjamin, 1736, m. Mary Colby; Samuel, 1740, m. Joanna Brown and wid. Anna (Sibley) Stevens; and Eastman, m. Martha Clough. JOHN F., son of 1st Moses, m. Bethiah S., d. of Barnabas Holmes, and had Deborah A., 1837, m. Cornelius Bartlett; John F., 1841, m. Sarah Blake; Moses O.; Frances, m. Hosea Bradford; Bethiah F.; Charles W., m. Anna Pierce; Elizabeth D., m. Winslow Jones of Abington and Emily Gorham. JONATHAN, son of 3d John, m. Sarah Shepard, 1753, and wid. Elizabeth (Eastman) Currier, and Phebe Marshal, and had Israel, 1754; Jonathan, 1756, m. wid. Hannah (Briggs) Aldrich; Levi, 1759; Sarah, 1761, m. Joseph Seavey; Enos, 1764; Phineas, 1766, m. Julia Ann Pinear; Benjamin, 1770, m. Sally Whipple; and Daniel, 1773. JOSEPH, son of 2d John, by wife Dorothy, had John, 1703, m. Mary Eastman; Mehitabel, 1705, m. Jeremiah Flanders; Joseph, 1708, m. Ann Pettingill; Ezekiel, 1710, m. Rebecca Brown; Judith, 1712; Nathan, 1714, m. Mary Pettingill; Moses, 1716; and Dorothy, 1718. MOSES, son of 1st Israel, m. Joanna Luce, and had John F., Moses, and Crosby. He m., 2d, Betsey Luce, and had Betsey, 1823; Joanna; Nancy, m. Benjamin Holmes; Curtis, Deborah A., and Otis. MOSES, son of above, m. Deborah A. Everson, and had Charity, and Lavilla.

HUBBARD, ABRAHAM, from Braintree, m., 1822, Deborah Whiting. BENJAMIN, Holden, son of Elisha, m., about 1803, Polly Walker, and had Warren, 1804, m. Lucy Joslyn; Simeon, 1805, m. Caroline Bennett; Levi, 1808; Lucy, 1810, m. Samuel Brooks; Alona, 1813, m. William Rogers; Persis, 1815, m. Silas Howe; Benjamin, 1817; Eli, 1820, m. Sarah Watson; Margana, 1824, m. Charles Chandler. BENJAMIN, son of above, removed to Plymouth, and m., 1844, Ellen Perry of Sandwich, and had Geraldine E., 1846; Linden P., 1850, m. Ella, d. of Lionel Churchill; Ellen H., 1863. ELISHA, Holden, son of 2d Samuel, m. his cousin, Mercy Hubbard, and had John, 1768, m. Lydia Raymond; Sarah, 1771, m. Ethan Davis; Mary, 1773, m. Peter Hubbard; Benjamin, 1781; Samuel, 1783, m. Betsey Hubbard; Elisha, m. Abigail Allen; Azubah, 1776, m. Moses Hunt; Eli, 1799, m. Mehitabel Haskel. GEORGE, born in England about 1595, settled in Watertown, and removed to Wethersfield as early as 1636, and finally to Guilford. He m. Mary Bishop, and had George, 1620; Mary, 1625, m. John Fowler; John, 1630; Sarah, 1635, m. David Harrison; Hannah, 1637, m. Jacob Mellen; Elizabeth, 1638, m. Thomas Watts and John Norton; Abigail, 1640, m. Humphrey Spinning; William, 1642, m. Abigail Dudley; Daniel, 1644, m. Elizabeth Jordan of Guilford. HENRY M., m., 1836, Mary C. Lapham. JOHN, Wethersfield, son of George, had Mary, 1651; John, 1655, m. Mary Wright; Hannah, 1656; Jonathan, 1659; Daniel, 1661, m. Esther Rice; Mercy, 1664, m. Jonathan Boodman; Isaac, 1667, m. Mary Warner; Mary, 1669, m. Daniel Warner; Sarah, 1672, m. Samuel Cowles. JONATHAN, Hatfield and Concord, son of above, m. Hannah Rice, and had Mary, 1682; Jonathan, 1683, m. Rebecca Brown; Hannah, 1685; Samuel, 1687; Joseph, 1689; Elizabeth, 1691;

John, 1693; Daniel, 1694; Thomas, 1696; Eleanor, 1700. LEVI, son of 1st Benjamin, removed to Plymouth. He m. Lusilla Haskell, and had Frank; Mary; Sarah, m. John Day; Elizabeth, m. William Parsons; Hervey N. P., 1839, m. Marcia T., d. of Thomas N. Bartlett. SAMUEL, Concord, son of Jonathan, m. Mary Clark, and had Samuel, 1713; Isaac, 1723; David, 1725. SAMUEL, Holden, son of above, by wife Eunice, had Sarah, 1740, m. Samuel Chaffin; Samuel, 1741, m. Lucy Wheeler; Elisha, 1744. By 2d wife, Abigail, he had Abel, 1751; Benjamin, 1755; Mary, 1757; Eunice, 1759; Eli, 1761; Levi, 1765; Clark, 1767; Silas, 1768. SAMUEL, m., 1734, Hannah Polden.

HUMPHREYS, JOHN, pub., 1757, to Beck Wicket, Indians.

HUNT, ASA, by wife Sarah, had Asa, 1744; Ziba, 1746; Buzi, 1748; Sarah, 1750.

HURST, JAMES, by wife probably named Catherine, had Patience, m. Henry Cobb; and perhaps others.

HUSTON, or HUESTON, NATHANIEL, son of 2d William, m., 1808, Nancy Harlow. WILLIAM, m., 1755, Elizabeth Wait, and had William, 1755. WILLIAM, son of above, m., 1778, Mary Churchill, and had William; Hannah, m. Henry McCarty; Nathaniel, 1786; Elizabeth, m. Thomas Covington; and Priscilla, m. Edward Morton. WILLIAM, son of above, m., 1803, Lucy Finney.

HUTCHINSON, ELISHA, son of Governor Hutchinson, m., about 1770, Mary, d. of George Watson. JOHN, m., 1778, Jane Kirk. ROBERT, from Scotland, m., 1811, Deborah, d. of Job Brewster, and had Susan A., 1812, m. a Rogers; Deborah Brewster, 1814, m. Benjamin Barnes; Robert, 1816, removed to New York; Lydia D., 1818, m. James Reed and a Clemmons of California. He m., 2d, Elizabeth, d. of Joshua Brewster, and had Betsey E., 1822, m. Thomas Rider; Joshua B., 1824; Emeline A., 1832, m. Lewis Holmes Whitten; Adeline, 1839, m. John Perry.

IRISH, CHARLES B., son of Sanford, m., 1828, Sarah L. Main of Marblehead, and had Charles S., 1829; Sarah M., 1830. EDWARD, Newport, son of 3d John, m. Joanna Bancroft of New Jersey, and had Hannah, 1764, m. Lawrence Clark; Sanford, 1766; Margaret, 1768, m. a Browning; Thankful, 1770, m. a Hitt; Sally, 1773, m. an Eddy; Ephraim, 1775, m. a Devol; Mary, 1777, m. an Oatley; Betsey, 1792, m. a Sanford. ELIAS, Taunton, son of 1st John, m., 1674, Dorothy, d. of William Witherell. JOHN, Duxbury, Bridgewater, and Little Compton, by wife Elizabeth, had John and Elias. JOHN, Middleboro', son of above, by wife Elizabeth, had David; Elizabeth, 1674; Jonathan, 1678; Joanna, 1681; Sarah, 1684; Priscilla, 1686; Jedediah, 1688; Content, 1691; Mary, 1695; John, 1699. He m., 2d, 1708, Deborah, d. of Richard Church. JOHN, perhaps Little Compton, son of above, had Edward, 1721; and John, 1722. SANFORD, Newport, son of Edward, m., 1797, Hannah Stanhope of Newport, and had Hannah, 1798, m. Elisha Thrasher; Charles B., 1800; Ephraim, 1802, m. a Melville; Abigail, 1805; Joanna, 1807; William Stanhope, 1809, m. Louisa Kimball; Emily, 1812, m. Isaac Sherman of Newport.

IVEY, JOHN, of Boston, m. Mercy, d. of Robert Bartlett, 1668.

JACK, JACK, a slave of Thomas Holmes, m. Patience, slave of Barnabas Churchill, 1739.

JACKSON, ABRAHAM, m., 1657, Remember, d. of Nathaniel Morton, and had Lydia, 1658, m. Israel Leavitt and Preserved Hall; Abraham; Nathaniel; Eleazer, 1669; and John, m. Abigail Woodworth. ABRAHAM, son of above, m. Margaret, d. of Samuel Hicks, 1685, and had Abraham, 1686; Samuel, 1689; Sarah, 1691, m. Thomas Hatch; Israel, 1693, m. Mercy Dunham; Seth, 1698, m. Esther Dunham; Lydia, 1699. ABRAHAM, son of above, by wife Rebecca, had Isaac, m. Sarah Bridget of Scituate; Mary, Margaret, and Abraham. ABRAHAM, son of above, m., 1741, Mary, d. of James Whiton of Plympton, and had Mary, 1742; Abraham, 1744. He m., 2d, Bethiah, d. of same, 1744, and had Isaac, 1745; Margaret, 1748. ABRAHAM, son of 1st Daniel, m. Harriet Otis, d. of John Goddard, 1818, and had Abraham, 1821; John Goddard, 1823; Thomas Otis, 1825; Horace W., 1828; George Hinckley, 1830; Isaac Carver, 1832; Isaac Winthrop, 1834; Edward Herbert, 1835; Harriet Otis, 1837. ABRAHAM, son of 1st Isaac, m., 1788, Lydia Ellines, and had Lucinda, 1789; Abraham, 1791; Olive, 1794; Robert, 1796. ALEXANDER, son of 4th Isaac, m., 1849, Caroline, d. of Nathaniel Reeves, and had Isaac, 1850, m. Elizabeth, d. of Edward Parrish of Philadelphia; Alexander, 1853, m. Abby Warren, d. of William T. Davis; Nathaniel Reeves, 1857. BENJAMIN, Halifax, son of Eleazer, had Sarah, m. John Bosworth; Susanna; and Hopestill, m. Micah Gurney. CHARLES, son of 2d Thomas, m. Lucy, d. of John Cotton, 1794, and had Charles, 1794; Thomas, 1795; Lucy, 1798, m. Charles Brown; Charles Thomas, 1801; Lydia, 1802, m. Ralph Waldo Emerson; Charles Thomas again, 1805, m. Susan Bridge of Charlestown; and John Cotton. CORNELIUS SAMPSON, son of 4th Thomas, m. Nancy B., d. of Benjamin Crandon, and had Lucy Ann, 1814, m. Asa Law of Medford. DANIEL, son of 2d Thomas, m. Rebecca Morton, 1784, and had Daniel, 1787; Rebecca, 1789, m. Josiah Robbins; Abraham, 1791; Jacob, 1794; William Morton, 1796; Thomas Taylor, 1798; Isaac Carver, 1799, and William Morton again, 1802. DANIEL, son of above, m. Elizabeth, d. of David Turner, 1809, and had Elizabeth Morton, 1813, m. Sebastian F. Streeter; Daniel Lothrop, 1817, m. Eleanor, d. of Charles Brewster; Rebecca, 1819, m. Phineas A. Stone; Sarah Taylor, 1821, m. James Allen Danforth; Susan Turner, 1823; Charles, 1825, m. Lucy B., d. of Caleb Rider of Plymouth and Emily F. Ross of Belfast; Isaac, 1827. He m., 2d, wid. Mercy Bisbee, and had Franklin, 1839; Mercy R., m. Elijah Winslow Cobb; Alfred, Theodore, and Hahneman. DAVID BARNES, son of 1st William, m., 1820, Deborah Crombie, and had William Kimball, and George Leonard. He m., 2d, 1848, Sarah Wright. EDWIN, son of Henry, m. Judith Stetson of Kingston, and had Henry H., 1845; Mary E., 1849; and Elizabeth. ELEAZER, son of 1st Abraham, m., 1690, Hannah Ransom, and had John, 1692; Eleazer, 1694; Joanna, 1696, m. William Harlow; Mercy, 1697, m. a Fuller; Hannah, 1698, m. a Pomeroy; Mary, 1701, m. a Cushman; Abigail, 1702, m. a Chandler; Deborah, 1704, m. a Brewster; Content, 1705, m. a Weston; Susanna, 1706; Ransom, 1708; Benjamin, 1710; Experience, 1713; Ephraim, 1714. GEORGE HINCKLEY, son of 5th Abraham, m. 1878, Hattie B. Robinson, and had George H., 1879.

HENRY, son of 3d Nathaniel, m., 1798, Huldah, d. of Eliphalet Holbrook, and had Henry Foster; Elizabeth A., m. Rufus B. Bradford; and Edwin. He m., 2d, Rebecca (Calder) Sargent, d. of Robert Calder of Charlestown. HEZEKIAH, son of 1st Thomas, m., 1765, Elizabeth, d. of John Thacher of Barnstable, and had Elizabeth, 1768, m. Thomas Sturgis. ISAAC, son of 4th Abraham, m., 1764, Lydia Barrows, and had Robert, 1765; Abraham, 1766; Isaac, 1769; Hosea, 1771; Hannah, 1773, m. Levi Lucas; Ransom, 1775; Israel, 1777; Lydia, 1779, m. Sylvanus Bisbee and Josiah Cotton; Olive, 1782; Nancy, 1784, m. John Churchill; Sally, 1787, m. Calvin Richmond. ISAAC CARVER, son of 1st Daniel, m. Abby, d. of Oakes Rundlett of Alna, Me., 1850, and had Isaac Morton, 1852; Gustavus R., 1856. ISAAC W., son of 5th Abraham, m., 1864, Lucretia L., d. of Sylvanus H. Churchill, and had Jennie E., 1865; Mary Taylor, 1870; Horace W., 1877. ISAAC, Boston, son of 3d Joseph, m. Sarah Thomas, and had Sarah; Isaac Newton, m. Nancy B. Webb of Weymouth; Isabella, m. Frederick Lovett of Beverly; Mary, m. Thomas H. Bacon of Boston; Alexander, 1819; John, Fanny, and Annie. JACOB, son of 1st Daniel, m., 1824, Joanna Holmes, and had Joanna, 1829, m. Lewis Gould Lowe of Bridgewater; Levantia, 1831; Sophia G., 1833; Gustavus; Lydia; Mary Ann; Andrew, 1839; Marcia E., 1843, m. Samuel P. Gates of Bridgewater. JEREMIAH, from Boston, m., 1702, Hannah, d. of Samuel Rider, and had Thomas, 1704, who removed to North Carolina; Jeremiah removed to Boston; Hannah m. James Nicolson; and Faith, m. James Shurtleff. JOHN, Middleboro', came from England, m. Mary, d. of John Smith, and had John and Cornelius, and died 1731. JOHN, Middleboro', son of above, m., 1735, Joanna, d. of Joseph Bates, and had Joseph, John, and Solomon, and removed to Vassalboro' before the revolution. JOSEPH, son of 1st Nathaniel, m. Remembrance Jackson, 1724, and had Joseph, 1725; and Lois, m. Gideon Gifford. JOSEPH, son of above, by wife Mary, had Remembrance, 1743. JOSEPH, Middleboro', son of 2d John, m., 1777, Rebecca, d. of Jacob Green, and had Solomon, Sarah, Joseph, Isaac, John; Rebecca, m. Jacob Smith; and Samuel. JOSEPH, Middleboro', son of above, m. Hannah Leonard, and had Caroline, m. Luke Perkins; Susan, m. Bradford Harlow; and Joseph. LEMUEL, son of 2d Nathaniel, m., 1735, Esther, d. of Thomas Savery, and had Jacob, 1736; Lemuel, 1738; David, 1740; Lemuel again, 1752. LEAVITT TAYLOR, Brunswick, Me., son of 1st William, m., 1820, Betsey Hall of Norton, and had Anna Barnes, 1820; William Francis, 1824. NATHANIEL, son of 1st Abraham, m., 1686, Ruth, d. of Samuel Jenney, and had Nathaniel; Joseph; Samuel; Ruth, 1700, m. David Turner; Thomas, 1703; and Ann, m. a Jones; and Joseph Tribble. NATHANIEL, son of above, by wife Abigail, had Lemuel, 1713; Nathaniel, 1716. He m., 2d, Rebecca Poor, 1720, and had Lydia, 1721, m. Benjamin Delano; Abigail, m. David Gorham; Hannah, m. Benjamin Bagnell; Rebecca m. Nathaniel Morton; Elizabeth, m. Samuel Bartlett; and Molly. NATHANIEL, son of 1st Thomas, m., 1768, Elizabeth, d. of Thomas Foster, and had Nathaniel, m. Deborah Harlow; Hezekiah, 1770, m. Sarah Nicolson ; Betsey, m. William Harlow ; and Henry, 1774. He m., 2d, 1776, Martha Bartlett. NATHANIEL, Lunenburg, son of above, m. Deborah, d. of William Harlow, and had William Harlow,

1801, m. Caroline Robinson; Lucy, 1806; Joseph, 1809; Edwin, 1812, m. Lovina Smith; Nathaniel, 1812, Mary, 1816; Eliza, 1819. NATHANIEL, Middleboro', who died 1768, by wife Patience, had Eunice, m. a House; Nathaniel, William, and Barnabas. RANSOM, son of Eleazer, m., 1736, Eleanor Doten of Middleboro', and had Hannah and John. RANSOM, son of 1st Isaac, m., 1799, Sarah Faunce, and had Hosea, 1800; Luther, 1801. SAMUEL, son of 2d Abraham, by wife Elizabeth, had Joanna, 1713; Elizabeth, 1716; Samuel, 1718; Sarah, 1722. SAMUEL, son of 1st Thomas, m., 1753, Experience, d. of John Atwood, and had Thomas, 1754; Samuel, m. Hannah Southworth; Experience, m. John Cotton; Mary, m. John Russell; Elizabeth, m. Samuel Brooks; Deborah, 1766, m. William Crombie; George, m. Susan Willard; Naomi, m. Calvin Crombie; Hannah, 1777, m. Zacheus Bartlett. SALISBURY, son of 1st William Hall, m., 1801, Sally, d. of John Goodwin, and had Louisa Salisbury, 1803; Deborah Salisbury, 1804; Sally Gorham, 1806, m. William Kapsur; Evelina Goodwin, 1809, m. Eleazer Stephens Bartlett; Samuel Salisbury, 1811; William Hall, 1819; Salisbury, 1817. SAMUEL SALISBURY, son of Salisbury, m., 1833, Mary Ann, d. of Heman Cobb. He m., 2d, 1837, Harriet N. Tenney, and had Harriet Louisa, 1843. SETH, m., 1760, Ann May of Halifax. THOMAS, son of 1st Nathaniel, m., 1724, Hannah Woodworth, of Little Compton, and had Hezekiah, 1725; Thomas, 1729; Samuel, 1731; Ruth, 1733, m. Ebenezer Nelson; Hezekiah, 1738; Nathaniel, 1742; William Hall, 1744; Hannah, 1747, m. Joseph Penniman; Molly, 1749, m. Nathaniel Goodwin; and Elizabeth. THOMAS, son of above, m., 1751, Sarah, d. of Jacob Taylor, and had Sarah, 1752; Sarah, 1753, m. Thomas Witherell; Hannah, 1755, m. John Goodwin; Thomas, 1757; Lucy, 1759, m. Stephen Marcy; Daniel, 1761; William, 1763; Priscilla, 1765, m. Rosseter Cotton; Lydia, 1767; Lydia, 1768; Charles, 1770; Rebecca, 1772, m. Ward Cotton of Boylston; Woodworth, 1775. THOMAS, son of above, m., 1788, Sally May, and had Thomas, 1788; Edwin, 1790; Sarah, 1793. THOMAS, son of 2d Samuel, m., 1783, Lucy Sampson, and had Ezra, 1783; Cornelius Sampson, 1785; Desire, 1788; Frederick, 1791; Caroline, 1793; George, 1797; Thomas, 1799; Lucy, 1801. He m., 2d, Sarah LeBaron, 1805, and had Mary Ann, 1806; Priscilla Alden, 1809. THOMAS, son of above, m. Sophronia N., d. of Joseph Bishop of Rochester, and had Lucia S., 1838, m. George H. Griffin; George F., 1840, m. Hannah T., d. of Thomas Mayo; Betsey A., 1845, m. Edward E. Green; and Cornelius S., m. Emma L. Wright of Cambridge. He m., 2d, 1873, Mary Ann, wid. of Silas Shaw, and d. of Luke Perkins. THOMAS OTIS, son of 5th Abraham, m., 1864, Sarah Fuller, d. of Philip Washburn of Kingston, and had Thomas, 1865; Grace Otis, 1868, Philip, 1874; Hannah W., 1880. WILLIAM, son of 2d Thomas, m., 1788, Anna, d. of David Barnes of Scituate, and had Frances Leonard, 1789, m. Samuel Maynard; Leavitt Taylor, 1790; David Barnes, 1794. He m., 2d, 1795, Mercy, d. of John Russell, and had Frederick William, 1796; Frederick William again, 1798; Anna, 1799; William R., 1801. He m., 3d, 1804, wid. Esther (Phillips) Parsons. WILLIAM HALL, son of 1st Thomas, m., 1766, Deborah, d. of Benjamin Salisbury of Boston, and had William, 1766; Salome, 1768; Salisbury, 1772. He m., 2d, Sally Gorham of Barnstable. WILLIAM

HALL, son of Salisbury, m., 1837, Rebecca S. Walker of Duxbury, and had William Hall, 1842; Rebecca, 1849. WILLIAM MORTON, son of 1st Daniel, m., 1828, Sylvina, d. of Spenser Brewster of Kingston, and had Sylvina Augusta, 1828; William Spenser, 1830; Morton Spenser, 1836. WILLIAM FRANCIS, Roxbury, son of Leavitt Taylor, m., 1850, Abby Crocker West of Norton, and had William Leavitt, 1853; George West, 1858; James Marsh, 1863. WOODWORTH, son of 2d Thomas, m., 1800, Maria Morton, d. of John Torrey, and had Betsey Morton, 1801; Maria Torrey, 1804; John Torrey, 1814.

JAMES, RALPH, m., 1650, Mary Fuller.

JARVIS, THOMAS, from Boston, m., 1804, Judith Hedge.

JEFFREY, ACCALABA, m., 1734, Betty Simmons, Indians. AMOS, m., 1763, Phebe Sepit, Indians.

JENNEY, JOHN, from Norwich, England, came in the James, 1623. He m. in Leyden, 1614, Sarah Carey of Moncksoon, England, whom he brought, with children Samuel; Abigail, m. Henry Wood; and Sarah. He had here, John and Susanna. SAMUEL, son of above, m. Ann, d. of Thomas Lettice, and had Samuel, 1659; and Ruth, m. Nathaniel Jackson.

JENNINGS, JOSEPH, m. Polly Cotton, 1780. He m., 2d, Sarah Holbrook, 1795, and had Mercy, m. Truman Bartlett; Sarah, m. Daniel Rider; Mary, and Abby.

JENKINS, BENJAMIN, m. Sarah, d. of Isaac Cole, 1835, and had Sarah W., 1836, m. Ezra Thomas; Nancy T., 1840, m. George S. Ryder; Lizzie H., 1812, m. Charles W. Huff; Benjamin S., 1844, m. Annie H. d. of Hiram Delano of Duxbury. CALEB of Scituate, m. Elizabeth Tilson, 1790. JOHN, Plymouth, 1643, removed to Barnstable, m. Mary Ewer, 1653, and had Sarah, 1653; Mehitabel, 1655; Samuel, 1657; John, 1659; Mary, 1662; Thomas, 1666; Joseph, 1669.

JERMAN, WILLIAM, m. Eleanor Thomas, 1746.

JOB, HASADIAH, m. Betty Sepit, 1760.

JOHNSON, BRANCH, son of Joseph, m. Nancy Atwood, 1829, and had William Henry. CLARK, son of 2d Jacob, m. Sylvia Gibbs of Sandwich, 1802. JACOB, m. Sarah Clark, 1731, and had Sarah, 1732, m. Cornelius Morey; Jacob, 1734; Thomas, 1736; Josiah, 1738, m. Bathsheba Barrows. JACOB, son of above, m. Hannah Mason, 1759, and had Joseph, 1760; Thomas, 1762, m. Susanna Sylvester; Abigail, 1764; Mason, 1766; Jacob, 1768; and Clark. JACOB, son of above, m. Betsey Bates, 1793, and had Susanna, 1797. He m., 2d, Abigail Bates, 1800, and had Betsey, 1804; Sylvia, 1806; Abigail, 1809; Hannah Mason, 1812. JACOB, m. Eunice Cushman of Plympton, 1764. JAMES, m. Ann Cook, 1717. JOHN, m. Elizabeth Gould, 1720. JOSEPH, son of 2d Jacob, m. Betsey Blackmer, 1788, and had Hannah, 1790; Betsey, 1793, m. Samuel Doten Holmes; Josiah, 1795; Branch, 1801; Mary, 1801, m. Joseph Simes; Mercy Blackmer, 1804, m. a Wardwell. JOSIAH, probably son of 1st Robert, m. Patience Faunce, 1747, and had Josiah, 1748; Patience, 1752; Eleazer, 1755. JOSIAH, son of above, m. Bethiah Rider, 1772, and had Josiah. JOSIAH, son of above, m. Hannah Bramhall, 1807, and had Josiah, 1808; Thomas, 1811. RICHARD FRANCIS, from Kingston, m. Polly Turner, 1791. ROBERT, m. Elizabeth Cook, 1715, and had Jane, 1716; Joseph, 1718; Sarah, 1720; Caleb, 1722; and probably Josiah. ROBERT, m. Mary Cook, 1717, and had Elizabeth, 1718; Mary Carver, 1721; Robert Carver, 1723.

JONES, ADAM, by wife Mary, had Mercy, 1703; Remembrance, 1705. CLEMENT, m. Mary Dike, 1815. JOHN, m., 1740, Sarah Barnes, and had John, 1742; Thomas, 1744; Sarah, 1747; James, 1749. JOHN, m. Lydia Tinkham, and had John, 1759; John, 1763; Benjamin, 1767; Ebenezer, 1769; Lydia, 1771; Ebenezer, 1774.

JOSLIN, ISAAC, m. Mary Boylston, 1797. JACOB, m. Abigail Rider, 1795, and had William, 1796. SAMUEL, of Boston, m. Adaline Tinkham, 1827. SIMON of Pembroke, m. Betsey Delano, 1814.

JORDAINE, JOURDAINE, or JORDAN, JOHN, had Barack, 1650, m. Mary Wilder; and probably Thomas, m. Esther Hall and Jehosabeth, m. John Robbins.

JUDSON. See "Landmarks."

KEEN, SNOW, of Pembroke, m. Rebecca, d. of Timothy Burbank, 1756. TILDEN, son of 2d William, m. Joanna Pearson, 1817, and had Tilden Holmes, 1822, and Phebe Pearson, 1821. WILLIAM, probably a descendant from Joseph of Duxbury, who m., 1665, Hannah Dingley, m. Ruth Sargent, and had Elizabeth, 1744; Ruth, 1746; Grace, 1748. He m., 2d, 1755, Margaret, wid. of Seth Drew, and had William. WILLIAM, son of above, m., 1785, Lydia Holmes, and had William, m. Abigail, d. of Corban Barnes; Tilden; Margaret James, m. George Washburn; Charlotte W., m. Jabez Churchill and Isaac Perkins; Eliza, m. America Brewster Rogers; Lydia, m. Joseph Lucas; Abigail, m. Elisha Nelson; and Eleanor, m. John Fenno.

KEITH, JONAS, m., 1820, Mercy Ellis Bartlett.

KEMPTON, AMOS, Croyden, N. H., son of Jeremiah, m., 1825, Lois Stevens, and had Daniel M., 1827; Ira P., 1829, m. Ann J. Noyes and Pamelia Sargent; Henry M., 1831, m. Charlotte M. Swain of Nantucket; Obed, 1833, m. Harriet M. Leavitt of Chichester, N. H.; Lois B., 1835, m. William H. Flanders, of Concord, N. H.; Judson, 1838, m. Caroline E. Hobbs of Methuen; Dexter, 1841, m. Pamelia West of Chichester; Amos, 1844, m. Ellen Nutter of Farmington, N. H. He died, 1849, in Newport, N. H. CALVIN, Croyden, son of Jeremiah, m., 1818, Ruth Baxter, d. of Nathan Clark, and had Calvin Albert, 1819; Adelia Gordon, 1821, m, John S. Proctor of Claremont, N. H.; Nathan Clark, 1822, m. Vesta A. Pinkham; Calvin, 1824; Albert, 1825; Rollins, 1826, m. Maria J. Reed of Northfield, N. H.; Benjamin Franklin, 1828; Jeremiah Gordon, 1831; Benjamin Franklin, 1833; Baxter Clark, 1835. He m., 2d, 1837, Rachel Clough of Grantham, N. H., and had Rachel Ruth, 1838; Willard Clough, 1840; Viola, and Maria S. DAVID, Dartmouth, son of 1st Thomas, had Ruth; Esther, m. Elihu Aiken; Joseph; Deborah, m. Rufus Sherman; Aaron; Caleb; Charity, m. Thomas Aiken; Virtue, m. William Potter. EDWARD, Croyden, son of 6th Ephraim, by wife Ruth, had Warren Munroe, 1815, m. Emily Allen; Edward B., 1818, m. Mary Harris, and others. ELISHA, Croyden and Newport, N. H., son of Jeremiah, m. Harriet Vickery, and had Eunice, 1827, m. Ruel G. Bascom; Elisha Moody, 1831, m. Lucina E. Alden of Alstead, N. H.; Amanda, 1837; Jonathan Powers, 1840. EPHRAIM, appeared in Plymouth 1643, and had a son Ephraim, and died in 1645. EPHRAIM, Scituate, son of above, m. Joanna, d. of Thomas Rawlins, 1646, and had Joanna, 1647, m. George Morton; Patience, 1648; Ephraim, 1649; Menassah, 1652. EPHRAIM, son of above, m. Mary, d. of John Reeves of Salem, and had Ephraim, 1674, probably Stephen, 1676; Samuel, 1681. EPHRAIM, son of above, m., 1702, Patience, d. of Thomas Faunce, and had Ephraim, 1703; Thomas, 1705; William, 1707; Joanna, 1710, m. Joshua Drew. EPHRAIM, Uxbridge, son of above, m., 1740, Abigail Bolster, and had Ephraim, 1741; Stephen, 1743; Joseph, 1745; Mary, 1748. EPHRAIM, Uxbridge and Croyden, son of above, m., 1761, Hannah Battles of Uxbridge, and had Rufus, 1762, m. Abigail Breck of Sherburne; Abigail, 1764, m. Ebenezer Hurd of Croyden; Susanna, 1766; Jeremiah, 1768; Ephraim, 1770; Joseph, 1772; Mary, 1774, m. Thomas Billings of Croyden; Hannah, 1776, m. Giles Shurtleff; Thomas, 1778; Edward, 1780; Daniel, 1783; Rachel, 1787. EPHRAIM, Dartmouth, son of 1st Thomas, m. Elizabeth Tupper, and had Lydia, 1774; Mary, 1777, m. Paul Kempton; David, 1779, m. Joanna Wakefield; Thomas, 1783; Ephraim, 1789; Elizabeth, 1794. EPHRAIM, son of above, m., 1811, Mary Hillman, and had Horatio A., 1812, m. Caroline Thornton; and Mary H., 1823, m. William G. Taber. EPHRAIM, Uxbridge and Croyden, son of 6th Ephraim, m., 1793, Betsey, d. of Jonas Cutting, and had Ephraim Alexander, m. Francis W. Wilcox; Experience, m. Leonard Lawton; Thankful, m. Jacob Walker and Samuel Goldthwaite; Susan, m. Orren Perry; Dulcina, m. Moses Walker; Lucy A., m. Charles G. York; Darling, m. Sarah Webster; Ann, m. William Darling; Jonas Cutting; Warren F., m. Amanda Spiller; Hiram P., m. Mrs. Welthea S. Marsh; and Katharine H. P., m. Jacob Jeffers. JEREMIAH, Uxbridge and Croyden, son of 6th Ephraim, m., 1788, Esther Gordon, and had Calvin, 1791; Nancy, 1792, m. Chase Noyes; Obed, 1795; Amos, 1796; Jerusha Hall, 1798, m. Jonathan Powers; Elisha, 1800; Silas, 1802; Moody, 1804. JOHN, son of 1st Samuel, m. Elizabeth Randall, and had Jerusha, 1738, m. Joseph Trask; John, 1740; Elizabeth, 1742; Nathaniel, 1744; Hannah, 1747, m. Lemuel Cobb; Mary, 1749; Deborah, 1751; Samuel, 1753; Zacheus, 1754; Sarah, 1756; Joanna, 1758; Nathaniel, 1762. JOHN, son of above, m. Mary Hatch, 1763, and had Nathaniel Hatch, 1765; Charles, 1768; Seth, 1773; Zacheus, 1775; Lemuel, 1778; Mary, 1781; Samuel, 1783; Joseph, 1785; Stephen, 1787. JOHN, son of Zacheus, m. Abigail Diman, 1824, and had John, 1825; Samuel Hopkins, 1826; Ezra Diman, 1828; Edmund Payton, 1833; Elizabeth Morton, 1834; Nancy Dean, 1837. JONATHAN, Dartmouth, son of 1st Thomas, m. Lydia Wing, and had Mary, Humphrey, Hannah, Hepsa, Deborah, Sarah, Charles, and Abby. JOSEPH, Uxbridge and Croyden, son of 6th Ephraim, m., 1794, Polly Jones, and had Russell, 1795; Sargent, 1797; Mary, 1799, m. Zebulon Young; William A., 1802; Sabra, 1804; Hannah, 1807, m. Alvah Wakefield; Marion, 1810, m. Calvin Wakefield; Ephraim, 1812, m. Almira Fagg. JOSEPH, from Dartmouth, m. Mary Lothrop, 1759. MENASSAH, brother, probably, of 1st Ephraim, came in the Ann 1623, and m., 1627, Julian, wid. of George Morton, and d. of Alexander Carpenter, and probably left no issue. MENASSAH, Plymouth and Southampton, L. I., son

of 2d Ephraim, m. Mehitabel Holmes, and had Menassah, 1715; Ruth, 1718.
OBED, Croyden and Newport, son of Jeremiah, m., 1821, Nancy Noyes, and
had Leonard Noyes, 1822, m. Arvilla B. Emerson; Jeremiah, 1824, m. Eunice
Lincoln. OBED, from New Bedford, m. Abigail Carver, 1835. SAMUEL, son
of 3d Ephraim, m. Mercy Dunham, and had Mercy, 1707; probably Thomas;
Lois, 1710; Mehitabel, 1712; Samuel, 1714; John, 1716; Mercy, 1719; Sarah,
1721; Sarah, 1722; Sarah, 1724; Sarah, 1725; Rebecca, 1731. SAMUEL, son
of above, m., 1737, Mabel Soule of Duxbury, and had Samuel, 1738, m. Elizabeth Sampson; Mabel, 1740; Lydia, 1742; Oliver, 1743, m. Experience Ripley, and had Oliver, who m. Sarah Harlow, 1799. SILAS, Croyden, son of
Jeremiah, m., 1825, Mary A. Shedd, and had Emily, 1826; Josephine B.,
1828, m. Albro Emerson; Jerusha P., 1830; William S., 1834, m. Irena L.
Wright; Charles, 1838, m. Addie Haven; Emma J., 1843, m. Edwin Cotting.
THOMAS, son probably of 1st Samuel, m., 1731, Mary, d. of Richard Holmes,
and had Margaret, 1732; Mary, 1736; Richard, 1739. THOMAS, Plymouth
and Dartmouth, son of 4th Ephraim, m. Esther Throop of Bristol, 1730, and
had Esther, 1736; Thomas, 1740; Hepsibah, 1743; Ephraim, 1746; Mary,
1750; David, 1753; Jonathan, 1754. THOMAS, Dartmouth, son of above, m.
Ruth Bailey, and had Samuel, 1771. He m., 2d, Deborah Price, and had
William W., 1785; Thomas, 1788; Abigail G., 1791, m. Warren Cushing.
WILLIAM, son of 4th Ephraim, m., 1731, Mary Brewster, and had William,
1732; Ephraim, 1734. ZACHEUS, son of 1st John, m., 1782, Sally Robinson,
and had Sally, Woodworth, Charles, Zacheus, who m. two wives in Connecticut, and Abigail Cox in Plymouth, 1819; John; Nancy, m. Amos Dean; and
Eliza.

KENDALL, EZEKIEL, Sterling, son of 1st Samuel, had Abijah, Joseph,
David, Noah; Ezekiel, 1763; Elizabeth, and Hannah. EZEKIEL, Sterling,
son of above, m. a d. of James Kendall, and had Edward, Ezekiel; Samuel,
1792; Betsey, m. Jotham Bush; Harvey; Abigail, m. Almon Derby; Noah,
and Rufus. EZEKIEL, Sterling, son of above, m. a Bennett, and had
Charles Ezekiel of Boston; and Martha Jane, m. Weston Lewis. FRANCIS,
Woburn, 1640, m. Mary Tidd, 1644, and had John, 1646; Thomas, 1649; Mary,
1651; Elizabeth, 1653, m. Ephraim Winship; Hannah, 1655; Rebecca, 1657;
Samuel, 1659; Jacob, 1661; Abigail, 1666. HARVEY, Sterling, son of 2d Ezekiel, m. a Bailey, and had Henry, John; and Lucinda, m. Taylor Ross.
JAMES, Sterling, son of 1st Samuel, m. Sarah Richardson of Woburn, 1735,
and had Paul; a d. m. Ezekiel Kendall; and James, 1742. JAMES, son of
above, m. Elizabeth Mason of Lexington, and had Pierson, 1766, m. Catherine
Edes; Rev. James of Plymouth, 1769; Mary, 1772, m. John Porter of Sterling; and Lydia, m. Rev. Thomas Mason of Northfield. Rev. JAMES of Plymouth, son of above, m. Sarah Poor, and had Sarah, 1802; James Augustus,
1803; Hannah Poor, 1805, m. Rev. George Washington Hosmer; Lydia, 1807;
and Elizabeth, 1808. He m., 2d, Sally, d. of Paul Kendall, and had Mary
Elizabeth, 1811; Lydia Mason, 1813; Persis, 1815, m. Rev. William H. Lord;
Catherine, 1816; John Robinson, 1818; and Julia Parkhurst, 1823. PAUL,
Templeton, son of 1st James, had Sally, and perhaps others. SAMUEL,
Woburn, Townsend and Athol, son of Thomas, by wife Elizabeth, had

Samuel, 1708, minister of New Salem; James, 1710; Josiah, 1712; Ezekiel, 1715; Timothy of Leominster, 1717; Elizabeth, 1719, m. John Brooks of Leominster; Jonas, Leominster, 1721; Sarah, 1723, m. John Kendall, son of 2d Thomas; Susanna, 1724; Obadiah, Woburn, 1725; Jesse, Athol, 1727, m. Elizabeth Evans of Woburn; Seth, Athol, 1729; Abigail, 1731, m. Jacob Peirce of Woburn; Ephraim, 1732; Jerusha, 1735, m. Reuben Richardson of Woburn. SAMUEL, son of 2d Ezekiel, m. Emily, d. of John Porter, and his wife, Mary (Kendall) Porter, d. of 2d James Kendall, and had Amory Holman, 1843, m. Judith Sprague, d. of Gershom B. Weston, son of the late Gershom B. of Duxbury. THOMAS, Woburn, son of Francis, by wife Ruth, had Ruth, 1675; Thomas, 1677; Mary, 1680; Samuel, 1682; Ralph, 1685; Eleazer, 1687; Jabez, 1692. He m., 2d, Elizabeth Broughton, 1696. THOMAS, son of above, probably of Woburn, had a son John, m. Sarah, d. of 1st Samuel.

KENDRICK, ASA, m. Charlotte T. Morey, 1833, and had Reuben R., 1838, m. Mary B., d. of William Morse; and Elizabeth F., 1841. He m., 2d, Sarah V., d. of Nathaniel Harlow. JAMES, brother of above, m. Sally K. Raymond, 1840, and had James F., m. Susan M. Westgate; and Sarah E., m. Samuel N. Holmes. He m., 2d, Deborah Morey, 1850, and had Walter H., m. Elizabeth C. Shurtleff; and Mary E., 1854, m. Freeman P. Kinsman of Cohasset. He m., 3d, Ellen Coyle, 1857, and had Hattie B., 1864.

KENNEDY, or CANNEDY, ALEXANDER, by wife Elizabeth, had Hannah, 1678, m. Eleazer Pratt; Elizabeth, 1682; Jean, 1685; William, 1689; Sarah, 1693; Annable, 1698; John, 1703. JOHN lived in Plymouth, 1821, and bought in that year a lot in South street.

KENT, SAMUEL, of Marshfield, by wife Desire, had Samuel, 1729; Nathaniel, 1732; Desire, 1735; Hannah, 1737; John, 1739; Sarah, 1741; Huldah, 1743; Ichabod, 1744.

KEYES, BENJAMIN, by wife Polly, had William, 1798; Benjamin, 1801; Samuel Norris, 1805; Jane Williams, 1808; Oliver, 1811. OLIVER, probably brother of above, m. Lydia, d. of Benjamin Bagnall, 1796, and had Lydia, 1798; Oliver, 1799; Oliver Shurtleff, 1801.

KIMBALL, HENRY WARE, son of Putnam, m. Levina H. Webber of Braintree, and had Henry Putnam, 1865; Susan Mabel, 1867; Lothrop Foster, 1869. LOTHROP TURNER, son of Putnam, m. Elizabeth Eddy, d. of Barnabas Churchill, and had Mary Lizzie, 1863; Carrie Gibson, 1865; Barnabas Lothrop, 1868; and Emma Frances, 1870. PETER, born 1752, m. Ruth Turner, 1780, and had Samuel, 1781; Deborah Lothrop, 1782; Turner, 1785; Putnam, 1787. His wid. m. Jacob Foster, 1797, and had Deborah Lothrop, 1799. PUTNAM, son of above, m. Eleanor, d. of Robert Dunham, 1808, and had Eleanor Putnam, 1812, m. Benjamin Bagnall; Lydia Ann, 1814, m. William Gooding; Deborah Lothrop, 1816, m. Eleazer H. Barnes; Samuel, 1819; Putnam, 1822, m. Elizabeth T., d. of Thomas Torrey; Maria Elizabeth, 1828; Henry Ware, 1830; Lothrop Turner, 1835. RICHARD, m. Susanna Dunham, 1762. SAMUEL, son of Putnam, m. Betsey Ann Keith of West Bridgewater, and had Edward Pardon, 1847; Elizabeth Putnam, 1848; Fanny Sawyer, 1852; Ella Maria, 1856; Charlotte Lemist, 1858; Edith, 1861.

KING, BENJAMIN, m. Betty Lovell of Kingston, and had Betty, 1751, m. an Everson; Rebecca, 1753, m. John Phillips; Benjamin, 1758, m. Lydia Dunham; Susanna, 1759. ELEAZER, m. Ann Wilder, 1713. ISAAC, m. Thankful Barrows, and had Isaac, 1714; Lydia, 1716, m. Gershom Holmes; Mercy, 1717; Martha, 1719; Jonathan, 1721; Samuel, 1723. ISAAC, m. Mehitabel Bryant, 1690. ISAAC, m. Hannah Harlow, 1729. ISAAC B., m. Harriet Hoyt, 1840. JOHN, m. Hannah Pierce, 1751, and had Amaziah, 1752. JOHN, m. Polly Briggs, and had Elisha, 1802; Betsey, 1804; Sally, 1805; John, 1808; Polly, 1810; Phineas, 1811. JOHN, m. Thankful Holmes, 1764. JOHN, m. Elizabeth Harlow, 1775. JONATHAN, son of 1st Isaac, m. Deborah Carver, and had Nathaniel, 1746; Lydia, 1747, m. John Rickard; Jonathan, 1749; Lucy, 1752; Abigail, 1754, m. a Fuller; Mercy, 1756; Mary, 1761. JOSEPH, m. Elizabeth Bryant, 1690. JOSEPH, m. Mercy Dunham, 1701. JOSEPH, m. wid. Mercy Spooner, 1719. JOSEPH, m. Asenath Pratt, 1786. NATHAN, m. Joanna Vaughn, 1831, and had Eunice, 1832; William, 1835; Adeline, 1836; Mary Abba, 1838; Joanna, 1840; Nathan, 1842. OBADIAH, m. Hannah Clark, 1806, and had Hannah, 1807; Sophronia, 1810; Obadiah, 1813; Lothrop C., 1815; Nathaniel C., 1817; Stephen C., 1820; Kendall W., 1825. ROBERT, m. Sally Wing, 1804. ROBERT, by wife Sarah, had Rufus, 1824; Olive, 1827; Francis, 1830; Washington, 1833. SAMUEL, m. Mary Rowe, and had Seth, 1736; Mercy, 1739; Mary, 1739; Elizabeth, 1742; Susanna, 1744. SAMUEL, owner of an estate in Plymouth, had Samuel, 1649; Isaac, 1651. WILLIAM, m. Susanna Harlow, 1770, and had Susanna, 1771.

KNAPP, JOSEPH, died on expedition to Canada, 1690, leaving brothers Samuel and Moses.

KNEELAND, JOSHUA, m. Harriet, d. of James Harlow, 1820, and had John, m. 1st, Elizabeth, d. of Isaac Sampson of Plymouth, and 2d, Mary Frances, wid. of Charles F. Fessenden of Boston, and d. of Albert Forbes Conant of Boston.

KNOWLES, JOHN, m. Mary Delano, and had Mary Delano, 1822; Lucy Merrick, 1823.

LAHORNE, ROWLAND, 1636, had a wife Flora.

LAKEY, JAMES, pub., 1754, to Margaret Beard.

LANE, MARSHAL, m., 1810, wid. Elizabeth Rogers.

LANGMORE, JOHN, came in the Mayflower, and soon died.

LANGFORD, WILLIAM, m., 1807, Betsey Morton, and had Mary Ann, m. Ebenezer Nickerson; Nancy; Betsey, m. Henry Finney; William; and John.

LANMAN, or LANDMAN, CHARLES H., son of 1st Nathaniel Cobb, m. Martha Freeman, and had Mary, Charles, Mary again, and Watson. EDWARD, son of James, m., 1754, Joan Tobey of Sandwich. He m., 2d, 1758, Abiah Bryant of Plympton, and had William, 1759. Either he or a son Edward, m., 1796, Martha Newcomb of Wellfleet, whose descendants are now living. ELLIS THOMAS, son of 3d Samuel, m. Jane, d. of Richard Jones, 1850, and had John Ellis, 1850, and John Ellis again, 1855. GEORGE FRANCIS, son of 3d Samuel, m. Abigail Barton, and had George F., 1835; and Sam-

uel Ellis, 1837. He m., 2d, Catherine McGuire, and had James. HENRY T.,
son of 2d Peter, m. wid. Olive (Goss) Pinkham, and had Delia S., 1852;
Alice A., 1855; Edward T., 1858. HIRAM JAMES, son of 4th Samuel, m.,
1864, Mary Gale Osborne, and had Mary Gale Osborne, 1867. JAMES, son
of 1st Thomas, m., 1714, Joanna, d. of Thomas Boylston of Boston, where he
had Mary, m. Isaac Doty; Samuel, 1722; and Peter, m. Sarah Coit, 1724;
removed to Norwich, and had a son Peter. He removed to Plymouth, and
had William, 1726, removed to Norwich; Thomas, 1728, m. Rebecca Kempton; Joanna, 1731, m. William Foster of Plymouth and John Baron of Barnstable; Edward, 1733. NATHANIEL COBB, son of 2d Samuel, m., 1817, Nancy
E., d. of Richard Bagnall, and had Nancy Ellis, 1818; Nathaniel Cobb, 1820;
Charles Henry, 1825; Nancy Ellis, 1828; William Rogers, 1830; Sarah H., 1832;
Lucy Ann, 1834, m. Eleazer Thomas and Alanson Thomas; Nancy Ellis, 1837,
m. Austin E. Luther. He m., 2d, 1851, Almira, wid. of Judson W. Rice, and
d. of William Weston. NATHANIEL COBB, son of above, m., 1844, Beulah, d.
of William Simmons, and had Charles, m. Mary, d. of Ephraim Holmes;
Emma; Alice; Sarah; Nathaniel, m. Louisa Bancroft; Mary; Frank; and
Arthur. PETER, son of 1st Samuel, m. Mary, d. of George Holmes, 1783,
and had Polly, 1784, m. George Savery; Peter, 1786; Sally, 1788, m. John M.
Nichols and Zebulon Bisbee; Peter again, 1790; Nancy, 1792; Isaac, 1794, m.
Jane, d. of Richard Holmes; Samuel, 1796; Thomas, 1798; Eliza E., 1801.
PETER, Kingston, son of above, m. Deborah Bisbee, and had Henry T.,
1827; Deborah, 1829; Harriet, 1832, m. Henry Barstow; Ann E., 1835, m.
Thomas Cole. SAMUEL, son of James, m. Elizabeth Ellis of Middleboro',
and had Samuel, 1752; Elizabeth, 1755, m. Cornelius Holmes; Rebecca, 1757,
m. George Bartlett; Peter, 1759; Thomas, 1763. SAMUEL, son of above, m.,
1780, Sarah (Holmes) Cobb, wid. of Nathaniel Cobb of Plympton, and had
Polly, m. Ansel Bartlett; Nathaniel Cobb; Elizabeth, m. Lewis Weston;
Rebecca, m. William Rogers; Samuel; and Lucy, m. Thomas Burgess.
SAMUEL, son of above, m., 1809, Content Thomas of Middleboro', and had
Ellis Thomas, 1812; George Francis, 1814; Sarah Holmes, 1817, m. John
Campbell and Oliver C. Vaughn; Elizabeth, 1821, m. Thomas Atwood; Samuel Ellis, 1819; Ellis Thomas again, 1824, m. Jane Jones. SAMUEL, son of
1st Peter, m. Charlotte Southworth, and had Samuel Thomas, 1827; Char-
lotte Almira, 1830, m. Winslow Bradford; Hiram James, 1833. SAMUEL
ELLIS, son of 3d Samuel, m. Ruth Bailey, and had William Wallace, 1844,
m. Mary McCarty. SAMUEL ELLIS, son of George Francis, m. Ellen Carr,
and had John E., 1859; Mary Ann, 1864; Ellie J., 1867; George F., 1870.
THOMAS, born in England, m. Lucy Elton and settled in Watertown, and
had James, and perhaps others. THOMAS, Kingston, son of 1st Peter, m.
Sophia McLaughlin and Eliza Soule; and had Thomas E., 1831, m. Mary Bradford; Charles, 1833; John M., 1834, m. Josephine Bosworth; Salina, 1839, m.
a Harrub and a Chandler.

LANGNELL, JOSEPH, m. Mary Thomas, 1722.

LAPHAM, ELISHA, m. Polly Fish, 1818.

LATHAM, WILLIAM, came in the Mayflower, and about 1640 went to
England, and then to the Bahamas, where he is said to have died.

LAWRENCE, DANIEL, m. Lydia Bartlett, 1784, and had Caroline, m. John Bartlett. JAMES, by wife Abigail, had Sarah, 1769.

LAZELL, or LASSELL, SIMON, m. Margaret Cooke, and had Joshua, 1719; Lydia, 1723. THOMAS of Duxbury, m., 1685, Mary Allen, and had, probably, Martha, m. Joseph Pratt.

LEACH, ALBERT, son of Finney, m. Eleanor, d. of Daniel Churchill, 1830, and had Albert B., 1830; George, 1831; George E., 1832; Robert B., 1834, m. Susan W., d. of William Hall; Charles P., 1835, m. Francilia A., d. of Elkanah Barnes; Louisa E., 1837; Ellen A., 1841; Rebecca B., 1844; Maria A., 1847; Elizabeth, 1850. CALEB, from Bridgewater, by wife Abigail, had Ebenezer, 1783; Abigail, 1785; and perhaps others. DAVID, son of 2d Lemuel, m. Nancy Harlow, 1828, and had David, 1828; and Allen, 1841. He m., 2d, Eliza, d. of Stephen Doten, 1847, and had Anna E., 1848, m. Calvin T. Howland. EZRA, son of 2d Lemuel, m. Hannah, d. of Stephen Doten, 1825, and had Ezra H., m. Nancy W., d. of Rufus Sampson, and Margaret N. Morton. He m., 2d, Jane, d. of Stephen Doten; and, 3d, Ellen, d. of Caleb Morton. FINNEY, son of 1st Lemuel, m. Mercy, d. of Ephraim Bartlett, 1800, and had David, 1801; Marcia, 1805; Phineas, 1807; Robert B., 1809; Albert, 1811; and Josiah, 1819. LEMUEL, came to Plymouth, perhaps from Bridgewater, and m. Sarah Holmes, 1766, by whom he had Naomi, m. Samuel Allen; Lemuel; and Finney, 1774. LEMUEL, son of above, m. Susanna Harlow, 1791, and had Ezra, Lemuel, David, Reuben; Susan, m. Henry Howland; Sarah, m. Jeroboam Swift; and Betsey, m. Stephen Doten. LEMUEL, son of above, m. Lucy, d. of Elkanah Finney, 1826, and had Louisa; Lemuel, m. Susan Baker, d. of Ellis Morton; and Betsey L., m. Benjamin H. Griffin. PHINEAS, son of Finney, m. Sally B., d. of Robert Dunham, 1829, and had Phineas A., 1831; Franklin S., 1835. He m., 2d, Mary P. Ellis, and had Louisa; Robert B.; George E., 1846; Herbert C., 1848; Phineas, 1853; and Mary, 1857. REUBEN, son of 2d Lemuel, m. Mary F. Morton, 1835, and had Reuben; Phebe L., m. Frederick E. Churchill; Mary Susan, m. John W. Sampson; and Betsey.

LEBARON, BARTLETT, son of 1st Lazarus, m., 1762, Mary Easdell, and had Mary, 1762; Hannah, 1764; Lydia, 1767, Rebecca, 1774; Betsey, 1776; John, 1778; James, 1780. He m., 2d, 1786, Lydia Doggett, and had Nancy, 1787; Lucia, 1788; Nancy 1789; Esther, 1791, m. Solomon Davie; Mira, 1793, m. Lewis Drew; Harriet, 1795. CYRUS, Middleboro', son of 2d Joseph, m., 1834, Angeline Thomas, and had William O., 1837; Cyrus A., 1839; Eldora A., 1846; Sylvanus T., 1848. FRANCIS, came to Plymouth from France in 1694 by the way of Buzzard's Bay, where he was wrecked in a French vessel. He m., 1695, Mary, d. of Edward Wilder of Hingham, and had James, 1696, Lazarus, 1698; Francis, 1701. He died 1704, and his wid. m., 1707, Return Wait. His grandchild, Elizabeth, who m. Ammi Ruhuma Robbins of Norfolk, Conn., was often heard by her grandchild, Mrs. James Humphrey of Brooklyn, now living, to say that he was a Huguenot. FRANCIS, son of above, m., 1721, Sarah, d. of Joseph Bartlett, and had Francis, 1722; Mary, 1723; Isaac, 1725; Sarah, 1728, m. Lemuel Barnes; Francis, 1731. His wid. m., 1737, Joseph Swift. FRANCIS, Middleboro', son of 1st James, died 1745,

leaving two children, Francis and Joshua. JAMES, Middleboro', son of 1st
Francis, m., 1720, Martha Benson, and had James, 1721; John, 1724; James,
1726; Joshua, 1729; Martha, 1732; Francis, 1734; Mary, 1737; David, 1740;
Lydia, 1742. JAMES, Middleboro', son of above, m. Hannah Turner, and
had James, 1748; Japhet, 1750; Elizabeth, 1752; Martha, 1754, m. Daniel
Tinkham; William, 1757; James, 1759, m. Elizabeth Washburn; Francis,
1762; Isaac, 1764; Hannah, 1766, m. Elkanah Shaw; Abigail, 1768; Lazarus,
1771. JAMES, Middleboro', son of 2d Lazarus, m. Lucinda Morton, and had
James Sullivan, 1829; Abigail, 1832; Phineas, 1834; Amanda, 1838; Harriet,
Betsey, George Boutwell. ISAAC, son of 1st Lazarus, m., 1774, Martha, d.
of Consider Howland, and had Isaac, 1777; Martha, 1778, m. Nathaniel
Russell; Francis, 1781; Mary Howland, 1786, m. John B. Thomas. ISAAC,
son of above, m., 1811, Mary Doane of Boston, and had Caroline Eliza,
1812, m. Gustavus Gilbert; Isaac Francis, 1814; Frederick, 1816; Mary Jane,
1817; Isaac, 1819; Ann Doane, 1821; Francis, 1824; Martha Howland, 1829,
m. Delano E. Goddard of Boston. JAPHET, Middleboro', son of 2d James,
m., 1773, Sarah Holmes, and had Joseph, 1775; Japhet, 1777; Sarah, 1788.
JAPHET, Fairhaven, son of above, m., 1811, Thankful Macomber, and had
Albert, 1812; Marcus B., 1814. JOHN, Middleboro', son of 1st James, m.,
1748, Mary Raymond, and had Abisa, 1749; John, 1750, m. Repentance
Lucas; Zebulon, 1752, m. Elizabeth Lucas; Eunice, 1761, m. Timothy Shurtleff; Joshua, 1763; Levi, 1765; Chloe, 1773, m. John Macomber; Mary, 1775,
m. Timothy Shurtleff. JOHN, Middleboro', son of Levi, m., 1814, Bethany
Rider, and had Sally Burt, 1815; John Burt, 1817; Ziba, 1823; Hannah, 1833.
JOHN BURT, Middleboro', son of above, m. Kesiah Baylies, and wid. Mary J.
Rose, and had John Baylies, Maria, and Eugene. JOHN ALLEN, Matta-
poisett, son of Lemuel, m., 1807, Martha Phillips, and had Lemuel, 1809;
James, 1811; Horatio G., 1813. JOSEPH, son of 1st Lazarus, m., 1747,
Sarah, d. of Nathaniel Leonard, and had Joseph, 1748; Sarah, 1749, m. Wil-
liam Hazen. JOSEPH, Middleboro', son of 1st Japhet, m., 1798, Margaret
Morse, and had Cynthia, 1799; Joanna A., 1801; Mercy M., 1803; Otis, 1805;
Cyrus, 1808; Joseph, 1810; Sally Burt, 1812. JOSHUA, Middleboro', son of
Levi, m. Hannah Cushing, and had Sarah, 1839; Charles E., 1844. He m.,
2d, Rhoda Morse, and had Adelaide, 1854. LAZARUS, son of 1st Francis,
m., 1720, Lydia, d. or Joseph Bartlett, and had Lazarus, 1721; Joseph, 1722;
Lydia, 1724, m. Nathaniel Goodwin; Mary, 1731, m. William Bradford;
Hannah, 1734, m. Benjamin Goodwin; Teresa, 1736; Bartlett, 1739. He
m., 2d, Lydia, wid. of Elkanah Cushman and d. of David Bradford, 1743, and
had Isaac, 1744; Elizabeth, 1745, m. Ammi Ruhama Robbins; Lemuel, 1747,
m. Sarah Allen; Francis, 1749; William, 1751; Margaret, 1755; Priscilla,
1753, m. Abraham Hammatt. LAZARUS, son of above, m., 1743, Margaret
Newsom of Barbadoes, and had Lazarus, 1744. He m., 2d, 1756, Mary
(Thomas) Lothrop, wid. of Ansel, and had Elizabeth Warren, and Mary
Lothrop. LAZARUS, Middleboro', son of 2d James, m., 1797, Abigail
Maxim of Rochester, and had Thomas M., 1808; James, 1810, Hannah, 1814;
Edmund, 1817. LEMUEL, Mattapoisett, son of 1st Lazarus, m., 1774, Eliza-
beth Allen of Martha's Vineyard, and had Lemuel, 1775; Ann, 1778; Lemuel,

1780; John Allen, 1782; Elizabeth, 1784; William, 1786; Lazarus, 1789; Sally, 1791; James, 1794. LEVI, Middleboro', son of 1st John, m., 1787, Temperance Morse of Rochester, and had John, 1787; Ziba, 1789; Waitstill, 1792; Joshua, 1794; Temperance, 1796; Elizabeth, 1798, m. Abraham Thomas; Temperance, 1801; Levi, 1803; Mary, 1805; Lucy, 1807. THOMAS M., Middleboro', son of 3d Lazarus, m., 1830, Sarah E. Morse, and had Emily Desire, 1836; William Edwin, 1834; Simeon M., 1840; Thomas J., 1848; Theophilus B., 1850. WILLIAM, Fairhaven, son of 1st Lazarus, m., 1774, Sarah, d. of John Churchill, and had William, 1775; Sarah, 1776, m. Thomas Jackson; Mary, 1778; Lucy, 1778, m. Thomas Mayo; Priscilla, 1781, m. Gideon S. Alden of New Bedford; Eliza, 1785; William, 1787. WILLIAM, son of Lemuel, m., 1810, Eliza, d. of William LeBaron, and had Sarah Ann, 1811; William, 1814; Eliza, 1816; Thomas R., 1818; Lucy G., 1821; Charles Henry, 1823. WILLIAM EDWIN, New Bedford, son of Thomas M., m., 1859, Eunice S. Morse, and had Nellie F., 1860; Anna S., 1862.

LEE, JOHN, m. Olive Thomas, 1836. PHILIP, m. Elizabeth Jackson, 1726.

LEISTER, EDWARD, came, a young man, in the Mayflower, and afterwards went to Virginia, where he died.

LEMOTE, GEORGE, son of Matthew, m. Catherine Nicholson, and had Francis, 1766; Mercy, 1768. MATTHEW, m. Mary Billington, 1729, and had Matthew, 1730; Joseph, 1732; Abigail, 1733; Mercy, 1734, m. William Barnes; Susanna, 1736, m. William Chambers; Matthew, 1738; Mary, 1739, m. Daniel Pappoon; George, 1741; Abigail, 1743.

LEONARD, ABNER, from Middleboro', born 1807, m., 1830, Zilpha Morton, and had Clarinda, 1831; Betsey M., 1833; Eliza A., 1834; Abner, 1837; Sumner, 1839, m. Isabella, d. of Barnabas Ellis; Charles H., 1841, m. Mary, d. of Charles Tilson; Abner, 1843, m. Eliza Robbins of Falmouth; Clarinda, 1845, m. Henry F. Gibbs; Foster, 1848. BENJAMIN, Taunton, son of James, m., 1679, Sarah Thrasher, and had Sarah, 1680; Benjamin, 1684; Hannah, 1685; Jerusha, 1689; Hannah, 1691; Joseph, 1693; Henry, 1695. ELKANAH, Middleboro, son of 1st Thomas, by wife Charity, had Joseph, 1705; Rebecca, 1706; Abiah, 1707; and Elkanah. EPHRAIM, son of 2d Philip, m., 1804, Elizabeth Churchill, and had George Churchill, 1806; Ephraim, 1808; Richard Warren, 1810. GEORGE, Taunton, son of 1st Thomas, m., 1695, Ann Tisdale, and had George, 1698; Nathaniel, 1700; Abigail, 1703; Ephraim, 1706. JAMES, born in Pontypool, England, son of a Thomas, came with a brother Henry, settled in Lynn, and Philip settled in Marshfield, and appeared in Providence, 1645, Taunton, 1652, and afterwards in Lynn and Braintree. He had Thomas, 1641, m. Mary Watson; James, m., 1st, a wife Hannah, and 2d, Lydia Gulliver; Abigail; Joseph, m. Mary Black of Milton; Benjamin; Hannah, m. Isaac Deane; Uriah; John, 1662, m. Elizabeth, d. of Thomas Caswell. He had a 2d wife, Margaret, without children. JOSEPH, son of Benjamin, had a son Philip. JOSEPH N., son of ˉ3d Nathaniel, m. Abby, d. of Benjamin Crandon, and had Benjamin Crandon, Mary Ellen, and Sarah. NATHANIEL, Norton and Plymouth, son of George, m., 1724, Priscilla Rogers, and had Sarah, 1724, m. Joseph LeBaron; Anna, 1728; Mary, 1729; Nathan-

iel, 1730; Priscilla, 1732; George, 1742; Thomas, 1744; and Phebe. NATHAN-
IEL, son of above, m., 1761, Bethiah Rider, and had Nathaniel, 1765; William,
1767; Thomas, 1770. NATHANIEL WARREN, son of 2d Philip, m., 1795,
Mary Warren, and had James Easdell, 1796, m. Abby Bishop; Mary W., 1799,
m. Zebidee Leonard of Middleboro'; Nathaniel W., 1801, m. Eunice Finney;
Joseph Nelson, 1804; Eleanor Warren, 1806, m. George Bramhall; William
M., 1809, m. Susan Morton. PAUL, from Raynham, m., 1759, Mary Rider.
PHILIP, Marshfield, son of Thomas of Pontypool, by wife Lydia,
had Phebe, m. Samuel Hill of Duxbury. PHILIP, son of 1st Joseph,
had Philip. PHILIP, son of above, m., 1766, Hannah Warren, and
had Nathaniel Warren, 1768; Ephraim; Hannah, m. Caleb Morton; Mary;
Phebe, m. Caleb Finney. SAMUEL, Norwich, son of Solomon, m. Abigail,
d of John Wood of Plymouth, and had Elizabeth, m. Thomas Clark, and
others. SOLOMON, Duxbury, 1637, afterwards Bridgewater, had Solomon, Samuel, John, Jacob, Mary, and Isaac. THOMAS, Taunton, son of James, born in
England, m., 1662, Mary Watson of Plymouth, and had Mary, 1663; Thomas,
1666; John, 1668, m. Mary King; George, 1671; Samuel, 1674, m. Catherine,
d. of Thomas Dean; Elkanah, 1677; James, 1679; Seth, 1682; Phebe, 1684;
Elizabeth, 1686. THOMAS, son of 2d Nathaniel, m., 1793, Sally Babb, and
had Priscilla, 1793; Abigail, 1795, m. Henry Hollis; Nathaniel, 1797; Sally
Thomas, 1799; Thomas, 1802. His wid. m. John Ridgebi, and had Bethiah
Johnson, m. Isaac Austin. WILLIAM, son of 2d Nathaniel, m., 1791, Rebecca
Bartlett, Susanna Bartlett, 1805, daughters of Ephraim, and Abigail, d. of
Richard Holmes and wid. of Ephraim Bartlett, 1812, and had Eleanor, m.
John Macomber; and Rebecca, m. Olive Weston.

LESTER, TERRIT, m. Sarah Little, and had Sarah, 1760.

LETTICE, THOMAS, Plymouth, 1638, by wife Ann, had Thomas, Ann, m.
Samuel Jenny; Elizabeth, m. William Shurtleff, Jacob Cook, and Hugh Cole;
and Dorothy, m. Edward Gray and Nathaniel Clarke.

LEWIN, JOSEPH, m. Hannah Rogers, and had John, 1727, m. Sarah
Holmes; and Meriah, 1730, m. Isaac Morton.

LEWIS, DANIEL, son of William, m., 1809, Lucy Sampson, and had
Daniel J., and others. DANIEL J., Fairhaven, son of above, m. Sarah, d. of
Lewis Weston of Plymouth, and had James Augustus, 1833; Albert, 1835;
William, 1839. GEORGE, from East Greenwich, England, m., about 1634,
Sarah Jenkins, and had Mary, Thomas, George, James, John, Joseph, and
Nathaniel. JACOB, m., 1729, Bathsheba Mallis. JAMES, m., 1822, Cynthia
Manter. JESSE, m., 1820, Deborah Bagnall. JOHN, m., 1809, Elizabeth
Foster Dunham. NATHANIEL, m., 1791, Hannah Drew, and had Hannah,
1792; Lucy Shaw, 1794; Edward Hutchinson, 1796. SAMUEL, son of William,
m., 1810, Mercy, d. of Stephen Doten, and had Samuel Williams, 1811;
Hannah Doten, 1815; Jesse James Hawkes, 1816; Mercy Doten, 1818. He m.,
2d, 1819, Mercy, d. of Willard Sears, and had Edwin, 1821; Christiana White,
1823; Wealthy Sampson, 1825; William, 1827. STEPHEN, m., 1829, Rebecca
Holmes. THOMAS, by wife Sarah, had Thomas, 1771. WILLIAM, m. Christiana, d. of Jesse White of Marshfield, and had Samuel, 1788; and Daniel.

LIBERTY, FRANCIS, m. Sarah Newport, 1791, Indians.

LINCOLN, BENJAMIN, from Taunton, m. Mercy Carver, 1755. ELIJAH, from Raynham, m., 1815, Patience Bates.

LING, THOMAS, m. Elizabeth Macklam, 1745.

LISCOM SAMUEL, m., 1818, Elizabeth Westgate.

LITCHFIELD, NICHOLAS, m. Bathsheba Clark, 1705.

LITTLE, CHARLES, son of 1st Isaac, m. Sarah, d. of James Warren, and had Sarah, 1711; Bethiah, 1715; Charles, 1717; Lucy, 1719; Sarah, 1721; Charles, 1723. EPHRAIM, son of 1st Thomas, m. Mary, d. of Samuel Sturtevant, 1672, and had Ephraim, 1673; Ruth, 1675, m. an Avery; David, 1681; John, 1683; Ann, m. Thomas Gray; and Mary, m. an Otis. EPHRAIM, minister at Plymouth, son of above, m. Sarah, d. of William Clark, 1698, and had no children. FOBES, Marshfield, son of John, by wife Sarah, had Lucy, 1734; Fobes, 1736. ISAAC, Marshfield, son of 1st Thomas, by wife Bethiah, had Thomas, 1674; Dorothy, 1676; Isaac, 1678; Bethiah, 1681, m. Thomas Barker; Charles, 1685, m. Sarah, d. of James Warren; Nathaniel, 1690; William, 1692. ISAAC, Marshfield, son of above, by wife Mary, had Mary, 1704; Isaac, 1710; Otis, 1712; Mercy, 1716; Nathaniel, 1722. ISAAC, son of 2d Thomas, m. Sarah Church, 1726, and had Joseph, 1728; George, 1730; Sarah, 1732, m. Territ Lester. JOHN, Marshfield, son of 1st Ephraim, m. Constant Fobes, and had Anna, 1708; Ruth, 1710; Mercy, 1711; Fobes, 1713; John, 1714; Anna, 1716; Thomas, 1717; Ephraim, 1718; Thomas, 1719; William, 1720; Lemuel, 1724. NATHANIEL, of Tiverton, probably grandson of 1st Ephraim, through his son John, m. Kesiah Adams, 1755. SAMUEL, son of 1st Thomas, m. Sarah, d. of Edward Gray, 1682, and had Thomas, 1683; Sarah, 1685; Samuel, 1691. THOMAS, Plymouth, 1630, m., 1633, Ann, d. of Richard Warren, and had Isaac, 1646; Thomas; Ephraim, 1650; Samuel, 1656; Hannah, m. Stephen Tilden; Mercy, m. John Sawyer; Ruth, and Patience. THOMAS, son of 1st Isaac, m., 1698, Mary Mayhew, and had Thomas, 1701; Isaac, 1704; Mayhew, 1707; Mary, 1709, m. Jonathan Bryant; George, 1712. WILLIAM of New Bedford, m. Jane C. Holmes, 1829.

LITTLEJOHN, HENRY, m. Sarah Pratt, and had Hannah, 1722, m. William Harlow; William, 1724; James, 1728. ORSANUS, of Middleboro, m. Elizabeth Swift, 1828.

LOBDELL, ISAAC, by wife Sarah, had Sarah, 1682; Martha, 1684; Samuel, 1687. THOMAS I., m. Hannah, d. of William Sturtevant, 1817.

LOCKE, JOHN, from Ashby, m. Hannah Goodwin, 1799. JOSEPH, from Billerica, m. Lydia Goodwin, 1803.

LOMBART, THOMAS, owned an estate in Plymouth, 1800.

LONG, MILES, came to Plymouth from North Carolina, and m., 1770, Thankful Clark. His children were Betsey, m. John Clark; and Thomas. ROBERT, came in the Ann, 1623, but disappeared before 1627. THOMAS, Buckfield, Me., son of Miles, m. Bathsheba Churchill of Plymouth, and had Betsey, about 1796, m. Isaac Ellis; Thomas, about 1798; Zadoc, 1800; Sally, about 1802, m. Lucius Loring; George Washington, died in infancy; Bathsheba, m. Isaac Bearse; Harriet, died in infancy; Miles, m. Ann Budgham; Thankful, died in infancy; Washington, about 1811; Harriet; Thankful C., m. William W. Bacon. THOMAS, son of above, m., 1822, Mary Ann, d. of

Robert Dunham of Plymouth, and had Robert Thomas, 1823; George W..
1825. ZADOC, Buckfield, son of 1st Thomas, m., 1824, Julia Temple Davis,
and had Julia Davis, 1825, m. Nelson D. White; Persis Seaver, 1828, m. Per-
cival T. Bartlett; Zadoc, 1834, m. Ruth A. Strout; John Davis, 1838, m. Mary
W. Glover of Hingham.
LORING, BENJAMIN, Duxbury, son of 4th Thomas, m., 1739, Ann, d. of
John Alden, and had Mary, 1739; Sarah, 1744; Benjamin, 1745; Samuel,
1747; Judah, 1749; Daniel, 1751; John, 1752; Seth, 1755; and Lucy, 1758.
CALEB, son of 2d Thomas, m. Lydia, d. of Edward Gray, and settled in
Plympton. His children were Caleb, 1697; Hannah, 1698; Ignatius, 1699;
Polycarpus, 1701; Lydia, Jacob, Joseph, John, and Thomas. EZEKIEL,
Plympton, son of 3d Thomas, m. Hannah, d. of Elisha Stetson, and had
Thomas, John, Sarah, Friend, Lydia, Seth, Lewis, Ezekiel, Charles, Sophia,
Clyntha, Leonice, and Isaac. EZEKIEL, Plympton, son of above, m., 1807,
Lydia, d. of Elijah Sherman of Plymouth, and had Seth Lewis, m. Laura
Ann Thomas of Marshfield; Mary Ann, m. Oliver Churchill of Plympton;
Thomas of Plymouth, m. Lucy, d. of Jonathan Parker of Plympton; Clyntha,
m. William L. Bradford of Homer, N. Y.; Lydia Sherman, m. Thomas Cur-
tis of Homer; Maria Morton, m. James T. Barstow of Haverhill, N. H.;
Eveline Kimball, m. Albert G. Burr of Cortland, N. Y.; and John Thomas.
HENRY W., of Plymouth is a son of Henry and Lucy (Loring) Loring of
Pembroke, grandson of Nathaniel, great-grandson of Nathaniel, great-great-
grandson of Nathaniel, who was son of 3d Thomas. ISAAC of Plympton, m.
Eliza Morton, 1825. JOHN, m. Abigail Thomas, 1812. PEREZ, Duxbury,
son of 5th Thomas, m., 1758, Sarah Freeman, and had Mary, Braddock,
Freeman, Deborah, Barak, Belinda, Sarah, Perez, and Levi, 1775, m. Joanna
Joslyn. SAMUEL, Duxbury, son of Benjamin, m. Prudence Chapman, 1777,
and had Anna, 1778; Hannah, 1780, m. Nathaniel Winsor; Benjamin, 1784;
Prudence, 1789, the 1st wife of Richard Soule; Lydia, 1790, the 2d wife of
Richard Soule; and Samuel. SAMUEL, Duxbury, son of above, m. Nancy
Sprague, 1819, and had Samuel, m. Laura Ann, d. of Samuel and Lucy
(Delano) Loring, granddaughter of William and Alathea (Alden) Loring,
great-granddaughter of Nathaniel, who was son of 3d Thomas; Harrison of
Boston; Seth Loring, Sprague, Julia, Ann, Martha, Emily, Prudence,
Charles, and Abbot. THOMAS came from Axminster, England, 1635. He
m., in England, Jane Newton, whom he brought with him, together with
two children, Thomas and John, and settled in Hingham. He had, after
arrival, Isaac, Josiah, Joshua, and Benjamin. THOMAS, Hull, son of above,
m., 1657, Hannah, d. of Nicholas Jacob, and had Hannah, 1664, m. Rev.
Jeremiah Cushing and John Barker; Thomas, 1668; Deborah, m. John
Cushing; David, 1671; Caleb, 1674; and Abigail, 1679. THOMAS, Plympton,
son of Caleb, m. Sarah, d. of Ebenezer and Mercy (Standish) Lobdell, and
had Ezekiel. THOMAS, Duxbury, son of 2d Thomas, m., 1699, Deborah, d.
of John Cushing, and had Thomas; Joshua, 1701; Nathaniel, Benjamin,
Deborah, and Hannah. THOMAS, Duxbury, son of above, m., 1724, Mary
Southworth, and had Thomas, Simeon, Perez, 1729; Levi, Joshua, and
Deborah. WILLIAM of Plympton, m. Lucy Rider, 1768.

LOTHROP, ANSEL, son of 2d Thomas, m. Mary Thomas, 1736, and had Joseph, 1737; Mary, 1739, m. Elkanah Cushman; Betty, 1741, m. William Warren; Ansel, 1743; Joseph, 1745; William, 1748; Lydia, 1750, m. William Beadle. BARNABAS, Barnstable, son of 1st John, m. Susanna Clark, 1658, and had John, 1659; Abigail, 1660; Barnabas, 1663; Susanna, 1665; Nathaniel, 1669; Bathshua, 1671; Ann, 1673; Thomas, 1675; Mercy, 1676; Sarah, 1680; Thankful, 1682, m. John Hedge; James, 1684; Samuel, 1685. He m., 2d, 1698, Abigail, wid. of Joseph Dodson, and d. of Robert Button. BARNABAS, Barnstable, son of above, m. Elizabeth Hedge, 1687, and had Mercy, 1689; Elizabeth, 1690; Barnabas, 1692; Nathaniel, 1694; Lemuel, 1695; Barnabas, 1698; Susanna, 1699; Thankful, 1701, Sarah, 1703; Mary, 1705; Kembel, 1708. BARNABAS, Barnstable, son of 2d Joseph, m. Bethiah Fuller, 1706, and had John, 1709; Hannah, 1712. BENJAMIN, Barnstable, son of 1st John, by wife Martha, had Martha, 1652, m. John Goodwin; Hannah, 1655, m. Henry Swain; Benjamin; Mary, 1661, m. William Brown; Sarah, Elizabeth, Rebecca, Mercy, and John. He removed to Charlestown. BENJAMIN, Barnstable, son of 3d Samuel, m. Experience, d. of Thomas Howland of Plymouth, 1727, and had Hannah, 1729; John, 1731; Benjamin, 1733; Thomas, 1735; Thomas, 1736; Nathaniel, 1738; Joseph, 1741; Thomas Howland, 1743. By a 2d wife, Ruth, he had James, 1758; Elizabeth, 1758, m. Josiah Thatcher of Yarmouth; and Sarah, 1759, m. William Barker. DAVID, Barnstable and Plymouth, son of 2d John, m., 1770, Bathsheba, d. of John May of Plymouth, and had Bathsheba, 1773, m. William Nelson. DAVID, Bridgewater, died 1808, leaving a wife Mary, and a d. Eleanor, m. a Perkins. HOPE, Barnstable, son of 1st Joseph, m. Elizabeth Lothrop, 1696, and had Benjamin, 1697; John, 1699; Solomon, Hannah, John, Rebecca, Joseph, Sarah, Ebenezer, Elizabeth, Mary, Maltiah, and Ichabod. ICHABOD, son of Hope, had Solomon, and Hope. ISAAC, son of Maltiah, m., 1698, Elizabeth, d. of Jonathan Barnes, and had Maltiah, 1701; Elizabeth, 1705, m. Thomas Witherell and Samuel Bartlett; Isaac, 1707. ISAAC, son of above, m. Hannah, d. of Edmund Freeman, 1729, and had Freeman, 1730. He m., 2d, Priscilla (Thomas) Watson, wid. of John, 1733, and had Isaac, 1735; Nathaniel, 1737, m. Ellen, d. of Noah Hobart, and Lucy Hammett; Thomas, 1740; Caleb, 1742; Priscilla, 1747, m. Gershom Burr of Fairfield. ISRAEL, son of 1st Samuel, m. Rebecca Bliss, and had Martha, Mary, Jabez; Samuel, m. Elizabeth Waterman; John, m. Elizabeth Abell; William; Benjamin, m. Martha Adgate; Ebenezer, m. Elizabeth Leffingwell; Rebecca, and Israel. ISRAEL, son of above, m. Mary Fellows, and had Mary, Ezekiel, Israel, Prudence, Simon, Catherine, Ephraim, and Jedediah. JOHN, born in Elton, East Riding, Yorkshire, son of Thomas of Cherry Burton, and grandson of John Lowthorpe of Lowthorpe, Yorkshire, first settled in Egertown in Kent, and afterwards succeeded Henry Jacob as pastor of the Southwark Church in London. He came over in the Griffin 1634, and settled first in Scituate, and then in Barnstable, 1639. By a 1st wife, he had, in England, Thomas, Benjamin; Jane, m. Samuel Fuller; Barbara, m. an Emerson; Samuel, about 1620; and Joseph. By a 2d wife he had Barnabas, 1636; Abigail, 1639, m. James Clark; Bathsheba, 1642; John,

1645. JOHN, Barnstable, son of Hope, had Thatcher, David, John, and Jonathan. JOHN, Barnstable, son of 1st Barnabas, had Elizabeth, 1692; Barnabas, 1694. JOHN, son of 1st Benjamin, m., 1695, Hannah, wid. of John Fuller, and had Bathsheba, 1696; Phebe, 1701; Benjamin, 1704. JOHN, Bridgewater, son of 4th Samuel, had Susanna and Sarah, and died 1743. JONATHAN, Bridgewater, died 1819, leaving Lemuel, Libbeus; Sarah, m. David Alger; and Chloe, m. Jacob Fisher. JOSEPH, son of 1st John, m. Mary Ansel, 1650, and had Joseph, 1652; Mary, 1654, m. Edward Croswell; Benjamin, 1657; Elizabeth, 1659, m. Thomas Fuller; John, 1661; Samuel, 1664; John, 1666; Barnabas, 1669; Hope, 1671; Thomas, 1674; Hannah, 1676. JOSEPH, Barnstable, son of 1st Samuel, m. Elizabeth Scudder, and had Joseph, m. a Hartshorn; Abigail, Barnabas, Solomon, and Elizabeth. He m., 2d, Ann Wartrous, and had Esther, Mehitabel, Temperance, and Zeruiah. JOSEPH, Springfield, son of Solomon, m. Elizabeth Dwight, and had Dwight, m. Lord Stebbins; Samuel; Joseph, m. Rowena Wells; Seth, m. Anna Abbott; Solomon; and Samuel, m. Mary McCracken. JOSHUA, son of 4th Thomas, m. Mercy Eells, and had Joshua, Lydia, Daniel, and Thomas. MALTIAH, Barnstable, son of 1st Thomas, m., 1667, Sarah Farren, and had Thomas, 1668; Tabitha, 1668; Isaac, 1673; Joseph, 1675; Elizabeth, 1677; Ichabod, 1680; Shubael, 1682; Sarah, 1684. MARK, Salem, Duxbury, and Bridgewater, according to family tradition, brother of 1st John, died in Bridgewater, 1686, leaving children, Elizabeth, m. Samuel Packard; Mark, Samuel, and Edward. MARK, Bridgewater, son of above, died 1691, probably unmarried. NATHANIEL, Barnstable, son of 1st Barnabas, by wife Bethiah, had John, 1696. SAMUEL, Barnstable, son of 1st John, m., 1644, Elizabeth Scudder, removed to New London, 1648, to Norwich, 1668, and had John, 1645, m. Ruth Royce; Samuel, 1650; Israel, 1659, m. Rebecca Bliss; Joseph, 1661, m. Elizabeth Scudder; Elizabeth, m. Isaac Royce; Ann, m. William Hough; Sarah, probably m. Nathaniel Royce; Abigail, and Martha. SAMUEL, Norwich, son of above, m., 1675, Hannah, d. of Thomas Adgate, and had Hannah; Thomas; Elizabeth, m. John Waterman, whose d. Hannah was d. of Benedict Arnold; Nathaniel, m. Ann Backus; Simon, 1689, m. Martha Lothrop, and Samuel, m. Deborah Crow. He m., 2d, 1690, Abigail, d. of John Doane of Plymouth. SAMUEL, Barnstable, son of 1st Joseph, m., 1686, Hannah Crocker, and had Mary, 1688; Hannah, 1690; Abigail, 1693; Benjamin, 1696; Joseph, 1698; Samuel, 1700. SAMUEL, Bridgewater, son of 1st Mark, m. Sarah Donner, and had Mary, 1683, m. Josiah Keith; Samuel, 1685; John, 1687; Mark, 1689; Sarah, 1693; Joseph, and Edward, and died 1724. SAMUEL, Bridgewater, son of above, by wife Elizabeth, had Jonathan, Samuel, and Mark, and died 1777. SETH, Bridgewater, died 1804, leaving children, Susanna, m. Calvin Kingsley; Seth; and Mehitabel, m. Alpheus Fobes. SETH, Bridgewater, son of above, by wife Abigail, had Barsillai, Cyrus, and Bettie. SIMEON, Bridgewater, died 1808, leaving wife Margaret and children, Hannah, m. William Miller; and Kesiah. SOLOMON, son of 2d Joseph, m. wid. Martha (Perkins) Todd, and had Martha and Joseph. THOMAS, Barnstable, son of 1st John, m. Sarah, wid. of Thomas Ewer, and d. of William Larned, and had Mary, 1640; Hannah, 1642; Thomas, 1644; Maltiah, 1646;

Bethiah, 1649, m. John Hinckley; and Mary, m. John Stearns, and William French, and Isaac Mixer. THOMAS, son of 1st Joseph, m., 1697, Experience Gorham, and had Deborah, 1699; Mary, 1701; James, 1703; Thomas, 1705; Ansel, 1707; Joseph, 1709; Seth, 1712; Mehitabel, John, and Lydia. He m., 2d, Deborah Loring. THOMAS, son of 2d Isaac, m., 1773, Lydia, d. of Nathaniel Goodwin, and had Caleb; and Harriet, m. Chandler Robbins. THOMAS, son of 2d Samuel, m. Lydia Abell, and had Lydia, Daniel, and Joshua. THOMAS, son of Joshua, had Lydia, Joshua, and Jerusha.

LOUD, HUGH, from Sydney, Nova Scotia, m. Catherine Chesnut, 1852, and had William D., 1858; Allen, 1865; and Walter H., 1867. JACOB, Hersey, son of Thomas of Hingham, born in 1802, came to Plymouth 1825. He m. Elizabeth Loring Jones of Hingham, and had Sarah, 1830, m. Dr. Edward H. Clark of Boston; Thomas Hersey, 1835; Hersey Jones, 1838; and Arthur Jones, 1846. Thomas, the father of Jacob, was the son of John, who was the grandson of Francis of Weymouth, who m. Honor, sister or niece of Thomas Prince the annalist. Francis was the son of Francis who appeared in Sagadahock in Maine as early as 1675. JOSHUA B., from Abington, m. Lillis B. Churchill, 1837. PHILIP W., brother of Hugh, m. Hannah Howland, 1854, and had Flora Ann, 1856.

LOUDEN, ISAAC, of Pembroke, m. Anna Holmes, 1804.

LOVELL, EZEKIEL, m. Patty Cahoon, 1807. JOSEPH, m. Elizabeth Harlow, 1761. LEANDER, m. Mercy, d. of James Bartlett. NATHANIEL, of Sandwich, m. Sarah Holmes, 1816. ROBERT, of Barnstable, m. Jerusha Bartlett, 1815. THOMAS, by wife Mary, had Elizabeth, 1687; Joshua, 1689; Thomas, 1691; Mary, 1693; Hannah, 1696; Sarah, 1699.

LUCAS, ABIJAH, Plympton, son of 2d Samuel, m. Mary Robbins, and had Rebecca, 1782, m. Edmund Sears; Hosea, 1784, m. Hannah Lucas; Abigail, 1786; Mary, 1788, m. Josiah Cobb; Abijah, 1790, m. Hannah Shurtleff; Eleanor, 1792, m. Eliab Wood; Harvey, 1794; Elizabeth, 1798; Martin Luther, 1801. ABIJAH, Carver, son of above, m. Hannah Shurtleff, and had Mary R., 1818; Horatio A., 1820; Mary R., 1822; Abigail S., 1828; and Lot Shurtleff, 1831. ABNER, son of Barnabas, m. Ruth Rickard, 1822. ANSEL, son of 1st Joseph, m. Susanna Dunham, and had Ansel. ANSEL, son of above, m. Mary B., d. of Ezekiel Rider, 1827. BARNABAS, Plympton, son of 2d Joseph, had Nehemiah, Elijah, Barnabas, Ephraim, Consider, Seth, Caleb, Meltiah, m. William Whitten, Joanna, Molly, Elizabeth, and Hannah. BARNABAS, Plympton, son of above, by wife Betsey, had Barnabas, 1783, m. Lucy Bryant; Asaph, 1785; Sampson, 1787; Ephraim, 1789; Betsey, 1792; Charles, 1795; Warren; Abner, 1797, m. Ruth Rickard; Jemima, 1800. BELA, son of 1st Benjamin, m., 1781, Hannah, d. of John Lucas, and had Benjamin, 1783; Hannah, 1786; Zillah, 1789, m. Winslow Bradford; Ezra, 1791. BENJAMIN, son of 1st William, m., 1755, Lydia, d. of Theophilus Crocker, and had Bela, 1757; Isaac, 1759; Abigail, 1761; Ezra, 1763; Lucy, 1765, m. Andrew Sturtevant; Lydia, 1767, m. Joseph Holmes; Naomi, 1770. BENJAMIN, son of Bela, m., 1806, Persis, d. of John Lucas, and had Benjamin, 1808; Erastus, 1811; Isaac, 1813; Zilpha Winslow, 1815; John Bela, 1818; Persis Shaw, 1820. BENONI, son of Thomas, by wife Repentance, had

Mary, 1684, m. John Wright; Samuel, 1689; Joanna, 1691; Sarah, 1692; Elisha, 1699; Bethiah, 1704. BEZALEEL, Carver, son of 2d Samuel, m. Sally Sears, 1793, and had Oliver, 1794; Willard Sears, 1796; George, 1798. He m., 2d, Rhoda Shurtleff, and had Hazael, 1801; Sally, 1802; Ruth Shaw, 1803; Edward, 1804. CALVIN, Carver, son of 3d Joseph, by wife Ruth, had James, 1794, m. Cynthia Manter; Oliver, 1797; Ruth, 1801; Calvin Luther, 1807; Ruby Fuller, 1812. DAVID, Kingston, son of 2d John, m. Lydia Wright, and had Nathan, m. Priscilla Sampson; David; Doten; Sarah, m. Ward Bailey; Deborah, m. Joseph McLaughlin; and Hannah, m. Hosea Lucas. DAVID, Kingston, son of above, had David, Mary, and others. ELISHA, Plympton, son of Benoni, by wife Margaret, had James, Samuel, Elkanah, Benoni, and Elisha. EPHRAIM, Carver, by wife Azubah, had Mary, 1792; Isaac, 1794; Cynthia, 1796; Joanna, 1798. EPHRAIM, by wife Sally, had Abner, 1824; Sarah, 1828; Betsy C., 1832; Louisa B., 1835; Ephraim T., 1839. EZRA, son of Bela, m., 1821, Betsey, d. of Asa Barrows, and had Ezra, 1823; Betsey, 1825; Francis Winslow, 1827; Benjamin Franklin, 1833. FRANCIS WINSLOW, son of above, m., 1852, Caroline Bradley, and had Carrie Orinda, 1857; and Caroline F., 1862. He m., 2d, Mary Jane, wid. of Frank A. Thomas, and d. of Benjamin Bullard. HARVEY, Carver, son of 1st Abijah, m. Sarah Atwood, and had Horatio Atwood, 1827; and Eleanor, 1830. ISAAC SHAW, Plympton, son of 2d Samuel, m., 1st, a wife Martha, and, 2d, Lydia Jackson, and had Asenath, 1779; John, 1780; Oliver, 1781; Joel, 1784; Amasa, 1787; Willard, 1789; Olive, 1794; Martha, 1797. ISSACHAR, Carver, son of 1st John, m. Nancy Russell, and had John, 1807; Edward Fuller, 1809; Deborah, 1811. ISAAC JACKSON, son of Levi, m. Catherine, d. of Jacob Howland, 1819, and had Isaac J., 1830, m. Mary Ann Chapman, and Hannah J., 1827, m. John B. Washburn. He m., 2d, B. Flora, wid. of William Robinson, 1866. JOHN, son of 2d John, m. Lydia Lucas, and had Rhoda, 1771; Persis, 1782; Issachar, 1784. JOHN, Plympton, son of 2d Joseph, by wife Lydia, had Persis, 1742, m. a Cobb; Joseph, 1742; John, 1744; David, 1746; Lydia, 1748; Hannah, 1750; Susanna, 1752; William, 1755. JOHN SHAW, Carver, son of 3d Samuel, m. Mary Bartlett, and had David B., 1817; Hiram, 1820; Edwin, 1823; John, 1826. JOSEPH, son of 1st William, m. Mary Rickard, 1753, and had Benjamin, 1755; Phebe, 1757, m. George Dunham; Louisa, 1759; Elnathan, 1762, m. Lydia Cornish; Ansel, 1764, m. Susanna Dunham; Molly, 1766, m. Jeremiah Holmes; and Lazarus. JOSEPH, Plympton, son of 1st Samuel, m. Persis, d. of Jonathan Shaw, and had John, 1715; Hannah, 1717; Samuel, 1719; Patience, 1723. He had a 2d wife, Meletiah, and had Barnabas, 1729. JOSEPH, Plympton, son of 2d John, by wife Ruby, had Levi, 1768; Calvin, 1770; Luther, 1772; Olive, 1775; Huldah, 1777; Anna, 1780; Alden, 1782, m. Deborah Barnes; Joseph, 1785; Ruby, 1788; Ebenezer, 1789; Oliver, 1802. JOSEPH, son of above, m. Lydia Keen, 1823, and had Augustus Henry, 1824, m. Eliza, d. of Solomon Sylvester; Catherine Amelia, 1825; Frederick William, 1831, m. Angeline, d. of Solomon Sylvester. LAZARUS, son of 1st Joseph, m. Mary Cole, 1797. LEVI, son of 3d Joseph, m. Hannah Jackson, 1794, and had Allen of New Bedford; Levi; and Isaac Jackson, 1797. He m., 2d, Betsey Davie, 1802.

MARTIN LUTHER, Carver, son of 1st Abijah, m. Mary Shurtleff, and had Ebenezer Shurtleff, 1831, m. Eliza H. Walker of Westboro'; Rebecca Bartlett, 1834; Henry Martin, 1836; Elisha Shaw, 1839; William Shurtleff, 1839; Sarah Ellis, 1841, m. Nelson H. Fuller of Halifax; and Eldora C., m. Silas Poole of Jamaica Plains. NATHAN, Kingston, son of 1st David, m. Priscilla Sampson, and had Martin, Alvin, George, Eliza, and Roxanna. SAMUEL, son of Thomas, m. Patience Warren, and had John, 1688; Joseph, 1689; William, 1692; Patience, 1696, m. Nathaniel Harlow. SAMUEL, Plympton, son of 2d Joseph, m. a wife Abigail, and had Isaac, 1750; Abigail, 1752; Samuel; Isaac Shaw, 1756; Abijah, 1759; Abigail, 1762; Patience, 1766, m. a Robbins; Elizabeth, 1768; Bezaleel, 1771; Zilpha, 1773. SAMUEL, Plympton, son of above, m. Jemima Robbins, and had Rebecca, 1777; Lois, 1779; Daniel, 1781, Samuel, 1783, m. a Mitchell; Ezra, 1786; Jemima, 1788; Job, 1791, m. Mary Morse; John Shaw, 1793; Jesse, 1796, m. Deborah Bagnall; Stephen, 1798. SAMUEL, Plympton, perhaps son of 1st Samuel, by wife Elizabeth, had Molly, 1723; Repentance, 1726, m. Arthur Bennet. By a 2d wife, Abigail Shaw, 1732, he had Samuel, 1732; Elizabeth, 1735, m. John Shaw; Abiel, 1737; and Samuel again. STEPHEN, son of 3d Samuel, m. Rebecca Holmes, 1820, and had Rebecca, 1825, m. Alexander G. Nye. THOMAS, came to Plymouth from the west of England, and by a wife, whose name is unknown, had John, 1656; Mary, 1658; Benoni, 1659; Samuel, 1661; William, 1663. He was killed in King Philip's war. WARREN, son of Barnabas, m. Charlotte Hathaway, 1827, and had Asenath, 1831. WILLIAM, son of 1st Samuel, m. Mehitabel Doty, 1722, and had William, 1723; Phebe, 1725; Priscilla, 1727, m. Eleazer Robbins; Joseph, 1729; Benjamin, 1731; Isaac, 1733; William, 1734; Mehitabel, 1738. WILLIAM, of Middletown, perhaps a brother of Thomas, m. Esther Clark, 1666, and had William, 1667; John, 1669; Mary, 1672; Thomas, 1676; Samuel, 1682. WILLIAM, son of 2d John, by wife Desire, had John, 1784; William, 1786; Sarah, 1790; Desire, 1791; Abraham, 1793; Ivory, 1794; Zephaniah B., 1796; Lydia, 1798; and Calvin. ZEPHANIAH B., son of above, m. Eliza Blackmer, 1818, and had Emily H., 1820; and Ivory B., 1822, m. Mary G. Walker.

LUCE, ALDEN, m. Deborah Barnes, 1804. CROSBY, son of 1st Seth, m. Elizabeth, d. of Thomas Totman, 1775, and had Elkanah, 1779; Crosby, 1780; Elizabeth, 1782; Joanna, 1784, m. Moses Hoyt; Crosby, 1786, m. Betsey Doten; Thomas, 1788, m. Olive Delano of Duxbury; Elizabeth, 1790; Anna, 1792; Freeman, 1794; Nancy, 1796, m. Nathaniel Carver. EBENEZER, son of 1st Seth, m., 1777, Lydia Harlow, and had Lydia, m. Meletiah Howard and Jacob Taylor Morton. He m., 2d, 1779, Sarah Holmes. EPHRAIM, son of 1st Seth, m., 1769, Ruth Morton, and had Hannah, 1772, m. Benjamin Goddard. SETH, from Wareham, m. Hannah Morton, 1740, and had Anna, 1741; Ephraim, 1742; Seth, 1744; Ebenezer, 1747; Crosby, 1749; Hannah, 1751, m. Ezra Finney and Naaman Holbrook; Elizabeth, 1754, m. William McLaughlin; Deborah, 1756, m. Noah Curtis of Pembroke. SETH, son of above, m. Sarah Blackwell, 1769, and had Seth, m. Jedidah Barnes; and Sally, m. Samuel W. Holmes.

LUNENBURG, CHARLES, m. Elizabeth M. Haskins, 1831.

LUNT, WILLIAM PEARSON, m., 1829, Ellen Hobart, d. of Barnabas Hedge.

LYFORD, JOHN, came over 1624 with, probably, wife Ann and children Ruth, m. James Bates; and Mordecai. He removed to Nantasket, thence to Cape Ann, and finally to Virginia.

MACKEEL, JOHN, m. Susanna Sampson, and had Abigail, 1757.

MACKIE, ANDREW, by wife Amelia Bradford, had Andrew, 1823; John Howel, 1826. ISAAC, m. Sarah Harlow, and had Isaac, 1764; William, 1765; Mary, 1767; Martha, 1768; Hannah, 1770.

MACOMBER, ELIJAH, probably a descendant from John of Taunton, who m. Anna Evans, 1678, and had a son John, who had a son Elijah, born 1718, came to Plymouth about 1800, with a wife, whose maiden name was Chloe Smith, and had Elijah, John, Warren S.; Lucia, m. Samuel Robbins; Ann, m. William Drew; Betsey, and Nancy and Hannah, twins. ELIJAH, son of above, m. Deborah Thomas, 1819, and had Deborah, 1819; Nancy T., 1821; Elijah, 1823; John C., 1825; Hannah L., 1828; Francis H., 1836; Laura A., 1839. JOHN, son of 1st Elijah, m. Eleanor, d. of William Leonard, 1822, and had Eleanor, 1825; Betsey Ann, 1827; Augusta Jane, 1830; Emeline, 1832; John Alfred, 1835. WARREN S., son of 1st Elijah, m., 1846, Jeanette T., d. of Benjamin Weston, and had Annie Warren, and Walter Spooner.

MAGLATHLIN, MCGLATHLA, or MCLAUTHLIN, BARTLETT, Duxbury, son of 1st Daniel, m., 1817, Maria W., d. of Nathan Chandler of Kingston, and had Henry Bartlett, 1819; Nathan Chandler, 1821; Edward Doten, 1825; Daniel S., 1828; Sydney S., 1831; Mercer E., 1834; Mary D., 1836, m. Levi Ford; Isabel S., 1840, also m. Levi Ford. CHARLES C., Watertown, son of Lewis, m., 1855, Mary Bacon, and had Mary E., 1856; Lewis, 1857; Howard O., 1859; Hattie F., 1861; Rufus H., 1865; Wallace H., 1867; Nellie F., 1872. DANIEL, Duxbury, son of 1st John, m., 1779, Asenath Stetson of Pembroke, and had Daniel Stetson, 1779; Polly, 1780, m. Benjamin Prior; Sophia, 1785, m. Levi Sampson; Asenath, 1786, m. Joseph Ford; Simeon Hall, 1791; Prudence, 1792; Lucy, 1794; Bartlett, 1797; Prudence, 1801, m. Joshua W. Hathaway of Duxbury. DANIEL S., Duxbury, son of Bartlett, m. Lucy White of Duxbury, and had Daniel Herbert, 1854; Bartlett White, 1856. DANIEL STETSON, New Sharon, Maine, son of 1st Daniel, m., 1816, Susan Richardson, and 1828, wid. Mary Shaw, and had Mary Elizabeth, 1837, m. Henry M. Howes of Farmington. ELISHA, Kingston, son of 1st Robert, m. Olive Bryant of Pembroke, and had Olive, 1792, m. Ira Hayward of Kingston; Polly, 1793, m., 1st, Peleg Simmons, and 2d, Solomon Thompson; Elisha, 1795; Harvey, 1797; Luranna, 1799, m. Martin McLaughlin of Bridgewater; Judith, 1801; Robert B., 1803, m. Betsey Lincoln of Hanover; Rebecca, 1806, m. Samuel Soule. ELISHA, Kingston, son of above, m. Abigail, d. of John Wright of Plympton; and had Nancy H., 1822; Almira B., 1823; Elisha, 1825; Abigail W., 1827, m. Edward Lyon of Halifax; Almira B., 1829, m. Nahum Simmons; Olive M., 1831, m., 1st, T. W. French; and, 2d, Cephas Washburn of Halifax; Sarah B., 1833, m. Charles P. Lyon of Halifax; George W., 1834, m. Amelia W. Faunce; Amanda A., 1837, m. Cephas Washburn; Sophia W., 1840, m. Algernon S. Chandler. He m., 2d, wid. Nancy Fish. EDWARD

DOTEN, Boston, son of Bartlett, m. Persis Walker of Pembroke, and had Sydney E., 1849; Edward Bartlett, 1852; Persis Doten, 1855; Abbot, 1858; Persis Selina, 1862. GEORGE W., Kingston, son of 2d Elisha, m. Amelia W. Faunce, and had Hannah R., 1857; Elisha, 1859; George Walter, 1869. GEORGE I., son of Lewis, m. Mary B. E. Church of Hanover, and had Irving, Morris Copeland, Albert Irving, and Clarence. HENRY BARTLETT, son of Bartlett, m., 1854, Elizabeth, d. of Dura Wadsworth of Duxbury, and had Abbie, 1855, m. George F. Lane of Kingston; Arthur, 1857, m. Eudora Lobdell; Alice, 1862. HIRAM WEST, Lynn, son of 1st Joseph, dropped the family name. He m. Abigail P. Oliver of Salem, and had Hiram Augustus, 1826; Sarah Maria, 1829; Abby Ann, 1832. He m., 2d, Elizabeth Caldwell, and had Abby Jane, 1837; Faustina Elizabeth, 1838; Hiram Murray, 1841; Mary Abby, 1843; Jane Augusta, 1846; Emma Frances, 1850. HIRAM LEWIS, Pembroke, son of 2d Joseph, m. Hannah Drake, and had Margaret F., 1843, m. Herbert M. Cummings of N. H.; Mary, 1844, m. Melvin E. Peterson of Kingston. He m., 2d, Estella Frost, and had Hattie Lewis, 1876. He m., 3d, Nancy H. White of Duxbury. JOHN, according to family tradition, was the son of Robert and Isabella (Sampson) Maglathlin, or McGlathlea of Glasgow, born 1695. There was a Robert Macklathlin who came to New England about 1650, and settled in Brookfield, and John may have been a relative. John settled in Duxbury after a short residence in Maine, and m. Margaret Miller, said to have been born in the County of Antrim, Ireland, by whom he had John, 1737, m. Jedidah Sampson; Robert, 1740; Daniel, 1744; William, Thomas; Jane, m. Samuel Sampson of Kingston; Margaret, 1748; Joseph, 1754; Polly, 1756; and Nathaniel. JOHN, Duxbury, son of above, m., 1763, Jedidah Sampson, and had John, 1769; Sally, m., 1st, Oliver Sampson of Duxbury, and, 2d, Joshua Brewster of same. JOHN, Kingston, son of above, m. Rizpah Chandler, and had Sally, 1812, m. Edward D. Chandler; Angeline, 1814, m. Peter W. McLaughlin; Almira, 1816, m. Joseph Holmes; Augusta, 1819. He m., 2d, Lydia, wid. of Hezekiah Simmons, and had Alden, 1822. JOHN, Shrewsbury, son of 1st Joseph, m. Pamelia, d. of Robert Maglathlin, and had John, and Pamelia Ann. JOSEPH, Pembroke, son of 1st John, m. Jane West of Kingston, and had Joseph, 1778; Miller, 1780; Lydia, 1782, m. Nathaniel Bonney of Plympton; Margaret, 1784; Peter West, 1786; John, 1789; Samuel W., 1791; Jane, 1792; Lewis, 1796; Pamelia, 1798, m. Joseph Ford; Martin, 1800; Hiram West, 1803. JOSEPH, Pembroke and Kingston, son of above, m. Deborah Lucas of Kingston, and had Sophia, 1805, m. Thomas Lanman; Margaret, 1807, m. Harvey Ransom; Sophronia, 1809; Deborah, 1812, m. Ezra Mitchell; Polly, 1813, m. John Bonney; Joseph Warren, 1815; Hiram Lewis, 1818; Lydia W., 1820; Selina W., 1821, m, Nathan Chandler McLaughlin; Mahala, 1824. JOSEPH L., son of Lewis, m., 1853, Sarah A. Learned of Watertown, and had Emma H., 1856. JOSEPH WARREN, Chelsea, son of 2d Joseph, took the name Joseph Way, and m., Sarah A. Barker, and had Henry, Herbert, and Everett. LEWIS, Pembroke, son of 1st Joseph, m. Polly, d. of Rufus Hathaway of Duxbury, and had Judith W., 1821, m. Sylvanus Smith of Duxbury; Joseph L. and Rufus H., 1823, twins; Jane W., 1825, m. John Bradford of Duxbury; Walter S., 1829;

Charles C., 1831; George I., 1835; John T., 1838, m. Lucy F. Lincoln of Quincy; Mary E., 1840. MARTIN, East Bridgewater, son of 1st Joseph. m., 1823, Hannah Howard, d. of Jesse Reed of Marshfield, and had Roxilana Reed, 1824; Martin Parris, 1825; George Thomas, 1826, m., 1st, Clara Matilda Holden, and, 2d, Matilda Hull; Hannah Reed, 1831; Mary West, 1833. He m., 2d, 1849, Susanna McLaughlin of Kingston. MARTIN PARRIS, East Bridgewater, son of above, m., 1866, Elizabeth Pease, d. of Ambrose Vincent of New Bedford, and had Elizabeth Rena, 1867; George Vincent, 1868; Martin Bernard, 1871; Ambrose Vincent, 1874; Parker Reed, 1877; Sarah Louisa, 1879. MILLER, son of 1st Joseph, m. Betsey Fish of Kingston, and had Charles Henry, and Nathaniel Miller. NATHAN CHANDLER, Kingston, son of Bartlett, dropped the family name. He m. Selina W., d. of Joseph McLaughlin, and had Hattie Maria, 1846, m. Lloyd G. Bartlett of Kingston. PETER WEST, son of 1st Joseph, m. Hannah B. Weston of Marshfield, and had Peter W., 1810. PETER WEST, Kingston, son of above, m. Angeline, d. of John McLaughlin, and had Harvey, 1834, m. Harriet Crapo of Bridgewater; Augusta, 1836, m. Nathan Ford of Duxbury; Ann, 1838. He m., 2d, Marcia Bradford of Maine, and had Philemon W., 1844, m. Mahala Bonney of Kingston; Onslow, 1846, m. Harriet Bradford of Maine; Edwin L., 1849, m. Almira Simmons of Kingston; Horace B., 1851, m. Eleanor Ford of Duxbury; Angie L., 1854, m. Eliott W. Blanchard; Helen A., 1856, m. Barker Baker of Pembroke. ROBERT, Duxbury and Kingston, son of 1st John, m. Mary Keen of Pembroke, and had Rebecca, 1764; Elisha, 1765; Polly, 1768, m. Abner Stetson of Pembroke; Robert, 1770; Ruth, 1772; Peggy, 1775; Judith, 1778, m. Spencer Holmes of Kingston. ROBERT, Kingston, son of above, m. Pamelia, d. of Joseph Holmes of Kingston, and had Pamelia, 1806, m. John McLaughlin and Allen C. Streeter; Ann, 1808; Mary J., 1810, m. Spencer Holmes; Lucia, 1812, m. James W. Holmes; Ann, 1815, m. Pelham Brewster. RUFUS H., son of Lewis, m., 1752, Fanny W. Corthell of Rochester, and had Helen L., 1853; Lewis, 1855; James C., 1856; Fanny C., 1859; Alice L., 1870. SAMUEL W., Kingston, son of 1st Joseph, m. Hannah B., wid. of Peter West McLaughlin, and had Hannah B., 1816, m. Thomas Adams of Kingston; Christiana H., 1819, m. John Johnson; Samuel, 1822, m. Hannah B., d. of Jeremiah Snell of Brockton; Simeon Weston, 1826, m. Frances A. Bradford. SAMUEL, son of above, m. Hannah B. Snell of Brockton, and had Charles W., 1848; George W., 1850; Hattie E., 1855; Frank A., 1859. SIMEON HALL, New Sharon, Maine, son of 1st Daniel, m., 1821, Mary Richards, and had Horace, 1823; Harriet B., 1825, m. Stephen Howes; Susan R., 1827; Asenath, 1829; Daniel W., 1831; Henry A., 1834; Lucy A., 1836; Augusta, 1838; Charles E., 1841. SIMEON WESTON, Kingston, son of 1st Samuel, m. Frances A. Bradford of Kingston, and had Herbert W., 1854; Frances, 1861; Lydia L., 1862. THOMAS, son of William, m. Lovica, d. of Seth Thomas of Middleboro', 1806, and had Thomas, 1808; Freeman T., 1809, m. Harriet Thomas of Middleboro; Seth, 1812, m. Priscilla, d. of George Raymond of Plymouth; Lovica T., 1815; Mercy W., 1817, m. Eleazer S. Raymond. THOMAS, Duxbury, son of 1st John, m. Saba Ames of Marshfield, and had Jane, 1775, m. Daniel Ripley of Kingston. WALTER S., son of Lewis, m. Abby C. Learned, and had Walter S., 1860. WILLIAM, son of 1st John, m. Elizabeth Luce of Plymouth, 1773, and had Thomas; Jedidah, m. George Paulding of Plymouth; and Deborah, m. George Burgess of Plymouth.

MAGOON, EDWARD, m. Mary Covill, 1789.

MAHOMMEN, SIMON, of Sandwich, m. Mary Swift, 1749.

MALLISE, ALEXANDER, m. Bathsheba Hill, 1725.

MANCHESTER, ISAAC, from New Bedford, m., 1815, Harriet Bartlett.

MANGE, HENRY, m., 1832, Wealthea Wadsworth.

MANN, CHARLES G., m., 1832, Jerusha Cornish.

MANTER, BELCHER, came to Plymouth from Wareham, and had, by a 1st wife, George, about 1768, m. Nancy Richmond; Grafton, about 1770, m. Lydia Leach; James, and Alden. He m., 2d, Rebecca Palmer, and had Belcher and Prince. By a 3d wife, Mehitabel, he had Rebecca. BELCHER, son of above, m. Sarah Wright, 1799, and had Freeman, m. Naomi, d. of Branch Pierce; Nancy, m. David Sears; Sarah, m. Adoniram Whiting; Rebecca, m. Otis Harlow; William, m. Lucy B. Wright; Charlotte, m. Lewis Peterson; Deborah, m. Joseph Davie; and Prince. GEORGE, son of 1st Prince, m. Sally Sampson, and had George, 1824, m. Ruth S. Sampson; Sally, 1823, m. Ebenezer Pierce; Servia, 1828; David, 1827; Lucy B., 1831, m. Nathan B. Sampson. DAVID, son of 1st Prince, m. Betsey, d. of Elkanah Finney, and had David L., 1844, m. Lucy, d. of Joseph Morton; Horace I., 1856; Edward Russell, 1858, m. Mary, d. of Ebenezer Nickerson. PRINCE, son of 2d Belcher, m. Lucy Besse, and had Sally, m. Josiah Morton; George; Thomas, m. Naomi Clark, and Mary, d. of Lemuel Morton; Prince; Cynthia, m. Jonathan Thrasher; Lucy, m. Elijah Morey and Branch Pierce; Parnell, m. George Godfrey of Taunton; Timothy, m. Susan Benson; David, m. Betsey Finney. He m., 2d, Lydia Douglass, and had Preston, 1821, m. Ruth, d. of Branch Pierce; William, 1824, m. Sarah Swift; John, 1826, m. Jeanette Burgess; Belcher, 1830, m. a Finney of Plympton; and Lydia, 1839. PRINCE, son of above, m. Wealthea, d. of William Burgess, and had Maria Frances, m. Ivory Blackmer; Prince, 1831, m. Sarah H. Rogers of Ipswich; and Augusta, m. Alvin Nightingale and Albert Mortimer Watson.

MARCY, CHARLES, son of Stephen, m. Abigail Packard of Bridgewater, and had Susan Packard, m. Oliver Orr of Bridgewater; and James. He m., 2d, Charlotte Warren, and had James Warren, 1818, m. Helen Munroe of Boston; and Mary Ann, m. Charles White. JOSEPH, son of Stephen, m. Charlotte Eaton of Boston, and had Charlotte, m. Henry G. Capen. STEPHEN, from Woodstock, Vt., m. Lucy, d. of Thomas Jackson, 1783, and settled in Plymouth as a physician. His children were Hannah, m. Joseph Sanger of Bridgewater; Stephen, m. Temperance Dunbar of Woodstock; Charles, Joseph, William, Lucy, Edward; Mary T., m. Horace R. Rolfe; and Thomas.

MARGESON, EDMUND, came, unmarried, in the Mayflower, and died 1621.

MARRENCE, ANTHONY COAST, pub. to Elizabeth Brown, 1729.

MARSH, THOMAS, by wife Mercy, had Thomas, 1798; Perez, 1801; Mary, 1804; Lillis, 1805; Warren, 1807; and Hannah, 1809. THOMAS, son of above, m. Lydia, d. of Ezra Burbank, 1822.

MARSHAL, Bartlett, son of 3d Samuel, m. Ruth Doten, 1777, and had Ruth, 1778; Bartlett, 1780; Samuel, 1783. He m., 2d, Bathsheba Doten, 1792. JOHN, Duxbury, m. Mary, d. of Rev. Ralph Partridge, 1631, and had Robert, John, and perhaps others. ROBERT, son of above, m., 1659, Mary, d. of John Barnes, and had John; Robert, 1663; and perhaps Samuel. SAMUEL, Barnstable, perhaps son of above, by wife Sarah, had Sarah, and perhaps Samuel. SAMUEL, son of above, m. Priscilla Finney, and had Elizabeth, 1718; Samuel, 1719; Mary, 1722, m. Benjamin Carter; John, 1726, m. Jerusha Watkins. SAMUEL, son of above, m. Susanna Bartlett, 1748, and had Bartlett; Priscilla, m. Barnabas Holmes; and others.

MARSTON, NYMPHAS, m. Elizabeth Cooper, 1782.

MARTIN, CHRISTOPHER, came in the Mayflower with his wife, and both died soon. JOHN CHARLES, m. Sarah Holmes, 1791. STEPHEN of Dartmouth, m. Abigail McFarland, 1775.

MASON, STEVENS, m., 1766, Lydia Simmons, and had Stevens, 1769; Lydia, 1772; Polly, 1773; Susanna, 1774.

MASTERSON, RICHARD, from Sandwich, England, m. at Leyden, 1619, Mary Goodall of Leicester, and had Nathaniel; and Sarah, m. John Wood. He probably came over 1629.

MATTHEWS, THOMAS, born in South Shields, England, 1725, had a wife Desire, born 1732, and owned an estate in Plymouth, 1764, which at his death, in 1807, he gave to Thomas Lambert, a relative of his wife.

MAY, CHARLES, son of 6th John, m. Mary Ann Williams of Taunton, and had Harriet W., m. Russell Tomlinson; Mary W.; Abby W.; and Charles T., m. Harriet E., d. of Johnson Davie. EDWARD died 1691, leaving a son Edward. ISRAEL, died in Plympton, 1709. JOHN, Roxbury, 1640, came from Mayfield, England, and by wife Sarah, had John and Samuel. JOHN, Roxbury, son of above, m., 1656, Sarah Brewer, and had Mary, 1657; Sarah, 1659; Eleazer, 1662; John, 1663; Mehitabel, 1665; Naomi, 1667; Elisha, 1669; Ephraim, 1670. JOHN, Roxbury, son of above, m., 1684, Prudence Bridge; and had John, 1685; John, 1686; Samuel, 1689; Ebenezer, 1692; Prudence, 1694; Hezekiah, 1696; Sarah, 1698; Nehemiah, 1701; Mehitabel, 1703; Eleazer, 1705; Benjamin, 1708. JOHN, son of above, came to Plymouth and m., 1712, Ann Warren, and had Mary, 1713; John, 1722; Sarah, 1724. JOHN, son of above, m., 1745, Bathsheba Blackwell, and had John; Anna, m. Thomas Witherell; Bathsheba, m. David Lothrop; and Sarah, m. Thomas Jackson. JOHN, son of above, m. 1778, Mercy, d. of Thomas Foster, and had John, 1778; George, 1782; Lucy, 1784; William, 1788; Charles, 1791; Edwin, 1793; Sally; Thomas, m. Cordelia Howard. JOHN, son of Nicholas, m., 1748, Ann, d. of Joseph King of Plympton. NICHOLAS died 1713, leaving a wife Rebecca, and two children, Abigail and John.

MAYFIELD, THOMAS, from Connecticut, pub. to Millicent Barrows, 1775.

MAYHEW, THOMAS, perhaps son of Jonathan of Chilmark, m., 1740, Mary, d. of Thomas Witherell, and had Mary, 1742; Thomas, 1744; Anna, 1746, m. John Thomas; Elizabeth, 1748; William, 1751; Sarah, 1753, m. Thomas Nicolson; William, 1755; Betty, 1757; and Lucy, 1760.

MAYNARD, SAMUEL, m. Frances L., d. of William Jackson, 1821, and had Frances L., and George. SOLOMON, m., Betsey Swift, 1807.

MAYO, DANIEL, m. Mary Bartlett, 1789. NATHANIEL, son of 1st Thomas, m. Hannah Bartlett, 1808. SETH, son of 1st Thomas, m. Elizabeth Atwood, and had Sally Crosby, m. Thomas Hobbs; Eliza, m. Curtis Bisbee; Betsey Doane, m. Wendell Hall; Seth; Mary, m. Joel Randall of Easton; Bathsheba, m. Joseph Thayer; Molly, m. Levi Dame of Boston; and Thomas A., 1821. THOMAS of Cape Cod, m. Sally Crosby and had Mercy, m. James Snow and Thomas Holmes; Nathaniel, Thomas, Seth and Matthew. THOMAS, son of above, m. Lucy, d. of William LeBaron, and had William Thomas, m. Triphosa Fessenden of Sandwich. THOMAS ATWOOD, son of Seth, m. Hannah Stillman, and had Seth, John, George, Hannah, and Etta.

MAXIM, DAVID, m., 1819, Sally Burgess. EDMUND, Plympton, living 1740, had a wife Abigail, and children Edmund, John, Thomas, Jabez, and Ellis, removed to Coleraine. EZRA, m., 1813, Polly Reed. JACOB, Rochester, son of 2d Samuel, died 1789. He mentions in his will a cousin Thomas, and Ruth, d. of Thomas; also Nathan and Samuel and Jacob, his sons; also David and his d. Dinah, and Dinah, wife of Andrew Sturtevant. JOSEPH, m., 1816, Nannie Simmons. LEVI, m., 1810, Ruby Hall. SAMUEL, Rochester, died 1762, and left a wife Elizabeth, and children Samuel, Ezra, Elizabeth, Caleb, Nathan, who probably m. Martha Chubbuck. SAMUEL, Rochester, either son or father of above, died 1763, leaving wife Hannah and children Jacob, Freelove, Thaddeus; Dinah, m. Andrew Sturtevant; Samuel, Edward, Adonijah, and John.

McCARTER, JOHN, m., 1777, Mary Sampson, and had John, 1777; Mary, Sarah; and Henry, m. Hannah Hueston.

McFERSON, Paul, pub., 1747, to Hannah Thomas.

McMAHON, CHARLES, from New Jersey, m., 1836, Hannah L. Marsh.

MEHURIN, JOSIAH, m., 1799, Patience Burgess.

MELICK, John, pub., 1799, to Polly Jackerman.

MELVIN, RUFUS, from Chelmsford, m., 1824, Eunice S. Warren.

MENDALL, ELLIS, son of Seth, by wife Hannah, had Polly, 1793; Lucy, 1794; Seth, 1796. JABEZ, from Plympton, m. Meriah Churchill, and had Samuel, 1747. SETH, by wife Mary, had John; Phebe, m. a Swift; and Ellis. ZACHEUS, from Sandwich, brother of Seth, m., 1749, Mary Swift.

MENDLOVE, MARK, in Plymouth, 1637. WILLIAM, in Plymouth, 1633.

MERCER, STEPHEN, from Bradford, m., 1783, Lucy Jackson.

MERRIFIELD, FRANCIS, m., 1734, Constant Billington.

MERRY, RALPH, m., 1673, Lucy Cobb.

MEVIS, JOHN, pub., 1798, to Sarah Quam.

MILLER, EDWARD, m., 1817, Caroline Nicolson. STEPHEN, from Milton, m., 1763, Hannah Dyer.

MILLIGEN, WILLIAM, pub., 1778, to Eunice Howard.

MINTZ, JOHN, m., 1838, Priscilla, d. of Thomas Pope, and had Mary Williams, 1839; Thomas Pope, 1841.

MITCHELL, EBENEZER, son of 2d Joseph, m. Joanna Rogers, 1798, and had Elizabeth, 1798; Nancy, 1802. EXPERIENCE, came in the Ann 1623, removed to Duxbury, and m. Jane Cook, and a 2d wife, Mary, by whom he had Elizabeth, m. John Washburn; Thomas; Mary, m. James Shaw; Edward, m. Mary Hayward and Alice Bradford; Sarah, m. John Hayward; Jacob, John; and Hannah, m. Joseph Hayward. JACOB, son of above, m. Susanna Pope, 1666, and had Jacob; Thomas, m. Elizabeth Kingman; and Mary. JACOB, son of above, m. Deliverance Kingman, 1696, and had Jacob, 1696. He m., 2d, Rebecca Cushman, and had Susanna, 1703; Rebecca, 1704; Seth, 1706; Mary, 1708; Lydia, 1710; Noah, 1712; Isaac, 1715; Sarah, 1717; Elizabeth, 1722. JOHN, Duxbury, son of Experience, m. Mary Bonney, 1675, and had Experience, 1676. He m., 2d, Mary Lothrop, 1679; and 3d, Mary Prior, 1682, by whom he had Mary, 1682; Hannah, 1683; Joseph, 1684; Elizabeth, 1685; Elizabeth, 1686; John, 1689; Sarah, 1690; Esther, 1692. JOSEPH, son of John, m. Bathsheba Lambert, and had Sarah, 1711; Hannah, 1713; Joseph, 1714; John, 1716; Mary, 1718; Sarah, 1719; Bathsheba, 1721; Alice, 1723; Joseph, 1725; Benjamin, 1728; Martha, 1731, m. Japheth Rickard; and Ruth. JOSEPH, son of above, m. Mary Tinkham, 1760, and had Joseph, 1760; James, 1763; Ebenezer, 1765; Mary, 1768. THOMAS, m. Elizabeth Totman, 1756. TIMOTHY, from East Bridgewater, m. Melissa Alden Raymond, 1825.

MOORE, or MORE, GEORGE, in the family of Edward Doty, 1630, and died in Scituate, 1677. JASPER, a boy in the Mayflower, who soon died. JOHN, m., 1726, Mary Shattuck. JOSIAH, m., 1831, Rebecca W., d. of William Sturtevant. RICHARD, came in the Mayflower in the family of William Brewster. He removed to Scituate, and had Nathaniel, 1646; Thomas, 1650; Richard, 1652; Josiah, 1654.

MOREY, BENJAMIN, son of 2d Jonathan, by wife Thankful, had Mary, 1716, m. Josiah Swift; Maria, 1719; Mercy, 1721, m. William Fish; Benjamin, 1727; John, 1729, m. Jerusha Swift. CORNELIUS, son of 2d Jonathan, m. Sarah Johnson, 1751, and had Mercy, 1754, m. Silas Valler; Sarah, 1756, m. Elisha Nye; Elijah, 1759; Cornelius, 1761; Josiah, 1763; and Sylvanus. He m., 2d, Ruth, wid. of Zacheus Holmes. CORNELIUS, son of above, m. Jerusha Harlow, and had Elijah, 1784; Sarah, 1786; Cornelius, 1789, m. Sally Harlow, William, 1791; Jerusha, 1794, m. Benjamin Clark; and Josiah, 1797. He probably m., 1st, without issue, Mercy Bates, 1782. ELIJAH, son of Joseph, m. Rebecca West, 1763, and had Silas, 1764, and probably Elijah. ELIJAH, son of above, m. Grace Cornish, and had Elijah, 1801, m. Lucy Manter; Grace, 1805; Diploma, 1810; Abigail, m. Ansel Lucas; and Lucy Ann, m. Thomas Rogers. ELLIS, m. Rebecca Clark, 1819. GEORGE came in the Truelove in 1635, and settled in Duxbury, where he died, 1640, leaving one son, Jonathan. ICHABOD, son of Silas, m. Mary Churchill, and had Mary Ann, 1820, m. Mendall Peirce; Ichabod, 1822; Lucy, 1823, m. Henry J. Raymond; Caroline, 1825, m. David Vining Pool; Deborah, 1827, m. James Kendrick; George C., 1831; Susan G., 1833; William, 1836; and Charles H., 1839, m. Annie M., d. of Perez S. Wade. JOHN, m. Jerusha Swift, 1751. JONATHAN, son of George, m., 1659, Mary, wid. of Richard Foster and d. of Robert Bartlett, and had Jonathan. JONATHAN, son of above, m. Hannah Bourne of Sandwich, and had Benjamin, 1690; Maria, 1692; Mary, 1694; Thankful, 1696, m. Thomas Swift; Jonathan, 1699; Reliance, 1702; Cornelius, 1706; Silas, and Joseph. JONATHAN, son of above, m. Elizabeth Swift, 1728, and had Jonathan, 1730; Thomas, 1732; Elizabeth, 1734. JOSEPH, son of 2d Jonathan, m. Mary Swift, 1733, and had Abigail, 1733; Joseph, 1737; Mary, 1739; Elijah, 1741; Philemon, 1743; Hannah, 1745. JOSIAH of Plympton, m. Nancy Holmes, 1839. SILAS, son of 1st Elijah, m. Eunice Dunham, 1786, and had Sylvanus, 1789; Rebecca 1791; Silas, 1792; Eunice, 1794, m. Horace Chandler; Ichabod, 1796; Deborah, 1798, m. Amasa Morton; Bartlett, 1801; Nancy, 1803, m. Micah Holmes; Charlotte, 1807. WILLIAM, son of 2d Cornelius, m. Polly Edwards, 1812, and had William, 1813, m. Susan, d. of Sylvanus Rogers; John Edwards, 1815; Thomas, 1817; Cornelius, 1820; Mary E., 1822; Charles, 1825; Edwin, 1827; Henry, 1833, and Helen M., m. Lemuel B. Bradford.

MORGAN, BENNETT, came in the Fortune 1621, and disappeared before 1627.

MORANG, JOHN, m., 1794, Hannah Nicolson.

MOROPE, JOHN MICHAEL, m., 1796, Sally (Gould) Holmes.

MORRELL, SAMUEL A., m., 1835, Elizabeth S. Bates.

MORRIS, PATRICK, m. Mary Vincent, and had John, 1758; James, 1761.

MORSE, ANTHONY, Newbury, came in the James in 1635, and by wife Mary, had Anthony, Benjamin, Sarah, Hannah, Lydia, Mary, Esther, and Joshua. ANTHONY, Newbury, son of 1st Joshua, m. Judith, d. of Dr. Caleb Moody, and had Anthony and others. ANTHONY, son of above, Salisbury, m. Martha Merrill, and had Humphrey, and others. ANTHONY, Plymouth, son of Humphrey, m. Nancy, wid. of Branch Johnson, and d. of William Atwood, and had Charles P., 1839. EDWARD, Plymouth, son of 2d Joshua, m. Anna Holmes, 1805. HUMPHREY, son of 3d Anthony, m. Lydia Parsons, and had Anthony of Plymouth, and others. ISAAC, Middleboro', m. Joanna Swift, 1788. JOHN, m. Nancy, d. of Nathaniel Doten, and had Nancy A., 1839; and John A. JONATHAN, son of 1st William, had Joshua, and Jonathan. JOSHUA, Newbury, son of 1st Anthony, by wife Joanna, had Hannah, 1681; Joshua, 1686; Anthony, 1688. JOSHUA, Plymouth, son of Jonathan, m. Elizabeth Doty, and had Joshua, 1699; Elizabeth, 1701; Edward, 1704; Joseph, 1706; Newbury, 1709; Abigail, 1711; Theodosius, 1714. MELTIAH of Rochester, m. Joanna Swift, 1788. NOAH, of Middleboro', m. Patience Bryant, 1805, and had William Bryant, 1811. WILLIAM, Newbury, came, with his brother Anthony, in the James 1635, and, by wife Elizabeth, had Elizabeth, Ann, Jonathan, Joseph, Timothy, Abigail, and Edward. WILLIAM B., by wife Mary, had Mary B., 1840.

MORTON, AMASA, son of 6th Josiah, m. Deborah, d. of Silas Morey, 1818, and had Amasa, m. a d. of Ephraim Lucas; Ellis, m. Mary Hodges; and Betsey m. Charles Little Hathaway of North Bridgewater; and Edwin. BENJAMIN, son of 1st Samuel, m., 1753, Hannah Faunce, and had Lydia, 1754; Hannah, 1755; Hannah, 1758, m. Abner Baker; Barnabas, 1759; Benjamin, 1763, m. Rebecca Swift; Bartlett, 1766. CALEB, son of 1st Ezekiel, m., 1786,

Rebecca Warren, and had William Warren, 1787; Rebecca, 1791; Joseph, 1793; Abigail, 1795. CALEB, son of 2d Ezekiel, m., 1800, Hannah Leonard, and had Joseph M.; Caleb, m. Mary Lucas; Ezekiel; Hannah, m. Stephen Doten; Mary and Ellen, m. Ezra Leach. CORNELIUS, Kingston, son of 5th Ephraim, m. Fear Johnson, and had Cornelius, 1740; Joshua, 1743; Sarah, 1746; Deborah, 1752. EBENEZER, son of 2d Ephraim, m. Hannah Morton, and had Mary, 1711; Edward, 1713; Patience, 1716; Zacheus, 1718. He m., 2d, 1720, Mercy Foster, and had Solomon, 1727. EBENEZER, Kingston, son of 5th Ephraim, m., 1743, Susanna Holmes, and had Kenelm, 1744; Ebenezer, 1746; Zenith, 1749. EDWARD, son of 4th Ephraim, m., 1778, Sarah Morton, and had George; Eunice, m. Thomas Holmes; Ellen; Edward. EDWARD, son of above, m., 1810, Priscilla Hueston, and had Edward, 1810, m. Susan Spear; William H., 1816, m. Mary S., d. of Lemuel Simmons; Nathaniel H., 1818; Frederick, 1820; Henry M., 1823; Ellis H., 1827; Eunice, 1833. EDWIN, son of 2d Ichabod, m. Betsey T., d. of John Harlow, and had Edwin, 1832; Helen, 1834; Margie, 1836; Hannah, 1838; Maria, Frank, and Theodore. ELEAZER, son of 1st Ephraim, m., 1693, a wife Rebecca, and had Eleazer, 1693; Ann, 1694, m. Robert Finney; Nathaniel, 1695; Rebecca, 1703. ELEAZER, son of above, m.,1724, Deborah Delano, and had Ambros, 1725; Nathaniel, 1727. ELEAZER, son of Zephaniah, m., 1776, Jemima, d. of Jacob Taylor, and had Lazarus S., 1778; William, Zephaniah, Amasa, Jemima, Jerusha, Jane, Eleazer, and Jacob Taylor. ELISHA. son of 1st Samuel, m., 1760, Elizabeth Mitchell, and had Elisha, 1761; Elizabeth, 1764. ELKANAH, Dartmouth, son of 5th Ephraim, m., 1724, Elizabeth Holmes, and had Ephraim, 1725; Elisha, 1728; Elkanah, 1731; Phebe, 1734; Betty, 1739, m. William Tallman; Lazarus, 1742. ELLIS, son of 6th Josiah, m. Polly Nickerson, and had Josiah, m. Harriet B. Tallman; Abby Warren, m. George Finney; Susan Baker, m. Lemuel Leach; Ruth Chatman, m. Edwin W. Hoxie; Lucy, m. George Blanchard; Ebenezer, and Mary Abbot. EPHRAIM, son of 1st George, m., 1644, Ann Cooper, and had George, 1645; Ephraim, 1648; Rebecca, 1651; Josiah, 1653; Mercy, Nathaniel, Eleazer; Thomas, 1667; Patience, m. John Nelson. He m., 2d, 1692, Mary, wid. of William Harlow, and d. of Robert Shelley of Scituate. EPHRAIM, son of above, by wife Hannah, had Hannah, 1667, m. Benjamin Warren; Ephraim, 1678; John, 1680; Joseph, 1683; Ebenezer, 1685. EPHRAIM, son of above, m., 1712, Susanna Morton, and had Susanna, 1713; Hannah, 1715; Sarah, 1718, m. Nathaniel Warren; Ephraim, 1722; Abigail, 1724, m. Ezekiel Morton; Ichabod, 1730. EPHRAIM, son of above, by wife Sarah, had Ephraim, 1747; Osborn, 1751; Edward, 1753; Ichabod, 1756; Rebecca, m. Daniel Jackson. EPHRAIM, son of 2d George, by wife Hannah, had Samuel, 1699; Elkanah, 1702; Benjamin, 1705; Elisha, 1711; Cornelius, 1713; Ebenezer, 1715. EPHRAIM, son of 1st Ichabod, m., 1797, Sarah Howland, and had Isaac; Henry; Ephraim, m. Sarah Swift; Sarah m. Perez Peterson; Betsey m. John Gooding; Zilpha, m. Abner Leonard, Hannah; and Eliza. EZEKIEL, son of 1st George, m., 1746, Abigail Morton, and had Mary, 1747; Ezekiel, 1749; and Caleb. EZEKIEL, son of above, m., 1776, Faith Churchill, and had Freeman; Caleb, m. Hannah Leonard; Mary, m. Amasa Clark; Lucy, m. Elkanah Finney; Hannah, m.

Ephraim Bradford. FREEMAN, son of above, m., 1806, Rebecca Harlow, and had Freeman, m. Jane Burgess; Alvin G., m. Catherine Holmes; and Remember. GEORGE came in the Ann, 1623. He m. in Leyden, 1612, Julian, d. of Alexander Carpenter of Wrentham, England, and had Nathaniel, 1613; Patience, 1615, m. John Faunce; John, 1616; Sarah, 1618, m. George Bonum; Ephraim, 1623; and perhaps George, who had a wife Phebe. GEORGE, son of 1st Ephraim, m., 1664, Joanna, d. of Ephraim Kempton, and had Hannah, 1668, m. John Dyer; Manasseh, 1669; Ephraim, 1671; Joanna, 1673, m. Thomas Holmes; Ruth, 1676, m. Stephen Barnaby; George, 1678; Timothy, 1682; Rebecca, 1684, m. Nicholas Drew; Elizabeth, 1686; Thomas, 1690. GEORGE, son of above, m. Rebecca Churchill, and had Zephaniah, 1715; William, 1717; George, 1720; Rebecca, 1724. GEORGE, son of above, m., 1746, Sarah, d. of Timothy White of Scituate, and had George, 1747; Sarah, 1753; John, 1756; Eli, 1758; Rebecca, 1761. GEORGE, son of Jonathan, m. Mary Lemoine, and had John Lemoine; James; Rebecca, m. Jacob Tinkham; Hannah, m. James Bell; Susan, m. a Smith; Polly, and Betsey. HENRY, son of 6th Ephraim, m., 1823, Rebecca Whitney, and had Almira T., 1827; Henry, 1829; Ephraim S., 1837; Lucy T., 1840. ICHABOD, son of 3d Ephraim, m., 1758, Zilpha Thayer, and had Ephraim, 1759; Ichabod, 1761; Hannah, 1762, m. Amasa Clark; Polly, m. Joseph Whiting; Zilpha, m. Samuel Bartlett; Susan, m. Thomas Sears. ICHABOD, son of above, m., 1787, Sarah Churchill, and had Sarah, m. Lemuel Stephens; Ichabod, Hannah; Mary, m. Elkanah Bartlett; Abigail; Betsey, m. Joseph Whiting and William Clark; Edwin; Maria, m. William Churchill. ICHABOD, son of above, m. Patty, d. of Coomer Weston, and had Abigail, 1821. He m., 2d, Betsey, d. of Gideon Holbrook, and had George E., 1829; Nathaniel, 1831; Ichabod, 1833; Austin, 1834; Howard, 1836. ICHABOD, son of 2d Nathaniel, m., 1748, Deborah Morton of Middleboro', and had Eleazer, Elisha, Ichabod, John, Nathaniel, and Mordecai. ISAAC, son of 6th Ephraim, m., 1826, Betsey Everson, and had Betsey L., 1828; Sarah A., 1830; Adeline, 1832; Isaac, 1834; Margaret, 1842. ISAAC, son of 2d Thomas, m. Meriah Lewin, and had Hannah, 1747; Hannah, 1749, m. Ichabod Thomas; Sarah, 1752, m. Isaac Churchill; Isaac, 1754, m. Ruth Tinkham; Alvin, 1758. JACOB TAYLOR, son of 3d Eleazer, m. Lydia, d. of Ebenezer Luce and wid. of Meltiah Howard, 1812, and had Joanna B., 1813; Lazarus S., 1819; Jacob Taylor, 1821. JAMES, son of 5th George, m., 1815, Betsey Coin, and had George, Abraham; James, 1817; Betsey D., m. Thomas Cooper Holmes; Mary, m. John H. Harlow. JAMES, son of above, m., 1846, Mary B. C., d. of Isaac Davie, and had George S., m. Lucinda, d. of Leavitt Finney. JOB, Carver, son of 1st Silas, m. Patience Crocker, and had Job, 1790; Patience, 1790; Abigail, 1793; Eliza Crocker and Mary, 1799, twins. He m., 2d, Molly Dunham. JOB, Carver, son of above, m. Caroline Chandler, and had Caroline, 1833; Charles Henry, 1842. JOHN, son of 1st George, came from England with his father, and, by wife Lettice, had John, 1649; John, 1650; Deborah, m. Frances Coombs; Mary, Martha; Hannah, m. John Fuller; Esther; Manasseh and Ephraim, twins, 1653. JOHN, son of 2d Ephraim, m., 1706, a wife Reliance, and had John, 1706; Jonathan, 1708; Josiah, 1710; James, 1714, m. Mehitabel Churchill; David, 1716, m. Rebecca Finney.

JOHN, son of 1st John, by wife Phebe, had Joanna, 1682; Phebe, 1685, m. John Murdock. He m., 2d, Mary Ring, and had Mary, 1689; John, 1693; Hannah, 1694, m. John Cook; Ebenezer, 1696; Deborah, 1698, m. Caleb Stetson; Perez, 1700. JOHN LEMOINE, son of 5th George, m., 1815, Lilly Russell Torrence, and had John, m. Hannah A. Bates of Scituate; Sarah E., m. George H. Harlow. JONATHAN, son of 2d Thomas, m., 1749, Rebecca, wid. of William Witherell, and had Cary Harris, 1750, m. Sarah Bolce; Jonathan, 1753; George, 1757. JOSEPH, son of 2d Ephraim, m., 1709, Mary Chittenden, and had Joseph, 1711; Hannah, 1713, m. Jonathan Diman; Ezekiel, 1718. JOSEPH, son of above, m., 1738, Amiah Bullock of Rehoboth, and had Diman, Perez, Joseph, Ephraim, and Abigail. JOSEPH, son of 2d Caleb, m. Sabria N. Ellis, and had Shalman Ellis, 1831; Joseph Nye, 1834; Mary Grabrant, 1836; Ann Harlow, 1838; Gideon S., 1840. JOSEPH, Roxbury, son of 2d Joseph, had Mary Hersey, m. George Thompson; Joseph, Ephraim; William Saxton, m. Jane Woodbury Gremis of Francestown, N. H.; Sarah Bradford, Caroline Stimson, and Abigail. JOSIAH, son of 1st Ephraim, m., 1686, Susanna Wood, and had Susanna, 1687; Josiah, 1688; Susanna, 1690, m. Ephraim Morton; Henry, 1692. JOSIAH, son of above, m., 1710, Elizabeth Clark, and had Henry, 1711; Josiah, 1713; Elizabeth, 1716, m. David Diman; Ruth, 1718, m. Thomas Clark; Elizabeth, 1730, m. Daniel Diman. JOSIAH, son of 2d John, m. Meletiah Finney of Barnstable, and had Seth, 1735; Benjamin, 1737, m. Hannah Faunce; Rebecca, 1740, m. David Holmes; Martha, 1742, m. Nicholas Drew; John, 1744; Mary, 1746, m. Sylvanus Finney; John, 1748; Josiah, 1752; Sarah, 1755; and Reliance. JOSIAH, son of 2d Josiah, m., 1743, Experience Ellis, and had Simeon, 1743; Sarah, 1746; Thomas, 1748; Elizabeth, 1752, m. Samuel Dunham; Josiah, 1756; Amasa, 1758, m. Hannah Morton; William, 1761, m. Eunice Bartlett; Ruth, 1763. JOSIAH, son of 3d Thomas, m., 1804, Lucy Burgess, and had Josiah Ellis; John Thomas; Harriet, m. John Courtenay. He m., 2d, Sally Morton, and had Sarah Warren, m. George Godfrey; Lucy L., m. Abiathar Hoxie; Experience, m. Josiah H. Swift. JOSIAH, son of 3d Josiah, m., 1785, a wife Mary, and had Levi, 1785; Ellis, 1788; Mary, 1791; Elizabeth, 1795; Amasa, 1798. LEMUEL, son of 4th Nathaniel, m., 1788, Azubah Cushman Rickard, and had Nathaniel, 1789; Lemuel, 1792; Elizabeth Cushman, 1795; Mary Ellis, 1799; Nancy, 1801. LEMUEL, son of above, m., 1818, Hannah, d. of Charles Gibbs, and had Charles Gibbs, 1818, m. Lucy N. Sherman of Carver. He m., 2d, Hannah Symmes Holmes, and had Hannah Symmes, 1824; Martha Brewster, 1833; Margaret D., 1838, m. James Cornish; and Quincy. MANASSEH, New Bedford, son of 2d George, by wife Mary, had Elizabeth, 1704; Zephaniah, 1707; Ruth, 1714; Seth, 1722. MARCUS, Taunton, son of 10th Nathaniel, m., 1807, Charlotte, d. of James Hodges of Taunton, and had Maria, m. William T. Hawes; Lydia Mason, m. Henry Lee; Charlotte, m. Samuel Watson; Sarah Cary, m. Willard Lovering; Marcus, m. Abby, d. of George Hoppin of Providence; Nathaniel, m. Harriet, d. of Francis Baylies; James, m. Elizabeth, d. of George Ashman of Springfield; Frances W., m. Charles Henry French of Andover; Susan Tillinghast; and Emma Matilda. NATHANIEL, son of 1st George, came with his father in the Ann 1623, and

m., 1635, Lydia Cooper, by whom he had Remember, 1637, m. Abraham
Jackson; Mercy, m. Joseph Dunham; Lydia, m. George Ellison; Elizabeth,
1652, m. Nathaniel Bosworth; Joanna, 1654, m. Joseph Prince; Hannah, m.
Benjamin Bosworth; Eleazer, and Nathaniel. He m., 2d, 1671, Ann, wid.
of Richard Templar of Charlestown. NATHANIEL, son of 1st Eleazer, m.,
1720, Rebecca Ellis, wid. of Mordecai, and d. of Thomas Clark, and had
Elizabeth, 1720; Nathaniel, 1723; Eleazer, 1724; Ichabod, 1726. NATHAN-
IEL, Freetown, son of above, m., 1749, Martha Tupper, and had Rebecca;
Nathaniel, 1753; Martha, Elizabeth, Job. NATHANIEL, by wife Rebecca,
had Nathaniel, 1741. By a 2d wife, Mary, he had Nathaniel, 1747;
Nathaniel, 1749; Lemuel, 1757. NATHANIEL, son of 1st Thomas, m. Mary
Shaw, and had Mary, 1734. NATHANIEL, son of 1st Ephraim, m., 1706, Mary,
d. of Joseph Faunce, and had Nathaniel, 1706. NATHANIEL, son of above, m.
Meriah Clark, and had Nathaniel, 1731. NATHANIEL, son of above, m., 1753,
Rebecca, d. of Nathaniel Jackson, and had Josiah, 1754; Meriah, 1758, m.
John Torrey; Rebecca, 1762, m. William Davis; Betty, 1770. He m., 2d,
Joanna, d. of Nathan Delano. NATHANIEL, m. Mary Ellis, 1740. NA-
THANIEL, Freetown, son of 3d Nathaniel, m., 1782, Mary, d. of Eleazer
Cary of Bridgewater, and had Marcus, 1784; Mary, 1785, m. Elijah Dexter
of Freetown, father of Henry M. Dexter. OSBORN, son of 4th Ephraim,
m., 1781, Patience Cobb, and had Ephraim, 1782, m. Dorcas Brown; Martha,
1784; Osborn, 1785; David Cobb, 1788; Patience, 1792; Osborn, 1794; Sarah,
1797; Nehemiah, 1802. SAMUEL, son of 5th Ephraim, m., 1724, Lydia
Bartlett, and had Lydia, 1725, m. John Phillips; Samuel, 1726; Benjamin,
1728; Ephraim, 1731; Elisha, 1734; Hannah, 1734; Barnaby, 1735; Ephraim,
1739; Sarah, 1741, m. John Black. SAMUEL, son of above, m. Ruth, d. of
Thomas Rogers, and had Ruth, 1749, m. Ephraim Luce; Rebecca, 1751, m.
David Holmes; Sarah, 1755, m. Isaac and Charles Churchill; Priscilla, 1759,
m. Charles Bradford; Samuel, 1763, m. Mary Washburn. SETH, son of 3d
Josiah, m., 1761, Mercy Sampson, and had Mercy, 1762, m. Joshua Besse;
Elizabeth, 1765, m. Lothrop Turner; Mary; Josiah, m. Nabby Winsor; Seth.
SETH, son of above, m., 1797, Mercy Savery, and had Seth, 1797; Mercy,
1800, m. Antipas Brigham; William, 1802; James, 1806, m. Pamelia D. Robbins; Betsey, 1808; Harriet, 1811, m. William Atwood; Henry, 1815; Caroline, 1818, m. Richard W. Holmes. SETH, son of above, m., 1825, Catherine,
d. of Lemuel Brown, and had Seth, 1825; Catherine B., 1827, m. William
Bishop; William H.; Lemuel B., 1834; and Mary Ann, m. Thomas D.
Shumway. SETH, New Bedford, son of Manasseh, m. Elizabeth, d. of William Allen, 1746, and had Sarah, 1748; Hannah, 1750; Ruth, 1752; Timothy,
1754. SILAS, son of Timothy, m., 1748, Martha Morton, and had Hannah,
1749; Silas, 1752; Timothy, 1754; Martha, 1757, m. Nicholas Drew; Job,
1760; Oliver, 1763, removed to North Carolina; Thomas, 1765, removed to
Hebron, Maine; Ezra, 1768; Hannah, 1770; Lemuel, 1775. SILAS, Hanover,
son of above, m., 1792, Elizabeth Foster, and had Elizabeth Foster, m.
William P. Ripley; Silas; Caroline, 1796, m. Robert Briggs; George Washington, m. Sarah Davis; Mary Ann; Sarah Foster, m. William C. Barstow;
Lucia Davis, m. a Folsom; and Harriet, m. Caleb C. Gilbert of Boston.

SYLVANUS, son of 2d Thomas, m., 1752, Mary Stephens, and had Abigail, 1753; James, 1755. THOMAS, son of 1st Ephraim, m., 1696, Martha Doty, and had Thomas, 1700; Lydia, 1702, m. Benjamin Bartlett; Lemuel, 1704; Sarah, 1706, m. Joseph Bartlett; Nathaniel, 1710; Mary, 1712, m. a Nelson. THOMAS, son of 2d George, m., 1722, Abigail Pratt, and had Ruth, 1723, m. William Holmes; Isaac, 1725; Jonathan, 1726; Thomas, 1728; Sylvanus, 1730; Abigail, 1732, m. Stephen Sampson; Hannah, 1733, m. Billings Throop of Bristol; Abiel, and Joanna. THOMAS, son of 4th Josiah, m. Ruth Warren, and had Thomas, Josiah; Sarah, and Lucy, the 1st and 2d wives of George Bramhall; Jane, m. Chandler Burgess; Betsey, m. William Langford; and Susan. THOMAS, son of above, m., 1802, Nancy, d. of Levi Paty, and had Thomas, m. Harriet B. Holmes; Levi Paty, m. Sarah L. Swift; Hannah, m. Clark Holmes; Susan, m. William Leonard; Nancy Paty, m. Lothrop C. King; Elizabeth Warren, m. Harrison Field; Lucy m. Calvin Bearse. THOMAS, son of 1st Thomas, m., 1726, Hannah Nelson, and had Bathsheba, 1727, m. John Rickard; Martha, 1730, m. Silas Morton. THOMAS, son of 2d Thomas, m., 1754, Mary Morton, and had Nathaniel, 1754; Thomas, 1757; William, 1759; Jesse, 1761; Mary, 1763; Andrew, 1765; Martha, 1767; Taber and Andrew, 1770, twins. THOMAS, came in the Fortune 1621, and either died or returned before 1627. THOMAS, perhaps brother of 1st George, came with him in the Ann 1623. TIMOTHY, son of 2d George, m., 1712, Mary Rickard, and had Charles, 1714, m. Mary Shattuck; John, 1716; Job, 1719, m. Mary Barnes; Mary, 1722, m. Thomas Foster; Silas, 1727; Elizabeth, 1732. He m., perhaps Sarah Wilson, 1737. WILLIAM, son of 3d George, m., 1749, Mary Warren, and had William, 1751. WILLIAM, son of 6th Thomas, m. 1787, Pamelia Howland, and had Pamelia, 1795; Anna, 1797; Lewis, 1809; William, 1810. ZEPHANIAH, son of 3d George, m., 1748, Jerusha Doten, and had Zephaniah, 1749, m. Rebecca Pierce; George, 1750; Eleazer, 1753; Sarah, 1758; William, 1757; Rebecca, 1760.

MOSES, DAVID, m., 1798, Sarah Cowit. SIMON, m., 1750, Sarah Adams.

MULLINS, WILLIAM, came in the Mayflower, 1620, with wife, son Joseph, and daughter Priscilla, who m. John Alden.

MUNDO, DOLPHIN, m. Cate Quandy, 1786.

MURDOCK, or MURDOCH, BARTLETT, Plympton, son of 3d John, by wife Lucy, had Bartlett, Elisha, William; Lydia, m. a White; Ruth; Phebe, m. a Standish; and Elizabeth, m. a Bent. BARTLETT, Plympton, son of above, m. Deborah, d. of Joshua Perkins, and had John, 1775; Chloe, 1777, m. a Bonney; Jesse, 1779; Deborah, 1781; Bartlett, 1783; Sarah, 1786; Thomas, 1788; Abigail, 1791; and Thomas again, 1793. BARTLETT, Carver, son of above, m. Hannah Atwood, and had Warren, 1808; Rachel, 1810; Hiram, 1812; Abigail, 1814. ELISHA, Carver, son of 1st Bartlett, m. Martha, d. of Joshua Perkins, and had Ira, 1789; Lydia, 1791; Sarah, 1793; Lothrop, 1795; Martha, 1798; Thompson, 1800; Elisha, 1802; Hannah, 1804; Alfred, 1806, who, by a wife Harriet, had Alfred, 1837; Elizabeth, 1808; Phebe, 1811; Rebecca, 1813; Elijah, 1817. IRA, Carver, son of above, m. Waitstill, d. of Nathaniel Shaw, and had Harriet, 1812; Jason, 1814; George Shaw, 1816; Henry Clay,

1818; Albert Gallatin, 1820; Lydia, 1822; John, 1825; Ira, 1828; and Waitstill, 1828. JAMES, Plympton, son of 2d John, by wife Hannah, had John, 1742; Deborah, 1744; Jeanette, 1746; Hannah, 1752; James, 1754; Andrew, 1758, who, by wife Meribah, had Edward, 1782, and Andrew, 1784; Huldah, 1760; Edward, 1763. By a 2d wife, Faith, he had Mehitabel, 1767; and Samuel, 1770. JESSE, Carver, son of 2d Bartlett, m. Susannah Ellis, and had Jesse, 1806; and Susanna Ellis, 1812. JOHN, Carver, son of 2d Bartlett, m. Azubah Sears, and had Philip, 1798; Bartlett, 1799; Chloe, 1801, m. Blaney Phillips; Sally, 1802; Azubah Sears, 1804; Deborah, 1806. JOHN came from Scotland, and m. Lydia Young, by whom he had John, 1687; Jeanette, 1689; John, 1691; James, 1693; James, 1695; Robert, 1697; Robert, 1699; and Thomas, 1701, m. Elizabeth Doggett. He m., 2d, Phebe, d. of John Morton of Middleboro', 1719, and had Phebe, 1723, m. William Bowdoin of Boston. He probably had a brother, Robert, who settled in Roxbury. JOHN, son of above, m. Ruth, d. of Benjamin Bartlett, and had Ruth, m. John Wall; James, and Bartlett. THOMPSON, Carver, son of Elisha, m. Lucy Atwood, and had Mary Atwood, 1822; Thompson, 1826, Elisha, 1829; Eliza Ann, 1834. WILLIAM, Carver, son of 1st Bartlett, had Seabury, Elisha; Polly, m. Israel Thomas; and William. WILLIAM, son of above, m. Zilpah, d. of Peleg Savery, and had Abigail, 1818, m. Rufus C. Freeman; and William, 1820, m. Maria Frances Evans of Baltimore. WILLIAM, son of above, m. Maria Frances Evans of Baltimore, 1850, and had William B., 1852; William B., 1854; Francis Wyman, 1856.

MURPHY, MICHAEL, by wife Jane, had William James, 1812; Hannah Jane, 1814; Polly Holmes, 1818.

NASH, GILES, m., 173 , Remember Jackson.

NED, GOLIGHTLY, pub., 1737, to Esther Lawrence, Indians.

NELSON, ALEXANDER O., m., 1847, Hannah, d. of Ezekiel Rider. CHARLES, son of 2d Ebenezer, m. Lucy, d. of Peabody Bartlett, and had Lucy T., 1830, m. Curtis Davie; Charles, 1833; Elisha T., m. Sarah C. Savery and Anna H., d. of Richard W. Holmes; Addie E., m. John F. Hall; Mary T., 1840; and Harriet E., m. John N. Prouty. EBENEZER, son of 1st Samuel, m., 1754, Ruth Jackson, and had Ebenezer, 1756; Samuel; Lemuel, 1771; Cynthia Cobb; Hezekiah; Elisha, 1775; Ruth; Hannah, 1769; William, 1767; Thomas, 1766. EBENEZER, son of above, m., 1786, Lydia Robbins, and had Ebenezer; George, 1795; Elisha, and Charles. EBENEZER, son of above, m., 1812, Polly Holmes, and had Ebenezer, 1814; Eliza H., 1815, m. George A. Hathaway; Lewis, 1818; Mary Bryant, 1822, m. Francis Hastings of Weston; Ebenezer, 1824, m. Helen Warner of Boston. ELISHA, son of 2d Ebenezer, m., 1823, Abigail Keen, and had George William, 1823, m. Catherine S., d. of Nathaniel S. Barrows; Harriet Thomas, 1828, m. Thomas Dunning of Portland. GEORGE, son of 2d Ebenezer, m., 1825, Ruth Cobb Holmes, and had Ruth, 1827, m. Gamaliel Thomas; George, 1830, removed to New Bedford. HEZEKIAH, son of 1st Ebenezer, m., 1788, Abigail Holmes, and had Polly, m. John Kempton Cobb; Abigail, m. David Diman; Samuel, and Ruth. John, son of 1st William, m., 1667, Sarah, d. of Henry Wood, and had John and Martha. He m., 2d, Lydia, wid of James Barnaby, and

d. of Robert Bartlett, and had Samuel, 1683; Joanna, 1689. He m., 3d, Patience, d. of Ephraim Morton, 1693, and had Lydia, 1694; Sarah, 1695. JOHN, son of 1st Samuel, m., 1732, Mary Morton, and had Mary, 1733; Lydia, 1734; Hannah, 1737; Samuel, 1739; Thomas, 1741; John, 1748. SAMUEL, son of 1st John, m., 1704, Hannah Ford. He m., 2d, Bathsheba Nichols, and had Hannah, 1707; John, 1712; Samuel, 1714; Sarah, 1716, m. Seth Cobb. He m., 3d, 1718, Sarah Holmes, and had Bathsheba, 1719, m. Abner Holmes; Samuel Nichols, 1721; Ebenezer, 1723; Patience, 1724. SAMUEL, son of 1st Ebenezer, m., 1787, Lucy Ellis, and had Lucy. SAMUEL, son of Hezekiah, m., 1823, Sarah, d. of Peter Holmes, and had Samuel, 1824, m. Eliza A. Bartlett and Lydia Briggs; Hezekiah, 1828; Cyrus, 1831, m. Susan Williams, d. of Martin Perkins of Plympton. SAMUEL NICHOLS, son of 1st Samuel, m., 1744, Elizabeth, d. of Joseph Warren, and had Samuel, 1747; Patience, 1749; Sarah, 1754; Alathea, 1758; Joseph Warren, 1761, m. Alathea Warren; Priscilla, 1765; Betty, 1768. STEPHEN S., pastor of the Baptist Society in Plymouth, by wife Emeline, had Caroline Elizabeth, 1821. THOMAS, son of 1st Ebenezer, m., 1791, Abigail Holmes, and had Martha, 1794. WILLIAM, the ancestor, m. Martha, d. of wid. Ford, who came in the Fortune 1621, and had Martha, m. John Cobb; John, 1647; Jane, 1651, m. Thomas Faunce; and William. WILLIAM, son of 1st Ebenezer, m., 1792, Bathsheba Lothrop, and had William, 1796; and Mary Lothrop, m. Jesse Harlow. WILLIAM, son of above, m., 1821, Sarah, d. of Josiah Carver, and had William Henry, 1830, m. Hannah Coomer, d. of Coomer Weston; Thomas Lothrop, 1833, m. Susan A. Warren of Exeter, N. H., and Mary Stratton of Atchison, Mo.; and Sarah Elizabeth, 1838, m. William K. Churchill. WILLIAM, son of 1st William, had a son Thomas, who m. Hope Higgins of Barnstable, and died 1782, at the age of 105. Thomas had a d. Ruth, a son Thomas; and a 'son William, who m. Elizabeth Howland, and had Samuel, William, Ebenezer, and Abner. Of these, Samuel was settled in Middleboro' as a minister, and there died 1822. William was ordained at Norton, 1772; Ebenezer was ordained at Norton, 1790; and Abner was a farmer in Maine. Ebenezer had a son Ebenezer, who settled over the Baptist Church in Lynn, and died in Middleboro', 1863.

NEWBERRY, JAMES, m. Susanna Perry, and had James, 1773; Lemuel, 1775.

NEWCOMB, JOSHUA, by wife Hannah, had Ruth, 1741; Joseph, 1745; Sarah, 1747.

NEWMAN, JOHN H., of Exeter, m. Eliza A. Symons, 1828.

NICKERSON, ISRAEL, by wife Rebecca, had Joseph M., 1815; John W., 1818; Israel F., 1821; George Y., 1824; Charles H., 1827; Lorenzo J., 1830; Emeline R. Y., 1834. ISRAEL F., son of above, by wife Tamsen, had William Dana, 1844. JAMES, m. Sylvia Raymond, 1824, and had James W., 1824; Hiram, 1826; Ivory H., 1829; Maria, 1831; Frederick W., 1833; Sylvia W., 1835; Miranda R., 1838; Andrew T. J., 1841; James T., 1844. JOHN, son of 3d Seth, m. Lydia, d. of Jacob Howland, 1817, and had John, 1819; Jacob Howland, 1825; Marcia, 1829; Seth, moved to New York; Sarah, m. a Wadsworth; Mary, m. James Beal; Anna, m. a Holbrook; and Lydia, m. George

M. Collins. JOHN, son of above, m. Sophronia, d. of Samuel Alexander, 1840, and had George A., 1850, m. Eliza J. Grover. SETH, called in the records Nicholson, came from Harwich, and m., 1743, Margaret Moore, by whom he had Seth, 1746. SETH, son of above, called both Nicholson and Nickerson, m. Lydia Holmes, 1767, and had Seth, 1769. SETH, called Nicson, son of above, m. Meriah Harlow, 1791, and had Seth, John, Maria, and William. WILLIAM, son of 3d Seth, m. Mary B., d. of Thomas Marsh, and had Maria H., 1826; Warren M., 1830; Maria A., 1832; William T., 1838. He m., 2d, Betsey, d. of Joseph Barnes, 1841, and had Maria A. m. Warren Rickard; Mary E., m. Samuel C. Wright of Plympton; Charles H., and Ambrose E. He m., 3d, Joanna (Barnes) Bradford, wid. of Joseph Bradford, 1856; and, 4th, Betsey, d. of William Rogers, 1871.

NICHOLAS, AUSTIN, came in the Fortune 1621, and nothing more is known of him.

NICHOLS, EBENEZER, m. Elizabeth Holmes, 1787. EDWARD, m. Polly, d. of William Rogers, 1811. JAMES W., of Charlestown, m. Joanna H. Savery, 1827. JOHN of Freetown, m. Sarah Bramhall, 1812. JOHN of Freetown, m. Hannah Johnson, 1820. MOSES, m. Bethiah Nelson, 1822. OTIS, m. Sarah Clark, 1814, and had Hannah, 1818; Sarah, 1824; Otis, 1829; Susan, 1834; Gertrude, 1837.

NICOLSON, JAMES, m., probably in Boston, Hannah, d. of Jeremiah Jackson, and removed to Plymouth, where he had Elizabeth, 1746, m. Jonathan Tufts; Thomas, 1748. THOMAS, son of above, m., 1771, Sarah, d. of Thomas Mayhew, and had Sarah, 1771; Hannah, 1773, m. John Morong; Polly, 1775, m. John Allen of Salem; Elizabeth, 1777; Lucy, 1778; Nancy, 1780; Thomas, 1782; James, 1784; and Anna, m. John D. Wilson of Salem. He m., 2d, Hannah, d. of John Otis, and had Samuel, 1791, m. Sarah Brinley; Hannah Otis, 1793, m. Daniel Spooner; Daniel, 1796; Caroline, 1798, m. Edward Miller.

NIGHTINGALE, ELLIS, from Sandwich, m., 1818, Hannah Swift. WILLIAM, m., 1816, Eliza Cahoon.

NORCUT, EBENEZER, by wife Susanna, had Ebenezer, 1745.

NORMAN, HUGH, m., 1639, Mary White, and had Elizabeth. He removed to Yarmouth.

NORRIS, BENJAMIN, son of Oliver, by wife Mary, had Sarah, 1718; Oliver, 1720; Mary, 1723; Abigail, 1725; Samuel, 1728; Elizabeth, 1731. BENJAMIN, m., 1806, Mehitabel Cahoon, and had Israel Bumpus, 1807; Benjamin, 1808; Asa Raymond, 1811. OLIVER, by wife Margery, had Nathan, John, Oliver, Thomas, Benjamin, Samuel, and Hannah. PHINEAS, m., 1820, Susan Saunders. SAMUEL, from Ware, m., 1772, Jedidah Swift.

NOTT, GEORGE, m. Mary Howland, and had Charles, 1720; George, 1723; Elizabeth, 1726.

NUMMUCK, MOSES, m., 1739, Sarah Deerskins.

NUTE, SAMUEL, from Bridgewater, m., 1804, Mary Weston.

NUTTING, RICHARD, by wife Mehitabel, had Richard, 1768; Joseph and Benjamin, 1773; Mehitabel, 1775; John, 1777.

NYE, ABRAHAM W., from Sandwich, m., 1818, Abigail C. Cornish. EBE-

NEZER, from Falmouth, m., 1776, Hannah Cotton. ELIAS, from Plympton, m., 1786, Elizabeth Bartlett. ELISHA, from Sandwich, m., 1779, Sarah Morey. GORHAM H., m., 1829, Lydia R., d. of Atwood Drew, and had Lydia G., m. Allen Bradford. NATHANIEL, m., 1815, Deborah Clark. Seth F., from Sandwich, m., 1813, Sally, d. of Nathaniel Carver. THOMAS S., from Wareham, m., 1825, Ruth W. Holmes. WILLIAM, from Sandwich, m. Lucy Sylvester, 1805, and had Hannah, m. Benjamin Hathaway, and Lucy W., m. Rufus Churchill.

O'BRIEN, JOSEPH, pub. to Deborah Gault, 1798.

OLDHAM, JOHN, came in the Ann 1623, returned to England 1628, came back 1629, and settled in Watertown. JOHN, from Sumner, m. Sarah S. Churchill, 1820. THOMAS, from Duxbury, m. Betsey Brewster, 1819.

OLIVER, JONATHAN, m. Mehitabel Stetson, 1767.

OLNEY, ZABEN, m. Rebecca Morton, 1816, and, 2d, Olive P. Walcott, 1862.

OSBORNE, OBADIAH, from Rhode Island, m. Jerusha Kempton, 1756.

OTIS, BARNABAS, son of 1st Joseph, m., 1781, Polly Rickard of Plymouth, and had Henry, 1782; Barnabas, 1785, m. Fanny Totman; Henry, 1787; Mary, 1790, m. Elias Williams of Taunton. JAMES, Barnstable, son of 3d John, m. Mary, d. of Joseph Allyne of Wethersfield, and had James, 1725, the patriot, who m. Ruth Cunningham; Joseph, 1726; Mercy, 1728, m. James Warren of Plymouth; Mary, 1730, m. John Gray; Hannah, 1732; Nathaniel, 1734; Martha, 1736; Abigail, 1738; Elizabeth, 1739; Samuel Allyne, 1740; Sarah, 1742; Nathaniel, 1743. JOHN, from Barnstable, England, born 1581, settled in Hingham about 1635. By a 1st wife, Margaret, he had in England, John, 1620; Richard; Margaret, m. Thomas Burton; Hannah, m. Thomas Gill; Ann, and Alice. After 1654 he removed to Weymouth, where he m. a 2d wife, and died 1657. JOHN, Scituate, son of above, by a 1st wife, had Mary, m. John Gowin; Elizabeth, m. Thomas Allyne and David Loring; John, 1657; Stephen, 1661. He m., 2d, Mary, d. of Nicholas Jacob, 1663, and had James, 1663; Joseph, 1665, m. Dorothy Thomas; Job, 1667. JOHN, Barnstable, son of above, m. 1683, Mercy Bacon, and had Mary, 1685; John, 1687; Mercy, 1693; Solomon, 1696; Nathaniel, 1690, m. Abigail, d. of Jonathan Russell; James, 1702. JOHN, Barnstable, son of above, m. Grace Hayman of Bristol, R. I., and had John, 1714. JOHN, Barnstable, son of above, m. Temperance Hinckley, and had John, 1742; John, 1743; Hayman, 1747; Hayman, 1748. JOHN, Plymouth, son of above, m. Hannah, d. of Stephen Churchill, 1765, and had Temperance, 1766; Hannah, 1768, m. Thomas Nicolson; Abigail; Grace Hayman, m. John Goddard; and John. JOSEPH, Boston, son of Stephen, m. Lucy Little, and had Joseph, 1734, m. Abigail Otis; John, 1736; Barnabas, 1739; and Charles. STEPHEN, Scituate, son of 2d John, m., 1685, Hannah Ensign, and had Ensign, 1691, m. Hannah, d. of Samuel Barker, and Hannah, d. of Jeremiah Cushing; John, 1694, m. Leah, d. of Samuel Stodder of Hingham; Hannah, 1696; Mary, 1697; Isaac, 1699; Stephen, 1707; Joseph, 1709; Joshua, 1711. (See Otis Genealogy).

OZMENT, WILLIAM, m., 1758, Elizabeth Dunham.

PACKARD, ELIJAH, m., 1754, Mary Rider, and had Abigail, 1755; and

Elijah. ELIJAH, son of above, by wife Thankful, had Alpheus, 1793. ZADOCK, from Bridgewater, m., 1800, Rebecca Phillips. ZIBEON, from Easton, m., 1814, Sally Dike.

PACKER, BENJAMIN, m., 1818, Molly Young.

PADDOCKE, PADDUCK, or PADDOCK, ICHABOD, perhaps son of Zechariah of Barnstable, m., 1712, Joanna, d. of Thomas Faunce, and had Jane, m. Gideon Bradford; and others. ROBERT had Zechariah, 1636; Mary, 1638; Alice, 1640; John, 1643.

PADDY, WILLIAM, came over 1635, and m., 1639, Alice, d. of Edward Freeman, and had Elizabeth, 1641; John, 1643; Samuel, 1645; Thomas, 1647; Joseph, 1649; and Mercy. He m., 2d, in Boston, where he removed, Mary (Greenough) Payton, wid. of Bazalael, 1651, and had William, 1652; Nathaniel, 1653; Hannah, 1656; Benjamin, 1658; and Rebecca.

PAINE, DAVID, m. Charlotte Hathaway, 1807. JOHN SAMPSON, son of 1st Stephen, m., 1815, Deborah, d. of Elnathan Holmes, and had Reuben Churchill, 1815. He m., 2d, Susan, wid. of Charles Holmes of Nantucket, and had Stephen; Hannah Sherman, 1836; John Sampson, 1838. SETH, from Eastham, m., 1767, Mrs. Sarah Sears. STEPHEN, prob. a descendant from Moses of Braintree, 1641, through his son Stephen of Braintree, and grandson Stephen of Rehoboth, by wife Mehitabel, had Samuel, Mary, Sarah, Mehitabel, and Stephen. He m., 2d, 1787, Hannah Sampson, and had John Sampson. STEPHEN, son of above, m. Susanna Bates, and had Stephen, 1801; Susan, 1803, m. Anthony Sherman Allen; Stephen, 1806. His wid. m. Joshua Torrey.

PALMER, WILLIAM, came in the Fortune 1621, with son William, who m., at Scituate, 1633, Elizabeth Hodgkins. His wife, Frances, came in the Ann 1623. He m. a 2d wife, and had Henry, and Bridget.

PAPPOON, DANIEL, m., 1759, Mary Lemote.

PARKER, EBENEZER GROVESNOR, m. Rebecca Morton, d. of William Davis, 1835, and had Henry Grovesnor, 1836, m. Lucy Josephine, d. of William Brown of Boston. JONATHAN, from Plympton, m., 1748, Lydia Bartlett. SETH, from Falmouth, m., 1776, Sophia, d. of John Cotton.

PATTISON, THOMAS, m. Susanna Beale, 1746.

PATY, EPHRAIM, son of 2d John, m., 1804, Betsey Fuller, and had Betsey, 1805, m. Kendall Holmes; Ephraim, 1806. He m., 2d, Martha Morton, 1819, and had Martha Ann, 1820, m. William Paty; Thomas Morton, 1822, m. Mary E. Swift; George Winslow, 1834; Elvira Cordelia, 1836, m. Francis Ambler; Seth W., 1839, m. Sarah E. Whiting. EPHRAIM, son of above, m., 1830, Sally Cole, and had Ephraim T., m. Susan E., d. of Caleb Holmes; Sarah G., 1835; Lizzie F., 1840; William A,, 1846; Willie A., 1849; Deborah J., m. Samuel Briggs; and Carrie C., m. Albert T. Finney. JOHN, from some place unknown, settled in Plymouth, and m., 1757, Margaret Finney, and had Ann, 1758; John, 1759; Levi, 1761; Ephraim; Sylvanus, 1765; Hannah, m. Francis Tully; Margaret, m. Thomas Farmer; and Thomas. JOHN, son of above, m., 1780, Deborah Fish, and had John, 1781; Ephraim, 1783; Deborah, 1785; Seth, 1787, m. Phebe Barnes; Sylvia, 1796, m. Joseph Cooper; Meriah, 1797; Thomas, 1798; Henry, 1800. JOHN, son of above, m.,

1802, Asenath Churchill, and had Asenath, 1802, m. James G. Gleason;
Caroline, 1805, m. Edward Taylor Cooper; John, 1807; Henry, 1809; Sylvia,
1811; William, 1814. JOHN, son of above, m., 1831, Martha Ann Jefferson
of Charlestown, and had John, 1835; John Henry, 1840, m. Juliet Bolles;
Mary Francisca, m. Henry M. Benson; and Emma Theodora, m. Isaac I.
Yates of Schenectady, U. S. N. LEVI, son of 1st John, m., 1785, Elizabeth
Finney, and had Nancy, m. Thomas Morton; Betsey, m. Bartlett Holmes.
SYLVANUS, son of 1st John, m., 1786, Hannah Barnes, and had Levi, and
William. THOMAS, son of 1st John, m., 1795, Jerusha, d. of Zacheus
Barnes, and had Thomas; Jerusha Thomas, 1802, m. Ellis Harlow and Sam-
uel Talbot; Nancy, 1804. THOMAS, son of 2d John, m., 1822, Maria Bemis,
and had Frances Maria, 1824; Harriet Ann, 1833, m. Phineas Pierce. WIL-
LIAM, son of Sylvanus, m., 1822, Jane Ellis, and had Hannah Curtis, 1822;
William, Caroline, and Jane. WILLIAM, Sandwich Islands, son of 3d
John, m., 1839, Martha Ann, d. of Ephraim Paty, and had Ellen D.,
m. John Matt Smith; Caroline F., Francis W., Caroline Louisa, and Charles
Morton.

PAULDING, or POLDEN, ALBERT, son of 1st William, moved from Ply-
mouth to New Bedford, where he m. Sylvia Benson, and had William Albert,
and Ellen. FRANCIS, brother of above, m. Catherine B., d. of Samuel N.
Holmes, 1837, and had Harriet Thomas, 1837; and Lydia F., m. James
Lewis. He m., 2d, Phebe S., d. of Thomas Savery, 1845, and had Edward
F., 1847. He m., 3d, Maria L. Lull of Kingston, 1850, and, 4th, Hannah B.
Lull, 1853. GEORGE, son of Jonathan, m., 1797, Jedidah, d. of Thomas Mc-
Claughlin, and had Lydia, m. Charles Westgate; Betsey, m. David V. and
John J. Wade; Hannah m. Perez Wade; Nancy, m. Philip Donnels; Polly, m.
William Douglass. JAMES, son of 1st Thomas, m., 1761, Elizabeth Beal,
and had William, 1761; James, 1764; Elizabeth, 1766; Hannah, 1770.
JAMES, son of above, m. Bethiah Dunham, 1784, and had James, m. Lucy
Holmes of Kingston; John, William, Nancy, and Sally, m. David Straffin.
JAMES T., son of 1st William, m. Nancy, d. of George Thrasher, 1841, and
had James H., 1845, m. Harriet N. Harlow; Lucy S., 1847, m. Charles W.
Johnson; Grace D., 1848; Eugene Herbert, 1851. He m., 2d, Catherine
Martin, 1872. JOHN BROWN, brother of above, m. Marian W. Churchill of
New Bedford, 1852, and had Herbert Russell, 1853; Elizabeth B., 1855; and
John Irving. JONATHAN, son of 1st Thomas, m. Mary Ward, 1765, and had
Mary, 1766; Jonathan, 1770, m. Sarah Rogers; Thomas, 1774, m. Triphosa
Westgate; George, 1776. SYLVANUS, son of 1st William, m. Alexina C., d.
of Elkanah Barnes, 1835, and had Harriet, Sylvanus; Clarabel, 1846; and
Alexina, 1850. SYLVANUS, parentage unknown to writer, by wife Catherine
Harriet, had Harriet Eliza, 1818. THOMAS, the first comer in Plymouth, m.
Deborah Spooner, 1735, and had Thomas, 1735; William, 1738, m. Susanna
Lee; Rebecca, 1740; James, 1742; Jonathan, 1744; Lydia, 1747, m. Ebenezer
Ward; Elizabeth, 1750; Hannah, 1752. WILLIAM, son of 2d James, m.
Eunice Sturtevant, 1810, and had William, Sylvanus, Francis, Albert,
James T., and John Brown. WILLIAM, son of above, m. Jane B., d. of
Solomon Holmes, 1832, and had William Crocker, 1833; Daniel Holmes,

1834, m. Lydia A. Dunham; Mercy J., 1836, m. Edward L. Robbins; Eunice Sturtevant, 1839; and Emily B., m. Winslow A. Wright.

PEACH, JOSEPH, m. Lydia Jeffrey, 1731.

PEAK, DANIEL, m. Rhoda Beal, 1748.   GEORGE of Providence, m. Jerusha Bartlett, 1754.

PEARSON, WILLIAM BENDICK, m., 1753, Phebe, d. of Joseph Holmes, and had Phebe, 1755, m. Lemuel Doten; Susanna, m. Joseph Wright; and William.   WILLIAM, son of above, m., 1784, Abiah Thrasher, and had Abiah, m. Nathaniel Bartlett; and William.

PECKHAM, GEORGE, from Providence, m. Jerusha Bartlett, 1754.   JOHN, Newport, son of Philip, had a 1st wife named Ellis.   He m., 2d, Tabitha, d. of Samuel Howland, and had Robert, Abigail, Samuel, Tabitha, William, Sally, and Josiah.   JOSEPH, from Easton, m., 1827, Sally, d. of Benjamin Seymour, and had Sarah, and William.   PHILIP, Newport, a descendant of a John of Newport, 1639.   He m., Sarah Black, about, 1710, and had John, 1714, and probably others.   ROBERT, Westminster, son of William, m. Ruth, d. of Joseph Sawyer of Bolton, and was the father of Rev. Joseph of Kingston, now living.   THOMAS G., from New York, m. Thankful Holmes, about 1825, and had George T. of Plymouth, m. Caroline E. Odell; Oliver Dean; Susan M., m. Frank Winton of St. Johns, N.F.; Charles F.; and Frances E., m. John Scofield of Stamford, Conn.   WILLIAM, son of John, born in Bristol, R. I., m., Elizabeth Knapp, and had Robert, Samuel Howland, and others.

PELHAM, EDWARD, of Hastings, in Sussex, England, a member of Parliament, 1597.   He was admitted at Gray's Inn, 1563, called to the bar 1579, knighted and made Lord Chief Baron of the Exchequer of Ireland, and died 1606.   His son, Herbert, of Michelham Priory, was admitted to Gray's Inn 1588, and his son, Herbert, bore his father's arms in the Hastings muster-roll 1619.   The 2d Herbert, born in 1601, graduated at Oxford 1619, and came to Massachusetts 1638, preceded by a daughter, Penelope, in 1635, and a son.   He had a 2d wife, Elizabeth, wid. of Roger Harlakenden, and d. of Godfrey Basseville, by whom he had Mary, 1640; Frances, and probably Waldegrave; Edward, and Henry.   He was the 1st Treasurer of Harvard College, and returned to England 1649, where he died 1673.   His wid. died 1706, and was buried in Marshfield; Edward, m. either Godsgift or Freelove, d. of Gov. Benedict Arnold of R.I., or both, and died in Newport 1720, leaving children Elizabeth, Edward, and Thomas; Penelope, born 1619, m. Josiah Winslow, and the mention in his will of his aunt, Elizabeth Pelham, suggests the inquiry whether Elizabeth, buried in Marshfield, was not a sister of Herbert instead of his wife.   The Pelham house in Hastings, built in 1611, was standing in 1862, the oldest house in the town.

PENNIMAN, JOSEPH, of Bradford, m. Hannah Jackson, 1771.

PENISS, NOAH, pub., 1740, to Abigail Chummuck, Indians.

PERIAS, FRANCIS, m., 1843, Mary Thomas.

PERKINS, ABRAHAM, Hampton, by wife Mary, had Mary, m. Giles Fifield of Charlestown; Abraham, baptized 1639, m. Elizabeth, d. of Thomas Sleeper; Humphrey, 1642; James, 1644; Timothy, 1646; James, 1647; Jonathan, 1650; David, 1653; Abigail, 1655; Timothy, 1657; Sarah, 1659; Humphrey, 1661; Caleb; Luke, 1666. ALVIN, Carver, son of Sampson, m. Priscilla Dunham, and had Elizabeth M., 1827; Alvin S., 1834; Albert W., 1839. CHARLES ANDERSON SIMEON, son of Martin, m., 1851, Eliza, d. of Stephen P. Brown of Plymouth, and had Charles Franklin, m. Cynthia Hopkinson of Brookline; Ann Eliza, Laura L., and Anderson. CYRUS, Woodstock, Vt., son of 6th John, m. Martha Child of Barnard, and had Semiramis, Joseph, Martha, Lucy, Betsey, Sarah, Munroe, Henry, and Vanness. DANIEL, son of 3d John, m. Louisa Barrows, and had Sally A., Joseph B., Mary L., Daniel W., and Abby B. DAVID, Beverly and Bridgewater, son of Abraham, m. Martha, d. of John Howard of Bridgewater, 1699, and had John, 1700; Mary, 1702, m. Gideon Washburn; Martha, 1704, m. Joseph Byram; Elizabeth, 1707, m. Solomon Leonard; Susanna, 1709, m. Samuel Allen; David, 1711; Jonathan, 1714; Abraham, 1716, and Sarah. DAVID GARDNER, son of 6th John, m., 1797, Deliverance Curtis of Hardwick, and had Mercy, 1798, m. Daniel Angell of Barnard, Vt.; Ichabod, 1802; Hosea, 1804, m. Elizabeth Cady of Bridgewater, Vt.; Almira, 1812, m. Timothy Lucas of Barnard; Lucia P., 1815. He m., 2d, Sally Russell of Stockbridge, Vt., and had Lucretia R., 1827. ELISHA PADDOCK, Woodstock, Vt., son of 6th John, m. Hannah Taft, and had Alvora, 1801, m. Sarah Boutwell; Orson, 1802, m. Hannah Rust; Sylvia, 1804, m. John Boutwell; Emily, 1806, m. Elias C. Smith; Hannah A., 1807, m. Earl Vaughn; Elisha Paddock, 1809, m. Louisa Beard; Caroline, 1811; Mahala, 1813, m. Increase B. Howes; Thankful, 1815, m. William C. Bement. GAIUS, Woodstock, Vt., son of 6th John, m., 1798, Millison Curtis of Barnard, and had Gardner, 1799; Elisha, 1801; Lyman, 1803; Hiram, 1806; Millison, 1807; Jerome, 1809; John, 1816; Roxana, 1828. GEORGE, son of 1st Gideon, m., 1800, Experience, d, of Samuel Battles, and had George, m. Rebecca Bartlett; Thomas S., m. Betsey, d. of Samuel Sampson; Rebecca, m. Samuel Sampson; Experience, m. Ezekiel Cushing Turner; William, 1810; Sarah, m. John Carver; Jane, m. Zacheus Stephens; Hannah, 1816; Betsey Williams, m. Israel W. Thompson of Middleboro'. GIDEON, Carver, son of 1st Joshua, by wife Desire, had Seth, 1772; Hannah, 1774; Cornelius, 1775; George, 1778; Rebecca, 1780; Patience, 1783; Gideon, 1786; Sarah, 1789. He m., 2d, Meribah Eaton, and had Betty, 1790; Seabury, 1792; Sylvia, 1794; John C., 1795; Josiah, 1801. GIDEON, son of above, m., 1809, Joanna, d. of David Drew of Plymouth, and had Joanna Drew, m. William Pearson; Ellis Atwood, m. Elnathan Wilbur of Middleboro'; Gideon, m. Deborah W. Burgess; Arad, m. Rhoda Goodwin of Fall River and Abby R., d. of Alonzo Scudder of Plymouth; David Drew, m. Lucy Atwood of Carver; Hiram, m. Lucy Davis of Boston; Almira A., m. Lloyd Perkins of Middleboro'; and Emily F. ISAAC, son of 4th Luke, m. Ruth Ingalls, and had Joseph; William A., m. Elizabeth Holmes, and Charlotte, wid. of Jabez Churchill, and d. of William Keen; Catherine, m. George W. Cobb; and Isaac. He removed to Conn., where he m. a Perkins, and had Maria, Elizabeth, Cornelia, Amos, and John. ISAAC, Plympton, son of 1st Josiah, m., 1771, Molly, d. of Barnabas Shurtleff. JAMES, Woodstock, Vt., son of 6th John, m., 1819, Hannah Lyon, and had Mary, 1820, m. Adriel Huntley of East Machias; Belinda Bard and Orinda H., twins, 1822; James S., 1824, m. Lizzie Lyons of Marion, Maine; William H., 1826; Hannah G., 1828, m. John Cook of East Machias; Susan K., 1830; Charles W., 1833, m. Camantha Denison of Cutler, Maine, and Julia E. (Simpson) Waters of Simpsonville, Md.; Ellery D., 1835, m. Priscilla Cates of Cutler; Francis M., 1838; Alonzo W., 1841, m. Annie Lyons; Leverett A., 1846. JAMES A., m., 1836, Betsey A. Burgess. JOEL, m., 1806, Lucy Barnes, and had Isaac H., 1807. JOHN, Plympton, son of 1st Luke, m., 1721, Mercy Jackson, and had John, Mercy, Eleazer, and Elizabeth. JOHN, Plympton, son of 1st Josiah, m. Mehitabel Shaw. JOHN, Kingston, son of 3d Luke, m., 1784, Sarah, d. of Joshua Adams and had Joshua, 1786; Betsey, 1790, m. Nathaniel Sylvester of Halifax; Charles, 1792; Thomas, 1796, m. Phebe Curtis of Scituate; John of Plymouth; Daniel, 1803; Sally A., 1807, m. Darius Holmes of Halifax; Beza, 1809. JOHN, son of above, m., 1825, Adaline Tupper of Kingston, and had Eliza B., Ronald H., and Priscilla. JOHN, Middleboro', son of 1st John, m., 1745, Patience Paddock, and had John, 1748; and Patience, m. Simeon Cushman. JOHN, Middleboro', son of above, m., 1772, Hannah Gardner, and had John; David Gardner, 1775; Gaius; Elisha Paddock, 1782; Patience, m. Stephen Taft of Woodstock, Vt.; James, Cyrus, Thomas; Joseph, 1795; Polly, m. Abner Buckman of Barnard; Simeon, 1798. JOHN, Barnard, son of above, m., 1795, Amelia Eastman, and had Hannah, Timothy, Zilpha, John, Millison, Lucy, Daniel, and Gaius. JOSEPH, Plympton, son of 2d Josiah, m., 1780, Sarah, d. of Isaiah Cushman, and had Susanna, 1781, m. Philip Caldwell; Oliver P., m. Sarah Elmes; Sarah, 1785, m. Ephraim Washburn and Simeon Staples; Joseph, 1788, m. Sally Perkins; Isaiah, 1791, m. Matilda Peterson; Maria, 1793, m. N. D. Andrews; Luther, 1796, m. Mary Bullen; Hiram, 1802, m. Ruth Megguien. JOSIAH, Plympton, son of 1st Luke, m. Deborah, d. of Nehemiah Bennett of Middleboro', and had Nathan, 1723; William, 1724; John, 1726; Martha, 1727; Joshua, 1729; Abner, 1731; Josiah, 1732; Luke, 1733; Abner, 1735; Deborah, 1737; Hannah, 1740; Zephaniah, 1742; Isaac, 1744. He m., 2d, Rebecca, sister of Rev. Jonathan Parker. JOSIAH, Plympton, son of above, m. Deborah, d. of Ebenezer Soule, and had Joseph, 1754; Ebenezer, 1757; Josiah, 1759; Oliver, 1760; Susanna, 1762; Calvin, 1763; Deborah, 1766; Rebecca, 1768; Sylvia, 1770. JOSIAH, Plympton, son of 1st Nathan, had Josiah, 1796, m. Deborah Hall of Middleboro'; Polly, 1798; Martin, 1800, Nathan, 1805. JOSHUA, Plympton, son of 1st Josiah, m. Hannah, d. of George Sampson, and had Gideon, 1751; Sarah, 1753, m. Andrew Barrows; Deborah, m. Bartlett Murdock; Abigail, m. John Shaw; Joshua Lothrop, 1761; Hannah, 1763, m. Peleg Savery; Rebecca, 1765; Martha, m. Elisha Murdock; Betty, 1769; Drusilla, m. Eliab Ward; Luke, 1773; Sampson, 1777. JOSHUA, son of 3d John, m., 1811, Elizabeth Morton, and had Betsey M., 1811; James R., 1814; Marcia, and Charles T., 1818. LEVI, Plympton, son of 4th Luke, m. Jane Sturtevant, 1807, and had Jane, Levi, Eliza; and Charles Henry, m. Susan R., d. of Thomas Holmes. LUKE, Plympton, son of Abraham, m. Martha, d. of Lot Conant, and had Josiah, Luke, Mark, John, and Martha. LUKE, Plympton, son of above, m., 1716, Ruth, d. of Robert Cushman, and had Ignatius, 1720; Hannah, 1723, m. Nathaniel Shaw; Mary, 1726. LUKE, Carver, son of 1st Joshua, m. Kesiah Bennett, and had Jacob Thompson, 1799; Hannah, 1801; Luke, 1804; Kesiah, 1807. LUKE, son of 1st Josiah, m. Elizabeth, d. of Isaac Churchill, and had Daniel and John. He m., 2d, Abigail, wid of George Little, and had George, 1766; Elizabeth, 1767, m. Andrew Ring; Abigail, 1770, m. Benjamin Eaton, and had Judith, who m. Franklin B. Cobb of Plymouth; Bena, 1772; Luke, 1774; Levi, 1776; Isaac, 1780. LUKE, son of above, m. Hannah Harlow, and had Stephen, m. Joann Lucas; Abigail S., m. William S. Burbank; Hannah Harlow, m. Elijah Walker; Mary Ann, m. Cyrus Shaw and Thomas Jackson; Ansel, m. Margaret Kittel of Schenectady; Calvin, m. Betsey Barrows; Nancy Bartlett, m. Lewis S. Wadsworth; George, m. Abby Sweetser. MARK, North Bridgewater, son of 1st Luke, m. Dorothy Whipple, and was the ancestor of the Brockton line. MARTIN, Plympton, son of 3d Josiah, m., 1827, Susan W., d. of Simon Richmond, and had Charles Anderson Simeon, 1828; Josiah Frederick, 1830; Susan Wm. Richmond, 1832; Lucien Leonidas, 1835; Sarah Jane Wayne, 1837, m. Willis K. Dickerson; Rebecca Whitman, 1839; William Martin, 1841; Marcia Sampson, 1844; Lydia Anderson, 1846; Edward Sampson, 1849. NATHAN, Plympton, son of 1st Josiah, m. Mary, d. of Jonathan Sampson, and had Priscilla, 1745, m. Thomas Waterman; Abner, 1747; Lydia, 1749, m. Jonathan Barrows; Josiah, 1751; Bennett, 1753; Mary, 1755, m. Caleb Thompson; Bennett, 1760; Joanna, 1762, m. John Soule of Middleboro'; Thomas, 1765. NATHAN, Plympton, son of 3d Josiah, m., 1829, Mary Holmes, d. of Asaph Soule, and had Olive Bisbee, 1830; Pamela James, 1835; Mary Isabella, 1838; Robert Cowin, 1848. SAMPSON, Carver, son of 1st Joshua, m. Rebecca Clark, and had Alvin, 1803; Sampson, 1806; Rebecca, 1808; Stillman, 1811. He m., 2d, Susanna Shaw, and had William; and Luke of Plymouth, m. Caroline, d. of Joseph Jackson of Middleboro'. SETH, Plympton, son of Zephaniah, m. Mary, d. of Joshua Adams, and had Nathaniel Sampson, 1792; Saba Adams, 1795; Ezra, 1798, m. Lydia Cook; Hannah, 1800, m. George Briggs and Shaffit Reed; Nancy Godfrey, 1806, m. Albert Howland; Seth, 1808, m. Elizabeth B. Prince and Eliza B. Lucas; William, 1812. SIMEON, Barnard, son of 6th John, had Esther, Horatio, and Matilda. THOMAS, Woodstock, Vt., son of 6th John, m. Lucinda Marsh, and had Adaline, Lucy, Cynthia, Mary, Charles, and Edwin. TIMOTHY, m., 1793, Rebecca Dunham. WILLIAM, Plympton, son of 1st Josiah, by wife Eliza, had Ambrose, 1746; Mary, 1748. WILLIAM, Plympton, son of Zephaniah, m., 1816, Sophia, d. of John Bradford, and had Sophia Bradford, 1817, m. Darius White; Rebecca, 1820, m. Ebenezer Taylor Dean and Alonzo Wright; William, 1824, m. Anginette, d. of Simeon Churchill. ZEPHANIAH, Plympton, son of 1st Josiah, m., 1763, Patience, d. of William Ripley, and had Hannah, m. Isaac Bonney; Seth; Rebecca, 1768, m. Salah Bosworth of Halifax; William, 1772; Daniel, 1773; Patience, 1784, m. John Bradford.

PERO, PERO, and Hannah, slaves of John Murdock, m., 1756.

PERRIGO, ROBERT, m. Susanna Holmes, 1754.

PERRY, ABNER, perhaps son of Benjamin of Scituate, by wife Joanna, had Joseph and Benjamin, twins, 1733. BENJAMIN, Scituate, probably son of William, m. Ruth Bryant, 1711, and had Samuel and Abner. DANIEL of Sandwich, m. Phebe, d. of Zacheus Bartlett, 1785. ELISHA of Sandwich, m. Susanna Clark, 1786. HENRY, Pembroke, son of Samuel, m. Bethiah Baker of Duxbury, 1760, and had Samuel B., m. Ann Bates; Henry, 1764, m. Content Barker; John and James, twins. JOHN, Pembroke and Plymouth, son of above, m. Rhoda Barker, and had Polly, John, Lewis; and Rhoda, m. Isaac Davie. JOHN, son of above, m., 1829, Ruth, d. of Sylvanus Sampson, and had John Barker, m. Clarissa Ward of New Bedford; and Lucinda, m. James Pease of New Bedford. JUDAH, m. Betsey Anderson, 1819. LEWIS, son of 1st John, m. Sarah, d. of David Drew, 1824. SAMUEL, Pembroke, son of Benjamin, m. Eunice Witherell, 1734, and had Henry; Mary, m. Howland Beal; Samuel; Noah, m. Jane Hobart; Israel; Betsey, m. Amos Turner; Seth, and Adam. THOMAS, Scituate, 1647, m. Sarah, d. of Isaac Stedman, and had probably Thomas, William, Henry, Joseph, and John. WILLIAM, Scituate, son of above, m. Elizabeth Lobdell, 1681, and had Amos, m. Ruth Turner; and Benjamin. WILLIAM, m. Lydia, d. of Stephen Barnaby, 1719. He was perhaps son of 1st William.

PETERS, THOMAS, m. Rebecca Shepard, 1721.

PETERSON, CHARLES, son of 2d Reuben, m., 1810, Thankful, d. of John Clark, and had John Clark, 1811; Betsey Thomas, 1815; Charles Henry, 1817; David Lewis, 1819; Sylvester Holmes, 1822; Daniel Porter, 1826; George Soule, 1830; Ichabod B., 1833; Sarah, 1833, m. David H. Babcock; Laura Clark, 1835. CHARLES HENRY, son of above, m., 1842, Lucy, d. of Ezra Clark, and had James Clark, 1843; Phebe Stephens, 1845, m. J. Augustus Potter; Charles Wallace, 1849; Charles Leslie, 1851, m. Abbie S. Wentworth of Middleboro'; Clara Washburn, 1854, m. George W. King; Josiah Lyman, 1856, m. Ella Coy of Boston; Betsey Thankful, 1859; a son, 1861; Mattie Putnam, 1863. He m., 2d, 1868, Ellen, wid. of Charles Washburn, and d. of Henry Lee, and had William Henry, 1869; Lucy Ellen, 1870. DANIEL PORTER, son of 1st Charles, m., 1853, Jerusha M., d. of Benjamin Clark, and had Elias Wells, 1854, m. Mary J. Hopper of Honolulu; Charles Allen, 1856; Arthur Porter, 1858; Adrianna Brown, 1867. DAVID LEWIS, son of 1st Charles, m., 1842, Rachel T., d. of Simeon Valler, and had Helen Frances, 1845, m. Hiram T. Delano of Duxbury; Medora Lewis, 1850, m. Jonathan F. Turner of Duxbury. ELIJAH, Duxbury, son of 1st Reuben, m., 1765, Abigail Whittemore of Marshfield, and had Jabez, Judah, Joel, Reuben, Packard, Whittemore, Olive, and Betsey. GEORGE SOULE, son of 1st Charles, m., 1854, Elizabeth, d. of Thadeus Faunce, and had Lizzie Warner, 1855; George Clifton, 1857; Lizzie Frances, 1864; Arthur Warner, 1870; Mary Ann Gilbert, 1872. ICHABOD B., son of 1st Charles, m., 1865, Henrietta C., d. of James Austin of Honolulu, and had Henrietta Thankful, 1866; James Austin, 1867; Charles Frederick, 1870; William, 1871; Robert, 1873; Sarah Elizabeth, 1875; David Lewis, 1878. JOHN CLARK, son of 1st Charles, m., 1835, Lucy G., d. of Seth Holmes, and had Caroline Matilda, 1836. He m., 2d, Roxanna L., d. of Joseph Howard of Holden, and had Edwin Howard, 1839, m. Hannah Sophia, d. of Francis H. Weston; Lucy Caroline, 1841; John Henry, 1843, m. Ella P., d. of Caleb B. Holmes; Frank Russell, 1845; Louise Franklin, 1847, m.

Charles H. Mignault of Boston; Flora Adelaide, 1850, m. Henry A. Thomas;
Frank Russell, 1852, m. Lucy T., d. of Israel Clark; Harriet May, 1856, m.
George W. Holmes of Duxbury; Mary Goodridge, 1858, m. Henry Dodge.
JONATHAN, Duxbury, son of Joseph, m. Lydia Thacher, and had John, 1701;
Hopestill, 1703, m. Joshua Delano; Jonathan, 1706; Reuben, 1710. JOSEPH,
Duxbury, had Jonathan; Benjamin, 1670; David, 1676; Isaac; John, 1710.
LEWIS, son of 4th Reuben, m., 1833, Charlotte, d. of Belcher Manter and had
Lewis; Mary J., m. Isaiah H. Ware; Augusta, Robert; and William F., m.
Irene F., d. of Nehemiah Savery. LORIN, Boston, son of 4th Reuben, m.,
1836, Jane D., d. of Elijah Sherman of Plymouth, and had Jane B., 1839;
Harriet E., 1844; Cynthia T., 1846. PEREZ, m., 1823, Sarah H. Morton.
REUBEN, Duxbury, son of Jonathan, m., 1732, Rebecca Simmons, and had
Elijah, Mary, Nehemiah; Abigail, m. Zenas Thomas; Sarah, m. Cornelius
Delano; Lydia, Thadeus; Luther, m. Priscilla Cushman; and Reuben.
REUBEN, Duxbury, son of above, m. Abigail Soule of Duxbury, and had
Samuel G., 1779; Ichabod, 1781; Charles, 1788; Reuben, 1791; Thomas, 1786,
m. Sally Sampson; Abigail, 1783, m. a Chandler; Lucy, 1799, m. Ephraim
Bradford; Sally, 1797, m. Ichabod Barstow; Clark, 1793, m. Lydia, d. of Seth
Clark, and Eliza Kent of Duxbury. REUBEN, son of above, m. Deborah, d. of
Seth Clark, 1817, and had a son Reuben, and perhaps others. REUBEN, son
of Elijah, m., 1812, Mary, d. of Benjamin White of Hanover, and had Lewis,
and Lorin. SYLVESTER HOLMES, son of 1st Charles, m., 1850, Matilda, d. of
David Scattergood of Philadelphia, and had John Mershon Scattergood, 1852,
m. Ella J. Mason of Philadelphia; Willie Sylvester Holmes, 1854; Charles
Augustus Barstow, 1855, m. Stella A., d. of George Gifford of New Bedford; Louise Matilda Scattergood, 1862. THOMAS, m., 1746, Susanna Beal.

PHILLIPS, ABSALOM, Pembroke, son of Christopher, m., 1804, Abigail
Barker, and had Gideon Barker, 1805; Abigail, 1806; Almira, 1808; James
Cushing, 1810; Betsey, 1811; Ann J., 1813; Charles B., 1816; Thomas H.,
1818; William, 1820; Nathaniel, 1822; Zavem, 1823; Albert, 1826. AMES,
from Reading, m., 1821, Betsey C. Robbins. BENJAMIN, Marshfield, son of
2d John, m., 1682, Sarah, d. of John Thomas, and had John, 1682; Joseph,
1685; Benjamin, 1687, m. Eleanor Baker; Sarah, 1689; Thomas, 1691; Hannah, 1693; Jeremiah, 1697, m. Sarah, d. of John White; Abigail, 1699; Isaac,
1703; Bethiah, 1705. BENJAMIN, Marshfield, probably son of above, m.,
1716, Eleanor Baker, and had Jeremiah, 1717; Benjamin, 1719; John, 1721.
He m., 2d, Desire Sherman, 1728, and had Desire, 1729; Eleanor, 1731; Penelope, 1735; Alice, 1744. BLANEY, Duxbury and Pembroke, son of 2d
Thomas, m., 1733, Christian, d. of Christopher Wadsworth of Duxbury, and
had Samuel, 1734; Blaney, 1736; Samuel, 1738; Christian, 1740, m. Philip
Chandler; Mercy, 1744, m. Mark Phillips; Alice, 1747, m. David Beal; Seth,
1749; Christopher, 1753; Lot, 1755; Betty, 1757. BLANEY, Fitchburg, son of
above, by wife Mary, had Olive, 1763, m. Robert Sampson; Eunice, 1764;
Samuel, 1766; Eunice, 1768; Mary, 1769; Huldah, 1771. By a 2d wife, he had
Joshua. BLANEY, son of Lot, m., perhaps, 1819, Chloe, d. of John Murdock of Carver, and had Louisa, 1819; Sally B., 1822; Deborah M., 1824;
Deborah M., 1826. CHRISTOPHER, Pembroke, son of 1st Blaney, m., 1775,

Priscilla Cushing, and had Edmund, 1776; Christopher, 1777; Edmund, 1780; Absalom, 1782; Lewis, 1785; Priscilla Cushing, 1788; Savan, 1793; Savan, 1795. EDMUND, Pembroke, son of above, m., 1802, Celia, d. of James Bourne, and had Theophilus Cushing, 1803; Lydia Barker, 1805, m. John Jordan; Edmund, 1808; Priscilla, 1810. EDMUND, Hanson, son of above, m., 1826, Mehitabel Cushing, d. of Samuel W. Josslyn, and had Edmund, 1827; Aaron, 1828; Calvin, 1830, m. Louisa, d. of Charles Bourne. He m., 2d, 1845, Joanna, d. of Allen Richmond of Lakeville, and had Allen R., 1846; George Lewis, 1848; Nancy Bourne, 1850, m. George W. Turner; Mary Maria A., 1852, m. William F. Howland; Sarah Rosilla, 1854, m. Wallace House; Charles Edward, 1861. ELISHA, Marshfield, son of 1st Joseph, by wife Mary, had Mary, 1757; Elisha, 1758; Joseph, 1761; Mercy, 1764. EZRA, Hanson, son of Lot, m., 1808, Mehitabel, d. of Joseph Allen of Bridgewater, and had Ezra, 1810; Mehitabel, 1811, m. Charles Beal of Turner, Me. He m., 2d, 1814, Lucy, d. of Josiah Chamberlain, and had a son, 1815; Lucy Pratt, 1818; George, 1824. He m., 3d, 1833, Nabby, wid. of Jonathan Pratt, and d. of Mark Phillips of East Bridgewater, and had Lot, 1841, m. Sarah Elizabeth Barker. EZRA, Hanover, son of above, m., 1834, Catherine Hitchcock, d. of Dr. Calvin Tilden of Hanover, and had Calvin Tilden, 1836, m. Maria Eveline, d. of Algernon Josslyn of Hanson; Catherine, 1842; Morrell Allen, 1844, m. Sophia Richmond, d. of Perez Simmons of Scituate; Charles Follen, 1846; Abigail Tilden, 1849. ISAAC, Marshfield, son of 1st Benjamin, m., 1727, Sarah White, and had David, 1731; Sarah; Isaac, 1728; Anna, 1737; James, 1739; Rebecca, 1742, m. Jabez Dingley; Solomon, 1750. IVERS, Fitchburg, son of 2d Samuel, m., 1828, Rebecca Carter of Leominster, and had Mary Ann, 1829; Ivers Carter, 1831; Harriet Rebecca, 1833; Sarah Thurston, 1836. JEREMIAH, Marshfield, son of 2d Benjamin, by wife Hannah, had Joseph, 1753; Hannah, 1759; Persis, 1760. JOHN, Plymouth, Duxbury, and Marshfield, born in England, 1602, had, by a wife unknown, John, Samuel, Benjamin, and Mary. He m., 2d, 1667, Faith, wid. of. Edward Doty, and d. of Tristram Clark. JOHN, Duxbury and Marshfield, son of above by a 2d wife, Grace, wid. of William Holloway, m., 1654, had Grace, 1654; Hannah; Joseph, 1656; Benjamin, 1658; and Jeremiah. JOHN, m., 1752, Lydia Morton. JOHN, by wife Elizabeth, had Elizabeth, 1752; John, 1755; Samuel, 1757. JOHN, m., 177–, Rebecca King. JOHN, Marshfield, m., 1677, Ann Torrey. JOHN, Marshfield, son of 1st Benjamin, m., 1710, Patience Stevens, and had Nathaniel, 1713. JOSEPH, Marshfield, son of 1st Benjamin, m., 1711, Mercy, d. of Anthony Eames, and had Naomi and Elizabeth, twins, 1711; Elisha, 1713; Eggatha, 1716; Jerusha, 1721; Mercy, 1725. JOSEPH, Marshfield, son of Elisha, m. Ruth Macomber, and had Ruth, 1787; Polly, 1788; Mercy, 1791. JOSEPH, Duxbury, m., 1829, Sarah Whiting of Plymouth. LEWIS, son of Christopher, m., 1807, Nancy, d. of Noah Bonney, and had Daniel Lewis, 1808; Oreb Williams, 1810; LaRoche, 1812; Mary Ann, 1815. LOT, Pembroke, son of 1st Blaney, m., 1779, Diana, d. of Rouse Howland, and had Ezra, 1779; Mehitabel, 1783; Lydia, 1786; Sally, 1788; Diana, 1791; Christian Wadsworth, 1793; Blaney, 1797. NATHANIEL, Marshfield, son of last John, m. Joanna White, and

had John, 1739; Nathaniel, 1742; Joanna, 1744; Patience, 1747; Daniel, 1752.
SAMUEL, Taunton, perhaps son of 1st John, m., 1676, wid. Mary Cobb, and
had Mehitabel, 1676; Samuel, 1678; and perhaps Thomas. SAMUEL, Fitchburg, son of Seth, had Ivers, 1805. SETH, Fitchburg, son of 1st Blaney, m.,
1777, Betty, d. of Eleazer Hamlin, and had Betty, 1778; Samuel, 1781; Lydia,
1785; Seth, 1787. THOMAS, by wife Mary, had Elizabeth; Rebecca, m.
Thomas Sturney, 1722; Merriam, m. a Dunham; Margaret, m., probably,
Samuel Chandler; and perhaps Thomas. THOMAS, Marshfield, perhaps son
of 1st Samuel, m., 1702, Rebecca, d. of John Blaney of Charlestown, and had
Rebecca, 1704, m. Philip Chandler; Thomas, 1705; John, 1707, who had a
wife Mary; Samuel, 1709; Blaney, 1711: and perhaps Mary, who m. Reuben
Carver. THOMAS, Duxbury, son of above, by wife Jedidah, had Mary, 1731;
Rebecca, 1732, m. Thomas Dawes; Abigail, 1733; and Thomas. He perhaps
m., 2d, 1745, Lydia Carver of Marshfield. THOMAS, Bridgewater, supposed
by Mitchell to be son of 1st Benjamin, m., 1724, Mary, wid. of John Sherman, and d. of Mark Eames, and had Abiah, 1729, m. Benjamin Taylor;
Thomas, 1731, m. Mary, d. of David Hatch; Mary, 1733; Lydia, m. Zebulon
Cary; Mark, 1736, m. Mercy, d. of Blaney Phillips; and Deborah, 1739. He
m., 2d, Hannah, wid. of Micah Allen. THOMAS, Duxbury, son of 3d Thomas,
m., 1771, Abigail, d. of Thomas Chandler, and had Abigail, 1774; Rebecca,
Luther, Mary, Chandler, and Silvia. THOMAS, pub. to Abigail Rider, 1722.
THOMAS, pub. to Phebe Holmes, 1747. THOMAS, Marshfield, died 1778,
leaving wife Lydia, and children Thomas, Amos, Lydia; Mary, m. a Mitch-
ell; Rebecca, m. a Swift; and Abigail, m. a Swift. TOMSON, probably from
Connecticut, m., 1725, Hannah, d. of Josiah Cotton, and had Hannah, 1728;
and George. Wadsworth Phillips, now living, says his great-grandfather,
Thomas, of Bridgewater, was born 1712. If so, he could not have been, as
Mitchell supposed, son of Benjamin, as that Thomas was born 1691. Of
those above recorded, four were killed by lightning; the 1st wife of the 1st
John, with a son, in 1666; the 2d John in 1658; and the 1st Ezra in 1856.

PIERCE, or PEIRCE, ABNER, by wife Mary, had George F., 1844; and
Marianna, 1851. ABRAHAM, Plymouth, 1623, by wife Rebecca, had Abra-
ham, 1638; Rebecca, m. a Wills; Mary, m. a Baker; Alice, m. a Baker; and
Isaac. ABRAHAM, Duxbury, son of above, had by a 1st wife, John, m.
Susanna Newland of Bridgewater; Samuel, m. Mary, d. of John Sanders;
and Abigail Pool. He probably m., 2d, Hannah Glass of Duxbury, 1695,
and had Abraham, m. Abigail Peterson; and Hannah, m. Joseph Newell of
Bridgewater. AMERICA, m. Violet Saunders, 1815, and had Hannah D., m.
John Williams; Margaret, m. William Francis; and James S., m. Mary C.
Williams. ASA S., m. Eliza C., d. of Joseph Davis, 1839, and had Amanda
Stephens, 1839. BENJAMIN, of Duxbury, m. Polly Sampson, 1801, and had
Judith, 1802; Melzar, 1804, m. Abby F. Morse; Lucy, 1807; Benjamin F.,
1812, m. Mary E. Drew; and Mendall, 1815. BENJAMIN, of Wareham, m.
Mary Kendrick, 1825. BENJAMIN N., by wife Mary, had Charles W., 1841;
Lucy Thomas, 1843; William T., 1844; Adeline F., 1847. BRANCH, son of
Jesse, m. Rebecca, d. of Joseph Bates, 1810, and had Sophronia, 1811, m.
George Pierce of Rochester; Caroline, 1813, m. Wallace Taylor; Branch,

1815; Moses, 1817; Thomas, 1819; Rebecca, 1824, m. Levi Sampson; Ezra, 1827; Ruth, 1829, m. Preston Manter; Naomi, 1830, m. Freeman Manter; and David, 1832. BRANCH, son of above, m. Abiah Douglass, 1837, and had Branch Henry, 1839; and Mary T., 1841, m. Nelson Sampson. He m., 2d, Lucy Manter, wid. of Elijah Morey, and, in 1851, m., 3d, Ruby J. Valler, by whom he had Caroline, m. Leander Mitchell; David, m. Nellie Benson; Ezra, 1857; and Charles. DENNIS, son of William, m. Melintha Raymond, 1815, and had Deborah, m. Moses Pierce, Eliza, Dennis, Moses, and Melintha. EBENEZER, son of 1st Ignatius, m. Sally, d. of George Manter, and had Louisa, 1843; Charles H., 1846; Ebenezer N., 1851; and Sarah E., 1858. ELNATHAN, m. Lucy Maxim, 1840. EZRA, son of 1st Branch, m. Deborah T., d. of Silas Valler, 1852, and had Hepsy, 1854; Elnora; Ida, m. Joshua Douglass; William T.; and Nellie. GEORGE, m. Deborah Turner, 1848. IGNATIUS, son of Jesse, m. Betsey Besse, 1804, and had Ignatius; Betsey, m. Caleb Raymond; Mary, m. William Churchill; Martha, m. Benjamin Bates; Nelson, living in San Francisco; Lucy, Ebenezer, and Stillman. IGNATIUS, son of above, m. Susanna W. King, 1836, and had Lucy, 1840. He m., 2d, Maria Shaw, d. of John Atwood, 1842, and had Maria E., 1847; Ignatius F., 1848; and Emma Frances, 1853. ISAAC, son of 1st Abraham, by wife Alice, had Isaac, m. Judith, d. of John Booth of Scituate; Thomas; Mary; Lydia, m. John Heyford of Bridgewater and Aaron Seekel; Mercy, m. Joseph Trovant of Bridgewater; Sarah, m. a Macomber; and Rebecca, m. Samuel Hoar of Middleboro'. JESSE, Middleboro', son of 1st Richard, m. a wife Ruth, and had David, Rachael, Kesiah, Ignatius, Branch, Jesse; and Mary, m. George Douglass. JOHN, m. Betsey Warren Morton, 1805. JOHN, m. Rebecca Dunham, 1725. JOHN, m. Deborah Burgess, 1831. JOHN, by wife Lucretia, had Moses N., 1840. JOSEPH, by wife Elizabeth, had Hannah, 1723; and Joseph, 1725. JOSEPH, son of above, m. Rebecca Eames, 1748, and had Joseph, 1749; Elizabeth, 1751; Rebecca, 1753. MENDALL, son of 1st Benjamin, m. Mary Ann Morey, 1841. He m., 2d, Adrianna, d. of Truman Sampson, 1847, and had Charles M., 1847; George Lewis, 1852; George Frederick, 1855; and Judith A., 1861. MOSES, son of 1st Branch, m. Deborah, d. of Dennis Pierce, and had Augusta, m. Nelson Sampson; Almeda; Mercy; Susan, m. Seth Holloway; Moses, George, William, Samuel, and Elizabeth. PHINEAS, brother of Asa, born in 1804, m. Dorcas M., d. of Caleb Faunce, 1828, and had Rebecca Jane, m. John Morse, 1829; and Phineas, 1834. PHINEAS, son of above, married Harriet A., d. of Thomas Paty, 1856, and had Francis Augustus, 1860; Henry Hitchcock, 1864; Edgar, 1870. RICHARD, son of 1st Thomas, Middleboro', m. Mary Simmons of Freetown, 1745, and had Zilpa, 1746, m. Michael Mosher; Jesse, 1747; Richard, m. Lydia Booth and Sarah Booth of Middleboro'. RICHARD, of Boston, m. Abigail Barnes, 1779. RICHARD, m. Mary W. Burt, 1844. SAMUEL, m. Elizabeth Hersey, 1762, and had Experience, 1764; Elizabeth, 1765; Sarah, and Samuel. THOMAS, son of Isaac, m. Naomi Booth of Middleboro', 1714, and had Thomas, m. Rebecca Jones of Yarmouth; Shadrach, 1717, m. Abigail Hoskins of Taunton; Naomi, 1719, m. Josiah Jones; Jonathan, 1723; Richard, 1725; and Hilkiah, 1727, m. Hannah, d. of Timothy Briggs of Taunton. THOMAS, son of

1st Branch, m. Roxanna, d. of John Pierce, and had Meribah, m. Simeon Nickerson; John, and Ruth. THOMAS, Rochester, son of William, m. Nancy Freeman of Rochester, and had Lemuel, m. Florina Leonard; Sarah, m. P. R. W. Pierce; Thomas, m. Mary, d. of George Douglass; Charlotte, m. Anthony K. Whittemore; Mary, m. Arthur O'Neil; Sophronia, m. Leander Sanford; Weldon S., m. Lucy Nightingale and Jane W. Raymond; and Anthony L., m. Helen Thrasher. THOMAS, son of above, m. Mary, d. of George Douglass, and had Mary S., 1846, m. Colman B. Chandler; Philip R., 1848; Laura, 1850, m. Thomas G. Savery; Meriba, 1852; Sarah Thomas, 1853; Charles M., 1856; Thomas J., 1860; and Nellie A. C., 1867. WILLIAM, Rochester, had Thomas; William, m. Cynthia Wing; Dennis; George m. Sophronia, d. of Branch Pierce; John, m. Meriba Gurney; and Robert, m. Lucy Swift,

PITMAN, THOMAS F., m. Nancy F. Bates, 1832.

PITT, WILLIAM, came in the Fortune 1621, and either removed or died before 1627.

PITTS, THOMAS, m. Mary Howard, 1744, and had Mary, 1748.

PLASKET, JOSEPH, born 1746, came to Plymouth with wife Tabithy, and died 1794. His wid. died 1807, leaving a son Joseph living in Nantucket.

POCKNOT, JOSHUA, m., 1754, Sarah Adams, Indians.

POLLARD, JOHN, m., 1702, Lydia Tilson, and had John, 1702; Elizabeth, 1703; Mary, 1706; William, 1708; Lydia, 1710; Thomas, 1712; Hannah, 1719; Benjamin, 1721; Thankful, 1725; William, 1727.

POMPEY, POMPEY, m. Barbara, 1788.

POMROY, EBENEZER, m., 1793, Eliza Mitchell.

PONTUS, WILLIAM, Plymouth, 1633, had Mary, m. James Glass and Philip Delano; Hannah, m. John Churchill and Giles Rickard.

POOL, JOSEPH, Abington, m. Mehitabel Jackson about 1770, and had Perez, m. Lydia Vining; Mary, m. Samuel Reed; Sarah, m. John Wilkes; Mehitabel, m. Thomas Hunt. PEREZ, son of above, removed to Plymouth. He m. Lydia Vining of Abington, and had Calista, m. Samuel Churchill; Mehitabel Jackson, m. Richard Rogers; Lydia Vining, m. Samuel Rogers; Joseph; Perez; Gridley T., m. Elizabeth Cassady; David Vining, m. Caroline, d. of Ichabod Morey.

POPE, ELISHA of Sandwich, m. Lydia Cotton, 1809. RICHARD, son of Thomas, m. Eunice, d. of Rufus Churchill, 1821, and had Richard, 1823; Richard Thomas; William Wallace, 1826; Lydia Covington, 1829, m. John Lawrence; Eunice, 1832, m. Thomas N. Eldridge; Lucy Ann, 1835, m. Thomas Atwood; Rufus H., 1838, m. Hattie P. Williams of Woonsocket; Addie F., m. Charles P. Hatch. THOMAS came to Plymouth, probably from Sandwich, and m., 1793, Mary Howland. He m., 2d, Priscilla Mitchell, 1797, and had Richard, 1798; Thomas, 1800; James; Thomas again; Sally, m. Stephen Turner; and Priscilla, m., 1st, John Mintz, and, 2d, John Dawes of Roxbury, where she now lives. THOMAS had Susanna, m. Jacob Mitchell; Seth, 1647; Thomas, 1651; John, 1652.

PORTER, ASAHEL, m. Harriet Hueston, 1821. JOHN of Abington, m. Eleanor Doten, 1801.

POULDARD, JOHN, m. Lydia Tilson, 1702.

POWERS, ASBURY, from Philadelphia, m. Jane Dey, 1820. SAMUEL, m. Hannah Scott, 1820.

PRATT, BENAJAH, Plymouth, 1654, prob. son of 2d Joshua, m., 1655, Persis Dunham, and had Abigail, 1657; and prob. John, Joseph, Benajah, and Eleazer. BENAJAH, son of above, by wife Mary, had Mary, 1695; Sarah, 1697; Deborah, 1698; Priscilla, 1701; Abigail, 1703. DANIEL, m., 1701, Esther Wright, and had Joshua, and Sarah. He m., 2d, 1706, Mary Washburn. DANIEL, m. Lydia Cobb, and had Lydia, 1760; Hopeful, 1761; William Cobb, 1764; Daniel, 1765; Ruth, 1768; Joshua, 1770. ELEAZER, son of 1st Benajah, m., 1697, Hannah, d. of Alexander Kennedy, and had Hannah, 1699; David, 1702. JOHN, son of 1st Benajah, by wife Margaret, had Benajah, 1686; Ebenezer, 1688; Joanna, 1690; Benajah, 1692; Samuel, 1693; John, 1696; Margaret, 1700; Patience, 1701; Thomas, 1703; Mehitabel, 1705. JONATHAN, perhaps brother of 1st Benajah, m., 1664, Abigail Wood, and had Abigail, 1665; Bathsheba, 1667; Jonathan, 1669; Hannah, 1671; Jabez, 1673; Meletiah, 1676; Bethiah, 1679. JOSEPH, son of 1st Benajah, m. Martha Lazell, and had Persis, 1704. JOSHUA, m., 1806, Ellen Boice. He m., 2d, 1838, Mary Ann Ferguson. Joshua came in the Ann 1623, and by wife Bathsheba had Hannah, m. William Spooner; Benajah, and Jonathan. PHINEAS came, 1622, and settled in Weymouth. He afterwards came to Plymouth, and m. a d. of Cuthbert Cuthbertson, and died in Charlestown 1680, aged 87.

PRENCE, THOMAS, came to Plymouth in the Fortune 1621, son of Thomas of Lechlade, in Gloucestershire, and m., 1624, Patience, d. of William Brewster. His children were Thomas, who went to England; Robert; Rebecca, m. Edmund Freeman; Hannah, m. Nathaniel Mayo and Jonathan Sparrow; Mercy, m. John Freeman; and Sarah, m. Jeremiah Howes of Yarmouth. In 1635, he m., 2d, Mary, d. of William Collier of Duxbury, where he lived for some years, and had Jane, 1637, m., 1661, Mark Snow; Mary, m. John Tracy; Elizabeth, m., 1667, Arthur Howland; and Judith, m. Isaac Barker of Duxbury. In 1662, he m., 3d, Mercy, wid. of Samuel Freeman, and d. of Constant Southworth, and died 1673, aged 72.

PRICE, GEORGE, m., 1773, Abigail Thomas, and had James, 1773; Sarah, 1775; George, 1777. He m., 2d, Susanna Farmer, 1786.

PRIEST, DEGORY, m., 1611, at Leyden, Sarah, wid. of John Vincent, and sister of Isaac Allerton. He came in the Mayflower 1620, and died soon after landing. His wid. m. Cuthbert Cuthbertson, and came to America with her children, Mary and Sarah, and 2d husband, in the Ann 1623. SEWELL, m., 1807, Mary Pitsley.

PRINCE, JAMES, son of Thomas of Kingston, m., 1780, Eunice Foster, and had Polly, 1784; Thomas, 1786; Lydia, 1788, and removed to Providence.

PROCTOR, ISAAC W., m. Elizabeth Drew, 1835.

PROWER, SOLOMON, came in the Mayflower, and died soon.

PULSIFER, ABIEL, m., 1733, Bethiah Cotton, and had Joseph, 1733; Abiel, and Bethiah.

PURDY, JOHN, m., 1811, Deborah Hathaway.

QUACKOM, SAMUEL, m. Kate Shanks, 1734, Indians.

QUAMONY, QUAMONY, slave of Josiah Cotton, m. Kate, slave of John Murdock, 1732. QUAMONY, m. Mary Hampshire, 1732.

QUASH, QUASH, slave of Lazarus LeBaron, m. Phillis, slave of Theophilus Cotton, 1756.

QUOY, QUOY, m. Mercy Peniss, 1742, Indians.

RAFE, JOSHUA, m., 1736, Nab Shanks.

RAMSDEN, DANIEL, son of Joseph, by wife Sarah, had Samuel, 1690; Joseph, 1693; Benjamin, 1699; Hannah, 1700. JOSEPH, m. Rachel, d. of Francis Eaton, 1646, and had Daniel, 1649. He m., 2d, 1661, Mary Savery.

RAND, JAMES, came in the Ann 1623, and disappeared before 1627. SAMUEL, m., 1798, Susanna Atwood.

RANDALL, DOUGHTY, grandson of 2d William, m., 1746, Elizabeth Tilson, and had Enoch, and perhaps others. ELIAS, m., 1832, Sylvia Johnson. ENOCH, son of Doughty, m., 1766, Phebe, d. of Ebenezer Tinkham, and had Enoch, 1767; Phebe, 1769, m. a Bryant; Lucy, 1771, m. a Bryant; William, 1773; Mercy, 1777, m. a Bonney. ENOCH, son of above, m., 1788, Ruth, d. of Robert Dunham, and had Enoch, 1790; William, Sally, Josiah. ENOCH, son of above, m., 1812, Nancy, d. of Thomas Farmer, and had Margaret Paty, 1813, m. Henry Matta; William Thomas, 1814, m. Mary Foster of Canterbury and wid. Sarah Jane Ladd, d. of Joseph Pervier of Franklin, N. H.; Jane, 1817, m. Abner H. Harlow; Enoch, 1819. JOHN, m., 1769, Nancy Bearse. JOSIAH, son of 2d Enoch m. Princis (Bryant), wid. of William Holmes of Duxbury, and had Princis Bryant, 1825; Josiah, 1827; Samuel Thomas, 1829; Judith, 1832. WILLIAM, Rhode Island, 1636, Marshfield, 1637, Scituate, 1640, by wife Elizabeth, had Sarah, 1640; Joseph, 1642; Hannah, 1644; William, 1647; John, 1650; Elizabeth, 1652; Job, 1655; Benjamin, 1656; Isaac, 1658. WILLIAM, Scituate, son of above, by wife Sarah, had Mary, William, John, Abigail, Hannah, Elizabeth. One of these moved to Plympton, and was the father of Doughty above mentioned. WILLIAM, son of 1st Enoch, m., 1801, Hannah Thomas of Kingston. WILLIAM, son of 2d Enoch, m., 1819, Patience, d. of Heman Churchill, and had William, 1820; George, 1822; Charles, 1824; James, 1826. WILLIAM, son of above, removed to Guaymos, Mexico, where he m. Mercedes Basozerval, and had William and Charles.

RANSOM, BENJAMIN, m. Rebecca Finney, 1791. EBENEZER, m. Rebecca Harlow, 1753. JOSHUA, m. Mary Gifford, 1686. JOSHUA, m. Susanna Garner, 1692. ROBERT, by wife Ann, had Abigail, 1691; Robert, 1695; Lydia, 1700; Ebenezer, 1702; and Mary. SAMUEL, m. Mercy Dunham, 1706. SAMUEL, m. Content Merrifield, 1753.

RATTLIFFE, ROBERT, came in the Ann, 1623, with wife and child, and removed or died before 1627.

RAYMOND, ALLEN, son of Caleb, m. Fear Chubbuck, 1816, and had Shadrack A.; Abigail, m. Isaac Swift, and afterwards Nelson W. Brown. ASA, m. Mercy Norris, 1791. CALEB, m. Deborah Harlow, 1782, and had

Caleb, Allen, Isaiah, Calvin; Diana, m. Lemuel Vaughn; Deborah, m. Ellis Shaw; Melissa, m. Dennis Pierce; and Hope, m. a Hartshorn. CALVIN, son of above, m. Polly Cahoon, and had Allen, 1823; Calvin, 1825; Weston, 1829; Seth S., 1831; Micajah, 1832; Josiah, 1834; Cordelia, 1837; and Margana, 1838. He m., 2d, Sarah Douglass, and had Dora and Samuel. CALVIN, by wife Betsey, had Lewis, 1833; Lucy, 1840. CHARLES, m. Jerusha Clark, 1818. CHARLES, son of 1st George, m. Eunice Morton Atwood, and had Charles Anthony. CLARK, m. Sarah Hall, 1797. EDGAR C., son of 1st George, m. Mary Grace Hughes, and had Mary Ellen, m. Edwin L. Edes and William Hughes. ELEAZER SEABURY, son of 1st George, m. Mercy Warren, d. of Thomas McLaughlin, and had Adelaide, m. Charles Barnes; Priscilla; Robert N.; and Joseph E., m. a Bird. EZEKIEL, m. Sarah Perkins, 1778, and had Perkins. GEORGE, born 1782, from Boston, m. Priscilla Shaw of Middle-boro', and had George, 1804; Charles, 1806; William S., 1807; Eleazer Seabury, 1809; Newell, 1811; Priscilla, 1813, m. Seth McLaughlin; Harvey S., 1815; Phebe S., 1818, m. Jonathan Douglass Dike; Anna R., 1820, m. Joseph M. Bradford of Falmouth; Charles, 1823; and Edgar C., 1825. GEORGE, son of above, m. Lydia A. Atwood, 1829, and had Frederick Augustus Sumner, m. Maria Brewster of Duxbury; George LeBaron, m. Mary Hall of Boston; Hannah Wheatley, Charles Moore, Margaret Hodge, and Benjamin Gleason. HARVEY S., son of 1st George, m. Betsey Allen, d. of Anthony Dike, and had George Anthony, m. Nellie Reed. ISAIAH, son of Caleb, m. Jane Nickerson, and had Adoniram, m. Betsey Swift; James, m. a Swift; Isaiah, m. Sarah Valler; Otis H., m. Almira Hall; Emeline, m. Shadrack A. Raymond; Susan, m. Stephen Cahoon; Jane, m. Wheldon Pierce; and Lucinda, m. Joseph Hathaway. LEMUEL, m. Betsey Caswell, 1819. NEWELL, son of 1st George, m. Celia Nye Bradford of Falmouth, and had Cordelia A., m. Leander Baker of Falmouth; Mary C., Joseph N., Edgar C. He m., 2d, wid. Anna (Richardson) Thomas of Freetown, and had Anna Newell. PERKINS, son of Ezekiel, by wife Elizabeth, had Eliza, 1803; Melissa, 1805; Lucy, 1808; Lewis, 1811; Sally, 1814; Samuel Abbot, 1818; Irena; 1822; David Drew, 1824; Eunice Sturtevant, 1827. STEPHEN, m. Elizabeth Holmes, 1785. WILLIAM S., son of 1st George, m., 1829, Mary C., wid. of Samuel Churchill, and had William Francis and Emily Jane, both of whom went with their father to Illinois.

READ, or REED, JAMES, by wife Lucy, had Betsey, 1789; James, 1791; Polly, 1794; Ruth, 1796; Lemuel Fish, 1800, m. Eunice Holmes; Samuel, 1803; Hezekiah, 1805; Henry, 1808; Sally, 1811. JAMES, son of above, m., 1812, Sally, d. of Silas Hathaway, and had James Hathaway, 1813; Silas, 1815; Silas, 1817; Lemuel, 1819; Lucy, 1820; Joseph Allen, 1822; Sarah J., 1825. JOHN, from Boston, m. Mercy, d. of Nathaniel Goodwin, 1780. LEVI, m., 1798, Lucy Doten. NATHAN, m., 1793, Lydia Bartlett, and, 1796, Rebecca Morton.

REDING, MOSES, m. Sarah Jones, 1766, and had Sarah, 1767; Brace, 1769; and Bennet, 1771. He m., 2d, Priscilla Rider, 1776.

RENELLS, JOEL, m. Polly Bartlett, 1824.

RENOFF, CHARLES, of Rehoboth, m. Mercy Doten, 1780.

REVIS, JAMES, m. Deliverance Abrahams, 1703.

REYNER, JOHN, came over 1635. He m. in England a Boyes, by whom
he had Jachin; and Hannah, m. Job Lane of Malden. He m., 2d, 1642,
Frances Clark, and had John; Joseph, 1650; Elizabeth, Dorothy, Abigail, and
Judith.

RICE, JUDSON W., m., 1829, Almira, d. of William Weston.

RICH, ISAAC B., from Charlestown, m. Sarah Holbrook, d. of Isaac Tribble, 1831, and had Louisa Azubah, 1833, m. Albert Hobart of Braintree;
Helen Baker, 1835; Sarah Holbrook, 1840; Mary Covington, 1843. JERE-
MIAH, m. Jane S. Taylor, 1814. WALTER, by wife Rebecca, had Elizabeth,
1734; Nathaniel, 1735; Eleazer, 1737; Rebecca, 1739; Ebenezer, 1741; Ann,
1745. He m., 2d, Experience Totman, 1751.

RICHARDS, JOHN, probably son of William, by wife Mary, had Mary, 1677;
Lydia, 1681; John, 1681; Josiah, 1683; Mary, 1687; Joanna, 1691, Abigail,
1694; Rebecca, 1699. THOMAS, Dorchester, 1630, removed to Weymouth,
and died about 1650, leaving a wid., Wealthian, and children James and
John, born in England, the latter of whom m. Elizabeth, wid. of Adam Winthrop, and d. of Thomas Hawkins; Samuel; Joseph; Benjamin, m. Hannah,
d. of William Hudson; Mary, m. Thomas Hinckley; Ann, m. Ephraim
Hunt; Alice, m. William Bradford of Plymouth; and Hannah. WILLIAM,
perhaps brother of Thomas, Plymouth, Scituate, and Weymouth, by wife
Grace, had John; Joseph; James, 1658; and Benjamin, 1660.

RICHMOND, ALPHEUS, son of 1st Simon, born about 1785, m. 1806, Abigail
Simmons, and had Alpheus, 1806, m. Ruth Dupee; Abigail Simmons, 1809,
m. Henry Eddy; William R., 1814; and John A., 1818, m. Isabella N. Towns.
CALVIN, son of 1st Simon, m., 1808, Sally Jackson, and had Olive Shaw,
Elijah, Sylvanus Bisbee, and William Briggs. ELIAB, probably brother of
1st Simon, came to Plymouth about 1770, and m. Hannah Holmes, 1773.
MICAH, nephew of Solomon, and belonging to a distinct branch from that of
Simon, though perhaps both find their root in the early Taunton family,
came to Plymouth from Weymouth about 1820, m. Emily, d. of William
Bradford, and had Hannah Sumner, Henry Bradford, Lucy Palmer, and
William. SIMON, came to Plymouth about 1770, with wife Salome, and had
Alpheus, Nathan; Henry, m. Submit Wetherell, 1795; Simon, Calvin, Wil-
liam; Nancy, m. George Manter; Deborah; Hannah, m. John Atwood, 1806,
and, 2d, Joseph Burgess; Sally, m. Joseph Burgess; and Mary, m. Reuben
Richmond, 1817. SIMON, son of above, m., 1800, Lydia A. Simmons, and
had Anderson Simmons, 1803; and Susan Williams, 1806. SOLOMON, uncle
of Micah, came to Plymouth early in this century, m., 1823, Anna, d. of William Bradford, sister of Emily, the wife of his nephew, and had Thomas
Hinckley, Anna, and Betsey Reliance. WILLIAM R., son of Alpheus, m.
Ellen Ishmael, and had Mary Ellen, 1847; William H., 1847; Mary Ellen,
1849; John A., 1851; Anderson, 1854.

RICKARD, ABNER, son of 2d Eleazer, by wife Susanna, had Lemuel, m.
Abigail Shurtleff, 1803, and lived in Croyden, N. H.; Ezra, 1770, of Vermont,
m. Susanna Barrows; Elijah; Abner, 1777, m. Lydia King of Plymouth;
Susan, 1775, m. Elijah Hall, 2d, a Hart, and, 3d, a Sawins; Sally, 1772, m.

Samuel Sawins. ABNER, son of above, m. Lydia King, 1797, and moved to
Canada, having Abner, Simeon, Lydia, Sophia, and perhaps others. AN-
SELM, m. Margaret, d. of Benjamin Drew, 1795, and had Anselm, 1798, m.
Cynthia Lucas, 1820. ELEAZER, son of 2d Giles, by wife Sarah, had Sarah,
1688; Judith, 1701; Lydia, 1704; Tabitha, 1707, m. James Barrows; Joanna,
1709; Eleazer, 1712. ELEAZER, Plympton, son of above, by wife Mary, had
Mercy, 1740, m. James Wright; Mary, 1747, m. Consider Chase; Sarah,
1749, m. Perez Wright; Kesiah, 1753, m. Joseph Ransom; Deborah, 1758;
Eleazer; Abner; and Elijah, 1756. ELIJAH, son of above, moved to New
Hampshire, and had Eleazer, 1790; Ira; Jonathan, 1787; Hannah; and Deborah, 1788. ELIJAH, son of 1st Abner, lived in New Hampshire, m. Content,
d. of Joseph Ransom of Carver, and had Mary, m. Josiah Osborne of Westmore-
land, N. H., and Winthrop Gilman Torrey of North Barton, N. H.; Miranda;
Ransom; Freeman W. of Plymouth, m. Adeline W. Hart; Warren; and Winslow of Plymouth, m. Cordelia Hart. He m., 2d, Lucy Durkee of Newport, N. H.
EZRA, son of 1st Abner, m. Susanna Barrows of Vermont, and had Levi,
Polly, Salmon, Charity, Cyrus, Rosamond, Alvira, Durancy, Susan, and Persis, all of whom lived in New Hampshire. GILES, 1637, Plymouth, by wife
Judith, had Giles, John, and Sarah, who, perhaps, m. George Paddock. He
m., 2d, 1662, Joan Tilson, and, 3d, 1669, Hannah, wid. of John Churchill,
and d. of William Pontus. GILES, son of above, m., 1651, Hannah, d. of
John Dunham, and had John, 1652; Giles, Eleazer, Henry; Samuel, 1662;
Abigail, m. a Whiting; Hannah, m. Ebenezer Eaton; Mercy; Judith, m.
Joseph Faunce; and Josiah. GILES, son of above, m. Hannah, probably d.
of Nicholas Snow, 1683, and appears by his will to have only had an adopted
child, Desire Doten. GILES, Kingston, son of Josiah, by wife Mary, had
Nathaniel, 1725; Hannah, 1727; Susanna, 1730; Solomon, Mary, Lucy, Cor-
nelius, Rebecca, and John. HENRY, Plympton, son of 2d Giles, m. Mercy
Morton, 1708, and had Henry, Elkanah; Judith, m. James Fuller; Bethiah, m.
John Chandler of Duxbury; and Mercy, m. Jonathan Weston. HENRY,
son of 1st Samuel, by wife Alice, had Samuel, 1724; Judah, 1725; Isaac, 1728.
ISAAC, Plympton, son of 1st Lemuel, m. Lydia, d. of Daniel Vaughn of Car-
ver, and had Lydia, 1778; Elizabeth, 1780; Mary, 1782; Isaac, 1784; Persis
Harlow, 1786; Lazarus, 1788; Elizabeth, 1791; Lemuel, 1792; Isaac, 1794;
Daniel Vaughn, 1797; Warren, 1800. ISAAC, Plympton, son of above, m.
Nancy, wid. of Lemuel Rickard, and had Isaac, 1829; Henry, 1831, m. Zilpa
Sherman of Carver; Giles, 1833; Nancy Bagnall, 1834, m. Isaac T. Hall of
Plymouth; Martin, 1836, m. Priscilla Churchill of Plympton; Lemuel, 1838;
and Warren, 1841, m. Maria, d. of William Nickerson of Plymouth. JAMES,
probably son of 2d John, m. Hannah Howland, 1720, and had James, 1721;
John, 1723; Benjamin, 1726; Lothrop, 1731; William, 1733; Hannah, 1737.
JOHN, son of 1st Giles, m., 1651, Esther, d. of John Barnes, and had John,
1657; Mary, m. Isaac Cushman; and Lydia. JOHN, son of above, by wife
Mary, had John, 1679; Mercy, 1682, m. a Cushing; John, 1684; Esther, 1691;
James, 1696; and Elizabeth, m. Eben Doggett. JOHN, son of above, by wife
Sarah, had James, 1706; Margaret, 1708; Mary, 1709; Meriah, 1711. JOHN,
son of 2d Giles, had Mary, 1677; John, 1681; Joseph, 1683; Mary, 1687, m.

an Eddy; Lydia, 1682, m. a Tilson; Johanna, 1691, m. a Dunham; Abigail, 1694; and Rebecca, 1699, m. a Pratt. JOHN, son of James, m. Bathsheba Morton, 1748, and had Bathsheba, 1750; John Howland, 1752; Mary, 1754; Benjamin, 1756; Thomas, 1758. JOHN, m. Lydia King, 1769. JOHN, m. Lucy Haskins, 1806. JONATHAN, Plympton, son of Simeon, m. Susanna, d. of Lemuel Cole, and had Jonathan, 1829; James Cole, 1830; Phebe Ann, 1833; Simeon, 1841. JOSEPH, Plympton, son of 4th John, m. Deborah Miller, 1707, and had Deborah, 1707; Priscilla, 1710; Mary, 1711; Joseph, 1713; John, 1715; Silas, 1717; Solomon, 1719: William, 1720; Japhet, 1723; Abigail, 1724; Jacob, 1726; Sabia, 1731. JOSIAH, Plympton, son of 2d Giles, m. Rebecca, d. of Benjamin Eaton, 1699, and had Giles, 1700; Benjamin, 1702; Josiah, 1703; Desire, 1706, m. a Frasier; Rebecca, 1708; David, 1711; and Deborah, m. an Ellis. LAZARUS, son of 2d Samuel, m. Molly Everson, and had Samuel, 1755. LAZARUS, son of 1st Isaac, m. Lucy, d. of John Dunham of Carver, and had Lucy Faxon, 1813; Lazarus Warren, 1815; Hiram, 1818; Louisa, 1821; Isaac Winslow, 1824; Naomi Lucas, 1826; Benjamin Crocker, 1829; Lydia, 1832. LEMUEL, Plympton, son of 2d Samuel, m. Persis, d. of James Harlow, and had Content, 1751, m. Nathaniel Pratt and Joseph Atwood; Mehitabel, 1752, m. Nehemiah Cobb; Isaac, 1754; Abigail, 1756, m. Ambrose Shaw. LEMUEL, son of 1st Abner, m. Abigail Shurtleff of Carver, 1803, moved to Croyden, New Hampshire, and had Alvin, Abigail, Ruel, Louisa, and Freeman, who was a physician in Woburn. LEMUEL, son of 3d Samuel, m. Nancy, d. of Nicholas Spinks Bagnall, and had Samuel, 1819, m. Lois Davis; and Deborah, 1821, m. Isaac S. Holmes. SAMUEL, Plympton, son of 2d Giles, m. Rebecca, probably d. of Nicholas Snow, 1689, and had Rebecca, 1691; Hannah, 1693; Samuel; Bethiah, 1698; Henry, 1700; Mary, 1702; Elkanah, 1704, m. Keturah Bishop; Mehitabel, 1707; Eleazer, 1709. SAMUEL, son of above, by wife Rachel, had Lemuel, 1722; Theophilus, 1726; Samuel, 1728, m. Ruth, d. of Robert Cushman; Lazarus, 1730; Elizabeth, 1732; Rachel, 1736; and Rebecca, 1740. SAMUEL, son of Theophilus, m. Priscilla, d. of Cornelius Holmes, 1786, and had Lemuel, 1788; Theophilus, 1789; Priscilla, 1791; Hannah, 1792; Samuel, 1795; Betsey, 1796; Ruth, 1798. SIMEON, son of Theophilus, m. Rebecca, d. of William Bartlett, and had Sylvia, 1794, m. Charles Cobb of Carver; Rebecca, 1795; Simeon, 1797; Hannah Harlow, 1799; Hannah Harlow again, 1801; Jonathan, 1804; Rachel, 1807; Abigail Harlow, 1809; Eliza, 1811. THEOPHILUS, son of 2d Samuel, m. Hannah, d. of James Harlow, and had Mary, 1749; Hannah, 1751, m. Timothy Cobb; Jonathan, 1753; Betty, 1754, m. Elijah Rickard; Lemuel, 1757: Rebecca, 1759, m. Ebenezer Doten of Carver; Sylvia, 1761, m. Daniel Vaughn; Theophilus, 1763; Samuel, 1764; Simeon, 1766; Ruth, 1768. WILLIAM, son of James, had James and John.

RIDER, AMOS, son of 1st Benjamin, m., 1743, a wife Ruth, and had Thomas, 1744; and Amos, m. Mehitabel Oliver. BENJAMIN, son of 2d Samuel, m. Hannah Rider, and had Amos, 1720; Lydia, 1722; Hannah, 1723; Benjamin, 1724; Abigail, 1726; Elizabeth, 1727; Stevens, 1728; Jesse, 1731; William, 1732; Mary, 1733, m. a Packer; Sarah, 1735, m. Ebenezer Rider. BENJAMIN, son of above, m., 1749, Betty Bartlett, and had Stephen, 1750;

Betty, 1752; Mary, 1754; Priscilla, 1756; Jesse, 1758. BENJAMIN, son of
1st Joseph, m., 1775, Patience, d. of John Howland, and had Patience, 1777,
m. George Sampson; Abigail, 1779, m. Jacob Joslin. CALEB, son of 1st
George, m., 1817, Harriet, d. of William Holmes, and had Caleb, George,
James, and Deborah. He m., 2d, Rosamond, d. of Alden Washburn.
CHARLES, son of 1st John, by wife Rebecca, had Lucy, 1742; Jean, 1744;
Charles, 1748; Rebecca, 1750, m. Thomas Sears; Elkanah, 1752. DANIEL,
son of 1st Job, m., 1810, Lydia, d. of Nathaniel Clark, and had Daniel, m.
Sarah H., d. of Joseph Jennings; and Rebecca. EBENEZER, son of 1st John,
m., 1726, Thankful, d. of Joseph Sylvester, and had Lydia, 1729, m. William
Sutton; Ebenezer, 1731, m. Sarah Rider; John, 1733, m. Priscilla Churchill;
Thankful, 1735. EZEKIEL, son of 3d Samuel, m., 1737, Margaret Churchill,
and had Keziah, 1737; Joseph, 1739; Deborah, 1740; Samuel, 1741; Lemuel,
1743; Patience, 1744; Lemuel, 1745; Ezekiel, 1746; Margaret, 1749; Ezekiel,
1751; Sarah, 1752; Joshua, 1755, m. Hannah Howland; Ezra, 1757. He m.,
2d, 1762, Lydia Atwood, and had Seth, 1765; Ezra, 1766. EZEKIEL, son of
6th Samuel, m., 1803, Polly Holmes, and had Ezekiel, m. Hannah Everson;
Harriet, m. Curtis Hoyt; Phebe Thomas, m. Eliab Wood. GEORGE, son of
6th Samuel, m., 1791, Deborah Chandler, and had Caleb, George; Lucia W.,
m. Nathan Bacon Robbins. GEORGE, son of above, m., 1831, Jane Church-
ill, and had Sarah Jane, 1832; Helen Maria, 1833; George Sylvester, 1835;
William E., 1838; and Charles. JESSE, son of 1st Benjamin, m., 1754,
Bethiah Thomas, and had Bethiah, 1755; James, 1756. JOB, son of 1st
Joseph, m., 1772, Rebecca W., d. of Daniel Diman, and had Joseph, 1773;
Rebecca, 1777; Elizabeth, 1779; Job, 1782; Daniel, 1784; Southworth, 1787;
Merrick, 1789; David, 1793; Thomas, 1797. JOB, son of above, m., 1808,
Sally, d. of William Cassidy, and had Sally, 1809, m. John C. Bennett; Lydia
Wm., 1811, m. Stephen C. Drew; Joseph, 1813, m. Joanna Drew; Job, 1815;
Betsey, 1817; Thomas, 1821, m. Betsey Hutchinson; Henry Cassidy, 1825.
JOB, son of above, m., 1838, Sally, d. of Ebenezer Holmes, and had Anna R.,
m. James Johnson and William A. Loveland; Samuel T., m. Eva L. Pooley.
JOHN, son of 1st Samuel, by wife Hannah, had Sarah, 1694; Mercy, 1696, m.
William Harlow; Samuel, 1698; Jolin, 1700; Ebenezer, 1702. By a 2d wife,
Mary, he had Hannah, 1707; John, 1709; Sarah, 1712, m. Jonathan Freeman;
Elizabeth, 1714, m. Sylvanus Cobb; Mary, 1716, m. John Harlow; Charles,
1718; Jerusha, and Rebecca. JOHN, son of above, m., 1734, Mary Drew, and
had Micah, 1737; Hannah, 1738; Elizabeth, 1740; Mary, 1742; Seth, 1745;
Nathaniel, 1747; William; Micah, 1752; Phebe, 1755, m. Rufus Sherman of
Plympton. JOSEPH, son of 2d Samuel, m., 1722, Abigail, d. of Benjamin
Warren; and had William, 1723; Abigail, 1726; Joseph, 1729; Hannah, 1731;
Benjamin, 1733; Tilden, 1736. He prob. m. 2d, 1740, Elizabeth Crosman,
and had Hannah, 1740, m. Joseph Barnes; Mary, 1741, m. a Leonard; Nathaniel, 1744; Job, 1746; Elizabeth, 1748, m. Lemuel Drew; Bathsheba, 1750, m.
Zadock Churchill; Sarah, 1753; Desire, 1755, m. Thomas Goodwin; Phebe,
1757; Huldah, 1760. JOSEPH, son of above, by wife Thankful, had Samuel,
1752; Samuel, 1754, m. Anna Dunham; Hannah, 1760, m. Sylvanus Sturtevant. JOSEPH, son of 1st Ezekiel, m., 1767, Abigail, d. of John Atwood,

and had Joseph, 1768; William, 1772; Michael, 1775; Margaret, 1777; Abigail, 1779; Benjamin; Joanna, 1781; William, 1784. JOSEPH, m., 1709, Mary Southworth. JOSIAH, son of 2d Samuel, by wife Experience, had Lemuel, 1723; Experience, 1725, m. a Barnes; Ruth, 1727, m. a Robinson; Sarah, 1728; Mary, 1732, m. a Sargent; Isaac, 1734, m. Bridget Nash; Lydia, 1737, m. an Elmes; Mercy, 1740; Josiah, 1742; Thomas, 1744; Caleb, 1746, m. Hannah McFarland. MERRICK, son of 1st Job, m., 1815, Lucy Delano, and had Lucy Merrick, 1817; Elizabeth Lyman, 1825; Arabella, 1835. SAMUEL, Yarmouth, 1643, m., 1656, Sarah, d. of Robert Bartlett of Plymouth, and had Samuel, 1657; John, 1663. By a 1st wife, he had Mary, 1647; and Elizabeth, m. John Cole. SAMUEL, son of above, removed to Plymouth, and m., 1680, Lydia, d. of Joseph Tilden, and had Hannah, 1680, m. Jeremiah Jackson; Sarah, 1682, m. John Bramhall; William, 1684; Lydia, 1686, m. Elisha Cobb; Samuel, 1688; Elizabeth, 1690; Joseph, 1691; Benjamin, 1693; Mary, 1694; Elizabeth, 1695; Josiah, 1696; Abigail, 1700. SAMUEL, son of above, m., 1713, Ann Eldreden, and had Keziah, 1714; Ezekiel, 1715; Samuel, 1717. SAMUEL, son of 1st John, m., 1722, Mary, d. of Joseph Sylvester, and had Meriah, 1724; Hannah, 1726; Mary, 1728; Sarah, 1730, m. Ezra Stetson of Rochester; Lois, 1732; Samuel, 1735; Martha, 1737; Deborah, 1741. SAMUEL, Rochester, who died 1762, by wife Rebecca, had Samuel, Seth; Rebecca, m. a Jackson; John; Bethiah, m. a Jenney; Esther, m. a Tobey; Lydia, m. a Dexter; Hannah, m. a Jenney. SAMUEL, son of 1st Ezekiel, m. Jane Swift about 1765, and had George, Samuel, and Ezekiel. SAMUEL, West Bridgewater, son of 2d Joseph, m., 1794, Ann, d. of George Dunham, and had Samuel, Lewis, William, and others. SETH, son of 1st Ezekiel, m., 1787, Hannah Bartlett, and had Seth, 1788; Hannah, 1789. He m., 2d, 1790, Sally Bartlett, and had Mary, 1792; Esther, 1794; John, 1797; Nathaniel, 1801. WILLIAM, son of 1st Joseph, m., 1749, Betty Bartlett, and had Hallet, 1760. WILLIAM, son of 2d John, m., 1780, Lydia Churchill, and had Lydia, m. Atwood Drew; Mary, m. Richard Holmes. WILLIAM, Brockton, son of 7th Samuel, m., 1834, Mary R., d. of Seth Snow, and had William Snow, 1835. He m., 2d, Lucretia, d. of Lewis Ames of West Bridgewater, and had William, 1844; Walter Brooks, 1849; Henry Herbert, 1853.

RIDGEBI, JOHN, m., 1806, Sarah Leonard.

RIGDALE, JOHN, came in the Mayflower with wife Alice, and both died the first winter.

RING, ANDREW, came from England with a widowed mother, sister Elizabeth, m. Stephen Dean, and perhaps brother William, prob. about 1629, m. Deborah, d. of Stephen Hopkins, 1646, and had William, Eleazer; Mary, m. a Morton; Deborah, Susanna; Elizabeth, 1652, m. a Mayo of Eastham; Samuel. He m., 2d, Lettys, wid. of John Morton. ANDREW, Kingston, son of Eleazer, by wife Zerviah, had Andrew, 1727; Mary, 1725; Susanna, 1730. DANIEL, Kingston, son of Francis, m. Sally E. Soule, and had Daniel, and Lydia. ELEAZER, son of 1st Andrew, m., 1687, Mary Shaw, and had Eleazer, 1688; Andrew, 1689; Phebe, 1691, m. Ichabod Standish; Samuel, 1694; Andrew, 1696; Deborah, 1698, m. John Fuller; Mary, 1700, m. a Sampson; Jonathan, 1702; Susanna, 1705, m. a Bosworth; Elkanah, 1706; Elizabeth, and Lydia. FRANCIS, Kingston, son of 3d Samuel, m. Mary Morton, and had Samuel, Daniel; Andrew, 1773; Rufus, 1774; Mary, 1776; Lucy, 1781; Francis, Ruth Sylvester, and Susan. GEORGE, Kingston, son of 3d Samuel, m. Lucy Chipman, and had Louisa, 1748; Samuel, 1750; Lucy, 1751; George; Marcus, 1760; Sherah. JONATHAN, Kingston, son of Eleazer, m., 1748, Sarah Mitchell, and had Andrew, 1748; Eleazer, 1749; Joseph, 1751; Sarah, 1754; Jonathan, 1757; Molly, 1760; Elkanah, 1762. JOSEPH, m. Mercy Dunham, and had Nathaniel, 1735. SAMUEL, son of 1st Andrew, by wife Sarah, had Sarah, 1670; Joanna, 1672; Samuel, 1674; Mehitabel, 1676; Bethiah, 1678; Joseph, 1680; John, 1683; Eleazer, 1685; Isaac, 1688; Martha, 1694. SAMUEL, son of above, m. Bethiah King, and had Joanna, 1697; Joseph, 1699; Rebecca, 1700; Lydia, 1704. SAMUEL, Kingston, prob. son of Eleazer, m. Ruth Sylvester, and had George, 1726; Grace, 1730, m. Samuel Bradford; Lydia, 1730, m. William Ripley; Mary, 1732; Samuel, 1734; Elizabeth, 1736, m. Samuel Hunt; Francis, 1738; Louisa, 1740; Eliphas, 1743, m. Rebecca Weston; Eleazer, 1744. SAMUEL, Kingston, son of Francis, m. Lydia Freeman, and had Mary, Elizabeth, Samuel. WILLIAM, son of 1st Andrew, m., 1693, Hannah Sherman, and had Deborah, 1696; Hannah, 1697; William, 1699; Elizabeth, 1701, m. a Prince; Eleazer, 1705; Deborah, 1708.

RIPLEY, ALEXANDER, m. Hannah S. Flemmons, 1816. CALVIN, son of 1st Luther, m. Betsey, d. of Timothy Allen. DAVID, Jr., of Plympton, m. Hannah W. Cuff, 1804. JOHN, m. Lucy Doten, 1787. JOSEPH SHURTLEFF, m. Phebe Persons, 1809. LEVI of Kingston, son of Jairus of Pawtucket, m. Mary Covington, 1804. LUTHER, son of Jairus of Pawtucket, m. Polly Simmons, and had Luther, 1807; and Calvin, 1808. LUTHER, son of above, m. Lydia, d. of William Barnes, 1832. NEHEMIAH, perhaps son of Nathaniel of Hingham, m. Sarah Atwood, 1728, and had Peter, 1729; Nehemiah, 1733; Nathaniel, 1743; Experience, 1747. NATHANIEL, son of above, m. Elizabeth, Bartlett, 1766, and had Nathaniel, 1767; Elizabeth, 1773; William Putnam, 1775; Levitt, 1787. RUFUS of Kingston, m. Mary Shurtleff, 1763. SYLVANUS of Plympton, m. Sally Sherman, 1818. THADDEUS, m. Mary Shurtleff, 1787. URIAH, m. Sarah King, 1795. WILLIAM, m. Chloe Thrasher, 1812. WILLIAM PUTNAM, son of Nathaniel, m. Mary Briggs, and had William Zebina, m. Adeline B, Cushman. He m., 2d, Anna, d. of Nathaniel Winslow of Hanover, and had Ann Eliza, m. Andrew March; Nancy Winslow, 1815; and Winslow. He m., 3d, Elizabeth Foster Morton of Pembroke, and had Betsey Foster Morton, m. Charles Nichols of Boston. He m., 4th, wid. Nancy March, and had no children. ZENAS, son of Jairus of Pawtucket, m. Lydia Simmons, 1807, and had Lydia, m. John Chase.

ROBBINS, AMMI RUHAMA, Norfolk, Conn., son of Philemon of Branford, m., 1762, Elizabeth, d. of Lazarus LeBaron, and lived in Norfolk. He had Philemon, 1763; Philemon, 1764; Elizabeth, 1766; Mary, 1767; Ammi Ruhama, 1768; Elizabeth, 1770; Nathaniel, 1772; Francis LeBaron, 1775; Thomas, 1777; Sarah, 1779, m. Joseph Battell; James Watson, 1782; Samuel, 1784; Francis LeBaron, 1787. ANSEL, son of Ebenezer, m., 1791, Hannah, d. of Lemuel Cobb, and had Ansel, 1791; James, 1793; Stephen, 1795; Harvey, 1797; Lemuel, 1799; Betsey, 1801; Thaddeus, 1803; Levi, 1806; Hannah,

1808; John Flavel, 1810, m. Margaret E. Harvey; Milton, and Fear Cobb. ANSEL, son of above, m. Joanna, d. of Benjamin Seymour, and had Fanny, m. Josiah Bartlett; and Joanna. BENJAMIN, son of 1st Rufus, m., 1789, Esther, d. of John Allen, and had Esther Allen, 1791; Betsey, 1792; Benjamin, 1795; Sally, 1797; Nancy, 1799; William Allen, 1802, m. Martha Washburn of Kingston. CHANDLER, pastor of First Church, son of Philemon of Branford, came to Plymouth 1760. He was pub., 1760, to Mrs. Thankful Hubbard of Guilford, Conn. He m., 1761, Jane Prince, and had Chandler, 1762, m. Harriet, d. of Thomas Lothrop; Jenny, 1764, m. Francis LeBaron Goodwin; Hannah, 1765; George, 1767; Hannah, 1768, m. Benjamin J. Gilman of Marietta; Isaac, 1770; Philemon, 1777; Samuel Prince, 1778, settled in Marietta; Peter Gilman, 1781. CHANDLER, son of Lemuel, m., 1816, Eleanor, d. of Peter Holmes, and had Mary Atwood, m. S. Dexter Fay of Westboro'; Ellen, m. Plympton R. Otis of Westboro'; Chandler, Mercy Ann, and John Brooks. CHANDLER, Carver, son of 1st Joseph, m., 1822, Sarah, d. of John Burgess, and had Chandler, 1824, m. Bathsheba Williams; Sarah B., 1830, m. Charles Shaw; John Sprague, 1832; Joseph S., 1835, m. Lucy Ripley; Benjamin W., 1835, m. Lydia Hammond; Alfred B., 1836. CHARLES, son of 1st Rufus, m., 1793, Mary, d. of Nathan Bacon, and had Charles, 1795; Nathan Bacon, 1797; Leavitt Taylor, 1799. CONSIDER, Carver, son of Ebenezer, m. Abigail Bartlett, and had Hammatt, 1793; Saba, 1795; Bartlett, 1798; Abigail Finney, 1800; Constance, 1802; Isaac, 1804; Ebenezer, 1806; Eleazer, 1808. DANIEL JACKSON, son of 1st Josiah, m. Elizabeth C., d. of James Ruggles of Rochester, 1854, and had Catherine R., m. James Warren of New York; and Charles S., 1859. EBENEZER, son of 2d Jeduthan, m. Eunice Fuller of Kingston, 1760, and had Levi, 1761; Ebenezer, 1762; Thaddeus, 1764; Consider, 1766; James, 1767, m. Olive King; Ansel, 1769; Levi, 1771. He m., 2d, Mercy (Harlow) Doten, wid. of Elisha, 1781, and had Ebenezer, m. Mercy Bartlett; George H.; Betsey, m. Sylvanus Smith; Benjamin, m. Betsey Thomas of Middleboro'. EDMUND, son of William, m., 1830, Nancy B., d. of John B. Chandler, and had Edmund, 1831, m. Rosilla B. Oldham; Nancy W., 1832, m. Charles Beal; William T., 1835, m. Martha Jane Batchelder, and wid. Martha Jane (Goodwin) Daniel, both of Maine; Francis Henry, 1837, m. Sarah J. B., d. of Isaac S. Holmes; Charles Augustus, 1839, m. Mercy C., d. of Nathaniel Carver Barnes; Lucilla M., 1841; George F., 1843; Herbert, 1845, m. Abbie F. Cole; Hannah C., m. Jacob Atwood. ELEAZER, Plympton, son of 2d Jeduthan, m. Rebecca Jackson, 1747, and had Rebecca, m. John Fuller; Consider; Sarah, m. Willard Sears; Seth, Sylvanus, Eleazer; Jemima, m. Samuel Lucas; Mary, and Elizabeth. ELEAZER, Carver, son of above, by wife Sarah, had Ruth, 1777; Olive, 1779; Sarah, 1781; Lois, 1783; Rebecca, 1783; Abigail, 1785; Charlotte, 1789; Jeduthan, 1791; Eleazer, 1793; Melinda, 1797. FREDERICK, son of 1st Samuel, m. Jane, d. of Ebenezer Davie, and had Mary Jane, 1828; Charles Frederick, 1830; Isabella Graham, 1834. FREDERICK W., son of 1st Josiah, m. Mary D. Wade of Charlestown, 1850, and had Frederick W., 1852; Mary Wade, 1854; John Wade, 1855; George J., 1858, m. Nettie H. Thomas; Eugene, 1859; Annie E., 1861; Annie, 1862; and Abby. GEORGE H., son of

Ebenezer, m. Betsey Churchill, 1806, and had George Edwin, 1809; Thomas; Elizabeth, 1812, m. Isaac L. Wood; Harriet Newell, 1814, m. Levi Robbins; Samuel B. Franklin, 1818; George Edwin again, 1820, m. Sarah Byron of Taunton; and Amasa, 1822, m. Susan Bates of Braintree. GEORGE T., son of 1st Josiah, m. Lydia J. Cotton of Leominster, and had George E., 1861. HEMAN C., son of Jesse, m. Mary Ann, d. of Thomas Spear, 1832, and had Mary Elizabeth, 1833; Almira F., 1834, m. John T. Oldham; Jesse L., 1836, m. Mary C. Holmes; Caroline A., 1837, m. Stimson Dunton; Charles Henry, 1839; Heman, 1841, m. Harriet E. Eddy; and Clarissa, 1844. HENRY, son of 1st Samuel, m., 1816, Margaret Harper Banks, and had Francis H., 1821, m. Nancy, d. of William Bradford. He m., 2d, Betsey, d. of Amaziah Churchill, 1831, and had Edward L., 1836, m. Mercy J., d. of William Paulding; Martha Churchill, 1839, m. Charles T. Holmes; Henry H., 1840, and Margaret H., 1843, m. Frederick L. Holmes. HENRY HOWARD, son of 2d Rufus, m. Mercy, d. of John Eddy, and had Charles Henry, m. Mary, d. of James Buffington of Fall River; Mercy, 1841; Margaret, 1844; Augusta, Jane, Fanny, and John. HORATIO, son of 2d Samuel, m. Mrs. Mary Dilloway, 1837, and had Ann Maria, 1838; Pamelia, 1840; and Pamelia again, 1841. ISAAC, son of 1st Samuel, m. Elizabeth, d. of Thomas Rogers, 1826, and had Isaac Marshall, 1826, m. Eliza T., d. of James Haskins; James Hewett, 1830, m. Abby, d. of Stephen Westgate; Curtis Holmes, 1832; Sarah Elizabeth, m. Samuel B. Chandler, and Albert R. JEDUTHAN, Plympton, son of John, m. Hannah Pratt, 1694, and had Jeduthan, 1694; Esther, 1695; John, 1696; Nicholas, 1698, m. Elizabeth Thomas; Persis, 1699, m. Jonathan Wood; Hannah, 1702, m. Barnabas Wood; Elizabeth, 1708; Mehitabel, 1713; Lemuel, 1715, m. Esther Dunham; and Abigail, 1718. JEDUTHAN, Plympton, son of above, by wife Rebecca, had Joseph, 1719; Mary, 1721; Sarah, 1723; Eleazer, 1724; James, 1727; Rufus, 1729; Benjamin, 1732; Rebecca, 1733; and Ebenezer. JESSE, son of 1st Samuel, m. Betsey Churchill, 1804, and had Heman C.; Betsey Otis, m. James Burgess; and Augustus, m. Mary C., d. of Ezekiel C. Turner. JOHN, son of Nicholas, m., 1665, Jehosabeth Jourdaine, and had Jeduthan; and Jonathan, m. Hannah Pratt. JOSEPH, m. Elizabeth, d. of Edward Stephens, and had Joseph, 1779; Mercy, 1781; Lemuel Stephens, 1783; Betsey, 1785. By a 2d wife, Elizabeth, he had Abigail, 1787; Hannah, 1790; Ephraim, 1793; Joseph, 1796; Chandler, 1801; Patience, 1805. JOSEPH, Carver, son of above, m., 1818, Rebecca, d. of John Burgess, and had Sarah B., 1821; Patience D., 1823; Sarah B. again; Joseph P., 1829; Anna T., 1832; Abigail B., 1836; Ephraim P., 1842. JOSIAH, son of 1st Samuel, m., 1806, Experience Morton, and had Experience Morton, 1807. He m., 2d, 1811, Ann Gray, d. of Zachariah Cushman, and had Pella M.; Josiah Adams, 1816; and Ann Gray Cushman, 1817. He m., 3d, Rebecca, d. of Daniel Jackson, 1818, and had Rebecca Jackson, m. Elnathan Haskell of Rochester, and Frederick A. Fiske; Ann Cushman, Josiah Adams, Frederick W., Daniel Jackson, and George T. JOSIAH ADAMS, son of above, m. Rebecca W., d. of John B. Atwood, 1851, and had William Thompson, 1852, Rebecca Jackson, 1853, m. Charles E. Chamberlin of Worcester; John B., 1855; Josiah T., 1857; Herbert A., 1859; Alexander A., 1862; Charles Bartlett, 1864; Gordon,

1868; and Walter J., 1870. JOSIAH P., Carver, son of 2d Joseph, m. Susan W., d. of Nathan Burgess, 1850. LEAVITT TAYLOR, son of Charles, m. Lydia, d. of Ephraim Fuller of Kingston, 1831, and had Lydia Johnson, 1833, m. Noah P. Burgess of Portland; Elizabeth Fuller, 1834, m. Nathaniel Morton; Leavitt Taylor, 1837, m. Louisa, d. of Lewis G. Bradford; Lemuel Fuller, 1839; Helen F., m. Edward G. Hedge; and Sarah B., 1850. LEMUEL, son of 1st Rufus, m. Mary Atwood, 1779, and had Rufus, m. Margaret Howard; Chandler, and Lemuel, m. Hannah Bailey. LEWIS, son of 1st Samuel, m. Betsey T. Backus of Plympton, and had Lewis C.; Sylvester H.; Arabella, m. Ebenezer Sears of Halifax; and Thaddeus Parker, moved to New York. LEVI, son of 1st Ansel, m. Harriet Newell, d. of George H. Robbins, and had Harriet Newell, 1832; Maria; Elizabeth, m. Ivory H. Clark; Mary L., m. Elias T. Benson; Emma F., 1846, m. William H. Green; Annette; Alice, 1850; and Ada L., 1857. NATHAN BACON, son of Charles, m. Lucia W., d. of George Rider, 1819, and had Lucia Rider, 1824; Mary Bacon, 1826. He m., 2d, Lucia Ripley of Kingston, 1830, and had Hannah Tilden, 1831; and Nathan Bacon, 1834. NATHANIEL, Cambridge, son of Richard, by wife Mary, had Nathaniel, 1670, and Mary. NATHANIEL, Cambridge, son of above, m. Hannah Chandler, and had Philemon, 1709. NICHOLAS, Duxbury, 1638, by wife Ann, had John, Mary, Hannah, and Rebecca. PHILEMON, Branford, Conn., son of last Nathaniel, m. Hannah Foot and Jane Mills, and had Philemon, 1736; Chandler, 1738; Ammi Ruhama, 1740; Hannah, Rebecca, Irene, Sarah, Hannah Rebecca, and Rebecca Hannah. RICHard, Charlestown, 1639, had a wife Rebecca, removed to Boston, and Cambridge, and had John, 1640; Samuel, 1643; Nathaniel, 1649; and Rebecca. RUFUS, son of 2d Jeduthan, had Lemuel, William, Charles, Seth, Benjamin; Samuel, 1752; Nathaniel; Rufus, m. Temperance Otis; Lois, m. James Collins; Sally, m. Abraham Whitten; Lydia, m. Ebenezer Nelson; and Remember, m. Joseph Bramhall; RUFUS, son of Lemuel, m., 1803, Margaret, d. of John Howard, and had Rufus, 1804, m. Alice Soule of Duxbury; Lemuel; and Henry Howard, 1811. SAMUEL, son of 1st Rufus, m. Sarah, d. of Zacheus Holmes, 1776, and had Henry; Josiah, 1786; Frederick, Samuel, Jesse, Isaac, Lewis, and Sally C., 1803. SAMUEL, son of above, m. Pamelia Dunham, 1800, and had Sally H., 1801; Edward, 1802; Samuel, 1804; Ann T., 1807, m. Robert Cowen; Pamelia, 1809; Josiah Dunham, 1811, m. Mary Ann Thomas of Wareham; Horatio, 1813; Adoniram, 1814; Daniel, 1816, m. Mary E. Trufant of Charlestown; Lewis Frederick, 1823. He m., 2d, 1834, Hannah T., wid. of Job Churchill. SAMUEL, son of above, m. Lucia, d. of Elijah Macomber, 1830, and had Lucia, m. Albert C. Vaughn of Wareham; and Alice S., 1846. SETH S., m. Mary James Sampson, 1846. THOMAS, son of George H., m. Eleanor Frances, d. of Samuel Andrews, and had Francis L., 1846; Frances C., 1848; and William S., m. Rebecca B., d. of Samuel Sampson. WILLIAM, son of 1st Rufus, m., 1783, Lois Doty, and had Theophilus, 1784; Lois, 1786, m. Thomas Witherell; Thomas Cooper, 1787; William, 1790; Nathaniel, 1796; Rufus, 1799; Alexander, 1802; Julia Ann, 1804, m. Thomas C. Angel; and Edward, 1809.

ROBERTS, ROBERT, born in England, 1743, m., 1753, Margaret Decosta, and had John, 1757. He m., 2d, 1769, Sarah Weston, and had Mary, 1769, m. John Clark; Robert, 1771; Sarah, 1773. ROBERT, son of above, m., 1798, Elizabeth, d. of Sylvanus Harlow, and had Sylvanus H., 1809; Robert of Medfield, m. Helen Brown, and a 1st wife unknown.

ROBERTSON, ALEXANDER, by wife Abigail, had Alexander, 1752; Micah, 1755. THOMAS, by wife Ruth, had Nancy, 1760, m. Jeremiah Holmes; Sarah, 1762. The name Robinson was corrupted into Roberson and Robertson, and it is suggested that the above may have been son of Gain Robinson, who came from Ireland in the first half of the 18th century, and is known to have had, by wife Margaret Watson, a son Alexander. A David Robertson, from Nova Scotia, where it is known one or more of the family of Gain Robinson went, and who may be also a descendant, m., in Plymouth, Eliza Cornish, 1826, and had Eliza, 1828; Mary, 1832; Samuel Franklin, 1835; David, 1837. WILLIAM of Litchfield, Maine, m. Christiana Sampson, 1833.

ROBIN, DANIEL, m., 1745, Sarah Saunders.

ROBINSON, ISAAC, son of Rev. John, born in Holland 1610, came, with his mother, in 1630, and settled, 1st, in Plymouth, and afterwards in Duxbury and Barnstable. He m., 1636, Margaret Hanford, and had Susanna, 1638; John, 1640, m. Elizabeth Weeks; Isaac, 1642, m. Elizabeth, d. of John Faunce of Plymouth; Fear, 1645, m. Samuel Baker; Mercy, 1647, m. William Weeks. He m. a 2d wife, and had Israel, 1651; Jacob, 1653, and perhaps Peter, and Thomas. THOMAS, an Englishman, m., 1756, Ruth, wid. of Nathaniel Hatch, and had Sally, m. Zacheus Kempton.

RODGERS, a minister, baptismal name unknown, came to Plymouth 1628 to settle, but was found to be of unsound mind, and sent back.

ROGERS, BENJAMIN, m. Phebe Harden, 1732, and had John, 1732; and Hannah, 1735. ELEAZER, son of 3d Thomas, by wife Ruhamah, had Elizabeth, 1698; Thomas, 1701; Hannah, 1703; Experience, 1707, m. Samuel Totman; Eleazer, 1710; Willis, 1712; Abijah, 1714; Meriah, 1716; and Ruth, 1718. ELEAZER, son of 1st Thomas, by wife Bethiah, had Bethiah, 1758; Thomas, 1765; Samuel, 1767; Priscilla, 1769. GEORGE, son of 1st John, m., 1798, Sally Harlow, and had George; and Bartlett, m. Elizabeth Winsor of Duxbury. GEORGE, son of above, m. Betsey Lewis, d. of Lewis Weston, and had George Henry, Elizabeth Lewis, George Lewis, Herbert; Charles Henry, m. Martha, wid. of William E. Barnes, and d. of David Turner; Edwin Eugene, m. Mary W. Burbank of Taunton. ISAAC, by wife Lucy, had Isaac Thomas, 1811. JOHN, son of 1st Thomas, m. Mary Holmes, and had John, 1762, m. Mary Wright; Thomas, m. Elizabeth Barnes; William, George, Sylvanus. JOHN, Plymouth, 1631, son of 2d Thomas, by wife Frances, perhaps d. of Robert Watson, had John, Joseph, Timothy; Ann, m. John Hudson; Mary, and Abigail. JOHN, son of above, m., 1666, Elizabeth, d. of William Pabodie, and had Hannah, 1668, m. Samuel Bradford; John, 1670; Ruth, 1675; Sarah, 1677; Elizabeth. JOHN, m. a wife Susan, 1838, and had Deborah B., 1839. JOSEPH, Duxbury, son of 2d Thomas, had Sarah, 1633; Joseph, 1635; Thomas; Elizabeth, 1639; John, 1642; Mary, 1644; James, 1648; Hannah, 1652, and removed to Sandwich. RICHARD, son of 3d Samuel, m., 1833, Mehitabel J. Pool, and had Mehitabel Jackson, 1838. SAMUEL, son of 1st Thomas, m. Hannah Bartlett, and had Priscilla, 1751; Samuel, 1752, m. Abigail Churchill; Hannah, 1754, m. Solomon Bartlett; and Sarah, 1756. SAMUEL, son of above, m. Abigail Churchill, 1775, and had Betsey, m. Eleazer Holmes; Samuel, m. Betsey Babb; Ruth, m. a Simmons; Stephen; and Abigail, m. John Chase. SAMUEL, son of above, m. Betsey Babb, 1798, and had Betsey; Samuel, m. Lydia Pool; Richard, m. Mehitabel J., d. of Perez Pool; and Lewis, m. in Boston. SAMUEL, son of 2d Eleazer, m. Joanna Sampson, 1790, and had Stephen Sampson, 1791. STEPHEN, son of 2d Samuel, m. Polly (Simmons) Ripley, wid. of Luther Ripley, 1813, and had Betsey, 1814, m. William Baker; Mary, 1818, m. John B. Wilson; Hannah B.; Angeline, 1821; Stephen, 1824; Angeline, 1825; Samuel, 1828; Sally Ann, 1829. SYLVANUS, son of 4th Thomas, m. Jane F. Lucas, 1819, and had Thomas Otis, m. Lucretia Hanneman, d. of Elijah Morey of Orland, Maine; Sylvanus Watson, m. Annie Jane Crosby of Marshfield; George H., m. Linda, d. of James M. Stillman; Eliza B., m. Josiah D. Baxter; and Jane. SYLVANUS, son of 1st John, m. Sally Finney, 1794. He m., 2d, Polly Mason, 1798, and had Sylvanus, Mason; Susan, m. William Morey, and Mary. THOMAS, son of 1st Eleazer, m. Priscilla Churchill, and had Ruth, 1722; Priscilla, 1723; Desire, 1725; Willis, 1727; Samuel, 1728; Thomas, 1730, m. Elizabeth Ward; Hannah, 1734; Eleazer, 1736; Priscilla, 1739; John, 1740. THOMAS came in the Mayflower 1620, with son Joseph, and, according to Bradford, other children, including John, came over afterwards. THOMAS, Eastham, son of Joseph, m., 1665, Elizabeth Snow, and had Elizabeth, 1666; Joseph, 1668; Hannah, 1670; Thomas, 1671; Thomas again, 1672; Eleazer, 1673; and Nathaniel, 1676. THOMAS, son of 2d Eleazer, m. Elizabeth Barnes, 1794, and had Thomas, 1794; Sylvanus, 1797; Sylvanus, 1798; Elizabeth, 1800, m. Isaac Robbins. WILLIAM, son of 1st John, m., 1787, Elizabeth Bartlett, and had William, 1788; Mary, 1794, m. Edward Nichols, Joseph Davis and Ezra Clark; John, 1799; Ichabod, 1803; Nancy Bartlett, 1806; Ellis, 1809, m. Melinda Thrasher; and Francis Edward, 1812. WILLIAM, son of above, m. Rebecca, d. of Samuel Lanman, 1808, and had America Brewster, m. Eliza Keen; Rebecca, m. Ebenezer S. Griffin; and Betsey, m. William Nickerson.

ROLFE, HORACE H., m., 1828, Mary T. Marcy.

ROWLEY, HENRY, Plymouth, 1632, m., 1633, Ann, wid. of Thomas Blossom. By a first wife he had, born in England, Sarah, m. Jonathan Hatch.

RUGGLES, JOSEPH, m. Hannah Cushman, 1743.

RUSSELL, ANDREW LEACH, son of 1st Nathaniel, m. Laura Dewey of Sheffield, 1832, and had Laura Dewey, 1833. He m., 2d, Hannah White, d. of William Davis, 1841, and had George Briggs, 1843, m. Jennie, d. of Gen. C. C. Augur; Andrew Howland, 1846; and Martha LeBaron, 1849. BRIDG-HAM, son of 3d Jonathan, m. Betsey, d. of Jeremiah Farris of Barnstable, and had Elizabeth Bridgham, 1829; and John Bridgham of San Francisco, m. Sarah Ann French of Boston. CHARLES, Medford, son of 5th John, m. Elizabeth Hacker, d. of Henry W. Abbot of Andover, and had Edwin,

James, Mary, Charles, Elizabeth; and Edwin F., m. Wilhelmina Letitia Barrington of Woburn. ELLIOTT, Boston, son of 2d Nathaniel, m. Sarah Lincoln, d. of Spencer Tinkham of Boston, 1860, and had Catherine Elliott, 1860. FRANCIS H., Boston, son of 2d Nathaniel, m. Emily, d. of Abiel and Abigail (Archer) Stevens of Lawrence, 1858, and had Mary Howland, 1860. GEORGE, Kingston, son of 4th John, m. Betsey Foster, d. of William Drew, 1798, and had Mercy Foster, 1799, m. James Nicholas Sever; Betsey, 1801, m. Martin Brewster and Josiah W. Powers; George, 1802, m. Sarah Lewis Thomas; and Nancy, 1805. He m., 2d, Amelia Drew, 1806, sister of 1st wife, and had Nancy, 1807, m. Edmund B. Whitman; Thomas, 1809, m. Sarah Ellis, d. of Ellis Bradford, and Sarah Ann Goodridge; Amelia, 1811; Catherine, 1814; Julia, 1817, m. Daniel Wight, Jr., of Scituate; Jane, 1819, m. Charles W. Gelett; and Mary Homer, 1822, m. Joseph Peckham. GEORGE, owner of an estate in Plymouth, 1637. JAMES, son of 4th John, m. Experience, d. of Ichabod Shaw, 1786, and had Lucia Shaw, 1787, m. Thomas Somes; James, 1789; William S., 1792. JOHN, Cambridge, 1636, came over with two sons, John and Philip. He removed to Wethersfield, and m., 1649, Dorothy, wid. of Henry Smith. JOHN, Wethersfield, son of above, m., 1649, Mary, d. of John Talcott of Hartford, and had John, 1650; Jonathan, 1655. He m., 2d, Rebecca, d. of Thomas Newberry of Windsor, and had Samuel, 1660; Eleazer, 1663; Daniel, 1666, and removed to Hadley. JOHN, Barnstable, son of 2d Jonathan, m. Elizabeth Bridgham, 1754, and had Jonathan. JOHN, came from Scotland and settled in Plymouth, where he m., 1757, Mercy, d. of Nathaniel Foster, and had John, 1758; James, 1760; Thomas, 1761; Mercy, 1763, m. William Jackson; Abigail, 1766; Nancy, 1767, m. John Sever of Kingston; Nathaniel, 1769; Jane, 1773, m. James Sever of Kingston; George, 1776; and Charles. A Thomas Russell came from Scotland about the same time, and settled in Weymouth, where he m. Abigail, d. of Thomas Vinton, and had Mary, m. Isaac Alden; Betsey, m. James Barrell; Abigail, m. William Keith; and Agnes. Was he a brother of John? In the receipt-book of John, in the possession of the writer, there are receipts signed by Thomas of Braintree, probably the same person, which indicate that he may have been. JOHN, son of above, m. Mary, d. of Samuel Jackson, 1786, and had John, 1786; Thomas, 1788; Charles, 1790; Mary, 1792, m. Thomas J. Lobdell; Nancy, 1795; Charles again, 1798; and James. JOHN, son of above, m. Deborah, d. of Nathaniel Spooner, 1816, and had Mary Spooner, m. James T. Hodge; John J.; Helen, m. William Davis and William H. Whitman; and Laura. JOHN J., son of above, m. Mary A., d. of Allen Danforth, 1855, and had Helen, 1857; John, 1860; and Lydia, 1863. JONATHAN, Barnstable, son of 2d John, m. Martha, d. of Joshua Moody, and had Rebecca, 1681, Martha, 1683; John, 1685; Abigail, 1687; Jonathan, 1690; Eleazer, 1692, Moody, 1694; Martha, 1697; Samuel, 1699; Joseph and Benjamin, twins, 1702; and Hannah, 1707. JONATHAN, Barnstable, son of above, m., 1725, Mary, d. of John Otis, and had John, 1730. JONATHAN, Barnstable, son of 3d John, m., 1784, Rebecca, d. of David Turner of Plymouth, and had Mercy, 1787; Betsey, 1790; Bridgham, 1793; Hannah, m. Charles Crocker of Barnstable; Deborah, m. William Wright; Abigail, 1797, m. Charles

Churchill of Plymouth; Rebecca, 1800; and Lucy. NATHANIEL, son of 4th
John, m., 1800, Martha, d. of Isaac LeBaron, and had Nathaniel, 1801; Mary
Howland, 1803; Andrew Leach, 1806; Mercy Ann, 1809; Francis James,
1811; LeBaron, 1814; Lucia Jane, 1821, m. George W. Briggs. NATHANIEL,
son of above, m., 1827, Catherine Elizabeth, d. of Daniel Roberts Elliott of
Savannah, and had Elliott, 1828; Martha LeBaron, 1830; Francis H., 1832;
Anna, 1835, m. Alexander M. Harrison; Nathaniel, 1837; and Catherine
Elliott, 1840, m. William Hedge. THOMAS, son of 5th John, m., 1814, Mary
Ann, d. of William Goodwin, and had Elizabeth, 1815; Lydia Goodwin, 1817,
m. William Whiting of Roxbury; Mary, m. Benjamin Marston Watson; Wil-
liam Goodwin, 1821; Thomas; and Jane Frances, m. Abraham Firth of
Boston. THOMAS, Boston, son of above, m., 1853, Mary Ellen, d. of Edward
T. Taylor of Boston, and had Mary Ann, 1855; Ellen Taylor, 1858, m., 1877,
Alejandro Ybarra of Venezuela, and had Elena Dolores del Carmen, 1879;
Alejandro Tomas (Simeon Mariano de las Mercedes), 1880; Dora Walton,
1861. THOMAS, from Boston, m. Elizabeth, d. of George Watson, 1788.
THOMAS, from Boston, m. Sarah, d. of William Sever of Kingston, 1784, and
had Sarah, m. Richard Sullivan of Boston. WILLIAM GOODWIN, Boston,
son of 1st Thomas, m. Mary Ellen, d. of Thomas Hedge, 1847, and had
Lydia Goodwin, 1854, m. Roger N. Allen of Boston; Thomas, 1858; and
Marion, 1865. WILLIAM SHAW, son of James, m. Mary Winslow, d. of
Nathan Hayward, 1820, and had William James, 1821, m. Flora Metz of
Brooklyn and Helen Richmond of Taunton; Edward Winslow, 1824; Mary
Winslow, 1826; Joanna Hayward, 1828; Elizabeth Hayward, 1831; and Susan
Hayward, 1833.

SACHEMS, MOSES, m. Kate Deerskins, 1745, Indians. MOSES, m. Sarah
Nummuck, 1751, Indians. PHILIP, m. Esther Peach, 1735, Indians.

SAFFIN, JOHN, m. Martha, d. of Thomas Willet, 1658, and had John,
1658; John again, 1662; Thomas, 1664; Simon, 1665; Josiah, 1668; Joseph,
1670; Benjamin, 1672; Joseph, 1676. He afterwards removed to Boston,
where he m., 2d, 1680, Elizabeth, wid. of Peter Lidget. He m., 3d, Rebecca, d.
of Samuel Lee of Bristol. His son Thomas went to England, and there died
in 1687.

SAMPSON, AARON, son of 2d Sylvanus, m. Judith, d. of Nathan Burgess,
1832, and Asenath, wid. ot Solomon Holmes, and d. of Vinal Burgess, 1869,
and had an adopted son Nelson (Leland) Sampson, m. Mary T. Pierce and
Deborah A. Ellis of Sandwich. ABNER, son of Abner of Duxbury, a descendant from 1st Abraham, through Abraham and Nathaniel, m. Ruth, d. of
Nathaniel Burgess, 1781. ABRAHAM came from England about 1629, and
settled in Duxbury, and is supposed to have been a brother of Henry. He m.
a d. of Samuel Nash, and is supposed, by Winsor, to have had a 2d wife. His
children were Samuel, born about 1646, m. a wife Esther; George, 1655, m. a
wife Elizabeth; Abraham, 1658, m. Sarah, d. of Alexander Standish; and
Isaac, 1660, m. Lydia Standish, sister of Sarah. If he had two wives, it is
probable that the three last children were of the second. ABRAHAM, Duxbury, son of above, m. Sarah, d. of Alexander Standish, and had Nathaniel,
about 1682, m. Keturah Chandler; Abraham, 1686, m. Penelope Sampson;

Miles, 1690, m. Sarah Studley; Rebecca; Ebenezer, 1696, m. Zeruiah Soule; Sarah, m. Joseph Sampson and John Rouse; and Grace. ALVAN, son of 3d George, m. Susan, d. of Benjamin Crandon, 1815, and had Susan Crandon, 1816, m. Lewis Baird of Lynn; William Boyd, 1819; and Mary Bishop, 1821, m. Daniel Newhall of Lynn. BARNABAS, Plympton, son of 1st Isaac, m. Experience Atkins, and had Barnabas, 1731; Experience, 1734; Elizabeth, 1734 BENJAMIN, Duxbury, son of 1st Stephen, m. Rebecca, d. of Jacob Cook of Kingston, 1716, and had Micah, 1717, m. a wife Deborah; Deborah, about 1720, m. Rev. Samuel Veasie of Duxbury; Cornelius, m. Desire Crocker; Rebecca, 1726; Benjamin, 1729, m. Deborah Cushing and Esther Weston; and Josiah, 1731. BENJAMIN, Kingston, son of above, m. Deborah Cushing of Pembroke, 1759, and had Benjamin, 1759, m. Priscilla Churchill; Deborah, 1762; Croade, 1763, m. Bethany Dawes. He m., 2d, 1770, Esther Weston, and had Micah, 1773, m. Mary Croswell; and Priscilla, 1776, m. a Nye. BEN- JAMIN, Kingston, son of above, m. Priscilla Churchill of Plymouth, 1786, and had James, 1787; Isaac, 1789, m. Elizabeth, d. of William Sherman of Ply- mouth; George, about 1792; and Deborah, 1794. BENJAMIN, Plympton, son of 1st George, m. Margaret Parker, 1710, and had Thomas, 1711, m. Lydia Bryant, Benjamin, 1712, m. Mary Williamson; Ruth, 1716, m. John Faunce of Plymouth and David Darling of Pembroke; Nathaniel, 1718, m. Martha Per- kins; and Philemon, 1720, m. Rachel Standish. BENJAMIN, Plympton, son of above, m. Mary Williamson, and had George, 1739; Margaret, 1741; Ben- jamin, 1746. CALEB, son of Henry, Duxbury, m. Mercy, d. of Alexander Standish, and, according to accurate John Adams Vinton, probably had David, 1685, m. Mary Chaffin; Lora, m. Benjamin Simmons; Rachel, m. Moses Simmons; Priscilla; Alexander, m. Rebecca Shattuck of Boston; Caleb; Joshua; and Jerusha, 1704, m. Ebenezer Bartlett. DAVID, Duxbury, son of above, m. Mary Chaffin of Marshfield, 1712, and had Lydia, m. Nathaniel Bosworth; Charles, m. Mary Church; Ebenezer, m. Hannah Harlow; David; Mary, m. John Little; Jonathan, m. Sarah Drew; Mercy, m. Timothy Hutch- inson; Elizabeth, m. Peter Pineo; Deborah; Chaffin, m. Elizabeth Clifts; and Eleanor, m. Joseph Farnum. EBENEZER, Plymouth, son of above, m., 1739, Hannah, d. of William Harlow, and had Ebenezer, 1740; Elizabeth, 1741, m. Ephraim Bartlett; Hannah, 1744, m. Richard Cooper; John, 1746, m. Hannah Sherman; George, 1748, m. Mary Kempton; Sarah, 1751; Lydia, 1753; Mary, 1755, m. Lemuel Bradford; Benjamin, 1757; Benjamin, 1760; Caleb, 1762; and Ebenezer again, 1764, m. Susanna Finney. EBENEZER, whose parentage is unknown by the writer, m. Priscilla Pratt of Middleboro', 1761. EBEN- EZER, son of 1st Ebenezer, had Olive, m. Perry Griffin; and Ebenezer. ELLIS, son of 2d Sylvanus, m. Sarah H. Ballou, 1830, and had Sarah H., m. Jackson Warren and Seth W. Burgess; Pelham, m. Emily C. Douglass; Rebecca F., m. Solomon M. Holmes; Ellis; Andrew, Aaron; and Jesse E., m. Deborah B. Manter. EPHRAIM, parentage unknown, of Middleboro', m. Polly Covill, 1808. EPHRAIM, Plympton, son of 1st Isaac, m. Abigail, d. of Humphrey Howel, and had Abigail, 1729, m. Ephraim Bryant; Elizabeth, 1732, m. Silas Sturtevant; Susanna, 1734; Eunice, 1737; Sarah, 1743; Mary, 1745, m. Isaac Bonney; Priscilla. GEORGE, son of 1st Abraham, Duxbury and Plympton, m., about 1678, a wife Elizabeth, and had Joseph, 1679, m. Ann Tilson; Abigail, 1680, m. Experience Bent; Judith, 1683; Ruth, 1684; m. Nehemiah Sturtevant; Benjamin, 1686, m. Margaret Parker; Martha, 1689, m. Nathaniel Fuller of Plympton; George, 1691, m. Hannah Soule; Elizabeth, 1692, m. Allerton Cushman; William, 1695, m, Joanna Vaughn; Seth, 1697, m. Ruth Barrows, and a 2d wife, Thankful (Sproat) Bennett. GEORGE, son of above, Plympton, m., 1718, Hannah, d. of Benjamin Soule of Plympton, and had Gideon, 1719, m. Abigail, d. of Israel Cushman and Rebecca Soule; Sarah, 1721; Deborah, 1725, m. Elijah Bisbee of Plympton; Zabdiel, 1727, m. Abigail Cushman and Abiah Whitmarsh; Hannah, 1730, m. Joshua Perkins; George, 1733; Rebecca, 1735, m. Jeremiah Kelly; and Elizabeth, 1737, m. Joseph Cushman. GEORGE, Plympton and Plymouth, son of 1st Zabdiel, m., 1780, Hannah, d. of Richard Cooper, and had Zabdiel, 1781, m. Ruth Lobdell; George, 1783, m. Sally Bartlett; Marston, 1785, m. Leonice Holmes and Caroline Bartlett; John, 1788, m. Priscilla Bramhall; Alvan, 1791, m. Susan Crandon; Joseph, 1794, m. Harriet Rider of Plymouth; Schuyler, 1797, m. Mary Ann Bartlett and wid. Sarah Taylor Bishop; Hannah, 1799, m. Boswell Ballard; and Caroline, 1801. GEORGE, son of above, Plympton, Plymouth, and Duxbury, m. Sally, d. of Sylvanus Bartlett of Plymouth, 1803, and had Sally Bartlett, 1804, m. Daniel L. Winsor; George W., 1806; Lloyd Granville, 1808, m. Mary Winsor; Hannah Cushing, 1810, m. Hiram Hunt; Lucia Ann, 1812, m. Samuel Knowles; Joseph Allen, 1814, m. Mary T. Soule; Betsey Parker, 1817. GEORGE, Plymouth, m. Patience Rider, 1796, and had Harriet, 1797; and Patience Howland, 1799. HENRY came in the Mayflower 1620, settled in Duxbury, and m. Ann Plummer, 1636, by whom he had Elizabeth, m. Robert Sproat; Hannah, m. Josiah Holmes; John, m. Mary Pease; Mary, m. John Summers; a d. who m. John Harmon; and Dorcas, m. Thomas Bonney; James, Stephen; and Caleb, m. Mercy Standish. HIRAM, son of 2d Sylvanus, Plymouth, m. Experience, d. of Nathaniel Clark, and had Hiram, m. Maria J. Cox; and Polly. He m., 2d, 1854, Ruth (Nickerson) Finney, wid. of Seth Finney, and previously wid. of Isaac Howland. ICHABOD, Plymouth, son of 1st Samuel, m. Mercy, d. of Thomas Savery, 1734, and had Thomas, 1735; Mercy, 1736; Esther, 1738; Elnathan, 1740; Ichabod, 1742; Samuel, 1745. ISAAC, Plymouth, son of 1st Abraham, m. Lydia, d. of Alexander Standish, and had Isaac, 1688; Jonathan, 1690; Josiah, 1692; Lydia, 1694; Ephraim, 1698; Priscilla, 1700; Peleg, 1700, m. Mary Ring; and Barnabas, 1705, m. Experience Atkins. ISAAC, Plymouth, son of 3d Benjamin, m. Elizabeth, d. of William Sherman, 1822, and had Elizabeth, 1824, m. John Kneeland; George, 1825, m. Rebecca Frances, d. of Henry A. Hovey of Boston; and Isaac, 1830. ISAAC, Plympton, son of 1st Isaac, by wife Sarah, had Hannah, Uriah, Sarah, and Margaret. JOHN, Middleboro', son of Obadiah, m. Elizabeth Cobb, and had Samuel, 1764, m. Lydia Holmes; Obadiah, 1766; Elizabeth, 1768; Elizabeth, 1769; Mercy, 1770; Rebecca, and Nathan. JOHN, Plymouth, son of 3d George, m. Priscilla, d. of Benjamin Bramhall, 1811, and had John A., 1812; Charles, 1817; Priscilla, 1819; Caroline Elizabeth, 1824. JONATHAN, Plympton, son of 1st Isaac, m., 1721, Joanna Lucas, and had Mary, 1722, m. Nathan Perkins; Joanna, 1723; Priscilla, 1726; Abigail, 1727, m. Jabez Prior;

Jonathan, 1729, m. Deborah, d. of Elisha Bradford of Kingston; Bethiah, 1731, m. Joseph Sampson; Josiah, 1735. JOSEPH, Plymouth, son of 1st Sylvanus, m. Sarah Manter, 1792, and had Joseph, m. Hannah Burgess; Sylvanus, m. Nancy Deadley; and Rufus, m. Nancy Whiting. He m., 2d, 1798, Zerviah, d. of Nathaniel Burgess, and had Marston, m. a.Simmons; and Sally, m. George Manter. JOSEPH, son of above, m. Hannah, d. of John Burgess, 1815, and had Mary, m. Eleazer Faunce of Kingston; and Joseph, m. Amelia Leonard of Bridgewater. JOSEPH, Plympton, son of 1st George, m. Ann Tilson, and had Deborah, 1706; Judith, 1708; Wealthea, 1712; Jedediah, 1714; Susanna, 1716. JOSEPH, Plympton, son of 1st Thomas, m., 1753, Bethiah, d. of Jonathan Sampson of Plympton, and had Peleg, 1754; Phebe, m. Samuel Ripley; Lucy, 1761, m. Isaac Waterman of Halifax; and Lydia. LAZARUS, Plymouth, parentage unknown, m. Jemima Holmes, 1726, and had Jemima, 1731. He m., 2d, Abigail, d. of William Shurtleff, and had Susanna, 1735; Ephraim, 1736; Lazarus, 1738; Mary, 1741; William, 1743; and Lazarus again, 1746. LEVI, son of 2d Sylvanus, m. Rebecca Pierce, 1841, and had Rebecca T., m. Philip M. Snow; Sophronia P., m. George A. Manter; Henry, m. Addie Johnson; Stillman R., m. Susan Raymond; and Lewis. MARSTON, Plympton, son of 3d George, m. Leonice, d. of Elnathan Holmes of Plymouth, 1810, and had Leonice Marston, 1811, m. Joseph W. Moulton of Roslin, New York; William Marston, 1815; Almira, 1817; Zabdiel, 1819. He m., 2d, Caroline, d. of Ansel Bartlett of Plymouth, 1821, and had Caroline Marston, 1823, m. George Frazier of Duxbury. MARSTON, son of 1st Joseph, m. a Simmons, and had Roscoe M., m. Ellen J. Warren. NATHANIEL, Dux-bury, son of 2d Abraham, m., 1703, Keturah Chandler, and had Noah, 1705, m. Jemima Rider of Plymouth; Perez, 1706; Fear, 1708, m. Benjamin Simmons; Robert, 1712, m. Alice, d. of Miles Sampson; Nathaniel, 1716, m. Mary Holmes; Keturah, 1719; Anna, 1723, m. Anthony Sampson; Abner, 1726. NATHAN-IEL, Plympton, son of 4th Benjamin, m., 1747, Martha, d. of Josiah Perkins, and had Deborah, 1748. NOAH, Plymouth, son of 1st Nathaniel, m. Jemima Rider of Plymouth, 1734, and had Southworth, 1735; Desire, 1738, m. Sylvanus Harlow; Elizabeth, 1740, m. Jesse Harlow. OBADIAH, Marshfield and Mid-dleboro', son of 2d Samuel, m., 1731, Mary Soule, and had Ruth; Israel; Samuel, 1735; Mary, Martha; Obadiah, 1739; John, 1741; Ezekiel, 1744; Esther, 1749. PELEG, Pembroke, Plympton, and Kingston, son of 1st Isaac, m., 1722, Mary Ring, and had Mary, 1724; Peleg, 1726; Mercy, 1731; Simeon, 1736; Priscilla, 1739. Mr. Vinton adds to these Jonathan, 1733; and Ephraim. PELEG, Plympton, son of 4th Joseph, m,, 1798, Sarah, d. of John Macfarlin, and had Lydia, 1799, m. William Shaw of Middleboro'; a d., 1801; Bethiah, 1803; Joseph, 1806; John, 1808. PHILANDER, Plymouth, son of Constant of Duxbury, who was descended from 1st Abraham, through Abra-ham, Miles, and Miles, m. Sarah Chandler about 1836, and had Albert, Sarah, John Thomas; and Ann Maria, m., 1866, John Addie of Charlestown. PHILEMON, Plympton, son of 4th Benjamin, m., 1742, Rachel, d. of Moses Standish, and had Philemon, 1743; Newland, 1744; Lydia, 1749, m. Francis Holmes; Moses, 1751; Benjamin, 1753; Jere-miah, 1755. RUFUS, Plymouth, son of 1st Joseph, m. Nancy Whitney,

1824, and had Elizabeth, m. Nathaniel C. Hoxie; Nancy W., m. Ezra H. Leach; Rufus, m. Nancy E. Morton and Esther Jordan; and John W., m. Mary S. Leach. SAMUEL, Duxbury, son of 1st Abraham, by wife Esther, had Samuel, 1670, m. Mercy Eddy; and Ichabod. SAMUEL, Middleboro', son of above, m. Mercy, d. of Obadiah Eddy, and had Obadiah, Gershom, Ichabod, Esther, and Mary. SAMUEL, Middleboro', son of 1st John, m. Lydia Holmes of Plymouth, 1788, and had John, 1789; Samuel, 1791; Holmes, 1793, m. Sally, d. of Elisha Murdock of Carver; Lydia, 1795, m. Simeon Staples; John, 1798, m. Margaret J. Williams and Stella M. Holton, Mercy, 1800, m. Seth Leach; Polly, 1803; Betsey, 1806, m. Seth Leach; Jane, 1808; Richard, 1811; Ira, 1819. SAMUEL, Plymouth, son of above, m. Abigail, d. of Solomon Bartlett, and had Lydia, 1812, m. Winslow Cole; Abby Mercy, 1817; Samuel, 1819; Betsey Bartlett, 1820, m. Dr. Thomas Spencer Perkins of Boston; and Solomon, 1824. SAMUEL, son of above, m. Rebecca, d. of George Perkins, 1840, and had Rebecca Bartlett, m. William S. Robbins; Alice Bradford, Mary Allerton, and Elizabeth Williams. SCHUYLER, Plymouth, son of 3d George, m., 1823, Mary Ann, d. of Amasa Bartlett, and had Mary Ann Bartlett, 1825, m. George G. Dyer. He m., 2d, 1827, Sarah Taylor (Bartlett) Bishop, sister of 1st wife, and wid. of William Bishop, and had Sarah Taylor Bartlett, 1829; George Schuyler, 1833; and Hannah Bartlett, 1835, m. Rev. Isaac C. White. SETH, Plympton, son of 1st George, m., 1724, Ruth Barrows. SIMEON, Kingston and Plymouth, son of Peleg, m. Deborah, d. of Seth Cushing of Hingham, 1759, and had Lydia, 1762; Lydia Cushing, 1763, m. William Goodwin; Simeon, 1766; Deborah, 1768, m. Rev. Ephraim Briggs and William Goodwin; Isaac, 1771; Mary, 1775; Mercy, 1777, m. Levi Bradford; Martha Washington, 1779; George Washington, 1781, m. Hannah C. Shaw; and Maria A., 1784, m. Rev. Daniel Johnson. SOLOMON, Plymouth, son of 4th Samuel, m. Maria Swift Benson, 1846, and had Maria Louisa. STEPHEN, Duxbury, son of Henry, by wife Elizabeth, had Benjamin, 1686, m. Rebecca Cook; John, 1688, m. Priscilla Bartlett; Cornelius, Hannah, Mary, Elizabeth, Dorcas, and Abigail. STEPHEN, Duxbury, m. Deborah, d. of David Turner, 1749. STEPHEN, Plymouth, son of Abraham of Duxbury, who was a descendant from 1st Abraham through his son Abraham, m. Abigail Morton, 1749, and had Stephen, 1751; James, 1753, m. Sarah Swift; Abigail, 1754; William, 1757; Enoch, 1759; Penelope, 1761, m. Judah Delano; Rufus, 1764; Henry, 1766. SYLVANUS, Plymouth, son of 1st Thomas, m. Mary, d. of Joseph Wright of Plympton, 1772, and had Sylvanus, m. Ruth Burgess; Thomas, m. Mercy Burgess; Joseph, m. Sarah Manter and Zerviah Burgess; Mary m. Benjamin Pierce; Sally, m. Consider Clark; Sophia, and Susan, both m. John Burgess; Lydia, m. Nathaniel Clark; and Lucy m. Daniel Lewis; and Levi. SYLVANUS, son of above, m. Ruth, d. of William Burgess, 1800, and had Truman, m. Ruth Burgess; Hiram, m. Experience Clark and wid. Ruth (Nickerson) Finney; Ellis, m. Sarah H. Ballou; Levi, m. Rebecca Pierce; Aaron, m. Judith Burgess and wid. Asenath Holmes; Ruth, m. John Perry of Plymouth and Nathaniel Perry; Christiana, m. William Robinson; Lucy, m. Seth D. Bennett; Sophia, m. Ebenezer Bryant; and Susan. He m., 2d, 1832, Thirza, d. of James Doten. SYLVA-

nus, Plymouth, son of 1st Joseph, m. Nancy Deadley of Virginia, and had
Sylvanus, m. Lydia C., d. of Vinal Burgess; Christopher, m. Susan M. Hayward; Joseph M., m. Susan M., wid. of Christopher; Susan A., m. William
J. Harlow; Harvey M., m. Edith P. Hayward; Deborah H., m. Barsillai
Holmes; Lydia A., m. Orin W. Bennett; and Henry H., m. Camille J. Warren. THOMAS, Plympton, son of 4th Benjamin, m. Lydia, d. of Samuel Bryant, 1730, and had Joseph, 1732, m. Bethiah, d. of Jonathan Sampson; Ruth,
1734, m. Adam Wright; Thomas, 1737, m. Ruth Bryant; Levi, 1740; Lydia,
1744; Sylvanus, 1747, m. Mary Wright. THOMAS, Plympton, son of above,
m. Ruth, d. of John Bryant, and had Olive, 1763, m. Onesimus Randall; Abigail, 1776, m, Moses Thompson of Middleboro'; Thomas, 1767; Molly, 1769,
m. Levi Harlow; Oakes, 1774, m. Abigail Lobdell; Sophia, 1777; Sophia,
1779, m. Josiah Diman of Plymouth; Ruth, 1782, m. Aaron Soule. THOMAS,
son of 1st Sylvanus, Plymouth, m. Mercy, d. of William Burgess, 1810, and
had Lucia Ann; Serena; Lydia, m. Ephraim B. Holmes; Wealthea B., m.
Thomas P. Osborn of East Bridgewater; Mercy W.; and Thomas, m. Eunice
Green of Woodstock, Me., though not in the order named. TRUMAN, son
of 2d Sylvanus, Plymouth, m. Ruth, d. of Nathan Burgess, 1825, and had
Ruth S., 1833, m. George Manter; Adrianna, 1830, m. Mendall Pierce; Truman, 1827, m. Olive Shepard of Vermont; Gustavus G., 1830, m. Esther C.,
d. of Vinal Burgess; Nathan B., 1832, m. Lucy R. Manter and Anna R.
Pierce; Miranda R., 1835, m. Melanci J. Pierce; Deborah Weston, m. Walter
Scott Dixon; and Levi R., 1840. WILLIAM, Plympton, son of 1st George, m.,
1721; Joanna Vaughn, and had Zerviah, 1736, m. Benjamin Cushman; William, 1727; Deborah, 1731, m. James Bishop; Zilpha, m. Joseph Bryant; and
Israel. ZABDIEL, Plympton, son of 2d George, m., 1747, Abigail, d. of Ben-
jamin Cushman, and had Sarah, 1749, m. William Bent of Middleboro'. He
m., 2d, Abiah, d. of Richard Whitmarsh of Abington, and had Zabdiel,
1754; George, 1755, m. Hannah Cooper; William, 1757; Abigail, 1758, m.
Gideon Bradford; Gideon, 1760, m. Lydia Ripley; Hannah, 1762, m. Richard
Cooper; Abiah, 1764; Philemon, 1766, m. Fanny Drew; and Issachar, 1768.
ZABDIEL, Plympton and Plymouth, son of 3d George, m., 1804, Ruth, d. of
Ebenezer Lobdell of Plympton, and had Milton Lobdell, 1805; Eudora Rowland, 1807, m. Francis L. Alden; Algernon Sydney, 1809; Marcia Lobdell,
1811, m. John H. Coggshall of New Bedford and John Hornby of Pough-
keepsie; Maria Louisa, m. Daniel Ricketson of New Bedford; Algernon Syd-
ney, 1815, m. Adeline Lombard; Ruth Lobdell, 1819, m. Daniel Hathaway of
Fairhaven; Zabdiel Silsbee, 1821, m. Helen M. Bird; Judith Lobdell and
Nancy Ripley, 1827, twins, the last of whom m. James L. Baker of Hingham.
(See Sampson Genealogy.)

SANGARELE, JAMES, m., 1721, Mrs. Mary Thomas.

SANGER, JOSEPH, m., 1812, Hannah Marcy.

SARGENT, WILLIAM, perhaps a descendant from William, Charlestown,
1638, who is thought to have moved to Sandwich. He m., 1749, Mary Rider,
and had Experience, 1750, m. Josiah Whittemore; Ruth, 1751, m. Benoni
Shaw; Mary, 1754; Elizabeth, 1756; Lydia, 1758, m. Joseph Holmes; Elizabeth again, 1760, m. Zenas Sturtevant of Plympton; Sarah, 1762; Hannah,
1764; and perhaps William, who m. Abigail Faunce.

SAUNDERS, ABRAHAM, m., 1810, Anna Morey. BILLY, m., 1795, Phebe
Holmes. HENRY, by wife Ann, had Amah, 1701; Sarah, 1703; Abigail, 1705;
Jonathan, 1713; and probably Henry. HENRY, son of above, m., 1742, Mary
Hambleton. JOHN, from Sandwich, published to Patience Bates, 1775.
JOHN, born in Dover, N. H., settled in Plymouth, and m., 1819, Betsey, d. of
Thomas Sherman, by whom he had John Calderwood, 1820; William, 1822;
Elizabeth, 1826, m. John C. Barnes; Lucia Ann, 1828, m. George Y. Loring,
Robert Thomas, 1833; Thomas S., 1834; Priscilla Simmons, 1838, m. William
Williams. JOHN CALDERWOOD, son of above, m. Eleanor, d. of John Sher-
man of Carver, and had George Eugene, 1847, m. Mary D. Baker of Dennis;
Horace Melvin, 1850, m. Catherine Sybeline, d. of Edwin Lewis; Albert
Francis, 1853. JONATHAN, son of 1st Henry, m., 1741, Elizabeth Tinkham,
and had Mary, 1742; Elizabeth, 1744; Jonathan, 1747. WILLIAM, Stockton,
Cal., son of 1st John, m. Martha, d. of Thomas Oldham of Duxbury, and
had Martha Davis, 1844, m. George E. Weller; Elizabeth Ann, 1846; William
Edwards, 1855; Clarence, 1857; Elizabeth, 1863.

SAVERY, ANTHONY, Rochester, probably son of 1st Thomas, m., 1703,
Margaret Price, and had Ruth, 1704; Joseph, 1706, m. Experience Hiller;
Anthony, 1708. DANIEL, Middleboro', son of 3d John, m. Huldah Soule,
and had John, 1795; Daniel, 1797; Huldah, 1798; William Soule, 1800;
Lydia, 1801; P. White, 1803; Sarah Briggs, 1805; Betsey, 1812; George Sim-
mons, 1816. GEORGE HOLMES, son of 2d William, m., 1804, Mary, d. of
Peter Lanman, and had Eliza Ellis, m. Nahum Johnson of Bridgewater;
Sally, Hiram; Mary N., m. Solomon Hardy and George Holmes. GEORGE
HOLMES, son of above, m. Diantha Gurney of Abington, and had Mary Eliz-
abeth, m. Stephen Hawes. ISAAC, Rochester, son of 4th Thomas, m., 1772,
Deliverance Clifton, and had Deborah, 1772, m. Lemuel Gurney; Timothy,
1773, m. Elizabeth Swift; Sarah, 1775, m. Lot Bumpus; Meribah, 1778, m.
Reuben Briggs; Deliverance, 1780, m. Richard Gurney; Uriah, 1781, m. Jane,
d. of Barnabas Ellis of Plymouth; Sylvia, 1784, m. Caleb King; Isaac, 1786;
Samuel, 1788; Benjamin, 1790, m. Lydia Whitlock of New Jersey; Phineas,
1792, m. Hannah, d. of George Cornish of Plymouth; Polly, 1795, m. Jacob
Swift. ISAAC, Rochester, son of above, m., 1808, Temperance, d. of George
Cornish of Plymouth, and had Hannah, 1809; Adelia, 1811; Samuel, 1813;
Clarissa, 1814; George Cornish, 1816; Temperance, 1818; Louisa Matilda,
1820; Sarah N., 1823; Lucinda B., 1825; Isaac P., 1827; Amanda W., 1831;
Mary T., 1833. JAMES, son of 3d Thomas, m., 1774, Mercy, d. of Timothy
Burbank, and had Mercy, 1776, m. Seth Morton; James, m. Olivia Shurtleff;
Priscilla m. a Churchill; Mary, m. Stephen Greenleaf; Ruth, m. Levi Morse.
JOHN, Middleboro', perhaps son of 1st Samuel, had John, 1706, m. Martha,
d. of Thomas Parlow; and Elizabeth and Thomas. JOHN, Middleboro', son
of above, m. Mary Thomas, and had Martha, 1731; John, 1735; Perez, 1737;
Nehemiah, 1740; Mary; Martha, 1743; Joanna, 1745; Lydia, 1747, m. a
Tinkham. JOHN, Middleboro', son of above, m., 1764, Thankful Cobb, and
had Daniel and Nehemiah. JOHN, Carver, son of 1st Peleg, m. Mary
Atwood of Middleboro', and had William, m. Mary Vanscaich of Albany;
Polly, m. Alexander Law; Hannah, m. P. A. Shurtleff; Waitstill, m. George

P. Bowers; and John. JOSEPH B., son of 6th Thomas, m., 1843, Betsey A., d. of George Thrasher, and had Thomas G., 1843, m. Laura A., d. of Thomas Pierce. LEMUEL, son of 3d Thomas, m., 1786, Elizabeth Davidson, and had John, 1786; Betsey, 1788, m. Isaac Dunham; William, 1790; Lemuel, 1792. LEMUEL, son of above, m., 1816, Bispha Thomas of Middleboro', and had Cordelia; Emily William, m. William Walker and Silas Dean; William T., m. Sylvia C., d. of Samuel Alexander; Elizabeth S., m. Henry Rider; Samuel M., m. Nancy R., d. of Ansel Bartlett; and Ann Maria. NATHAN, Wareham, son of 1st Uriah, m., 1770, Elizabeth Nye, and had Patience, 1772; Nathan, 1774. He removed to Nova Scotia, and m. Diadema, d. of Jeremiah Sabin, by whom he had Sabin, 1788, m. Olivia Marshal; Uriah, 1799; Nathan, 1809. NEHEMIAH, son of 3d John, m., 1794, Sarah, d. of Benjamin Cornish, and had Elizabeth, 1794; Thomas, 1795; Nehemiah, 1797; Mary, 1799; Winsor, 1800; Sarah C., 1804, m. Lewis Robbins. He m., 2d, Deborah Smith of Middleboro', 1806, and had Deborah, 1807, m. Joseph Wade and George W. Fisher; Louisa, 1810, m. David Cobb Holmes; Zenas, 1811; Mercy, 1813; Cordelia, 1817. NEHEMIAH, son of above, m., 1841, Phebe Cotton, d. of William Stephens, and had Nehemiah L., 1842, m. Wealthea E., d. of Charles Cobb; Irene F., 1848, m. William F. Peterson; Esther S., 1846, m. Alexander A. Bartlett; Sarah S., m. Edward Thompson of Brockton; Mary S., 1850; and James Everson. PELEG, Carver, son of 4th Thomas, m. Hannah Perkins, and had Thomas, 1787; John, 1789, m. Mary Atwood; William, 1791; Zilpha, 1793, m. William Murdock; Mary, 1797, m. Benjamin Ellis; Hannah, 1799, m. Bartlett Bent; Drusilla, 1802, m. Gamaliel Fuller; Peleg B., 1805. PELEG B., Carver, son of above, m. Julia Concklin of Albany, and had Charles, William, Mary E., Mary A., Alanson P. PHINEAS, Wareham, son of 1st Isaac, m. Hannah, d. of George Cornish, and had Mercy, 1798; Phineas, 1800; Lemuel, 1802; Cyrus, 1804. SAMUEL, Wareham, died 1812, had by wife Lois, Samuel, Phineas; Mehitabel, m. Ebenezer Clark; Lydia, m. David Swift; Elizabeth, m. Jeremiah Bumpus; and Mercy. SAMUEL, son of 1st Thomas, removed to Rochester, and had Mary, 1678; Judah, 1680; Thomas, 1681; Susan, 1690; Samuel, 1695; and probably John and Anthony. SAMUEL M., son of 2d Lemuel, m. Nancy, d. of Ansel Bartlett, and had William H., 1847; Jamie Cronacan, 1854; Samuel M., 1862. SAMUEL, Wareham, son of 2d Thomas, m. Elizabeth Bump of Rochester, and had Mehitabel, 1741; Lydia, 1744; Benjamin, 1746; Samuel, 1748; Benjamin, 1755; Phineas, 1757; Elizabeth, 1759; Mercy, 1760; Abigail, 1764. SAMUEL, Wareham, son of above, m. Ruth Gibbs, and had Lucy, 1772; Esther, 1774; Temperance, 1776; Ruth, 1778; Arathea, 1781; Polly, 1783. THOMAS, came in the Mary and John 1634, with a brother William, and by a wife Ann, had Mary, m. Joseph Ramsden; Moses, 1650; Samuel, 1651; Jonathan, 1653; Moses again; Mara, 1654; Anthony, Aaron; and Benjamin, 1644. THOMAS, son of 2d Samuel, m. Esther, d. of Henry Saunders, and had Mercy, 1706, m. Ichabod Sampson of Duxbury; Uriah, 1708; Thomas, 1710; Lydia, 1712, m. Thomas Bates; Esther, 1715, m. Lemuel Jackson; Samuel, 1718; Mehitabel, 1721. THOMAS, son of above, m. Priscilla, d. of Ichabod Paddock, and had Bethiah, 1735, m. a Rogers; Thomas, 1736; Priscilla, 1739, m. Ezra Burbank; William, 1744;

Esther, 1747, m. John Allen and William Stephens; Ruth, 1749; James, 1752; Ruth, 1755, m. William Coye; Lemuel, 1757. THOMAS, son of above, m., 1760, Zilpha, d. of George Barrows, and had Mary, 1761, m. Job Cole; Thomas, 1764; Peleg, 1764. He m., 2d, Hannah Bennett, and had Zilpha, 1766, m. William Cushman of Plympton; Mercy, 1768, m. Thomas Adams. He m., 3d and 4th, Mary Crocker and Mary Shurtleff, and had Samuel, Nathan, and Isaac. THOMAS, son of 1st Peleg, m. Betsey Shaw, and had John, 1815; Thomas, 1819; Elizabeth, 1828. THOMAS, son of 2d William, m., 1790, Abigail Everson of Kingston, and had Lydia Holmes, 1792, m. Bartlett Faunce; Sally, 1794, m. Thomas Faunce and a Harlow; Abigail T., 1796, m. Thomas Spinney; George, 1798. He m., 2d, 1806, Joanna, d. of Ezra Burbank, and had Sophia, 1807, m. John R. Spinney; Joanna H., 1808, m. James Nichols; Thomas, 1810, m. Fanny G. Smith; Mary, 1814, m. Henry Dunster, John Alexander, Charles Soule, and Aaron Sampson; William, 1816; Priscilla, 1819, m. William McDonald of Pembroke; Joseph B., and Phebe S. THOMAS, son of 4th Thomas, had Rufus of Rochester. TIMOTHY, Wareham, son of 1st Isaac, m. Eliza Swift, and had Eliza, 1802; Cyrus, 1805; Sarah, 1809; Timothy, 1811; Benjamin, 1816. URIAH, Wareham, son of 2d Thomas, m., 1738, Deborah Bump of Rochester, and had Thomas, 1739; Isaac, 1743; Mercy, 1741; Samuel, 1746; Nathan, 1745; and Esther. URIAH, Wareham, son of 1st Isaac, m., 1806, Jane, d. of Barnabas Ellis, and had Barnabas Ellis, 1807; Ruth Ellis, 1808; Robertson, 1810; Deborah, 1812; Isaac, 1814; Uriah, 1816. WILLIAM, son of 1st Peleg, m. Abigail T. Fearing of Wareham, and had William Curtis, 1818; Abigail Tobey, 1821; Mary Ellis, 1823, m. Joseph A. Bartlett; Thirza Tobey, 1825, m. Sturgis Chaddock of Boston; Hannah P., 1827, m. John K. Robinson of Falmouth; Bartlett M., 1830; William, 1832; Abigail C., 1836. WILLIAM, son of 3d Thomas, m., 1766, Lydia, d. of George Holmes, and had William, 1769; Thomas, George Holmes, Sally, and Joey. WILLIAM, son of 6th Thomas, m. Ruth Ann Barrett, and had Augusta S., m. Lorenzo F. Simmons; and Emeline P., m. Russell T. Bartlett. WINSOR, son of 1st Nehemiah, m., 1836, Fanny G., wid. of Thomas Savery, and had Winsor T., 1845, m. Almira F., d. of Charles Cobb; Sarah C., 1848, m. Elisha T. Nelson.

SAVIL, EDWARD, pub. to Huldah Hall, 1812.

SAWYER, THOMAS, m., 1749, Margaret Cotton.

SCARRET, THOMAS, m., 1728, Alice Ward, and had a son, 1729; and Joanna, m. Joshua Totman.

SCOTT, ELIAS C., m., 1832, Eliza R. Dunham.

SCUDDER, ALONZO, m., 1833, Mary D., d. of Richard Holmes.

SEARS, BARSILLAI, of Sandwich, m. Patty Ellis, 1825. DANIEL, son of Eleazer, m. wid. Belinda (Hall) Hamilton, 1844, and had Andrew, m. Mary McNeil; Frederick W., 1845; Daniel F., 1847; Julia F., 1849, m. Thaddeus Faunce; Eliza A., 1851; Daniel W., 1853; m. Louisa C. Holsgrove; Lucy J., 1856; and Lucy J. again, 1857. DAVID, son of Willard, m. Nancy Manter, 1819, and had Sarah P., 1820; Nancy, 1822; David, 1824; Stephen, 1827; Albert M., 1827, m. Mary Ann Mead. He m., 2d, Jane Doten, 1830, and had Ruth W., m. Abraham Whitten; and Anna M., m. Charles Whitten.

EDMUND, son of Willard, m. Rebecca Lucas of Carver, 1807, and had Edmund Thomas; and Rebecca, m. Timothy M. Benson. ELBRIDGE, son of 5th Thomas, m. Lydia Vaughn, 1847, and had Anna, 1850; Lydia F., 1854; Ellen, and Carrie. ELEAZER, son of Willard, m. Polly Morton, 1805, and had William, Hiram B., Daniel; Winslow, m. Nancy H., wid. of Homer Bryant, and d. of Seth Mehuran; Mary Ann, Harriet Newell, Lucy, and Eunice. HIRAM B., son of above, m. Lydia W., d. of Joseph Davie, 1842, and had Hiram B., 1845; Robert D., 1849, m. Sarah W. Howland; Emma; Harriet N., m. Elkanah Bartlett; and Bartlett, m. Augusta King. HORATIO, son of 5th Thomas, m. a wife Hannah, and had Sarah A., m. Pascal White; Andrew, Frederick, Hannah, and Horatio N. JAMES, son of 5th Thomas, m. Almira W. Hodges, 1838, and had Julia A., 1839, m. Howard K. Swift; James F., 1840, m. Harriet Stickney; Georgianna, m. Adam Stevens; Mercy D., m. H. K. Nash; Nathaniel T., 1851; Hattie A.; Almira W., 1854; Laura, 1856; Laura A., 1859; and Morrill. JOSEPH, son of Willard, m. Hannah Robbins of Carver, 1808, and had Leander, and Thomas. OTIS, son of 5th Thomas, m. Sarah M. Gibbs, and had William. PAUL, Yarmouth, son of 1st Richard, m. Deborah Willard, and had Samuel, Paul, and John. PAUL, Dennis, son of above, m. Mercy Freeman, and had Ebenezer, Paul, Elizabeth, Thomas, Rebecca, Mercy, Deborah, Ann, Joshua, Edward, Hannah, and Daniel. RICHARD, said to have been son of John Bourchier Sayer and Marie L. Egmond, born about 1590, appeared in Plymouth 1630, and m., 1632, Dorothy Thatcher, as is perhaps erroneously stated in the genealogy prepared by Edward H. Sears. He moved to Yarmouth, and his children were Knyvet, 1635; Paul, 1637; Silas, 1639; and Deborah, m. Zechariah Paddock. RICHARD, son of Silas, m. Bathsheba Harlow, 1696, and had Silas, 1697; Seth, 1699; Mary, 1703; James, 1705; John, 1707. SILAS, son of 1st Richard, Yarmouth, had Silas, Thomas, Richard, Hannah, Joseph, Josiah, Elizabeth, and Dorothy. THOMAS, son of 2d Paul, m. Elizabeth Bartlett, 1734, and had Thomas, Willard, Betty, Rebecca, Chloe, Sarah. He m., 2d, 1752, Mehitabel Fish, and had Mercy, or Mary, 1755. THOMAS, son of above, m. Rebecca Rider, 1770, and had Thomas; Bartlett, m. Patty Ellis; and Rebecca, m. Nicholas Smith. THOMAS, son of above, m. Susanna Morton, 1797, and had Thomas B.; Fanny, m. a Rowell of Oregon; Susan; and Bathsheba Drew, m. Francis Thompson. THOMAS B., son of above, m. Louisa H., d. of Amasa Churchill, 1831, and had Louisa Frances, 1831; Thomas Bartlett, 1834; Amasa Churchill, 1836; Walter Herbert, and Francis Dana. THOMAS, son of Willard, m. Rebecca Collins, 1815, and had James, Horatio, Elbridge; Otis, m. Sarah M. Gibbs; and Augustus. WILLARD, son of 1st Thomas, by wife Sarah, had Eleazer, David, Edmund, Willard, Joseph, Thomas; Mercy, m. Samuel Lewis; and Betsey, m. Eliab Wood. WILLIAM, son of Eleazer, m. Mercy, d. of Jabez Churchill, and had William Henry, 1833; Andrew Churchill, 1836; Everett H., m. Angelina R. Tripp; Herbert, 1841; Charlotte M., 1846.

SEKINS, EZEKIEL, m. Ann Raymond, 1798.

SELLER, JAMES, m. Rebecca Cobb, 1765.

SEPITT, DAVID, m. Joanna Stoke, 1740. MICAH, m. Mary Sepitt, 1756.

SEVER, or SEAVER, CALEB, Roxbury, son of Robert Seaver, dropped the letter "a" in his name. He m. Sarah, probably d. of John Ingoldsby of Boston, 1671, and had Caleb, 1673; Elizabeth, 1676; Nathaniel, 1677; Nicholas, 1680; Thomas, 1682; and Sarah, 1686. CHARLES SEVER, son of 1st John, m., 1827, Jane A. E., d. of Daniel Roberts Elliott, and had Catherine Elliott, John; Jane E., m. Alexander M. Harrison; and Charles, m. Mary Webber of Cambridge. JAMES SEVER, Kingston, son of 1st William, m., 1796, Jane, d. of John Russell of Plymouth, and had James Warren, m. Ann Carter of Boston; Thomas Russell, Jane Russell, Elizabeth Parsons, and Sarah Ann Warren. JAMES NICHOLAS SEVER, Kingston, son of 1st John, m., 1819, Mercy Foster, d. of George Russell, and had George Russell, James Nicholas, Winslow Warren, Charlotte, and Nancy. He m., 2d, Jane Nichols of Kingston. JOHN SEVER, Kingston, son of 1st William, m., 1790, Nancy, d. of John Russell of Plymouth, and had William R., John, James Nicholas; Winslow Warren, m. C. Freeman; Sarah Winslow, m. William Thomas of Plymouth; and Charles. JOHN SEVER, Kingston, son of above, m. Ann Dana, and had Ann Dana, Mary, Emily; Ellen, m. Rev. Theodore Tibbets and George S., Hale, and Martha. JOSHUA SEAVER, Dorchester, son of Robert, m. Mary, wid. of Joseph Pepper, 1678, and had Joshua, 1679; Mary, 1683. By a 2d wife, Mary, he had Mary, 1684; Ebenezer, 1687; John, Sarah, Jemima, Robert, and Jonathan. JOSHUA SEAVER, son of above, m. Mercy Cooke, and had Joshua, Mercy, Samuel, Elizabeth, and William. NATHANIEL SEAVER, son of 4th William, m. Hannah Loco of Boston, and had Horace, now living in Boston, and probably others. NICHOLAS SEVER, Kingston, son of Caleb, m., 1728, Sarah, wid. of Charles Little, and d. of James Warren, and had John, m. Judith Cooper; James, and William. He m., 2d, 1757, Susanna Winslow of Boston. ROBERT SEAVER came in the Mary and John 1634, and settled in Roxbury, where he m. Elizabeth Ballard, or Allard, 1634, and had Shubael, 1640; Joshua, 1641; Caleb; Elizabeth, 1643; Nathaniel, 1646; Hannah, 1648; Hannah again, 1650. WILLIAM SEVER, Kingston, son of Nicholas, m., 1755, Sarah, d. of James Warren, and had Sarah, m. Thomas Russell; William, m. Mary Chandler; James, m. Jane, d. of John Russell; Ann Warren, and John. He m., 2d, 1798, Mercy, wid. of John Russell, and d. of Nathaniel Foster, 1798. WILLIAM, son of above, m., about 1755, Sarah, d. of James Warren, and had Penelope W., m. Levi Lincoln; William James, m. A. Trask; Ann W., m. John Brazier. WILLIAM SEAVER, son of 2d Joshua, m. Patience Trescott of Dorchester, and had William, Ebenezer, Sarah, Rebecca, Ruth, Jonathan, Elizabeth, Patience, Mary, and Robert. WILLIAM SEAVER, Taunton, son of above, m. Molly Foster of Dorchester, and had Molly Foster, m. Samuel Caswell. He m., 2d, wid. Thankful Stetson of Braintree, and had John, Nathaniel, Hannah, Benjamin, Samuel; and William, who m. Lydia Presbry of Taunton, and was the father of Lydia, who m. Allen Danforth of Plymouth. (See Seaver, or Sever Genealogy).

SEYMOUR, or SEYMORE, BENJAMIN, came from Chatham, England, with wife Naomi, and had Benjamin, Henry, Joseph, Edward D., Naomi, Sally, m. Joseph Peckham; Frances, m. Thomas Hadaway; Webster, Portia, William, Mary S.; and Joanna, m. Ansel Robbins. BENJAMIN, son of above, m.

Mary W. Cuffs, 1823. EDWARD D., son of 1st Benjamin, m. Mrs. Julia Kingman of Wareham, 1833. HENRY, son of 1st Benjamin, m. Nancy Morton,
1826, and had Nancy Seely, 1827; Margaret Augusta, 1831; and Henry J., m.
Susan S., d. of Thomas Hadaway. He m., 2d, Mary, d. of Nathaniel
Bartlett.

SHATTUCK, ROBERT, perhaps son of William of Watertown, m. Mary
Pratt, and had Mary, 1720; Robert, 1721; Randall, 1723.

SHAW, ABRAHAM, Dedham, 1637, had Joseph, John, Mary, Martha, and
probably Susanna, m. Nicholas Byram. BENJAMIN SHURTLEFF, Boston, son
of 2d Southworth, m., 1856, Amelia Copeland, d. of Walter S. Tribou, and
had Allerton, 1858; Helen Southworth, 1861. BENONI, son of 1st Jonathan,
m. Lydia, d. of John Waterman, and had Lydia, 1697, m. Ebenezer Lobdell;
John, 1699, m. Abigail Perry; Mary, 1700, m. Benjamin Churchill; Margaret,
1702; Elkanah, 1703, m. Mehitabel Churchill; Moses, 1705; Jonathan, Benoni;
Benjamin, m. Mary Atwood, and Hannah, twins, 1715; Rebecca, m. Samuel
Lucas and Nathaniel Atwood, and Abigail, twins; and Phebe. BENONI, son
of 1st Samuel, m., 1772, Ruth, d. of William Sergeant, and had Ruth, 1774.
CHRISTOPHER, Plympton, had Ellis, about 1788; Gaius, and Hosea. CYRUS,
son of 1st William, m. Mary Ann, d. of Luke Perkins, 1825, and had Hannah
Drew, 1827, m. John A. Burgess; William Henry, 1829; Nancy L., 1833; Mary
Ann, 1835; Elizabeth Frances, 1838. DEFOREST, son of 2d Ellis, m. Susan
Rickards of Sharon, and had George, m. Lizzie Dickson; Mary A., 1846;
Lizzie, m. William Bartlett; Laura A., 1848, m. Charles Holmes; Sylvia M.,
1851, m. John Spear of Augusta; Benjamin, m. Nellie Smith; Weston, m.
Anna Oldham of Wareham; Frederick, and Clara. ELKANAH, Plympton,
son of Benoni, m. Hannah Cushman, 1725, and had Elkanah, m. Joanna
King, 1745. ELIAS, Carver, m. Lydia Faunce, 1796. ELLIS, son of Chris-
topher, m. Deborah Raymond, 1811, and had Deforest; Deborah, m., 1st,
Samuel Turner, and 2d, George Pierce of Rochester; Lyphena, m. Frank
Drake of Sandwich; Fanny, m. Benjamin Hathaway of Wareham; and
Hope, m. Albert Morey of Halifax. GEORGE SHATTUCK, Boston, son of 2d
Southworth, m., 1852, Georgiana Henshaw, and had Edward Sargent, 1853;
Caroline Churchill, 1855. ICHABOD, son of 1st Samuel, m., 1757, Priscilla,
d. of John Atwood, and had Priscilla, 1758; Mary, 1760, m. Nathaniel Har-
low; Experience, 1762, m. James Russell and Beza Hayward; Desire, 1765;
Lydia, 1767; Ichabod, 1769; Southworth, 1772; Lucy, 1773; Southworth,
1775; Sally, 1778, m. Benjamin Shurtleff; Nancy, 1781, m. Thomas Witherell;
John Atwood, 1783; Samuel, 1785; and Sarah Ann Maria, m. Russell Hallet.
ICHABOD, son of above, m., 1st, Betsey, d. of Ichabod Holmes, 1795, and
had Elizabeth Holmes, 1795. He m., 2d, her sister Esther, 1800. JAMES,
son of 1st John, m., 1652, Mary, d. of Experience Mitchell, and had James,
1754, and two daughters. JOHN came over before 1627, followed by wife
Alice and children John, who returned unmarried; James, Jonathan; and Abigail, m. Stephen Bryant. JOHN, Weymouth, son of Abraham, born in England, by wife Alice, had Elizabeth, 1656; Abraham, 1657; Mary, 1660;
Nicholas, 1662; Joseph, 1664; Alice, 1666; Hannah, 1668; Benjamin, 1670;
Abigail, 1672; Ebenezer, 1674; and John. JOHN, Bridgewater, son of

Joseph, m. Ruth, d. of Samuel Angier of Watertown, and had Oakes, 1736, father of Chief-Justice Lemuel Shaw; Besaliel, 1738; William, 1741; Eunice, 1743; Ruth, 1744, m. Nathaniel Goodwin of Plymouth; Ezra, 1746; John, 1748; Samuel, 1750. JOHN, Plympton, son of Benoni, m. Abigail, d. of William Perry of Scituate, and had Isaac, m. Persis, d. of James Harlow; Abigail, Zilpha; and Jemima, 1736, m. William Sturtevant. JONATHAN, son of 1st John, born in England, m., 1657, Phebe, d. of George Watson, and had Hannah, m., 1678, Thomas Paine of Eastham; Jonathan, 1663; Phebe, m. John Morton; Mary, m., 1687, Eleazer Ring; George; Lydia, m. Nicholas Snow; Benjamin and Benoni, twins, 1672. He m., 2d, Persis (Dunham) Pratt, wid. of Benajah, and d. of John Dunham. JONATHAN, Plympton, son of above, m. Mehitabel Pratt, 1687, and had Jonathan, 1689, m. Elizabeth Atwood; Phebe, 1690, m. Thomas Shurtleff; Persis, 1692, m. Joseph Lucas; Mehitabel, 1694, m. Zachariah Weston; James, 1696; Hannah, 1699, m. James Harlow; Elizabeth, 1701, m. a Lucas; Priscilla, 1702, m. a Bosworth; Abigail, 1705, m. a Lucas; and Samuel. He m., 2d, Mary Darling, and had Rebecca. JONATHAN, Plympton, son of above, m. Elizabeth Atwood, and had Nathaniel, 1714; Mary, 1716; Nathaniel, 1718, m. Hannah Perkins; Elizabeth, 1719; Sarah, 1724; Jonathan, 1728. JONATHAN, m. Sally Bartlett, 1797. JOSEPH, Bridgewater, son of 2d John, m. Judith, d. of John Whitmarsh, and had Elizabeth, 1687, m. Noah Washburn and Isaac Harris; Joseph, 1691; Judith, 1693; Abigail, 1695, m. Daniel Alden; Ruth, 1698, m. James Snow; Martha, 1700, m. Eleazer Alden, Sarah, 1702, m. James Carey; Hannah, 1704, m. Isaac Snow and John Whitman; Ebenezer; 1706, m. Mary, d. of Samuel Reed; John, 1708; Zechariah, 1711. JOSEPH, Bridgewater, son of 2d Zechariah, m., 1805, Olive, d. of Samuel Dike, and had Samuel Dike, 1813. JOSHUA, son of 1st Samuel, m., 1765, Margaret Atwood, and had Hannah, 1765; Elizabeth, 1767; Joshua, 1769; Joshua, 1772. LUCAS, m. Mehitabel Manter, 1803, and had Sylvanus, 1804; Sally, 1806; Lucas C., 1809; William Manter, 1811. NATHANIEL, Plympton, son of 3d Jonathan, m. Hannah, d. of Luke Perkins, and had Mary, 1741, m. Francis Shurtleff and Thomas Savery; Elizabeth, 1744; Nathaniel, 1747; Joseph, 1749; Hannah, 1751; Ruth, 1753; Sarah, 1756; Jonathan, 1758; Deliverance, 1760; James, 1764; Zilpha, 1765. SAMUEL, son of 2d Jonathan, m. Desire, d. of Ichabod Southworth of Middleboro', and had Samuel, 1731; Ichabod, 1734; Elijah, 1736; William, 1738; Joshua, 1741, m. Margaret Atwood; James, Desire, Benoni, and Samuel. SAMUEL DIKE, son of 2d Joseph, m. Betsey Hayward of Bridgewater. He m., 2d, Wealthea S. Estes of Brunswick, Maine, and had Henry W., 1840; and John J. of Plymouth, 1842, m. Persis R. Kingman of Keene, N. H., and Edith L. Aldrich of Riverport, R. I. SAMUEL, son of 1st Southworth, m. Mary Gibbs, d. of Simeon Dike, and had William Prince, 1833; George Atwood, 1836; Rebecca Harlow, 1838, m. Franklin Washburn; Isabella Frances, 1842; Emma Louise, 1845, m. Charles H. Frink; and Alberto Merritt, 1847. SOUTHWORTH, son of 1st Ichabod, m., 1798, Maria, d. of Stephen Churchill, and had Betsey, 1799; Southworth, 1801; Ichabod, 1803; Betsey, 1805, m. William Bramhall; Samuel, 1808; Maria, 1811; George Atwood, 1813; George Atwood, 1816; and James R., 1820, m. Susan, d. of Ephraim Finney. SOUTH-

WORTH, Boston, son of above, m., 1826, Abby Atwood, d. of Benjamin Shurtleff, and had Benjamin Shurtleff, 1827; George Shattuck, 1829; Ann Maria, 1830, m. Watson Freeman; Henry Southworth, 1833, m. Louisa Towne; Abby, 1837; Franklin Allerton, 1839; Edward Lothrop, 1841; Sarah, 1843, m. Samuel Craft Davis; Adela, 1845. STILLMAN, of Carver, m. Eliza Cole, 1830. SYLVANUS, m Rebecca Dunbar, 1780. WILLIAM, of Middleboro', m. Ruth Thomas, and had Harvey, m. Cynthia Thomas; Cyrus, m. Mary Ann Perkins, 1825; William; Sally, m. John Cleale; Polly, m. Joshua Standish; Priscilla, m. George Raymond. WILLIAM, son of above, m. Lydia, d. of Joseph Sampson, and had Francis Marion, 1823; Eleazer, 1825, m. Hannah N. Dunham; Sarah Jane, 1827; Joseph Bryant, 1830, m. Mary Dixon; and Asa, 1833, m. Cynthia Thomas. ZECHARIAH, Bridgewater, son of 1st Joseph, m., 1733, Sarah, d. of Daniel Packard, and had Sarah, 1734; Ruth, 1738, m. Joseph Snow; Martha, 1740; Daniel, 1742; Elizabeth, 1744, m. Obadiah Reed; Judith, 1749, m. John Edson; Zechariah, 1751; Nehemiah, 1753. ZECHARIAH, Bridgewater, son of above, m. Hannah, d. of Samuel Bisbee, 1777, and had Joseph, 1779; Sarah, 1782; Alvin, 1785.

SHEPARD, ARTHUR, m., 1754, Mary Morton. DAVID, m., 1699, Rebecca Curtis.

SHERIVE, or SHRIEVE, THOMAS, by wife Martha, had Thomas, 1649, and probably John, m., 1686, Jane, d. of John Havens of Rhode Island.

SHERMAN, ABIEL, Marshfield, son of Elisha, m., 1781, Lucy Sylvester, and had Lucy, 1782; Margaret, 1784; Lucy, 1786; Betsey, 1788; Stephen, 1791, Peter, 1793; Nathan, 1795. ANDREW, Carver, m. Calista Vaughn, and had Phebe Ann, 1833; Marietta, 1836; Hannah, 1838. ANTHONY, Carver, son of 7th John, m. Hannah, wid. of Bradford Cole, and d. of Thomas Tilson, and had Lydia Doten, m. Thomas M. Leach of Plympton; and John. m. Maria A. Cook of Boston. ANTHONY, East Bridgewater and Rochester, son of a John, m., 1746, Silence Ford, and had Mary, 1747, m. Eleazer Allen; Lemuel, 1748; Hannah, 1749; Jane, 1751; Anthony, 1753; Thomas, 1754; Lydia, 1756; Lois, 1758; Ruth, 1760; John, 1765; Betsey, 1768. ARTHUR, Marshfield, son of 2d Gershom, m. Henrietta Church, and had Marietta, 1813; Hannah, 1816. ASA, Carver, son of 6th John, m. Polly, d. of Edward Stephens, about 1780, and had Joseph, 1785, m. a Bradford; Polly, 1786, m. Jonathan Parker; Lucy, 1788, m. a Cushing; Asa, 1789, m. a Bradford; Zacheus, 1794, m. Nancy Bartlett of Plymouth; Nathaniel, 1795, m. in Boston; Charles, 1802; George, 1803, m. Betsey, d. of Nicholas Drew of Plymouth. ASA, Marshfield, son of Ignatius, m. Polly Kent, and had Polly, 1799; Asa, 1801; Wealthea, 1803; Abigail, 1806; Alice W., 1810; William, 1813. CALEB, son of 2d Ebenezer, by wife Rebecca, had Young, 1746; Ring, 1749; Hannah, 1751; Sarah, 1753; Ebenezer, 1755. CORNELIUS, Rochester, son of 8th William, m. Dilly Handy, and had Temperance, 1784; Martin, 1790; Dilly, 1794; Love, 1798; Bartlett, 1801; Roxanna, 1805. EBENEZER, Carver, son of 7th John, m. Abigail Morton of Carver, and had Lavina, 1815, m. Benjamin Cobb; Lucinda, 1818, m. Lothrop Barrows; Lucy N., 1821, m. Charles Gibbs Morton and Edward Hathaway, both of Plymouth; Abigail; Maria Ann, 1825; and Marcia Ann, 1826, m. Everett T. Manter; Marcus M., 1831; Ebenezer, 1835. EBEN-

EZER, Marshfield, son of 2d William, m., 1702, Margaret, d. of Valentine Decro, and had Eleazer, 1702; Rachel, 1703, m. Seth Joyce; William, 1704; Elizabeth, 1706, m. a Witherell; Joseph, 1709; Abigail, 1710, m. a Carver; Caleb, and Elisha. He m., 2d, Bathsheba Ford, and had Robert, Ebenezer; and Bathsheba, m. a Walker. EBENEZER, Marshfield, son of above, m., 1749, Elizabeth Wormall, and had Huldah, 1750; Deborah, 1752; Keziah, 1755; Ichabod, 1758; Ebenezer, 1760. EBENEZER, Marshfield, son of Elisha, m., 1773, Mary Simmons, and had Aaron, 1773; Sarah, 1775; Elisha, 1777; Lydia, 1779; Mary, 1782, m. Jonathan Hatch; Ebenezer, 1785, m. Grace Hatch; Isaac, 1788; Betsey, 1790; Beulah, 1794, m. Amos Damon. EDWARD, Middleboro', son of Elnathan, by wife Lucy, had Job, Nathan; Anna, m. William Bryant; Experience, m. Joseph Williams; Lucy, m. Job Shaw; Rhoda, m. Noah Winslow; and Rebecca. ELIJAH, son of 3d Samuel, m. Hannah (Morton), wid. of Ichabod Thomas, and had Elijah, 1788; Isaac Morton, 1790; and Lydia, 1785, m. Ezekiel Loring of Plympton. ELIJAH, son of above, m. Cynthia Fish, 1811, and had Cynthia Thomas, 1812, m. Thomas Tribble; Jane Doten, 1814, m. Lorin Peterson; William Doten, 1816, m. Sophia S., d. of Thomas Diman; Elijah, 1718, m. Lucy Ann Washburn; Adaline, 1820, m. Josiah Goodwin from Maine; Thomas F., 1823, m. Priscilla Morton, d. of Zephaniah Bradford; Hannah, 1825; Francis, 1828. ELISHA, Marshfield, son of 2d Ebenezer, m., 1744, Lydia Walker, and had Margaret, 1745; Abiel, 1747; Ebenezer, 1748. ELNATHAN, Middleboro', who died about 1785, had Simeon, Seth, Edward; Sarah, m. Benjamin Haskell; and Alathea. GERSHOM, son of 1st Samuel, m. Sarah Stevens, and had Lucy, 1742; Gershom, 1744; and Sarah. GERSHOM, Marshfield, son of above, m., 1779, Elizabeth Howland, and had Elizabeth, 1780, m. Samuel Holmes; Gershom, 1781; Arthur, 1785; Susanna, 1792; Jerusha, Luther, and Judah. GERSHOM, Marshfield, son of above, m. Huldah Carver, and had Huldah, 1810; Luther, 1813; Sophia, 1814; Susan, 1817; Eliza H., 1819; Wealthea, 1821; Jacob B., 1824; Gershom, 1826; Joseph P., 1828. HENRY, Carver, son of 7th John, m., 1832, Hannah Nelson Crocker, and had Nelson, 1841, m. Mary A. Wilbur of Plympton; and Hannah C., 1842, m. Joseph W. Sherman. He m., 2d, Christian Crocker. ICHABOD, Marshfield, son of 3d Ebenezer, m., 1783, Sarah Joyce, and had Ruth, 1784; Ebenezer, 1787; Mark J., 1789; Ichabod, 1792; Elizabeth, 1794; Rachel, 1796, Josiah, 1799; Sally, 1802; Mary, 1803; Benjamin, 1810. IGNATIUS, Marshfield, son of 2d Samuel, by wife Abigail, had Joseph, 1754; Abigail, 1756, m. William Thomas; Nathan, 1760; Lydia, 1766; Asa, 1773. ISAAC, Carver, son of Rufus, m. Zilpha Dunham, and had Isaac, 1819; Earl, 1823; Phebe, 1825; Zilpha, 1829; Hannah, 1835. ISAAC MORTON, son of 1st Elijah, m. Hope Doten, 1812, and had Betsey Doten, 1814; Isaac Morton, 1816; Winslow B., 1818, m. Sarah Ann Bent; Mary D., 1821; Hannah T., 1823, m. Cyrus N. Williams: Abby L., 1826, m. Ellis P. Thayer; Leander Lovell, 1829. He m., 2d, 1833, Sarah (Holmes), wid. of William Drew, and d. of Ephraim Holmes, and had George, 1834. JABEZ, Carver, son of 1st Nathaniel, m. Polly Barrows, and had Jabez, 1802; Nathaniel, 1805; Andrew, 1808; Polly, 1810; Sally, 1813; Lucy, 1815; Catherine, 1819. JABEZ, Carver, son of above, m. Mary E. Doten, and had Deborah C., 1827; Juliett; Edward,

1830. JACOB, Middleboro', who died about 1780, by wife Margaret, had David, Henry, Jacob, Nehemiah, Job; Alma, m. a Handy; Lydia, m. a Vail; Abigail, m. a Faunce; Mercy, m. a Bump; and Margaret. JOHN, Marshfield, son of 1st William, m., 1677, Jane, d. of Walter Hatch of Scituate, and had Bethiah, 1678, m. Israel Thomas; Abigail, 1679; John, 1682; Hannah, 1685; Samuel, 1686; Deborah, 1689; Lois, 1691; William, 1693; Eunice, 1696, m. a Lapham. JOHN, Marshfield, by wife Susanna, had Elisha, Urana; Martha, m. a Curtis; Priscilla, m. a Hall; and Mercy, m. a Pratt. JOHN, Rochester, son of 1st John, m. Sarah Baker, 1712, and had Sarah, 1714; Jane, 1716; Alice, 1719; John, 1721; Abigail; Bethiah, 1724; William, 1726; Lois, 1728; Samuel, 1730. JOHN, Rochester, son of above, m. Mercy Lucas, 1745, and had John, 1746; William, 1748; Samuel, 1750; Bethiah, 1753, m. Cornelius Clark; Nathaniel, 1755; Thomas, 1756; Micah, 1757; Joshua, 1760; Deborah, 1763; Mercy, 1765. He perhaps, also, m. Deborah Winslow. JOHN, Rochester, by wife Ruth, had John; Lucy, m. an Allen; Charity, m. an Ashley; Job, and Elizabeth. JOHN, Marshfield, perhaps son of 3d William, m. Elizabeth Dingley, 1746, and had Nathaniel, 1748; Ruth, 1750, m. Josiah Bisbee of Pembroke; Rufus, 1754; Asa, 1756; Betsey, 1758, m. William Finney of Plymouth; John, 1762. JOHN, Plymouth and Carver, son of above, m. Lydia, d. of Ebenezer Doten, and had Ebenezer, 1788; John, 1791; Reuben, 1797; Henry, 1806; Anthony, 1809. JOHN, Carver, son of above, m. Eleanor, d. of William Barnes of Plymouth, 1813, and had Lydia, 1814, m. Elkanah Churchill; Mercy, 1817, m. Thomas Vaughn; Ellen, m. John C. Saunders; Betsey W.; Sally, m. George W. Sherman of Plymouth; and John, m. Sarah Wright. JOSEPH, Marshfield, son of 6th William, m., 1760, Alice Shurtleff, and had Alice; Samuel, 1761; Huldah; Joseph, 1772; William; Amos, 1783. JOSEPH RANSOM, Carver, son of Micah, m. Betsey W. Cobb, and had Joseph William, 1832; Ann Janette, 1834; Frederick Cobb, 1835. JOSHUA, son of 1st Samuel, m. Deborah Croade, 1735, and had Joshua, 1736; Nathaniel, and Deborah. JOSHUA, Rochester, son of 4th John, m. Sarah Pope, and had Dennis, 1797, Charles P., 1799; Sarah P., 1802; Mercy, 1805; and Uriah, 1809. LEVI, Carver, son of 1st Nathaniel, m. Lydia, d. of Heman Crocker, and had Eleazer Crocker, 1817; Lydia Clark, 1820, m. P. M. C. Jones; Levi, 1828; Maria, 1834. MICAH, Carver, son of Rufus, m. Mercy Ransom, and had Joseph R., 1805; Rufus, 1806; Polly, 1808; Lucy, 1811; Micah, 1814; William M., 1816; Eliza, 1819; Lydia, 1823; Sarah, 1824; Albert A., 1829. MICAH, Orleans, son of 4th John, m. Lydia Taylor, and had Samuel, Jonathan, Deborah, Richard, Mercy, and Micah. NATHANIEL, Plympton, son of 6th John, m. Maria, d. of James Clark of Plymouth, and had Betsey, 1770; Nathaniel, 1771; Polly, 1776; Jabez, 1778, m. Polly Barrows; Sally, 1780; Anna, 1783; Levi, 1788; and three of the daughters m. John Prince and Launcelot Burgess of Kingston, and Joshua Barrows. REUBEN, Carver, son of 7th John, m. Priscilla P. Hammond, and had Elizabeth D., 1822, m. Wilson Barrows and William Tilson; Priscilla, 1824, m. Barnabas Hedge of Plymouth; Reuben, 1834. ROBERT, Marshfield, son of 2d Ebenezer, m., 1740, Mary Eames, and had Sarah, 1741; Valentine, 1743. RUFUS, Plympton, son of 6th John, m., 1775, Phebe Rider of Plymouth, and had Rufus, 1775, m. Lucy,

d. of Nathaniel Carver of Plymouth; Hannah, 1778, m. John Waterman; Phebe, 1781, m. Ebenezer Cobb; Micah, 1783, m. Mercy Ransom; Isaac, 1786, m. Zilpha Dunham. SAMUEL, Marshfield, son of 1st William, m. Sarah Daggett, and had Sarah, Prudence; and Susanna, m. John White. By a 2d wife, Hannah, he had Hannah, 1688; Samuel, 1689; Mercy, 1691; Joshua, 1693; Desire, 1695; Patience, 1698; William, 1699; Gershom, 1700; Caleb, 1703, m. Deborah Ring. SAMUEL, Marshfield, son of above, m. Mary Williamson, 1724, and had Samuel, Joseph, Nathaniel, Sarah, Ignatius, Manoah; and Mary, m. a Washburn. SAMUEL, son of above, m. Experience Branch, 1750, and had Samuel, 1751; Elijah, 1753; Lydia, 1755. He m., 2d, Betty Sears, 1761, and had Thomas, 1762; William, 1764; Andrew, 1767; and Betsey, m. Lewis Holmes. He m., 3d, 1770, Jerusha Morton. SAMUEL, son of above, m. Lydia Doten, 1789, and had Lydia, 1790; Samuel, 1791; Thomas Branch, 1794. SAMUEL, son of above, m., 1813, Eleanor Covington, and had Samuel, 1814; Eleanor, 1819; Triphena, 1822; Everett F., 1826, m., 1st, Elizabeth, d. of Samuel Talbot, and, 2d, Sarah, d. of Coomer Weston; Samuel again, 1828; Lydia Doten, 1831, m. James W. Blackmer. SAMUEL, Rochester, son of 1st John, had, by wife Charity, Samuel, 1724. SAMUEL, Ware, perhaps son of above, m. Mary Snow, and Jerusha Davis, and had Thomas, 1751; Prince, 1753; Reuben, 1759; Samuel, 1762; Mary, 1764; Ebenezer, 1768. THOMAS, son of 3d Samuel, m., 1790, Priscilla Calderwood, and had Thomas, 1791, m. Betsey Sears; Priscilla, 1793, m. Lemuel Simmons; Sally, 1795, m. Sylvanus Ripley; Betsey, 1797, m. John Saunders; William, 1799, m. Irene Standish of Halifax. He m., 2d, Deborah Kingman of Marshfield, and had Lucy Ann, m. Albert Bishop of N. Y. THOMAS BRANCH, son of 4th Samuel, m., 1832, Susan Durfey, and had Mary H.; Susan Doten, 1834, m. Nathaniel Holmes, Jr.; Samuel, 1836. THOMAS, Rochester, son of 4th John, m. a Winslow, and had Azuba, 1786; John, 1788. He m., 2d, Deborah Winslow, and had Zephaniah, 1792; Otis, 1794; Sarah, 1796; Sylvanus, 1798; Hannah, 1798; Leonard, 1800; Deborah, 1802; Thomas, 1804. THOMAS, East Bridgewater, son of 2d Anthony, m., 1781, Betsey Keith, and had Anthony, 1783; Daniel, 1785; Thomas, 1787; Lydia, Naomi, Betsey, Martin, and Hannah. WILLIAM, Plymouth, 1632, and afterwards Marshfield, m., 1639, Prudence Hill, and had Samuel, William; and John, 1646. WILLIAM, son of above, m., 1667, Desire Doty, and had Hannah, 1668, m. William Ring; Elizabeth, 1670; William, 1672; Patience, 1674; Experience, 1678; Ebenezer, 1680. WILLIAM, son of above, m., 1697, Mercy, d. of Peregrine White, and had Thankful, 1699; Sarah, 1701; Mercy, 1711; Abigail, 1711; John, 1720; Anthony, 1722. WILLIAM, son of 3d Samuel, m. Elizabeth Drew, 1794, and had Elizabeth, m. Isaac Sampson. WILLIAM, Marshfield, son of 1st John, m., 1719, Mary Eames, and had Sarah, m. Adam Hall; Thankful, m. a Polden; Mary, and Abigail. WILLIAM, Marshfield, son of 2d Ebenezer, m., 1732, Elizabeth Lapham, and had Eleazer, Joseph, Betty, Lydia, Abigail, Hannah, and Desire. WILLIAM, Rochester, who died 1816, by wife Hannah, had Rebecca, Nancy, and Hannah, m. Henry Pierce. WILLIAM, Rochester, son of 3d John, m. Abigail Handy, and had Jabez, 1754; Cornelius, 1756; Abigail, 1758; Alice, 1761; Sarah, Susanna, William, Jerusha, and Keziah. The family of Sher-

man, to which Gen. William T. Sherman belongs, is descended from John of
Watertown, born in Dedham, England, 1613, and so far as known is not connected with the old colony stock.

SHUMWAY, JEREMIAH, Oxford, son of 1st Peter, by wife Experience, had
Jeremiah, 1731; Experience, 1733; Peter, 1735; Mary, 1737; Martha, 1738; Elizabeth, 1740; Isaac, 1742; William, 1744; Solomon, 1747; Samuel, 1749; Benjamin,
1752; Mary again, 1757. NOAH, Oxford, son of 2d Peter, m. Lucy Dike, and
had Jeremiah; Lucy Dike, m. Pitts Sayles of Putnam; Thomas, m. Mary
Blackstock of Oxford; Noah, m. Elizabeth Stiness of Killingley, Conn.; Daniel, m. Rebecca Stiness, and Abiel Leavens. By a 2d wife, named Aldrich, he
had Jeremiah, m. an Albee; Nancy, m. a McDonough; Rufus, Ruth, and
George. NOAH, son of above, had, with others, Thomas D., of Plymouth, m.
Mary Anna, d. of Seth Morton. PETER, came from France about 1690, and
settled in Danvers, where he m. a Smith, and had Oliver, 1701; Jeremiah,
1703; Daniel, 1705; John, 1707; Jacob, 1709; Samuel, 1711; Abel, 1713.
PETER, Oxford, son of Jeremiah, m. Rebecca Leavens, 1759, and had Martha,
1760; Zeviah, 1762; Elijah, 1764; Rebecca, 1766; Elizabeth, 1768; Noah, 1770;
Leavens, 1772; Perly, 1774; Peter, 1779; Rebecca again, 1780; Zinah, 1788;
Polly, 1790.

SHURTLEFF, ABIEL, son of 1st William, m., 1696, Lydia, d. of Jonathan
Barnes, and had James, 1696; Elizabeth, 1698, m. Joseph Vaughn and Jonathan Shaw; Lydia, 1701, m. Barnabas Atwood; David, 1703; Hannah, 1705,
m. Caleb Cooke; John, 1707; Benjamin, 1710; William, 1713; Joseph, 1716;
Abiel, 1717. ABIEL, son of above, m., 1740, Lucy, d. of Samuel Clark, and
had Abiel, 1741; Abiel, 1742; Clark, 1745; Noah, 1747; Lucy, 1750, m. Timothy Goodwin; Levi, 1754; Samuel, 1759. ABIEL, Plympton, son of 1st David,
m., 1756, Mary, d. of James LeBaron, and had David, 1756; Timothy, 1760;
Gideon, 1762; Levi, 1765; James, 1768; Jael, 1771; Enoch, 1773; Abiel, 1776;
Enoch, 1779. When he died, in 1826, he had living 350 descendants.
ALBERT, Carver, son of Gideon, m. Lucy Thomas, and had Albert Tilson,
1837; Lucy Ann, 1839. AMASA, Plympton, son of 3d William, m. Sarah, d.
of Nathaniel Harlow, and had Sarah, 1784. ANSEL, Carver, m. Betsey
Atwood, and had Ansel, 1813. BARNABAS, Plympton, son of 2d William,
m., 1727, Jemima Adams, and had Susanna, 1728, m. Nathaniel Atwood;
Jemima, 1730, m. Ebenezer Lawrence; Barnabas, 1733; Molly, 1735; Francis,
1738, m. Mary Shaw; Caleb Loring, 1740; Elizabeth, 1743, m. Hezekiah Cole;
Molly, 1747, m. Isaac Perkins; Barnabas, 1750, m. Phebe Harlow. BARNA-
BAS, Carver, m. Zilpha Cole, and had William, 1806; Polly Savery, 1808;
Barnabas, 1812; Lothrop, 1814; Zilpha B., 1823. BENJAMIN, Plympton, son
of 1st Abiel, m. Hannah Diman. He m., 2d, 1745, Susanna, d. of Josiah
Cushman, and had Hannah, m. an Ellis; Benjamin, 1748; Susanna, 1751;
Ruth, 1753. BENJAMIN, Plympton, son of above, m., 1773, Abigail Atwood,
and had Benjamin, 1774; Nathaniel, 1776, m. Betsey Bumpus and Abigail
Barrows; Stephen, 1777; Barsillai, 1780, m. Dorothy Locke; Abigail, 1782,
m. Francis Atwood; Flavel, 1784, m. Elizabeth Cole and Lucy Allen; Ruth,
1787; Lot, 1789; Charles, 1790, m. Hannah Shaw; Samuel Atwood, 1792, m.
Lliza Carleton; Hannah, 1794, m. Abijah Lucas; Milton, 1796, m. Polly Fitz-

patrick and Mary Barnes. BENJAMIN, Carver and Boston, son of above, m., 1803, Sally, d. of Ichabod Shaw of Plymouth, and had Abby Atwood, 1804, m. Southworth Shaw; Benjamin, 1806; Sally, 1808, m. Benjamin Freeman; Nathaniel Bradstreet, 1810, m. Sarah Eliza Smith; Ann Shaw, 1812. BENJAMIN, Chelsea, son of above, m., 1830, Cynthia Bryant, and had Benjamin, 1831, m. Juliette Pickering; Elizabeth, 1834, m. Alexander Edward Savage; Josiah Bryant, 1838, m. Mary J. Hall; Sarah Shaw, 1842, m. Henry W. Dale, BENJAMIN, Napa City, Cal., son of Charles, m., 1853, Ann M. B. Griffith. and had George C., 1854; Charles A., 1857; Benjamin E., 1867. CHARLES, Carver, son of 2d Benjamin, m., 1815, Hannah Shaw, and had Samuel A., 1816, m. Hannah Savery; George A. C., 1819, m. Mary Jane Nye; Benjamin, 1821; Eliza Carleton, 1826. DAVID, son of 1st Abiel, m , 1731, Bethiah, d. of Benoni Lucas, and had Abiel, 1734, and David. DAVID, Plympton, son of above, by wife Mary, had Chloe, 1778; Joseph, 1780; Martha, 1782; William, 1784; Mary, 1786; David, 1788; Zenas, 1790; Abiel, 1793, Susanna, 1795; Lydia, 1797. DAVID, Carver, son of above, m. Waitstill Hammond, and had Harriet, 1813; Martha, 1815; Daniel W., 1817; Mary A., 1819; Jared, 1821; Anna, 1823. EBENEZER, Carver, m. Mary Shaw, and had Ruth Barrows, 1804; Ebenezer, 1807; Mary, 1810. FRANCIS, Plympton, son of 1st Barnabas, m. Mary, d. of Nathaniel Shaw, and had Zilpha, 1761; Caleb, 1763; Francis, 1765; Olivia, 1769; Lothrop, 1772; William, 1775; Nathaniel, 1776; Mary, 1779; Zilpha, 1782; Susanna, 1785. FRANCIS, Carver, son of above, by wife Elizabeth, had Nathaniel, 1786; Hannah, 1790, GIDEON, Carver, son of 3d Abiel, by wife Lucy, had Phebe, 1786; Lenomi, 1788; Gideon, 1789; Luther, 1790; Saba, 1792; Bethiah, 1793; James, 1795; Melinda, 1797; Eames, 1797; Robert, 1799; Levi, 1801; Lucy, 1803; Betsey, 1805; Alice, 1807; Albert, 1809; Mary, 1812; Amanda, 1817. ICHABOD, Carver, son of 1st Thomas, by wife Mercy, had Rebecca Holmes, 1827; Lucy Williams, 1830; Joseph Thomas, 1832; William Francis, 1834; Peter, 1837. JABEZ, son of 2d William, m. Mary, d. of Return Wait, and had Mary, 1717; Jabez, 1719. JAMES, son of 1st Abiel, m. Faith, d. of Jeremiah Jackson, 1734, and had Lydia, 1735, m. John Cornish; Elizabeth, 1837, m. Ephraim Spooner; Hannah, 1740, m. James Baker, Molly, 1741; Faith, 1745, m. Robert Slocum; and James. JAMES, m., 1744, Joanna Tupper, and had James, 1745, m. Priscilla Torrey. JAMES, Carver, m. Elizabeth Thomas, and had Mary W , 1819; Perez T., 1821; Elizabeth T., 1821. JOHN, Plympton, son of 2d William, m. Sarah, d. of Benoni Lucas, and had Susanna, 1727; William and Benoni, twins, 1730; Mary, 1732; Lothrop, 1735; Lucy, Amos; Jonathan, 1741, m. Abigail Lord; Lemuel, and John. JOHN, son of 1st Abiel, m., 1734, Abigail Fuller, and had Sylvanus, 1735; Silas, 1737; James, and Drusilla. JOSEPH, son of 1st Abiel, m., 1742, Sarah, wid. of Seth Cobb, and had Mary, 1743, m. Rufus Ripley; Joseph, 1746; Bathsheba, 1752, m. Simeon Chandler. JOSEPH, son of above, m. Olive Ripley, and had Joseph, 1770; Hezekiah, 1773; Clark, 1776. JOSEPH, pub. to Sylvina Battles, 1795. LEVI, Carver, m. Mary Chandler, and had Phebe, 1826; Josiah, 1828; Levi, 1829; Mary Jane, 1832; Ruth Cole, 1835; Abiel T., 1837; Isaac Chandler, 1839. LOTHROP, Carver, m. Betsey White, and had Lydia White, 1797; Mary Shaw, 1800; Betsey

White, 1804. LUTHER, Carver, son of Gideon, m. Hannah Fuller, and had
Roswell, 1816; Luther, 1818; George, 1820; Phebe, 1821; Gideon, 1824;
Hannah F., 1826; Robert, 1827. NATHANIEL, son of 2d William, m. Lydia
Branch, 1739, and had Nathaniel, 1739; Lydia, 1741; Thomas Branch, 1743;
Sarah, 1745; Mercy, 1747; Thankful, 1749; Nathaniel, 1751; William, 1753;
Sarah, 1755; Mary, 1759; Patience, 1762. NATHANIEL, Carver, m. Hannah
Shaw, and had Francis, 1812; Isaac Shaw, 1815. NATHANIEL, Carver, m.
Azubah Tilson, and had Alvin, 1811; Tilson, 1812; Nathaniel, 1814; Susanna,
1816. NATHANIEL BRADSTREET, Boston, son of 3d Benjamin, m., 1836,
Sarah Eliza Smith, and had Nathaniel Bradstreet, 1838; Hiram Smith, 1841;
Sarah, 1842; Priscilla, 1845; Anna, 1846; Benjamin, 1847; Mary, 1861. PETER,
Carver, son of 3d William, m. Rebecca Holmes, and had Sylvanus, 1769; Rebec-
ca, 1771; Thomas, 1773; Mary, 1775; Lydia, 1777; Deborah, 1781. ROBERT,
Carver, son of 3d William, by wife Molly, had Susanna, 1776; Huldah, 1778;
Priscilla, 1780; Nathaniel, 1784; Mary, 1787; John, 1789; Sarah, 1793.
SAMUEL, Plympton, son of 2d William, by wife Abigail, had Joseph, 1736;
Samuel, 1738; Alice, 1740, m. Joseph Sherman; Huldah, 1742; Abigail, 1745;
and Lucy, m. Joseph Lapham. SAMUEL ATWOOD, Roxbury, son of Charles,
m., 1842, Hannah Savery, and had Abbie Frances, 1843; Charles Allerton,
1848; Anna Louise, 1852; Hannah Savery, 1855; Grace Allerton, 1858.
SETH, Carver, had Andrew Gibbs, 1828; Elizabeth Swift, 1830; Seth Addison,
1832; Henry Lewis, 1835; Franklin Atwood, 1837; Micah Gibbs, 1839; James
Frederick, 1842; Almanda Partridge, 1844. STEPHEN, Carver, m. Lydia
Atwood, and had Susan, 1808; Serena Gerry, 1810; Phebe, 1811; Stephen,
1814; Lydia A., 1816; Obedience, 1818; Ansel, 1821; Mary Frances, 1823;
Sarah Shaw, 1826. THOMAS, Carver, by wife Polly, had Ichabod, 1802; Re-
becca, 1805; Sylvia, 1813. THOMAS, Plympton, son of 2d William, m., 1708,
Phebe, d. of Jonathan Shaw, and had Mary, 1709; Susanna, 1712; Thomas,
1714, m. Mercy Warren; Mehitabel, 1716; Phebe, 1718; William, 1723; Eliz-
abeth, 1725; Thankful, 1726; Barnabas; and Jonathan, 1727; and Ichabod.
Savage says he m., 2d, 1713, Sarah Kimball. WILLIAM, Plymouth and
Marshfield, m., 1655, Elizabeth, d. of Thomas Lettice, and had William, 1657;
Thomas; Abiel, 1666. WILLIAM, son of above, m., 1683, Susanna, d. of
Barnabas Lothrop, and had Jabez, 1684; Thomas, 1687; William, 1689, m.
Mary Atkinson; Susanna, 1691, m. Josiah Cushman; John, 1693; Barnabas,
1696; Ichabod, 1697; Jacob, 1698; Elizabeth, 1699; Mary, 1700; Sarah, 1702,
m. Ignatius Loring; Samuel, Abigail, and Nathaniel. WILLIAM, Carver,
son of 1st Abiel, m., 1732, Deborah Ransom, and had Lydia, 1734; Ebenezer,
1736, m. Mary Pratt; Peter, 1738, m. Rebecca Holmes; Sarah, 1741, m. Benjamin Bagnall; William, 1743, m, Ruth Shaw; Anna, 1745, m. Jabez Maxim;
John, 1747, m. Mercy Goward; Isaac, 1750; Robert, 1753; Deborah, 1755;
Priscilla, 1757; and Amasa.

SILAS, SILAS, slave of Daniel Diman, m. Venus, slave of Elizabeth
Edwards, 1772.

SILVERA, JOSEPH, m., 1836, Hannah M. Johnson.

SKIFF, EBENEZER, m., 1791, Deborah Ellis. ELLIS, m., 1820, Abigail
Blackwell. RUFUS, m., 1817, Lois Swift.

SIMES, JOSEPH, Portsmouth, Boston, and Plymouth, m. Mary, d. of Joseph Johnson of Plymouth, and is now living. He is descended from John Simes, who came from England 1736 and settled in Portsmouth, where the family, of which one member has been mayor of the city, has always occupied a prominent position.

SIMMONS, AARON, Duxbury, son of Isaac, m. Sarah Holmes of Marshfield, 1749, and had Abraham; Mary, 1755, m. Ebenezer Sherman of Marshfield; and Jesse, 1760. AARON, Scituate, son of Thomas, m. Mary Woodworth, 1677, and had Rebecca, 1679; Moses, 1680; Mary, 1683; Elizabeth, 1686; Ebenezer, 1689; Lydia, 1693. ALDEN S., m. Elizabeth T. Bartlett, 1833. EBENEZER, Scituate, son of 2d Aaron, m. Lydia Kent, 1714, and had Abigail, 1715; Joshua, 1717; Lydia, 1719; Elizabeth, Samuel, Reuben, Peleg, Ebenezer. EBENEZER, son of Elisha, also of Scituate, m. Sophia Richmond of Providence, and had Perez of Scituate, now living, who m. Adeline Jones of Scituate. He m., 2d, Mary (Hitchcock) Curtis, wid. of Stephen, and had Ebenezer. ELISHA, son of Joshua, m. Martha Hersey, and had William, m. Lucia Hammatt of Plymouth; Ebenezer, Martha, Elisha; Benjamin H., who removed to New Orleans; George W., Elizabeth; Joanna, m. Thomas Stephenson; and Franklin. GEORGE, son of 1st Lemuel, m. Mercy, d. of David Bates, 1804, and had Marcia B., m. Ichabod Simmons; George, 1805; Moses, 1808; William Davis, 1811; Augustus F., 1813; Lorenzo, 1815; Isabella, m. Samuel Harmon Davie; Victorine A., m. Gideon Holbrook; John Brooks, m. Harriet Sampson; and Joanna White, 1826. GEORGE, son of above, m., 1828, Fanny Fox Wilkins of Boston, and had George Augustus, 1829; Lorenzo Frederick, 1831; Fanny Wilkins, 1833; Isabella, 1836; Moses, 1838; Albert, 1841; William Wilkins, 1843; Washington, 1846; Washington, 1847; Washington, 1849. He m., 2d, Temperance Phinney Chase of Barnstable, 1849. ICHABOD, son of Isaac, had a 1st wife Lydia, and m., 2d, Mercy Sprague. His children were Consider; Noah, m. Sylvia Southworth; Lemuel, Abigail, Nathaniel; and Ichabod, m. Urania Holmes. ICHABOD, son of Nathaniel, m., 1828, Marcia B., d. of George Simmons, and had Marcia, 1830; Ichabod, 1831; Joanna Adelaide, 1834; Victoria Annette, 1837. ISAAC, son of John, had Isaac, m. Lydia Cushing; Ichabod, and Aaron. JAMES, m. Susan W. Holmes, d. of Nathaniel, 1838. JESSE, son of 1st Aaron, m. Lucy Weston, and had Weston, 1783, m. Lucy Tolman; Ruby, 1786, m. Eden Howland; Martin, 1788, m. Abigail Magoon and Rebecca Thomas; Sally, 1791; Aaron, 1797, m. Lucy Magoon and Sally Chandler; Lyman, 1807, m. Mary Louden of Duxbury. JOHN, son of 2d Moses, m. Mercy Pabodie, 1669, and had John, 1670, m. Experience Picknell; William, 1672; Isaac, 1674; Martha, 1677, m. Ebenezer Delano. JOSHUA, son of 1st Ebenezer, m. Elizabeth Dillingham, and had Joshua, Elizabeth, Lydia, Ebenezer; Mary, m. John H. Thacher of Barnstable: Samuel, Elisha, and William. LEMUEL, son of 1st Ichabod, m. Abigail Pierce, and had Polly, m. Robert Straffin; Moses; Beulah, m. Daniel Goddard; Anderson, 1776; Lydia H., m. Simon Richmond and Avery Dean; George, 1782; Abigail, 1784, m. Alpheus Richmond; Eunice Terry, 1787, m. a Churchill; Lemuel, 1790; and Cynthia Davis, 1794, m. Elkanah Barnes. LEMUEL, son of above, m. Priscilla, d. of Thomas Sherman, 1818, and had

Priscilla C., 1819, m. William H. Morton; Mary S., 1821, m. Albert L. Churchill; Eunice Terry, 1824, m. Robert Brown; and Lemuel, 1826. MOSES, called Symondson, came in the Fortune 1621, and had Moses and Thomas. MOSES, Duxbury, son of above, by wife Sarah, had John, Aaron; Mary, m. Joseph Alden; Elizabeth, m. Richard Dwelley; Sarah, m. James Nash. NATHAN, by wife Lydia, had Nathan, 1755; and Bennett, m. Sarah Cooper. NATHAN, m. Nancy Simmons, 1809. NATHANIEL, son of 1st Ichabod, m. Lydia Sprague, and had Barthena, 1781; Sarah, 1784; Anna, 1786; Nathaniel, 1788; Rebecca, 1791; Alathea, 1793; Lydia, 1795; Lucy and Nancy, twins, 1798; Ichabod, 1801; Mary, 1804; Joshua, 1807. THOMAS, son of 1st Moses, lived in Scituate, and had Moses, m. a wife Patience; and Aaron. WILLIAM, of Duxbury, m. Beulah, d. of Daniel Goddard, 1822, and had Sarah H., m. Lysander Dunham; and Beulah Goddard, m. Nathaniel Cobb Lanman. WILLIAM DAVIS, son of 1st George, m. Harriet, d, of Samuel Doten Holmes, and had William Davis, 1833, m. Mary S., d. of Johnson Davie. Frederick Augustus, 1837; Harriet Louisa, 1839, m. Stephen P. Basford.

SLOCUM, ROBERT, m., 1760, Faith Shurtleff.

SMALL, JOHN, from Provincetown, m., 1728, Hannah Barnaby.

SMALLEY, JOHN, had Hannah, 1641, m. John Bangs; John, 1644; Isaac and Mary, twins, 1647.

SMITH, ABIATHAR, born about 1785, had Howard; Fanny G., m. Thomas Savery and Winsor Savery; and Pamelia, m. Oliver Holmes. BENJAMIN, m., 1757, Sarah Doten. BENJAMIN, m., 1749, Sarah Tinkham. JOHN, called Senior, Plymouth, 1641, had a wife Lydia, and a 2d, Jael Packard of Bridgewater, and moved to Eastham. His children were Hannah, 1641, m. Francis Curtis; John, 1644, m. Hannah Williams; Isaac, 1647; Mary, 1647. JOHN, called Junior, Plymouth, 1643, m., 1649, Deborah, d. of Arthur Howland of Marshfield, and had Hasadiah, 1650; John, 1651; Joseph, 1652; Eleazer, 1654; Hezekiah, 1656. JOHN, m., 1819, Sally Haskell. JOSEPH, m., 1738, Lydia Barnes, and had Sarah, 1739; Lydia, 1744. NICHOLAS, m., 1770, Susanna Churchill, and had Nicholas. NICHOLAS, son of above, m., 1808, Rebecca Sears. PERO, m., 1785, Betty Thompson. PETER, m., 1824, Rebecca Bartlett. PETER W., m., 1827, Jane Faunce. RALPH, came over 1629, settled in Plymouth as pastor, and m., about 1634, Mary, wid. of Richard Masterson. RICHARD had Thomas and Hannah, twins, 1647. SAMUEL, m., 1791, Hope Doten. STEPHEN, from Sandwich, m., 1762, Deborah Ellis. SYLVANUS, m., 1820, Betsey B. Robbins. THOMAS, from New Hampshire, m., 1820, Sarah Finney.

SNOW, ANTHONY, m., 1639, Abigail, d. of Richard Warren, and had Josiah, Lydia, Sarah, Alice, and Abigail, m. Michael Ford. LEONARD, son of James, came from Barnstable County, and m. Meriah, d. of Benjamin Holmes, and had Priscilla H., m. John, son of Ebenezer Davie; James, 1823, m. Laura Newman of Portland; Hannah, 1826, m. Isaac Leavitt of Randolph; Benjamin Franklin, 1829, m. Frances Lane and Elizabeth Bumstead; Janette, 1833, m. Isaac Swift and Edward R. Bartlett; George, 1836, m. Abby Horton; and Leonard, 1838. NICHOLAS, came in the Ann 1623, m. Constance, d. of

Stephen Hopkins, and had Mark, 1628; Hannah, m. Giles Rickard; Rebecca, m. Samuel Rickard; and many others. He removed to Eastham, 1654.

SOULE, BENJAMIN, son of 1st John, m. Sarah Standish, and had Zachariah, 1694; Hannah, 1696, m. George Sampson; Sarah, 1699; Deborah, 1702; Benjamin, 1704; Sarah and Deborah, m. Edward Weston and Adam Wright. GEORGE, came in the Mayflower, removed to Duxbury before 1643, and m. Mary Becket, by whom he had George, Zachariah; John, 1632; Nathaniel, Benjamin, Patience, Elizabeth; and Mary, m. John Peterson. JOHN, Duxbury, son of above, by wife Esther, had John, Joseph; Joshua, 1681; Josiah, 1682; Benjamin; and two daughters. JOHN, Middleboro', son of above, had Martha, 1702; Sarah, 1703; John, 1705; Esther, 1707.

SOUTHER, NATHANIEL, Plymouth, 1636, by wife Alice, had Mary, m., 1653, Joseph Shaw, and afterward John Blake. He m., 2d, wid. Sarah Hill, and died in Boston, 1655.

SOUTHWICK, WILLIAM, published to Hannah Churchill, 1800.

SOUTHWORTH, BENJAMIN, Bridgewater, son of 5th Edward, m., 1763, Mary Smith, and left no children. BENJAMIN, Duxbury; son of 2d Edward, m., 1715, Rebecca Delano, and had Hannah, m. Hezekiah Harrington of Marshfield; Thomas; John, m. Sarah Clark; Constant, Obed, Jasper, Elizabeth; Deborah, m. Reuben Delano. He had a 2d wife, Martha. BENJAMIN, Duxbury, son of 3d Constant, m. Mary, d. of Thomas Hunt of Hanover, and had Sylvia, m. Noah Simmons; Cynthia, m. Asa Phillips; Abigail, 1742; Honor, m. Jonathan Soule; Olive, m. Asa Soule; and Submit. CONSTANT, son of 1st Edward, came from England 1628, with brother Thomas. His mother, Alice, d. of Alexander Carpenter, came in the Ann 1623, and became the 2d wife of William Bradford. He m., 1637, Elizabeth, d. of William Collier of Duxbury, and had Edward; Nathaniel, 1648; William, 1660; Mercy, m. Samuel Freeman of Eastham; Alice, m. Benjamin Church; Mary, m. David Alden; Elizabeth, m. William Fobes; and Priscilla. CONSTANT, Bridgewater, son of 5th Edward, m., 1734, Martha, d. of Joseph Keith, and had Betsey, 1735, m. Joseph Cole; Nathaniel, 1737, m. Catherine, d. of David Howard; Ezekiel, 1739, m. Mary Newman; Martha and Mary, 1741, twins; Desire, 1742; Jedediah, 1745; Constant, 1747; Sarah, 1749; Ichabod, 1751. CONSTANT, Duxbury, son of 2d Edward, m., 1715, Rebecca Simmons, and had William, Benjamin; Mercy, m. Micah Soule. EBENEZER, Middleboro', died 1751, leaving Sarah, Peleg, Laurana, and Ebenezer. EDWARD, England, son of a Thomas and his wife Jane (Mynne) Southworth of Wells in Somersetshire, m., 1614, Alice, d. of Alexander Carpenter, and had Constant, 1615; Thomas, 1616. EDWARD, Duxbury, son of 1st Constant, m., 1669, Mary, d. of William Pabodie, and had Elizabeth, 1672, m. Samuel Weston; Thomas, 1676; Constant; Mercy, m. Moses Soule; Benjamin, 1680; John, 1687; Priscilla, 1693. EDWARD, Duxbury, son of 2d William, m., 1769, Mercy Thomas, and had James, 1769; Edward; Mary, m. Sealey Baker; George, 1780; John, 1782; Jacob, 1785; Seth, and William. EDWARD, Duxbury and Plymouth, son of above, m., 1799, Ruth Ozier, and had Nancy, 1800, m. John Taylor and William G. Dunham; Francis, 1802, m. Polly, d. of Benjamin Goddard; Edward, 1804, m. Margaret Sands; Eli, 1807; George,

1810; Ruth B., 1814; Marcia Ellen, 1820, m. John Pearce; and Jacob William, 1822. His wid. lived to the age of 101. EDWARD, Middleboro', son of 1st Nathaniel, m. Bridget Bosworth, and had Constant, Edward, Lemuel, and Benjamin, all of whom settled in Bridgewater. EDWARD, Bridgewater, son of above, m., 1750, Lydia, d. of John Packard, and had Uriah, 1751; Perez, 1754; Desire, 1756; Edward, 1758; Abiah, 1760; Bridget, 1762; Lydia, 1764; Avis, 1768; Fear, 1770. ICHABOD, Middleboro', son of 1st Nathaniel, had Desire, m. Samuel Shaw; Priscilla, m. Nathaniel Macomber; Mary, m. Rowland Hammond; and Abigail. JACOB, Duxbury, son of 3d Edward, m. Cynthia Peterson, 1811. JAMES, Duxbury, son of 1st Jedediah, m., 1762, Sarah, d. of Perez Drew, and had Jedediah, 1764; Abigail, 1769, m. John Foster of Scituate; Thomas, 1771, m. Sarah James of Scituate; John, 1773; Hannah, 1776; Nathan, 1778; Sarah, 1780; James, 1782. JAMES, Duxbury, son of 3d Edward, m., 1797, Betsey Ozier, and had Joseph, 1797; Betsey, 1798, m. Francis Drew; Charlotte, 1800, m. Samuel Lanman of Plymouth; Hiram, 1803; Thomas, 1804; James, 1810. JASPER, Marshfield, son of 2d Benjamin, m. Rumah, d. of William Southworth, and had Deborah, m. Tabor Cowin; William of Waldoboro'; Francis of Machias, 1767; Lucy Ann, 1772, m. Asa Joyce of Duxbury; Charles, m. Deborah Vinal of Abington; James, m. Lucy Wheaton of Bristol. JEDEDIAH, Duxbury, son of 2d Thomas, m. Hannah Scales of North Yarmouth, Me., and had Sarah, 1729, m. Nathan Soule; Susanna, 1731, m. John Bartlett of North Yarmouth; John, James; Lydia, 1738, m. Seth Bradford. JEDEDIAH, Duxbury, son of 1st James, m., 1804, Elizabeth, d. of Peleg Thomas, and had Hannah, 1805, m. Micah Blanchard of Weymouth; Mary, 1807, m. William Paulding; Nathan, 1809, m. Elvira Soule; James, 1811, m. Lucy Benner; Sarah, 1813; Thomas, 1815; Abigail, 1817, m. Zack Damon of Hanover; Lydia, 1820; Charles, 1822; Henry, 1824; William, 1826, m. Amelia Pratt. JOHN, Duxbury, son of 3d Edward, m. Lucy Ozier, and had Catherine, 1807; Augusta, 1809; Martin, 1811; Lucy, 1816; Elizabeth, 1820, m. Edward B. Weston and William Faunce; Seth, 1818; Sarah, 1824; Cynthia, 1814; Alexander, 1826. JOHN, North Yarmouth, son of 1st Jedediah, m. Joanna Mitchell, and had fifteen daughters and three sons. JOHN, Duxbury, son of 1st James, m., 1809, Frances Allen of Boston, and had John, James, and Mary. LEMUEL, Bridgewater, son of 5th Edward, m., 1757, Patience West, and had Mehitabel, 1758; Hannah, 1760; Patience, 1763. NATHANIEL, son of 1st Constant, m., 1672, Desire, d. of Edward Gray, and had Constant, 1674; Mary, 1676, m. Joseph Rider; Ichabod, 1678; Elizabeth, m. James Sproat; Nathaniel, 1684, m. Jael Howland; Edward, 1688, m. Bridget Bosworth. NATHANIEL, Middleboro', son of above, had Fear, 1709, m. a Leonard; Gideon, Nathaniel, Samuel; and Hannah, m. a Sproat. NATHANIEL, Bridgewater, died 1778, leaving wife, Tenny, and children Simeon, Nathaniel, David, Catherine, and John. NATHANIEL, Marshfield, son of 2d William, m., 1782, Deborah Hatch of Pembroke, and had Martin; Sally, m. Chandler Oldham; Ruth m., also, Chandler Oldham; William, and Nathaniel. THOMAS, son of 1st Edward, came with his brother Constant, 1628, and m., 1641, Elizabeth, d. of John Reyner, by whom he had Elizabeth, m. Joseph Howland. THOMAS, Duxbury, son of 2d Edward, by wife Sarah, had Jedediah, 1702; Mary, 1703, m. Thomas Loring. THOMAS, Scituate, son of 1st James, m. Sarah, d. of Elisha James, and had James, Lucy, Nathan, Thomas, Temperance, and George. THOMAS, Duxbury, son of 2d Benjamin, by wife Anna, had William, 1763; Constant, 1764; Lydia, 1766, m. Ezra Briggs; Hannah, 1769; Anna, 1770, m. Curtis Brooks. WARREN, from Chelsea, m., 1829, Olive Robbins. WILLIAM, Duxbury, Little Compton, and Tiverton, son of 1st Constant, m., about 1680, Rebecca Pabodie, and had Benjamin, 1681; Joseph, 1683, m. Mary Blake; Edward, 1684, m. Mary Fobes; Elizabeth, 1686; Alice, 1688; Samuel, 1690; Nathaniel, 1692; Thomas, 1694; Stephen, 1696, m. Lydia Warren; Gideon, 1707, m. Priscilla Pabodie; Andrew, 1709. WILLIAM, Duxbury, son of 3d Constant, m. Betty, d. of Samuel Fullerton, and had Mary; Rumah, 1742, m. Jasper Southworth; Edward, 1747, m. Mercy Thomas; John, 1753; Nathaniel, 1757; William, 1759; Alice, 1764, m. Jacob Weston.

SPARHAWK, JOHN, perhaps son of Samuel of Cambridge, m. Hannah Jacobs of Scituate, and had Sarah, 1726; Hannah, 1728; John, 1730, Hannah, 1732; John, 1738.

SPARROW, EDWARD, m. Jerusha Bradford, 1741. RICHARD, Plymouth, 1632, came from England with wife Pandora and son Jonathan. He afterwards had John, sold his lands in Plymouth in 1656, and moved to Eastham either a little before or about that time.

SPEAR, JAMES H., son of 1st Thomas, m. Sarah Shurtleff, and had Linda M., 1867; Etta H., 1871; William H., 1874. JOHN K., by wife Sylvia M., had Mary S., 1874; Lizzie A., 1876; Lizzie L. SAMUEL T., son of 1st Thomas, m. Sarah E., d. of Seth Luce Holmes, and had Sarah, 1848. THOMAS, born in Bridgewater, m. Ciarissa, d. of James Harlow, 1804, and had Clarissa, 1805, m. John Battles; Mary Ann, 1807, m. Heman C. Robbins; Caroline, 1809; Susan, 1811, m. Edward Morton; Jane, 1813; Thomas, 1815; Samuel, 1818; Caroline again, 1819, m. James L. Leclerq and Nahum Thomas; Jane again, 1822; Relief T., Samuel T., James H., and Hannah. THOMAS, son of above, m. Elizabeth R., d. of Harvey Raymond, and had Ida Elizabeth, Thomas Irving, Ida Elizabeth again, and George H., 1862.

SPINKS, NICHOLAS, m., 1732, Mary Jackson.

SPOONER, ALLEN CROCKER, son of 2d Nathaniel, m. Susan Harlow, 1840, and had Anna. BOURNE, son of 1st Nathaniel, m. Hannah Bartlett, 1813, and had Nathaniel Bourne, 1818; William T.; Charles Walter, 1824; John Adams, 1826; and Edward Amasa, 1830. CALEB ALEXANDER of New Bedford, m. Nancy Simmons, 1805. EBENEZER, son of 1st William, Marshfield, m. Mercy Branch, and had Thomas, 1694; Ephraim of Abington, m. Sarah Pratt, Ruth Whitcomb, and Mary Jackson; John moved to North Carolina, and had a son Staunton; Bethiah, m. John Churchill; Susanna, m. Ichabod Bartlett. He m., 2d, Mercy, perhaps d. of Anthony Rose, 1708. EBENEZER, Middleboro', son of 1st Thomas, m. Mary Morton, 1743, and had Lucy, m. Job Alden; Bethiah, m. John Winslow; Phebe, m. Andrew Oliver; and Ebenezer. EDWARD AMASA, Philadelphia, son of Bourne, m. Hannah, d. of George Adams, and had Louisa Marice. EPHRAIM, son of 1st Thomas, m. Elizabeth Shurtleff, 1763, and had Elizabeth, 1765; Ephraim, 1767,

Ephraim, 1771; Sarah, 1772; Thomas, 1775; James, 1777; Ebenezer, 1779. EPHRAIM, son of James, m. Mary Elizabeth Spooner, 1830, and had James Walter, m. Frona E. Smith of Concord; and Esther S., m. Horace S. Shepard of Dorchester. HORATIO NELSON, son of 1st Nathaniel, m., 1837, Jerusha Weston, d. of John and Polly (Brewster) Mackenzie of Duxbury, and had Mary Holmes, 1839, m. John Walter Cushing of Duxbury; William Francis, 1843; Horatio Weston, 1850, m. Polly Alma, d. of Howard Marshal of Brockton; Martha Washburn, 1846, m. Mosés N. Pierce; Augusta Lovering, 1855, m. Charles Herbert Everson of Kingston. ISAAC, Dartmouth, son of 1st William, one of the original proprietors of that town, with his brothers John, Samuel, and William, by wife Alice, had Simpson, 1700; Edward, 1701; Mercy, 1707. JAMES, son of 1st Ephraim, m. Margaret Symms, 1801, and had James, 1802; Ephraim, 1804; Margaret, 1808; George Washington, 1811, m. Martha Pipes. JOHN, son of 1st William, Dartmouth, had John, 1668, and, by a 2d wife, William, 1680; Jonathan, 1681; Elizabeth, 1683; Eleanor, 1685; Phebe, 1687; Nathan, 1689; Rebecca, 1691; Deborah, 1694; Barnabas, 1699. JOHN ADAMS, son of Bourne, m. Lydia Sylvester, and had John Bourne, 1853; Ida Woodbury, 1854. NATHANIEL, son of 2d Thomas, m. Mary Holmes, 1784, and had Nathaniel, 1785; Mary, 1787; Bourne, 1790; William, 1792; Deborah, 1795, m. John Russell; John Adams, 1797; Charles Walter, 1799; Thomas, 1802; Mary Elizabeth, 1804, m. Ephraim Spooner; Horatio Nelson and Esther, twins, 1806, the last of whom m. Amasa Bartlett. NATHANIEL, son of above, m. Lucy Willard of Boxboro', 1811, and had Allen Crocker, and Nathaniel. NATHANIEL, son of above, m. Ethelinda Virgin, 1839, and had Florence, m. Benjamin T. Robbins of Kingston; Alice, 1844; and Mary B., 1850. NATHANIEL BOURNE, son of Bourne, m. Zilpha Washburn Harlow, and had Wendell Berkeley, 1854; and Ruth Harlow, 1858. SAMUEL, Dartmouth, son of 1st William, by wife Experience, had William, 1688; Mary, 1690; Samuel, 1692; Daniel, 1693; Seth, 1694; Hannah, 1696; Jabesh, 1698; Ann, 1700; Experience, 1702; Beulah, 1705; and Wing. THOMAS, son of 1st Ebenezer, m. Sarah Nelson, 1717, and had Ebenezer, 1718; Patience, 1720, m. John Howland; Joseph and Benjamin, twins, 1723; Thomas, 1724; Sarah, 1727, m. Nathaniel Bradford; Jean, 1729, m. Robert Bartlett; and Ephraim, 1735. THOMAS, son of above, m. Deborah Bourne, 1746, and had Nathaniel, 1748; Anna; Sarah, 1754; Thomas, 1756; Nathaniel, 1758; John, 1760. THOMAS, son of 1st Nathaniel, m. Mary Brewster, 1844, and had Arabella J., 1846; and Charles W., 1848. He m., 2d, Lucy Bonney of Pembroke, 1854, and, 3d, Maria Cornish, 1861. WILLIAM came from Colchester, England, 1637, and died in Dartmouth, 1685. He m. Elizabeth Patridge, and had John. He m., 2d, Hannah Pratt, 1652, and had Sarah, 1653, m. John Sherman; Samuel, 1655; Martha, m. John Wing; William, Isaac, Hannah, Mercy, and Ebenezer. WILLIAM, Dartmouth, son of above, m. wid. Alice Blackwell, d. of Nathaniel Warren, and had Benjamin, 1690; Jabesh, 1692; Joshua, 1693; Sarah, 1700; Abigail, 1702. WILLIAM, son of 1st Nathaniel, m. Hannah Otis, d. of Thomas Nicholson, 1818, and had Daniel Nicholson, m. Susan, d. of Charles Torrey of Boston; Caroline Miller, Catherine, and Ellen Otis. (See Spooner Genealogy).

SPRAGUE, ANTHONY, m. Elizabeth, d. of Robert Bartlett, 1661, and had Anthony, Benjamin, John, Elizabeth; Sarah, m. Caleb Bates; Samuel, James, Josiah, Jeremiah, Richard, and Matthew. FRANCIS came, with wife and child, in the Ann 1623, and had, at his death, John, Ann, Mary; and Mercy, m. William Tubbs.

SQUIB, JEREMIAH, m. Mary Scake, 1748.

STACEY, HUGH, came in the Fortune 1621, and had a d. Hannah, and removed to Dedham. JOSEPH, m. Patience Warren, 1721.

STACKPOLE, DAVID, m. Jean Reed, 1748.

STAFF, JOHN, m. Rebecca Stierney, 1738.

STANDISH, ALEXANDER, Duxbury, son of 1st Miles, m. Sarah, d. of John Alden, and had Miles; Ebenezer, 1672; Lorah, m. Abraham Sampson; Lydia, m. Isaac Sampson; Mercy, m. Caleb Sampson; Sarah, m. Benjamin Soule; Elizabeth, m. Samuel Delano. He m., 2d, Desire, double wid. of Israel Holmes and William Sherman, and d. of Edward Doty, and had Thomas, 1687; Desire, 1689, m. Nathan Weston; Ichabod, m. Phebe Ring; and David. DAVID, son of 1st Thomas, m., 1746, Hannah Magoon, and had Mary, Samuel, James; Olive, m. a Josselyn; Hannah; Priscilla, m. a Josselyn; David, and Lemuel, who removed to Bath. EBENEZER, Plympton, son of Alexander, m. Hannah, d. of Samuel Sturtevant of Plymouth, and had Zachariah, 1698; Moses, 1701; Hannah, 1704, m. Seth Staples; Zeruiah, 1707, m. Andrew Ring; Sarah, 1709, m. Jabez Newland; Ebenezer; Mercy, 1710, m. Ebenezer Lobdell and Benjamin Weston. EBENEZER, Plympton, son of 1st Zachariah, m. Averick, d. of Isaac Churchill, and had Mary, 1740; Ebenezer, 1741; Averick, 1744, m. Zadock Thomas; Shadrach, 1746. EBENEZER, Plympton, son of 2d Moses, m., 1784, Lydia, d. of Thomas Cushman, and had Thomas Cushman, 1785; Ebenezer, 1786. ELLIS, Plympton, son of 1st Shadrach, m. Polly Bradford, and removed to Sumner, Maine, where he had four daughters and two sons, one of whom was Miles, born 1804. ICHABOD, Halifax, son of Alexander, m. Phebe, d. of Eleazer Ring of Plymouth, 1719, and had Mary, Phebe; and Desire, m. David Hatch. ISAIAH, Rochester, son of 2d Zachariah, had Zachariah, Rebecca, Sally, and Isaiah. JAMES, an owner of land in Manchester 1640. JOB, Pembroke, son of 1st William, m. Ruth Witherell, and had Lydia, 1803, m. Dyer Robinson; Job, 1806; Judith, 1809, m. Ansel Robinson; Rebecca, 1811, m. Albert Williams; David, 1814, m. Julia Sharp; Margery, 1818; Stephen, 1821, m. Elizabeth Studley; Otis, 1824, m. Huldah Bates. JOB, Bridgewater, son of above, m., 1829, Hannah Jones, and had Charles Lewis, 1830; Mary Barker, 1833. JOHN, Halifax, son of 1st Moses, m. an Ellis, and had John, 1783, m. Jane Churchill. JOHN, Plympton, son of Nathaniel, m. Sarah Fuller, and had Sarah; and Angeline, m. Isaiah Churchill. JOHN, Plympton, son of 1st John, m. Jane, d. of Elias Churchill, and had Elias Ellis, 1806; John Ellis, 1808; Alexander, 1809; Erastus Warren, 1812; Miles, 1813; Jane Ellis, 1816; William Henry, 1818; Joseph Warren, 1820; Benjamin, William; Lewis Weston, 1822; Laura Ann, 1823; George Washington, 1826. JOHN AVERY, New Bedford, son of Levi, m., about 1806, Emeline, d. of Joseph Bourne, and had Emma B., m. George T. Stearns; John Avery, Levi Rose; and Miles, 1847. JONATHAN, Plympton, son of 2d

Moses, m. Irene Shaw, and had Jonathan, Soranus, William, Fanny, Irene, Polly, and Betsey. JOSIAH, Duxbury, Norwich, and Preston, son of 1st Miles, m., 1654, Mary, d. of John Dingley, and had by her, and by a 2d wife, Sarah, d. of Samuel Allen of Braintree; Miles, m. Mehitabel Adams; Josiah, Samuel; Israel, m. Elizabeth Richards; Mary, m. James Cary; Lois, m. Hugh Calkins; Mehitabel, Martha, and Mercy. JOSHUA, Plympton and Middleboro', son of 2d Moses, m. Susanna Cobb, and had Joshua, Josiah, Joseph, and John Cobb. JOSHUA, Middleboro' and Plymouth, son of above, m. Mary, d. of William Shaw of Middleboro', and had Susanna Cobb, 1815, m. Ichabod T. Holmes; Joshua, 1817; Ruth Shaw, 1819; Ethan Allen, 1822, m. Susan Ford of Bucksport; Mary Shaw, 1824, m. Robert H. Aldrich of Uxbridge; Ruth, 1826, m. Frederick Gleason of Boston; Miles, 1831; Winslow Brewster, 1834, m. Sylvia M., d. of Joseph Maybury of Plymouth. JOSHUA, son of above, m. Lydia Oldham, 1838, and had Miles, m. Ellen, d. of Charles Westgate; Lydia Ann; and James C., m. Lizzie C., wid. of Nathan Haskins, and d. of Robert Torrence, and, 2d, Mercy A. Clark. LEMUEL, Bath, son of David, m. Rachel Jackson, and had David, 1777; and Lemuel. LEVI, Westport, son of 1st Shadrach, m. Lucy Randall about 1805, and had John Avery; Angeline, m. Edmund Wright of Boston; and Lucy, m. George A. Bourne of New Bedford. MILES, Plymouth and Duxbury, came in the Mayflower 1620, with wife Rose, who died soon after arrival. By a 2d wife, Barbara, who probably came in the Ann 1623, he had Alexander, Miles, Josiah, Charles, Lorah, and John. He is supposed to have been born about 1586. MILES, Boston, son of above, m. Sarah, d. of John Winslow, and was lost at sea, leaving no children. MILES, Duxbury, son of Alexander, m. Experience Sherman, or Holmes, d. of his mother-in-law, by one of her earlier husbands, and had Sarah, 1704, m. Abner Weston; Patience, m. Caleb Jenny of Dartmouth; Priscilla, m. Elisha Bisbee; Miles, 1714; Penelope, 1717. MILES, Duxbury, son of above, m., 1738, Mehitabel Robbins, and removed to Bridgewater. His children were Miles, m. Naomi, d. of Daniel Keith, who removed to Pennsylvania; Penelope, Lydia; Experience, m. Simeon Ames; Hannah, 1746, m. Daniel Fobes; Sarah, 1748; and Priscilla. MILES, Pembroke, who died about 1805, perhaps son of Thomas, by wife Sarah, had Miles, Thomas, John C., Sarah, and Ruth. MILES, Pembroke, son of 1st William, m. Sarah Keen, and had Sarah, m. Daniel French; Miles, Thomas, Ruth, and John. MOSES, Plympton, son of 1st Ebenezer, m., 1723, Rachel Cobb, and had Moses, John; Rachel, 1726; Abigail, 1724, m. Philemon Sampson and Amos Fuller; Zerviah; Rebecca, m. Zachariah Weston; Sarah, Aaron; Zerviah again, m. Zebediah Thompson of Halifax; Sarah, m. a Tinkham, and, 2d, Adam Wright. MOSES, Plympton, son of above, m. Mary, d. of Zachariah Eddy of Middleboro', and had Ebenezer; and Hannah, m. Jonah Washburn; Moses, Nathaniel, Joshua, John, Jonathan; Olive, m. Abner Curtis; and Polly, m. a Hammatt. NATHANIEL, Plympton, son of above, m. Phebe Murdock, and had Phebe, Sally, Olive, Harriet, and John. SAMUEL, Preston, Conn., son of Josiah, m., 1710, Deborah, perhaps d. of George Gates of East Haddam, and had Deborah, 1711; Samuel, 1713; Lois, 1715; Abigail, 1717; m. Rufus Rood; Sarah, 1719; Israel, 1722, m. Content Ellis and Dorcas Bel-

lows; Thomas, 1724, m. wid. Sarah Williams. SHADRACH, Plympton, son of
2d Ebenezer, m. Mary, d. of David Churchill, and had Averick, 1772, m. John
Avery Parker of New Bedford; Ellis, 1774; Jane, 1777; Shadrach, 1779; Levi,
1779; Abigail, 1781; Mary, 1783; Sarah, 1788. SHADRACH, Plympton, son of
above, m. Mehitabel, d. of Ebenezer Clark, and had Averick Parker, 1799;
Eliza Savery, 1801; Mary Bradford, 1804; Clarissa Lovett, 181°; Shadrach,
1814; Jane, 1820. SORANUS, Plympton and Middleboro', son of Jonathan,
m. Fanny, d. of William Whitmarsh of Plymouth, and had Mary Frances;
Martin Parris, m. Elesener Thayer, d. of James Cole of Middleboro'; Sarah
Emily, m. Jason Wilbur; and George Eddy, m. Julia Maria, d. of William
Cole of Randolph. THOMAS, Pembroke, son of Alexander, m. Mary, d. of
William Carver, and had David, m. Hannah Magoon; Amos; Mary, 1733;
Thomas, 1735; William, 1737; Betty, 1739. THOMAS, son of above, m., 1748,
Martha Bisbee. THOMAS CUSHMAN, Plympton, son of 3d Ebenezer, m.
Bethiah Sampson, d. of Isaac Waterman of Halifax, and had Lydia Ann,
1811, m. Thomas Ellis Loring; Phebe Waterman, 1820, m. Nelson Campbell
Curtis; and Thomas Cushman, 1822, m., 1st, Sally Soule, d. of James Bos-
worth, and, 2d, Maria B. Tilson. WILLIAM, Pembroke, son of 1st Thomas,
m., 1763, Abigail Stetson, and had Miles, m. Sarah Keen; William, Abigail,
and Job. WILLIAM, Pembroke, son of above, m. Ruth Barstow, and had
Ruth, m. Melzar Sampson; William, m. Huldah Lowden; George Barstow,
m. Emeline Loring; Benjamin, m. Betsey Little; Mary, m. Sullivan Sawin;
Lucy, Elizabeth, Miles; Abigail, m. Peleg Cook. ZACHARIAH, Plympton,
son of 1st Ebenezer, m. Abigail, d. of Ebenezer Whitman of Bridgewater, and
had Ebenezer, 1721; Hannah, 1723, m. Elkanah Cushman; Sarah, 1729, m.
Josiah Cushman; Abigail, 1731, m. Samuel Wright; Peleg, 1734; Zachariah,
1739. ZACHARIAH, Plympton, son of above, by wife Olive, had Sarah, Rebecca, Isaiah, Oliver; Peleg, 1761; Zachariah, 1763.

STEELE, SAMUEL, m., 1714, Sarah Cooper.

STEENBECK, SAMUEL, m. Abigail Joyce, 1826.

STEPHENS, EDWARD, Marshfield, 1665, had Edward, William, Elizabeth;
and Patience, m. John Phillips. EDWARD, son of above, m., 1708, Mary, d.
of Eleazer Churchill, and had Mary, 1710; Hannah, 1712, m. Benjamin Bartlett; Sarah, 1715; Lemuel, 1716; Elizabeth, 1719; m. Benjamin Harlow;
Edward, 1721; Eleazer, 1723. He probably m., 2d, 1729, Mercy, wid. of
Joseph Sylvester, and d. of Elisha Holmes. EDWARD, son of above, m.,
1747, Phebe, d. of William Harlow, and had Edward, 1748; William, 1752;
Sylvanus, m. Betsey, d. of John Allen, and wid. of James Doten; John, m.
Elizabeth Battles; Samuel, m. Desire, twin sister of Noah Harlow, and
moved to Maine; Lemuel, Benjamin, Zacheus; Sally, m. Isaac Bonney;
Phebe, m. George Ellis; Mary, m. Asa Sherman; Elizabeth, m. Joseph Rob-
bins. EDWARD, son of above, m. Betsey Crocker, without issue, and 2d,
1802, wid. Lucy Nelson, and had a son Edward, who, after removal to New
York, m. Anna Winterbottom. EDWARD, son of 3d William, m. Mary D.
Wormwell, and had Nannie E., m. William P. Gooding; Ella M., m. Weston
C. Vaughn; and Edward. ELEAZER, son of 2d Edward, m., 1747, Sarah, d.
of Joseph Sylvester. He m., 2d, Susanna (Cobb) Sylvester, 1766, and had

Susanna, 1766, m. Lothrop Turner. He m., 3d, Elizabeth (Thacher) Jackson, wid. of Hezekiah, 1772, and had Hannah; and Sarah, 1772, m. Freeman Bartlett. GEORGE, from Providence, m., 1755, Elizabeth Dunham. JOHN, son of 3d Edward, m., 1788, Elizabeth, d. of Samuel Battles, and had John, Zacheus, Sally, Elizabeth, and Benjamin. LEMUEL, son of 2d William, m. Sally, d. of Ichabod Morton, and had Sarah, 1810, m. Charles Burton; Lemuel, 1812. LEMUEL, Philadelphia, son of above, m. Anna Maria Buckminster of Framingham, and had Anna Buckminster, Mary Morton, and Edward. LEVI, from Boston, m., 1740, Mary Marshal. PELEG, m. Sarah Wright, 1760, and had Asa, 1760; William, 1761. WILLIAM, Marshfield, son of 1st Edward, by wife Hannah, had Hannah, 1692, m. a Rider; William, 1694, m. Patience Jones; Josiah, 1695; Lydia, 1697, m. Ebenezer Cobb of Kingston; John, 1699, m. Eleanor Jarman; Abigail, 1702; Bethiah, 1703, m. Caleb Oldham, Edward, 1706; Elizabeth, 1709; Patience, 1712. WILLIAM, son of 3d Edward, m. Esther, d. of Thomas Savery, and wid. of John Allen, and had William, 1785; Lemuel, 1786; Phebe, 1790, m. Thomas Jackson Cotton. WILLIAM, son of above, m., 1808, Nancy Everson, and had Nancy, William; Phebe Cotton, m. Nehemiah Savery; Esther, James; Mary Ann, m. Charles B. Rice; Edward, 1821; and Charles. WILLIAM, son of above, m., 1836, Jane, d. of Nathaniel Doten, and had Jane E., m. Horace C. Whitten; William, m. Almeda F., d. of Lemuel Bradford; George, m. Lucy Cook; Mary; Samuel, m. Alice Cook; and Emma. ZACHEUS, son of John, m. Jane Perkins, and had Zacheus, 1827; John Francis, 1839.

STEPHENSON, JASPER HALL, son of John, by wife Rebecca, had William, 1790. JOHN, by wife Elizabeth, had John, 1757; Elizabeth, 1760; Jasper Hall, 1766; and William.

STETSON, BARSILLAI, son of 1st Caleb, m. Ruth Kempton, 1742, and had Barsillai, 1742; Jedediah, 1745; Sarah, 1749; Mehitabel, 1751. CALEB, by wife Sarah, had Abisha, 1706; Elizabeth, 1709; Barsillai, 1711, m. Ruth Kempton; Joshua, 1714; Jerusha, 1716; John, 1718; Jedidah, 1721. CALEB, by wife Abigail, had Caleb, 1755; Bradford, 1757. CALEB, m. Deborah Morton, 1732. ELISHA, m. Abigail Brewster, 1707. EZRA of Rochester, m. Sarah Rider, 1757. LOT, m. Hannah Rider, 1808. SETH, had Seth, 1802; Daniel, 1806; Clement, 1809; Sarah Drew, 1811; Prudence, 1816.

STEWART, JAMES, came in the Fortune 1621, and died before 1627, or removed.

STODDARD, ISAAC NELSON, son of Elijah of Upton, came to Plymouth in 1833, and m., 1836, Martha LeBaron, d. of John B. Thomas. His children have been Isabella, 1837; John Thomas, 1838; George N., 1841; Charles Brigham, 1842; Francis Russell, 1844, m. Mary F., d. of Jacob Baldwin; William Prescott, 1846; Mary, 1848, m. Charles G. Hathaway; Martha, 1850, m. Dr. James B. Brewster; Ann Thomas, 1853, m. William S. Morissey; Laura; George Howland, 1856; and Ellen J., 1858. Elijah Stoddard, father of Isaac Nelson, was the son of Ezekiel and grandson of Jeremiah, who was the son of Samuel. Samuel was son of Daniel and grandson of John, who was the son of Anthony, who appeared in Boston in 1639. JOHN THOMAS, son of Isaac Nelson, m. Elizabeth Carver, d. of Jeremiah Farris, 1864, and had Henry Farris, 1866, and Mary Carver. WILLIAM PRESCOTT, brother of John Thomas, m. Anna, d. of Jeremiah Farris, 1870, and had Prescott F., 1871; Mary C., 1873; Elizabeth C., 1876; and Ellen Janette, 1880.

STOOPS, DAVID, from Taunton, m. Margaret Merrifield, 1762.

STORY, ELIAS, came in the Mayflower, and died the first winter.

STRAFFIN, DAVID, son of 2d William, m. Harriet Otis of Scituate and Sally Paulding of Plymouth, and had Charles A., m. Martha A., d. of Sylvanus Holmes; Sarah, David, and Ann E. GEORGE, son of 1st William, m., 1797, Mary Simmons, and had George, 1798, m. Eliza Rogers; Robert, 1800. WILLIAM, m., 1770, Susanna Kimball, and had William, 1770; George, 1771; Lucy, 1773. WILLIAM, son of above, m., 1794, Prudence Turner, and had David and William S. WILLIAM S., son of above, m., 1821, Sophia Bartlett, and had William, 1824, m. Olive L. Kendrick; Sophia B., 1825, m. Pelham Whiting.

STREETER, SEBASTIAN F., m., 1833, Elizabeth Morton, d. of Daniel Jackson.

STUDLEY, JOHN, m., 1730, Elizabeth Doten.

STURGIS, THOMAS, from Barnstable, m., 1786, Elizabeth, d. of Hezekiah Jackson.

STURNEY, THOMAS, m. Rebecca, d. of Thomas Phillips, and had Dennis, 1725, m. Elizabeth Cook; Thomas, 1730.

STURTEVANT, ANDREW of Savoy, m. Mary Lucas, 1808. CALEB, son of 1st James, m., 1739, Patience, d. of Ichabod Cushman, and had Joanna, Betsey, Susan, Fear; Sarah, m. Josiah Whitman and Jacob Mitchell of Bridgewater; Patience, and Jabez. CORNELIUS, Plympton, son of Nehemiah, by wife Elizabeth, had Silas, 1730. DAVID, son of 3d Joseph, m. Sarah Holmes, 1725, and had David, 1725; David, 1726; Bethiah, 1729; Benjamin; 1731; Sarah, 1732; Amos, 1734; Jane, 1737; Elijah, 1741, m. Mary Bartlett. DAVID, Wareham, perhaps son of above, by wife Mary, had Heman, m. Betsey Bartlett of Plymouth; Lot, Joseph, Abisha, Jonathan, and David. DAVID, Wareham, son of above, had Abisha, David, and Charles. ELIJAH of Kingston, m. Mary Bartlett, 1774. HEMAN, m. Betsey Bartlett, 1783. JAMES, son of 2d Samuel, Plympton, m. Susanna, d. of Francis Cook of Kingston, and had Francis, 1712; Caleb, 1716, m. Patience Cushman of Plympton; James, 1718, m. Hazadiah Fuller of Plympton; Susanna, 1721; Lydia, 1724. JAMES, Plympton, son of above, m. Hazadiah Fuller, and had Hazadiah, 1744. JOHN, son of 1st Samuel, m. Hannah, d. of Josiah Winslow, and wid. of William Crowe, and had Hannah, 1687, m. Josiah Cotton. JOHN, m. Sarah Bartlett, 1725, and had John, 1726. JOHN, m. Mrs. Mary Haskell, 1711, perhaps wid. of William Haskell of Gloucester. JOSEPH, m. Ann Jones, 1803. JOSEPH, m. Mercy Cornish, 1812, and had Joseph, 1814. JOSEPH, son of 1st Samuel, m. Ann Jones, and had Joseph, 1695; David, 1697; Amah, 1699; Jonathan, 1702; Ephraim, 1704; Mary, 1708. JOSIAH, m. Lucy Clark, 1805, and had James Clark, 1806; Thomas, 1808; Josiah, 1810; and Zachariah, 1812. JOSIAH, by wife Ruth, had John Sherman, 1813. JOSIAH, Halifax, son of 2d Samuel, m. Hannah, d. of Nathaniel Church, 1719, and had Josiah, 1720, probably m. a Croade and wid. Lois

Foster of Plymouth, 1757; Charles, 1721; Zadock, 1724, m. Priscilla Howes; William, 1726; Hannah, 1727, m. Rev. John Cotton; Church, 1730; Mercy, 1732, m. Timothy Tilson; John, 1734, m. Faith Shaw; Lucy, 1737, m. George Hammond; Dependence, 1739; Samuel Stafford, 1745, the father of the late Stafford of Halifax, m. Priscilla Palmer. MOSES, Plympton, son of 2d Samuel, m. Elizabeth Howell, 1720, and had Abigail, 1721; Joseph, 1723; Moses, 1725; Mercy, 1728; and Consider. NEHEMIAH, son of 2d Samuel, m. Ruth, d. of George Sampson, and had Cornelius, 1704; Mercy, 1706; Paul, 1708; Nehemiah, 1710, m. Fear, d. of Benjamin Cushman; Noah, 1713; Ruth, 1715, m. John Loring; Noah, 1717, m. Susanna Harlow; Abiah, 1720, m. Simeon Holmes; George, 1725, m. Jerusha, d. of Benjamin Cushman; Susanna, 1728, m. John Waterman. SAMUEL, Plymouth, 1643, by wife Ann, had Ann, 1647, m. John Waterman; John, 1650; Mary, 1651, m. Ephraim Little; Samuel, 1654; Hannah, 1656; John, 1658; Lydia, 1660; James, 1663; Joseph, 1666. SAMUEL, son of above, by wife Elizabeth, had Samuel, James, Moses, Josiah, William, John, Nehemiah; Hannah, m. a Standish; and Mary or Mercy, m. a Bosworth. SAMUEL, Plympton, son of above, m. Mary Prince, 1707, and had Desire, 1709; Samuel, 1711; Samuel, 1716. SYLVANUS, m. Hannah Rider, 1786. WILLIAM, Carver, son of 3d Josiah, m. Jemima, d. of John Shaw, and had Lucy, 1757, m. Ezra Thomas of Middleboro'; John, 1759; William, 1761; Zilpha, 1763, m. Barnabas Faunce of Plymouth; Isaac, 1765, m. Elizabeth Darling of Middleboro'; Amos, 1767; Hannah, 1769; Gamaliel, 1771; Abigail, 1773, m. Barnabas Faunce; Ruth, 1775, m. Ephraim Harlow of Plymouth; and Jemima, 1779. WILLIAM, son of above, m. Sally, d. of Benjamin Warren, 1791, and had William W., 1792; Jane, 1794; Hannah, 1796, m. Thomas J. Lobdell; Sarah, 1799; Lucy, 1802; Rebecca, 1805, m. Rev. Josiah Moore, settled in Duxbury; and William, 1809. WILLIAM, Plympton, son of 2d Samuel, m. Fear, d. of Isaac Cushman, and had Isaac, 1708, m. Sarah, d. of Nathaniel Fuller of Plympton; Hannah, 1711, m. a Ripley of Halifax; Rebecca, 1715; and Fear, m. John Waterman, and Elizabeth, twins, 1719. ZENAS, m. Elizabeth Sargent, 1791.

SUTTON, JOHN, m. Abigail Clark, 1692. WILLIAM, m. Lydia Rider, 1751.

SWIFT, ASA, m., 1808, Sarah Cornish. BENJAMIN, from Ware, m., 1700, Hannah Cornish. ELEAZER, m., 1825, Betsey Harlow, ELISHA, m., 1818, Betsey Clark. EZRA, m., 1825, Ruth Ellis. HENRY, m., 1814, Mary Morton. JABEZ, m., 1813, Eunice Thomas Dunham. JACOB, m., 1784, Remember Ellis, and had Thomas and Jacob. JEREBOAM, m., 1817, Sarah Leach, and had Samuel, 1820; Bathsheba, 1823; George, 1825; Sarah, 1827; Flavel, 1834; Robert, 1836. JOHN, from Sandwich, m., 1752, Desire Swift. JOHN, m., 1826, Betsey Howland. JOHN, m. Penelope Rickard, 1794. JOSEPH, m. Mary LeBaron, wid. of Francis, 1738, and had Mary, 1738. JOSEPH, m. Lucy Holmes, 1788. JOSHUA, m. Jane Faunce, 1739, and had Abigail, 1739, m. a Cornish; Joseph, 1742; Jean, 1744, m. a Rider; John, 1746; Susanna, 1749; Joshua, Joanna, Rebecca, and Mercy. JOSHUA, son of above, m. Mary Cornish, 1780. MICAH, of Ware, m. Abigail Swift, 1759. NATHANIEL, of Sandwich, m. Betsey Ellis, 1785. NATHANIEL, m. Lucy Valler, 1823, and had Phineas, 1825; Nathaniel, 1826; Samuel, 1828; Eliza J., 1829; Edward, 1831; Warren, 1833; Charlotte, 1835; William R., 1837; Lucy A., 1841. NATHANIEL, by wife Alice, had Rufus, 1734. PHINEAS, son of 1st Thomas, by wife Rebecca, had Jedediah, 1753; Abiah, 1756. SAMUEL, by wife Abigail, had Elizabeth, 1718; James, 1721; Samuel, 1724. SETH, by wife Maria, had Mary, 1723; Seth, 1724, m. Desire Holmes; Hannah, 1727. STEPHEN, m. Phebe Mendall, 1783. THOMAS, m. Thankful Morey, and had Lydia, 1718; Deborah, 1720; Elizabeth, 1723; Thomas, 1725; Jerusha, 1727; Phineas, 1732; Rhoda, 1734; Thankful and Lemuel, twins, 1738. THOMAS, son of above, m. Rebecca Clark, 1746, and had Jonathan 1747. THOMAS, by wife Lois, had Isaac B., 1810; Jacob, 1811; Cynthia, 1813; Thomas, 1815; Louisa, 1817; Joanna E., 1818; Seth E., 1820; Eleazer E., 1822; Elisha B., 1824; William, 1825; Emily B., 1828; Abigail G., 1830; Nathan, 1832; Drusilla, 1836. THOMAS, m. Louisa Briggs, 1808. WILLIAM, probably brother of Samuel, and grandson of William, who was born in England and settled in Sandwich, m. a wife Lydia, and had Solomon, 1715; William, 1719. WILLIAM, m. Betsey Holmes, 1820. ZEPHANIAH, by wife Lydia, had Lydia, 1728; Alice, 1731. WILLIAM, by wife Mary, had Mary F., 1823; Betsey H., 1829; William, 1834; Cordana, 1827; Clark F., 1841.

SWINBURN, ROBERT, from England, m., 1837, Kesiah Davis (Wade) Haskins, wid. of Nathan H. Haskins, and d. of David Wade, and had Jane, 1838, m. David M. Brownell of Raynham; Margaret M., 1841, m. Samuel Phillips of Taunton; and Elon Smith, 1845.

SWINERTON, an offspring from the family, in Salem in 1637. JAMES, m. Martha Battles, 1744, and had William, 1745; Martha, 1747, m. Isaac Harlow; and Timothy, m. Hannah Curtis.

SYLVESTER, ABNER, son of 1st Solomon, m., 1748, Jedidah Harlow, and had Nathaniel, 1749. He m., 2d, 1753, Abigail Washburn, and had Caleb, 1754; Abner, 1756; Jedidah, 1763, m. Solomon Davie; Lydia, m. Samuel Harmon Cole and Barnabas Churchill; Mercy, m. Judah Bartlett and Jabez Churchill; Polly, m. Edward Taylor and John Blaney Bates; Martha, m. Amaziah Churchill; and John, m. Lydia Edwards. ABNER, son of 1st Nathaniel, m., 1823, Hannah Davie, and had Abner and Mary. EBENEZER, son of 1st Solomon, by wife Mary, had Ebenezer, 1756; Lemuel, 1758; Caleb, 1760; Joseph, 1763; Solomon, 1764. GEORGE, m. Mary Lanman, 1805. JAMES AUGUSTUS, son of 1st Nathaniel, m. Charlotte S., d. of Nathan Churchill, and had Catherine and Charles. JOHN, son of 1st Abner, m. Lydia Edwards, and had Abigail Washburn, 1801; Abigail Washburn, 1803; Lydia, m. James Wadsworth; John; and Abby. JOHN, son of above, m., 1823, Sally Burbank, and had Sarah W., 1825, m. Nathaniel L. Hedge; Lydia E., 1828, m. John Adams Spooner; John, 1831, m. Lydia A. Ellis. JOHN, Marshfield, son of Richard, by wife Sarah, had Sarah, 1671; John, Joseph, Samuel, Lydia, and Hannah. JOSEPH, Scituate, son of Richard, by wife Mary, had Joseph, 1664; Mary, 1666; Naomi, 1668; Ann, 1669; Benjamin, 1672; Amos, 1676; David, 1682. JOSEPH, son of above, removed to Plymouth, m. Hannah, d. of Joseph Bartlett, and had Solomon, 1690; Hannah, 1692, m. Eleazer Holmes; Joseph, 1695; Mary, 1697, m. Samuel

Rider; Thankful, 1703, m. Ebenezer Rider; Content, m. James Holmes; and
Ebenezer. JOSEPH, son of above, m. Mercy, d. of Elisha Holmes, and had
Sarah, 1721, m. Eleazer Stephens; Joseph, 1723. JOSEPH, son of 1st Solo-
mon, m., 1755, Susanna Cobb, and had Joseph, 1755; John, and Sarah.
JOSIAH, son of 1st Nathaniel, m. Lydia T. Chandler, and had Lydia and
Allen. NATHANIEL, son of 1st Abner, m., 1794, Elsie Finney, and had
Elsie, m. William Bradford; Nathaniel, Abner, Solomon; Polly, m. Thomas
Diman; William, George, Josiah, and James Augustus. NATHANIEL, son
of above, m., 1823, Phebe Holmes, and had Phebe Atwood, 1824; Elizabeth
Rand, 1827; Charles Thomas, 1829; Mary Harlow, 1836. RICHARD, Wey-
mouth, 1630, m., 1632, Naomi Torrey, and had Lydia, 1633; John, 1635;
Peter, 1637; Joseph, 1638; Dinah, 1642; Elizabeth, 1644; Richard, 1648;
Naomi, 1649; Israel, 1651; Esther, 1653; Benjamin, 1656. SOLOMON, son of
2d Joseph, m. Elizabeth, d. of Samuel Rider, and had Reuben, 1720; Nathaniel, 1721; Elizabeth, 1722, m. Amaziah Churchill; Abner, 1723; Caleb, 1725;
Lydia, 1726, m. Lemuel Churchill; Reuben, 1729; Ebenezer, 1730; Joseph,
1732; Solomon, 1733; Bartlett, 1735, m. Thankful Washburn; Hannah, 1737,
m. John Bates of Hanover. SOLOMON, son of above, m., 1758, Hannah
Churchill, and had Hannah, 1759; Elizabeth, 1762, m. Seth Churchill; Solomon, 1764; George, 1766; Lucy, 1768. SOLOMON, son of 1st Nathaniel, m.,
1823, Mary Ann Alexander, and had Eliza, 1827, m. Augustus H. Lucas;
Angeline, 1832; Fanny and Solomon, twins, 1834; George, 1835; William,
1837. THOMAS, m. Martha Tinkham, 1750, and had Thomas, 1751; Sarah,
1753; Hannah, 1756. He m., 2d, Elizabeth Dunham, 1766. WILLIAM, son
of 1st Nathaniel, m. Mary B. Harlow, and had William A., Mary H., and
William.

SYMMES, ISAAC, son of 3d Zechariah, m. Hannah Davis of Charlestown,
about 1752, and had Hannah; Grace, m. Ellis Holmes of Plymouth; Martha,
and Elizabeth. He m., 2d, Hannah Cobb of Plymouth, 1764, and had
Hannah, 1766; Isaac, 1767; Lucy; Margaret, m. James Spooner; Sarah, m.
Pelham Brewster of Kingston; and Lazarus, Nancy H., and Zachariah P. He
m., 3d, Joanna Holland, 1784. ISAAC, son of above, m. Mary Whitman,
1797, and had Isaac, Hannah, Mary Whitman, Martha, Daniel, and William,
now living in Kingston. LAZARUS, son of 1st Isaac, m. Mary, d. of William
Weston, 1802, and had Eliza, William, Columbus, Washington, Harriet, and
Mary. THOMAS, Bradford, son of 2d Zechariah, m. Elizabeth, d. of Thomas
Blowers of Beverly, and had Thomas, Andrew, John, William, Elizabeth,
Zechariah, and Anna. He m., 2d, Hannah, d. of John Pike of Dover, N. H.,
and had Abigail, and Sarah. He m., 3d, Eleanor, d. of Benjamin Thomp-
son, and wid. of Eleazer Moody of Dedham. WILLIAM, a distinguished
Protestant in the reign of Queen Mary, the father of a son William. WIL-
LIAM, son of above, ordained to the ministry 1588, who had a grandson
Zechariah. ZECHARIAH, grandson of above, born at Canterbury 1599, came
to America 1634, and settled in Charlestown. By wife Sarah, he had Sarah,
William, Mary, Elizabeth, Huldah, Hannah, Rebecca, Ruth, Zechariah, Deborah, and Timothy. ZECHARIAH, Bradford, son of above, m., 1669, Susanna,
d. of Thomas Graves of Charlestown, and had Sarah, 1672; Zechariah, 1674;

Catherine, 1676; Thomas, 1678; William, 1680; and Rebecca, 1681. ZECH-
ARIAH, Charlestown and Plymouth, son of above, m. Grace, d. of Isaac
Parker of Charlestown, and had Zechariah, William, John, and Isaac. He
m., 2d, Elizabeth, d. of Francis Locke of Medford, and had Elizabeth,
Thomas, Abigail, Sarah, and Grace.

TABER, LEMUEL, m., 1772, Hannah Atwood. THOMAS, m., 1700, Rebecca
Harlow.

TALBOT, MOSES, at Plymouth at an early date, was killed at the Kenne-
beck Trading Station 1634. SAMUEL, son of a George of Milton, came to Ply-
mouth, and m., 1821, Jerusha, d. of Robert Davie, and had Samuel, m.
Martha J., d. of Bradford Barnes; Sarah Ann, m. Ellis Holmes of Duxbury;
Jerusha; and Elizabeth E., m. Everett F. Sherman. He m., 2d, 1832, Jerusha
T., d. of Thomas Paty, and wid. of Ellis Harlow, and had Robert D., 1834;
George W., 1838; Nancy Ellis; Jerusha, 1845, m. Darius F. Eddy of Dorches-
ter; Mary P., 1848, m. Lewis Eddy of Dorchester. He m., 3d, 1858, Rebecca
A., d. of Samuel Doten, and wid. of Nathaniel Brown Faunce.

TAYLOR, EDWARD, Barnstable, m., 1664, Mary Menks, and had Ann,
1664; Judith, 1666; Isaac, 1669; Jacob, 1670; Experience, 1672; Mary, 1674;
Sarah, 1678; John, 1680; Abraham, 1684; Mehitabel, 1688. EDWARD, son of
3d Jacob, m., 1789, Mary, d. of Abner Sylvester, and had Jane Sampson,
1790, m. Jeremiah Rich; Jacob, 1792; Abner Sylvester, 1795, m. Susan, d. of
James Bartlett; Edward, 1797; Mary Edward, 1798. JACOB, Barnstable, son
of 1st Edward, m., 1693, Rebecca Weeks, and had Jacob; Hannah, 1695;
Rebecca, 1697. JACOB, son of above, m., 1729, Mary, d. of John Atwood,
and had Jacob, Sarah, Rebecca, Leavitt, Mary, Edward, Lydia, and Hannah.
JACOB, son of above, m., 1756, Jemima Sampson, and had Jemima, 1757, m.
Eleazer Morton; Mary, 1759, m. James Bartlett; Joanna, 1761, m. Samuel
Bartlett; Jacob, 1763; Edward, 1765; Sarah, m. Amasa Bartlett; Elizabeth;
Lucy, m. Joseph Cooper. JOHN, m. Mary Bryant, 1787, and had John.
JOHN, from Liverpool, England, son of John and Catherine, m. Nancy, d. of
Edward Southworth, and had John, 1821; Nancy Catherine, 1827, m. John
Glazier of Abington. JOHN, son of a William of Barnstable, who m. Desire
Thacher, m., 1799, Lucia, d. of John Watson, and had Lucia Watson,
1800; William John, 1801; Jeanette, 1802, m. Pelham Winslow Warren; Wil-
liam, 1804, m. Elizabeth Robbins Vila.

TENCH, WILLIAM, came in the Fortune 1621, and disappeared before
1627.

TESSIER, JOHN MICHAEL, m., 1806, Waite Shurtleff.

THATCHER, or THACHER, ANTHONY, came from Salisbury, in England,
1635, with a 2d wife, Elizabeth Jones. He settled, 1st, in Marblehead, and
then in Yarmouth. His children were Mary; Benjamin, 1634; Mary, Edith,
Peter, Judah; John, 1639; Bethiah, m. Jabez Howland, and perhaps
Rodolphus. JAMES THACHER, son of 3d John, a surgeon in the revolution,
settled in Plymouth, and m. Susanna, d. of Nathan Hayward of Bridgewater,
and had Betsey Hayward, 1785, m. Daniel Robert Elliott of Savannah and
Michael Hodge of Newburyport; Susan, 1788; James, 1790; James Hersey,
1792; Susan, 1794, m. William Bartlett; and Catherine, 1797. JOHN THATCHER,

Yarmouth, son of Anthony, m., 1664, Rebecca, d. of Josiah Winslow, and had Peter, 1665; Josiah, 1667; Rebecca, 1669; Bethiah, 1671; John, 1675; Elizabeth, 1677; Hannah, 1679; Mary, 1682. He m., 2d, 1684, Lydia, d. of John Gorham, and had Lydia, 1685; Mary, 1687; Desire, 1688; Hannah, 1690; Mercy, 1692; Judah, 1693; Mercy, 1695; Ann, 1697; Joseph, 1699; Benjamin, 1701; Mercy, 1703; Thomas, 1705. JOHN THATCHER, Yarmouth, son of above, m., 1698, wid. Desire (Sturgis) Dimmock, and had Abigail, 1699; Elizabeth, 1701; John, 1703, who dropped the letter "t" in his name; Lot, 1705; Fear, 1707; Rowland, 1710. JOHN THACHER, Yarmouth, son of above, m. Content, d. of Samuel Norton of Chilmark, and had James, 1754; Elizabeth, m. Hezekiah Jackson of Plymouth; Fear, m. John Goodwin. JOSIAH, Yarmouth, born 1736, m. Elizabeth, d. of Benjamin Lothrop of Kingston, and had Benjamin Lothrop. PETER, Milton, son of Thomas, m., 1677, Theodora, d. of John Oxenbridge, and had Theodora, Bathsheba; Oxenbridge, 1681; Elizabeth, Mary; Peter, 1688; John; Thomas, 1693. He m., 2d, Susanna, wid. of John Bailey, and, 3d, Elizabeth, wid. of Joshua Gee, and d. of Judah Thatcher. PETER, Middleboro', son of above, by wife Mary, had Mercy, m. Nathaniel Foster of Plymouth; Susanna, John, Oxenbridge, Mary, and Samuel. RODOLPHUS, or RALPH, Duxbury, Chilmark, Lebanon, and Groton, Conn., son of a Thomas, m., 1770, Ruth, d. of George Partridge of Duxbury, and had Thomas; Peter, m. Abigail (Lindon) Hibbard of Lebanon; Lydia, m. John Deane, and was the mother of Silas, one of the Commissioners to France with Franklin. ROWLAND, Wareham, son of 2d John, died 1775, leaving children Martha, m. a Howland; Jerusha, m. a Gibbs; Sylvia, m. a Crocker; Desire, m. a Nye; Abigail, Hannah, Fear, Elizabeth, Lot, Rowland, and John. SAMUEL, Middleboro', son of 2d Peter, m., 1758, Sarah Kent. THOMAS, son of Peter, Rector of St. Edmund's, Salisbury, England, and Anne, his wife, came, with his Uncle Anthony, 1635. He 1st went to Scituate, m., 1643, Elizabeth, d. of Ralph Partridge of Duxbury, and afterwards settled in Weymouth and Boston. His children were Thomas, Ralph; Peter, 1651; Patience, m. William Kemp; Elizabeth, m. Nathaniel Davenport and Samuel Davis. He m., 2d, about 1665, Margaret, wid. of Jacob Sheafe, and d. of Henry Webb of Boston.

THAYER, CORNELIUS, Boston, son of 1st Nathaniel, by wife Lydia, had Nathaniel and others. He m. about 1705. NATHANIEL, Boston, son of 1st Richard, by wife Deborah, had Nathaniel, 1671; Nathaniel again, 1681; Zechariah, 1683; Cornelius, 1684; John, 1687; John again, 1688; Ebenezer, 1690; Deborah, 1691. NATHANIEL, son of Cornelius, by wife Ruth, had Ebenezer, father of the late Rev. Nathaniel of Lancaster; Deborah, m. Miles Whitworth; and Eliab. RICHARD, Boston, 1640, came from England with children Richard, m., 1651, Dorothy Pray; Deborah; Sarah, m. Samuel Davis; Cornelius, m. Abigail Hayden; Nathaniel, and Zechariah.

THOMAS, ABRAHAM, from Middleboro', m., 1793, Mercy Doten. ADONIRAM, son of Levi, m. Eliza Bryant, and had Eliza Jane, m. John Burt. ANTHONY, Marshfield, son of 6th John, by wife Abigail had John, 1748. ASA, son of Eleazer, m. Lucy, d. of Ezra Thomas of Middleboro', about 1820, and had Gamaliel, m. Ruth, d. of George Nelson; Eleazer, m. Lucy

Ann, d. of Nathaniel Cobb Lanman; Alanson, m. the wid. of Eleazer; Ezra, m. Sarah, d. of Benjamin Jenkins; Fanny, and Asa. BENJAMIN, m., 1773, Lydia Faunce. BENJAMIN, Middleboro', by wife Elizabeth, had Benjamin, Perez, Eli, James, Ezra, Zenas, Zeruiah, Susanna; Eunice, m. a Dunham; Betty, m. a Hammond. He died about 1800. CALEB, Marshfield, son of 2d Nathaniel, m. Priscilla Capen, and had Priscilla, m. John Watson and Isaac Lothrop and Noah Hobart of Fairfield, the last of whom m. a 1st wife, Ellen Sloss, by whom he had Ellen, m. Nathaniel Lothrop of Plymouth, and John Sloss, the successor of Aaron Burr in the U. S. Senate. ELEAZER, Middleboro', m., about 1790, Bispha Bryant, and had Lucinda, m. Elias Thomas; Asa; Susan, m. Jacob Dunham of Plymouth; Eleazer, m. Eunice Shurtleff of Carver; Bispha, m. Lemuel Savery of Plymouth; Asenath, m. Harvey Shaw and a Williams. ELIAS, son of Levi, m., about 1805, Lucinda, d. of Eleazer Thomas, and had Bathsheba, m. Seth Benson; Elias, m. Deborah Freeman of Duxbury; Lucinda, m. Albert Finney; Hannah, m. David Dickson. EZRA, Middleboro', m. Lucy, d. of William Sturtevant of Carver, and had Elizabeth; Lucy, m. Asa Thomas; Ezra, Eunice; Abigail, m. a Keith, and John Sturtevant. EZRA, son of above, m. Hannah, d. of Job Cole, and had Charlotte, m. Phineas Sprague Burgess; Ezra, Isaac S., Elizabeth, and Hannah. GEORGE NELSON, son of 1st Joab, m. Lucy, d. of Nathaniel Holmes, and had George Nelson, 1829; Nathaniel T., 1831; Lucy M., 1833; James A., 1835; Isaac D., 1837. ICHABOD, son of 2d John, m., 1771, Hannah, d. of Isaac Morton, and had Mary, 1778, m. Samuel N. Holmes; Abigail, 1773, m. John Loring of Plympton; Maria, 1775, m. Benjamin Holmes. ISAAC, Marshfield, son of 2d Nathaniel, m., 1711, Ann Thompson, and had Isaac. ISAAC, son of above, m., 1748, wid. Mary Hatch, and had Isaac and Joshua, 1750, twins. ISAAC, perhaps son of above, m., 1793, Hannah Barnes, and had Isaac, 1795; Hannah Barnes, 1797; Fanny LeBaron, 1800. ISRAEL, Middleboro', son of 1st John, m., 1698, Bethiah Sherman of Marshfield, and had Gershom, Amos; Bethiah, m. Israel Hatch; Kesiah, m. John Dingley; Abigail, m. Thomas Waterman; Sybil, Deborah, Israel, Nehemiah; Jane, m. Thomas Ford. ISRAEL, son of above, by wife Abigail, had Jane, Sylvia, Sarah, Abigail, Levi, Finney. JACOB, Middleboro', died about 1796, leaving a wid. Content, and a son Seth. JAMES, Marshfield, son of 1st John, m. Mary, d. of Stephen Tilden, and had John; James, m. Deborah Sherman; Ebenezer, Mary, Ezekiel, Peleg, and Hannah. JAMES, son of 2d John, m. Priscilla, d. of Anthony Winslow, and had James, 1751; Jonathan, 1752; Priscilla, 1754; and Deborah. He m., 2d, probably 1760, Hannah Barnes. JAMES, Middleboro', brother of 2d Benjamin, had Joab, Stephen; Lois, m. Samuel West Bagnall; Minerva, m. Samuel West Bagnall; Hope, m. Levi Shaw; Benjamin, Hannah, Patty, Polly, Sarah, Justus, James, and Zeruiah. JEREMIAH, Middleboro', son of 1st Nathaniel, by wife Mary, had Nathaniel, 1686; Sarah, 1687; Jeremiah, 1689; Elizabeth, 1690; Mary, 1692; Lydia, 1694; Thankful, 1695; Jedediah, 1698, m. Lois Nelson; Bethiah, 1701; Ebenezer, 1703; Priscilla, 1705; Sophia. JOAB, son of above, m. Lois, d. of James Doten, and had George Nelson, Nahum; Lois, m. Nelson Holmes; Joab; Betsey, m. John T. Hall; and Mary, m. George Fuller. JOAB, son of above,

m. Jerusha, d. of John Kempton Cobb, and had Jerusha, William J., Frederick, Mary Anna, Susan, Loring, and Joab. JOHN, Marshfield, came an orphan in the Hopewell from London 1635, and m.', 1648, Sarah, d. of James Pitney, by whom he had John, 1649; Elizabeth, 1652; Samuel, 1655, m. Mercy, d. of William Ford; Daniel, 1659, m. Experience, d. of Thomas Tilden; Sarah, 1661, m. Benjamin Phillips; James, 1663; Ephraim, 1668; Israel, 1670, m. Bethiah Sherman. JOHN, son of 1st James, m. Abigail, d. of Micajah Dunham, 1726, and had John, 1727; James, 1729; Jonathan, 1733; Nathaniel, 1735, m. Margaret Newcomb; Mary, 1738; Susanna, 1741; Abigail, 1743; William, 1744; Ichabod, 1748; Ephraim, 1752. JOHN, son of above, m. Abigail Clark, and had Abigail, 1748; Sarah, 1752; Jonathan, 1759. JOHN, son of 4th Nathaniel, m. Anna Mayhew, and had Mary Anna, 1774; John, 1775; Nathaniel Gardner, 1777; Frederick, 1779. JOHN BOICE, son of Joshua, m. Mary, d. of Isaac LeBaron, and had Martha, 1816, m. Isaac N. Stoddard; Hannah, 1815; John S., 1818; Hannah Stevenson, 1821, m. Charles G. Davis. JOHN, son of Samuel, m. Lydia Waterman, 1714, and had Zeruiah, 1714, m. James Bradford; Ann, 1717; Anthony, 1719, m. Abigail Alden; John, 1724; Sarah, 1726, m. Jeremiah Kinsman; Kesiah, 1730. JOHN, Kingston, son of above, known as General Thomas of the revolution, m. Hannah, d. of Nathaniel Thomas of Plymouth, and had Nathaniel, 1769; John, 1766; and Hannah, 1762, m. Zephaniah Willis. JOHN, Kingston, son of above, m., 1791, Waity, d. of Wait Gray, and had Augustus, m. Sally Brewster; Saba, 1792; William Appleton, 1800; and John. He m., 2d, 1805, Judith, wid. of Joseph Sampson, and d. of James Drew, and had Hannah, m. Theodore Cunningham. JOHN, New York, son of above, m. Hannah, d. of Barnabas Hedge of Plymouth, 1823, and had Eunice Burr, 1824, m. John Earl Williams; and William Appleton, 1829, m. Anna Corliss Morton. JOSHUA, son of 3d William, m. Isabella Stevenson of Boston, and had John Boice, 1787; William, 1788; and Joshua. LEVI, Middleboro', perhaps son of 2d Israel of same, or of Noah, m. Hannah Weston about 1775, and had Otis, m. Susan Hilman of New Bedford; Spencer; Zachariah, m. Beulah Peterson of Duxbury; Abiel, m. Hannah Murdock of Carver; Adoniram, m. Eliza Bryant of Bridgewater; Jane, m. Freeborn Cogswell of New Bedford; Sarah, m. John Taber of New Bedford; and Elias. NAHUM, son of 1st Joab, m. Ruby Chandler, and had Nahum, m. Nellie Joslynn. He m., 2d, Abby, wid. of Oliver Kempton, and d. of Josiah Carver; and, 3d, Caroline, wid. of James Leclerq, and d. of Thomas Spear. NATHAN, Marshfield, son of Samuel, m. Alice Baker, 1713, Abiah Snow, 1717, and Sarah Bartlett, 1719. NATHANIEL, son of 1st William, by a wife unknown, had William, 1638; Nathaniel, 1643; Mary, m. Simon Ray; Elizabeth, 1646; Jeremiah, and Dorothy. He came from England with his father, and brought his wife and son William. NATHANIEL, Marshfield, son of above, m., 1664, Deborah, d. of Nicholas Jacob of Hingham, and had Nathaniel, Joseph, Deborah, Dorothy; William, 1671; Elisha, Joshua, Caleb, Isaac, and Mary. He m., 2d, Elizabeth, the wid. of William Condy, 1696, whose maiden name was Dolbery. NATHANIEL, son of above, m., 1694, Mary, d. of John Appleton of Ipswich, and had Nathaniel, 1695; John, 1696, m. Mary, d. of Simon Ray of New London;

Nathaniel, 1700; Joseph, 1702; Mary, 1709. He m., 2d, Anna (Tisdale)
Leonard, wid. of George, 1730. NATHANIEL, son of above, m. Hope, d. of
James Warren, and had Nathaniel, 1724; and Nathaniel again, 1727. He
m., 2d, Hannah, d. of Rev. John Robinson of Duxbury, and had Hannah,
1730, m. Gen. John Thomas. He m., 3d, Elizabeth, d. of Rev. James
Gardner of Marshfield, and had Nathaniel, 1742; John, 1745; and
Lucy. NATHANIEL, son of 3d William, m. Priscilla Shaw, 1781, and had
William, Nathaniel; Mary Ann, 1804, m. George W. Calloway; Harriet
T., 1805, m. Samuel J. Jones; Deborah, m. Elijah Macomber; and Nancy.
NATHANIEL, m. Mary Allen, 1734. NOAH, Middleboro', by wife Mercy,
had Daniel, Abiel, Job, Elias; Lucy, m. an Alden; Fear, m. a Shaw;
Mary, Hannah, and Priscilla. RANSOM, Middleboro', m. Deborah Dunham,
1786. SAMUEL, Marshfield, son of 1st John, m. Mercy, d. of William Ford,
1680, and had John, 1684; Nathan, Samuel, Joseph, Gideon, Josiah; Bethiah,
m., perhaps Jesse Rider; and Sarah. SETH, Middleboro', son of Jacob, had
Louisa, m. Thomas McGlathlen; Content, m. Samuel Lanman; Hope; Sorena, m. Jabez Williams; Joanna, Jacob, John, Nathaniel, and Samuel. SOL-
OMON of Middleboro', m. Sarah Harlow, 1774. STEPHEN, son of 3d James,
m. Susan, d. of Nathaniel Bartlett, and had Stephen, m. Almira Thomas.
He m., 2d, Sarah Everson, and had Nancy Everson, 1827, m. Joseph Avery
Dunham; Justus, 1829; Charles, 1833, m. Catherine E., d. of Edward Winslow Bradford; Sarah Ann, 1836, m. John Quincy Adams Waldron of Boston;
Susan Frances, 1838; Hannah, 1841. WILLIAM, one of the merchant adven-
turers of London, born about 1573, came from Yarmouth, England, in the
" Marye and Ann," 1637, and settled in Marshfield with his son Nathaniel, born
1606. WILLIAM, son of 2d Nathaniel, m. Abigail Henchman, d. of Samuel
Ruck, 1701, and Anne Breck, wid. of John, and d. of Richard Patershall,
1717, removed to Boston, and had William, 1718; and Margaret, m. John
Breck. WILLIAM, Boston and Plymouth, son of above, m. Mary, d. of
Peter Papillon of Boston, and had William, Ann, Elizabeth, and Peter. He
m., 2d, wid. Mercy Logan, d. of Joseph Bridgham of Boston, and removed
to Plymouth, where he had Joshua, 1751; Margaret, 1753, m. William Breck
of Boston; Joseph, 1755; Nathaniel, 1756; John, 1758, m. a wife Gertrude in
Poughkeepsie, where he lived and died; and Mary, 1759. He m., 3d, Mary,
d. of Consider Howland, 1771. WILLIAM, son of above, by a wife Rebecca,
had Dorothy, 1762; William, 1765, and removed to North Carolina. WIL-
LIAM, son of Joshua, m. Sally W., d. of John Sever of Kingston, 1816, and
had Ann Sever, m. William H. Whitman of Plymouth.

THOMPSON, THOMSON, or TOMSON, ANDREW, m. Elizabeth Murdock,
1755. EDWARD, came in the Mayflower, and died before landing. JOHN,
said by Ignatius Thomson, the family genealogist, without sufficient evidence,
to have come over in the Ann or Little James in 1623. He m. Mary, d. of
Francis Cooke, 1645, and had Adam; John, 1648; Mary, 1650, m. a Taber;
Esther, 1652, m. Jonathan Reed; Elizabeth, 1654, m. Thomas Swift; Sarah,
1657; Lydia, 1659, m. James Soule; Mercy, 1671. ISAAC, pub. to Sarah
Pierce, 1733. JOHN, son of Edward, m. Mary Tinkham, and had John, m.
Elizabeth Thomas; Ephraim, 1682, m. Joanna Reddington; Thomas, 1684,

m. Martha Soule; Shubael, 1685, m. Susanna Parker; Mary, Martha, Francis, Peter, Jacob, 1710, m. Mary Howard; and Ebenezer. JOSIAH, from Abington, m. Mary Webquish, 1783. PETER, son of 1st John, by wife Sarah, had Sarah, 1699; Peter, 1701; James, 1703; Joseph, 1706.

THRASHER, AZARIAH, m. Mary Withered, 1777. DANIEL, m. Lydia Swift, 1778. DAVID, son of 1st Jonathan, m. Susanna Swift, and had Nancy, 1815; and Lewis W. GEORGE, m. Rachel Holmes, 1784. GEORGE, m. Content Cornish, 1818, and had Nancy, 1819; George, 1821; Betsey Ann, 1822, Jerusha and Israel, 1824; Susan, 1829, Mary Jane, 1831; Content, 1833. JONATHAN, m. Nancy Swift, 1784, and had Joshua, 1786; Jonathan, 1786, David, 1789; Rhoda, 1792; Stephen, 1794; Betsey, 1796. JONATHAN, son of above, m. Ruth Lucas, 1822. JOSHUA, son of 1st Jonathan, m. Deborah Gammon, 1811, and had Joshua, 1811; and Melinda, 1815, m. Ellis Rogers. JOSHUA, by wife Cynthia, had Ruth, 1829; Lucy J., 1830; Angeline, 1832; Lorenzo, 1833; Maria, 1835; Maria, 1837; Jonathan, 1840.

THROOP, or THORP, BILLINGS, from Bristol, m., 1758, Hannah, d. of Thomas Morton, and had Billings. JOHN, had a wife Alice, and died 1653. JOSEPH, Rochester, living 1749, had a wife Charity. ZEBULON, died 1717.

THURBER, JAMES, son of George, m. Elizabeth, d. of Asa Danforth of Taunton, 1831, and had Elizabeth, 1832; James Danforth, 1839. He came to Plymouth in 1832. His father m. Lois, d. of Moses Leonard of Middleboro', and was son of Caleb, who m. Lucretia Collins of Stonington. CALEB was son of John and grandson of Thomas, who was son of John of Swansea, 1669. JAMES DANFORTH, son of above, m., 1862, Mary Ann, d. of Amasa Bartlett, and had Elizabeth, 1866; William Bartlett, 1868; Mary Tyler, 1874.

THURSTON, DAVID, from Rowley, m., 1776, Mary Bacon.

TILDEN, THOMAS, came in the Ann 1623, with wife and child, and perhaps returned to England.

TILLEY, EDWARD, came in the Mayflower with wife, and both died the first winter. JOHN, perhaps brother of above, came in the Mayflower, with wife and d. Elizabeth, m. John Howland. There was a Thomas in Plymouth 1643, who may have been his son.

TILLSON, EDMUND, appeared in Plymouth 1643, and had Mary, m. James Cole; Ephraim, Elizabeth, m. Benajah Dunham; and Joan, m. Giles Rickard. EDMUND, probably son of 1st Ephraim, m. Elizabeth Waterman, 1691, and had John, 1692; Edmund, 1694; Joanna, 1696; Mary, 1698; Elizabeth, 1700; Ruth, 1705. He m., 2d, Hannah Orcut, 1706, and had Samuel, 1712; James, 1714. He m., 3d, a wife Deborah, and had Stephen, 1717; Hannah, 1720. EDMUND, son of above, m. Elizabeth Cooper, 1722, and had Hannah, 1723: and Perez, 1725. EPHRAIM, son of 1st Edward, m. Elizabeth Hoskins, 1666, and probably had John; Lydia, m. John Polland; Ephraim; and Edmund. EPHRAIM, Plympton, son of above, by wife Mercy, had Samuel, 1711; Hannah, 1713; Mercy, 1716; Content, 1718; Lois, 1721; Waitstill, 1723; Abigail, 1729. EPHRAIM, Plympton, son of 1st John, m. Deborah Ransom, 1744. HAMBLIN, son of Isaiah, m. Susanna Bradford, 1803, and had Henry, 1804, m. Jerusha B. Paty; Susanna Bradford, 1807; Abigail Winslow, 1809, m. Winslow Drew; Anna Winslow, 1813; Rebecca, 1816; Mary William,

1818; and Hamblin. ISAIAH, Plympton, son of 2d John, m. Phebe Crocker, 1766, and had Luther, 1766; Calvin, 1769; Rebecca, 1771; Isaiah, 1773; John, 1775; Daniel, 1778; Hamblin, 1780; Timothy, 1783; Eleazer, 1784; Anna, 1790. ISAIAH, Plympton, son of above, m. Sarah, d. of Levi Bradford, 1802, and had Martin Luther, 1804; Phebe Crocker, 1807; Elizabeth Lewis, 1810, Sylvanus, 1812; Sally, 1814; Isaiah, 1817; Mercy Winslow, 1819. By a 2d wife, Hannah, he had Calvin, 1821; Charles Edwin, 1825; and Lucy Doten, 1826. ι JOHN, son of 1st Ephraim, m. Lydia Rickard, and had John, 1713; Jonathan, 1715; Patience, 1718; Mary; Ephraim; and Lydia. JOHN, Plympton, son of above, m. Ann Hamblin, 1737, and had Timothy, 1738; Ezra, 1741; Isaiah, 1744. JOHN, son of 2d Edmund, by wife Joanna, had Joseph, 1714; Benjamin, 1716; Mary, 1719; Joanna, 1725; John, 1725; Ephraim, 1728; Mary, 1729, m. Abner Cushman. JOHN, from Halifax, m. Desire Shaw, 1791. JONATHAN, Plympton, son of 1st John, by wife Martha, had Eunice, 1739. He m., 2d, Lucy Cobb, 1748, and had Lydia, 1749; Lucy, 1753; Molly, 1755; Martha, 1758. JONATHAN, Plympton, perhaps son of above, m. Sarah Doten, 1785. PEREZ, son of 3d Edmund, m. Sarah Witherell, 1764. SAMUEL, Plympton, son of 2d Edmund, m. Hannah Nye, 1740, and had Edmund, 1741; Sarah, 1744. STEPHEN, son of 2d Edmund, m. Jeanette Murdoch, 1740, and had William, 1741; John, 1742, m. Ruth Barrows: Stephen, 1747, m. Waitstill Shaw; Ichabod, 1750; Jeanette, 1753. TIMOTHY, Plympton, son of 2d John, m. Silence Whiting, 1761, and removed to Dutchess County, N.Y. WILLIAM, Plympton, son of Stephen, m. Mary Ransom, 1762.

TIMBERLAKE, JAMES, m. Lydia Boult, 1775, and had Sarah, 1775.

TINKHAM, CALEB, son of 1st Hezekiah, m. Mercy Holmes, and had Mercy, 1726; Patience, 1729; Fear, 1781; Sarah, 1733; Nathaniel, 1736; Caleb, 1738. EBENEZER, son of 1st Hezekiah, by wife Mary, had Sarah, 1733; Ebenezer, 1736. He m., 2d, 1736, Jane Pratt, and had Mary, 1737; Mary, 1739, m. Joseph Mitchell; Ebenezer, 1741; James, 1744; Phebe, 1746, m. Enoch Randall; Susanna, 1748, m. Thomas Farmer; Priscilla, 1755, m. William Anderson. EBENEZER, son of 1st Ephraim, m., 1679, Elizabeth Liscomb, and had Jeremiah, and others. He lived in Middleboro'. EDWARD, Kingston, son of John, by wife Lydia, had Salumis, 1743; Rebecca, 1745. EPHRAIM, Plymouth, 1643, by wife Mary, had Ephraim, 1649; Ebenezer, 1651; Peter, 1653; Hezekiah, 1656; John, 1658; Mary, 1661, m. a Thompson; John, 1663; Isaac, 1666, m. Sarah King. EPHRAIM, Middleboro', son of above, by wife Esther, had Ephraim, and Isaac. HEZEKIAH, son of 1st Ephraim, by wife Ruth, had Hezekiah, 1685; Mary, 1687, m. Ebenezer Curtis; John, 1689; Jacob, 1691, m. Hannah Cobb; Caleb, 1693; Sarah, 1696; Ebenezer, 1698; Ruth, 1701, m. Ebenezer Cobb; Peter, 1706. HEZEKIAH, son of above, by wife Elizabeth, had Hannah, 1710; Elizabeth, 1713, m. Joshua Saunders of Ware; Isaac, 1715, m. Remembrance Cooper; Sarah, 1718, m. Benjamin Smith; Jedediah, 1721; John, 1723; Mary, 1724; Martha, 1726; m. Thomas Sylvester; Ruth and Lydia, twins, 1729; Ebenezer, 1732; Lydia, 1735. ICHABOD, m., 1772, Mary Gorham, and had Mary, 1773. ISAAC, son of 2d Hezekiah, had Briggs, 1740; Elizabeth, 1743; Isaac, 1745. JACOB, son of 1st Hezekiah, m., 1721, Hannah Cobb, and had Mercy, 1722; Jacob, 1724. JACOB, son of above, m. Lydia,

Dunham, and had Hannah, 1747; Lydia, 1749; Mary, 1751; Jacob, 1754, m. Rebecca Morton. JOHN, son of 1st Hezekiah, m., 1714, Ann Gray, and had Mary, 1718, m. Benjamin Eaton; Edward, 1720; Ephraim, 1724; Ann, 1726; Joseph, 1728. LAZARUS, from Sandwich, m., 1821, Mary Rogers. PETER, son of 1st Hezekiah, by wife Mary, had Jacob, 1738; Arthur, 1742. ZEDEKIAH, m,, 1767, Mercy Tinkham, and had Sarah, 1768.

TINKER, THOMAS, came in the Mayflower with wife and one child, and all died the first winter.

TISDALE, ABRAHAM, m., 1765, Experience Totman, and had Samuel, Abraham; Isaac, 1768. SAMUEL T., from New York, m., 1825, Lucy B., d. of Benjamin Ellis.

TOBEY, JONATHAN, from Sandwich, m., 1740, Deborah Swift. WILLIAM was an owner of real estate in Plymouth 1729.

TORRANCE, THOMAS, pub. to Betsey Harris, 1788.

TORREY, HAVILAND, son of 1st William, by wife Elizabeth, had Haviland, 1716; John, 1717; Nathaniel, 1721; Thomas, 1723; William, 1725; Joseph, 1727; Josiah, 1729, m. Mercy Atwood; and Deborah. JAMES, Scituate, 1640, m., 1643, Ann, d. of William Hatch, and had James, 1644; William, 1647; Josiah, 1649; Damaris, 1651; Jonathan, 1654; Mary, 1656; Josiah, 1658; Sarah, 1660; Joanna, 1663; Bethiah. JAMES, Scituate, son of above, m., 1666, Lydia, d. of William Wills, and, 2d, 1679, Elizabeth, d. of Nathaniel Rawlins, and had Ann, 1680; James, 1682; William, 1683; Nathaniel, 1686, m. Hannah Tilden; David, 1687; Elizabeth, 1689; Samuel, 1691; Rachel, 1693; Joseph, 1694, Stephen, 1696; Lydia, 1698. He m., 3d, Eunice, wid. of Jonas Deane, 1701, and had Eunice, 1701. JOHN, son of Haviland, m. 1751, Mary Tilley of Boston, and, probably, a 1st wife, Deborah Reed, 1741. By his 2d wife, he had Haviland, 1752; John, 1754; Elizabeth, 1756; Mary, 1759, Elizabeth, 1762; George, 1765. JOHN, son of above, m., 1777, Meriah, d. of Nathaniel Morton, and had John, 1778; Maria, 1780, m. Woodworth Jackson. He m., 2d, Elizabeth d. of Jesse Harlow, 1783, and had Harlow, 1784; Elizabeth, 1786; John again; Jesse Harlow, 1793; George Washington, 1800. JOHN, son of above, m. Marcia Otis, d. of Henry Warren, 1813, and had Henry Warren of Harvard University; and Elizabeth. JOSIAH, Scituate, son of 1st James, m., 1684, Isabel, wid. of Samuel Witherell, and had Mary, 1685; Josiah, 1687. He m., 2d, 1692, Sarah Mendall, and had Ruth, 1694; Caleb, 1695; Jemima, 1696; Keziah, 1702. JOSHUA, m., 1798, Sarah Doten, and, 1828, Susan, wid. of Stephen Paine. NATHANIEL, son of Haviland, m., 1747, Anna Leonard, and had Elizabeth, 1748; Nathaniel, 1750; Priscilla, 1754; Anna, 1756; Sarah, 1758; Daniel, and John. SAMUEL, m., 1754, Deborah Torrey. THOMAS, son of Haviland, m., 1747, Abigail Thomas, and had Thomas. THOMAS, son of above, m., 1786, Elizabeth Holmes, and had Isaac, m. Olive Hatch; Abigail Thomas, m. Thomas Goodwin; and Thomas. THOMAS, son of above, m., 1821, Lydia, d. of Ebenezer Davie, and had Lydia Ann, 1822, m. Isaac Lewis Davie; Elizabeth Thomas, 1824, m. Putnam Kimball; Lucy Haviland, 1828, m. George A. Kimball of Greenfield. WILLIAM, son of 1st James, removed to Plymouth, and had a son Haviland. WILLIAM, son of Haviland, m., 1748, Mary Turner, and had Mary, 1749, m. Cornelius Bramhall; William, 1751; Anna, 1753; Joseph, 1755.

TOTMAN, ELKANAH, son of Stephen, m., 1727, Sarah Churchill, and had Priscilla, 1728; Joshua, 1730; Elkanah, 1732. By 2d wife, Elizabeth, he had Elkanah, 1734; Sarah, 1735; Elizabeth, 1738, m. Thomas Mitchell; Joseph; Dorothy, 1744; Abiel, 1736. JOHN, son of 2d Thomas, by wife Elizabeth, had John, 1759; Reuben, 1766; Asaph, 1769. JOSEPH, son of Elkanah, m. Elizabeth Curtis, 1764, and had Sarah, 1765; Hannah, 1767; Joseph, 1770. JOSHUA, son of Elkanah, m. Joanna Scarrit, 1752, and had Joshua, 1753; Betty, 1756; Elkanah, 1758; Thomas, 1760. SAMUEL, son of Stephen, m. Deborah Buck, 1714, and had Simeon, 1716. He probably m., 2d, Experience Rogers, 1727, and had Joshua, 1727, m. Elizabeth Rogers; Samuel, 1729; Deborah, 1732, m. Moses Barrows; Hannah, 1734; Joshua, 1737, m. Elizabeth Sutton; Experience, 1744, m. Walter Rich. STEPHEN, Scituate, son of 1st Thomas, m. in Scituate, and had Samuel, 1693; Stephen, 1695; Mary, 1696; Christian, 1699. He moved to Plymouth, and by 2d wife, Dorothy, had Elkanah, 1703; Thomas, 1705; Lydia, 1708; Stephen, 1711. THOMAS, Plymouth, moved to Scituate, 1660, by wife Mary, had Stephen, and perhaps others. THOMAS, son of Stephen, m. Lucretia Rose, 1729, and had Ebenezer 1731; John, 1733, m. Elizabeth Harlow; Mary, 1734; and Elizabeth, m. Crosby Luce.

TOTO, GEORGE, from Kingston, m. Zilpha Buckley, 1764.

TOWNS, SIMEON, of Andover, m., about 1822, Eliza (Kingsbury) Eaton, wid. of Timothy, and had Joseph F. of Plymouth, m. Sarah Royal, d. of Nathan H. Haskins; Lydia, Janette; and Matilda, m. William H. Pettee of Plymouth.

TOWNSEND, SOLOMON, from Providence, m., 1827, Fanny Lee, d. of George Drew, and had Fanny Glover, 1830; Eugene Lee, 1831.

TOXE, ROBERT, pub., 1739, to Mrs. Hannah Clark.

TRACY, STEPHEN, came in the Ann, 1623, with wife Tryphosa, m., at Leyden, 1621. He brought also daughter Sarah, and had, after arrival, Rebecca, Ruth, Mary; and John, m. Mary, d. of Thomas Prence.

TRASK, ELIAS, possibly grandson of Elias of Salem, who was son of John, and grandson of William, who came over 1626, by wife Abigail, had Abigail, 1746; John, 1751; Samuel, 1753. JOSEPH, perhaps brother of above, m., 1758, Jerusha Kempton, and had Joseph, 1758; Thomas, 1760; Priscilla, 1761; William, 1763; Jerusha, m. Robert Davie and John Bartlett.

TRENT, JAMES, pub., 1798, to Bethiah Johnson.

TREVORE, WILLIAM, came in the Mayflower as a sailor, and returned in the Fortune 1621.

TRIBBLE, HIRAM, Kingston, son of 4th Joseph, m., 1832, Abigail T., d. of Daniel Ripley, and had William Robert, Mary Holmes; William Thomas, m. Angeline Sampson; Maria Thomas, Irene, Harriet, Hiram, Otis. ISAAC, son of 3d Joseph, m., 1810, Lois, d. of Gideon Holbrook, and had Sarah Holbrook, m. Isaac B. Rich; Gideon Holbrook; Augustus, m. Frances A., d. of James G. Gleason; and Jennie Wellington. JAMES, son of 3d Joseph, m., 1804, Susanna Holmes, and had James and Sylvanus. JAMES, son of above, m. Mary Bartlett, d. of Ebenezer Holmes; Elizabeth Bennett, 1837, and Harriet A. Thomas, 1862. By the 1st wife, he had Susan H., m. Lorenzo M. Bennett; Jeanette, m. Asahel W. Handy. JOHN, son of 3d Joseph, m., 1803, Bathsheba, d. of Elnathan Holmes, and had Christiana D., 1805; Albert, 1807; Winslow M., 1811, m. Thankful S. Chandler; Gustavus, 1812; Marcia, 1814. He m., 2d, 1816, Polly, wid. of Ephraim Holmes, and d. of Lemuel Bradford, and had Albert R., m. Lydia, d. of George Harlow; Levantia, 1821; and Marcia. JOSEPH, the first settler of the name in Plymouth, m., 1729, Anna Jones, a wid., and d. of Nathaniel Jackson, and had Joseph and John. JOSEPH, son of above, m., 1750, Sarah, d. of James Howard, and had Joseph, 1752; Sarah, 1754, m. Thomas Covington; Mary, m. Sylvanus Dunham; Lydia, 1762, m. Thomas Burgess; Anna, 1765, m. John Burgess; Elizabeth, 1766, m. Joseph Barnes. JOSEPH, son of above, m., 1772, Sarah Dunham, and had Joseph, John, James, William, Isaac; Polly, m. Wait Atwood; Sally, m. William Barnes. JOSEPH, son of above, m., 1794, Polly, d. of Ephraim Holmes, and had Thomas; Hiram, m. Abigail T. Ripley of Kingston; William, m. Lucia W., d. of Daniel Goddard; Robert F.; Mary, and George, THOMAS, son of above, m., 1821, Maria Paty, d. of Samuel Alexander, and had Maria. He m., 2d, 1850, Cynthia T., d. of Elijah Sherman. WILLIAM, son of 3d Joseph, m., 1807, Elizabeth, d. of Josiah Bradford, and had Francis; William Bradford, m. Desire d. of Thomas Goodwin; Betsey W., m. Nathaniel Carver Barnes; Caroline, m. David Drew; Emily, m. William Churchill; Lorenzo, m. Nancy Churchill, d. of John Atwood.

TRUANT, or TROWANT, CHURCH CLIFT, son of Samuel, m. Lucia Sampson of Waldoboro', and had Church Clift, Samuel, Charles Sampson, Lucy Sampson; and Sarah, m. John C. George of Boston. JOHN, Marshfield, son of Maurice, had Prudence; Hannah, m. a Ford; Mary, and John. He died about 1730. JOHN, Marshfield, son of above, by wife Mary, had Samuel, Mary, Lydia, and John, and died 1749, when his children were all minors. JOHN, Marshfield, son of above, by wife Elizabeth, had Betsey Church, m. a Hall, and Joseph; and died 1811. JOSEPH, Middleboro', by wife Mercy, had Nathan; Hannah, m. a Simmons; and a d. m. a Holloway. MAURICE, Duxbury, 1643, born 1606, by wife Jane, had Joseph; Hannah, m. Jonathan Eames; Mehitabel, m. John Doggett; John, Mary, Jane, and Elizabeth. SAMUEL, Marshfield, son of 2d John, by wife Rhoda, had Church Clift, m. Lucia Sampson of Waldoboro'; Huldah, m. Joel Hatch; and Samuel.

TUCKER, LEMUEL, pub., 1778, to Sarah Black.

TUFTS, JONATHAN, a descendant from Peter, who came to Charlestown about 1650, m., 1772, Elizabeth, d. of James Nicolson, and had Elizabeth, 1782, m. Thomas Atwood. He m., 2d, 1789, Priscilla, d. of James Drew, and had William Drew, 1791; Sarah, 1794; Priscilla, 1797; James, 1799; Charles, 1803. The daughters died unmarried, and the sons removed to Boston.

TUPPER, ELIAKIM, by wife Mary, had Ruth, 1741; Mary, 1743; Charles, 1748. ENOCH, from Sandwich, m., 1786, Martha Battles. NATHANIEL, m., 1761, Susanna Blackmer.

TURNER, DANIEL, Scituate, son of 1st Humphrey, m. Hannah Randall, and had Lazarus, Hannah, Amasa, Mary, Abner, Elizabeth, and Rachel.

DAVID, Scituate, son of 2d John, m. Elizabeth, d. of Charles Stockbridge, and had David, 1693, and Humphrey. DAVID, son of above, moved to Plymouth, where he m., 1719, Ruth, d. of Nathaniel Jackson, and had David, m. Deborah Lothrop. He m., 2d, Rebecca (Doty) Warren, 1756. DAVID, son of above, m., 1753; Deborah, d. of James Lothrop of Barnstable, and had Ruth, 1754, m. Peter Kimble; Deborah, 1756, m. Zacheus Curtis; Sarah, 1757; Lothrop, 1762; David; Rebecca, m. Jonathan Russell of Barnstable; Mary, m. Richard F. Johnson; and Hannah, m. Jesse Harlow. DAVID, son of above, m. Lydia Washburn, 1793, and had David; Lydia, m. David Crocker; Mercy; Deborah Lothrop, m. Washburn Bursley; Maria, and Lydia. DAVID, son of Lothrop, m. Martha L. Annable, and had Lothrop, 1836; Arabella, 1837; and Martha L., 1839, m. William E. Barnes and Charles H. Rogers. He m., 2d, Ruth (Freeman) Drew, wid. of Nicholas Henry. EDWARD, came to Plymouth with a brother Stephen, and m., 1830, Sally King. ELEAZER STEPHENS, son of Lothrop, m. Laura Ann, d. of Samuel Doten, 1835, and had Susan Stephens, 1837; Francis W., 1839; Laura S., 1844; and Stephens, 1849. EZEKIEL CUSHING, son of Thomas, m. Experience, d. of George Perkins, and had Mary C., 1828, m. Augustus Robbins. HUMPHREY, came to Plymouth 1628, with wife Lydia Gamen, and a son John, m. Mary Brewster. He afterwards had a 2d John, called young John, m. Ann James; Thomas, m. Sarah Hiland; Joseph; Daniel, m. Hannah Randall; Nathaniel, m. Mehitabel Rigby; Mary, m. William Parker; and Lydia, m. James Doughty. HUMPHREY, Scituate, son of 1st David, m. Mary Faunce, and had Mary, 1694; Experience, 1697; Humphrey, 1699; Joseph, 1702; Priscilla, 1707; and Bethiah, 1709. JAPHET, Scituate, son of 2d John, m. Hannah Hudson, and had Ann, 1679, m. Thomas Bicknell; Joshua, 1681, m. Mary Perry; Japhet, 1682, m. Hannah Hatch; and Ruth, 1685, m. a Clark. JESSE, Scituate, son of Jonathan, m. Lydia Neal, and had Seth, Mercy, David, Nabby, Lydia, Jonathan, Seth, Elisha, and John. JESSE, son of Seth, m. Elizabeth Rider, 1814, and had Jesse Humphrey, 1816. JOHN, the elder, son of 1st Humphrey, Scituate, m. Mary, d. of Jonathan Brewster, 1645, and had Jonathan, 1646; Joseph, 1648; Joseph, 1650; Ezekiel, 1651; Lydia, 1653; John, 1654; Elisha, 1657. JOHN, the younger, son of 1st Humphrey, m. Ann James, 1649, and had Japhet, 1650, m. Hannah Hudson; Ann, 1652, m. Joseph Green; Israel, 1654, m. Sarah Stockbridge; Miriam, 1658, m. Nathan Pickles; Sarah, 1665, m. Ichabod Holbrook; Jacob, 1667, m. Jane Vining; David, 1670, m. Elizabeth Stockbridge; Philip, 1673, m. Elizabeth Nash; and Ichabod. JOHN came in the Mayflower with two sons, and all died the first winter. JOHN, from Scituate, m. Persis Washburn, 1795. JONATHAN, Scituate, son of 1st John, m. Martha Bisbee and Mercy Hatch, and had Deborah, Kesiah, Jonathan, Mary, Jemima, Ruth, Isaac, Ignatius, Jesse, and Martha. JOSHUA, Scituate, son of Japhet, m. Mary Perry, and had Rebecca, Hannah, Mary; John, m. Mary Randall; and Joshua. JOSHUA, son of above, Scituate, m. Sarah Winslow, and had Joseph, Joshua, and Jesse. JOSHUA, son of above, m. Betty Barker, and had Betty, Peterson; Cela, m. a Leavitt; Winslow; Thomas, 1779; Deborah, m. Jacob Peterson; Joshua, m. Hannah Simmons;

Ezekiel, and Joseph. LOTHROP, son of 3d David, m., 1784, Elizabeth Morton, and had Elizabeth Morton, m. Daniel Jackson. He m., 2d, Susanna, d. of Eleazer Stephens, 1790, and had Lothrop, m. Marie de Verdier; Sarah, 1796; David, 1803; Susan, Deborah, John Standish, Stephens, Patience C.; and Eleazer Stephens, 1805. SAMUEL, from Sandwich, m. Deborah Shaw, 1836. SETH, son of 1st Jesse, m. Mary Stetson, and had Humphrey, Charlotte, Jennings, Francis Small, Harvey, Seth, Jesse, Mary, Hannah, and Esther. STEPHEN came to Plymouth from Cape Cod with his brother Edward, and m., 1822, Sally Pope, by whom he had Stephen, 1822; Sally, 1824; Mary Ann, 1826; Lydia D., 1828; Benjamin Franklin, 1832; Martha Thomas, 1833; Emeline Francis, 1836; and Laura Maria, 1839. THOMAS, son of 3d Joshua, m. Mercy, d. of Benjamin Parris, and wid. of David Sturtevant, and had Winslow of Missouri, 1802, m. Sarah Palmer and Emily Pollard; Almira Keith, 1804, m. Elisha W. Tilson; Ezekiel Cushing, 1805; Marina, 1807, m. Isaiah Bearse of Hanson, and Mercy Parris, 1809, m. Hector Munroe of Halifax. (See Turner Genealogy).

TWINEY, JABEZ, pub. to Mary Simons, 1737, Indians.

UNQUIT, MATTHEW, pub. to Sarah Acquit, 1737, Indians.

VAIL, JOHN, from Carver, m., 1826, Rebecca D. Barrows.

VALENTINE, SIMON, m., 1804, Bathsheba Wicket.

VALLER, JOHN, m. Mary May, and had Sarah, 1734; Ann, 1736; John, 173); Sylvanus, 1742; Silas, 1744; Ann, 1746; Simeon, 1748; Lois, 1752. SILAS, son of above, m., 1770, Mercy Morey. SILAS, by wife Deborah, had Saul, 1827; Simeon, 1829; Eliza, 1833. SIMEON, son of John, m., 1781, Ruth Holmes. SYLVANUS, m., 1836, Hannah M. Johnson.

VAUGHN, ALVIN, from Carver, m., 1816, Sarah S. Ripley. DANIEL, from Newport, m., 1678, Susanna, d. of Samuel Grimes of Plymouth, and had John, 1679; Ann, 1683; Daniel, 1685; David, 1687; Samuel, 1690. HOSEA, m., 1803, Jedidah Harlow. JOSEPH, m., 1720, Elizabeth Shurtleff. LEVI, from Carver, m., 1803, Phebe Dunham. OLIVER, m., 1808, Sally Churchill. OLIVER C., m. Sarah Holmes, wid. of John Campbell, and d. of Samuel Lanman, and had Eliza S., 1850, m. William E. Baker, and Mary D., 1854.

VAY, STEPHEN, m., 1816, Bathsheba Hollis.

VEAZIE, SAMUEL, from Duxbury, m., 1742, Deborah Sampson.

VERMAYES, BENJAMIN, m., 1648, Mercy, d. of William Bradford, and removed to Boston.

VINCENT, PHILIP, from Yarmouth, m., 1744, Philippa Rider.

VIRGIN, GEORGE WILLIAM, son of 1st John, m., 1816, Mary, d. of Isaac Barnes, and had George William, m. Caroline, d. of Charles Brewster; Ethelinda, m. Nathaniel Spooner; Sally Barnes, m. Benjamin Hathaway; and John. JOHN, brother of 1st Samuel, m., 1791, Priscilla, d. of Richard Cooper, and had John, William Henry, and George William. His wid. m. Ezra Weston of Duxbury. JOHN, son of above, m., 1816, Abigail Davie, and had Abbie Davie, 1818, m. Samuel H. Doten. SAMUEL, brother of 1st John, m., 1801, Esther, d. of Richard Cooper, and had Mary Henderson, 1802; Priscilla Cooper, 1804; Adeline, 1805, m. Arioch Thompson of Abington;

Samuel, 1808. SAMUEL, Boston, son of above, m. Melissa Cobb Hammond of
Carver, and had Charlotte Augusta, 1839; Samuel Henderson, 1842. SAMUEL
HENDERSON, New York, son of above, m., 1868, Isadora F. Blodgett of
Boston, and had Mabel Hammond, 1871; Frederic Oakman, 1873; Edith
Meriam, 1877.
VOSE, JOSEPH, from Boston, m., 1815, Deborah Churchill.
WADE, DAVID, came from North Carolina to Plymouth, having there m.
Siley Bell, and had Kesiah Davis, 1807, m. Nathan H. Haskins and Robert
Swinburn; Sarah Royal, 1810; and David V., 1811. He m., 2d, Deborah
Johnson of Rochester, and had Siley Bell, m. Samuel Doten, Joshua S.
Pratt, and Harvey Bumpus; George Washington, Perez S., John J.; Eliz-
abeth, m. James O'Neil; William, and Charles. DAVID V., son of above, m.
Betsey Polden, 1829, and had Betsey Taylor, 1830, m. Nathan S. Torrence.
JAMES, of Bridgewater, m. Anna Clark, 1754. JOHN J., son of 1st David,
m. Betsey, wid. of David V., 1838, and had Mary Elizabeth, 1838; Deborah
J., m. George W. Gardner; and John, m. Adeline Parker. JOSEPH, m.
Deborah Swift, d. of Nehemiah Savery, 1828. PEREZ S., son of 1st David,
m. Hannah Polden, 1835, and had David, 1835; Hannah P., 1838, m. Isaac
T. Oldham and Sydney Besse of Wareham; and Anna M., m. Charles H.
Morey. He m., 2d, Elizabeth A. Harrington, 1866; and, 3d, Betsey, wid. of
Allen Hathaway, 1875.
WADSWORTH, ABIAH, Duxbury, son of Elisha, by a wife Mary, had
Lenity, 1743, m. Henry Seaver; Joseph, 1745; Irene, 1748; and Lowly.
CEPHAS, Duxbury, son of 1st Peleg, m. Molly Cook about 1770, and moved
to Kingston, where he had Cephas, Alfred, Peleg, John; Levinia, m. a Wood-
worth of Maine; Lucy, m. a Lewis; Polly, m. a Cook; and Welthea, m. Con-
stant Sampson. CEPHAS, son of above, m. Lucy Sylvester, and had William;
Lewis Sylvester of Plymouth, m. Nancy Bartlett Perkins; Lucy Sampson, m.
a Beal of Brockton; Eveline, m. Nathaniel W. Stoddard; Augusta, m. Samuel Winslow of Duxbury; Hannah, m. Charles P. Stoddard; Cephas, m. Mary
Jane Woodworth; and William Alexander m. Margaret Cushman. CHRIS-
TOPHER, Duxbury, 1632, had by wife Grace, Joseph; John, 1638; Samuel;
and Mary, m. an Andrews. DURA, Duxbury, son of 1st Peleg, m. Lydia
Bradford, and had Dura, 1788; Peleg, 1791; Seth, 1792; John, 1794, m. Lydia
Perry; Hannah, 1796, m. Stephen Churchill Bradford; Susanna, 1797; Zilpah,
1800; Lydia, 1802; Uriah, 1808. DURA, Duxbury and Plymouth, son of
above, m. Mercy Taylor, and had Mercy, m. Thomas N. Bartlett. He m., 2d,
Abigail Cushman, and had Lucy, m. Isaac B. Holmes; Henry, m. Abby Winsor; Abigail; Gamaliel, m. Mary Freeman; Dura, m. Olive Wentworth; Elizabeth Briggs, m. Henry B. McLaughlin; Julia Thomas; William; and Zilpah,
m. Charles Sears. ELISHA, Duxbury, son of Joseph, m. Elizabeth Wiswell,
and had Elizabeth, 1695; Alice, 1697, m. Thomas Burton; Ann, 1700; Abiah,
1703; Patience, 1706, m. Samuel Gray of Kingston; Fear, 1709; Wait, 1714.
JAMES, son of 2d Wait, m. Lydia, d. of John Sylvester, and had Susan
Edwards, 1822; George, 1825; Charles E., 1832; and Sylvester D. JOHN,
Duxbury, son of Christopher, m. Abigail Andrews, 1667, and had Mary,
1668; Abigail, 1670; John, 1671; Christopher, 1685; Ichabod, 1687; Isaac,

Lydia, Sarah; Grace, m. William Sprague; Hopestill, m. William Brewster; and Mercy, m. Joshua Cushman. JOHN, Duxbury, son of above, m. Mercy Wiswell, 1704, and had John, 1706; Uriah, 1708, m. Eunice Bradford; Dorothy, 1710, m. Joseph Bartlett; Ichabod, 1712, m. Ann Hunt; Peleg, 1715. He m., 2d, wid. Mary Verdie of Boston, 1718, and had Mary, 1721, m. Elisha Phillips. JOSEPH, Duxbury, son of Christopher, m. Abigail Waite, and a 2d wife Mary. His children were Elisha, Samuel, Joseph, Mehitabel, Ruth, and Bethiah. PELEG, son of 2d John, Duxbury, m. Susanna, d. of John Sampson, and had Zilpah, 1742; Cephas, 1743; Jeptha, 1745; Zilpah, 1746, m. Perez Drew; Peleg, 1748; Uriah, 1751, m. Eunice Bradford; Ira, 1757; Welthea, 1759, m. an Alden; Dura, 1763; and Lucy. PELEG, Duxbury and Plymouth, son of above, m. Elizabeth, d. of Samuel Bartlett of Plymouth, and had Charles Lee; Zilpah, m. Stephen Longfellow; Henry, and Alexander Scammel. PRINCE, of Duxbury, m. Zilpah Ellis, 1766. ROBERT, son of 2d Wait, m. Welthea Delano, about 1800, and had Wait of Plymouth; George, m. Catherine Alexander; James, m. wid. Pamelia (Robbins) Morton, d. of Samuel Robbins, Rebecca, m. Charles Cobb; and Welthea, m. Henry Mange. WAIT, Duxbury, son of Elisha, m., 1748, Abigail Bradford, and had Abigail, 1749, Joseph, 1750, m. Ann Drew; Ahira, 1751; Seneca, 1753; Wait, 1754; Cynthia, 1756, m. Ezekiel Soule; Robert, 1757, Eden, 1749; Beulah, 1762, m. Arthur Howland; Celanah, 1763, m. William Keen of Bristol, Elisha, 1765; Zenith, 1766; Abigail, 1768, m. Prince Howland, and Wiswell. WAIT, Duxbury, son of above, m. Julia Bartlett Robinson, 1774, and had Robert, 1774; Matilda, 1776, m. James Chandler; Sylvia, 1781, m. Ziba Hunt; Lucinda, 1785, m. Zenas Winsor; Jerusha, 1789, m. Zenas Faunce; James, 1792, m. Lydia, d. of John Sylvester; Waity, 1797, m. Nathan Sampson; Caroline, 1802, m. Allen Hunt and Daniel Bradford; Lewis L., 1804, m. Maria Hall; and Jane, 1809, m. John Mange.

WAIT, RETURN, prob. son of Return of Boston, m. Mary (Wilder) LeBaron, wid. of Francis, 1707, and prob. had no children. He m., 2d, 1738, Martha Tupper. RICHARD, prob. brother of above, m., 1706, Elizabeth Kennedy. He m., 2d, 1722, Mary Barnes, and had Mary, 1823, m. Asa Hatch; Lydia, 1725; Martha, 1727, m. Ephraim Dexter of Rochester; Elizabeth, 1729; Abigail, 1731; Elizabeth, 1734, m. William Hueston; Sarah, 1735; Thomas, 1739; Thomas again, 1741; Hannah, 1743; Richard, 1745.

WALKER, ELIJAH, by wife Hannah, had Antoinette, 1832; Elizabeth B., 1837; Paulina Ross, 1839. JOHN, pub., 1735, to Remembrance Nash.

WALL, JOHN, m., 1754, Ruth Lucas, and had Ruth, 1756.

WALLEN, RALPH, came in the Ann 1623, with wife Joyce.

WALLINS, JAMES, m., 1771, Ruth Dunbar.

WALLIS, THOMAS, owned an estate in Plymouth 1639.

WAMPUM, JACOB, pub. to Jean Atkins, 1762, Indians. JOSEPH, pub. to Patience Deerskins, 1733, Indians.

WARD, BENJAMIN, Plympton, son of Ephraim, m. Mary Shaw, and had Eliab, 1769; Benjamin, 1771; Ebenezer, 1775; Ephraim, 1778; Sarah, 1782;

Benjamin, 1785. BENJAMIN, Carver, son of above, m. Hannah Atwood, and had Luther, 1806; Sibilla, 1807; Sibilla, 1808, m. Orin Atwood; Hiram, 1810; Benjamin, 1812; Joseph Atwood, 1815; Eliab, 1817; Hannah, 1819, m. Allen Atwood; Benjamin, 1821; Betty, 1823, m. Welcome Shaw; Horatio, 1824; Adeline, 1826, m. Harrison Shurtleff; Julia Ann, 1828, m. a Carlton. EBE-NEZER, son of Thomas, m. Lydia Polden, 1765. ELIAB, Carver, son of 1st Benjamin, m. Elizabeth Tillson, and had Stillman, 1813; Polly, 1815; Elizabeth, 1817; Benjamin, 1820; Eliab, 1823; Austin, 1826; Elizabeth Tillson, 1828. EPHRAIM, son of Nathan, m. Sarah Dunham, 1743, and had Benjamin, 1744; and Sarah. NATHAN, m. Elizabeth Pope, 1706, and had Thomas, 1706; Mercy, 1708; Alice, 1710; Benjamin, 1713, who died in Virginia; Ephraim, 1720; John, 1725; and Hannah. STILLMAN, Carver, son of Eliab, m. Mary Bent, and had Henry T., 1837; Stillman W., 1839; Mary Elizabeth, 1841. THOMAS, son of Nathan, m. Joanna Dunham, 1730, and had Ebenezer, 1731; Elizabeth, 1733; Jonathan, 1735; Joann, 1737; Mary, 1740; Hannah, 1744; Thomas, 1745; and Ebenezer again, 1748.

WARREN, BENJAMIN, son of 1st Joseph, m., 1697, Hannah Morton, and had Benjamin, 1698; Abigail, 1700, m. Joseph Rider; Hannah, 1704, m. Eleazer Faunce; Nathaniel, 1709; Priscilla, 1712, m. Lemuel Drew; and Patience. He m., 2d, Esther, wid. of Elkanah Cushman, and d. of Jonathan Barnes, 1716, and had Joseph, 1717; Mercy, 1721, m. James Howard. BEN-JAMIN, son of above, m., 1738, Rebecca Doty, and had Benjamin, 1740. BEN-JAMIN, son of above, m. Jane Sturtevant, 1761, and had Benjamin, 1766; Rebecca, 1768, m. Josiah Finney; Sally, 1769, m. William Sturtevant; and David. He m., 2d, 1797, Lois Doten; 3d, 1803, Patience, wid. of Daniel Dimon, and, 4th, 1821, Phebe (Persons) Doty, wid. of Lemuel. BENJAMIN, son of above, m., 1789, Sarah, d. of Daniel Young, and had Benjamin, 1792, m. Sarah Wright; David Young, 1794; Jane, 1796, m. Elisha Doten and David Sears; Solomon, 1798; David, 1799; Lois, 1801, m. Ansel Barrows; Eunice Smith, 1804, m. a Melville; and Patience, m. Benjamin Holmes. CHRISTO-PHER, England, m. Alice, d. of Thomas Webb of Sidnam, in Devonshire, and had Robert, m. Margaret Burgess; John, who came to Massachusetts 1630; Thomas, Richard; Christopher, m. Sarah, d. of Nicholas Opie of Plymouth, England; William of London, who m. Mary, d. of William Cuttney; and Ann, m. John Richards. DAVID, son of 3d Benjamin, m., 1796, Sally Dunham, and had Sally Sturtevant, m. William Martin Brewster; David, m. Sally C. Brewster; Lucy W., m. George Bates; John Clement; Robert Clement, m. Sarah Harding and Margaret Hersey; Eliza Ann, m. Willard Fobes. GEORGE, New York, son of Henry, m., 1840, Elizabeth, d. of Barnabas Hedge, and had Anna White; Charles, m. Anna Nightingale of Providence; James, m. Catherine R., d. of Daniel Jackson Robbins of Plymouth; George, Pelham Winslow, and Lothrop. HENRY, son of 3d James, m., 1791, Mary, d. of John Torrey; Winslow, 1795; Pelham Winslow, 1797; Charles Henry, 1798, m. Abby, d. of Barnabas Hedge; James, 1801; Mary Ann, 1803; Richard, 1805; George, 1807; Edward J., 1809, m. Mary Coffin of Boston. JAMES, son of 1st Nathaniel, m., 1687, Sarah, d. of Edward Doty, and had John, 1688, m. Naomi Bates; Edward, 1690; Sarah,

1692, m. Charles Little and Nicholas Sever; Alice, 1695, m. Peleg Ford; Patience, 1697, m. Joseph Stacy; James, 1700; Hope, 1702, m. Nathaniel Thomas; Mercy, 1705, m. Sylvanus Bramhall; Mary, 1707; Elizabeth, 1711, m. Thomas Murdock and a Thompson. JAMES, son of above, m., 1724, Penelope, d. of Isaac Winslow, and had James, 1726; Ann, 1728; Sarah, 1730, m. William Sever; Winslow, 1733; Josiah, 1736. JAMES, son of above, m., 1754, Mercy Otis, sister of the patriot, and had James, 1757; Winslow, 1759; Charles, 1762, died in Spain; George, 1766, removed to Maine; Henry, 1764. JOHN, Scituate, son of 1st James, m. Naomi Bates, and had James, 1714; Hope, 1716, m. Caleb Torrey; John, 1719; Nathaniel, 1721. JOSEPH, son of 1st Richard, m. Priscilla, d. of John Faunce, about 1654, and had Mercy, 1653, m. John Bradford; Abigail, 1655; Joseph, 1657; Patience, 1660, m. Samuel Lucas; Elizabeth, 1662, m. Josiah Finney; Benjamin, 1670. JOSEPH, son of above, m., 1692, Mehitabel Wilder, and had Joseph, 1694; Priscilla, 1696. JOSEPH, son of above, m., 1722, Alathea Chittenton, and had Joseph, 1724, m. Mercy Atwood; Elizabeth, 1726, m. Samuel Nichols Nelson; Mary, 1730, m. William Morton; Priscilla, 1733; William, 1737. JOSEPH, son of above, m., 1763, Mercy Torrey, and had Joseph, 1765, who removed to South Carolina. NATHANIEL, son of 1st Richard, m., 1645, Sarah Walker, and had Richard, m. in Middleboro'; Jabez; Sarah, 1649; Hope, 1651; Jane, 1652, m. Benjamin Lombard; Elizabeth, 1654, m. William Green; Alice, 1656, m. John Blackwell and William Spooner; Mercy, 1658, m. Benjamin Lombard and Ebenezer Burgess; Mary, 1661; Nathaniel, 1662, m. Phebe Murdock; John, 1663; James, 1665. NATHANIEL, son of 1st Benjamin, m., 1734, Sarah Morton, and had Hannah, 1736, m. Philip Leonard; Nathaniel, 1740; Sarah, 1742, m. Seth Harlow; Hannah, 1744; Susanna, 1746, m. Ezra Harlow; John, 1748; Abigail, 1753; Ruth, 1758, m. Thomas Morton of Greenwich, England. PELHAM WINSLOW, son of Henry, m. Jeanette, d. of John Taylor, and had Henry Pelham and John Dutton, twins. RICHARD, son of Christopher, came in the Mayflower 1620. His wife, who was wid. Elizabeth (Jouatt) Marsh, came in the Ann 1623, with five daughters; Mary, m. Robert Bartlett, 1628; Ann, m. Thomas Little, 1633; Sarah, m. John Cooke, Jr., 1634; Elizabeth, m. Richard Church, 1636; Abigail, m. Anthony Snow, 1639. Two sons, Nathaniel, and Joseph, were born in Plymouth. RICHARD, son of 1st Nathaniel, m. in Middleboro', and had James, 1680; James, 1682; Samuel, 1683; and Hope, m. David Torrey and John May. RICHARD, New York and Boston, son of Henry, m. Angelina Greenwood of Boston, and had Mary W., Emma G., Henry, and Angelina. He m., 2d, Susan Gore of Roxbury, and had Edward Winslow, and Susan. SAMUEL, son of 2d Richard, had Priscilla, 1704; Jabez, 1706; Samuel, 1707; Benjamin, Josiah; and Cornelius, m. Mercy Wood. WILLIAM, son of 3d Joseph, m., 1764, Rebecca Easdell, and had Rebecca, 1765, m. Caleb Morton; Alathea, 1767, m. Joseph W. Nelson; William, m. Elizabeth Lothrop; Mary, m. Nathaniel W. Leonard. WINSLOW, son of Henry, m., 1835, Margaret, d. of Zacheus Bartlett, and had Mary Ann; Winslow, m. Mary, d. of Spencer Tinkham of Boston; and Caroline.

WASHBURN, ABIEL, Kingston, son of 2d Jabez, m. Rebecca Adams, and removed to Ohio. He had Cornelia, 1808, m. Albert G. Mallison; Lorinda, 1810; Leander, 1811, m. Eliza Upson; Keziah, 1813, m. Charles Mallison; Rebecca A., 1816, m. Henry S. Hampson and John W. Wilbur; Daniel B., 1814, m. Mildred A. Adams. ALDEN, Bridgewater, son of Eleazer, m. Sally Gannett, and removed to Tantworth, N. H. He had Oliver, m. a Stephenson; Alden, Eleazer, Ephraim; Sally, m. Nicholas Ham; and Abigail. ALDEN, Tamworth, son of above, m. Sarah Pease, and had Zadock, m. Catherine Wakefield; Alden; Rufus, m. Josephine Quimby; Sally, m. a Howry of Lebanon, Ohio; and Rosamond, m. Caleb Rider and William Allen, both of Plymouth. BARNABAS, Kingston, son of 2d John, m. Hannah Sears, and had Barnabas, 1746; Elkanah, 1751, m. Mercy Foster; Elizabeth, 1754. BILDAD, Kingston, son of 2d Jabez, had Betsey, 1785; Judith, 1786; Ira, 1788, m. Abigail Emerson; Sophia, 1790, m. John Adams; Alvin, 1792, m. Margaret Noble; Nathaniel; Elias, 1796, m. Lydia Allen; Nancy, 1798, m. Benjamin Faunce; Eliza, 1800, m. Azel Wood; Francis, 1801, m. Judith Sampson; Jabez, 1803, m. Mary A. Wood of Ohio; Mary, 1803, twin, m. Franklin White; Lucy K., 1806, m. George Bryant; Julia A., 1811, m. Lyman Clark. EBENEZER, Kingston, son of 2d John, m. Lydia Faunce, and had Lydia, 1733, m. Nicholas Davis; Ebenezer, 1735, who had a wife Sarah; Simeon, 1738. ELEAZER, Bridgewater, son of Noah, m., 1738, Anna, d. of Ebenezer Alden, and had Susanna, 1740; Zenas, 1741; Anna, 1742, m. Amos Whitman; Eleazer, 1746, Asa, 1749; Levi, 1752; Oliver, 1755; Alden, 1758; Isaac, 1760. ELISHA, Kingston, son of 2d John, m. Martha Perkins of Plympton, and had Lydia, 1729; Martha, 1732; Elisha, 1735. ELISHA, Kingston, son of 2d Jabez, m., 1780, Deborah Prince, and had Mary, 1781, m. Seth Drew; Kimball, 1784, m. Mary Stephenson; Job, 1786, removed to Thomaston, and m. Sarah D. Clough and Mrs. Betsey Carlton; Lucy, 1795, m. Abner Rice of Thomaston; Sarah Prince, 1799, m. Robert Snow of Thomaston; Deborah Prince, 1802, m. George Stetson. ELKANAH, Kingston, son of Barnabas, m., 1786, Mercy Foster, and had a d. m. Sylvanus Bryant; Nathaniel; Mercy, m. Samuel J. Nutter; and Lusanna. EPHRAIM, son of 1st Seth, m., 1822, Mary Lucas. EPHRAIM, Kingston, son of 2d John, m. Egloth Washburn, and had Ezekiel, 1733, m. Priscilla Chipman; Deborah, 1735; Mary, 1738; Ephraim, 1741; Elizabeth, 1743; Eunice, 1746; Nehemiah, 1749; Sarah, 1752. FRANCIS, Kingston, son of Bildad, m. Judith Sampson, and had Azel W., 1822, m. Hannah T. Adams; Elizabeth H., 1831, m. Lothrop Holmes; Josephine C., 1834; Lucy M., 1838; Eliza W., 1842, m. Solomon Davie. ICHABOD, Kingston, son of 2d John, m. Bethiah Phillips, and had Bethiah, 1729; Ichabod, 1731; Malatiah, 1733; Sarah, 1737. ICHABOD, Kingston, son of 1st Seth, m. 1793, Sylvia Bradford, and had Pamelia, m. a Warren of Portland; Ichabod and Charles of Worcester, 1798, twins. JABEZ, Kingston, son of 2d John, m., 1731, Judith, d. of John Faunce, and had Jabez, 1733, m. Mary Sherman; Elisha, 1735; Susanna, 1737; John, 1739; Molly, 1742; Rebecca, 1744; Judah, 1746. By a 2d wife, Deborah, he had Thomas, 1755; Susanna, 1762. JABEZ, Kingston, son of above, m. Mary Sherman, and had Elisha, 1758; Molly, 1759; Elias, 1761; Judith, 1771, m. Seth Kingman; Lucy, 1769, m. Abel Kingman; Abiel, 1775, m. Rebecca Adams; John, 1764, m. Jenny Drew; Bildad, 1762.

JACOB, m., 1833, Olive Stone. JOB, Kingston, son of 2d Elisha, removed to
Thomaston, and m., 1812, Sarah D. Clough. He had Antoinette C., 1813, m.
Lewis T. Fales; Harriet N., 1815, m. Enoch Eastman and Samuel D. Carlton;
Judson R., 1817, m. Sarah L. Biskey; John W.; Isabella P., 1821, m. Ebe-
nezer Elbridge Carlton; Sarah E., 1823; Lucy R., Mary S.; Job K., 1828; Wil-
liam H., 1829; Abby P., 1832. He m., 2d, Mrs. Betsey Carlton of Camden.
JOHN, Duxbury, 1632, perhaps son of Anthony of Wichingford, England,
had two sons, John, and Philip. JOHN, Kingston, m. Lydia Billington, and
had John, 1699; Ichabod, 1701, m. Bethiah Phillips; Mercy, 1702, m. Robert
Cushman and John Fuller; Elisha, 1703; Ephraim, 1705; Barnabas, 1707;
Jabez, 1708; Ebenezer, 1709; Thankful, 1715, m. John Adams. JOHN, Bridgewater, son of 1st John, m., 1645, Elizabeth, d. of Experience Mitchell, and
had John, m. Rebecca Lapham; Thomas, m. Abigail, d. of Jacob Leonard,
and Deliverance, d. of Samuel Packard; Joseph, m. Hannah, d. of Robert
Latham; Samuel, m. Deborah, d. of Samuel Packard; Jonathan, m. Mary, d.
of George Vaughn; Benjamin; Mary, 1661, m. Samuel Kinsley; Elizabeth, m.
James Howard and Edward Sealey; Jane, m. William Orcutt, Jr.; James,
1672; and Sarah, m. John Ames. JOHN, Kingston, born about 1672, m. We-
borah, d. of Joseph Bumpus, and Mehitabel Wright, and had Barnabas, and
Ephraim. JOHN, Kingston, son of 2d John, m. Abigail Johnson, and had
John, 1730; Abigail, 1732, m. Abner Sylvester; Mary, 1734; Mercy, 1736;
Seth, 1738; Philip, 1739; Thankful, 1742. JOHN, son of above, m., 1755,
Lydia Prince, and had John, 1755, m. Olive Finney; Abiel, 1757; Benjamin,
1761, m. Bathsheba Churchill and Abigail Bartlett; Prince, 1763; Lydia, 1765;
Thomas, 1767. JOHN, son of 2d Thomas, m., 1823, Nancy, d. of Bradford
Barnes, and had John Bradford, 1825; Nancy Barnes, 1829, m. Asa H. Moore;
Franklin, 1834, m. Rebecca, d. of Samuel Shaw. JOHN, m., 1777, Experience
Totman. JOHN, Kingston, son of 2d Jabez, had Dorothy, m. Caleb Bates;
and William D., m. Emily Chandler. JOSIAH, from Bridgewater, m., 1702,
Mercy Tillson. JUDAH, Kingston, son of 1st Jabez, m. Priscilla Sampson of
Middleboro', and had Rufus, 1769; Isaac, 1774; Thomas, 1779, m. Lucy, d. of
Joshua Delano; Priscilla, 1786, m. William Drew of Plymouth. KIMBALL,
Kingston, son of 2d Elisha, m., 1808, Mary Stevenson, and had Margaret
Prince, 1809, m. Willard Fales; Mary Rice, 1811, m. William Thompson;
Henry Stevenson, 1813, m. Maria Loring; Frances L., 1815, m. Ezra D.
Ewell; George K., 1817, m. Abigail K. Dunn; Elisha, 1819, m. Arabella King-
man and Elizabeth A. Kingman; Adeline S., 1822, m. Jonathan Grout;
Charles P., 1825. NATHANIEL, m., 1756, Mary Rider, and had Mary, 1758;
Nathaniel, 1760; Mary, 1764. NOAH, Bridgewater, son of Samuel, m. Elizabeth, d. of Joseph Shaw, 1710, and had Eleazer, and Noah. PHILIP, Bridgewater, son of 1st John, is thought to have had no children. PHILIP, Kingston, son of 5th John, m. Silence Davis, 1765, and had Sarah, 1766; Philip,
1767; Israel and Levi, 1770, twins. PHILIP, Kingston, son of above, m.
Patience Ransom, and had Thaddeus, Patience, Hervey; Mary, 1805, m. William Symmes; Martha, Charles, George, and Philip. PHILIP, Kingston, son
of above, m., 1833, Hannah Drew Fuller, and had Philip Madison, Hannah
Drew of Plymouth; and Sarah Fuller, m. Thomas Otis Jackson of Plymouth.

PRINCE, Kingston, son of 6th John, m., 1786, Ruth Stetson, and had Ruth, Lydia, Benjamin, and George. REUBEN, m., 1767, Meriah Holmes. SAMUEL, Bridgewater, son of 3d John, m. Deborah, d. of Samuel Packard, and had Samuel, 1668; Noah, 1682; Israel, 1684; Nehemiah, 1686; Benjamin; Hannah, m. John Keith. SETH, Kingston, son of 5th John, m. Fear Howard, 1765; and had Fear, 1766, m. James Foster; Persis, m. John Turner; Abigail, m. Zenas Churchill; Seth, 1769; Ichabod. He m., 2d, Ann Fullerton, and had Anna. He m., 3d, Mrs. Deborah Churchill, and had Ephraim of Plymouth. SETH, Kingston, son of above, m., 1792, Sarah Adams, and had Marcia, 1793, m. Nathaniel Faunce; Sally, 1796, m. Solomon Davie; Christiana Drew, 1799, m. Nahum Bailey; Hannah, m. Sewall Rice of Worcester; Judith, m. Francis Johnson; Amelia, m. Charles C. Faunce. THOMAS, m., 1721, Elizabeth Howland. THOMAS, son of 6th John, m., 1793, Hannah Smith, and had John, and Hannah. THOMAS, Kingston, son of Judah, m., 1802, Lucy, d. of Joshua Delano, and had Martha, m. William Allen Robbins; Edward, and Rebecca, WILLIAM DREW, Kingston, son of 9th John, m. Emily Chandler, and had William, 1818; Amelia, 1820, m. Harrison White of Bridgewater; George. 1821; Henry, 1823; Martin Parris, 1824; Jane D., 1826, m. George Prentice of Holyoke; Caroline, 1829; John, 1831; Mary Sherman, 1833; Julia, 1834; Sarah A., 1838; Albert, 1840; Martin Parris, 1842, m. Juliet M. Drew; Edward. (For other branches of the Washburn family, see Mitchell's History of Bridgewater).

WATERMAN, ELKANAH, son of 2d John, m., 1754, Mary West, and had Mary, 1755; Mercy, 1757. JAMES, son of 2d John, m., 1770, Joanna Wood, and had John. JOHN, Marshfield, son of 1st Robert, m., 1665, Ann Sturtevant, and had Samuel, 1666; Elizabeth, 1669; Ann, 1671; Lydia, 1678; Robert, 1681; John, 1685, m. Lydia, d. of Eleazer Cushman. JOHN, son of Samuel, m. Hannah, d. of Robert Cushman, 1731, and had Elkanah, 1733; John, 1735; Elizabeth, 1737; John, 1739; Hannah, 1742; John, 1744; James, 1745. JOHN, Kingston, son of James, had John, now living in Kingston. JOHN, Norwich, son of 1st Thomas, m., 1701, Elizabeth, d. of Samuel Lothrop, and had a large family, of whom Hannah was the mother of Benedict Arnold. JOSEPH, Marshfield, son of 1st Robert, m. Sarah Snow, and had Sarah, 1674; Joseph, 1677, m. Susanna Snow; Elizabeth, 1679; Abigail, 1681; Anthony, 1685; Bethiah, 1687; Lydia, 1689. JOSIAH, m. Fear Tinkham, and had Joshua, 1757; Josiah, 1760; Jerusha, 1763. ROBERT, Plymouth, 1638, m. in that year Elizabeth Bourne of Marshfield, and had Joseph, 1639; John, 1642; Thomas, 1644, m. Meriam, d. of Thomas Tracy; Robert, 1652. ROBERT, Hingham, son of above, m., 1675, Susanna Lincoln, and had Susanna, 1677; Elizabeth, 1682; Robert, 1684; Josiah, 1687. He m., 2d, Sarah, wid. of Thomas Lincoln, and d. of James Lewis of Barnstable, 1699, and had Lydia, 1700; Thomas, 1702; Hannah, 1704. ROBERT, Marshfield, son of 1st John, m., 1702, Mary, d. of Isaac Cushman, and had Isaac, 1703; Josiah, 1705, m. Joanna, d. of Samuel Bryant; Thomas, 1707; Rebecca, 1710, m. Joseph Holmes and William Rand; Robert, 1712, m. Martha, d. of Josiah Cushman; Mary, 1716, m. Jonathan Holmes; Samuel, 1718; Anna, 1720. He probably m., 2d, 1723, Elizabeth, d. of Elkanah Cushman; and 3d, 1729, Abigail

Dingley. SAMUEL, son of 1st John, had John, and perhaps others. THOMAS, Norwich, son of 1st Robert, m., 1668, Meriam, d. of Thomas Tracy, and had Elizabeth, m. John Fitch; Martha, m. Reinold Marvin; Meriam; Lydia, m. Eleazer Burnham; Ann, m. Josiah DeWolfe; Thomas, and John. THOMAS, Norwich, son of above, m., 1691, Elizabeth, d. of Robert Allyn, and had Elisha, Asa, Nehemiah, and others.

WATKINS JAMES. m., 1746 Jerusha Rider. JONATHAN, m., 1766, Lucy Dunham.

WATSON, ALBERT MORTIMER, son of 3d John, m., 1831, Abigail, d. of Nathan Burgess, and had James Marston, 1833; Edward Winslow, 1835, m. Alice F. Walker of Roxbury; Albert Mortimer, 1837, m. Augusta, wid. of Alvin Nightingale, and d. of Prince Manter; Nathan Burgess, 1844; Ellen Florence, 1851. BENJAMIN MARSTON, son of 3d John, m., 1804, Lucretia Burr, d. of Jonathan Sturges of Fairfield, Conn., and had Lucretia Ann, m. Rev. Hersey B. Goodwin; Elizabeth Miller; Benjamin Marston, 1820; and Jonathan Sturges. BENJAMIN MARSTON, son of above, m. Mary, d. of Thomas Russell, 1846, and had Benjamin Marston, 1848; Thomas Russell, 1850; Lucretia Sturges, 1851; Edward Winslow, 1853; Ellen, 1856. DANIEL, son of 3d John, m. Susan Sudler, and had Susan Augusta, m. Rowland Edwin Cotton. EBENEZER, Windsor, son of 2d Robert, m. Abigail Kelsie of Windsor, 1703, and had Mary, Samuel, Hannah, Abigail, Ebenezer. EBENEZER, Windsor, son of above, m. Ann Trumbull, 1743, and had Ebenezer, John, Robert, Nathaniel, Timothy, and Ann. ELKANAH, son of 1st George, m. Mercy, d. of William Hedge of Yarmouth, 1676, and had John, 1678; Phebe, 1681, m. Edmund Freeman; Mercy, 1685, m. John Freeman; Mary, 1688, m. Nathaniel Freeman; Elizabeth, m. John Bacon. His wid. m. Rev. John Freeman of Harwich, and the three daughters first named m. three of his sons. ELKANAH, son of 1st John, m., 1754, Patience, d. of Benjamin Marston of Manchester, and had Marston, 1756; Elkanah, 1758; Priscilla, 1760, m. Josiah Cotton; Patty, 1762; Lucia, 1765. He m., 2d, Fanny, wid. of John Glover, and d. of John Lee of Manchester, and had Charles Lee, 1793; and Lucia, 1795, m. Thomas Drew. ELKANAH, son of above, m. Rachel Smith, 1784, and had Emily M., 1791, m. George B. Larned of Pittsfield; George Elkanah, 1793, m, Lucy, d. of Nathan Willis of Pittsfield; Mary Lucia, 1797, m. Aaron Ward of New York; Charles Marston, 1799, m. Elizabeth B. Shankland, and lived at Port Kent, N.Y.; Winslow Cossoul, 1803, m., 1st, Frances, d. of Richard Skinner of Manchester, Vt., 2d, Susan Skinner, and, 3d, Elizabeth A. Patterson. He lived at various times in Providence, England, France, Pittsfield, Albany, and Fort Kent, founded by him, where he died. GEORGE, son of 1st Robert, was in Plymouth certainly as early as 1633, where he m., 1635, Phebe, d. of Robert Hicks, and had Phebe, m. Jonathan Shaw; Mary, m. Thomas Leonard of Taunton, John; Samuel; 1648, Elizabeth, twin, 1648, m. Joseph Williams of Taunton, Jonathan, 1652; Elkanah, 1656. GEORGE, son of 1st John, m., 1748, Abigail, d. of Richard Saltonstall, and had George, 1749, and a son unnamed, 1751. He m., 2d, 1753, Elizabeth, d. of Peter Oliver, and had Mary, 1754, m. Elisha Hutchinson; George, 1757; Sarah, 1759, m. Martin

Brimmer of Boston; Elizabeth, 1764; Elizabeth again, 1767, m., 1st, Thomas Russell of Boston, and, 2d, Sir Grenville Temple. He m., 3d, Mrs. Phebe Scott. Sir Grenville Temple Temple, son of Elizabeth, born 1799, m., 1829, Mary, d. of George Baring, brother of Lord Ashburton. GEORGE, Roxbury, son of 3d John, m., 1801, Elizabeth Leach, and had Elizabeth Leach, 1802, m. William Stevens, Lucia Marston, 1803; Anna Maria, 1804; Ellen, 1806; Caroline Lucretia, 1808; Sarah Brimmer, 1809; George, 1811, m. Susan A. Smith; Hannah Emily, 1816; John, m., 1st, S. M. Bicknell, 2d, Jane Holt; Jeanette Phebe, 1818; Henrietta Frances, 1822, m. Joseph Kittridge. JOHN, son of 1st Elkanah, m., 1715, Sarah, d. of Daniel Rogers of Ipswich, and had John, 1716; George, 1718. He m., 2d, Priscilla, d. of Caleb Thomas of Marshfield, 1729, and had William, 1730; Elkanah, 1732. JOHN, son of above, m., 1744, Elizabeth, d. of Joseph Reynolds of Bristol, and had Elizabeth, 1745, m. Edward Clark of Boston; John, 1747; Daniel, 1749. JOHN, son of above, m., 1769, Lucia, d. of Benjamin Marston of Manchester, and had John, 1769; George, 1771; Sally Marston, 1772; Benjamin Marston, 1774; Lucia, 1776, m. John Taylor; Daniel, 1779; William, 1783; Winslow, 1786; and Brooke. He m., 2d, 1796, Eunice, wid. of LeBaron Goodwin, and d. of John Marston of Boston, and had Edward Winslow, 1797; Eliza Ann, 1799; Albert Mortimer, 1801. JOHN, son of above, m. Pamelia Howard, 1794, and had Elizabeth, m. Melzar Brewster; Sally, m. Charles Mack; Lucia Marston; Daniel H., m. Betsey Weston; Eunice, and Nancy. JOHN, Connecticut, son of 2d Ebenezer, m. Ann Bliss, and had John, William, Mary, Ann, Henry, Sarah, and Harriet. JOHN, Connecticut, son of above, m. Ann Bliss, and had Ralph, Ann Bliss, Edward H., Laura H., and Mary H. JOSEPH, m. Mary Wadsworth of Duxbury, 1754. MARSTON, son of 2d Elkanah, m. Lucy, d. of John Lee of Manchester, 1779, and had Benjamin Marston, 1780, m., 1st, Elizabeth, d. of Theophilus Parsons, and, 2d, Mrs. Roxana Davis of Boston; Lucy, 1781; Martha Marston, 1782, m. Thomas Cushing of Boston; Lucy Lee, 1783; Sally Maria, 1784, m. Thomas Welsh of Boston, Laura A., 1786; Henry Monmouth, 1788; Horace Howard, 1789, m. Thirza Hobart of Hingham; Eliza Constantia, 1791, m. Thomas Cushing; Agnes Lee, 1793; Almira, 1795; John Lee, 1797, m. Elizabeth, d. of John West of Taunton, and lives in Orange, N. J.; and Adolphus Eugene, 1800, m., 1st, Louisa C. M. Stoughton of Boston, 2d, Eliza Mellen of Cambridge, 3d, Susan L. Ferguson. ROBERT, from London, came to Plymouth early, and settled finally in Connecticut. By wife Elizabeth he had, born in England, George, 1603, Robert; Samuel; and perhaps Frances, m. John Rogers. He died in 1637. ROBERT, Windsor, son of above, m., 1646, Mary, d. of John Rockwell, and had Mary, 1652; John, 1654; Samuel, 1656; Hannah, 1658; Ebenezer, 1661; Nathaniel, 1664; Jedediah, 1666. THOMAS, m. Sarah Lester, 1788. WILLIAM, son of 1st John, m., 1756, Elizabeth, d. of Benjamin Marston of Manchester, and had William, 1757; Eliza, 1759, m. Nathaniel Niles of Vermont; Benjamin, 1761; Ellen, 1764, m. John Davis. WILLIAM, Duxbury, son of 3d John, m. Huldah Delano, and had William; George, 1813, m. Hannah Stevens; Almeda, 1819, m. Henry T. Whiting. WINSLOW, son of 3d John, m. Harriet Lothrop, d. of LeBaron

Goodwin, 1812, and had Winslow Marston, 1812, m. Louisa Gibbons; and Elizabeth Gray.

WEBB, ADEY, Plymouth, 1631, owned a house and land in Plymouth, and probably had a family. WILLIAM, from Dedham, m. Sarah M. Brown, 1839.

WEBBER, RICHARD, by wife Priscilla, had Priscilla, 1741.

WEBSTER, MOSES, a schoolmaster, by wife Elizabeth, had John Armstrong, 1813.

WEED, FREDERICK G., from New Bedford, m. Matilda, d. of William Drew, 1839.

WEEKS, BENJAMIN, by wife Mary, had Isaac, 1722; Elizabeth, 1725; Jabez, 1729. JOHN, Plymouth, 1636. JOSHUA, m. Lydia Barrows, 1816.

WELLINGTON, GEORGE, from Fairfax, Me., m., 1815, Lucretia Bartlett.

WELLS, DANIEL S., son of Phineas, m. Mary E. Shaw of Carver, and had Isabella. PHINEAS, came to Plymouth from Maine, and m., 1828, Mercy, d. of George Ellis, by whom he had Mercy Ellis, 1828; William Gould Sewell, 1830; Daniel S., 1831; Phineas, 1833; Daniel S. again, 1836; George Ellis, 1838; Isabella, 1840; and Daniel S. again, 1845. WILLIAM GOULD SEWELL, son of above, m. Abby Phillips, d. of Thomas Diman, and had Anna, 1856.

WEST, JUDAH, m. Bethiah Keen, 1718, and had Charles, 1719; Charles, 1720; Judah, 1721; David, 1722; Bethiah, 1723; Lydia, 1725, m. George Holmes; William, 1726; Elizabeth, 1727; Bethiah, 1729; William, 1730; Samuel, 1731, m. Elizabeth Rich; Joshua, 1732; Josiah, 1734, m. Elizabeth Griffith. PETER of Kingston, m. Lydia Keen, 1743; and had Rebecca, 1744; Enos, 1746; Lydia, 1752; Samuel, 1754; Esther, 1755; Josiah, 1756; Jane, 1759; Peter, 1750, m. Tabitha Wright. SAMUEL of Dartmouth, m. Experience, d. of Consider Howland, 1768. SILAS, by wife Mary, had Sarah, 1733; Jean, 1734; Mary, 1736; Silas, 1738, m. Rebecca Wethered; John, 1739; Charles, 1742; Bethiah and William, twins, 1745.

WESTGATE, BENJAMIN, came to Plymouth from Rochester, where he had brothers, Thomas, William, and Joseph, and probably a sister Elizabeth, m. Luke Hall. His children were Charles; Elizabeth, m. Samuel Luscomb; Darius; Benjamin, born about 1790; Amos; Ruth, m. William Barrett and Martin Gould; and Lucy, m. James Haskins and Stephen Westgate. BENJAMIN, son of above, m. Lucinda (Maxim) Tinkham, wid. of Asaph, and a previous wid. of William Hall, 1813, and had Darius; and Lucinda, m. a Field. He m., 2d, Abigail Haskins, 1820, and had Abigail, m. Samuel Wood. CHARLES, son of 1st Benjamin, m. Lydia Polden, 1827, and had Charles H., 1832; Nancy P., 1835; Susan M., 1838; Ellen, 1841; Lydia, Ann, Edward, and William. DARIUS, son of 1st Benjamin, m. Laura Edson, 1828, and had Darius, Lydia, Benjamin; Susan, m. three husbands, the last of whom was Frederick Buck; Elizabeth, m. Alexander Haskins; and Laura, who m. three husbands, the last of whom was Charles Pierce. DARIUS, son of 2d Benjamin, m. Emily Frank, and had Lucinda, Emily Augusta, George Antoine. Flora, Rosina, and Benjamin. JONATHAN, m Mercy King, 1816. STEPHEN, a nephew of 1st Benjamin, m. Lucy, wid. of James Haskins, and d. of Benjamin Westgate, and had Lucy, m. Robert W. Holmes and William L. Churchill; and Abby, m. James H. Robbins.

WESTON, ASA, from Taunton, m. Hannah Morton, 1816. BENJAMIN, Plympton, son of 2d Edmund, by wife Hannah, had Benjamin, 1724; Joshua, 1725; Hannah, 1729. He m., 2d, Hannah, d. of William Coomer, 1731, and had William, 1732; Noah, 1734; Zadock, 1736; Hannah, 1738; Job, 1741. He m., 3d, Philemon Jones, and, 4th, Mercy, wid. of Ebenezer Lobdell. BENJAMIN, son of 1st Lewis, m. Joanna Washburn, 1807, and had Joanna, 1809; Henry, 1810; Mary, 1813; Nancy, 1815; Mary, 1817, m. a Tilden; Jeanette, 1819, m. Warren S. Macomber; Elizabeth C., 1823, m. Nathan P. Lamson of Boston; Catherine, 1825, m. Isaac N. Harlow; Bathsheba, 1828; and Sarah Nye, 1830. CHARLES H., son of 1st Harvey, m. Nancy Cotton, d. of Joseph Barnes, 1847, and had Nannie B., m. Dexter H. Craigg of Marblehead; and Jennie B., m. Maurice Livingston. COOMER, son of 1st William, m. Patty, d. of Isaac Cole, 1784, and had Coomer, 1784; Isaac, 1787, moved to Maine, and m. Mary Emmons of Portland; Thomas, 1788; Patty, 1791, m. Ichabod Morton; Lydia, 1794, m. Samuel Ellis. COOMER, son of above, m. Hannah, d. of Jabez Doten, 1804, and had Coomer, 1805; Francis Henri, 1807; Hannah Doten, 1809, m. Francis Borasso; Ann Maria, 1813; Lydia, 1818; Thomas, 1821; and Miles Standish, 1826. COOMER, son of above, m. Sally Sturtevant, d. of John Eddy, 1829, and had Sarah, 1831, m. Everett F. Sherman; Hannah Coomer, 1833, m. William Henry Nelson; Laura Ann, 1835, m. Edward Harlow; Harriet Davie, 1837, m. Albert E. Thayer of Hingham; Edmund, 1843, m. Florence A., d. of Nathaniel Wood. EDMUND, came in the Elizabeth and Ann to Boston 1635, and settled in Duxbury. He had Edmund, John; Mary, m. John Delano; and Elnathan. EDMUND, Duxbury, son of above, m., 1688, Rebecca, d. of John Soule, and had Nathan, 1688; Zechariah, 1690; Rebecca, 1693, m. Thomas Darling of Middleboro ; John, 1695, m. Deborah, d. of Thomas Delano; Edmund, 1697; Benjamin, 1701. He removed to Plympton, and there died 1727. ELNATHAN, Duxbury, son of 1st Edmund, by wife Jane, had Samuel, Joseph; Mary, m. Joseph Simmons; Sarah, m. Joseph Chandler; Abigail; and perhaps Thomas. FRANCIS, came to Plymouth with Roger Williams. and went with him to Rhode Island. He m. Margaret Reeves, 1640, and died, 1645, childless. FRANCIS HENRI, son of 2d Coomer, m. Anna W. Ellis, 1842, and had Anna, m. Charles Gleason and William Whiting; Hannah Sophia, m. Edwin H. Peterson; and Francis C., m. Mary C. Lamberton. GEORGE, son of 2d William, m. Polly, d. of Joseph Holmes, 1813, and had Mary Ann, 1814; Lydia Holmes, 1817, Emily W., 1820, m. Isaac Barnes; James H., 1822, George Francis, 1824, m. Hannah T., d. of Sylvanus D. Chase, Joseph Lewis, 1826, m. Esther, d. of Joseph Brown, and Abbie E., d. of Thomas Everett Cornish. HARVEY, son of 2d William, m. Lucy Harlow, 1816, and had William. He m., 2d, Sarah, d. of Daniel Churchill, and had Harvey W., 1822; Charles H., 1824; Frances D., 1828, m. William H. Myrick; Samuel N., 1831; Sarah E.; and Frederick L., 1837, m. Maria T. Tribble. HARVEY W., son of above, m. Martha, d. of Henry Gibbs, 1851, and had Robert T.; and Amie B., m. Herbert L. Washburn. HENRY, son of 2d Benjamin, m., 1835, Henrietta H., d. of Thomas Holmes and had

Henry Hersey, 1835; Hannah Harlow, 1837, m. William O. Harris; Benjamin H., 1842, m. Bessie H., d. of Joseph Churchill; Mercy T., 1844, m. William W. Burgess; Alfred P., 1847, m. Mary E., d. of Leavitt Finney; Sarah Elizabeth, 1847, m. Edmund M. Leach; John W., 1852. ICHABOD, Duxbury, son of 3d Thomas, m., 1769, wid. Mehitabel Soule, and had Mehitabel, m. Jabez Peterson; and Sophia, m. Abraham Simmons. JACOB, Duxbury, son of 3d Thomas, m., 1755, Deborah Simmons, and had Jacob; and Deborah, m. Nathaniel Kent. JAMES, from Middleboro', m., 1757, Abigail Dunham. JOHN, Duxbury, son of 2d Edmund, m. Deborah, d. of Thomas Delano, and had Deborah; and Eliphas, m. Priscilla Peterson. JOSEPH, Duxbury, son of Elnathan, m., 1721, Mercy Peterson, and had Thomas, Jacob, William, Zabdiel; Sarah, m. Thomas Hunt; and Abigail, m. Enoch Freeman. LEWIS, son of 1st William, m. Lucy Churchill, 1782, and had Benjamin, Hannah, Lewis; and Lucy, 1785. LEWIS, son of above, m. Martha Bartlett Drew, 1818, and had Sylvanus Bartlett, 1821; Edward L., 1828, m. Henrietta Willoughby of Romney, N. H.; Horace, 1825, m. Frances Preston of England; Sophia, 1831, m. Edward Baker. LEWIS, son of 2d William, m. Betsey Lanman, 1798, and had Lewis, 1802; Betsey Lewis, 1804, m. George Rogers; Mary, 1807; Marcia, 1809, m. William Davie; Sally, 1811, m. Daniel J. Lewis of Fairhaven; Harriet, 1816; Susan, 1818; William; and Lewis, 1822. MILES STANDISH, son of 2d Coomer, m. Lydia Hinckley, d. of Thomas Harris of Barnstable, 1853, and had William Eliot, 1855, m. Sarah Lemont of Somerville; and Miles Standish, 1857. NATHAN, son of 2d Edmund, m. Desire Standish, 1715, and had Nathan, 1723; and Isaac, 1725. OLIVER, a descendant from John of Salem, 1648, m. Rebecca, d. of William Leonard, 1820, and had Lycurgus Bartlett, 1821; Susan Rebecca, 1824; Sarah William, 1827; William Leonard, 1829; Oliver Emerson, 1830; Leander Lovell, 1832. SIMEON, Duxbury, son of 3d Thomas, had Levi, Asa; Anna, m. Charles Witherell; Sarah, m. Abel Chandler; Hannah, m. Nathaniel Holmes; Lucy, m. Elisha Sampson; and two other daughters, who m. Charles Simmons and a Howard. THOMAS, of London, sent a colony to Weymouth, 1622. He came over in 1624, was a short time in Plymouth, and returned to England. THOMAS, perhaps son of Elnathan, m., 1723, Mary Howland, and had Thomas, 1725, m. a wife Isabel, and lived in Boston. He m., 2d, Prudence, d. of Josiah Conant, 1730, and had Mary, m, William Weston; and Sarah, m. a Ball. THOMAS, Duxbury, had Thomas, 1717; Simeon, William, Jacob, Ichabod, Zabdiel, Jane, m. Thomas Hunt; Abigail, m. Enoch Freeman. THOMAS, Duxbury, son of above, m. Mary, d. of Constant Southworth, and had Joseph and Mary, twins, 1753; Thomas; Jane, m. Simeon Soule; Mercy, m. Isaiah Alden. He m., 2d, Martha Chandler, and had Mercy, Peleg; and Rebecca, m. Bradford Sampson. THOMAS, Bernardston, son of 2d Coomer, m. Lucinda Ralph Cushman of Bernardston, and had Mary Kay. THOMAS PRATT, by wife Alpha, had Thomas Miller, 1828. WILLIAM, son of 1st Benjamin, m., 1754, Mary d. of Thomas Weston, and had Lewis, 1754; Coomer, and William. WILLIAM, son of above, m., 1778, Mary Churchill, and had Lewis, 1778; Harvey; Almira, m. Judson W. Rice and Nathaniel Cobb Lanman; Polly, m. Lazarus Symmes; Betsey, m. Lewis Finney; William; and George, 1790. He m., 2d,

Polly Sampson Holmes, 1801. WILLIAM, son of 3d Lewis, m., 1845, Susan S., d. of Richard Bagnall, and had William L., 1848; Herbert; Hattie, 1853; Clara, 1857; and Mary L., m. Thomas P. Swift. WILLIAM, Duxbury, son of 3d Thomas, m., 1760, Ruby Chandler, and had Ichabod; Ruby, m. Abner Dingley; Lucy, m. Jesse Simmons; Nathaniel. He m., 2d, Kesiah Dingley, and had Sarah, m. Edmund D. Baker. ZABDIEL, Duxbury, son of 3d Thomas, m., 1769, Hannah Curtis, and had Olive, m. E. D. Baker; Sylvanus, Wealthea, m. Bartlett Sampson; Elkanah. He m., 2d, 1798, wid. Lydia Churchill of Plymouth. ZECHARIAH, son of 2d Edmund, m., 1717, Mehitabel Shaw, and had Jonathan, 1718; Zeruiah, 1720; James, 1723; Zechariah, 1726; and Mehitabel.

WETHERED. This name is supposed by some to have been corrupted from Wetherel. JOHN, son of Samuel, m. Remember Bates, 1732, and had Rebecca, 1733; Mary, 1735; Rebecca, 1737; Remember, 1739; Mercy, 1742, m. Barnabas Holmes; Samuel, 1745; and John. JOHN, son of above, by wife Submit, had Mary, 1777, m. Clark Finney. SAMUEL, m. Abigail May, 1708, and had John, 1708; Rebecca, 1711, m. Silas West.

WHARTON, ROBERT, m. Mary Burn, 1779.

WHITBECK, GEORGE W., m. Betsey C. Woodward, 1839.

WHITE, BENJAMIN, Hanover, son of 1st Cornelius, m., 1743, Hannah Decrow, and had Penniah, 1744; Robert, 1747; Hannah, m. Daniel Crooker of Pembroke; Benjamin, 1754; Cornelius, 1755. BENJAMIN, Hanover, son of above, m., 1780, Mary Chamberlain of East Bridgewater, and had Lewis, Cyrus; Mary, m. Reuben Peterson of Duxbury; Sylvia, m. Ezekiel Stetson; Benjamin, 1791; Benjamin, 1795, m. Mary Hall. BENJAMIN, Marshfield, son of 1st Daniel, m., 1714, Faith Oakman, and had Abigail, 1715; Tabitha, 1717; Lydia, 1719; Jedidah, 1721; Benjamin, 1724; and Joshua. BENJAMIN, Marshfield, son of above, by wife Mercy, had Benjamin, 1749; Tobias, 1753; Gideon, 1755; Luther, 1758. BENJAMIN, Marshfield, son of 2d Benjamin, m. Mary Hall, and had George, 1832; Mary H., 1833; Lewis E., 1835; Benjamin F., 1837; Harriet S., 1841. CORNELIUS, Marshfield, son of 1st Daniel, m., 1706, Hannah Randall, and had Lemuel, 1706; Cornelius, 1708; Paul, 1711, m. Elizabeth Curtis; Joanna, 1713, m. Nathaniel Phillips; Daniel, 1716; Gideon, 1717; Benjamin, 1721. CORNELIUS, Marshfield, son of above, m. Sarah Hewitt of East Bridgewater, and had Charles, 1740; Alice, 1742; Sarah, 1744; Ruth, 1746; Lucy, 1748; Cornelius, 1750; Cornelius, 1752; Olive, 1754; Cornelius, 1756; Warner, 1758; Polly, 1760. CORNELIUS, Shelburne, Nova Scotia, son of 2d Gideon, m., 1824, Agnes Crowell, and had Katharine Johnston, 1825; Elizabeth, 1827; Cornelius, 1830; Agnes, 1831; Gideon, 1833; Joann Davis, 1836; Sarah Jane, 1838; Mary Brinley, 1842; Cornelius, 1846. CORNELIUS, Hanover, son of 1st Benjamin, m., 1787, Sarah L. Hill of Pembroke, and had Cornelius, 1788. He m., 2d, 1801, Rebecca Bates, and had Albert, 1802, m. Lydia Bates. CYRUS, Hanover, son of 2d Benjamin, m., 1806, Ruth S. Keen of Pembroke, and had Sylvia, m. Leonard Green of Sharon; Lydia; Mary, 1810; Cyrus, 1811; Lewis, m. Catherine Gardner of Duxbury and Ann Bell; Deborah; and Benjamin, 1816. DANIEL, Marshfield, son of 1st Peregrine, m., 1674, Hannah Hunt, and had John, 1675, m. Susanna Sherman; Joseph, 1678,

m. Elizabeth Dwelly, and removed to Connecticut; Thomas, 1680; Cornelius, 1682; Benjamin, 1684; Eleazer, 1686; Ebenezer, 1691. DANIEL, Marshfield, son of 1st Cornelius, m. Abigail, d. of Samuel Turner, and had Daniel, Abigail, Catherine, Lewis, Urania, Samuel, Lydia, Temperance. DANIEL, Marshfield, son of above, by wife Margaret, had Nancy, 1786; Samuel, 1788; George, 1791; Sarah, 1793; Daniel, 1795; Cornelius, 1797; Eliza, 1799. EBENEZER, Marshfield, son of 1st Daniel, m., 1713, Hannah Doggett, and had Obdiaah, 1716; Rebecca, 1718; Hannah, 1721. ELEAZER, Marshfield, son of 1st Daniel, m. Mary Doggett, 1712, and had Nehemiah, 1714; Peregrine, 1715; Eleazer, 1717; Elkanah, 1719; Mary, 1721; Benaiah, 1724; Penelope, 1727; Thomas, 1729; Rebecca, 1731. GIDEON, son of 1st Cornelius, m. Joanna, d. of Thomas Howland, 1744, and had Cornelius, 1744; Elizabeth, m. Hamilton L. Earl of England, and had Elizabeth, wife of the late General Durnford of the English army; Hannah, 1747; Experience, 1755; Gideon, 1752; Polly; Thomas, 1758; Joanna, m. Pelham Winslow; Catherine, and Thomas. GIDEON, Plymouth and Shelburne, Nova Scotia, son of above, an officer in the English army, m., 1787, Deborah, d. of Miles Whitworth, and had Joanna, 1788, m. William Davis of Plymouth; Miles Whitworth, 1789; Deborah Foxcroft, 1791, m. Thomas Brattle Gannett of Cambridge; Nathaniel Whitworth, 1793; Gideon Consider, 1795; Cornelius, 1797; John Dean Whitworth, 1799, m. Maria Rowland of Shelburne, and lives in Philadelphia; Sarah Whitworth, 1801, m. Thomas Brattle Gannett; Thomas Howland, 1806. GIDEON CONSIDER, son of above, m., 1816, Rachel Crowell of Shelburne, and had Elizabeth Crowell; Cornelius; Agnes, 1822, m. John A. Gannett and Winslow Warren. JESSE, Marshfield, son of 1st John, m. Catherine Charlotte Wilhelmina Sybellina Warner, a native of Germany, and had Sybeline, 1744; William; Sybeline, 1748; Christiana, 1750, m. a Lewis, the grandfather of Daniel James Lewis, now living in Fairhaven. JOHN, Marshfield, son of 1st Daniel, m., 1700, Susanna, d. of Samuel Sherman, and had Hannah, 1702; John, 1704; Abijah, 1706; Sarah, 1710, m. Isaac Phillips; Rebecca, 1713; Sylvanus, 1718; Jesse, 1720. JOHN, Marshfield, son of above, m., 1729, Joanna Sprague, and had John, 1732; Lusanna, m. Ezekiel Young; James; Hannah, Andrew, and Nathan. JOHN, m. Ruth Shepard, 1726. JOHN, m., 1806, Sally Novent. JOHN, m., 1807, Lydia King. JONATHAN, Middleboro', son of 1st Peregrine, had previously lived in Yarmouth. JOSEPH, Marshfield, son of 1st Daniel, m. Elizabeth Dwelly, and had Deborah, 1712; Ruth, 1715; Elizabeth, 1721. JOSHUA, Middleboro', son of 3d Benjamin, had William, 1744; Joel, Zabdiel, Daniel, Polly, and Nabby. LEMUEL, Marshfield, prob. son of 1st Cornelius, m. Anna Little, and had Anna, 1739; Priscilla, 1740; Sylvanus, 1742; Abijah, 1745; Sarah, 1749; William, 1752; John, 1753; Susanna, 1756; Deborah, 1746; Abijah, 1747. LUTHER, Marshfield, son of 4th Benjamin, by wife Mary, had Benjamin, 1790; Thomas Foster, 1802. MILES WHITWORTH, Boston, son of 2d Gideon, m., 1812, Marcia, d. of John Davis of Boston, and had Ellen, m. Edward Baldwin; Thomas, and Miles Whitworth. PEREGRINE, son of 1st William, born in Provincetown harbor, 1620, m., 1648, Sarah, d. of William Bassett, and had Daniel; Jonathan, 1658; Sylvanus, Peregrine; Sarah, m. Thomas Young of Scituate; Mercy, m. William Sherman. PEREGRINE, Weymouth, son of above, by wife Susanna, had Benni, 1686, and others. REUBEN, from Wareham, m., 1816, Beulah King. RESOLVED, Scituate, son of 1st William, came with his father in the Mayflower 1620, and m., 1640, Judith, d. of William Vassall of Scituate, and had William, 1642; John, 1644; Samuel, 1646; Resolved, 1647; Ann, 1649; Elizabeth, 1652; Josiah, 1654; Susanna, 1656. ROBERT, Hanover, son of 1st Benjamin, m., 1771, Mary Crooker, and had Penniah, 1773. He m., 2d, 1777, Ann House, and had David, 1779; Martin, Richmond, Charles, Elijah. THOMAS F., from Marshfield, m., 1824, Hannah Clark. THOMAS HOWLAND, Shelburne, son of 2d Gideon, m., 1831, Cornelia Ogden, and had Cornelia, 1832, and Nathaniel Whitworth, 1837. TOBIAS, Marshfield, son of 4th Benjamin, by wife Hannah, had Mercy, 1778; Sarah, 1780; Gideon, 1783; Benjamin, 1785. WILLIAM, son probably of Bishop John White of England, came in the Mayflower 1620. He m. in Leyden, 1612, Anna, sister of Samuel Fuller, always called Susanna, He brought with him his wife and son Resolved, born 1615, and had Peregrine, born in Provincetown harbor after arrival. WILLIAM, New Bedford, son of Joshua, m. a Bryant of Middleboro', and had Charity, Cabel, and Joshua. He m., 2d, Hannah Stetson, d. of Theophilus Cushing of Pembroke, and had William, Cushing, Ann, and Lucinda. WILLIAM, from New Bedford, son of above, m., 1807, Fanny Gibbs, and had Arabella, m. Nathaniel Goodwin of Plymouth; Fanny, m. Hayden Coggshall; Peregrine, and John. WILLIAM, Marshfield, son of Jesse, had Sybil, John, Anna, and perhaps others.

WHITEHOUSE, JOHN, from Newport, m., 1766, Thankful Holmes.

WHITING, WHITTEN, or WHITON, ABRAHAM WHITTEN, Kingston, son of 2d Elisha, m. Sally Robbins, 1796, and had Abraham; Sally, m. Joseph Wright; Polly, m. Thadeus Washburn of Kingston; and Charles. ABRAHAM WHITTEN, son of above, m. Lucia H. Holmes, 1826, and had Francis L., m. wid. Augusta P. Cady; Horace C., m. Jane E., d. of William Stephens; and Orrin Brooks, m. Abby Cushing. AMOS WHITTEN, son of 2d Elisha, m. Priscilla, d. of Barnabas Holmes, 1803, and had Samuel Marshal, Amos; Priscilla, m. Jason Murdock of Wareham; and Lucia Ann, m. a Stetson of Kingston. ASA WHITING, Salem, probably son of 2d Joseph, m. Anna Thistle, and had John T., and Asa Alden. ASA ALDEN, son of above, m. Mary Millet Nichols, and had George A., 1838, m. Sarah Elizabeth, d. of Francis J. Goddard of Plymouth; Annie, 1840, m. Charles O. Churchill of Plymouth; Lucy, 1842, m. William A. Tarbell; John, m. Mary Winsor of Duxbury; and Sarah, m. William A. Munroe. BENJAMIN WHITING, son of 2d Elisha, m. Martha Harlow, and had Benjamin, m. Susan L. Finney; Ellis, m. Hannah C. Nickerson; John, Josiah; Martha, m. Ephraim F. Churchill; and Nancy, m. Rufus Sampson. BENJAMIN WHITING, son of above, m. Susan L. Finney, 1827, and had Benjamin, m. Lucy Hammond; and Josiah, m. Lydia C. White of Weymouth. CHARLES WHITTEN, son of 1st Abraham, m. Mary R. Holmes, 1827, and had Charles, m. Lydia N. Bradford, M. Anna Sears, and Charlotte A. Irving; Lewis Holmes, m. Emeline A., d. of Robert Hutchinson; Abraham, m. Ruth W. Sears; Rufus Robbins, m. wid. Pauline (Wheeler) Wellington; Elisha Cobb; and Edward W., m. Laura Diman. ELISHA

WHITON, son of 3d James, m. Joanna, d. of John Dunham, 1728, and had Elisha, 1729; Joanna, 1731; Alpheus, m. Ruth Grafton; Azariah, m. wid. Rebecca (Churchill) Holmes; and Mercy, m. Ebenezer Doten. ELISHA WHITON, son of above, m. Betsey Holmes, and had Levi, m. Ruth Finney and Mary Barden; Joseph, m. Sarah Morton and Polly Morton; Nathan, m. Rebecca Doten; Ephraim, m. Elizabeth Bartlett; Benjamin, m. Martha Harlow; Josiah, moved to Ohio; Mary, m. Josiah Morton; and Josie, all of whom assumed the name of Whiting. He m., 2d, Mary (Harding) Howard, wid. of Jesse, and had Abraham, Melzar, and Amos, all of whom assumed the name of Whitten. ELISHA WHITING, son of 1st Joseph, m. Almira Holmes, and had Caroline Augusta, m. William F. Spear; Mary Ellen, m. Winslow S. Holmes; Abby Iowa, Elisha; Joseph B., m. Laura T., d. of John T. Hall; and Fanny, m. William H. Moore, living in the state of New York. EPHRAIM WHITING, son of 2d Elisha, m. Elizabeth, d. of Ephraim Bartlett, 1795, and had Ephraim, m. Patience Everson; and Benjamin, m. Phebe R. Flemmons. GEORGE WHITING, son of 1st Joseph, m. Betsey P. Holmes, and had Emma, m. William H. Clark; and Georgianna. HENRY WHITING, son of 1st Joseph, m. Grace, d. of Ellis Holmes, and had Henry, 1816, m. Nancy, d. of William Burgess; Winslow, 1820, m. Abby Holmes; Pelham, 1823, m. Sophia B. Straffin. JAMES WHITON, the ancestor, was in Hingham 1647, where he m. in that year Mary, d. of John Beal, and had James, 1651; Matthew, 1653, m. Deborah, wid. of John Howard; John, 1655; David and Jonathan, twins, 1658; Enoch, 1659, m. Mary Lincoln; Thomas, 1662, m. Joanna Garnet; Mary, 1664, m. Isaac Wilder, and a 2d husband named Jordan. JAMES WHITON, Hingham, son of above, by wife Abigail, had Hannah, 1678, m. John King; James, 1680, m. Mercy, d. of Matthew Whiton; John, 1681; Samuel, 1685, m. Margaret Williams and Elizabeth Williams; Joseph, 1687, m. Martha Tower; Judith, 1689, m. James White; Rebecca, 1691; Benjamin, 1693, m. Sarah Tower; Solomon, 1695. JAMES WHITON, Hingham, son of above, m. Mercy, d. of Matthew Whiton, and had Mary, 1710; James, 1712, moved to Hartford; Matthew, 1714; Jael, 1718, m. Isaac Thayer; Nathan, 1721; Cornelius, 1723; and Elisha. JOHN, Plympton, son of 1st James, by wife Bethiah, had Azariah, 1711; Alice, 1713; Jedidah, 1714; Zacheus, 1716; Alpheus, 1718; Bethiah, 1720; John, 1722; Thomas, 1724. JOSEPH WHITING, son of 2d Elisha, m. Sarah Morton, 1789, and had Abigail, 1790, m. Rufus Gibbs; Joseph, 1792, m. Betsey, d. of Ichabod Morton; and Henry, 1794. He m., 2d, Polly Morton, and had Sarah, 1804, m. Joseph Phillips of Duxbury; Eleanor, 1806; James Harvey, 1808; Elisha, 1811; and George. JOSEPH WHITING, Bridgewater, son of 2d Solomon, m. Abigail, d. of Isaac Alden, 1778, and had probably Asa. LEVI WHITING, son of 2d Elisha, m. Ruth Finney, 1784, and had Levi, m. Deborah Morton. He m., 2d, Mary Barden, 1812. MELZAR WHITTEN, Kingston, son of 2d Elisha, m., 1805, Wealthea Delano and wid. Deborah Caswell, and had Melzar, m. Susan, d. of Benjamin Delano. NATHAN WHITING, son of 2d Elisha, m. Rebecca Doten, 1795, and had Nathan, 1797, m. Polly Finney; Elizabeth Doten, 1798, m. Seth Finney; Olive, 1800; Rebecca, 1803, m. Henry Morton; Adoniram, 1805, m. Lucy F. Ingalls and Sarah W. Manter; Stephen, 1807; Levi, 1808,

m. Betsey W. Hueston; Stephen, 1810; and Hannah, 1810, m. Abner Burgess. He m., 2d, Betsey Howland, 1817. NATHAN, son of above, m. Polly Finney, and had Polly F., 1818, John, 1822; Nathan, 1823; Albert, 1828; Edward, 1830; Lydia F., 1835; Harriet, 1837; Adoniram, 1840; Leavitt, 1842. SAMUEL MARSHAL WHITTEN, son of Amos, m. Harriet Bartlett, and had Abbie, m. Leonidas C. Jewett; Cora, m. John B. Wilson, Jr.; Alice, m. Albert T. Harlow; Harriet E., m. Josiah Russell Drew; Samuel A., m. Nellie Ellis; and Joseph B., unmarried. SOLOMON WHITON, Hanover, son of 2d James, m. Jael, d. of Joseph Dunham, 1721, and had Jael, 1722; Solomon, 1724; Ruth, 1726; Deborah, 1728; Mercy, 1730; Thankful, 1732; Silence, 1734; Comfort, 1736; Melea, 1739; Rebecca, 1741. SOLOMON WHITON, Hanover, son of above, m. Mary Campbell, 1746, and had Asa, 1747; Solomon, 1751; Joseph, 1754; Peleg, 1758; Jael, Ruth, Mary, and Betsey.

WHITMAN, DANIEL, son of a John of Bridgewater, who was son of Nicholas of same, and grandson of Thomas, mentioned below, m. Mary Doten, and had John, 1769; Mary, and Daniel. EBENEZER, Bridgewater, son of Thomas, m. Abigail Burnham, 1699, and had Abigail, 1702; Zechariah, 1704; John, 1707; Hannah, 1709; Ebenezer, 1713. JOHN, Weymouth, 1638, perhaps son of 3d Zechariah, by wife probably named Mary, had Thomas, 1629; John, m. Ruth Reed and Abigail Hollis; Abiah, m. Mary Ford; Zechariah, 1644, m. Sarah Alcock; Sarah, m. a Jones; Mary, m. John Pratt; Elizabeth, m. Joseph Green; Hannah, 1641, m. Stephen French; and Judith, m. a King. He had a brother Zechariah, who was in Milford as early as 1639. KILBORN, Pembroke, son of 2d Zechariah, m. Betsey, d. of Isaac Winslow of Marshfield, and had Isaac Winslow, m. a Miss Jenkins of New York; Charles Kilborn; Eliza Winslow, m. Samuel K. Williams of Boston; John Winslow, m. Sarah Powers of Providence; Sarah Ann, m. Benjamin Randall of Bath; Caroline; Maria Warren, m. Frederick Bryant of New Bedford; James Hawley, m. Harriet Briggs of Pembroke; Frances Gay, m. Jacob Hersey of New Bedford and William Henry. THOMAS, Bridgewater, son of John, born in England, m. Abigail, d. of Nicholas Byram, 1656, and had John, 1658, m. Mary Pratt; Ebenezer; Nicholas, m. Sarah Vining; Susanna, m. Benjamin Willis; Mary, m. Seth Leach; Naomi, m. William Snow; and Hannah. ZECHARIAH, Bridgewater, son of Ebenezer, m. Eleanor Bennet of Middleboro', and had Samuel, 1734; Abiah, 1735; Zechariah, 1738; Eleanor, 1739, m. a Chamberlain; Benjamin, 1741; Abigail, 1743; Ruth, 1746; Jonah, 1749; Ebenezer and Sarah, twins, 1752. ZECHARIAH, Bridgewater, son of above, m. Abigail Kilborn of Litchfield, Conn., and had Kilborn, 1765; Benjamin, 1768; Cyrus, 1773; Angelina, 1777; and Cassandra; Angelina, m. Curtis Barnes of Hingham; and Cassandra, m. Rev. Gaius Conant. ZECHARIAH, aged 60, came in the Truelove 1635, with children Sarah, aged 25, and Zechariah, 2. WILLIAM HENRY, son of Kilborn, m. Ann Sever, d. of William Thomas of Plymouth, 1846, and had Isabella Thomas, 1848; Elizabeth H., 1850; and William Thomas, 1853. He m., 2d, Helen, wid. of William Davis, and d. of John Russell, and had Russell, 1861; and Ann Thomas, 1862.

WHITMARSH, EZRA, m. Dorothy Gardner, 1741. THOMAS, m. Chloe Simmons, 1801. WILLIAM, m. Fanny Hathaway, 1801.

WHITTEMORE, JOSIAH, from Charlestown, m. Mary Hatch, 1743, and had Mehitabel, 1744; Thomas Hatch, 1747, m. Thankful Holmes: Josiah, 1749, m. Experience, d. of William Sargent; and Joanna, 1752.

WHITWORTH, MILES, Boston, 1750, a surgeon in the British Army, m. Deborah, d. of Nathaniel Thayer, and had Miles, about 1750, a surgeon in the English Navy; Nathaniel, Commissary-General in the Royal Army; Charles, also a Commissary; Deborah, m. Gideon White of Plymouth: and Sarah, m. John Foxcroft of Cambridge.

WHOOD, NATHAN, pub. to Rachel Jeffry, 1727, Indians.

WICKET, OBADIAH, m. Bathsheba Hammett, 1778, Indians.

WILCOCKES, DANIEL, m., 1661, Elizabeth Cooke.

WILDER, ROGER, came in the Mayflower 1620, and died the first winter.

WILKINS, JOHN M., m., 1835, Elizabeth P. Drew.

WILLARD, JACOB, prob. son of Simeon of Salem, and grandson of Simon of Cambridge, who came over 1634, by wife Sarah, had Sarah, 1703; Simon, 1706.

WILLET, THOMAS, came over about 1632. He m., 1636, Mary, d. of John Brown, and had Mary, 1637, m. Samuel Hooker; Martha, 1739, m. John Saffin; John, 1641; Sarah, 1643, m. John Eliot; Rebecca, 1644; Thomas, 1646; Esther, 1647, m. Josiah Flint; James, 1649, m. Elizabeth Hunt of Rehoboth; Hezekiah, 1651; Hezekiah again, 1653, m. Andia Brown of Swansea; David, 1654; Andrew, 1655; Samuel, 1658.

WILLIAMS, ELIAS, m., 1809, Mary Otis. JOHN, m. Eliza, d. of Samuel Holmes, and had Eliza Ann, 1829; John, 1831; Eliza Ann, 1833; John B., 1837. ROGER had a d. Mary born in Plymouth 1633. JOSEPH, m., 1667, Elizabeth Watson. THOMAS, m., 1743, Hannah Bagnall. THOMAS, m., 1804, Polly McCarter. WILLIAM, m., 1770, Thankful Thrasher.

WILLIS, BENJAMIN, Bridgewater, son of 1st John, m. Susanna, d. of Thomas Whitman, and had Thomas, 1694; Benjamin, 1696; Susanna, m. a Cobb; Elizabeth, m. Nathaniel Woodward. BENJAMIN, Bridgewater, son of above, m., 1719, Mary Leonard, and had Benjamin. BENJAMIN, Bridgewater, son of above, m., 1742, Bathsheba Williams of Taunton. He m., 2d, Sarah Bradford of Plymouth, 1761, and had Mary, 1762; Benjamin, 1765; Sarah, 1768, m. Simeon Pratt. DANIEL, Bridgewater, son of 4th John, m., 1756, Keziah, d. of Ebenezer Willis, and had Daniel and John, 1758; Jonah, 1764; Ebenezer, 1767. EDWARD, Kingston, son of 2d Jonah, m., 1843, Mary Ann, d. of Thadeus R. Washburn, and had Mary Helen, 1845, m. Josiah Churchill; Edward A., 1848, m. Abbie G. Peckham. GEORGE FREDERICK, son of 2d Jonah, m. Mehitabel Howland, and had George, and Forest. He m., 2d, Josephine Story, and had Emily. He had a 3d wife, Jennie. JOHN, Duxbury, 1637, and afterwards Bridgewater, m. Elizabeth Hodgkins Palmer, wid. of William, and had John, Nathaniel, Joseph, Comfort, Benjamin; Hannah, m. Nathaniel Hayward; Elizabeth, m. a Harvey; and Sarah, m. John Ames. JOHN, Bridgewater, son of above, m. Experience, d. of Nicholas Byram, and had John; Samuel, m. Margaret Brett; Experience, m. William Hudson; Mary, m. Israel Randall. JOHN, Bridgewater, son of above, m. Mary, d. of

Elihu Brett, and had Mary, 1699, m. Joseph Packard; John, 1701; Margaret, 1704, m. Nathaniel Harvey; Experience, m. John Randall; Martha, m. Samuel Harden and James Pratt; Mehitabel, m. James Stacy. JOHN, Bridgewater, son of above, m., 1724, Patience, d. of Samuel Hayward, and had Susanna, 1727, m. David Johnson; Daniel, 1732. JONAH, Bridgewater, son of Daniel, m., 1788, Abigail, d. of Jonathan Hayward, and had Abigail, 1790, m. Jacob Hayward; Jonah, 1792, now living in Kingston; Polly Hayward, 1795, m. Leonard Hill; Lyman, 1798. He m., 2d, 1800, Hannah, sister of 1st wife, and had Clement, 1801; Henry Williams, 1803; Nathan, 1806; Emeline Frances, 1808; Augustus, 1811; Benjamin, 1815. He m., 3d, 1816, Freelove, wid. of William Fobes. JONAH, Kingston, son of above, m. Abigail, d. of Nathaniel Foster, and had Edward, 1819; George Frederick, 1821; Foster, 1824, m. Adaline Eaton; Jonah, 1826; William Henry, 1828; Julia Parris Foster, 1831, m. Francis Oliver Leach; Abby A., 1834, m. Green Evans; Jonah, 1836; Angeline, 1839, m. Joseph Packard. JONAH, Kingston, son of above, m. Betsey A. Bagnall and Caroline Reach, and had Caroline. RICHARD, Plymouth, 1634, m., 1639, Ann Glass, and had Richard, who m. Patience Bonum, 1670. THOMAS, Bridgewater, son of 1st Benjamin, m., 1716, Mary, d. of Samuel Kingsley, and had Susanna, 1718, m. Ephraim Fobes; Thomas, 1721, m. Susanna Ames; Jonah, 1723; Mary, 1725, m. Isaac Johnson; Rhoda, 1727, m. Daniel Lothrop; Betty, 1731, m. James Howard; Zephaniah, 1733; Nathan, 1738. ZEPHANIAH, Bridgewater, son of above, m., 1754, Bethiah, d. of Thomas Hayward, and had Zephaniah, 1757. ZEPHANIAH, Kingston, son of above, m. Hannah, d. of John Thomas, and had John Thomas; Betsey, 1793; Sarah, and Bethiah.

WILSON, JOHN D., from Salem, m. Anna, d. of Thomas Nicolson, 1814. JOHN BARKLEY, son of John and his wife Clara Van Baker of the Hague, born in Antwerp, came to Plymouth about 1835, and m. Mary, d. of Stephen Rogers, by whom he had Elizabeth; John Barkley, 1849, m. Cora, d. of Samuel M. Whitten; Stephen Rogers, 1852, m. Alice, d. of Eleazer H. Barnes.

WING, JEDEDIAH, from Rochester, pub., 1734, to Elizabeth Gifford. REUBEN, from Warren, m., 1825, Mrs. Caroline Burgess.

WINSLOW, ANTHONY, Bridgewater, son of 2d Gilbert, m. Deborah, d. of William Barker, and had Priscilla, m. James Thomas; and Deborah, m. Nathaniel Clift. CHARLES, Hanover, son of 2d Thomas, m., 1827, Margaret L. Litchfield, and had Charles L., 1828; Rachel F., 1832; Helen, 1838. EDWARD, Droitwich, England, son of 1st Kenelm, m., probably, Eleanor Pellam of Droitwich, and had Richard about 1586. He m., 2d, 1594, Magdalene Ollyver, and had Edward, 1595; John, 1597; Eleanor, 1598; Kenelm, 1599; Gilbert, 1600; Elizabeth, 1602; Magdalene, 1604; Josiah, 1606. EDWARD, son of above, came in the Mayflower 1620. He m. in Leyden, 1618, Elizabeth Barker from Chatsun, or Chester, or Chesham, England, and brought her with him. He m., 2d, 1621, Susanna (Fuller) White, wid. of William, and had before 1627, Edward and John. After that date he had Edward again; Josiah, 1628; Elizabeth, m. Robert Roaks and George Curwin of Salem. EDWARD, son of 1st Isaac, m. Hannah, d. of Thomas Howland, and wid. of William Dyer, 1741, and had John, 1741; Penelope, 1743; Sarah,

1745; Edward, 1746. He was a loyalist, and removed to Halifax 1776, where he died 1784. EDWARD, son of above, m. Mary Symonds, and had Thomas Astor Coffin, Ward Chipman, Brooks Watson; Mary, m. Edward W. Miller; Edward; Sarah, m. Lawrence B. Rainsford; Hannah, Penelope, John Francis Wentworth, Daniel, Christian; Eliza Chapman, m. Dr. Sampson of the British army; and Catherine Wiltden. He was also a loyalist, and removed to New Brunswick in 1776, before his marriage, and died in Fredericton 1815. EDWARD, Boston, son of 1st John, m. Sarah Hilton, and had John, 1661; Sarah, 1663; Mary, 1665. He m., 2d, Elizabeth, d. of Edward Hutchinson, and had Edward, 1669; Catherine, 1672; Elizabeth, 1674; Ann, 1678. EDWARD, Duxbury, son of 9th Edward, m., 1755, Eleanor Pierce, and had David, 1756; Edward, 1761; Joshua, Thomas; Edward, 1769; George, Abigail. EDWARD, Duxbury, son of above, m. Rebecca Harlow of Plymouth, and had George, 1796; Betsey, 1798, m. Daniel Gale of Plymouth; George, 1800; Polly, 1802; Seth, 1805; Samuel, 1808; Rebecca, 1811. EDWARD, Rochester, son of 3d Kenelm, by wife Sarah, had Edward, 1703; Mehitabel, 1705, m. Thomas Winslow; James; Lydia, 1709, m. James Foster; Mercy, 1712, m. Chillingworth Foster; Sarah, 1707, m. Thomas Lincoln and James Whitcomb; Thankful, 1715, m. Josephus Hammond. EDWARD, Rochester, son of above, m. Hannah, d. of 6th Kenelm, and had Edward, 1729; Clark, 1731; Sarah, 1733; Enoch, 1735; Isaac, 1738; Hannah, 1740; Ezra, 1742; Bethiah, 1744. He m., 2d, 1746, Rachel, d. of 3d Josiah, and had Rachel, 1749; Tisdale, 1751; Josiah, 1753; Thankful, 1755; Benjamin, 1758; Mercy, 1763. He m., 3d, wid. Hannah Winslow of Dighton. EDWARD BYRON, Fredericton, N. B., son of John Francis Wentworth, m. Emma B. Orr, and had Wentworth Byron, Jasper Andrews, John James Frazier, and Jane Caroline. ELEAZER ROBBINS, Newton, son of Shadrach, m., 1813, Ann, d. of David Corbet of Boston, and had sixteen children, one of whom is Hon. John of New York and Brooklyn. FRANCIS EDWARD, Chatham, N. B., son of John Francis Wentworth, m. Constance Hansard, and had Edward Pelham, Warren Copley, Laura, Edith, and Charlotte. GEORGE, Duxbury, son of 6th Edward, m., 1781, Sarah G. Thomas. GILBERT, son of 1st Edward, came in the Mayflower 1620, returned to England after 1624, and died in 1650. GILBERT, Marshfield, son of 1st Nathaniel, m., 1698, Mercy, d. of Josiah Snow, and had Issachar, 1699; Barnabas, 1701; Gilbert, 1704; Anthony, 1707; Mercy, 1710; Rebecca, 1712; Job, 1715; Benjamin, 1717; Lydia, 1720. ISAAC, Marshfield, son of 2d Josiah, m., 1700, Sarah, d. of John Wensley of Boston, and had Josiah, 1701; John, 1702; Penelope, 1704, m. James Warren; Elizabeth, 1707, m. Benjamin Marston of Salem; Anna, 1709; Edward, 1714. ISAAC, Marshfield, son of 3d John, m., 1768, Elizabeth, d. of Benjamin Stockbridge of Scituate, and had Elizabeth, m. Kilburn Whitman; Isaac; Sarah, m. Ebenezer Clapp; Ruth S., 1771, m. Josiah C. Shaw and Thomas Dingley; John, 1774. He m., 2d, Francis, d. of Ebenezer Gay of Hingham. ISAAC, Charlestown, son of 1st John, m., 1666, Mary, d. of Increase Newell, and had Parnel, 1667; Isaac, 1670. ISAAC, Hingham, son of 4th John, m., 1848, Abby Frothingham, d. of Ebenezer Gay, and had Edward Gay, 1849. JAMES, Freetown, son of 3d Josiah, m., 1738, Charity Hodges, and had

Mehitabel, 1739, m. Jesse Bullock of Rehoboth; Ephraim, 1741, m. Hannah, d. of Thomas Gilbert; Margaret, 1743, m. David Talbot; Joseph, 1746, m. Mary Crane of Berkeley; James, 1748, m. Sarah Barnaby, and wid. Ruth Clark, d. of Ivory Hovey; Shadrach, 1750; Bethiah, 1753; Thankful, 1754, m. Benjamin Evans; Isaac, 1759. JAMES, Rochester, son of 1st Nathaniel, by wife Mary, had Seth, 1699; Mary, 1701; Bathsheba, 1705; James, 1709; Job, 1712; Nathaniel, 1715. By a 2d wife, Elizabeth, he had Peter, 1720. JOB, Freetown, son of 2d Kenelm, m. Ruth, d. of Daniel Cole of Eastham, and had James, 1687; John, and others. JOHN, son of 1st Edward, came in the Fortune, 1621, and m., about 1627, Mary, d. of James Chilton, who came in the Mayflower, 1620, and had Susanna, m. Robert Latham; Mary, 1630, m. Edward Gray; Edward; Sarah, m. Miles Standish and Tobias Payne and Richard Middlecot; John, Joseph, Samuel, 1641; Isaac, 1644; Anne, m. a LeBlond; Benjamin, 1653. In 1657 he removed to Boston, and died 1674. JOHN, Boston, son of above, by wife Elizabeth, had John, 1669; Ann, 1670. He m., 2d, a wife Judith. JOHN, known as General Winslow, son of 1st Isaac, m., 1726, Mary, d. of Isaac Little, and had Josiah, 1730; Pelham, 1737; Isaac, 1739. He m., 2d, a wid. Johnson, born Barker of Hingham, where he died 1774. JOHN, son of 2d Isaac, m. Susanna Ball, and had John, 1801; Elizabeth S., m. Seneca White; Frances Gay, 1805; Penelope Pelham, m. George W. Nichols; Pelham, 1809; Isaac, Edward, and Edward Josiah. JOHN, Rochester, son of 3d Kenelm, who died 1755, m., 1722, Bethiah, d. of Stephen Andrews of Rochester, and had John, 1722; Deborah, 1724; Jedediah, 1727; Nathaniel, 1730; Bethiah, 1732; Lemuel, 1734; Prince, 1737; Stephen, 1739; Elizabeth. JOHN, Rochester, son of above, who died 1774, m., 1745, Bethiah Sherman, and had Stephen, 1747; Bethiah, 1748, m. Increase Clapp; Abigail, 1750; Kesiah, 1752, m. Elijah Dexter; John, 1755; Lemuel, 1757; Zephaniah, 1760; Micah, 1761; Deborah, 1763; Elizabeth; and Sarah, 1768. JOHN, Wareham, son of 1st Jonathan, by wife Mary had William; Faith, m. a Randall; Eleanor, m. a Besse; Sarah; Mary, m. a Wood. JOHN, Rochester, son of 6th John, had John, Paul, Dorcas, Kenelm, and Nathan. JOHN, Bridgewater, m., about 1822, Emeline, d. of Edward Mitchell. JOHN FRANCIS WENTWORTH, Woodstock, N. B., son of 4th Edward, m. Jane C. Rainsford, and had Francis Edward, John Coffin, Mary; Elizabeth, m. John Jacobs; Thomas Bradshaw, Wentworth, and Edward Byron. JOHN COFFIN, Woodstock, son of above, m. Charlotte O'Donnell, and had John Norman, Minnie O'Donnell, Jesse K., and Pauline. JONATHAN, Marshfield, son of 1st Josiah, m. Ruth, d. of William Sargent of Barnstable, and had John, 1664. JOSIAH, son of 1st Edward, came in the White Angel to Saco 1631, and after a residence in Scituate removed to Marshfield. He m., 1637, Margaret, d. of Thomas Bourne, and had Elizabeth, 1637; Jonathan, 1638; Mary, 1640, m. John Tracy; Margaret, 1641, m. John Miller; Rebecca, 1642, m. John Thatcher of Yarmouth; Hannah, 1644, m. William Crow and John Sturtevant. JOSIAH, son of 2d Edward, m., 1651, Penelope, d. of Herbert Pelham, and had Elizabeth, 1664, m. Stephen Burton; Edward, 1667; Isaac, 1670. JOSIAH, Freetown, son of 3d Kenelm, m., 1695, Margaret, d. of James Tisdale of Taunton, and had Josiah, 1697, m. Sarah Hayward of Bridgewater; Mercy, 1700, m.

James Whitcomb of Rochester; Ebenezer, 1705, m. Esther Atwood, and had Benjamin of Berkley, m. Phebe Pierce; Edward, 1709; James, 1712; Margaret, 1716, m. John King of Norton; Mary, 1720, m. Daniel Hunt; Rachel, 1722, m. Edward Winslow. JOSEPH, Boston, son of 1st John, by wife Sarah, had Mary, 1674; Joseph, 1677. JOSHUA, Duxbury, grandson of 6th Kenelm, through his son Kenelm, m. Hannah Delano, 1772, and wid. Salome Delano, 1780. KENELM, of Kempsey, England, died in Worcester, England, 1607. He had, by wife Catherine, Edward, 1560. KENELM, son of 1st Edward, came over about 1629, and m. Eleanor (Newton) Adams, wid. of John, and had Kenelm, 1635; Ellen, 1637, m. Samuel Baker; Nathaniel, 1639; Job, 1641. KENELM, Yarmouth, son of above, m., 1667, Mercy, d. of Peter Worden, and had Kenelm, 1668; Josiah, 1670; Thomas, 1673; Samuel, 1674; Mercy, 1676; Nathaniel; and Edward, 1680. He m., 2d, Damaris, and had Damaris, m, Jonathan Small; Elizabeth, m. Andrew Clark of Harwich; Eleanor, m. Shubael Hamblin; and John. KENELM, Marshfield, son of 1st Nathaniel, m. Abigail Waterman, and had Kenelm, 1717, m. Abigail, d. of Sylvanus Bourne of Barnstable; Eleanor, 1718; Joseph; Sarah, m. a Smith; Abigail, m. a Lewis; Faith, m. Joseph Taylor; and Nathaniel. He prob. had a 2d wife. KENELM, Bridgewater, brother of 9th John, m. Orza, d. of Benjamin Pope, about 1822. KENELM, Yarmouth, son of 3d Kenelm, m. Bethiah, d. of Gershom Hall of Yarmouth, and had Bethiah, m. John Wing; Mercy, m. Philip Vincent; Rebecca, m. Samuel Rider; Thankful, m. Theophilus Crosby; Kenelm, m. Zerviah Rider; Thomas, m. Mehitabel Winslow; Mary, m. Ebenezer Clapp of Dorchester; Hannah, m. Edward Winslow; Seth, m. Thankful Sears and Priscilla Freeman. MICAH, Rochester, son of 6th John, had a wife Hannah. NATHANIEL, Marshfield, son of 2d Kenelm, m. Faith, d. of John Miller of Yarmouth, 1664, and had Faith, 1665; Nathaniel, 1667; James, 1669; Gilbert, 1673; Kenelm, 1675; Eleanor, 1677, m. John Jones; Josiah, 1681; and John. NATHANIEL, Marshfield, son of above, m. Lydia, d. of Josiah Snow, 1692, and had Lydia, 1693, m. Joseph Thomas; Thankful, 1695; Snow, 1698; Oliver, 1702; Deborah, 1708; Patience, 1710; Nathaniel, 1712, m. Susanna Bryant. He m., 2d, Deborah Bryant, 1716, and had Ruth, 1718; and Abiah. NATHANIEL, Marshfield, son of 4th Kenelm, by wife Lydia, had Ruth, m. a Wadsworth. NATHANIEL, Hanover, son of Oliver, m. Sarah Hatch, 1766, and had Nathaniel, 1767; Sarah, 1769, m. Thomas Waterman and Ebenezer Copeland; Walter, 1772; Joseph, 1774; Anna, 1776, m. William Putnam Ripley of Plymouth; Judith, 1780, m. Elisha Tolman; Lydia, 1786, m. Anthony Collamore of Pembroke; and William, 1788. NATHANIEL, Hanover, son of above, m. Clarissa, d. of Ebenezer Curtis, 1796, and had Josiah, m. Abigail, d. of Lemuel Curtis. OLIVER, Scituate, son of 2d Nathaniel, m. Agatha Bryant and Bethiah Prior, and had Oliver; Ruth, 1739; Nathaniel, 1741; John, 1743; Bethiah, 1751; and Joseph, 1753. PELHAM, son of 3d John, m. Joanna, d. of Gideon White, about 1770, and had Mary, 1771, m. Henry Warren; Joanna, 1773, m. Nathan Hayward; and Penelope Pelham. RICHMOND, Hanover, son of 2d Thomas, m. Harriet Howard of Duxbury, 1828, and had Samuel R., 1829, m. Elizabeth, d. of Clement Bates of Plymouth; James B., 1830; Rebecca H., 1832; Erastus B., 1834; John A., 1837; Joshua

S., 1740; Daniel W., 1842; Frederick R., 1848. SAMUEL, Boston, son of 1st John, m. Hannah, d. of Walter Briggs, and had Mary, 1678; Samuel, and Richard. SAMUEL, Rochester, son of 3d Kenelm, m., 1700, Bethiah Holbrook. He m., 2d, 1703, Mercy King, and had Mercy, 1705; Elizabeth, 1707; Anne, 1709; Thomas, 1711; Kenelm, 1712; Judith, 1716. He m., 3d, 1739, Ruth Briggs. SHADRACH, Freetown, son of 1st James, m., 1781, Elizabeth, d. of Eleazer Robbins of Foxboro', and had Betsey Peck, 1783; Eleazer Robbins, 1786; James, 1788; Isaac, 1791, m. Leonora, d. of Francis Jones of Raynham; Jesse, 1794, m. Caroline Ray of Newton; Samuel, 1797; Thomas Jefferson, 1800; Mary, 1802; Fanny, 1805, m. Samuel Billings Leonard; Joseph, 1807. SNOW, Marshfield, son of 2d Nathaniel, m., 1728, Deborah Bryant, and had Snow, Josiah, Lydia, and Deborah. THOMAS, a descendant from 1st Kenelm, m. Hannah Torrey, 1779, and had Thomas. THOMAS, Hanover, son of above, m. Ruth Grose, 1800, and had Thomas G., 1800, m. Susan W. Gardner of Hingham and a Pollard of Maine; Joshua, 1801; Charles, 1803; Richmond, 1804; Pelham, 1805; Lucy T., 1808, m. George Hildreth of Dorchester; Henry, 1810; William, 1812; Ruth G., 1814; Elizabeth, 1816; Eleanor J., 1816, m. Isaiah Jenkins; Samuel, 1818; Mary, 1819, m. David Freeman of Duxbury; Priscilla B., 1821; and Samuel L. F., 1825. (For other branches of the Winslow family, see Holton's Winslow Genealogy).

WINSOR, WILLIAM D., of Kingston, m. Hannah Howard, 1827.

WINTER, CHRISTOPHER, m., about 1635, Jane Cooper, and had John; Mary, m. John Reed; Naomi, m. a Turner; Anna, m. a Badson; Martha, m. John Hewitt. He had a brother Timothy at Braintree, who had a son Christopher.

WISWALL, DANIEL, Cambridge, son of Ebenezer, m. Lydia Tufts of Medford, and had George Ricks, 1776. EBENEZER, probably Dorchester, son of Enoch, m. Ann Capen, 1721, and had Ebenezer, 1722; Oliver, 1725; Noah, 1727; Daniel, 1729; Esther, 1732; Samuel, 1734; Elijah, 1738; Ann, 1740; Hannah, 1742; Ichabod, 1743. ENOCH, Dorchester, son of Thomas, m., 1657, Elizabeth, d. of John Oliver of Boston, and had John, 1658; Enoch, 1661; Hannah, 1662; Oliver, 1665; Elizabeth, 1667; Esther, 1669; Susanna, 1672; Enoch, 1675; Mary, 1677; Samuel, 1679; Enoch and Ebenezer, twins, 1683. GEORGE RICKS, son of Daniel, m. Salome Nickerson of Chatham, and removed from Provincetown, where he had lived after his father's death, to Plymouth, and had Lydia Tufts, 1779, m. John Foster Dunham; John, 1801; Salome, 1802, m. Seth Luce Holmes; Hannah, 1804, m. John Atwood; Rebecca, 1806; George R., 1808, m. Elizabeth Adams; Paulina, 1808; Rebecca, and Paulina again, 1814. ICHABOD, Duxbury, son of Thomas, m., 1679, Priscilla, d. of William Peabodie, and had Mary, 1680, m. John Wadsworth; Hannah, 1682, m. John Robinson; Peleg, 1684; Perez, 1686; Mercy; Priscilla, m. Samuel Seaberry; and Deborah. JOHN, son of George Ricks, m. Priscilla Perkins of Plymouth, and had Priscilla Thomas, 1828, m. Clifford Thompson of Halifax; and John Bradford, 1837. THOMAS, Cambridge and Dorchester, came from England about 1634, with a brother John, a wife Elizabeth, and son Enoch, born about 1633. He had afterwards Esther, m. William Johnson of Woburn; Ichabod, Noah; Mary, m. Samuel Payson of Dorchester; Sarah, m. Nathaniel Holmes; Ebenezer, 1646; Elizabeth, 1649.

WITHERELL, WETHERELL, or WITHERLE, JOHN, son of 1st William of
Scituate, had John, 1675; William, 1678; Thomas, 1681; Joshua, 1683. SAM-
UEL, Marshfield, m. Anna Rogers, 1698. THOMAS, son of John, moved to Plymouth, and by wife Rebecca, had Rebecca, 1713, m. James Easdell; Thomas,
1715; William, 1718; James, 1720; Mary, 1722, m. Thomas Mayhew, and her
gravestone is in the old pest-house grounds near Gallows Lane; John, 1725,
m. Sarah Crandon, died in Surinam; Mercy, 1727, m. Thomas Foster; Lemuel, 1729; Hannah, 1732. THOMAS, son of above, m. Elizabeth, d. of Isaac
Lothrop, 1738, and had Hannah, 1739; Lemuel, 1741; Thomas, 1742.
THOMAS, son of above, m. Ann, d. of John May, 1768, and had William,
1769; Ann May, 1771, m. Joseph Bartlett; Thomas, 1773; Elizabeth, 1775.
He m., 2d, Sarah, d. of Thomas Jackson, 1780, and had William, 1781; Isaac,
1783; Sarah, 1787, m. James Bartlett; Lucia, 1789; and Harriet, 1792.
THOMAS, son of above, m. Nancy, d. of Ichabod Shaw, 1799, and had John
May, 1800; Anna May, 1801; William Thomas, 1802; Eliza Ann, 1804, m.
William H. Whittlesey; Sarah, 1805, m. Horatio P. Blood; and Isaac, 1806,
m. Elizabeth P. Webster of Milton and Mary Louisa Quincy of Portland.
He m., 2d, Lois Robbins, 1812, and had Lothrop, Charles May, Nancy Shaw,
and Sylvanus James. WILLIAM, Scituate, 1644, came from Maidstone, Eng-
land, 1635, with wife Mary and three children, one of whom was Samuel.
He had born in this country John, Theophilus; Elizabeth, m. John Bryant;
Sarah, 1644, m. Israel Hobart; Hannah, 1646; and Mary, m. Thomas Oldham. WILLIAM, son of 1st Thomas, by wife Rebecca, had Hannah, 1740;
Rebecca, 1744; and possibly Sarah, who m. Perez Tilson, 1764. A branch of
this family, of which William Howe of Castine is a member, and which is
descended from Theophilus, son of 1st William, assumed the name of
Witherle.

WOOD, ABIEL, Middleboro', son of Henry, m. Abiah Bowen, and had
Elnathan, 1686; Abiah, 1689; Abiel, 1691; Timothy, 1693; Jerusha, 1695;
Ebenezer, 1697; Judah, 1700; Thomas, 1703. ALVAH, came to Plymouth
from Hanover about 1835, with wife Huldah, d. of Eells Damon, and children Alvah, m. Harriet N., d. of Samuel Eliot; Israel, m., 1844, Sabin Ann
Churchill; Samuel N., m., 1846, Abigail Westgate; and Elvira Jane, m.,
1849, James P. Jordan. DAVID, Middleboro', son of Henry, m. Mary, wid.
of Francis Coombs, and d. of Cuthbert Cuthbertson, and had John, 1686,
David, 1688; and Jabez, 1691, m. Hannah Nelson. DAVID, Middleboro', son
of above, m. Joanna Tilson, 1720, and had David, 1725; Francis, Edmund,
and Joanna. DAVID, Middleboro', son of above, m. Rebecca Pratt, 1746,
and had David, 1748; Joanna, m. James Waterman; Lydia, Rebecca, and
Kesiah. DAVID, Plymouth, son of above, m., 1770, Elizabeth Doten, and
had Azubah, m. Nicholas Drew; Zilpha, m. Caleb Dunham; Polly, m. John
Bailey; Elizabeth; Eliab, 1785, Oliver, 1791. EBENEZER, Middleboro', son
of Abiel, m. Lydia Lovell, and had Silas, Timothy, Sarah, 1734; Ebenezer;
Lydia, m. Abijah Nichols, Ebenezer Elms, and a Brown; Simeon, Levi, Abiel,
and Mary. EBENEZER, Middleboro', son of above, m. Sally Bennett, and
had Wilkes, Gorham, Horatio G., and Sally. ELIAB, son of 4th David, m.
Persis Rickard, and had Persis, m. David Holmes; Eliab, m. Betsey Sherman;

and Phebe, m. Thomas Rider; Elizabeth A., 1813, m. Benjamin Cooper Finney; Lydia, m. Bradford Faunce; Emily, m. in Middleboro'; Lemuel R., m. Lucy W. Burgess; and George K., m. Mary F. Davie. He m., 2d and 3d, Eleanor Lucas and Betsey (Sears) Sherman, wid. of Thomas, without children, and 4th, Mary Farmer Doten, and had David Brainard. HENRY, Plymouth, 1643, m., about 1645, Abigail Jenny, and had David, 1651; Sarah; Samuel, 1647; John; Jonathan, 1649; Isaac, and Abiel. ISAAC LEWIS, son of Oliver, m. Elizabeth Robbins, 1838, and had George F., 1839, m. Sarah E. Harvey; Charles T., 1842, m. Sarah Harris; and Agnes R., 1850. JAMES, m. Deborah Fish, 1735. JOHN, Plymouth, 1643. (See Atwood.) JOHN, son of Nathaniel. (See Atwood.) NATHANIEL, son of 1st John. (See Atwood.) NATHANIEL, came to Plymouth in early part of this century with wife Rhoda Colburn, and had Caroline Matilda, 1811, m. Lewis Henry Brown; Rhoda Ann, 1812, m. Lewis Finney; Nathaniel, 1814; Willard, 1817; Lewis Colburn, 1820; Harriet Maria, 1822, m. Henry M. Morton. NATHANIEL, son of above, m. Angeline Finney, 1837, and had Warren Colburn, 1840; and Florence A., 1847, m. Edmund Weston. He m., 2d, Betsey R., d. of Charles Churchill, 1854, and had Nathaniel Russell, 1856. OLIVER, son of 4th David, m. Betsey Torrence, 1811, and had Oliver Thomas, 1812; Isaac Lewis, 1814; Mary Elizabeth, 1825; Elizabeth Ann, 1829, m. Josiah C. Fuller. OLIVER THOMAS, son of above, m. Mary H. Holmes, 1832, and had Eudora Holbrook, 1834, m. Ezra Chandler; Oliver Everett, 1837, m. Abby S. Wadsworth; Mary Covill, m. Samuel Dow; William H., m. Emma Meade; and Emma Frances, m. Charles H. Holmes. He m. 2d, wid. Sarah A. Sampson, 1850, and had Elizabeth Ann, 1855. SAMUEL, Middleboro', son of Henry, by wife Rebecca, m. before 1679, had Henry, Ephraim, Samuel; Jabez, m. Mercy Fuller; Joanna, m. a Smith; Rebecca, m. a Smith; Ann, and Susanna. SAMUEL, Middleboro', son of above, by wife Joanna, had Abner, Susanna, Azubah, and Rebecca. STEPHEN, Plymouth, 1643, m., 1644, Abigail, d. of John Dunham, and had John, 1648; Hannah, 1649; Eldad, m. Ann Snow; and Medad. WILKES, Middleboro', son of 2d Ebenezer, m. Betsey Tinkham, and had Sally, m. James Leonard; Clarinda, m. Manning Leonard; and Betsey, m. Thomas N. Leonard. He m., 2d, Betsey W. Thompson, and had Cornelius B., m. Lucy Ann Washburn and Cornelia Snow; William H.; Charles W., m. Eliza Ann Bigelow and Catherine Lemist; Emily L., m. Thomas B. Crane; Joseph T., m. Ellen Taylor; Mary T., m. Russell L. Hathaway; and Betsey T. He m., 3d, Lucy (Nichols) Cushing, wid. of Christopher of Scituate. WILLIAM, m. Eliza Finney, 1742, and had Elizabeth, 1743. ZACHEUS, by wife Deborah, had Mary, 1809; Joshua, 1816; Sylvia, 1818.

WOODWARD, ELKANAH, m. Sally Nichols, 1815.

WOOTEN, JOHN, m. Elizabeth Sherman, 1775.

WRIGHT, ADAM, son of Richard, lived in that part of Plymouth which afterwards became Plympton. He m. Sarah, d. of John Soule of Duxbury, and had John and Isaac. He m., 2d, Mehitabel Barrows, and had Samuel, Moses, James, Nathan; Esther, m. Daniel Pratt; Sarah, m. Seth Fuller; Mary, m. Jeremiah Gifford; and Rachel, m. Ebenezer Barlow. He died 1724, about eighty years of age. ADAM, m. Rebecca Shaw, 1812. BENJAMIN, m.

Deborah Sampson, 1796. EDWARD, m. Elizabeth Decosta, 1746. ISAAC, son of Adam, m., 1717, Mary, d. of John Cole, and had Susanna, 1719; Joseph, 1721; Mary, 1726, m. Ebenezer Thompson of Halifax; Rachel, 1732; Isaac, 1736. He lived in that part of Plympton which is now Carver. ISAAC, Plympton, son of above, m., 1761, Faith, d. of Zebedee Chandler, and had Caleb, 1762; Billya, 1764, m. Patience Ellis; Isaac, 1766, m. Selah Ellis; Chandler, m. Susanna Ellis, and died in West Cambridge, 1824; Nathaniel, m. Lydia Holmes, and settled in Boston; Molly, m. Stephen Doten of Plymouth; Zebedee; Caleb, 1774, m. Hannah Tyler of Boston; Winslow, settled in Boston, and m., 1st, Sally Dunlap, 2d, Mary Wright, and 3d, Jane Melville; and Hannah, m. Stephen Doten of Plymouth. ISAAC, Plympton, son of above, m., 1788, Selah, d. of Joel Ellis, and had Southworth, 1789, m. Jane Stetson; Sophia, 1790, m. Josiah Thompson Ellis; Ellis, 1792, m. Bathsheba N. Holmes, and settled in Boston; Isaac, 1796, m. Marcia Randall; Selah, 1798; Hannah, 1800, m. John Sampson; Mary, 1807, m. Nathaniel Lucas. JOSEPH, Plympton, son of 1st Isaac, m. Sarah Brewster of Duxbury, and had Deborah, 1749, m. Nathaniel Churchill; Susanna, 1751, m. Abner Rickard; Mary, 1754, m. Sylvanus Sampson; Joseph, 1750; Joshua, 1758; and Thomas. He removed to Plymouth. JOSEPH, son of Joshua, m. Lucy Burgess, 1805, and had Joseph, m. Sally, d. of Abraham Whitten; and Joshua; and perhaps others. JOSHUA, son of 1st Joseph, m. Susanna Pearson, 1779, and had Joseph; Susanna, m. Nathan Burgess; Deborah, m. Abner Burgess; and perhaps others. MARTIN, m. Sarah Beale, 1749, and had Joseph, 1751; Sarah, 1759. RICHARD, perhaps son of 1st William, m., 1644, Hester, d. of Francis Cook, and had Adam, Esther, Mary, John, and Isaac. He died 1691, about eighty-three years of age. SAMUEL, from Plympton, m. Sarah Richmond, 1783. THOMAS, m. Abigail Rogers, 1738, and had Elizabeth, 1739; Elizabeth again, 1740; William, 1743. WILLIAM, perhaps the William who was baptized at Austerfield, England, 1588, came in the Fortune 1621, with wife Priscilla, d. of Alexander Carpenter, and perhaps a son Richard. WINSLOW, from Plympton, m. Mary Cole, 1827.

YOUNG, JAMES, m. Rebecca Shepard, and had Mary, 1723. JOHN, m., 1648, a wife Abigail, and had John, 1649. He removed to Eastham, and had Joseph, 1654; Nathaniel, 1656; Mary, 1658, m. Daniel Smith; Abigail, 1660, m. Stephen Twining; David, 1662; Lydia, 1664; Robert, 1667; Henry, 1669; and Henry again, 1672.

Part II.

ADAMS, " Hannah T. Brewer," wife of George, son of Ebenezer, should be " Hannah T. Brewster." "Nellie," daughter of 2d George, should be "Ellen B." After the marriage of 3d George to Lucy Nye, 1811, add, "and had George N., m. Desire T. Carver; Betsey, m. Jacob Sprague; Lucy Nye; Hannah, m. Andrew Burditt; and Benjamin Nye, m. Sophia, daughter of John Burgess." The third wife of Samuel should be "Abigail Bearce," not "Bruce." William, a foreigner, m., 1808, Sophia, widow of Seth Eddy.

ALBERTSON, POLLY, daughter of Rufus, m. George Dunham.

ALDERSON, ANDREW P., m., 1845, Sarah P., daughter of David Sears, and had Nancy Eldora, 1846, m. James W. Vaughan; Charles Lewis, 1847, m. Kate Dunning; Susan Parsons, 1850, m. George W. Bowker and George W. Graves; Walter David, 1852, m. Minnie Klucker; Emma Jane, 1854, m. Wm. F. Lander; Maria Sophia, 1857, m. Jerome McNeill; Victor Clifton, 1862, m., 1888, Harriott E. Thomas.

ALLEN, ADAM, m., 1761, Susannah Sachem. ANTHONY SHERMAN had a first wife, Susan, d. of Stephen Paine, by whom he had Hannah, who m. Richard W. Bagnall. By his second wife he had Sherman, who m. Sorena, d. of David Finney. JOHN, from Dartmouth, m., 1777, Sarah Langford, of Greenwich, R. I., and had Mary, 1779, m. Ezra Morton; William, 1782, m. Betsey Swinerton, of Cornish, N. H.; John, 1784, m. Hannah Goldthwaite, of Croyden, and Dolly Gove, of Cornish; Samuel, 1786, m. Naomi Leach; Gideon, 1788; Eliza, 1789, m. Wm. Marble, of Croyden; Joseph, 1791, m. Mary Webber, of Franconia; Thomas, 1793, m. Lydia Wright, of Cornish; Marmaduke, 1795, m. Mary Melendy, of Croyden; Hosea, 1798, m. Hannah Brown, of Grafton; Sarah, 1799, m. Stephen H. Thompson; Lydia, 1800. JOHN, the father, removed to Croyden in 1800. SAMUEL, son of above John, m. Naomi Leach, and had Naomi, 1812; Albert G., 1818; Marcia Maria, 1820. SAMUEL, son of 3d John in the text did not marry Naomi Leach.

ALLERTON, ISAAC, the 2d in the text, removed from New Haven to Wicomico, Va.

ALLYN, JOSEPH, in the text, had, at Wethersfield, Hannah, 1705; Samuel, 1707; Sarah, 1708; Martha, 1710. His d. Elizabeth m. Hezekiah Kilborn, of Wethersfield, in 1722; Hannah m. Rev. Ebenezer Wright of Stamford, and Joseph St. John of Norwalk, and Rev. Moses Dickinson of Norwalk; Samuel removed to Boston; and Sarah m. Capt. Nathaniel Stilman, of Wethersfield.

ANNABLE, ANTHONY, came in the *Ann*, 1663, with wife Jane and child Sarah, who m. Henry Ewell. He had born here Hannah, m. Thomas Freeman; Susanna, m. Wm. Hatch, of Scituate; and a daughter Deborah. He m., 2d, 1645, Ann Clark, and had Samuel, 1645, m. Mehitabel, d. of Thomas Allyn; Ezekiel, 1649. He m., 3d, Ann Barker, and had Desire, 1653, m. John Barker.

ATKINS, JOSEPH, m., 1822, Sarah, widow of Calvin Cooper and daughter of Eleazer Morton.

ATWOOD, ASAPH, son of William and Lydia (Tillson) Atwood, mentioned below, had Tillson and others. ELIJAH D., mentioned in the text, was son of John below. ANTHONY, son of Jesse R., mentioned in the text, should be Anthony T. JOHN, the 2d in the text, m. Sarah, d. of Israel, not Josiah, Leavett. JOHN, of Carver, had three wives, and by the 1st had Benjamin, Solomon, Reed and Eunice. By the 2d, Adoniram and Elijah D. JOHN, the 4th in the text, m. his 1st wife, 1765. JONATHAN, son of William below by wife Mary, had Lucy, m. Thompson Murdock and Ansel Gibbs. THOMAS, the 1st in the text, m. for his 3d wife Elizabeth (Avery) Holmes, and not Lydia (Savery). THOMAS C., mentioned in the text. The last d. was Martha B., and m. Willard C. Butler. WAIT, in the text, married Susanna Marshall, and had a d. Susanna; his d. Mary Wait was born 1803. WILLIAM, the first in the text. His son William was born 1808; Nancy E., 1809; Thomas C., 1815. WILLIAM, Plympton, son of John 3d in the text, m. Lydia, d. of Jonathan Tillson, and had Eli, William, Francis, Asaph, Jonathan and Lydia, m. John Shaw. WILLIAM, of Carver, son of Jonathan, had Miranda, Lucius and George W. WILLIAM, 3d in the text. His son William R. should be William P., and had also Frederick W., born 1857.

AVERY, JOSEPH, in the text, from Holden, son of Rev. Joseph, of Dedham.

BABB, RICHARD, in the text. His wife should be Maria, not Martha, and his children were Sally, m. Thomas Leonard; Abigail, m. Isaac Banks; and Richard, m. Grace Burns.

BACON, DAVID, in the text. His d. Abigail m. John Carpenter, of Foxboro, and his son Jacob m. Sarah Vose, and lived in Milton and Dorchester. GEORGE in the text. His daughter Mary was Mary T. JOHN in the text. His 1st wife was a d. of John Howes. His d. Hannah m. Ebenezer Morton; his son Nathaniel m., 1st, Anna Annable, and 2d, 1730, Thankfull Lumbert, and had Lemuel, Benjamin, Jabez, Hannah and Jane. John's 2d wife was the wid. of James Warren. John's son John m. Elizabeth Freeman, and had ten children. John's son Solomon m. Hannah Capron. NATHANIEL in the text. His d. Hannah m. Thomas Walley. His son John was born in 1665.

BAGNALL, BENJAMIN, 1st in the text, d. "Nellie" should be "Sally." NICHOLAS SPINKS in the text, son Ichabod P. m. Caroline E. Fisher. SAMUEL WEST, in the text, d. Martha James not Martha Jane.

BARDEN, STEPHEN, "Barden" not "Banden."

BANKS, ISAAC, in the text, his children were Maria, Elbridge Gerry and Margaret Harper, who m. Henry Robbins. LILLISTON, in the text, d. Sarah Cutton should be Sarah Cotton, and she m. Isaac Bartlett.

BARNES, BENJAMIN, 2d in the text, son Benjamin was born 1775, and d. Deborah 1785. BRADFORD, 1st in the text, d. Nancy C. was born in 1800. Bradford 2d, in the text, son Winslow Bradford m. a 2d wife, Marietta J. Kealing. BRADFORD, son of 1st Benjamin in the text, m. Sarah Howard and moved to Danby, Vt., in 1790. His children were Hosea, m. Hannah Brewster, of Paulet, Vt., and later removed to Ohio; Benjamin, m. Zilpha Gifford; Bradford, m. Rachel Austin, of Dorset, and in 1825 removed to Buffalo. CORBAN, 3d in the text, m. Susanna Bradford, d. of Hamblin Tilson, not Susan. HENRY, 1st in the text, his son Charles Henry m. Alice G. Howland. ISAAC, 2d in the text, wife, Betsey T., not Betsey. JOHN, 1st in the text, erase "Esther m. John Rickard." JOHN, 2d in the text, d. Mary, m. Richard Waite. JONATHAN, 2d in the text, d. Sarah, m. Thomas Doane; d. Rebecca, m. Ebenezer Finney;

d. Lydia, m. Joseph Smith. LEVI, in the text, son Albert, was born 1831. NA-THANIEL m., 1765, Lydia Curtis. NATHANIEL m., 1766, Jerusha Blackmer. SAMUEL, in the text, m., 1802, Lucy Stetson, not Perkins. WILLIAM, 4th in the text, son James, was born 1801; d. Lydia, 1809; d. Mary, 1806; d. Sarah 1804. WILLIAM, 5th in the text, son William was born 1796; Southworth, 1808; Nathaniel Carver, 1806. WILLIAM, 6th in the text, son Winslow C. m. Elizabeth, not Eliza, Diman, and son Charles C., m. Adelaide, d. of E. Seabury Raymond, not Alice G. Howland. WILLIAM BREWSTER, in the text, son Wm. E. was born 1835; Charles E., m. 1st, Eleanor M., wid. of Harvey Pratt and d. of Allen Chase, and 2d, Hannah S. Chadwick.

BARRETT, WILLIAM, in the text, m. in 1808, not 1812, son Benjamin W., born 1818.

BARROW, BARROWS. ASA, in the text, d. Lydia, m. Joshua Weeks; d. Mira should be Almira; d. Lucy B., m. Wm. Frieze; d. Deborah, m. Wm. T. Appling; d. Rebecca Drew, m. John Vail; d. Ann, m. James B. Ransom; d. Sally, m. Wm. Brown and John Chase; d. Jane, m. Azel Cole. JABEZ, son of 3d Robert, in the text, m. Sibbel Hall, and had Robert, 1739, who m. Joanna Porter, and had Mary, 1783, who m. Stedman Huntington Wright, who had Amanda Marsh, 1815, who m. Sylvester Barrows, as below. JOHN, 2d in the text, m., 1767, Sarah Manning, of Cambridge. ROBERT, in the text, had a d. Ruth, who married John Briggs. SAMUEL, 1st in the text, m. Desire, d. of Thomas Rogers; child Lazarus should be Lurany. THOMAS, son of 2d Robert in the text, m. Esther Hall. His son Thomas, born 1742, m. Eleanor Cross, and had John, born 1777, who m. Lucinda Willys, and had Sylvester, born 1801, who m. Amanda Marsh Wright, and had 1854, John Wright Barrows, of Denver, Col. THOMAS, of Carver, in the text, was son of Peleg.

BARTLETT, ABNER, in the text, daughter Olive, should be Olive H. ALLEN, son of William and Mercy, below, m., 1811, Abigail P. Haskell, of Portland, and had Flavel, 1812; Washington Allen, 1814; Warren Holmes, John Wesley, 1818; Abby P., m. Robert Keller, of Bangor; Mercy Ann, m. a Thornton; Francis Asbury, m. Ada Webb, Harriet, m. Samuel Warden, of Worcester. ANDREW, 1st in the text, had two children by his first wife, Lois, 1791; and Sarah, 1793, who m. David P. Reynolds. He m. 2d, 1797, Elizabeth Hammond, of Rochester, and had Eliza, 1799; Eliza again, 1802, m. Michael Howland; Hannah, 1804, m. Algernon S. Sylvester; Andrew, 1806; Winslow, 1808; Cordelia, 1812; Oren, 1815. ANSEL, 1st in the text, strike out the words, "and Alexander Dewsbury," and insert after "Marston Sampson" the words, "and William Dewsbury." ANSEL, 2d in the text; he was son of 5th Benjamin, not 6th. ANSEL, 3d in the text, m. Abigail R., d. of Thadeus Ripley; his son Kimbal R., was born in 1815 and his d. Mary was Mary E. BENJAMIN, 2d in the text, strike out "Elizabeth m. Ephraim Bradford" and change Ismael Bradford to Israel. CALEB, son of 1st Andrew in the text, m. Rebecca, d. of Seth Holmes, and had Mary Lucretia, who m. a Willington, of Bangor, and Nathaniel. CLEMENT, son of William and Mercy, below, m. Fannie Whittemore, of West Roxbury, and had Ann, Francis, Henry and Alfred. DIMAN, in the text; his son Lewis was born in 1803, and Ephraim in 1805. EBENEZER, 1st in the text; his son Ebenezer was born in 1694, not 1794. EBENEZER, 2d in the text; his d. Lydia, m. Lemuel

Delano. ELEASER STEPHENS, in the text; he m. 1831; and his son, Wm. Stephens, was born 1832. He m. his 2d wife 1834; and his son Francis Jackson was born 1838; his daughter Mary L. in 1841; and daughter Evelina Stephens in 1846. FRANCIS JACKSON, son of above, m., 1870, Lettie C. Shipley, of Laurel, Md., and had Mary Evelina 1871, m. James McIlvain Stokes, of Rancocus, N. J.; Helen Shipley, 1874; Francis Jackson, 1877, m. Marie E. Victor, of Philadelphia, and Clara Churchill, 1881. FLAVEL, son of William and Mercy, below, by wife Hannah had Allen Smith and Eva. FREDERICK HUNTER, of Buffalo, son of Frederick William, m. Alice May, d. of Charles W. Evans, of Buffalo. FREEMAN, in the text, had Freeman, 1798; Sarah, 1800, m. Lewis Copeland, of Milton; Mary, 1803; Eleaser Stephens, 1804; Elizabeth Thatcher, 1807, m. William Reed; Hannah, m. John Ransom, and William, 1805. HENRY, son of 1st Andrew in the text, m., 1791, Clarissa Harlow, and had Henry, 1792; Hosea, 1797; Abigail, 1794; Seth, 1802, m. Mary Bradford, of Duxbury. ICHABOD, 1st in the text, the father of the wife of his son Josiah was Zebulon Chandler and the wife of his son Seth was Charity Gulliver. ICHABOD, 2d in the text; his d. Laura Frances, m. Noah Kelrey, not Nelrey. ISAAC, son of 1st Isaac in the text, m., 1827, Mary Ann Ward, of Portland; and had Mary Elizabeth, Lucy Ellen, Ephraim, Lendall, 1836; George, 1838; Mary C., 1840; Fannie, 1845; Ellen L., 1848. ISAAC, 3d in the text, was son of 11th Joseph; and m. Sarah Cotton Banks. He had an additional child, Sarah Kimball. IZAIAH, son of 2d Sylvanus in the text, died in Ohio, in 1867; and had a son, P. M. Bartlett. JOHN, Duxbury, son of Nathaniel and Zenobie, below, m. Molly Bonney, and had Nathaniel, 1777; Margaret, 1779; Betsey, 1782; John, 1784; Ira, 1787; Daniel, 1789; Joseph 1791; Polly, 1794. He moved to Hartford, Maine. JOHN WESLEY, Boston, son of Allen, above, m. Mary Stockman, of Rockport, and had Frank Madaline, 1847, m. Nathan B. Hoyt, of New Haven; Horace M., 1849; Edith May; Effie; Edith Somes, 1856, m. John E. Levy, of Milltown, Maine; Louise F., 1859; Mabelle S., 1861; Clifton W. A., 1864. JONATHAN, 1st in the text; his son Jonathan, m. Mary Doten. JOSEPH, 1st in the text, m. Hannah, d. of Thomas Pope, not of Gabriel Fallowell. JOSEPH, 10th in the text; his son Cornelius A., m. Isabel, not Mabel Drew; and his daughter Lucy F., m. Peter Trott, not Pratt. JOSIAH, son of 1st Ichabod in the text, m. Mary Chandler and removed to Lebanon, Conn.; one of his sons, Dr. John, m. Lucretia Stewart, and had a son Telemachus, who m. Lydia Coffin, of Nantucket. LEMUEL, 1st in the text, had another child, Paren, born 1820. LEWIS, in the text, son of Diman, m., 1830, Sally Cornish, d. of Nehemiah Savery; and had Martha Ann, 1830; Lewis Thomas, 1833; Sarah Ann, 1834; Mary E., 1837, m. John Fairbanks, of Bridgewater. He m. 2d, 1844, Achsah H. (Kittridge) Brown, d. of Job Giddings, of Walpole, N. H., and wid. of Joseph Brown; and had Joseph Lewis, 1844; Sarah Achsah, 1847; Francis Kittridge, 1849; Ephraim Diman, 1853, m. Harriet Russell, d. of Jacob Dickson. LEWIS, son of 1st Ansel, in the text, m., 1825, Mary Corban Holmes, and had Charles Lewis, 1829; Martha Ann, 1830; Wm. Marston, 1832; Mary Jane, 1834. NATHANIEL, 3d in the text; his son Cornelius, m. Deborah A., wid. of Charles H. Chandler; and d. of John F. Hoyt. NATHANIEL, son of 2d Ebenezer in the text, m. Zenobie, d. of Christopher Wadsworth, and had Zenobie, 1743; Nathaniel, 1745; Mercy, 1746; Elizabeth, 1749; John, 1752. ROBERT, son of 3d Robert in the text, m., 1759, Lucy Woodworth. RUFUS, in the text, had besides the children mentioned, Lizzie, m. Kimball Harlow; Rebecca, m. George Ellis Blackmer and Timothy Allen; Nathaniel C., m, Hannah, d. of Samuel Bartlett and Clark. SAMUEL, in the text, d. Elizabeth m. Joseph Bartlett, not Ephraim Bradford. SOLOMON, son of 2d Solomon in the text, m. Abigail Torrey and Hannah Rogers. His sister Abigail, 1791, m. Samuel Sampson. SYLVANUS, 2d in the text, removed to Salisbury, Conn., and his son Loring had a son Egbert, of Ansonia, Conn. THOMAS, 3d in the text; his d. Phebe T. m. William S. Burbank, and d. Roxanna A. m. Isaac White. TRUMAN, 1st in the text; son Charles, was born 1814; son Stephen, 1802; d. Lucia, 1813; and d. Angeline, 1818. URIAH, 1st in the text; strike out the words "and a Leach" after "Jane Adams" and add the words "m. a Leach" after "Mahala, 1823." WASHINGTON ALLEN, son of Allen above, m. Ruth B. Bloom, of New York, and had Frances Amelia, m. Don Estaban St. C. De Ruda, of Havana. WILLIAM, 3d in the text; d. Betsey Thacher, should be Elizabeth Thacher, and d. Mary should be erased. WILLIAM, 4th in the text; his d. Mary was Mary Grayton. WILLIAM, son of 1st Lemuel in the text, m. Mercy Holmes and had Esther, 1780; Stephen, 1784; Emily, 1785; Allen, 1789; Flavel, 1794; Clement, 1796; Eliza, 1804; Jane H., 1800. ZACHEUS, 1st in the text; d. Phebe, m. a 2d husband, Branch Blackmer. ZACHEUS, 2d in the text; d. Caroline m. James, not George Pratt. ZACHEUS, 3d in the text; d. Sarah, born 1823, not 1828.

BASSETT, WILLIAM, 2d in the text; his son William born 1624, m. Mary, d. of Hugh Burt, of Lynn; his son Nathaniel, born 1628, m. Mary or Dorcas, d. of John Joyce, of Yarmouth; his son Joseph had a 1st wife before Martha; d. Sarah born 1630; d. Elizabeth born 1626; and also had a d. Ruth, m. John Sprague.

BATES, CLEMENT, 1st in the text; had also a son Samuel, born 1639. He was descended from Thomas, of Lydd, Parish of All Hallows, who died 1485, through John, Andrew, John and James. COMFORT, 4th in the text; his son Gustavus Davie in the text should be Gustavus Davis. DAVID, the 1st in the text, was son of Samuel in the text. JAMES, in the text; his d. Hattie should be Hattie E. JOSEPH, 4th in the text; his d. Rebecca, m. Branch Pierce. SAMUEL, Hingham, son of 1st Clement m., 1667, Lydia Lapham, d. of Thomas and Mary (Tilden) Lapham, of Scituate; and had Lydia, 1669; Mary, 1671; Sarah, 1673; Anna, 1676; Judith, 1678; Samuel, 1680; Thomas, 1682; David, 1684; Mary again, 1685.

BATTLES, JOHN, 2d in the text, was not son of 1st John.

BAXTER, JAMES, in the text; son James was James P., and m. Susan E. Cobb. He had also a son Robert.

BAYLEY, THOMAS, m. 1755, Sarah Langlee.

BEARSE, ICHABOD, m. 1768, Esther Holmes. THOMAS, in the text, m. 1825.

BENSON, MOSES, from Vermont, m. Experience Briggs and had Isaac; Susan, m. Timothy Manter; Lydia, m. Ezra Finney and others. SETH, in the text; the wife of his son George was Caroline Elizabeth, d. of Samuel Brown, of Boston. The husband of d. Bathsheba Thomas, should be Levi F. Tinkham.

BILLINGTON, FRANCIS, 2d in the text; d. Sukey should be Mercy.

BISBEE, ZEBULON, in the text; his wife Sally (Nichols) was d. of Peter Lanman.

BLACKMER, BRANCH, 2d in the text, m. Phebe (Bartlett) Perry, widow of Daniel Perry, and d. of Zacheus Bartlett. PETER, in the text, had also a son Stephen, born 1704.

BLISS, ALEXANDER, in the text, had William Davis, 1826, and Alexander, 1828.

BLOSSOM, THOMAS, in the text had a wife Anne, and his son Peter m., 1663, Sarah Bodfish.

BONHAM, BONUM, George 2d, in the text, m. 1681, not 1683.

BOSWORTH, ORIN, in the text, m., according to Church Records, 1824.

BOULT, CHARLES, in the text, m. 1755.

BOURNE, THOMAS, of Marshfield, from Kent, by wife Elizabeth had John; Martha, m. John Bradford and Thomas Tracy; Elizabeth, m. Robert Waterman; Ann, m. Rev. Nehemiah Smith; Margaret, m. Josiah Winslow; Lydia m. Nathaniel Tilden and others.

BRADFORD, ABRAM, son of Elijah below, Camden, Maine, m. Sarah Palmer and had Betsey, Ruth, Sarah, Elmira; Caroline, m. Levi Harding of Dixmont, Maine; and Charles. ALLEN TAYLOR SMITH, son of William and Mary (Smith) Bradford, below, m., 1833, Margaret Diman, and had Mary Abby, 1835, m. A. Winsor Gooding; Sarah, 1837; Allen T., 1840; Margaret Diman, 1843, m. George F. Stanton. BARTLETT, in the text, m. in 1807; son, Lewis G., was born 1810, and Eveline in 1812. BENJAMIN WRIGHT, son of 4th. Nathaniel in the text, m., 1831, Catharine Allen of New York. CALVIN, in the text, son Luther m. Lydia, not Ruth, Holmes. CORNELIUS, m. Elizabeth Hinckley, and had Cornelius, Ephraim, Rebecca, William, Josiah, Thankful, Betsey and Mary. CORNELIUS, son of above, m. Mary Bakin, and had Joseph M., and Celia Nye, who m. Newell Raymond, of Plymouth; the widow of Cornelius m. Francis Nye. DAVID, 1st in the text; it is claimed by some that he m. Elizabeth, d. of Josiah Finney, and that Elizabeth, d. of John Finney, m. William Bradford (for proof that this claim is incorrect, see the entry in this appendix under the head of Josiah Finney). DAVID, 2d in the text, had also a d. Desire H., 1823; his d. Lydia Holmes was born in 1835. EDWARD WINSLOW, in the text, m. 2d, Betsey Courtney (Dillard) (Kempton) Everett, widow of Isaac Kempton and Elisha H. Everett, and d. of Benjamin Dillard. ELIJAH, Belmont, Maine, m. Sarah Jones, and had Huldah and Abram. ELISHA, in the text; his 2d wife was Bathshua, not Bathsheba, and his d. Hannah was born 1720, not 1719. EPHRAIM, 1st in the text; his d. Susanna should be Lusanna. EPHRAIM, 2d in the text; his son, George, m. Ruth Ann, d. of James T. Ford. EPHRAIM, 4th in the text; d. Maria should be Marcia. EZEKIEL HERSEY, son of 8th William, m. Abby DeWolf and Abby Atwood, and had Hervey and Seraphine. GERSHOM, 2d in the text, of Bristol, m. 1st, Mary Reynolds, and the children mentioned were of both wives. ISAIAH, Duxbury, son of 5th Samuel in the text, m. 1801, Elizabeth, d. of Jabez Dingley, and had Lucia.

1802; Rebecca D., 1804; Betsey Ann, 1806, m. Briggs Peterson; William, 1807, m. Sarah Cushman; Lucia, 1809, m. Isaac Chandler; Lyman, 1812; Newton, 1813; Lyman, 1815; Charles, 1816, m. Rebecca Emerson, of Boston; George, 1819, m. Charlotte B. Shaw, of Weymouth. JOHN, 1st in the text, was son of 4th William, not of 2d. JOHN, Kingston, 2d in the text; the 2d husband of d. Alice, should be Joshua Hersey. JOHN, son of 8th William in the text, m. Jemima Wardwell, and had Ann, 1795, m. Nicholas Peck; Benjamin, 1797, m. Jemima G. Peck; LeBaron, 1799; Mary, 1801, m. Josiah Howland ; Eleanor, 1803, m. Thomas Church; Lydia, 1806, m. William Hatch; Jemima, 1808; Walter, 1809, m. Sarah W. Macomber; Hannah, 1811, m. George H. Reynolds; Harriet DeWolf, 1814, m. William R. Taylor; William, 1816, m. Ann W. Nooning. JONATHAN, 1st in the text; son Jonathan born 1798, not 1796, and besides children mentioned, he had Joanna, m. Francis Drew, of Kingston. JONATHAN, son of above, had David Thaxter, 1828, now of Atchison. JOSEPH, 2d in the text, m. Anna, d. of Rev. James and Priscilla (Mason) Filch, not Daniel. JOSIAH, son of 9th William in the text, m. 1803, Mary, d. of Lemuel Robbins, and had Josiah, 1806; Mary, 1808, m. Horatio Robbins; Jane Chandler, 1809. m. 1831, John Harlow; Ruth Ann., 1813, m. Maltiah Howard; Matilda, 1814, m. William Faunce; Katherine Warner, 1816, m. Henry Barnes. LUTHER, son of Calvin, in the text, of Plympton, m. Lydia Holmes and had Lydia, m. Jacob Barrows. He m. 2d Mary, d. of Jonathan Standish, and had Irene, m. Simeon Pratt of Middleboro; Ruth, m. Addison Pratt; Sarah, m. Benson Waterman, of Halifax; Caroline, m. Prince Penniman, of Middleboro; Mary Angie, m. Charles Swett, of Middleboro; Clara, m. Albert Hartwell of Brockton, Joseph Warren, Clinton, and William Harrison. NATHANIEL, 3d in the text; erase from 1818 to end of sentence. NATHANIEL, New York, 4th in the text, insert among children "Benjamin Wright." NATHANIEL GOVERNEUR, New York, son of Nathaniel Governeur in the text, m., 1853, Mary Abigail Sackett, of New York, and had Mary Estelle, 1854; Emily, 1856; Alice B. L., 1857. PEREZ, 2d in the text, m. Abigail Balch, not Belch. PETER JAMES, son of William and Betsy (James) Bradford, below, m., 1839, Lucretia S. Coit, and had William James, 1840, m. Mrs. Ma (Snow) Goodrich; and Mary E., 1843, m. William L. Wheaton. PRINCE, L bury, son of Samuel, below, m. Harriet Churchill, and had Gershom, 1816, m. Betsey Burt of Woodstock, Vt.; Peleg; Harriet; and Otis, m. Jane Hacket. ROBERT, Boston, died about 1680, had two wives, Martha and Margaret; his d. Martha, b. 1645, m. Peter Maverick, and son Moses by wife Elizabeth, had John, 1668; Robert, 1673; Thomas, 1678, and others. SAMUEL, Duxbury, 1st in the text; son Gershom m. Priscilla Wiswell; son Perez m. Abigail Balch, not Belch, and d. Elizabeth, m. Charles Whitney, not William. SAMUEL, 2d in the text; son Samuel born 1788, d. Lucy, 1787. SAMUEL, 3d in the text, m. 1817. SAMUEL, Plympton, 4th in the text, son William born 1728, and d. Phebe m. Shubael Norton. SAMUEL, Duxbury, son of 4th Samuel in the text, m. Lydia Bradford and had Prince; Eunice, m. Asa Weston; George; Samuel, m. Anna Sampson. SPENCER, Kingston, in the text, d. Francis Alden should be Frances Adelia. STETSON, Kingston, in the text; son William m. 1807, Nancy S. Brooks of Scituate; son Charles m. Mrs. Elizabeth P. Brown Clark, and

moved to Thomastown, Maine, and to Ohio. THOMAS, 2d in the text, m.
Anna, d. of Rev. Nehemiah and Ann (Bourne) Smith. WILLIAM, 4th in the
text; son Thomas m. Ann, d. of Rev. Nehemiah Smith. WILLIAM, 5th in the
text; his wife Rebecca was d. of Benjamin, not Joseph, Bartlett. WILLIAM,
6th in the text; his d. Jerusha also m. Josiah Carver. For proof that the
claim of some that he m. Elizabeth, d. of John Finney, and that David Bradford m. Elizabeth, d. of Josiah Finney is unfounded see the entry in this appendix under the head of Josiah Finney. WILLIAM, son of 8th William in
the text, m. Betsey B. James and· had Peter, 1790; Harry, 1787; John, 1793;
Mary, 1778, m. Elijah Willard; Sally, 1779, m. a Seymour; William, 1781;
Elizabeth, 1785, m. a Dearth. WILLIAM, son of above, m. Mary Smith of
Bristol, R. I., and had William Parnell, 1805; Edward James, 1806; Allen
Taylor Smith, 1808; Peter James, 1815, m. Lucretia S. Coit; Nancy Smith,
1811, m. Leonard Wright; Mary Smith, 1813, m. Albert G. Pearse. WILLIAM,
8th in the text: son John born 1768; son Ezekiel should be Ezekiel Hersey;
d. Lydia born 1773; d. Nancy born 1770; d. Mary born 1760, and her husband,
Henry Goodwin, was son of Benjamin and Hannah (LeBaron) Goodwin.
WILLIAM, 9th in the text: son Josiah was born 1782. WILLIAM, 10th in the
text: son William born 1797; d. Mercy born 1804. WILLIAM, 11th in the text, m.
Alice Sylvester, 1820. WILLIAM, Holmes, in the text; son George F. m. Arabella F., d. of Eleazer Barnes. WILLIAM JAMES, son of Peter James, above,
m. 1873, Mrs. Mary (Snow) Goodrich, and had William, 1876. ZEPHANIAH in
the text: strike out "and James B."

BRAMHALL, BENJAMIN, 2d in the text, moved to Boston, not Quincy.
CHARLES, in the text, m. 1819. GEORGE, 2d in the text, d. Sally, m. Israel
Richmond. GEORGE, 4th in the text, wife's name was Eleanor Warren Leon-
ard. JOSEPH, in the text, son Joseph, m. Remember Robbins. SYLVANUS, 1st in
the text, son Benjamin, born 1765, and he had also a d. Mercy, who m. Thomas
Marsh. SYLVANUS, 2d in the text, son Sylvanus, m., 1823, Mary Wait, d. of
Wait Atwood.

BREWSTER, BENJAMIN, Norwich, son of 1st Jonathan in the text, m., 1659,
Ann Dart, and had Mary, 1660; Ann, 1662; Jonathan, 1664; Daniel, 1667;
William, 1669; Ruth, 1671; Benjamin, 1673; and Elizabeth. BENJAMIN, 3d in
the text, d. Sarah, m. Hazen Nelson and Willis Fish; and son Washington, m.
Rebecca Oxton. BENJAMIN, 4th in the text, was son of Cyrus below, and not
of William. CHARLES, 1st in the text, son Martin, m. Emily M. Benson.
CYRUS, son of 10th William in the text, m. a Tappan, and had Benjamin and
others. DANIEL, of Preston, Conn., son of Benjamin and Ann (Dart) Brewster above, m. 1686, Hannah Gayer, and had Daniel, 1687, m. Elizabeth
Freeman; Hannah, 1690; Mary, 1692; John, 1695; Jerusha, 1697; Ruth,
1700; Bethiah, 1702; Jonathan, 1705. ELISHA, Kingston, 1st in the text, the
last three names in the list of children should be one name, "Earnest Wrestling Elisha." ELLIS, in the text, had two other children, William and Ellis.
ICHABOD, in the text, m., 1735, not 1725; his son Ichabod was born 1753. IRA,
1st in the text, m. 1796. IRA, 2d in the text; the d. Lovina should be Lorina;
and wife of son Edward B. should be Lucy A. Watts. JOHN, 1st in the text,
was son of 1st, not 2d, Wrestling, and the name of wife was Cotta. JONATHAN,

1st in the text, was born in Scrooby, August 12, 1593, and m., April 10, 1624, Lucretia Oldam, or, Oldham. He had William, 1625; Mary, 1627, m. John Turner; Jonathan, 1629; Ruth, 1631, m. John Pickett; Benjamin, 1633; Elizabeth, 1637; Grace, 1639. JONATHAN, Connecticut, son of Daniel above, m., 1725, Mary Parrish, and had Lucrista, 1727; Ruth, 1730; Ephraim, 1731; Jonathan, 1734; Mary, 1735; Lydia, 1739. JONATHAN, Duxbury, 2d in the text, moved to Windham, Conn., about 1728, had son Jonathan and others. JONATHAN, son of 2d Jonathan in the text, born 1737, m. 1766, Eunice Kingsley, and had Orson, 1767; Eunice, 1770; Ohel, 1771; Oramel, 1773; Joana, 1775; Lydia, 1779; Jonathan, 1781. JOSEPH, Belmont, Me. in the text; son Ira m. a Mariner; and d. Eunice m. a Dunnell. JOSHUA, 1st in the text; his d. Betsey E. m. Robert Hutchinson; d. Priscilla W. m. also a Tucker; and son William N. should be William M. JOSHUA, 2d in the text; d. Sarah, m. Joseph, not Joshua, Wright. JOSHUA, 3d in the text, d. Ruth born 1803, not 1810. JOSHUA, 4th in the text, son Joshua T., m. Marcia, not Maria Hunt. LEMUEL, Kingston, in the text, d. Rebecca, m. Maltiah Cobb. MOSES, son of Jonathan and Zipporah (Smith) Brewster, of Connecticut, m. Lucy Watts, and had Aurelia, 1794; Osmyn, 1797; Horace, 1796; Betsey, 1800; Martha, 1802; Ezra S., 1804; Moses, 1805; Lucy, 1809. NATHAN C., Duxbury, in the text, m. 1821. ORSON, son of 2d Jonathan, in the text, of Middletown, Vt., m. Zeruiah Loomis, and had Dorinda, 1795, m. 1815, and moved to Fairhaven, Vt., and to Bennington; Ohel, Harvey, Henry, Fitch and Fay. OSMYN, Boston, son of Moses above, m., 1824, Mary Soper Jones, and had Mary J., 1824; Martha A., 1825; Charles O., 1827; Sarah C., 1830; George T., 1832; Lucy W., 1834; Harriet, 1836; Emily, 1839; Kate, 1842. WILLIAM, 1st in the text (the whole re-written), came in the *Mayflower* with wife Mary and two sons, Love and Wrestling; his d. Fear, who m. Isaac Allerton, and d. Patience, who m. Thomas Prence, came in the *Ann*, 1623; son Jonathan came in the *Fortune*, 1621. WILLIAM, 2d in the text, had also a d. Mercy, who m. Edward Arnold. WILLIAM, 6th in the text, moved to Connecticut, son Daniel, born 1746; Nathaniel, 1748; Stephen, 1750. WILLIAM, 7th in the text, son Isaac, m. a Smith; son John M., m. a Gardner. WILLIAM N., 8th in the text, should be William M., and the husband of d. Catherine should be Porter C. Read, not Peter. WILLIAM, son of 1st Jonathan in the text, m., 1651, Mary Peame, of London. WRESTLING, 1st in the text, d. Mary, m. Ephraim Holmes; and d. Elizabeth, m. Ephraim Bradford; and d. Hannah, m. Benjamin Alden. ZADOCK, in the text; d. Sarah m. a Herrick. The discovery of what is called the Brewster Book adds to the confusion already existing concerning the date of the death of Elder Brewster. The entry there made by his son Jonathan makes it April 10, 1644. Bradford says he died, as has been usually quoted, about April 18, 1643, but the photographic copy of Bradford suggests that April 16th has been miscalled April 18th. The church records say April 16, 1644, and this must be considered the true date.

BRIGGS, ISAAC, in the text, son of Samuel, born 1781.

BROWN, JOHN, of Truro, m. Sarah Little. JOSEPH LASINBY, in the text; son is Arthur L. JOSEPH P., in the text; son Joseph A. m. Cynthia P. Douglass. STEPHEN P., in the text; d. Annie m. Charles Anderson Simeon Perkins; strike out the words "Caroline E. m. George Benson."

BRYANT, ICHABOD, in the text, m. 1702; son Philip was father of a Peter, and grandfather of William Cullen Bryant. JOHN, 1st in the text, had also a son Daniel. JONATHAN, in the text, had also a d. Ruth, who m. Consider Howland. SAMUEL, 1st in the text, m. Joanna Cole; son Josiah should be d. Joanna, and d. Abigail m. Josiah Finney. SAMUEL, son of above, m. Dorcus Ford and had Joseph, m. Zelpha, d. of William Sampson, 1756. SAMUEL, 2d in the text, m. 1758. STEPHEN, in the text, had also a d. Abigail, who m. John Bryant.

BULLARD, BENJAMIN, m., 1823, Mary Drew.

BUMPUS, EDWARD, in the text, had a wife Hannah; his d. Sarah m. Thomas Dunham. He had also sons Philip and Thomas. THOMAS, Barnstable, son of Edward in the text, m., 1679, Phebe, d. of John Lovell, and had Hannah, 1680, m. Samuel Parker; John, 1681; Mary, 1683; Samuel, 1685, m. Joanna Warren; Thomas, 1687; Sarah, 1688; Elizabeth, 1690; Abigail, 1693; John, baptized 1696; Benjamin, 1703.

BURBANK, DAVID, 2d in the text; son Asaph S. m. also Charlotte A. Peterson. EZRA, 2d in the text; son William S. born 1797. JOHN, 2d in the text, m. 1826. SAMUEL, in the text; d. Sally born 1803; son William should be William D.; d. Mary Ann born 1805; son Walter should be Walter D. TIMOTHY, in the text, was son of Timothy and Rebecca, of Boston. WILLIAM S., in the text; children Abigail and William should be one name.

BURGESS, ABNER, in the text, should be Abner S.; his son Abner was born 1808, and son Sydney in 1815. CHANDLER, in the text, m. in 1805. JAMES, 1st in the text; son James born 1809. JOHN, 2d in the text; son Nathan born 1792. JOSEPH WILLIAM, in the text; son James Kendall born 1843, not 1844, and Erford A., 1846, not 1847. NATHAN, 1st in the text; d. Ruth born 1803; d. Judith, 1806; d. Abigail, 1814. NATHANIEL, 1st in the text; d. Lucy m. also James Glass. THOMAS, 3d in the text; son Joseph born 1790; d. Irene Sanger, 1793; d. Betsey, 1797. VINAL, in the text; d. Experience should be Experience C.; son Seth m. Sarah H. Warren. WILLIAM, 1st in the text; son Abner S., born 1784; son William, 1791; son Vinal, 1797; d. Welthea, 1801. WILLIAM, 2d in the text; son Otis should be Otis W.

BURR, JEHUE, England, 1600, had Jehue and John, born in England. Jehue had Daniel and Peter. Daniel had Rev. Aaron 1716, father of Aaron Burr. Peter, born 1667, had Thadeus, 1700; m., 1725, Abigail, d. of Jonathan Sturgis. and had Thadeus, of Fairfield, Conn., 1735, m. Eunice, d. of James Dennie, and Gershom 1744, m. Priscella, d. of Isaac Lothrop, of Plymouth. Gershom, Fairfield, had Gershom; Eunice, m. Barnabas Hedge, of Plymouth; Priscilla, m. a Buckley and Lewis Burr Sturgis; Abigail, m. a Capers. John, son of 1st Jehue, had John, 1673, who had Andrew 1696, m. Sarah, d. of Jonathan Sturgis 1719, who had Ann, m. Samuel Sturgis, 1740, who had Jonathan, m. Deborah, d. of Lothrop Lewis, of Barnstable, and had Lucretia Burr, m. Benjamin Marston Watson, of Plymouth.

BURT, LABAN, m. 1806.

BUSHNELL, HARVEY, m., 1821, Susan Nichols.

CALDERWOOD, JOHN, in the text; wife d. of Ansel, not Isaac, Churchill.

CALLAWAY, GEORGE, W., m., 1828, Mary Ann, d. of Nathaniel Thomas.

CAMPBELL, CHARLES WILLIAM, son of John, a soldier at Waterloo, was born at the Cape of Good Hope; and m., 1804, Mary Fuller, d. of Kendall Holmes, and wid. of William Crocker Churchill. DUNCAN, in the text, m. 1773, Susanna McKeil. JOHN, in the text; d. Frances M. m. a third husband, Nathaniel M. Davis.

CANNON, NATHAN, of Rochester, m., 1829, Mary Ann Jackson.

CARVER, JOSIAH, 3d in the text; d. Eliza born 1805. NATHANIEL, 3d in the text; d. Elizabeth should be Mary. REUBEN, in the text, was son of 2d William.

CASE, WILLIAM, of Boston, m., 1761, Joanna Ward.

CASSIDY, JOHN, in the text, was born in Ireland, in 1784.

CHANDLER, EPHRAIM, Kingston, m., 1814, Deborah Rider. JOHN B., in the text, m. 1804; d. Nancy B. born 1811; son Samuel B., 1809; d. Lucy S., 1815; son John T., 1820; Lydia T., 1819; Thankful S., 1813; Hannah Brown, 1816; Hannah S., 1821; Lucy S., 1823; strike out Phineas and William. JOSEPH, 1st in the text, had a wife Mercy, and his son Edmund m. Elizabeth Alden, and had a d. Mercy, m. Josiah Bartlett. JOSEPH, 2d in the text, m. Martha, d. of Samuel Hunt. JOSEPH, 3d in the text, had also James and Joseph. SAMUEL, 2d in the text, m. Margaret, d. of Thomas Phillips. SAMUEL, 4th in the text, m. 1830; he had also Coleman B. m. Mary S., d. of Thomas Pierce. STETSON, m., 1816, Eliza Marston.

CHASE, CONSIDER, of Carver, by wife Molly had Levi; Lewis; Martha, m. a Ransom; Sarah, m. a Dunham; Lucy, m. a Washburn. JOHN, 2d in the text; son John was born 1804. LEVI, Carver, son of Consider above, by wife Hannah had Levi, Ezra, Benjamin, Consider, Isaac, Sylvanus, John, Eunice and Hannah, m, a Pratt. SYLVANUS D., in the text, was son of Levi.

CHIPMAN, JOHN, in the text, was born in Barnstable, England, in 1614 and came to Plymouth 1630. SAMUEL, in the text, m. 1815. SAMUEL, son of John above, m. Sarah Cobb, and had ten children, one of whom was John, born 1619, another Thomas, born 1687, who settled in Groton, Conn., and moved to Litchfield, Conn., and had five sons, Thomas, John, Amos, Samuel and Jonathan. Samuel, the son of Thomas, m. Hannah Austin, of Suffield, Conn., and had six sons, one of whom, Nathaniel, born in Salisbury, Conn., in 1752 removed to Vermont and m. Sarah Hill, of Tinmouth, Vt., and had seven children, of whom Henry, the oldest, removed to Detroit in 1824, and m. Martha Logan, of South Carolina. John Logan Chipman, son of Henry, born in Detroit, in 1830, died while a member of the 53d Congress.

CHUBBUCK, NATHANIEL, in the text, m. Margaret Joy, of Hingham. TIMOTHY, of Wareham, m. Lurany, d. of Samuel Barrows, and had Alice, Timothy, William, Silas and Lot, the last of whom m. Betsey, d. of Thomas and Mary Curtis Faunce, and had Stillman E., Harvey C. and Betsey.

CHURCH, BENJAMIN, in the text; his son Thomas had a d., who m. Sylvester Brownell, of Newport; his son Edward had Benjamin; and Abigail, who m. George Wanton, of Newport. CALEB, of Dedham and Hingham, son of 1st Richard in the text, born 1642; m. 1667, Joanna, d. of William Sprague, of Salem, and had a d. Rebecca, 1678. CHARLES, in the text; he had also children, Martha, and Elizabeth, who m. John Sampson. NATHANIEL, in the text; his son Richard m. Sarah Barstow, and he had also a d. Hannah, who m. Josiah Sturtevant. RICHARD, 1st in the text, born 1608, arrived 1630, m. 1632, and lived in Plymouth, Watertown, Charlestown, Sandwich, Hingham and Dedham, and died 1670; his son Caleb was born 1642.

CHURCHILL, ANSEL, 1st in the text, son of John, was born 1775. ASAPH, in the text, had also a d., Sarah, born 1816. BARNABAS, 1st in the text, m. 1711. BARNABAS, 4th in the text; son Robert Bruce, born 1841; and d. Mary Louise, m. Charles H. Cobb. CHARLES, 2d in the text, son Joseph, born 1804. DANIEL, 2d in the text, son Daniel O., born 1828. EBENEZER, 1st in the text, probably m. 2d, 1775, Patience, d. of Eleaser Faunce. EBENEZER, 3d in the text; strike out marriage and children. EBENEZER, 4th in the text, was son of Ichabod, and had additional children, Samuel, Jacob, Prince, Bathsheba and Lucy. EBENEZER, 5th in the text, had a wife, — Leach, and had additional children, Joanna and Eleazer. ELEAZER, 1st in the text, had an additional son, Jonathan. ELEAZER m., in Bridgewater, 1788, Lucy Otis. ELKANAH, 1st in the text, had an additional d., Lydia Ann, born 1837. ELKANAH, son of 1st Charles in the text, m., 1801, Eunice Finney. GEORGE, 2d in the text, m. Martha Cotton Holmes, 1826; son John, born 1828, m. Martha James Bagnall; and d. Martha, born 1835, m. for 2d husband John McAdams. ISAAC, 1st in the text, was son of Isaac and Sarah Cobb Churchill, below, and had additional children, Seth, 1790; Timothy, 1785; Rebecca, 1787; Nancy, 1792. ISAAC, 2d in the text, m. Meletiah, d. of Joshua Bradford. ISAAC, son of 1st Barnabas in the text, m. Sarah Cobb, and had ISAAC, 1757. JABEZ, 2d in the text; son Jabez, born 1835; son Sylvester, 1838. JAMES, 1st in the text; son James, m. Sarah d. of Ebenezer Soule; Clara, not James, 1782, m. 1st, Joel Ellis, and 2d, Peleg Chandler. JAMES CREIGHTON, son of Thomas and Alice Creighton Churchill, below, m. Eliza Walker Osborne, of Portsmouth, N. H., 1809. JOHN, 1st in the text, son Joseph, born 1649; son John, 1657. JOHN, 5th in the text; son George, born 1803; son John, 1805; d. Hannah J., 1801; d. Bethiah, 1807; d. Nancy, 1808. JOHN, 6th in the text, m., 2d, 1718, at Portsmouth, N. H., Mary Jackson, and had John, m., 1741, Mary Noble, and had John, 1743, m. Hannah Smith at New Hackensack, N. J. JOHN, 6th, m. 3d, Elizabeth Jackson Cotton. JOHN DARLING, in the text; son Josiah D., born 1853; he m. 2d, 1883, Julia A. Hawley. JOHN, son of 1st Barnabas, m., 1770, Molly Bradford. JOHN m., 1761, Hepzibah Pemberton, of Boston. JOHN m. 1767, Sarah Pratt, of Bridgewater. JOSEPH, Newmarket, N. H. son of 1st Thomas in the text, m., 1795, Sally Task, and had John Task, 1796, and eleven others. John Task m., 1817, Mehitabel Gilman Wiley, and had Nathaniel Wiley, of Boston Highlands, born 1827, and nine others. Nathaniel Wiley m. Martha, d. of Benjamin Wiggin, of Dover, N. H. JOSEPH, Boston, son of 2d Joseph in the text, m. Agnes Fettis. JOSEPH, 4th in the text; his d. Reenet E., born 1830; son Frederick Ellis, 1837; son Joseph Lothrop, 1842; d. Ann Maria, 1838; d. Hannah Nelson, 1834: d. Betsey Harlow, not Betsey alone. NATHANIEL, 3d in the text, had additional children by wife Susanna, Abigail, Lydia, Sylvanus and Susanna. OLIVER, in the text; Angeline, wife of son Isaiah, was d., not wid., of John Standish. RUFUS in the text; son Rufus, m., 1827, d. Eunice, born 1803. SAMUEL, 1st in the text; children born, Samuel, 1779; Caleb, 1782; Mendell, 1786; Lucy, 1788; Henry, 1790; Deborah, 1793, m., 1815, Joseph Vose; and Esther, m. Samuel

Avery Collins. SAMUEL, 2d in the text, m. Nancy, not Mercy, Covington. SETH, son of 2d Barnabas in the text, m. Elizabeth Sylvester; and Seth m. Sally Seabury Simmons. SETH, son of 2d Isaac in the text, m. Sarah S. Johnson, and had Eliza, m. Alfred Chubbuck; Benjamin, 1814, m. Betsey Bumpus; James W., m. Sarah Ann Carr; Augustus R., of Atlanta, Ga. STEPHEN, 3d in the text; children born, Heman, 1770; Daniel, 1772; Stephen, 1768; Peleg, 1769; Maria, 1778; Nancy, 1780; Polly, 1786; Sally, 1782; Hannah, 1776; Otis, 1774; Eleanor, 1783; Elizabeth, 1778. SYLVANUS, 1st in the text; son Josiah was Josiah W. SYLVANUS, 2d in the text; d. Abigail Holmes m. Ozen Bates; son Sylvanus m. Bella N., d. of Nelson Holmes. THADEUS, in the text, m. 1775. THOMAS, 1st in the text, m. 1757, and had additional children, Ichabod, 1764; Polly, 1762; Lydia, 1766; Thomas, 1768; Susanna, 1770; Desire, 1774; Thomas, 1764; Nathaniel, 1776: John, 1778; Joseph, 1772. THOMAS, son of Ist Thomas in the text, m. about 1776 Alice Creighton, of New Hampshire, and had James Creighton, 1787; Thomas, 1791; Elizabeth, 1799; all born in Newmarket, N. H. WILLIAM, 2d in the text; d. Hannah m. Hopestill Bisbee; d. Rebecca m. Amos Ford; Ruth m. Ebenezer Cole; Abigail m. John Bryant; Sarah m. Josiah Marshall. ZADOCK, son of 2d Stephen in the text, m. Bathsheba, d. of Joseph Rider, and had Bathsheba, 1776, m. Thomas Long, and other children.

CLARK, ANDREW, Harwich, son of 1st Andrew in the text, m., 1711, Elizabeth, d. of Kenelm Winslow, and had Mehitabel, 1712; Elizabeth, 1716; Thankful, 1721; Eunice, 1724, m. Samuel Foster; Hannah, 1726. BARNABAS, born in Harwich, 1771, m. Mollie Bassett, of Dennis, and moved to Westfield, Mass. He had George, 1798; Alvan, of Cambridge, 1804; Mary, 1809; Barnabas, 1799; Thankful, 1802; Samuel, 1805; Daniel, 1807; Abigail, 1812; William, 1814. CORNELIUS, in the text, was son of John, of Rochester, below. He had a 1st wife Elizabeth, by whom he had John, 1723; Jonathan, 1727; by Susanna his 2d wife, he had Lemuel or Samuel, 1733; Simeon, 1735; Ruth, 1737. EBENEZER, son of John, Jr., of Rochester, below, m., 1730, Mary Claghorn, and had Mary, 1733. EBENEZER, son of William and Martha Rider Clark, below, m., 1764, Elizabeth Dexter, and had William, 1765; Ebenezer, 1768; Elizabeth, 1770; and in Conway, Mass., Ebenezer, 1781; Mary, Joanna, Hannah, Seth, Thomas and Sarah, twins, Elisha and Martha. EBENEZER, son of above, m. 1808, Sarah Griffiths, and had Almira, Albert, Almira Griffiths, Rodolphus, Asa Bement, Aurora and Ebenezer Lincoln, now of Dubuque, Ia. ENDOR, son of Joshua, of New Salem, below, m., 1824, Nancy King, and had Rodolphus, 1825; Clara R., 1827; Frederick S., 1829; he m. 2d, Mary Ann Fasset, and had Sarah Maria, 1838, m., 1859, William H. Foster; Albert Baxter, 1840; he m. 3d, 1847, Hannah Holden, and had Lewis, 1848; Cora, 1851; Abby, 1853. ISRAEL, 2d in the text; son Israel born 1806. JAMES, 1st in the text; d. Susanna m. Samuel Cornish, and d. Abigail m. John Sutton, and d. Bathsheba m. Nicholas Litchfield, of Scituate. JOHN, 1st in the text, m. Rebecca Lincoln, 1695; son Joseph m. Elizabeth Alcock, of Boston; he had an additional d. Martha, m. Isaac Bates. JOHN, of Rochester, son of 1st Thomas in the text, had, by wife Sarah, John, 1709, m. Mary Tobey; Joseph, m., 1720, Thankful Stevens; Cornelius; Sarah, m. John Dexter; Mary, m. Timothy Stevens, and Elizabeth.

JOHN, son of Cornelius in the text, m., 1748, Epiphany Dexter, and had Eunice, 1749; John, 1752. JOHN, son of above, by wife Bethiah, had Eunice, 1781; Epiphany, 1783; Mary, 1785: Abigail, 1788; Bethiah, 1790; Sally, 1792; John H., 1796; Sarah, 1798. JOHN, JR., of Rochester, m. Mary Tobey, of Sandwich, and had Ebenezer, 1710, m. Mary Claghorn; Jean, 1712, m., 1733, Andrew Haskell; Sarah, 1714, m., 1734, John Crapo; William, 1717, m., 1741, Martha Rider; Mary, 1720; Mary, 1722. JOHN, son of William and Martha Rider Clark, below, m., 1766, Susa Harris, and had in Rochester, Hulda, 1767; Alden, 1770; and in New Salem, John, 1772; Israel, 1774; Susa, 1776; Hannah, 1778; Joshua, 1780; Joseph, 1782; Prudence, 1783; Susa, 1786. JONAS, in the text, m. 1767, not 1765. JOSEPH, son of John, of Rochester, above, m., 1720, Thankful Stevens, and had Isaac, 1721, m., Content Weeks; Katharine, 1723; Joseph, 1724; Thankful, 1727; Nathaniel, 1729; Willard, 1731, m., 1755, Jane Saunders. JOSEPH, son of above, m., 1750, Mary White, and had Joseph, 1751; Thankful, 1753; Lydia, 1755; Isaac, 1757; Lemuel, 1759. JOSHUA, New Salem and Wendell, Mass., son of John and Susa, above, m., 1800, Susanna Smith, and had Aurilla R., 1803; Parney, 1800; Endor, 1804; Florella, 1806; Collin, 1808; William S., 1812; Joshua G., 1820; Parney S., 1823. JOSIAH, 1st in the text, m., 1766. SETH, son of Thomas, of Harwich, below, had a son Seth, of Salisbury, who had a son Seth born in Salisbury, 1772, who m., 1797, Susanna Noyes. SETH, 2d in the text; son Samuel, born 1791, and son Seth, 1796. SETH, 3d in the text; 2d wife of son Seth Pope was Sarah L. Bartlett, d. Adeline m. Benjamin D. Finney, and d. Abby N. B. should be Abby A. B., who m. Nathaniel Cornish and Henry Morton. SIMEON, son of Cornelius in the text, m., 1755, Mercy Bumpus, and had Simeon, 1756. THOMAS, 1st in the text; son Andrew, born 1635; James, 1637; Susanna, 1641; William, 1639; Nathaniel, 1643. His 2d wife was wid. of Mordecai Nichols, of Boston. A part of his estate in Plymouth was called Saltash, a name borne by a district of Plymouth in England, where the author has found that the name Clark has prevailed during many generations. It seems fair to assume that Thomas Clark came from there. THOMAS, 2d in the text; d. Rebecca m. also Mordecai Ellis. He had an additional d. Rebecca, born 1698. THOMAS, Harwich, son of 1st Andrew, m. 1699, Patience (Hall) Rider, and had Thomas, 1700, m. Priscilla Paddock; Sarah, 1702, m. Edward Bangs; Robert, 1703, m. Lydia Dillingham; Mehitabel, 1704, m. Joshua Bangs; Susanna, 1705, m. Samuel Hallet; Hannah, 1706; Thankful, 1707, m. Thomas Hopkins; Seth, 1709, m. Huldah Doane; Isaac, 1710; Content, 1712; Elizabeth and Mary, twins, 1716. TRISTRAM, in the text, was born 1590. WILLARD, son of Joseph and Thankful, above, m., 1755, Jane Saunders, and had Huldah, 1757; Eunice, 1760; Willard, 1762. WILLIAM, 2d in the text, perhaps m. a 1st wife, Sarah Wolcott, in 1659, and had Thomas, 1660. WILLIAM, son of John Jr., of Rochester, above, m., 1741, Martha Rider, and had Ebenezer, 1742; John, 1743; Joshua, 1746; Joshua, 1747; Mary, 1751; Martha, 1753. WILLIAM, last in the text, m. 1767. ZOETH, 1st in the text; son John, born 1801. ZOETH, 2d in the text; son John Thomas m. Mary W. Fernside.

COADE, JAMES, in the text, m. 1762.

COBB, BENJAMIN, Barnstable, son of Eleazer, below, m., 1749, Anna Davis, and had Reliance, 1750; Eleazer, 1752; Benjamin, 1759, m. Persis Taylor; Joseph, 1763, m. Elizabeth Adams; Samuel, 1865. The son Benjamin m. in 1783, and had Enoch T. CHARLES, 2d in the text, born 1813; d. Welthea E. m. Nehemiah L. Savery. EBENEZER, 1st in the text; d. Mercy m. Cornelius Holmes; d. Sarah m. a Bartlett; and d. Mary, not Mercy, m. Silas West. EBENEZER, 2d in the text, m. 2d wife Martha, 1771. EBENEZER, son of Sylvanus, below, m. Lydia Churchill, of Middleboro, and had James, Ebenezer, Sylvanus, Bennie, Rebecca, Thankful and Lydia. EDWARD, son of Gershom and Mehitabel, below, m. 1778, Hannah Hallet, and had ten children. ELEAZER, Barnstable, son of Samuel in the text, m., 1724, Reliance Paine, and had Benjamin, 1725; Joseph, 1727; Reliance, 1728, m. Paul Crowell; Patience, 1731, m. Nathaniel Allen, of Barnstable. ELISHA, 1st in the text, had an additional son, Thomas. ELISHA, son of James and Elizabeth Hallet, below, m. Mary Harding. EPHRAIM, in the text, was son of John and Hannah (Lothrop) Cobb, below, and m. Margaret Gardner, 1730. FRANKLIN B., in the text; son Franklin B. m. for 2d wife Mary E. Chamberlin. GEORGE W., in the text, born in Vermont in 1812, the brother of Franklin B. above, and son of Binney and Azuba Cobb, had additional children, Ruth J., m. Lemuel B. Burgess; Emma and Alma. GEORGE, 1st in the text; insert "and had" before " George F " GERSHOM, Barnstable, son of 2d James in the text, m., 1703, Hannah Davis, and had John, 1704; Sarah, m. Nathaniel Bacon; Gershom, 1707; John, 1709; Hannah, 1711, m. David Childs; Thankful, 1714, m. David Dimmock; Anne, 1716, and Josiah, twin, 1716; Edward, 1718; Mary, 1721, m. Isaac Gorham and James Churchill. GERSHOM, son of above, m., 1732, Sarah Baxter, and had Gershom, who m., 1752, Mehitabel, d. of Job Davis, and had Edward, 1752, Gershom and Josiah. HENRY, 1st in the text; d. Mary, m., 1657, Jonathan Dunham; d. Patience, m. a 2d husband, William Crocker; d. Sarah, m., 1686, Samuel Chipman. HENRY, 2d in the text, removed to Stonington, and there had Ebenezer, 1705; Mary; Henry, 1710, who m. 1st a d. of Oliver Babcock, and 2d Prudence Champlin; and Hallet, 1719, who m. Bridget Champlin. JAMES, 2d in the text; d. Mary m. Caleb Williamson; Sarah m. Benjamin Hinckley; Patience m. James Coleman; Hannah m. Joseph Davis. JAMES, son of above, m., 1695, Elizabeth Hallet, and had James, 1698; Sylvanus, 1700, m., 1728, Mercy Baker; Elisha, 1702, m. Mary Harding; Jesse, 1704, m., 1734, Thankful Baker; Seth, 1707; Ebenezer, 1709; Jude, 1711; Nathan, 1713, m. Bethiah Harding. JAMES, son of above, m., 1724, Hannah Rich, of Truro, and had Elizabeth, 1726; Lois, 1729; Isaac, 1731; Ezekiel, 1734; Hannah, 1737; Dinah, 1740; Deliverance, 1742. JAMES, 3d in the text; son James m. Melatiah Holmes. JESSE, son of James and Elizabeth Hallet, above, m., 1734, Thankful Baker. JOB, 2d in the text; son Job born 1780; d. Patience, 1787. JOB, 3d in the text, moved to "Baltimore," not "Bateman." JOHN, 1st in the text, had an additional child, John, 1677. He married 2d, 1676, Jane Woodward, of Taunton. JOHN, Barnstable, son of 2d James in the text, m., 1707, Hannah Lothrop, and had Ephraim, 1708, m. Margaret Gardner, of Yarmouth; John, 1711; John, 1719. JONATHAN, Barnstable, son of Samuel in the text, m., 1715, Sarah Hopkins, of Harwich, and had Benjamin, 1726, m. Bethiah Homer; Samuel, 1728; Elkanah, 1731; Eleazer, 1734, m. Keziah, d. of Eleazer Crosby; Elizabeth, 1738, m.

a Crosby; and Jonathan. JONATHAN, son of above, m. Mary Clark, and had Elijah, Scotto, 1741; Isaac, 1745; John, Seth, Mary, Sally, Hannah, Betsey and Elkanah. JONATHAN, Barnstable, in the text, had additional child, Gershom, 1695. JONATHAN, Portland, son of above, by wife Betty had Lydia, 1720; Ebenezer, 1722; Mary, 1723; Deborah, 1725. LEMUEL, in the text; son John Kemptom was born 1786. MATTHEW, Barnstable, son of Thomas, below, m., 1751, Mary Garret, and had Matthew, of Portland, Daniel and others. NATHAN, in the text, was of Plympton; his d. Deborah m. Edward Cole, and he had an additional child, Ebenezer. NATHANIEL, Barnstable, son of Thomas, below, m., 1738, Susanna Bacon, and had Thomas, 1739; Oris, 1741; Samuel, 1744; Susanna, 1747; Nathaniel, 1749; Sarah, 1751. SAMUEL, in the text; d. Sarah m. Benjamin Bearse; Elizabeth m. Ebenezer Bearse; d. Experience m. Jasher Taylor; son Thomas m. Rachel Stone, of Sudbury; and son Samuel m. Sarah Chase and Hannah Cole. STEVENS, Kingston, in the text; d. Fanny m. John Fearo. SYLVANUS, son of James and Elizabeth (Hallet) Cobb, above, m., 1728, Mercy Baker, and had Mercy, 1729, m. James Churchill; Ebenezer, 1731, m. Lydia Churchill. THOMAS, Barnstable, son of Samuel in the text, m., 1710, Rachel Stone, of Sudbury, and had Abigail, 1711, m. Nathaniel Sturgis; Nathaniel, 1713; Elizabeth, 1715, m. Jonathan Lewis; Samuel, 1717: Matthew, 1719; David, 1721, m. Thankful Hinckley; Henry, 1724, m. Bethiah Hinckley; Thomas, 1726; Ebenezer, 1726, twin, m. Mary Smith ; Eunice, 1729; and Mary.

COLE, EPHRAIM, in the text, was son of 2d James. HEZEKIAH, son of James, below, born 1743, m., 1765,Elizabeth, d. of Barnabas Shurtleff, and had Hezekiah, 1777; Deborah, 1765; Betsey Shurtleff, 1766 ; James, 1768; Zilpha, 1770. HEZEKIAH, Carver, son of above, m., 1802, Jane, d. of Calvin Bradford, and had Elizabeth, 1803; Jane Bradford, 1804; James, 1807; Zilpha, 1809; Hezekiah, 1811; Bradford, 1813; Hezekiah and Jane again, twins, 1815; Harrison G., 1817; Lucy Fuller, 1819; Mary Morton, 1822. He married 2d, 1826, Lucy Prince, wid. of Frederick Cobb and d. of Perez Bradford, and had Margaret Jackson, 1826; Marcia, 1828; Laura Ann, 1830; the son, Harrison G., Carver, m., 1840, Lucy, d. of Levi Chase. EPHRAIM, in the text, was son of 2d James. HUGH, 1st in the text; son Hugh, m., 1681, Deborah Buckland. HUGH, 2d in the text, m. 2d Mary (Shelley) (Harlow) Morton, wid. of Samuel Harlow and Ephraim Morton, and had John and others. JAMES, 2d in the text; son John m. Patience Barber. He had additional children, Hannah, m. Elisha Bradford, and Ephraim. JAMES, son of 1st Ephraim in the text, had Hezekiah, 1743. JOB m. Rebecca Collier, 1634. He had brothers John and Daniel and sister Rebecca, all probably brothers and sisters of the 1st James in the text. JOSHUA, probably son of 2d John in the text, m. Elizabeth Lucas, and had Alfred, m. Fanny Bartlett; Azel, m. Jane Barrows; John Avery and Abigail. His son Alfred had Caleb Harvey; Alfred Bartlett, m. Lucetta Hatfield; Frances Olivia, m. George Freeman; John Avery, m. Ella Joslyn; Robert William, m. Ella Tappan; Louisa Frederika, m. Henry Ellis; Eliza Simmons, m. George H. Dunham ; Abby Forest, m. Herbert Robbins; and Harriet Newell, unmarried.

COLLIER, WILLIAM, a merchant from London, came in 1633, and settled in Duxbury. He had a d. Sarah, m. Love Brewster, and 2d, a Parks ; Rebecca, m.

Job Cole ; Mary, m. Thomas Prence ; and Elizabeth, m. Constant Southworth.

COLLINGWOOD, THOMAS, in the text, m. Martha A. Bates. WILLIAM, in the text, was born in England, 1780.

COLLINS, GAMALIEL, 2d in the text; son James T. born 1819. GEORGE M., in the text; 3d wife was Sarah R. Terry. JAMES, 1st in the text; son Samuel Avery m. Esther, d. of Samuel Churchill.

CONNELL, JEREMIAH, in the text, m. Elizabeth Engles, 1775.

CONNETT, JOHN, in the text, was m. 1814.

COOK, CALEB, in the text; son Caleb m. Abigail Howland, 1723. FRANCIS, in the text, was born in Yorkshire, 1577. JACOB, 1st in the text, had an additional child Sarah, who m. Robert Bartlett. JACOB, 2d in the text; son John m. Phebe Crossman 1730, and not Hannah Morton. JOHN, 2d in the text, m. 2d Hannah Morton.

COOMBS, JOHN, in the text; son Francis, of Middleboro, by wife Mary had a d., who m. Samuel Barnes.

COOPER, CALVIN, son of 2d Richard in the text, m., 1812, Sally or Sarah, d. of Eleazer Morton, and had Sally Winslow, 1813, and Betsey Taylor, 1818; Sarah, wid. of Calvin, m., 1822, Joseph Atkins. RICHARD, 2d in the text, had additional children, George, 1773 ; Lucia, 1782; Nancy, 1785 ; Calvin, 1788. The son John was born 1786, and d. Priscilla, 1767.

CORNISH, GEORGE, in the text; d. Hannah did not marry Phineas Savery. THOMAS, 1st in the text, m. his 2d wife 1756. THOMAS, 2d in the text; d. Content born 1799.

CORPSE, ABNER, in the text, should be "Corpe," not "Corpse."

COTTON, JOHN, 1st in the text; his wid. m. Richard Mather; his d. Elizabeth m. 1655; d. Mary should be Maria. JOHN, 2d in the text; Bray should be Brian; d. Elizabeth born 1663; additional children, Sarah, 1665; son Rowland, m. Elizabeth, wid. of Rev. John Dennison; d. Maria, m. Wymond Bradbury; d. Sarah, m. William Bradbury; son Theophilus, m. Elizabeth Dimond, and Mary, wid. of Dr. Gedney, of Salem. JOHN, 3d in the text, m., 1747, Hannah, d. of Josiah Sturtevant; d. Mary m. J. Jennings; d. Sophia did not marry Seth Parker; d. Elizabeth m. Lot Haskell. JOHN WINSLOW, in the text, m., 1825, Mary D. Arndt, and had John Rossiter, 1826 ; Elizabeth, m. C. R. Tyler; Priscilla Jackson, Mary Gordon and Charles Arndt. JOHN, the last John in the text, was the son of Theophilus, and had additional children, Theophilus, Thomas, John and Hannah. JOHN, son of 2d Josiah in text, m., 1815, Susan Buckminster, and had, 1816, Susan Buckminster, m. Talbot Bullard, of Indianapolis ; John Thomas, 1819, m. Sarah A. Fitzhugh, of West Virginia ; Josiah Dexter, 1822, m. Ann Stuce; Hannah Maria, 1825, m. H. B. Shipmàn, Charles Fiske and David Barnes m. Mary C. Slocumb, of Marietta, Ohio. JOHN ROSSITER, son of John Winslow in the text, m. Caroline A. Redfern, of Fulton City, Ill., and lives in Chicago. JOSIAH, 3d in the text; m. Temperance, wid. of Rufus Robbins, and d. of John Otis. ROSSITER, in the text; son Charles m., 1817, Mary Northam. ROWLAND EDWIN, in the text; m., 1828, Susan Augusta, d. of Daniel Watson, and had Daniel Watson, 1829. He m. 2d, 1831, Louisa Maria, d. of Emery Wells Sudlar, and had Rowland Edwin, Louisa, Emery Wells Sudlar, 1836, and Thomas E. Sudlar,

1838. He m., 3d, Hannah Hammond, and had Hannah, Sophia, Sarah Louisa, m. Wallace T. Miller, and Augusta Delfthaven. He m., 4th, wid. Sarah H. (Evans) Lovell, of Leominster. THEOPHILUS, in the text; strike out d. Polly and her marriage and d. Eliza and her marriage; son William Crow was born 1751; Josiah, 1753; and Edward, 1759. THOMAS E. SUDLAR, son of Rowland Edwin, m., 1860, Maria Antoinette, d. of Simeon Butterfield, of Chelsea, Mass., and had Edwin Simeon, 1861. WARD, son of 3d John in the text, m., 1800, Rebecca, d. of Thomas Jackson, and had John Thomas, 1801; Mary Atwood, 1802; Ward Mather, 1804; Lydia Jackson, 1806, m. Josiah Pope; Sally May, 1808, m. Charles Robinson; Hannah Sophia Phillips, 1810, m. Daniel S. Whitney. WARD MATHER, son of above, m., 1828, Elizabeth M. Lamson, and had Charles Ward, 1829, m. Ellen M. Graham, of Orange, Mass; Lydia Jackson, 1833, m. George T. Robbins, of Plymouth, and George C. Bixford; John Atwood, 1835, m. Lydia M. Cowdry; Thomas Jackson, 1847, m. Flora A. Colvin.

COVINGTON, THOMAS, 1st in the text; d. Eleanor born 1792; d. Eunice born 1777.

COWEN, ROBERT, in the text, was born in 1800.

COX, ELIAS, in the text; son Elias born 1798; son James, 1803; he m., 2d, Patience, d. of Ansel, not Isaac, Churchill. There was an Elias, son of Agnes, baptized in 2d Church, Boston, April 6, 1707, and had a brother Andrew, baptized February 13, 1714–15.

CRANDON; at the top of page 74, "Chandon" should be "Crandon." BENJAMIN, 1st in the text; d. Jane born 1802. EDWIN SANFORD, son of John Howland in the text, m., 1886, Cara Warren Howard, and had Lowell Drew, 1887; Evelyn Howland, 1889, and Emily, 1892. JOHN, in the text, first settled in Boston, not Dartmouth, and m. Jane Baast, not Bass. JOHN HOWLAND, in the text; d. Emma Agnes m. George E. Fay, and had Ruth Crandon, and d. Helen m. D. Frank Lord.

CROCKER, DAVID, of Barnstable, m., 1825, Lydia P., d. of David Turner, of Plymouth.

CROMBIE, WILLIAM, 1st in the text, came to Plymouth 1760, not 1762; he m. 2d in 1761.

CROSBY, THOMAS, m., 1759, Elizabeth Beal.

CROSWELL, ANDREW, 1st in the text, m. Rebecca, d. of Elisha Holmes. ANDREW, 2d in the text; 2d wife was d. of Samuel Palmer, and he had an additional child, Samuel Palmer. ANDREW, 3d in the text, m. Susan, d. of John Church of Farmington, and had Andrew, Samuel, Thomas, Emily and Susan C., who m., 1831, Admiral Henry Knox Thatcher. JOSEPH, in the text, was son of Rev. Andrew, of Boston, and by his wife Jerusha, d. of Joseph Bartlett, he had a son and daughter, unmarried. THOMAS came from Staffordshire about 1654, and settled in Charlestown, and m. Priscilla Upham; his son Caleb had Andrew and Joseph.

CROWELL, PAUL, of Sandwich, m., 1803, Lydia Ellis.

CUSHING, DANIEL, son of 1st Daniel in the text, m., 1680, Elizabeth, d. of John Thaxter, and had Daniel, 1681; Elisha, 1682; Lydia, 1684; Daniel, 1686; Elizabeth, 1688; Sarah, Ruth, Deborah, 1694; Abigail, 1700; Moses, 1704; EZRA, in the text, m. Betsey, d. of Timothy Allen, and had Sarah, m. Cornelius B.

Bradford, and Frederick. JEREMIAH, in the text; d. Hannah m. John, not Samuel, Barker. MATHEW, 1st in the text, was son of Peter, of Hingham, Eng., who m. 1585, Susan Hawes. MATHEW m. 1613. PETER was son of Thomas, of Hardingham, who was son of John, who was son of William, the son of Thomas, who lived in 1450. SETH, Plympton, son of Theophilus, below, m. 1729, Lydia Fearing, and had Mary, Seth, 1732; Ezekiel, 1734; Margaret, 1736; Deborah, 1738. THEOPHILUS, son of 1st Daniel in the text, m., 1689, Mary, d. of John Thaxter, and had Nehemiah, 1690; Mary, 1691; Adam, 1693; David, 1694; Abel, 1696; Rachel, 1698; Mary, 1701; Theophilus, 1703; Seth, 1705.

CUSHMAN, BENJAMIN, son of 2d Thomas in the text, m., 1712, Sarah Eaton, and had Jabez, 1713; Caleb, 1715; Solomon, 1717; Jerusha, 1719; Benjamin, 1722; Sarah, 1725; Abigail, 1727; Thomas, 1730; Jerusha, 1732; Huldah, 1735; he m., 2d, 1738–9, wid. Sarah Bell. ELKANAH, 6th in the text, was son of 4th Elkanah; his son Alexander m. Jane Ramsey of Edinboro. JOSEPH, 4th in the text; d. Hannah m. Churchill Thomas. MOSES, son of Eleazer in the text, m. Mary, d. of Eleazer Jackson, and had ten children. THOMAS, Plympton, son of Benjamin above, m. Anna, d. of Jacob Chipman, of Halifax, Mass., and had Job, 1753; Jerusha, 1755; Samuel, 1756; Thomas, 1758; Zachariah, 1761; Elizabeth, twin, 1761; Zebedee, 1763; Sarah, 1765; Lydia, 1767; Chipman, 1769; Polly, 1771; Bartholomew, 1776. THOMAS, New Gloucester, and Alfred, Maine, son of above, m., 1783, Ruth Ring, and had Asa, 1784; Israel, 1875.

DANFORTH, ALLEN, born 1796.

DAVIE, CURTIS, in the text, had Charles Nelson, not Nelson, and Nathaniel Curtis, not Nathaniel, EBENEZER, 1st in the text; d. Lydia born 1801; son Nathaniel Curtis, 1820; d. Deborah Curtis, 1810; son George, 1813; son John, 1809. ISAAC, 1st in the text; son Isaac Lewis born 1824. JOSEPH, in the text; d. Matilda born 1809, and d. Betsey F. born 1806. ROBERT, 3d in the text, m. 2d, 1828. SOLOMON, 1st in the text, m., 1st, 1812, Esther LeBaron. WILLIAM, 1st in the text; son Ebenezer born 1775; Isaac, 1786. WILLIAM, son of 1st William in the text, m., 1793, Experience Stetson, and had Deborah, m. a Dearborn; Ellen, m. a Sprague, and two d., both of whom married Whitmores.

DAVIS, CHARLES GIDEON, in the text; d. Joanna born 1855. JOHN, 2d in the text; d. Sarah born 1794. JOSEPH in the text; d. Mary Ann m. Adoniram J. Holmes, NATHANIEL MORTON, in the text; d. Elizabeth Bliss m. Henry G. Andrews. THOMAS, 1st in the text, when he removed to North Carolina, settled at Black Walnut Point, Bertie County. His son Robert lived in Tyrell County, and had Richard and Zephaniah. His son John had Thomas, John, Enoch, Benjamin, Anna, Rosa, Rebecca and Zilpha, and removed to Tennessee. THOMAS had a second wife, Mary, who was the mother of some of his children. WENDELL, 1st in the text, m. Caroline Williams Smith in 1802, and had Wendell B., 1803; Samuel, 1808; Thomas, 1809, besides those children mentioned in the text. WILLIAM, 2d in the text; d. Rebecca was Rebecca Morton. WILLIAM, Boston, who died 1676, and whose mother was Elizabeth, m. Sarah, d. of Zechariah Simmes, and had Thomas, Benjamin, William, John, Elizabeth, Maria, Rebecca, Huldah, Ruth, Margaret and Hannah. WILLIAM THOMAS, in the text; d. Catherine should be Katharine.

DEAN, AVERY, Plympton, m., 1817, Lydia Anderson Richmond.

DELANO, BENJAMIN FRANKLIN, in the text; d. Charlotte born 1845. BEN-JAMIN, 4th in the text; d. Lucy m. George Waterman. BENONI, Duxbury, son of Thomas, had Beriah, Lemuel, Hannah, m. a Harlow; Rebecca, m. Amasa Turner. BERIAH, in the text, was son of Benoni above. EDWARD HARTT, in the text, was m. in 1843, and had an additional child, William Edwards; his 2d wife was Avoline S. Frost, m. 1858. LEMUEL, in the text; son Icha-bod should be Beriah. PHILLIP, 1st in the text; d. Rebecca m., 1686, John Churchill and son Jonathan died at Acushnet, 1720, at age of seventy-two. THOMAS, in the text; son Josiah should be Joseph. WILLIAM HARTT, in the text; d. Emma should be Emma Louisa.

DEXTER, CHARLES, in the text, had additional child, Hannah, m. Barnabas Hiller, of Rochester. JOHN, son of above, m. Mary Soule, d. of Moores Rogers of Rochester, and had Moores Rogers, m. Mary Ann, d. of James Purrington, and Lizzie, m. Orzamus Winston, and Mary Jane, m. H. F. Colson.

DILLARD, BENJAMIN in the text; d. Betsey Courtney m. Isaac Kempton, Elisha H. Everett, Edward Winslow Bradford and Barnabas Dunham.

DIMAN, THOMAS, 3d in the text; d. Mary Harlow m. Job E. Luscomb, not John E.

DIXON, LYMAN, son of Timothy, below, m., 1864, Deborah Thomas, d. of John Harlow, and had Martha J., 1865. TIMOTHY, from Greenfield, m. Eme-line Hunt, and had Timothy, m. Annie Smith; Comfort, m. Mary Jane Valler; Walter, m. Deborah Sampson; Edwin, m. Nellie Waterson; Graham, m. Lydia J. Blanchard; Alanson, unmarried; Lyman, m. Deborah Harlow; Addie, m. Kimball Bartlett; Jane, m. Joseph Doten, and Elizabeth, m. George Shaw.

DOGGETT, SAMUEL, son of 1st Samuel in the text, born 1683, m., 1710, Bethiah Waterman, and had Amos, 1710; Silpha, 1714; Sarah, 1715; Noah, m. Marcy Clark, and Mary Allyne, and perhaps Samuel.

DOTY AND DOTEN, ELISHA, 1st in the text, m. Hannah Harlow, 1686. ELISHA, 2d in the text, m., 1809, Huldah Lamerce, and had Amasa; he m. 2d, 1819, Jane Warren. ISAAC, 2d in the text; son Thomas m. Jerusha Howes. ISAAC, m., 1764, Deborah Rider. JABEZ, in the text; d. Hannah born 1786. JACOB, m., 1758, Sarah Cobb of Kingston. JAMES, son of 2d Stephen in the text, m. Sarah Andrews, of Boston, and had Susan, m. Briggs Bennett. JAMES ROBBINS, m., 1811, Betsey Robbins. JOHN, 1st in the text, m. 1667. JOHN, 3d in the text; d. Sarah born 1796; d. Patience, 1797; d. Desire, 1799. JOHN, 4th in the text, m. Mary, d. of Isaac Wright. JOSEPH, 4th in the text, was son of 2d Stephen. JOSEPH, m., 1765, Deborah Rider. LEMUEL, 1st in the text; d. Betsey, without the Warren. NATHANIEL, 1st in the text; son Prince born 1780. NATHANIEL, 3d in the text; son Nathaniel born 1808. NATHANIEL, 4th in the text; d. Ezra J., should be Emma J. RICHARD, son of 2d Joseph in the text, m., 1814, Rosanna Hammond of Mid-dleboro. STEPHEN, 1st in the text, had additional children, James and Lucy. STEPHEN, 2d in the text, m. Abigail, wid. of Thomas Clark. STEPHEN, 4th in the text, m. Hannah, d. of Isaac Wright, of Plympton; d. Betsey Bartlett m. also Timothy Allen; he had another child, Marcia, m. John Finney, and another, Rebecca Olney, m. Nathaniel C. King. THOMAS, m., 1759, Abigail

Leach, of Boston. WILLIAM, 1st in the text, m. 1776; his d. Cynthia, born 1788, m. Thomas Fish and Elijah Sherman.

DOUGLASS, JOHN, 1st in the text, m., 1761, Mercy Holmes. JOHN, 2d in the text, m. Mary Southworth; son Joshua born 1794; son Ephraim, 1778. JOSHUA, in the text; son Nathan should be Nathan K.; son Warren is Warren S., and Martin born 1836, not 1828.

DREW, ABBET, in the text, m. Elizabeth, d. of Nathan Churchill; son Frances Abbet should be Francis Abbet. BENJAMIN, 1st in the text, m. Elizabeth Doggett, 1764. BENJAMIN, 3d in the text; strike out the comma between Helen and Eudora, making them one name. DAVID, 1st in the text; son Atwood born 1780. DAVID, 2d in the text; son Ellis, born 1805, m. 1828; son David born 1809; d. Lucinda born 1807; d. Sarah born 1803, and he had additional child, Solomon, 1813. GEORGE, 1st in the text; d. Fanny Lee m., 2d, John Sidney Jones, of Philadelphia, and son John Glover m. Phebe Mundy, of Fall River. JOSIAH, 2d in the text; he had also d. Mary, 1840. NATHANIEL, in the text; he had also Isabel, 1819, m. Cornelius A. Bartlett. SAMUEL, 4th in the text; his son Consider m. Jean Ellis. STEPHEN D., in the text; his d. Adelia m. Thaxter F. Burgess. STEPHEN CURTIS, in the text, had also Charles Henry, 1882. WILLIAM RIDER, in the text as corrected, son of Atwood, m., 1849, Susan, d. of Peter Holmes, and had William Brooks, 1850; Mary, 1852; William Holmes, 1855, m. Mary Caroline Hathaway; Annie, 1855, twin to William Holmes; Susan H., 1856, m. Dr. John F. Gaylord; and Emily Darling, 1858; he m. 2d, 1873, Emily, sister of his first wife. WILLIAM T., son of 1st William in the text, m., 1832, Lucinda, d. of David Drew, and had Lucinda T., 1834.

DUCY, WILLIAM, in the text, m. 1767.

DUNBAR, JOHN DANFORTH, in the text, was son of Elijah and Sarah (Hunt) Dunbar.

DUNHAM, ABRAHAM, 1st in the text; son Isaac Thomas m. Angeline, d. of Truman Bartlett. AMOS, in the text; strike out "m. Abigail Faunce," after "Amos, 1741"; add at the end of the sentence, "he m., 3d, Abigail Faunce." BARNABAS, 3d in the text; his 4th wife was Betsey Courtney, wid. of Isaac Kempton, Elisha H. Everett and Edward Winslow Bradford, and d. of Benjamin Dillard. CALVIN, of Carver, m., 1803, Hannah Harlow. CORNELIUS, 1st in the text, had also a d. Ruth. DANIEL, in the text, by a wife Hannah, had Hannah, 1670, m. Joseph Alden, and Mehitabel. DANIEL, son of Jonathan in the text, by wife Rebecca, had Jacob, Daniel, Zephaniah, Silas, Eleazar, Samuel, Matilda, Rebecca, Dinah, Sarah, Persis, Mary. DANIEL, son of Joseph, in the text, by wife Sarah, had Daniel, 1712; John, 1715; Sarah, 1718; Esther, 1720; Joseph, 1723; Benjamin, 1730; Mercy, 1727; Abigail, 1728; DANIEL, son of above, m., 1737, Abigail Hart, and had Daniel, 1738; John, 1740; Robert, 1742; Abigail, 1744; Benjamin, Sarah, Benajah, Esther, Martha, Almy, Joseph, Elizabeth, Patience; he m., 2d, 1776, Amy Murphy. DANIEL, son of above, m., 1759, Elizabeth Dunham, and had Elizabeth, 1761; Sarah, 1762; Daniel, 1764; Abigail, 1766; Jesse, 1768; Abigail, 1772. DANIEL, son of above, changed his name to Denham; he m., 1789, Alice Gladding, and had Jonathan, 1791; Daniel Chase, 1798; Alice, 1800. DANIEL CHASE

DENHAM, son of above, m., 1824, Sarah, d. of William Shearman, and had Charlotte W. S., 1825, m. G. E. Cranston; Sarah D. S., 1828, m. J. H. Atkinson; Daniel C., 1835; John D., 1837; Wm. S., 1843; Henry J., 1847, m. Ella Vose. DANIEL C., son of above, m., 1858, Cynthia R. Tuell, and had Lizzie D , 1866, m. Howard G. Ward. ELEAZER, 1st in the text; his wife Bathsheba was perhaps d. of Jonathan Pratt. ELEAZER, 2d in the text, m. Meriam, d. of Thomas Phillips. ELIJAH in the text; his d. Deborah m. Silas Hathaway and John Atwood; d. Eunice Thomas m. Jabez Swift; d. Elizabeth m. Edward Burt; son Benjamin m. Nancy Dunham. GEORGE, 2d in the text, m. 1778; son George m. 1806. JOHN, 1st in the text, was born, 1589; son John born 1636; son Thomas m. Sarah Bumpus; son Jonathan m., 1655, Mary, d. of Phillip Delano, and, 1657, Mary, d. of Henry Cobb. JOHN, 3d in the text; his wife Mary was d. of Rev. John Smith. His d. Desire, and d. Mercy, m. Samuel Stetson, and son Elisha m. Temperance Stewart. JONATHAN, in the text, had by 2d wife Daniel, Jonathan, Eleazer, Gershom, Samuel and Hannah. JOSEPH in the text; son Eleazar born 1662; son Daniel born 1688; LUCAS, in the text, was son of 2d, not 1st George, and m. Matilda Lovell, not Eldridge. LYSANDER, in the text; the 2d wife of son was Selissa (not Salissa) P. Meloon (not Melvin). NATHANIEL, 1st in the text, m. Anne Peterson, of Duxbury. SAMUEL, 4th in the text; son Chandler m. Judith, d. of Benjamin Pierce. SILAS m., 1764, Bethiah Bartlett. SILAS, son of 2d Sylvanus in the text, m. Mary Tilson, and had Patience, 1774, m. Nathaniel Rider of Middleboro; Elizabeth, 1777, m. John Fuller; Lucy Tilson, 1780, m. Joshua Bartlett; Silas, 1783; Tilson, 1786; Ira, 1789; Sally Tilson, 1792; Rebecca, 1795, m. Asa Cook of Kingston; Marcy, 1799, m. Benjamin Dunham. SILAS, son of above, m , 1805, Experience (Randall) Foster, wid. of David Foster, and had Silas, 1807; Mary Tilson, 1809; Charles Wheeler, 1811; Eliza, 1813. TILSON, brother of above, m., 1809, Anna Jenny Blankinship, of Rochester, and had Caroline Crocker, 1810, m. Cephas W. Chapman; Tilson Bourne, 1813, m. Rachel Gilbert Leach; James Ruggles, 1816, m. Roxanna W. Brown, of Newport; Ruth Delano, 1819, m. George W. Bird, of New Bedford; Joanna Blankinship, 1822; Maria Richmond, 1824, m. Francis Loring Parker; William Harris, 1837, m. Mary Fuller; Frederick Harper Delano, 1830. SYLVANUS, 2d in the text; d. Susanna m. Arthur Cobb; d. Molly m. John Morton; son Asa m. Lydia Cobb, and settled in Norway, Me.; son Eleazer m. Jane Bryant, of Plympton. WILLIAM, last in the text, m. Mercy, not Nancy.

DURFEY, PELEG, in the text, was son of Robert, of Tiverton, and grandson of Thomas. RICHARD, 1st in the text, was son of Benjamin and grandson of Thomas.

DYER, CHARLES, 2d in the text; son Charles born 1774. JOHN, 2d in the text; strike out "m. Hannah Morton."

EAMES, ANTHONY, 2d in the text, was son of Mark, and he m. Mercy, d. of John Sampson. MARK, of Marshfield, m. October 11, 1769, Priscilla, d. of Benjamin Howland, of Pembroke.

EATON, BENJAMIN, 2d in the text; his d. Hannah m. Benjamin Bryant; d. Sarah m. a Soule; and d. Elizabeth m. Cornelius Sturtevant. DAVID, in the text; d. Eunice, m. a Cook.

EDDY, DARIUS, in the text; son John Lodge, m. Effa, d. of Ellis Holmes. JOHN, 2d in the text, was of Taunton. LEWIS, in the text, m. Sarah W. Hersey. SAMUEL, Middleboro, m., 1783, Anna Morton, of Plymouth.

EDES, OLIVER, in the text, was born 1815.

EDWARDS, JOHN, 2d in the text, had Mary E., 1795, m. William Morey. Lydia E., 1777, m. John Sylvester.

ELLIOTT, DANIEL ROBERT, in the text; d. Jane A. was born 1805.

ELLIS, BARTLETT, in the text; strike out " of West Bridgewater " after "Ryder." GEORGE, FRANCIS, in the text; strike out "Louisa m. Edward G. Ditmar," and insert " Edward Gardner m. Louisa Ditmar"; d. Helen Maria m. Silas W. Dean, and add another child, Anne Warren. MATTHIAS, in the text, m. Mary Burgess; son Malachi m. Jane Blackwell. NATHANIEL B., in the text, had a d. Esther, m. Ichabod Carven; son Charles, m. Hannah, d. of Timothy Ellis, and d. Emma F., m. Charles D. Dunbar.

EWER, THOMAS, in the text, m. 1749, and had Thomas, 1750; Eleazar, 1752, m. Abigail Lothrop; Ansel, 1753; Seth, 1755; Lydia, 1758; Seth, 1760.

FALLOWELL, GABRIEL, had a d. Ann, m. Thomas Pope.

FARMER, JAMES, son of 1st Thomas in the text, was born 1780 and m., 1804, Elizabeth Webb, and had James Lawrence, 1811; William Burrows, 1816. JAMES LAWRENCE, son of above, m., 1843, Sarah Bridge Blanchard, of Marblehead, and had Anna Elizabeth, 1850, m. George P. Bradley, Surgeon U. S. Navy, and Eleanor Horton, 1854.

FAUNCE, CALEB, in the text; d. Jane born 1804. ELIJAH, in the text; strike out "twin of Lydia," and insert " and Mary twins." JOHN, 2d in the text, was son of 1st Thomas; son John m., 1733, Ruth Sampson, and had Mary, 1734, m. Amos Curtis, of Scituate. JOHN, 3d in the text, was son of 1st Joseph. PELEG, 1st in the text; d. Hannah born 1784; son Peleg, 1798. SOLOMON, 1st in the text; son Solomon born 1809, and son Lemuel Bradford, 1811. STEPHEN, 1st in the text; son William Shurtleff m. Salina F., d. of Edward Doten. THOMAS, 4th in the text; son Thomas m. 1769. THOMAS, 5th in the text, m. Sally Everson, 1816.

FINNEY, ALBERT, in the text; son Adelbert Thomas, m. a 1st wife, Pella T. Whitman, of St. Louis. BENJAMIN D., son of 1st Caleb in the text, m. Mary Ann Churchill and had Benjamin, m. Ruth Peterson; Lydia Covington, m. George Shurtleff; Caleb Morton; Mary Ann, m. Daniel W. Peterson; Sally, m. Seth Finney; Harvey and William Howland. He m., 2d, Adaline, d. of Seth Clark, and had Seth Clark, Caleb and Abbot Gardner. CLARK, 1st in the text; son Everett m. Susan W., d. of Henry Howland. CLARK, 2d in the text; son Clark, born 1845, m. Antoinette C. Bachelder, 1870, and son Elkanah, born 1850, m., 1874, Jennie S., d. of Chandler W. Doten, and d. Lucy M., born 1846, m. 1866, William S. Hadaway. DANIEL, in the text; son Benjamin Cooper born 1809; d. Sally C. born 1795; d. Lydia born 1806; d. Olive born 1799. ELKANAH, 1st in the text; son Elkanah born 1803; son Henry, 1807; d. Marcia, 1814. ELKANAH C., in the text; strike out children "Elkanah and Clarinda" and insert "Clara B., 1841, " m. John Franklin Churchill; Elizabeth Ann, 1843, m. Chandler Holmes, and Elkanah C., m. Florian Weston, of Duxbury. EPHRAIM, 2d in the text; strike out children " Caleb, Solomon and

Sylvanus." EzRA, 1st in the text; son Seth born 1780. He m. 2d in 1808. GEORGE, 1st in the text; son Ezra born 1812. JOHN, 2d in the text, m. Mary, d. of Joseph Rogers. JOSEPH, 1st in the text; d. Alice m. a Hamblin. He m., 2d, Esther West, and had Joseph; Pelatiah, m. Mercy Washburn; Mercy and Patience. JOSIAH, 1st in the text, was son of 1st John, not 1st Robert. It has been thought by some that his d. Elizabeth m. Daniel Bradford, and that Elizabeth, d. of John Finney, m. William Bradford. Aside from family tradition the marriages as stated in the text are confirmed by a deed recorded in the Plymouth Registry, Book 22, page 70, under date of June 6, 1727, in which William Bradford and wife Elizabeth, Samuel Marshal and wife Priscilla, Jonathan Barnes, Jr. and wife Phebe, quit claim to their brothers, Josiah and John Finney, all their interest in the real estate of their honored father, Josiah Finney. LEAVITT, in the text; add child Henry W., m. Mary Lemoine, d. of John H. Harlow; and son Leavitt Weston, m., 1861, Rebecca D., d. of William A. Robbins, of Kingston. LEWIS, in the text; son Lewis m. 1833; son Pelham born 1811; son Harrison born 1814. SETH, 1st in the text; son Elkanah C. born 1804. SYLVANUS, son of 3d John in the text, m. Mary Morton and had Caleb, Solomon and Sylvanus. WILLIAM, in the text; son William born 1807; son Albert born 1811; son Leavitt, 1813.

FISH, NATHAN, in the text, m. Deborah Barrows, not Barnes.

FISHER, LOWELL, from Francestown, N. H., m. Betsey Wilkins, of Deering, and moved to Boston. He had Caroline E., 1814, m. Ichabod P. Bagnell; Elizabeth, 1816, m. Andrew Simmons, of Newbury, N. H.; Hosea, 1818; Lyman, 1820, m. Eliza Buzzell, of Maine; Lucy, 1822, m. Abigail Drew; Mary, 1826, m. William Swift; Rhoda, 1828.

FORD, WILLIAM, in the text; son William, m. Sarah Dingley; son Michael, m. Bethiah Hatch, and had a son Thomas, who m. Ruth, d. of Josiah Bradish.

FOSTER, JOHN, 1st in the text; son Chillingworth born 1680; add child of 1st wife, a d. Deborah. He m., 2d, Sarah, wid. of John Thomas. JOHN, 2d in the text; d. Hannah m. George, not William Partridge; son Samuel m. Margaret Tilden; son Thomas m. Lois Fuller. RICHARD, in the text; add child Benjamin, born 1655. THOMAS, 1st in the text; son Thomas m. Sarah, d. of Robert Parker, of Cambridge; son Hopestill m. Elizabeth, wid. of Thomas Whittemore, and d. of Thomas Pierce, of Woburn; son Joseph m. Alice Gorton, of Roxbury; add d. Elizabeth, m. James Frost, of Billerica.

FOUNTAIN, BARNABAS, in the text; put 1756 not 1755.

FULGHAM, JOSEPH, in the text, was from Newport, Isle of Wight, England.

FULLER, AMASA, of Attleboro, m., 1817, Nancy Finney. CONSIDER, son of 2d John in the text, m. Lydia, d. of Samuel Bryant, and had Lydia, Ezra, Consider, Levi, and perhaps others. ELISHA, son of Joshua, below, m. Rebecca Waterman, and had John, who m. a Cotton or a Capen, Joshua, 1778; Susan, m. Dr. Younger; Isaac, m. Eleanor Jones; Ely, m. Jerusha Little; Joel, 1786, m. Phebe Jones; Asenath, m. Ashel Rood; Samuel, m. Mary Warner; Martha, m. Henry Starkie; Waterman, 1796, m., Sarah Abercrombie; Henry S., m. Esther Miller; Rebecca, m. John Carver; Zera, m. Caroline Wright. EzRA, 1st in the text, m. Elizabeth Cobb. JABEZ, in the text; son Jonathan, m. Lucy Ellis, of Middleboro. JOEL, son of Elisha, above, had Esther J.,

1807; Sarah, 1809; Levi J., 1814. JOHN, 3d in the text, m. 1768. JOSHUA, son of Young, below, of Ludlow, Mass., m. Mercy Lothrop, of Tolland, Conn., and had Elisha, 1754; Solomon L., Ezekiel, Sarah, Lydia, Benjamin and Olive. MATTHEW, 1st in the text; d. Mary m. 1655; add d. Ann, m. Samuel Fuller. ROBERT, of Salem, 1639, and later of Rehoboth, was not apparently connected with the Plymouth family. SAMUEL, 3d in the text; son Samuel, born 1638; add d. Elizabeth, m. a Taylor; d. Sarah, m. a Crow. SAMUEL, 4th in the text; son Thomas, m. Elizabeth, d. of Joseph Lothrop; son Samuel, m. Ruth, d. of Eleazer Crocker. SAMUEL, 6th in the text; son Matthew m. Patience Young; son Barnabas m. Elizabeth Young; son Joseph m. Thankful Blossom. YOUNG, son of 2d Matthew in the text, of Colchester, Conn., had Joshua, 1730; Caleb and David.

GAMBLE, ROBERT, in the text, m. 1759.

GIBBS, ANSELM, in the text, should be Ansel. His wife Lucy, was d. of William LeBaron.

GILBERT, DAVID, in the text, of Mansfield, not Marshfield; his son Gustavus born 1801. DAVID HUMPHREYS, in the text; son Walter L. m. Josephine I., not J. Peckham,

GLASS OR GLASSE, JAMES, in the text, had perhaps a brother Roger, in Barnstable.

GLOVER, GEORGE, in the text, m. 1757.

GODDARD, BENJAMIN, 2d in the text; d. Polly, born 1800; d. Ruth Rogers, born 1801. DANIEL, 1st in the text; son Benjamin born 1813. FRANCIS J., in the text; d. Lucy H. m. Arthur L. Trebble, and son Frank m. Fannie B. Keith. JOHN, 3d in the text; d. Harriet Otis born 1797. JOSEPH, 1st in the text; son Joseph m. Mary Perrin. WILLIAM, 2d in the text, m. Elizabeth Everton.

GOODING, BENJAMIN BARNES, in the text; d. Flora Leslie m. William G. Doten. JOSEPH, in the text; son John born 1780.

GOODWIN, BENJAMIN, of Boston and Easton, son of 2d John in the text, m., 1757, Hannah, d. of Lazarus LeBaron, and had Benjamin, 1758; Henry, 1760; Joseph, 1761; William, 1763; Charles, 1765; Daniel, 1767; LeBaron, 1769; Jane, 1770; Hannah LeBaron, 1771, m. Daniel Wheaton; Mercy Robie, 1773, m. D. Wheaton. DANIEL, son of above, m. Polly, d. of Timothy Lewis, and had Daniel LeBaron, 1800; and Irene Weatherton, 1775; James Briggs, 1806; Frederick Deane, 1804; Edward Byam, 1810; Thomas Shepard, 1817; Hannah LeBaron, 1814; Harriet Briggs Lewis, 1796; Abigail Potter, 1798; Henry Bradford, 1802; John, 1808; Benjamin Lewis, 1819; and Mary D., 1812. DANIEL LEBARON, son of above, m., 1825, Rebecca, d. of William Wilkinson, of Providence, and had ten children. FRANCIS LEBARON, son of Nathaniel, m., 1787, Jane Prince, d. of Chandler Robbins, and removed to Frankfort, Me. He had Francis, Chandler Robbins, Lazarus and William Bradford. FREDERICK DEANE, son of Daniel, above, went to Virginia. He m., 1837, Mary Frances, d. of Dr. Robert Archer, of U. S. Army, and had Fannie Archer, m. Dr. William Ribble, of Wytheville; Frederick Le Baron, of Clifton, Arizona, m., 1st, Maggie, of Alabama; John Francis, m. Miss Rutherford, of Richmond; Mary Baldwin,

m. Rev. Thomas H. Lacy; Susan Valentine; Sarah Anderson; Robert Archer, m. Sallie C. Bump; and Mary Arabella Harrison, Ella Rosa and Edward Louis. HENRY, son of Benjamin, above, m., 1781, Mary, d. of William Bradford, of Bristol, R. I., and had May, 1782, m. Charles DeWolf; Hannah, 1784, m. Simeon S. Goodwin; Charlotte, 1786, m. George DeWolf; Henry, 1789. ISAAC, in the text; son William Hammett born 1815; additional child, Francis Henry, 1817. JOSEPH son of Benjamin, above, of Lenox and Hudson, m., 1784, Susanna Keith, of Easton, and had Hannah, 1785; Joseph, 1788; Sarah, 1789, m. Ephraim Starr; Charles, 1791; Nancy, 1793, m. Henry Whiting; Benjamin, 1795; Harriet, 1797, m. Abram B. Vanderpool; Lewis, 1799; Henry, 1804. m. Sarah Finn; Susanna, 1806; Mary, 1789, m. Colonel Pinckney; and Archibald Watt NATHANIEL, 1st in the text; son-in-law Thomas Page should be Dr. Benjamin Page, of Hallowell. NATHANIEL, 6th in the text; son Thomas m. Elizabeth Gate. NATHANIEL, 7th in the text; d. Rebecca m. Robert Gouge; and additional children, Mary, 1740, m. Asa Fuller; Martha, 1743; Benjamin, 1745. THOMAS, 1st in the text; son Charles born 1792. WILLIAM, in the text, m. 1781; son Simeon Sampson m. Hannah DeWolf, d. of Henry Goodwin; d. Jane Frances was born 1799; d. Mary Ann, 1792. He m., 2d, 1817, Deborah, wid. of Rev. Ephraim Briggs, and d. of Simeon Sampson.

GORHAM, RALPH, of Benefield, Eng., was born 1575, and appeared in Plymouth 1637. He had John and Ralph.

GRAY, EDWARD, in the text; additional child, Samuel. EDWARD, in the text; d. Elizabeth m. Seth Arnold; and d. Sarah m. Samuel Little. JOHN, 1st in the text, was son of 1st Samuel; son Lewis born 1790. LEWIS, in the text, had Judith, 1813, m. Benjamin Diman, of Plymouth. THOMAS m. Anna Little, of Marshfield, in Boston, 1694.

GREEN, WILLIAM, 1st in the text, son of William and Elizabeth (Warren) Green, m., 1709, Desire, d. of John Bacon, of Barnstable, and had Mary, 1710; Warren, 1716; Desire, 1718; William, 1721; Sarah, 1723; Mary, 1725; John, 1726; James, 1728. He m., 2d, 1731, Mary, d. of Thomas Fuller. WILLIAM, last in the text, was born 1780.

GRIFFIN, GEORGE W., in the text, was son of Henry, and born 1805.

HADAWAY, Thomas, in the text, was born 1794; the name of the wife of his son William S. was Lucy M. His son, J. B. S., born in England, had Sarah S., m. Henry I. Seymour; Clara M., John B., Fannie E. and Katie. Thomas had also a d. Fanny, born in England.

HADEWAY, JOHN, in the text, m. Hannah d. of Andrew Hallet. He m., 2d, 1672, Elizabeth, d. of Edward Coleman, of Yarmouth.

HALEY, EDWARD, m., 1830, Clarissa, d. of William Barrett.

HALL, JOHN, 1st in the text; son John m. Priscilla, d. of Austin Bearse, of Barnstable; son Samuel m. Elizabeth. d. of Thomas Folland, of Yarmouth; son Benjamin m. Mehitabel Mathews, of Yarmouth; son Nathaniel m. Ann, d. of Rev. Thomas Thornton, of Yarmouth.

HALLET, ANDREW, in the text, by wife Mary had Andrew. Samuel, Hannah, Josias and Joseph. Andrew, his son, m. Ann Besse, and had Dorcas, 1646; Jonathan, 1647; John, 1650; Mehitabel, m. John Dexter; Abigail, 1644, m. Jonathan Alden; Ruhamah, m. Job Bourne.

HAMMATT or HAMMETT (rewritten), ABRAHAM, son of John m., 1748, Lucy, d. of Consider Howland, of Plymouth, and had Abraham, 1750; William, 1752; Lucy, 1754, m. Nathaniel Lothrop. ABRAHAM, son of above, m., 1774, Priscilla, d. of Lazarus LeBaron, and had Priscilla, 1775; William, 1778; Samuel Avery, 1780; Abraham, 1781; Sophia, 1784; Lucia, 1786, m. William Simmons; Eliza, 1789, m. Isaac Goodwin; Consider Howland, 1791; George, 1793; Henry, 1795. BENJAMIN, son of John, born at Newlin, Cornwall, in 1712, m., 1734, Mary Pierce, and had Catherine, 1735; John, 1738; Mary, 1742; Anna, 1745; Benjamin, 1746; Martha, 1748; Joseph, 1750; Elizabeth, 1723. He m., 2d, 1762, Mercy, wid. of Capt. Samuel Brown, and had Mercy, 1763; William; Lydia; Sally, 1769. It is thought that he came over in 1727. GEORGE, son of 2d Abraham, m. Mary Farley, and had Mary, Elizabeth and Howland. JOHN, of Newlin, in the Parish of St. Paul, Cornwall, m. Catherine, d. of J. James, and had John; Benjamin, 1712; Abraham, 1719; and William. WILLIAM, son of 1st Abraham, m. Elizabeth, d. of Josiah Barker, of Nantucket, and 2d, Mary, d. of Andrew Sigourney, of Boston, and wid. of John Cathcart, and had by one or both wives William, Abraham, Benjamin, John, Elizabeth, m. Abisha Delano; Lucy, m. a Chamberlin; and Ann Sigourney, m. George Bond, of Boston. WILLIAM, son of 2d Abraham, m., 1806, wid. Esther Phillips, and d. of William Walter Parsons, and had William Cushing, 1807, m. Mary Ann, d. of Samuel Holden Parsons; Hannah Phillips, 1809, m. Hazen Mitchell; Abraham LeBaron, 1812; Esther Jackson, 1815, m. Joseph Carr; Ann Frances, 1818, m. Edward F. Hodges. of Boston; Thomson Phillips, 1821; John Howland, 1824; Elizabeth Whiting, 1828.

HAMMOND, BRITTAN, a slave of John Winslow, m., 1762, Hannah, a slave of James Hovey.

HARDY, SOLOMON, m., about 1830, Mary Ann, d. of George Holmes Savery.

HARLOW, BRANCH, of Middleboro, son of 2d Jonathan in the text m. Lurana Keith, and had Hope Keith, 1816; Branch Blackmer and Bradford Greenleaf, twins, 1818; Lurana Keith, 1822; Ivory Hovey, 1824; Chester Isham, 1826; Elizabeth Sturtevant, 1829; Foster Alexander, 1831; Rufus Kendrick, 1834; Louisa Jane, 1837; Benjamin Franklin, 1838. ELEAZER, in the text, m. 1715. ELEAZER, son of above, m., 1739, Abigail Thomas, of Marshfield, and had Asaph, Thomas, Gideon, Abigail, William. He m., 2d, 1745, Abigail Clark. of Plympton, and had Arunah, Hannah, Elizabeth and Patience. ELIPHAS, Taunton and Rehoboth, son of Eleazer in the text, by wife Hopestill had Eleazer, 1740, m. Rhoda Alexander. ELLIS, in the text, m. Sarah Holmes, not Harlow. EZRA, 3d in the text, was of Middleboro. His wife was d. of William Ellis. His children, Joseph, born 1769; Ellis, 1771; Thomas, 1773; Lydia, 1774; Betsey, 1775; Ezra, 1777; William, 1779; Otis, 1781; Samuel, 1783; Hannah, 1785; Josiah, 1786; Patience, 1789; Sally, 1791; Ezra, 1793. GIDEON, Duxbury, son of Eleazer, above, m. Patience Ford, wid. of Abner Eames, and had Eleazer, Gideon, Lydia, Arunah, Thomas, 1775, and Abner. GIDEON, son of Thomas, of Shrewsbury, below, m. Harriet Howe, d. of Nathan, 1828, and had William, 1828; Thomas, 1830; Henry, 1835; Hiram, 1841; Harriet, 1843. IVORY, in the text; son Justus born 1811; d. Lucy, 1814, JABEZ m., 1823, Hannah Harlow. JAMES, 2d in the text; son Simeon died in Columbia,

Ill., 1846. JAMES, 4th in the text; his wife Hannah was d. of Jonathan Shaw; his son Barnabas m. Mary, d. of Peter West, of Kingston. JAMES, son of 2d James in the text, removed to Hallowell, Maine. He m. Martha Fitts, and had Woodward, James M., 1809; Olive and Olivia. JAMES M., Hallowell, son of above, removed to Kingston, and there died, 1866. He m., 1840, Catherine T. Daniels, of Plymouth. His brother Woodward lived for a time in Halifax, Mass. JAMES HENRY, son of John, below, m., 1858, Elsie Roxanna, d. of Alden Gee, of Fitzwilliam, N. H., and had Alice Holmes and John Bradford. JAMES HENRY, son of Stephen, below, m. Maria Louisa Dean, of Plympton. JOHN, son of 1st Lewis, m., 1831, Jane Chandler, d. of Josiah Bradford, and had John Bradford, 1832 ; James Henry, 1837; Martha Jane, 1839; Deborah Thomas, 1844, m. Lyman Dixon. JONATHAN, 2d in the text, add children Stephen, Branch, Betsey, m. Eliab Wood, and Lemuel ; son Lewis should be Lemuel. KIMBALL, son of Reuben in the text, m. Nancy, d. of Rufus Bartlett, and had Nancy, Ellis J. and Kimball. LEVI, 1st in the text, m. Mercy, not Mary, Barnes. LEVI, of Westminister, Vt., born 1767, son of Eleazer, the son of Eliphas, above, m. Elizabeth Ranney, and had Eleazer, 1797, who m., 1820, Ruth Owen, of Ashford, Conn., and had Henry Mills, 1821, who m. Louisa Stone Brooks, and was the father of Dr. George Arthur Harlow, of Boston. LEWIS, in the text; d. Lucy C. born 1804 ; d. Hannah born 1797; son John born 1808 ; add also child Otis. NATHANIEL, 1st in the text, m. Abigail Buck, not Burt. NATHANIEL, 2d in the text; son Nathaniel m. Sarah, d. of Isaac Bonney, and d. Susanna m. Noah Sturtevant, of Plympton. NATHANIEL, 3d in the text; d. Mary Olive born 1811. ROBERT, 1st in the text; d. Mary m. Nathan Thompson, not James Hovey. STEPHEN, Middleboro, son of 2d Jonathan, m. Patience Ellis, and had Sarah, m. Augustus Williams ; Stephen, m. Bethiah Keith; James Henry, m. Maria Louisa Dean, of Plympton; Betsey, m. John M. Soule ; Mary, Edward and Ivory. SYLVANUS, son of 1st Sylvanus in the text, m. Catherine, d. of Belcher Manter, and had fifteen children. SYLVANUS, son of above, moved West and had a son Noah, who had Alonzo. THOMAS, 1st in the text; son Jonathan m. Sarah, d. of Elisha Holmes. THOMAS, m., 1762, Anna Fuller, of Plympton. THOMAS, Shrewsbury, son of the first mentioned Gideon, above, m. Thankful, d. of Nathan Banister, of Boylston, and had Gideon, 1799; Nancy; Elmira, 1805; Abigail, 1810. WILLIAM, 1st in the text; d. Mary m. Samuel Dunham. WILLIAM, 2d in the text; son William born 1692. WILLIAM, 4th in the text; d. Rebecca m. Ebenezer Ransom. WILLIAM, 6th in the text, was son of 3d William; son Simon should be Simeon; son James m. Hannah, d. of Benjamin Bagnall. WILLIAM, 8th in the text, was son of 4th William. WILLIAM, 9th in the text, was son of 6th William. ZEPHANIAH, in the text; strike out "m. William Tribble."

HARMON, JOHN, in the text, was son of Francis, not James. He had also a d. Jane, who m., 1678, Samuel Doty.

HARRIS, OLIVER, in the text, was born 1798.

HART, JASON, in the text; son Orin F. m. Isabella Wells.

HARVEY, BENJAMIN, was from Norfolk, Va., and born 1810. SYLVANUS, in the text ; d. Eliza "S. V.," not "S. N."

HASKINS, NATHAN II., in the text; name of son-in-law was Horatio S. Cameron. WILLIAM, last in the text, m., 1677, Sarah Caswell.

HATCH, THOMAS, 1st in the text, was of Barnstable and Yarmouth, and had a wife, Grace; son Jonathan m. Sarah Rowley, and he had also Lydia, m. Henry Taylor.

HATHAWAY, ALANSON, in the text; son Benjamin born 1805; son Allen born 1802. BENJAMIN, in the text; d. Rebecca II. m. Isaac H. Eddy. SILAS, last in the text; son Charles born 1807.

HEDGE, ALBERT GOODWIN, in the text; d. Albertha born 1874. BARNABAS, 1st in the text; son Samuel should be Lemuel; son William born 1750. BARNABAS, 3d in the text, m., 1789, Eunice Dennie, d. of Gershom Burr, of Fairfield, Conn. ELISHA, in the text; son John born 1673. WILLIAM, 1st in the text, by 1st wife had Elizabeth, 1647, m. Jonathan Barnes, of Plymouth; Mary, 1648, m. a son of Edward Sturgis; Sarah, m. a Matthews; Abraham, Elisha, William, John, Lemuel, and Mercy. He m., 2d, 1655, Blanche, wid. of Tristram Hull.

HICKS, ABRAHAM, in the text, m. Bathsheba Dunham. ROBERT, 1st in the text, m., in England, Elizabeth Morgan, and had Elizabeth, Thomas, John, Stephen. His 2d wife was Margaret Winslow, by whom he had Samuel, Ephraim, Lydia and Phebe. JOHN, son of above, m., 1st, Hored Loring, and had Thomas, Hannah and Elizabeth. SAMUEL, in the text, son of Robert, had also Dorcas and Sarah, m. Joseph Churchill. THOMAS, son of John above, m., 1st, Mary Washburn, and had Thomas and Jacob. He m., 2d, Mary Doughty, and had Isaac, William, Stephen, John, Charles, Benjamin, Phebe, Charity, Mary and Elizabeth.

HIGHTON, HENRY, in the text, m. 1768.

HINCKLEY, SAMUEL, in the text; d. Susanna m. John Smith. THOMAS, son of above, m., 1641, Mary Richards, d. of Thomas, of Weymouth, and, 1660, Mary, wid. of Nathaniel Glover.

HOBART, NOAH, in the text, m., 1758, Priscilla, wid. of John Watson and Isaac Lothrop and d. of Caleb Thomas. He had by a 1st wife Ellen, m. Nathaniel Lothrop and John Sloss.

HODGE, JAMES THACHER, had also Mary, 1854. MICHAEL, of Salisbury, born 1683, m. Joanna, d. of William Titcomb, and had Charles, 1716, and five others. MICHAEL, in Newbury, 1748. MICHAEL, appointed Naval Officer of Newburyport, 1776.

HODGKINS, JOSEPH W., in the text, was born 1801.

HOLBROOK, ELIPHALET, 2d in the text; son Gideon born 1786. GIDEON, 1st in the text; son Eliphalet born 1831.

HOLLIS, HENRY, in the text, m. Abigail, not Deborah. NATHAN, Middleboro, by wife Lucy had Barsillai, 1770; Nathan, 1772; Jerusha, 1774; Joseph, 1783; Warren, 1786. SAMUEL, 3d in the text, had George F., m. Hannah E. Fry; Lucy, m. Otis Allen, of Taunton; Abby M., Samuel, James Henry and William.

HOLMES, ALBERT, in the text, m., 1844, Jerusha, d. of Henry Tilson, and had Albert Henry, 1844; Albert Truman, 1847; Charles Edward, Carrie Clifton, 1857; Hattie Gray, 1861. ALLEN, son of Chandler, m. Hannah, d. of Job

Churchill. ANSEL, 1st in the text, m. 1771; son Ansel born 1777. ANSEL, 2d in the text; d. Martha W., not Martha. ANSEL, 3d in the text, was son of 6th Joseph. BARNABAS, 1st in the text; d. Betsey born 1803. BARNABAS HINCKLEY, in the text, should be Barnabas Hopkins. BARSILLAI, in the text, was son of 3d Josiah. BENJAMIN, 1st in the text; d. Rebecca was Rebecca D. BENJAMIN, 2d in the text, m. 1756. CALEB, in the text, was of Dennis, Mass. CHANDLER, in the text, had Chandler, 1797; Phebe, 1799, m. Nathaniel Sylvester; Ichabod Shaw, 1801; Chandler, 1809; Ichabod Shaw again, 1805; Mehitabel, 1807; Esther, 1810; Allen, 1815; Susan, 1811; Atwood, 1813, m. Almira Ward. CORNELIUS, 2d in the text, had also Hannah, 1778, m. John Hall. DAVID, 2d in the text; son David born 1807; d. Rebecca born 1800. DAVID COBB, in the text (rewritten), m., 1831, Louisa, d. of Nehemiah Savery, and had David W., 1832, m. Sarah S. Braley; Andrew, 1833, m. Caroline F. Spear; Albert, 1833, twin, m. Elizabeth S. Millard; Louisa, 1835; Mary S., 1836, m. Charles F. Fleming; Nehemiah S., 1838, m. Nancy S. Carr; Cephas A., 1840; Edmund W., 1842, m. Clara Perkins; Gideon F., 1843, m. Helen A. Drew; Patience C., 1846, m. Charles Braley; Deborah S., 1848, m. Eldridge L. Brown; George A., 1850; Louisa, 1852. He m., 2d, 1856, Martha Millard. EBENEZER, 2d in the text; d. Phebe m. Thomas Hinckley. EBENEZER, 3d in the text; son Ebenezer m., 1756, Hannah Nelson. EBENEZER, 4th in the text; son David S. born 1801. ELISHA, 2d in the text; son Elisha m. Sarah, d. of Thomas Ewer. ELLIS, 1st in the text; son Ellis born 1795; d. Betsey, 1797; d. Grace, 1793; son Kendall, 1801; d. Rebecca, 1804; d. Hannah S., 1800; d. Deborah, 1808. ELLIS, 4th in the text, m. 1813. ELNATHAN, 2d in the text; son Elnathan born 1763. EPHRAIM, 3d in the text, m. 1768, not 1767; d. Joanna born 1803. GEORGE, 2d in the text; d. Bethiah born 1746. GERSHOM, 2d in the text; son Micah born 1800. ICHABOD SHAW, son of 1st Chandler, m. Tabitha Kingman, of Weymouth, and had James A., m. Anna Vinal, of Cambridge; William J., m. Lizzie Rice, of Worcester; Ruth White, m. E. A. Presbry, of Boston; Chandler, m. Elizabeth Ann, d. of Elkanah C. Finney. JOHN, 9th in the text; d. Mary G. m. Jabez N. Pierce. JOHN CALDERWOOD, m., 1823, Jane Avery Holmes. JOSEPH, 3d in the text; child Micah should be Meriah. JOSEPH, 5th in the text; d. Polly born 1791. JOSEPH, 6th in the text, m. 1769. JOSEPH, 7th in the text, m. 1775. JOSEPH, 8th in the text; d. Martha Cotton born 1803; son Joseph born 1815. JOSEPH, 10th in the text, was son of 4th Joseph. JOSEPH, 12th in the text; son Adoniram J. m. Mary Ann, d. of Joseph Davis. KENDALL, in the text; d. Mary Fuller m. William Crocker Churchill and Charles William Campbell. LEMUEL, 1st in the text, was son of 1st Eleazer. LEWIS, 1st in the text; d. Mary Sherman born 1795. MICAH, in the text; d. Almira born 1824. NATHAN, 1st in the text; son David Cobb born 1801. NATHAN, 3d in the text; son Henry B. born 1818; son Elisha born 1821. NATHANIEL, 5th in the text; d. Mary born 1802. NATHANIEL, 6th in the text; d. Marcia C. born 1794. PETER, 1st in the text; son Peter born 1778. PETER, 2d in the text; son Peter m. Almira Cobb, of Kingston, and wid. Sarah Reed, of Boston; son Charles H. m. Maria P. Holman, of Boston; d. Eliza m. Jesse Delano, of Marshfield; son Franklin B. born 1826. Add d. Emily, 1821, m. William Rider Drew. RICHARD, 2d in the text; d. Sarah born 1782. SAMUEL N., in the text; son Benjamin born 1802, and m. Maria Harris; son Isaac S. born 1813. SETH, 1st in the text; d. Mary m. a Bartlett; d. Rebecca m. Caleb Bartlett. SOLOMON, in the text; insert after child "Solomon, 1764," the words "He prob. m., 2d, 1768, Mary Delano, and had." SOLOMON, 2d in the text; d. Jane B. born 1811; son Daniel Crocker born 1809. SOLOMON MAYNARD, son of Barsillai in the text, m. Asenath, d. of Vinal Burgess, and had Ruth; Solomon Maynard, m. Rebecca F., d. of Ellis Sampson; Barsillai, m. Deborah F., d of Sylvanus Sampson. STEPHEN, in the text; son Clark m. Hannah, d. of Thomas Morton. THOMAS, 3d in the text; son Barnabas Hinckley should be Barnabas Hopkins. TRUMAN COOK, 1st in the text; son Curtis m. Susan Torrey, d. of Richard W. Bagnall. WILLIAM, 4th in the text, was son of 2d William. He had Mary Holbrook, m. Oliver T. Wood. He m., 2d, 1812, Bathsheba Doten, and had Betsey Doten, Bathsheba James, m. Ansel H. Harlow. WILLIAM, 5th in the text; strike out all relating to him. WILLIAM, son of 1st Jeremiah, m., 1801, Ruth, d. of Josiah Morton, and had Betsey, m. William Swift, and Ruth W., m. Thomas Nye, of Wareham. He m., 2d, Sarah, d. of Lothrop Clark. WILLIAM, Plymouth, 1633, leader of the expedition to the Connecticut River, moved to Duxbury and died in Boston, 1649. After he left Plymouth he appears to have gone to England and entered the royal service, as in his will he mentions arrears due him as soldier and commander in service of the king. He mentions also Margaret, Mary, Rachel and Bathsheba, children of deceased brother Thomas in London and Antigua, and gave a legacy of twenty pounds to his kind kinsman Job Hawkins. ZEPHANIAH, 2d in the text, m. Mercy Withered, not Bradford.

HOPKINS, STEPHEN, in the text, came in the *Mayflower* 1620. His 2d wife Elizabeth was d. of Francis Cooke; his son Damaris came in the *Mayflower*.

HOVEY, AARON, in the text; d. Frances born 1798. IVORY, 1st in the text, was also of Topsfield; son Ivory born 1714. IVORY, 2d in the text, born in Topsfield, 1739, m. Olivia, d. of Samuel and Hannah (Tristram) Jordan.

HOWARD, EBENEZER, 1st in the text; his wife was Thankful (Whittemore) Lemote. JAMES, 5th in the text; d. Hannah born 1805; d. Cordelia born 1810; son Curtis Cushman born 1816. MELTIAH, 2d in the text; d. Margare should be Margaret; son Josiah B. m. Cynthia T., d. of George W. Burgess and wid. of Phineas Burt. THOMAS, in the text, m. 1768.

HOWES, JEREMIAH, in the text; 2d marriage was in 1759.

HOWLAND, AARON, son of Charles, below, was the father of Henry E., of New York. ABRAHAM, 1st in the text; he had no d. who m. Jedediah Beals, but had a d. Anna who m. Solomon Beals. ABRAHAM, 2d in the text; d. Betty m. Elisha Hatch. ALLEN, in the text; d. Mahala m. Ambrose Parris; d. Lucy O. m. Nathan Stevens; d. Sally m. Amasa Edson. He had also children, David Oldham, 1811; Hiram, 1814; Urania Barker, 1817, m. John Polden, of Duxbury; Rebecca C., 1820. ALLEN, son of above, m. Ruth Ellis, of New Bedford, probably, and had Samuel Allen and Caleb Ellis. ANDREW BARTLETT, Titusville, son of Michael, m., 1801, Emily Ann Hill, and had Frank Parris, 1864; Harry Allen, 1869; Frederick Bartlett, 1873. BENJAMIN, 2d in the text; d. Priscilla m., 1769, Mark Eames, of Marshfield. CALVIN, 2d in the text; son

Calvin T. m. Annie Leach. CHARLES, son of a John, m. Elizabeth Hepzibah Crease, of Boston, and removed to Walpole, N. H. He had Aaron, 1801, and perhaps others. DAVID OLDHAM, Pembroke, son of 1st Allen above, m., 1838, Mary H. Ford, and had Augustus, Albion and a d. He m., 2d, Mrs. Martha Mason. EDWARD PAYSON, son of Southworth Allen, m. Elizabeth Holden, of Quincy, Mass., 1874. GARDNER GREENE, in the text; son Robert Shaw m. Mary E. W. Woolsey. HARRISON OTIS, in the text; d. Abby B., 1853. HENRY, Duxbury, 1st in the text; d. Abigail m. John Young or Richard Kirby. HENRY Stark, son of Jonathan and Lydia, below, m., 1852, in Oakville, Can., W. Cordelia Sophia, d of Thompson Smith, of Toronto, and had Harriet Julia, 1853; Henry Stark, 1855; Peleg, 1857; Fred N., 1859; Egbert Amos, 1861; Thompson Smith and William Pearce, twins, 1862; Mary May, 1865; Lydia and George W., twins, 1867; Frank, 1868; Horace, 1870. JACOB, 1st in the text; son Jacob born 1793. JACOB, 2d in the text; additional child, Bethiah. JACOB, 3d in the text, m. 1846. His children were Anna J., 1847, m. Rinaldo Alden; Warren C., 1849, m. Kate Van Pelt; Lizzie Page, 1856; Arthur L., 1859; Almon R., 1860. JACOB, 4th in the text; d. Catherine born 1800. JEDEDIAH, in the text, m. Susan, d. of Peter Crapo, of Dartmouth. His son James, of Lakeville, Mass., m., 1st, Anna Johnson, of Stockholm, and had seven sons. He m., 2d, Rosina Walker, of England, and had three d. and one son. JOHN, 4th in the text, was of Plympton, and m. Elizabeth Lewis. JOHN, 6th in the text; strike out the first marriage. JOHN, 8th in the text; son John was John F. JOHN, son of 1st Henry, m., 1685, Mary Walker. JOHN, son of 4th Nathaniel in the text, m. Mary, d. of John Cook, of Portsmouth, R. I., at the house of Thomas Connell, and had Israel, 1713, m. Drusilla Wood, and settled in Rawlings, N. Y.; Hannah, 1715, m. Joseph Gifford; Ruth, 1717; John, 1719; Nathaniel, 1721; and Prince, m. Deborah Slocum. JOHN, son of above, m., 1745, Deborah Shepherd, and had Ruth, 1746; Rebecca, 1748; Dorcas, 1750; Levi, 1752; John, 1755. JONATHAN, in the text; additional child, Caleb, 1806. JONATHAN, son of Peleg, below, m., 1803, Lydia Pearce, and had Matilda, 1804, m. John Van Slyck; Lillias Melinda, 1807, m. D. Pierce, of Utica; Peleg, 1809, of Toronto; William P., 1811; Sally H., 1814, m. Rev. Truman Hill, of Yorkville, Can.; Roxania G., 1816, m. Joseph Roger and James F. Starbuck, of Watertown, N. Y.; Harriet, 1819, m. W. W. Herrick; Elizabeth, 1821, Henry S., Toronto, 1824, m. Adelia Smith; Frederick A., 1827. MICHAEL, in the text, was of Pembroke. He m., 1828, Eliza Bartlett, and had Andrew Bartlett, 1830. NATHANIEL, 3d in the text, had additional children, Nathaniel, 1770; and Silas Atkins, 1772. NATHANIEL, 4th in the text; Deborah, wife of son James, was d. of John Cooke; Hannah, wife of son John, was d. of John Aiken; d. Content m. Weston Briggs. NATHANIEL, son of John and Mary (Cook) Howland, above, m., 1746, Joanna Ricketson, and settled in Rawlings, N. Y., and had Peleg, 1772; Nathaniel, 1756, m. a sister of Peleg's wife, and, 2d, Sarah White; Mary, 1749, m. Benjamin Ferris, Jr.; Meribah, 1747, m. Benaniel Shaw; Diadema, m. Shaddick Sherman; and Sarah. NATHANIEL, son of 12th John, settled in Duchess County, N. Y, and m. a gr. d. of Lord Edward Fitzgerald, and had Peleg, 1752; Nathaniel, 1756; Mary, 1749; and Meribah, 1717. PELEG, son of above, m. Elizabeth Aikens, and had Jonathan, 1781;

Joanna, Nathaniel, George and Ebenezer. PEREZ, in the text; d. Alice m.
Hezekiah Keen. His wid. m. Benjamin Keen. ROBERT, 2d in the text, m.
Ruth Crocker; son Robert born 1791; additional children, Urania, m. Thomas
Barker; Margaret, m. Edward Bates; Abigail, m. Ephraim Leonard. ROBERT,
Pembroke, son of above, m., 1814, Mary Balston, and had Robert, 1815; Mary
B., 1817; Margaret Sprague, 1820; Statira, 1821. ROUSE, in the text; addi-
tional child, Ann. SAMUEL, 1st in the text, m., 1678, Mary Merihew. SAMUEL,
2d in the text, m. Sarah Joy. SOUTHWORTH, in the text; additional children,
Harriet, 1806; and Mary Esther, 1823. WILLIAM, 7th in the text; additional
child, William, born 1743. WILLIAM EDGAR m. 1847, not 1747. WILLIAM
BAILEY, of Chatham, N. Y., son of Harrison O., in the text, m., 1873,
Ella May Jacobs, and had Karl Van Schaack, 1874; Harold Jacobs, 1877.
Mr. Charles Hervey Townshend has found a Parish Register in England, which
he does not disclose, in which the name of John Carver appears in several
generations, and in the next Parish are the names of Tilley, Sampson and
Robinson. After investigation the relations of Carver and Howland may be
learned.

HOYT, JOHN F., in the text; d. Deborah A. m. Charles H. Chandler. Moses,
1st in the text, m. 1803; son Curtis born 1818.

HUBBARD, DANIEL, m., 1820, Lucretia Stanford, of Boston.

HUMPHREYS, JOHN, in the text, m., 2d, 1759, Mary Paul.

HURST, JAMES, in the text, m. Catherine Thurston.

HUSTON, WILLIAM, 2d in the text; d. Priscilla born 1789.

HUTCHINSON, ROBERT, in the text, born 1789; d. Susan A. m., 2d, Job
Churchill.

JACKSON, ABRAHAM, 5th in the text; son Horace no middle name. ALEX-
ANDER, in the text, m. Cordelia A.; son Isaac m. Elizabeth Hunt Parrish.
DANIEL, 2d in the text, m. Elizabeth M., d. of Lothrop Turner. DAVID BARNES,
in the text, m. Deborah J. Crombie. ELEAZER, in the text; d. Mary m. Moses
Cushman. HENRY, in the text; son Henry Foster born 1801; son Edwin, 1812.
ISAAC, 1st in the text; d. Nancy m., 2d, Stephen Churchill. ISAAC, 4th in the
text; d. Sarah was Sarah Thomas; son-in-law Fred Lovett was Fred W.; addi-
tional children, Thomas, Ellen, Frances, Ann Eliza. JACOB, in the text; son
Gustavus born 1826. JOHN, 1st in the text; son John born 1716; son Cor-
nelius, 1718. JOSE H, 3d in the text; d. Caroline Frances, 1825; Susan, 1831;
Hannah, 1827. LI VITT TAYLOR, in the text; son William Francis m. Abby
Crocker West, of Norton. NATHANIEL, 2d in the text; wife Abigail was d. of
John Rickard. NATHANIEL, 4th in the text, m. 1799. SAMUEL m., 1808, Nancy
Cotton. SALISBURY, in the text; son William Hall born 1814. THOMAS, 4th
in the text; d. Mary Ann m. Nathan Cannon, of Rochester; son Alden m. a
Southworth.

JENNINGS, JOSEPH, in the text; d. Sarah H. born 1815.

JOHNSON, JOSIAH, 1st in the text; d. Patience m. Zephaniah Harlow. He
m., 2d, 1767, Bathsheba Barrows, of Plympton.

JONES, JOHN, in the text, m. 1756.

KEEN, JOHN, m., 1819, Sarah W. Churchill. WILLIAM, in the text, son
William born 1785; d. Abigail born 1804.

KEMPTON, EPHRAIM, 3d in the text; son Stephen m., 1705, Ruth Ingleden. OBED, in the text, had son Obed W., 1839. EPHRAIM, 7th in the text, was son of 2d Thomas, not 1st. OLIVER, son of Oliver and grandson of 2d Samuel in the text, m., 1799, Sarah Harlow, and had Eliza O., 1802, m. Elias Cox. ZACHEUS, in the text, had also Isaac, m. Betsey C. Dillard. ZACHEUS, son of above, m., 1st, Abigail Cox, in 1819. He m., 2d, Harriette Hollister, 1823, and had Elizabeth, 1826; Amos W., 1828; Lucy A., 1830; Marian D., 1832. He m., 3d, Emeline Higley, 1836, and had Emeline, 1837; Rebecca, 1841; Emily Louisa, 1846; Jennett Keeny, 1848.

KENDALL, THOMAS, last in the text, of Boston, m., 1708, Sarah Cheever.

KENNEDY, JOHN, in the text, m. Esther Allen, wid. of Benjamin Robbins, and had James and Nancy. His wid. m. John Osgood.

KENT, SAMUEL, in the text, was son of John and Sarah (Smith) Kent and m. Desire Barker.

KEYES, AMAZIAH, son of an Abijah, was born 1771 and probably lived in Boston, where he m., 1794, Nancy, d. of Edward Crafts. He removed to Palmyra, N. Y. BENJAMIN, in the text, brother of above, m., 1796, Polly Norris. OLIVER, in the text, brother of above; son Oliver Shurtleff should be William Shurtleff.

KING, ISAAC B., in the text, was son of 2d John. JOHN, 1st in the text, came from Maryland. JOHN, 2d in the text; son Elisha should be Elihu; add children Isaac B. and Joanna E., 1813, m. Reuben Hall. WILLIAM, in the text, m. Susanna, d. of Robert Harlow.

KNEELAND, JOSHUA, in the text, was born 1792.

LANMAN, CHARLES JAMES, son of James below, born in Norwich, 1795, m., 1816, Mary J., d. of Antoine Guy, and had son Charles, who was secretary of Daniel Webster. JAMES, son of Peter and Sarah (Colt) Lanman, born in Norwich, 1769, m. Maria Griswold Chandler and Mary Judith Benjamin, mother of Park Benjamin. PETER, 1st in the text; d. Polly m. George Holmes Savery. SAMUEL, 1st in the text; son Nathaniel Cobb born 1793. SAMUEL, 2d in the text, m. 1811; d. Elizabeth m. Thomas C. Atwood.

LEACH, FINNEY, in the text; son Albert was Albert G. LEMUEL, 2d in the text; son Ezra born 1799; son Lemuel born 1805; son David, 1807; Reuben, 1809.

LEBARON, BARTLETT, in the text, m. wid. Mary Easdell; son James m. Mary, d. of Caleb Fiske; d. Nancy m. Phillip Taylor, of Penn.; d. Lucy m. Thomas Mayo. DAVID, son of 1st James, m. Martha Chatfield and had Solomon, 1766, m. Zada Hare; Francis, 1769, m. Sabrah Kelsey; Huldah, 1771, m. a Curtis; Martha, 1773, m. Tilley Gilbert; David, 1775; Lydia, 1777, m. Philander Nettleton; Ruth, 1779, m. Silas Fordham; Naomi, 1781; James, 1783, m. Louisa Adams; Daniel, 1785, m. Esther Welsey; Hannah, 1788, m. Daniel Higgins. FRANCIS, the 1st in the text, was not a Roman Catholic as has been often stated. The author has a letter in his possession dated Norfolk, Conn., June 5, 1882, from Mrs. Maria Humphrey, a gr. d. of Elizabeth Robbins, who was a gr. d. of Francis LeBaron. Mrs. Humphrey says that her grandmother "related to her grandchildren often that he was a Protestant." ISAAC, 2d in the text; d. Martha Howland m. Delano A. Goddard. ISAAC, son of 2d

James in the text, Woodstock, Vt., and Calais, had Hannah, Nancy, Druzilla, Martha, Lucinda, Apollos and James. JAMES, 1st in the text; son Joshua m. Grace Bush; d. Mary m. Abiel Shurtleff. JAMES, 2d in the text; son William m. Lusanna Bennett. JAPHET, son of Joshua below, m. Elizabeth Prouty and Mary Huntington, and had Elijah, 1814. JEREMIAH, son of Joshua, below, m., 1807, Elizabeth Gary, and had Fanny, 1807; Nelson, 1808; Mahala, 1812; Benjamin, 1815; Mary, 1817; James B., 1819; Jane, 1821; Emeline, 1826. JOHN BURT, in the text, m., 1841, Mary J. Chase; son John Baylies born 1845; d. Maria born 1847. JOHN, son of 2d Joshua, below, m., 1806, Fanny Ludlow, and had Maria, 1806. JOSHUA, son of 1st James, m., 1761, Grace Bush, of Sheffield, and had Isaac, 1762; Jerusha, 1766, m. Simeon Sage; Mary, 1765, m. David Kellogg; Japhet, 1767; Pamelia, 1769, m. Amasa Marsh; John, 1771; Mark, 1774; Jeremiah, 1776; James, 1778, m. Sarah Hix; Laura, 1780, m. Richard Sutleff; Hosea, 1783. LAZARUS, son of 2d Lazarus in the text, m., 1767, Susanna Johonnet; 1775, Hannah Chase; 1783, Mary Chase, and 1812, Mary Woodbury, and had Susanna, 1767, m. Stephen Monroe, of Sutton. LEMUEL, son of Lemuel in the text, m., 1809, Martha Osgood, d. of Thomas Kittridge, of Andover, and had John Kittridge, 1810; William, 1814, m. Sarah Jarvis Carr, of Roxbury; Thomas Kittredge, 1819. He m., 2d, 1836, Lydia Holmes, of New Bedford. LEMUEL, in the text; son John Allen m. Martha Phillips; son Lazarus m. Priscilla Hammond; d. Sally m. Mathew May. LEVI, in the text; d. Waitstill m. Caleb Thomas, and d. Temperance m. Davis Thomas. NERO, a slave, enlisted June 2, 1780, on board ship *Mars*, Capt. Simeon Sampson, and served nine months, ten days. WILLIAM, 1st in the text; d. Mary m. Wyatt Hammond; d. Lucy m. Ansel Gibbs and Thomas Mayo; d. Priscilla m., 2d, Francis LeBaron Robbins, of Enfield, Conn.; d. Eliza m. William LeBaron. WILLIAM, 2d in the text; d. Sarah Ann m. Arvin Cannon; son William m. Jerusha C. Drisko; d. Eliza m. Phillip G. Hubbard.

LEMOTE, GEORGE, in the text, m. 1764, and m., 2d, 1776, Thankful Whittemore.

LEONARD, ABIEL, son of 1st Nathaniel in the text, m., 1765, Mary Green, and had Nathaniel, 1768, who had a son Abiel, of Oakwood, Mo. ABNER, in the text; d. Clarinda m. Harrison F. Gibbs. EPHRAIM, 1st in the text, was son of 3d Phillip. EPHRAIM, son of 2d Phillip in the text, m. Mary Pratt and had James; Jane, m. O. L. Perkins; Sarah, m. Orlando Thompson; and Betsey, m. J. Drake. NATHANIEL, 1st in the text; d. Phebe born 1740, and add children Abiel, Elizabeth, Ephraim and Margaret. NATHANIEL, 2d in the text; add children William, 1761; Priscilla, 1763. PHILIP, 1st in the text; add children George, Ephraim and Chloe, m. Eliphalet Elms. PHILIP, 2d in the text; add children Benjamin, Philip, Samuel and George. WILLIAM, in the text; add children William, Bethiah; d. Rebecca, born 1793, m. Oliver Weston. All the children were by 1st wife. WILLIAM, son of above, m., 1813, Ruth Carver, of Taunton, and had Jane; Bethiah, m. Thomas O. Moore, of Lawrence; Sarah, and Rebecca, m. Gervais Baillio.

LESTER, TERRIT, in the text, m. 1755.

LEWIS, NATHANIEL, in the text, m. Lucy Shaw, not Hannah Drew. SAMUEL, m., 1772, Hannah Drew.

Ling, Thomas, in the text, m. Elizabeth Mackson, not Macklam.

Litchfield, Nicholas, in the text, m. Bathsheba, d. of James Clark.

Little, Ephraim, 1st in the text; d. Ruth m., 2d, 1686, Rev. John Avery, of Truro. Isaac, 3d in the text; son George m., 1755, Abigail Soule, of Plympton. Thomas, 2d in the text; son Thomas was of Chilmark.

Littlejohn, Orsanus, should be Orsamus.

Lobdell, Thomas, in the text, m., 2d, 1819, Mary Russell.

Long, John Davis, son of Zadoc in the text, m., 1870, Mary Woodward, d. of George S. Glover, of Hingham, Mass., and had Margaret, 1873; Helen, 1875. He m., 2d, 1886, Agnes, d. of Rev. Joseph Dexter Peirce, of N. Attleboro, and had, 1887, a son Peirce. Thomas, 1st in the text; son Miles m. Ann Bridgham, not Budgham.

Loring, Thomas, 4th in the text; d. Deborah m. John Cushing, of Scituate.

Lothrop, Barnabas, 1st in the text; d. Abigail m. Thomas Sturgis; d. Susanna m. William Shurtleff; d. Bathshua m. a Freeman; d. Ann m. Ebenezer Lewis; d. Sarah m. a Skiff. Had child John, 1667. He m., 2d, 1698, Abigail, wid. of Joseph Dudson. Barnabas, 2d in the text, m., 2d, 1718, Hannah Chipman, and 1744, Thankful Gorham. By 2d wife had Jonathan, 1719; Barnabas, 1721; Samuel, 1728; and by 3d wife, Mary, 1747. Benjamin, 1st in the text; d. Sarah born 1664; Rebecca, 1666; Mercy, 1670, and son John, 1672. Hope, in the text; children, Solomon born 1710; Hannah, 1722; Elizabeth, 1712; John, 1709; Rebecca, 1701; Joseph, 1720; Sarah, 1703; Ebenezer, 1706; Mary, 1716; Maltiah, 1714; Ichabod, 1708; Benjamin, 1697. Ichabod, in the text, m. Abigail, d. of John Barker. Isaac, 1st in the text; son Nathaniel m., 2d, Lucy Hammatt. John, 1st in the text, m., 1610, Hannah Howse, of Eastwell, Kent; d. Ann born 1616; son John, 1618; d. Barbara, 1619; son Thomas, 1621; Joseph, 1624. He m., 2d, 1637, Ann Hammond; d. Bathsheba m. Alexander Marsh, and son John m., 1672, Mary Cole, and had John, 1673; Mary, 1675; Martha, 1677. John, 2d in the text; son David born 1748. John, 3d in the text, m. Elizabeth, d. of James Green, of Charlestown. Maltiah, in the text, m. Sarah Farrar; d. Tabitha born 1671, not 1668. Nathaniel, in the text; add children Joseph and Hannah. Seth, in the text, was born 1722. Thomas, 1st in the text, m. 1639. Thomas, 2d in the text; add children Elizabeth and Rebecca.

Loud, Jacob Hersey, in the text; strike out the comma between Jacob and Hersey. Thomas, in the text; Honor was cousin of Thomas Prince.

Lovell, Leander, in the text, m. 1825.

Lucas, Abijah, in the text; son Martin Luther born 1800. Abner, in the text; add children, Susan, m. Wilson Churchill; Cynthia, m. Anselm Rickard; Mary, m. Caleb Morton; Rebecca, m. Nathan Howland; Olive B., m. Ellis Battles. Ebenezer, Carver, son of Martin Luther in the text, m. Eliza H. Walker, of Westboro, and had Mary A., 1857; Hannah Adelia, 1858; Maria E., 1860; Henry E., 1862; Amelia T., 1863; Henry E., 1868; Mattie H., 1872; Helen E., 1873. Harvey, in the text; son Horatio Atwood m. Mary E. Leach. Joseph, 4th in the text; son Frederick William m. Mary, not Angeline. Lazarus, in the text, m. Mary Code, 1797, and had Nancy, m. John Howland;

Mary J., m. Daniel Clark; William Warren. MARTIN LUTHER, in the text, m. Mary, d. of Ebenezer Shurtleff; son Elisha Shaw m. Matilda (Unwin) Buffum, of Chicago; d. Sarah Ellis should be Sarah Ellen. WILLIAM WARREN, son of Lazarus in the text, of Sangerville, Me., m., 1st, Sally Latham, and had Benjamin, Lewelyn, Latham A., Sarah A., m. Osgood Martin and Charles W. Brodhead, of Wisconsin.

LUNT, WILLIAM PEARSON, in the text, should be William Parsons.

MACKIE, ANDREW, in the text, m., 1821, Amelia Bradford. ISAAC, in the text, m. 1763.

MACOMBER, ELIJAH, 1st in the text; son Warren S. born 1815.

MAGLATHLIN, McLAUTHLIN, etc., ARTHUR, Whitman, son of Henry Bartlett, m. Eudora Lobdell, and had Maria Weston, 1879, m. William Ripley, of Whitman; Clarence Weston, 1883; Chester Arthur, 1887; and Leona Gertrude, 1892. BARTLETT, in the text; d. Maria Weston; son Daniel Stetson; son Sydney Smith; d. Mercy Everett; d. Mary Dexter, m. Levi Ford, with the others named in the text. ELISHA, 1st in the text; d. Luranna should be Susanna. ELISHA, 2d in the text; d. Abigail W. m. Edwin Lyon. EDWARD DOTEN, in the text; son Elisha born 1857. JOHN, 1st in the text, m. Isabella (Samson) Maglathin, born in Scotland, 1695, and came over about 1712, settling in Duxbury about 1740; son William born 1742; son Thomas, 1747; d. Jane, 1748. JOHN, 2d in the text; son John born 1771; d. Sally born 1769. JOHN, 3d in the text; d. Angeline m. Peter W. Maglathlin. JOHN, 4th in the text; son John born 1827, m. Mary E. Latham; d. Pamelia Ann born 1829, m. William J. Sheldon, of Boston. JOSEPH, 1st in the text, m. Jane, d. of Peter West; d. Lydia m. Nathaniel Bonney, of Rochester. JOSEPH, 2d in the text; d. Selina W. m. Nathan Chandler Maglathlin. MARTIN, in the text; son George Thomas had no 2d wife. Martin m., 2d, Luranna McLauthlin. NATHAN CHANDLER, m. Selina W., d. of Joseph Maglathlin. PETER WEST, 2d in the text, m. Angeline, d. of John Maglathlin. ROBERT, 2d in the text; d. Pamelia m. John McLauthlin. RUFUS, in the text, m. 1852, not 1752. SAMUEL W., in the text; wife was wid. of Peter West Maglathlin. SIMEON HALL, in the text, m. Mary Richardson. SIMEON WESTON, in the text; d. Frances B., and d. Lydia S.

MANTER, BELCHER, 1st in the text; add children, Catherine, m. Sylvanus Harlow; and William. Erase the 3d wife. BELCHER, 2d in the text, m. Sarah, d. of Joshua Wright; son William born 1803. GEORGE, in the text, m. 1821. DAVID, in the text; d. Lucy A., son Horace I. born 1854. PRINCE, 1st in the text; son George born 1798; son Thomas m., 2d, Mary Ellis Morton; son Timothy born 1812; son John was John D., m. Jeanette D. Burgess; d. Lydia W., 1837, m. Warren S. Douglass.

MARCY, CHARLES, in the text, m. 1812. STEPHEN, in the text; d. Lucy born 1784; d. Mary T. m. Horace H. Rolfe.

MARSH, THOMAS, in the text, m. Mercy, d. of Sylvanus Bramhall. Add perhaps child Calinda.

MARSHAL, SAMUEL, in the text; add child Susanna, 1751.

MARSTON, JOHN, Boston, m. Elizabeth Greenwood, and had John; Eunice, m. Lazarus Goodwin; Eliza, Martha and William. JOHN, son of above, m.

Ann Randall, and had Nancy, m. Henry DeWolf; Louisa, John, Ward, Helen, Henry.

MASON, ALBERT, Chief Justice of the Superior Court of Massachusetts, m., 1857, Lydia F., d. of Nathan Whiting, of Plymouth. STEVENS, in the text, m. 1767.

MATTHEWS, THOMAS, in the text, m., 1758, Desire Gifford, of Rochester.

MAY, CHARLES, in the text; d. Harriet W. born 1820; d. Mary W., 1825; d. Abby W., 1828. EDWARD, in the text, had a wife Dorcas and child Israel and two daughters. JOHN, 1st in the text, was born 1590; had a 2d wife, Sarah; son John born 1631, and son Samuel m. Abigail Stansfall. JOHN, 2d in the text, m. Mary Bruce, not Brewer; d. Mary m. a Ruggles; d. Sarah m. Samuel Williams. JOHN, 3d in the text; son Ebenezer m. Abigail Gore. JOHN, 4th in the text, was probably son of Samuel, a son of 1st John, born 1670, and the John, son of John, of Roxbury, m., 1711, Elizabeth Child, of Brooklyn, Conn. The marriage of John 4th to Ann Warren is doubtful. JOHN, 5th in the text; d. Bathsheba born 1754. JOHN, 6th in the text; son Thomas born 1800.

MAYO, NATHANIEL, in the text; d. Mary born 1810. THOMAS, 2d in the text, m., 1807, Lucy Gibbs, d. of William LeBaron. THOMAS ATWOOD, in the text; son Seth T. m. Elizabeth A. Pippy; son John A. m. Margaret J. Cahill, of Boston.

MILLER, EDWARD, in the text, was of Quincy.

MITCHELL, EXPERIENCE, in the text; the children in the text were by 1st wife. JACOB, m., 1759, Mary Tinkham. THOMAS, from Bridgewater, m., 1757, Keziah Swift.

MOREY, JONATHAN, 1st in the text, had also children John and Hannah. JONATHAN, 2d in the text, m. Hannah, d. of Job Bourne. SILAS, in the text; d. Eunice m. Hosea Churchill.

MORRIS, PATRICK, in the text, m. 1761; son John born 1768.

MORSE, ANTHONY, 4th in the text; son Charles P. m. Julia A. Seavey. HUMPHREY, in the text; son Anthony born 1795. ISAAC, m., 1767, Jemima Pratt. JOSHUA, in the text; son Theodosius should be Theodorus.

MORTON, AMASA, in the text; son Amasa born 1824. CALEB, 1st in the text, was son of Seth, below, and m. Rebecca Wood, not Warren; d. Rebecca born 1799, m. Gideon Carpenter. CALEB, 2d in the text; son Caleb born 1803; son Ezekiel born 1807; d. Hannah L. born 1801. EBENEZER, 1st in the text, was son of 3d John, in the text, and m. Hannah, d. of John Bacon, of Barnstable; son Ebenezer born 1726, and Seth, 1732. EBENEZER, son of above, m., 1753, Sarah Cobb, and had Livy, of Middleboro, 1760, who m., 1788, Hannah Dailey, and had Daniel Oliver, 1788, who m. Lucretia Parsons, who had Levi Parsons, the late Vice-President, 1824, who m. Anna L. Street. Daniel Oliver was born in Winthrop, Me., and moved back to Middleboro 1793. He graduated at Middlebury, Vt., and preached at Shoreham, Vt., where Levi Parsons was born. EDWARD, in the text, m. Sarah, d. of Zephaniah Morton. EDWIN, in the text (rewritten), son of 2d Ichabod, m. Betsey T., d. of John Harlow, and had Edwin, 1832; Helen, 1834; Theodore W., 1836; Hannah, 1838; Frank T., 1840; Maria, 1844; Margaret Bradford, 1854. ELEAZER, 1st in the text,

m. Rebecca Marshal, of Boston. ELEAZER, 3d in the text; add child Sarah, 1790, m., 1st, Calvin Cooper, and 2d, Joseph Atkins. ELKANAH, son of Elkanah in the text, removed to Nova Scotia and had a son Elkanah, who moved to New Brunswick and again to Digby, N. S., and became Justice of the Inferior Court and Probate. He had a son John Elkanah, born 1793, in New Brunswick, who became Collector of the Customs in Digby and died 1835. EPHRAIM, 1st in the text, m. Hannah Finney. EPHRAIM, 3d in the text; strike out " Rebecca m. Daniel Jackson." EPHRAIM, 5th in the text; son Isaac born 1803; Henry, 1801; son Ephraim m. Sarah Ann Swift. EPHRAIM, m., 1803, Dorcas Brown. EZEKIEL, 2d in the text; d. Mary born 1791. EZRA, Plymouth, Enfield and Croyden, N. H., son of 1st Silas, m., 1795, Mary, d. of John and Sarah (Langford) Allen, and had Ezra, 1796, m. Nancy Wright; Sarah, 1798, m. James Carroll; Judith, 1800; Naomi, 1802. GEORGE, 1st in the text, m. Julian Carpenter, of Urington, Somersetshire. GEORGE, 2d in the text; strike out "m. John Dyer"; d. Elizabeth m. Haviland Torrey. HENRY, in the text, m. Rebecca Whiting, not Whitney; son Ephraim S. m. Ellen Cushman. ICHABOD, 2d in the text; d. Sarah born 1788; son Edwin born 1804. ICHABOD, 3d in the text, m. 1818. ISAAC, 2d in the text; strike out "Isaac Churchill and Ruth Tinkham." JOB, Carver, in the text; add child Annie, m. William A. Thomas. JOHN, 1st in the text; son John m. Phebe Shaw and Mary Ring. JOHN, 3d in the text, son of above; his wife Phebe was d. of Jonathan Shaw, and he m. Mary Ring, 1687. JOSEPH, 2d in the text, m. Anna Bullock; son Perez born 1751; add also children, Anne and Hannah. JOSIAH, 6th in the text; son Levi m. Susanna, d. of Ebenezer Cushman, of Kingston; d. Elizabeth m. Isaac Loring, of Plymptom. LEMUEL, 1st in the text; d. Mary Ellis m. Thomas Martin; add child Margaret Drew, 1808, m. James Cornish and Henry Seymour. LEMUEL, 2d in the text; he m., 2d, 1823; d. Margaret D. should be Margaret F., and strike out "m. James Cornish"; son Quincy born 1840. MARCUS, in the text; son Marcus born 1819. NATHANIEL, 1st in the text; d. Remember m., 2d, Preserved Hall. Ann Templar was d. of Richard Pritchard, who removed from Yarmouth to Charlestown. NATHANIEL, 5th in the text; d. Mary m. Thomas Morton. He m., 2d, 1740, Mary Ellis and had Nathaniel, 1747; Nathaniel, 1749; Lemuel, 1757; Mercy, m. James Cushman, of Kingston. NATHANIEL, 9th in the text; strike out the whole. NATHANIEL, son of 1st Ebenezer, in the text, m., 1757, Lucy Washburn, and, 2d, Rebecca, d. of Nathaniel and Martha Tupper Morton. His children were Nathaniel, 1758; Tempe, 1762; Abraham, 1765, by 1st wife, and by 2d wife, Lucy Braley, 1768; Abraham, 1769; Ruth Braley, 1771; Andrew, 1772; Rebecca, 1775; Martin Tupper, 1783; Hannah, 1786; Deborah, 1791. SETH, son of 1st Ebenezer, m. Lydia Hall and Hepzibah Packard, and had Caleb, 1758. SETH, 2d in the text; son Seth m. Eunice Doten. SILAS, in the text; son Silas born 1794; George Washington, 1798; d. Sarah Foster, 1800. THOMAS, 3d in the text; d. Hannah born 1808. TIMOTHY, in the text, m., 2d, Mrs. Mercy Wilson. ZEPHANIAH, in the text; d. Rebecca m. Daniel Jackson; add child Zacheus m. Sylvesta Akin.

MURDOCK, BARTLETT, 1st in the text; d. Phebe m. Nathaniel Standish.

JAMES, in the text; son Samuel should be Lemuel. JOHN, 3d in the text; add child Jeanette, m. Stephen Tilson.

NELSON, CHARLES, in the text, m. 1828. EBENEZER, 1st in the text; d. Ruth born 1757. EBENEZER, 2d in the text; son Elisha born 1802; add d. Bathsheba, m. Lemuel Bradford. ELISHA, in the text, m. 1824. GEORGE, in the text; d. Ruth was Ruth J. JOHN, son of 1st William, in the text, m., 1667, Sarah, d. of Henry Wood. He m., 2d, Lydia (Barnaby) Bartlett, and 3d, Patience, d. of Ephraim Morton. By 1st wife he had John and Martha; by the 2d, Samuel, 1683; Joanna, 1684; and by 3d, Lydia, 1694; Sarah, 1695. WILLIAM, 1st in the text, m. 1640. WILLIAM, 4th in the text; his gr. d. Ruth m. Henry Thomas; add to grandchildren Hannah, m. Jabez Wood; Lois, m. Jedediah Thomas; Eliza, m. Benjamin Cole; and Sarah.

NEWBERRY, JAMES, in the text, m. 1773.

NICKERSON, LEVI, of New Bedford, m., 1824, Patty Cahoon. SETH, 2d in the text; son John born 1795; son William, 1804.

NICHOLS, HAYWARD, of New Bedford, m., 1820, Susan Clark. JOHN M. m. Sarah, d. of Peter Lanman, 1806.

OLNEY, ANTHONY, m., 1813, Patty Crane, of Canton. ZABEN, in the text, was born 1793.

OTIS, JOHN, 5th in the text; d. Temperance m. Rufus Robbins and Josiah Cotton.

PADDY, WILLIAM, in the text; d. Elizabeth m. John Wensley. He died in Boston, 1658.

PAINE, STEPHEN, in the text; d. Mary m. Enos Churchill; d. Mehitabel m. Hayward Gardner. His son John Sampson was born 1889. STEPHEN, in the text, m. 1799.

PATY, EPHRAIM, 1st in the text; son Seth W. m. Nannie B. and Sarah E. Whiting. JOHN, 1st in the text; d. Meriah m. Melvin Bailey. LEVI, in the text; d. Betsey born 1787. SYLVANUS, in the text; son William born 1793.

PAULDING, GEORGE, in the text; d. Lydia born 1810. JAMES T., in the text, m. Nancy G. Thrasher. WILLIAM, 1st in the text; son William born 1811; James T., 1820.

PEARSON, WILLIAM BENDICK; d. Phebe m., 2d, Benjamin Warren; d. Susanna born 1756; son William, 1758. WILLIAM, in the text; d. Abiah born 1789, m. William Bartlett; son William, born 1800, m. Joanna Perkins and Betsey Ann, wid. of James A. Perkins and d. of Nathan Burgess. Add children Deborah; Phebe, 1787, m. Joseph S. Ripley; Joanna, 1791, m. Tilden Keen; Rosanna, 1793, m. Samuel Cheever.

PEABODY, WILLIAM, m. Elizabeth, d. of John Alden, and had Elizabeth, m., 1666, John Rogers.

PELHAM, HERBERT, in the text, Treasurer of Harvard College. His will proved in London, March 13, 1677, calls him of Ferrers in Bewers Hamlet, Essex, and speaks of Governor Bellingham as the husband of his sister. HERBERT, born 1546, m. sister of Lord Delaware and his son Herbert m. another sister.

PERKINS, GEORGE, in the text; d. Jane born 1805. GIDEON, 2d in the text; son Gideon born 1814; son Ellis Atwood should be d. Eliza Atwood. JAMES,

1st in the text, m. at Lubec, Me. JOEL, in the text, m. Lucy (Stetson) Barnes, wid. of Samuel Barnes. JOHN, 3d in the text; son John born 1799. JOHN, 4th in the text; d. Eliza B. born 1827; son Ronald H., 1829. JOHN came over in 1630 and settled in Ipswich. A son Jacob, who died in Ipswich in 1700, had Joseph and Jabez. Jabez had a son Jabez, who was the ancestor of Isaac Newton Perkins, of Liverpool, N. S., and New York. Isaac Newton was son of John, of Liverpool, who m., 1804, Eliza, d. of John Thomas a Loyalist from Plymouth. LUKE, 4th in the text; son Bena should be Beza. LUKE, 5th in the text; son Stephen born 1798. SETH, in the text; the wife of son Ezra was d. of Robert Cook.

PERRY, JOHN, 1st in the text; son Lewis born 1798; d. Rhoda born 1795.

PETERSON, LEWIS, in the text; son Lewis born 1836; add child Charlotte A., m. Asaph S. Burbank. REUBEN, 3d in the text; son Reuben m. Julia Beale and had Reuben, m. Josephine Davis. REUBEN, 4th in the text; son Lewis born 1812.

PHILLIPS, AMES, in the text, should be Amos. BENJAMIN, 1st in the text; son Isaac should be Israel. BENJAMIN, son of 2d Benjamin, in the text, m. Alice, d. of Nathan Thomas, 1743, and had Alice, 1745, m. William Baker; Benjamin and Nathan. He m., 2d, Elizabeth Bourne. ELISHA, in the text, m. Mary, d. of John Wadsworth; d. Mercy m. a Randall. ISAAC, in the text. should be Israel. JEREMIAH, in the text, m. Hannah Glover, of Milton; d. Hannah m. Prince Hatch. JOHN m., 1763, Patience Robbins — Indians. JOSEPH, 1st in the text; d. Mercy m. Benjamin Hatch. NATHANIEL, in the text; son John m. 1735; d. Joanna m. Thomas Turner, of Pembroke; son Daniel m. Abigail Thomas. THOMAS, 1st in the text; d. Elizabeth born 1687; d. Merriam m. Ebenezer Dunham; son Thomas born 1678. TOMSON, from Middletown, Conn., in the text; d. Hannah m. George Phillips, of Middletown.

PIERCE, or PEIRCE, ABNER, in the text, was son of 1st Ignatius, in the text. AMERICA, in the text, m., 1st, 1808, Catherine Ann, and 2d, 1816, Violet Saunders. BENJAMIN, 1st in the text, son of Benjamin, below. BENJAMIN, Duxbury, m., 1775, Lucia, d. of Nathaniel Burgess, and had John, Benjamin, Patience, m. Josiah Mehurin; and Melzar. BENJAMIN, 2d in the text, was son of Richard and m. Mary E. Kendrick. BENJAMIN N., in the text; add child Rebecca S., m. Elisha S. Doten. IGNATIUS, 1st in the text; son Ignatius born 1814; d. Martha born 1811; d. Lucy born 1822; son Ebenezer born 1826; add son Abner, born 1813. JESSE, in the text; son Ignatius born 1785; son Branch born 1789. JOHN, 1st in the text; erase the whole. JOHN, 3d in the text, was son of John, below. JOHN, Duxbury, son of Benjamin and Lucia, above, m. Betsey, d. of Lemuel Doty, 1805, and had John, 3d above, m. Deborah, d. of Nathan Burgess; Phebe, m. Leander Hathaway; William; Tilden, m. Mary, d. of Ephraim Washburn; Nancy, m. Seth Mehurin. He m., 2d, Lucretia Phillips, and had James and Hiram. JOSEPH, of Duxbury, son of 2d Joseph, in the text, by wife Olive had Joseph, 1774; Luther, 1776; Calvin, 1778; Seth, 1786. MOSES, in the text; son Moses m. Lydia K. Raymond. SAMUEL, in the text, was of Bristol, R. I., and son Samuel born 1769.

POOL, JOHN, m., 1759, Jean Allen. PEREZ, in the text; d. Lydia Vining born 1805; son Gridley T. born 1815; son David Vining born 1823. THOMAS,

2d in the text, m., 1637, Ann, d. of Gabriel Fallowell, and 1646, Sarah, d. of John Jenney; add children Joanna, m. John Hathaway, and Sarah, m. Samuel Hinckley and Thomas Hackers.

PRATT, JOSHUA, of Plympton, m., 1756, Eunice Jackson. JOSHUA, 2d in the text, m. Bathsheba Fay.

PRENCE, THOMAS, 1st in the text, was born about 1600. His 3d marriage is doubtful.

PULSIFER, ABIEL, in the text, m., 2d, Sarah Noyce, niece of Governor Belcher.

RANSOM, EBENEZER, in the text; add child Sarah, m. Benjamin Cobb, and perhaps others. ROBERT, in the text; add after d. Mary, "and probably Sarah, who m., 1738, Caleb Williamson." ROBERT, son of above, born 1695, m., 1729, Sarah Chyles, and had Mary, 1730; Lemuel, 1732 ; Deborah, 1734; Anna, 1736; Samuel, 1738; Ebenezer, 1740; John, 1742.

RAYMOND, CALEB, 1st in the text; son Isaiah born 1788. CALEB, son of above, m. a King and had Caleb, Lewis and Thomas H., m. 1st Phebe Pierce, of Rochester, 2d, a Howard, and 3d, Sarah Pierce, of Rochester. The children of Thomas II. were Robert H. m. Mehitabel Nightingale ; Betsey K. m. James Drew ; Lydia K. m. Moses Pierce. CALEB, son of above, m. Betsey, d. of Ignatius Pierce, and had Albert, m. Naomi, d. of Preston Manter; Lewis, and Lucy, m. Joshua Douglass. CHARLES, in the text; son Charles Anthony m. Alice, d. of Stephen P. Brown. ISAIAH, in the text; son Otis II. m. Almira D. Hall. JOHN, m., 1831, Jedidah Ann Morse. PERKINS, in the text, m. Elizabeth Drew.

READ or REED, JOSEPH S. m., 1819, Sally Goodwin. NATHAN, in the text, m. Lydia, wid. of Jonathan Bartlett and maiden name Ellis.

REYNOLDS, JAMES, m., 1757, Elizabeth Dunbar.

RICH, JEREMIAH, of Orrington, Me., in the text, had Jeremiah T., 1822, and probably Benjamin Taylor.

RICHARDS, THOMAS, in the text, m., in England, Wealthian Loring; son John m., 1st, 1654, and 2d, 1692, Mrs. Anne Winthrop.

RICHMOND, ALPHEUS, in the text, m. 1805; son William B. should be William H. MICAH, in the text; add child Emily F., 1845. SIMON, 1st in the text; son Nathan born 1787; d. Hannah born 1780. WILLIAM R. should be William II. His wife was d. of Robert and Ellen Ishmail, of Wales, born 1823.

RICKARD, ABNER, 1st in the text; son Elijah born 1784. ELEAZER, 2d in the text; son Eleazer born 1741. ELIJAH, 2d in the text; son Freeman W. born 1814. ISAAC, 1st in the text; d. Mary m. a Cushing; d. Persis Harlow m. Eliab Wood. JOHN, 2d in the text; d. Esther m. a kinswoman, not d. of John Barnes. JOHN, 4th in the text, had a wife Mary; the 4th d. Mary should be Marcy; d. Lydia m. Joseph Tilson; d. Abigail m. Nathaniel Jackson. JOSIAH, in the text; d. Deborah m. an Allen, not Ellis. SILAS, son of Joseph, in the text, m., 1746, Elizabeth Raymond, in Pomfret, Conn., and had Lucy, 1747; Hannah, 1748; Edna, 1755; Silas, 1758; Elizabeth, 1761. SILAS, son of above, of Pomfret, m. Eunice Hyde, 1794, and had Polly, 1795; George, 1796; Alfred, 1797; Eliza, 1802; George, 1806; Roswell Raymond, 1810. His son

George m. Sarah Clark Helme, of South Kingston, R. I., 1833, at Providence, and had Sarah Helme, 1835, m. Jonathan C. Randall, of Pomfret; James Helme, 1838, m. Abbie Smith Weld, of Woonsocket; Mary Alice, 1839; William, 1842; George Silas, 1841, m. Peninnah Jackson; Elizabeth Estelle, 1844; John B., 1846. SIMEON, in the text; d. Hannah Harlow m. Jonathan Standish; d. Rachel m. Elias E. Standish; d. Eliza m. Atwood Drew. WILLIAM, in the text; add son William m. Martha Tilley.

RIDER, DANIEL, in the text; son Daniel born 1820; add d. Lydia Ann m. Daniel P. Pates; and Francilia. GEORGE, 1st in the text; son Caleb born 1793; son George, 1804. GEORGE, 2d in the text; son George Sylvester m. Nancy T., d. of Benjamin Jenkins; son Charles should be Charles E. ISAAC, of Middleboro, m., 1757, Bridget Nash. JOB, 2d in the text; d. Anna R. should be Anna. JOHN m., 1760, Susanna Briant, of Plympton. SAMUEL, 1st in the text, was son of Samuel and wife, Ann, of Yarmouth. SAMUEL, 2d in the text, m. d. of Thomas, not Joseph Tilden; d. Sarah m. Joshua, not John Bramhall. SAMUEL, 4th in the text; d. Hannah probably m. Josiah Bradford. SAMUEL, 6th in the text, m. 1763. SAMUEL BLACK, born in Plymouth, 1774, moved to Vermont and m. Lucy Chase, of Bethel, Vt., and had Samuel Black; Abner, m. Sophronia Ziba; Eleanor; Penelope and John Stafford. SETH, in the text; d. Esther m. Joseph Holmes. WILLIAM, 1st in the text, m. 1745. He probably m., 2d, 1763, Martha Tilley.

RIDGEBI, JOHN, in the text, had child Bethiah, m. Isaac Austin.

RING, ANDREW, 1st in the text; his mother was Mary; d. Mary m. John Morton; d. Susanna m. Thomas Clark. ELEAZER, in the text; d. Lydia m. a Sturtevant. WILLIAM, in the text; d. Elizabeth m. a Pearce, not Prince. ZEBEDEE, born 1750, m. Hannah Estabrooks and had Theophilus, 1773; Sarah, 1774; Mary, 1776; Hannah, 1778; Jarvis, 1780; Deborah, 1782; Zebedee, 1784; Elizabeth, 1787; Olive, 1789; Jacob, 1791. He moved to New Brunswick and his son Jacob died at St. John, 1827, having had four children, Hannah Amelia, Zebedee, Jacob and Samuel, of whom Zebedee was father of Allen M., who, in 1838, lived in Arlington, Mass.

RIPLEY, JOHN, Hingham, had John, Joshua, Jeremiah, Josiah, Peter and Hezekiah, of whom Peter had Peter, Nehemiah and Ezra. JOSEPH, in the text, son of Thadeus, in the text, born 1785. LUTHER, 1st in the text, was son of Calvin. NEHEMIAH, in the text, was son of Peter, of Hingham. THADEUS, in the text, m. Mary, d. of Ebenezer Shurtleff, had Joseph Shurtleff, William, Abigail R., m. Ansel Bartlett; Sarah, m. Alvian Vaughn, of Carver; Hannah, Nancy. WILLIAM, son of above, had William, m. Roxanna B. Corliss, of Quincy; Joseph S., m. Mariah Winsor, of Duxbury; Harvey M., m. Naomi Manter. WILLIAM PUTNAM m. Mary Briggs, 1805. He m. 2d wife 1810, and 3d wife 1821; d. Eliza born 1812, m. Andrew S. March. His 3d wife was d. of Silas Morton, of Hanover. ZENAS, in the text, was son of Calvin.

ROBBINS, AMMI RUHAMA, in the text; son Ammi Ruhama m. Salome Robbins; d. Elizabeth m. Grove Lawrence; son Nathaniel m. Hannah Tibbets; son James Watson; son Samuel m. Fanny Osborne; son Francis LeBaron m. Priscilla Alden, d. of William LeBaron. BENJAMIN, in the text; d. Betsey m. James Doten; son Benjamin m. Betsey Thomas; d. Sally m. George Delano.

CHANDLER, 1st in the text; d. Jenny should be Jane Prince; d. Hannah m. Benjamin I., not L. Gilman. DANIEL JACKSON, in the text; d. Catherine R. born 1855. ˙HEMAN C., in the text; d. Mary Elizabeth m. Charles H. Perkins. JAMES WATSON, in the text, son of 1st Ammi Ruhama, m. Maria Eggleston, and had James, Maria, m. Dr. Schenck; Ammi, Thomas, Mary Eggleston, George E., and Edward. JEDUTHAN, 2d in the text; son Benjamin m., 1755, Abigail Cushman. JESSE C., in the text; son Heman C. born 1808. JOSIAH, 1st in the text; son Josiah Adams born 1826; son Frederick W. born 1823; son Daniel Jackson born 1828. He m., 3d, 1855, Mary T. Reynolds, of Portland. LEMUEL, in the text; add child Mary, m. Josiah Bradford. NATHANIEL, 1st in the text, m., 1669, Mary Brazier; son Nathaniel born 1678. NATHANIEL, 2d in the text, had eight other children. He m. 2d, 1718, Mrs. Mary Prentice. PHILEMON, in the text; d. Irene born 1747, m. George D. Thompson; d. Sarah born 1749, m. Rev. Peter Starr; d. Rebecca m. John Keith and Jahliel Woodbridge. RUFUS, 1st in the text, m. Bathsheba Joy. RUFUS, son of above, m. Temperance, d. of John Otis, and had John Otis and Hannah. Hannah m. Samuel LaForrest at Foxboro, in 1811. WILLIAM, in the text; son Edward should be Edmund.

ROBERTSON, THOMAS, m. Elizabeth Collins, 1755.

ROBINSON, WILLIAM, m., 1814, Rebecca Austin.

ROGERS, ELEAZER, 2d in the text, m., 1756, Bethiah Savery. GEORGE, 1st in the text; son George born 1803. GEORGE, 2d in the text; son Charles Henry m. Martha L. JOHN, 1st in the text, m. 1762. JOHN, 2d in the text; d. Ann m. also George Russell. JOSEPH, in the text; son Thomas born 1638; d. Elizabeth m. a Higgins; d. Mary m. John Finney. He removed to Eastham. JOSEPH, son of Joseph in the text, m. Susanna, d. of Stephen Dean, and had Bathsheba, 1666; Hannah, 1667; Micajah, 1669; Bethiah, 1672. SAMUEL, 2d in the text; son Stephen born 1791. SYLVANUS, 1st in the text; Thomas and Otis were two sons, and son Sylvanus Watson was born 1829 and d. Elizabeth B., not Eliza B., born 1819, m. Josiah D. Baxter. THOMAS, 1st in the text; son John m. Mary Holmes.

RUSSELL, ANDREW LEACH, in the text; son George Briggs m. d. of Gen. C. C. Auger, not Augur. BRIDGHAM, in the text, m. 1822. JOHN, 4th in the text, born 1728, had a sister Agnes who m., in Scotland, John Martin, in the parish of Shotts, Shire of Lenark, and her son settled in Shelburne, N. S. THOMAS, 1st in the text; d. Lydia Cushing, not Lydia Goodwin; son Thomas born 1825.

SAMPSON, AARON, in the text; his 2d marriage was in 1869. ABRAHAM, 1st in the text; son Abraham m. Lorah, not Sarah. GEORGE, 3d in the text; d. Hannah m. Roswell Ballard. ISAAC, 3d in the text, m., 1715, Sarah Barlow. He had a 2d wife, Elizabeth; he had Isaac, Elizabeth, Lydia, Anna, m. James Presho; Phebe and Jacob. JACOB, son of above, born 1742, m., 1761, Allis Clark, in Middleboro, and had Jacob, George, Clark, Allis, Deborah, Betsey and Polly. By a 2d wife he had Samuel and Liscomb. He moved to New Salem in 1772 and served in the Revolution. His son George born in Middleboro, 1745, m., 1787, Sally Smith, in New Salem, and had Abigail, 1788; Caleb, 1792; Sarah, 1794; Phebe, 1797; George, 1801. He moved, 1804, to Stamford, Vt., and had there John, 1805; Calvin, 1810; Caleb, the son of George, m., 1814, Fanny Page, of Stamford, Vt. JOSEPH, 1st in the text; son Sylvanus born 1803. JOSEPH, 2d in the text, m. 1817, not 1815. SAMUEL, 4th in the text, m. 1815; d. Lydia born 1815, m. Winslow Cole 1832. SYLVANUS, 1st in the text; son Sylvanus born 1780; son Thomas born 1790; d. Sophia born 1795. SYLVANUS, 2d in the text; son Truman born 1802; son Hiram born 1804. TRUMAN, in the text, m. 1826.

SANGARELE, or LANGARELE, JAMES, in the text, was perhaps Langarele.

SAVERY or SAVARY (entirely rewritten), ANTHONY, probably son of 1st Samuel, m., 1703, Margaret Price, and had Ruth 1704; Joseph, 1706, m. Experience Hiller; Anthony, 1708. DANIEL, Middleboro, son of 3d John, m., 1794, Huldah Soule, and had John, 1795; Daniel, 1797; Huldah, 1798; William Soule, 1800; Lydia, 1801; P. White, 1803; Sarah Briggs, 1805; Betsey, 1812; George Simmons, 1815. GEORGE HOLMES, son of 2d William, m., 1804, Mary, d. of Peter Lanman, and had Eliza Ellis m. Nahum Johnson, of Bridgewater; Sally, Hiram, Mary N. m. Solomon Hardy; Ann, 1812; and George Holmes. GEORGE HOLMES, son of above, m. Diantha Gurney, of Abington, and had Mary Elizabeth m. Stephen Hall. ISAAC, Rochester, son of 1st Uriah, m., 1772, Deliverance Clifton, and had Deborah, 1772, m. Lemuel Gurney; Timothy, 1773, m. Elizabeth Swift; Sarah, 1775, m. Lot Bumpus; Meribah, 1778, m. Reuben Briggs; Deliverance, 1780, m. Richard Gurney; Uriah, 1781, m. Jane, d. of Barnabas Ellis, of Plymouth; Sylvia, 1784, m. Caleb King; Isaac, 1786; Samuel, 1788, m. Sally Wadsworth; Benjamin, 1790, m. Lydia Whitlock, of New Jersey; Phineas, 1792, m. Hannah, d. of George Cornish, of Plymouth; Polly, 1795, m. Jacob Swift. ISAAC, Rochester, son of above, m., 1808, Temperance, d, of George Cornish, of Plymouth, and had Hannah, 1809, m. Barnabas Ellis Swift; Adelia, 1811, m. Wilson Gurney; Samuel, 1813; Clarissa, 1814, m. Wilson Doty; George Cornish, 1816, m. Rachel Porter; Temperance, 1818, m. Samuel Mitchell; Louisa Matilda, 1820, m. Allen Thrasher; Sarah N., 1823, m. James Homan; Lucinda, 1825, m. P. T. Rose and Rueben Tuck; Isaac P., 1827, m. Marie Blakeslee; Amanda W., 1831, m. Jacob H. Sexton; Marietta E., 1833, m. J. H. Talcot. JAMES, son of 3d Thomas, m., 1774, Mercy, d. of Timothy Burbank, and had Mercy, 1776, m. Seth Morton; James, 1778, m. Olivia Shurtleff; Priscilla m. Perez Churchill; Mary m. Stephen Greenleaf; Ruth, 1780, m. Levi Morse. JOHN, Middleboro, probably son of 1st Samuel, m. Martha Parlow, and had John, 1706, Elizabeth and Thomas. JOHN, Middleboro, son of above, m., 1729, Mary Thomas, and had Martha, 1731; John, 1735; Perez, 1737; Nehemiah, 1740; Mary, 1733; Martha, 1743; Joanna, 1745; Lydia, 1747, m. a Tinkham. JOHN, Middleboro, son of above, m., 1764, Thankful Cobb, and had Daniel, 1764; Nehemiah, 1769. JOHN, Carver, son of 1st Peleg, m. Mary Atwood, of Middleboro, and had William, 1815, m. Mary Van Schaack, of Albany; Polly, 1818, m. Alexander Law; Hannah Perkins, 1820, m. Samuel A. Shurtleff; Waitstill Atwood, 1822, m. George P. Bowers; and John. JOSEPH B., son of 6th Thomas, m., 1843, Betsey A., d. of George Thrasher, and had Thomas G., 1843, m. Laura A., d. of Thomas Pierce. LEMUEL, son of 3d Thomas, m., 1786, Elizabeth Davidson, d. of John Stephenson, and had John 1786, m. Abiah Butterfield; Betsey, 1788, m. Isaac Dunham; William, 1790; Lemuel, 1792; Samuel. LEMUEL, son of above, m., 1816, Rispah, d. of Eleazer Thomas, of Middleboro, and had Cordelia Bartlett, 1828, m. Robert Cole; Emily Williams m. Wm. Walker and Silas Dean; William T., 1820, m. Sylvia C., d. of Samuel Alexander; Elizabeth S. m. Henry S. Rider; Samuel M., 1825, m. Nancy R., d. of Ansel Bartlett, and Ann Maria. NATHAN, Wareham, son of 1st Uriah, m., 1770, Elizabeth Nye, and had Patience, 1772, m. George Douglass; Nathan, 1774, m. Elizabeth Gammons; Mercy m. Savery Bolles; Amelia m. Wm. Swift and a Drake; and Aaron. He removed to Nova Scotia in 1783 and m. 1785, Deidamia, d. of Jeremiah Sabin, and had Sarah, 1786, m. Charles Thibault and two others; Sabin, 1788, m. Olivia Marshal; Lemuel; Esther, 1792, m. James Smith; Susanna LaVallee, 1794, m. James Brown; Deidamia, 1796, m. George Worthy-lake; and Stanley Wright; Uriah, 1799, m. Alice Elizabeth Worthylake; Deborah, 1801, m. John Andrews; Aurilla, 1803, m. Wm. Warner; Lydia, 1806, m. Samuel Doty; Nathan, 1809, m. Phebe Dunbar; Mary Ann, 1813, m. Allen Shute. NEHEMIAH, son of 3d John, m., 1794, Sarah, d. of Benjamin Cornish, and had Elizabeth, 1794, m. a Pratt, of Weymouth; Thomas, 1795; Nehemiah, 1797; Mary, 1799, m. Joseph Smith; Winsor, 1800; Sarah C., 1804, m. Lewis Bartlett. He married 2d, 1806, Deborah Smith, of Middleboro, and had Deborah, 1807, m. Joseph Wade and George W. Fisher; Louisa, 1810, m. David Cobb Holmes; Zenas, 1811; Mercy, 1813; Cordelia, 1817. NEHE-MIAH, son of above, m., 1841, Phebe Cotton, d. of Wm. Stephens, and had Nehemiah L., 1842, m. Wealthea E., d. of Charles Cobb; Irene F., 1848, m. Wm. F. Peterson; Esther S., 1846, m. Alexander A. Bartlett; Sarah S. m. Edward Thompson, of Brockton; Mary S., 1850; James Everson, 1854; Emeline, 1855. PELEG, Carver, son of 4th Thomas, m. Hannah Perkins, and had Thomas, 1787; John, 1789; Wm., 1791; Zilpha, 1793, m. Wm. Murdock; Mary, 1797, m. Benjamin Ellis; Hannah Perkins, 1799, m. Bartlett Bent; Drusilla, 1802, m. Gamaliel Fuller; Peleg Barrows, 1805. PELEG BARROWS, Carver, son of above, m. Julia Concklin, of Albany, and had Charles, William, Mary E., Mary A., Alanson P. PHINEAS, Wareham, son of 2d Samuel, m. a 1st wife, Mercy, and, 2d, Hannah Swift, and had Mercy, 1798, m. Samuel Hatch; Phineas, 1800; Lemuel, 1802, m. Selina Gibbs; and Margaret R. (Nichols) Gorham; and Benjamin. PHINEAS, son of above, m. 1st, 1825, Hope Tobey; 2d, 1829, Nancy Messenger; 3d, 1853, Sarah Bailey. PHINEAS, son of 1st Isaac, m. Hannah, d. of George Cornish, and had Phineas, 1811; Richard Gurney, 1812, m. Cordelia Delano; Mary, 1814; Samuel, 1816, m. Sarah Peck; Henry, 1818, m. Martha Rogers; Ruby Ann, 1821, m. Sanford T. Samson; Clifton, 1823, m. Harriet Clarke; Uriah, 1825; Horace C., 1827, m. Nancy Hartwell; and Caroline Stanchel; Louisa, 1830, m, George H. Howland; Emily, 1832, m. Benjamin Mattison; Sarah, 1834, m. Jason Wade. SAMUEL, son of 1st Thomas, removed to Rochester, and had Mary, 1678; Judith, 1680; Thomas, 1681; Susan, 1690; Samuel, 1695; and probably John and Anthony. SAMUEL, Wareham, son of 2d Thomas, m. 1st Elizabeth Bump, of Rochester, and had Mehitabel, 1741, m. Ebenezer Clark; Lydia, 1744, m. David Swift; Benjamin, 1746; Samuel, 1748; Benjamin, 1755; Phineas, 1757; Elizabeth, 1759, m. Jeremiah Bumpus; Mercy, 1760; Abigail, 1764. He m., 2d., Lois Sturtevant, a wid. of Josiah Sturtevant, and d. of Thomas Foster, and had Mercy, and some of the children may have been hers. SAMUEL, Wareham, son of above, m. Ruth Gibbs, and had Lucy, 1772; Esther, 1774; Temperance, 1776; Ruth, 1778; Arathea, 1781; Polly, 1783; Lucinda, 1787; Samuel, 1789; Nabby, 1792; Wm., 1796. SAMUEL M., son of 2d Lemuel, m. Nancy, d. of Ansel Bartlett, and had Wm. H., 1847; Jamie Cronacan, 1854; Samuel M., 1862. THOMAS, Plymouth, 1633, by a wife Ann, had Benjamin, 1644; Mary, 1645, m. Joseph Ramsden,; Thomas, 1648; Moses, 1650; Samuel, 1651; Jonathan, 1653; Moses again; Mara, 1654; Anthony, 1655; Aaron, 1656. THOMAS, son of 1st Samuel, m., 1705, Esther, d. of Henry Saunders, and had Mercy, 1706, m. Ichabod Sampson, of Duxbury; Uriah, 1708; Thomas, 1710; Lydia, 1712, m. Thomas Bates; Esther, 1715, m. Lemuel Jackson; Samuel, 1718; Mehitabel, 1721. THOMAS, son of above, m. Priscilla, d. of Ichabod Paddock, and had Bethiah, 1735, m. a Rogers; Thomas, 1736; Priscilla, 1739 m. Ezra Burbank; William, 1744; Esther, 1747, m. John Allen; and Wm. Stephens; Ruth, 1749; James, 1752; Ruth, 1755, m. Wm. Coye; Lemuel, 1757. THOMAS, son of above, m., 1760, Zilpha, d. of George Barrows, and had Mary, 1761, m. Job Cole; Thomas, 1764; Peleg, 1764. He m. 2d, Hannah Bennett, and had Zilpah, 1766, m. Wm. Cushman; Mercy, 1768, m. Thomas Adams. He m., 3d and 4th, Mary Crocker and Mary Shurtleff. THOMAS, son of 1st Peleg, m. Betsey Shaw, and had John, 1815; Thomas, 1819; Elizabeth Shaw, 1828. THOMAS, son of 2d William, m. 1790, Abigail Everson, of Kingston, and had Lydia Holmes, 1792, m. Bartlett Faunce; Sally Everson, 1794, m. Thomas Faunce, and a Harlow; Abigail T., 1796, m. Thomas Spinney; George, 1798. He m. 2d, 1806, Joanna, d. of Ezra Burbank, and had Sophia, 1807, m. John R. Spinney; Joanna H., 1808, m, James Nichols; Thomas, 1810, m. Fanny G. Smith; Mary, 1814, m. Henry Dunster, John Alexander, Charles Soule and Aaron Sampson; Wm. S., 1816; Priscilla Paddock, 1819, m. Wm. McDonald, of Pembroke; Joseph B., 1820; and Phebe S. THOMAS, son of 1st Uriah, m. 1766, Elizabeth Randall, of Rochester, and had Hannah, 1767; Elizabeth, 1769; Mary, 1771; Mercy, 1772; Charity, 1775; Thomas, 1777; Peleg, 1779. THOMAS, son of above, m., 1807, Mary Rider, and had Stillman, 1809; Charity, 1810; Rufus, 1812; Eliza, 1816; Hannah, 1818. THOMAS, m., 1821, Penelope Swift. TIMOTHY, Wareham, son of 1st Isaac, m., 1798, Elizabeth Swift, and had Elizabeth, 1802; Cyrus, 1805; Sarah, 1809; Timothy, 1811; Benjamin, 1816; Corban Barnes, 1818. URIAH, Wareham, son of 2d Thomas, m., 1738, Deborah Bumpus, of Rochester, and had Thomas, 1739; Isaac, 1743; Mercy, 1741; Samuel, 1746; Nathan, 1748; and Esther. URIAH, Wareham, son of 1st Isaac, m., 1806, Jane, d. of Barnabas Ellis, and had Barnabas Ellis, 1807; Ruth Ellis, 1808; Robertson, 1810; Deborah, 1812; Isaac, 1814; Uriah, 1816; James, 1819; Elizabeth, 1821; Patience, 1825; Maria, 1827. WILLIAM, son of 1st Peleg, m., 1817, Abigail T. Fearing, of Wareham, and had Wm. Curtis, 1818; Abigail Fearing, 1821; Mary Ellis, 1823, m. Joseph A. Bartlett; Thirza Tobey, 1825, m. Sturgis Chaddock, of Boston; Hannah P., 1827, m. John K. Robinson, of Falmouth; Bartlett M., 1830; Wm., 1832; Abigail C., 1836. WILLIAM, son of 3d Thomas, m., 1766, Lydia, d. of George Holmes, and had Wm., 1769; Thomas, George Holmes, Sally and Joey. WILLIAM S., son of 6th Thomas, m. Ruth Ann Barrett, and had Augusta S. m. Lorenzo F. Simmons; Emeline P. m. Russell

T. Bartlett. Winsor, son of 1st Nehemiah, m., 1836, Fanny G., wid. of Thomas Savery, and had Winson T., 1845, m. Almira F., d. of Charles Cobb ; Sarah C., 1848, m. Elisha T. Nelson.

Sears, David, in the text, m. Nancy, d. of Belcher Manter. His d. Sarah P. m., 1845, Andrew P. Alderson, who is the father of Victor Clifton Alderson, professor of mathematics in the Armour Institute of Technology in Chicago. Richard, 1st in the text, m. Dorothy Jones, not Thatcher. Thomas, 3d in text; son Thomas B. was born 1809. Willard, in the text; son David born 1786 ; Thomas, 1789.

Sever or Seaver, Charles Sever, 1st in the text; d. Catherine Elliott born 1827 ; son John Elliott born 1829; d. Jane Elliott born 1831; son Charles W. born 1834. James Sever in the text; son James Warren born 1797; son Thomas Russell born 1798; d. Jane Russell, 1802; d. Elizabeth Parsons, 1803 ; Sarah Ann Warren, 1805. James Nicholas Sever, in the text; son George Russell born 1822; James Nicholas, 1828; Winslow Warren, 1832; d. Charlotte F., 1833; Nancy R., 1835; add children James Russell, 1823, Sarah, 1829. John Sever, 1st in the text; son William R. born 1791; John, 1792 ; James Nicholas, 1793; Winslow Warren, 1796; d. Sarah Winslow, 1798; Charles, 1795. John Sever, 2d in the text; d, Ann Dana born 1828; Mary, 1832 ; Emily. 1834; Ellen, 1835; add children John, 1826, Herbert, 1829, and Charles W, Nicholas Sever, in the text; son John born 1730; James, 1733; William, 1729. William Sever, 1st in the text; d. Sarah born 1757 ; son William, 1759; James, 1761; d. Ann Warren, 1763: son John, 1766. William Sever, 2d in the text (rewritten), son of above, m., 1785, Mary Chandler, and had Penelope W., 1786, m. Levi Lincoln, of Worcester; William James, 1793, m. a Trask; Ann W., 1789, m. John Brazier. William Seaver, 1st in the text, m., 1742; son William born 1743; Ebenezer, 1745; d. Sarah, 1746; Rebecca, 1749; Ruth, 1751 ; son Jonathan, 1753; d. Elizabeth, 1756; Patience, 1758; Mary, 1764; son Robert, 1766; add child Waitstill born 1761. William Seaver, 2d in the text, m., 1st 1767, and 2d 1771; son John born 1771; Nathaniel, 1773 ; Hannah, 1775; Benjamin, 1777; Samuel, 1781 ; William, 1779.

Seymour, Benjamin, 1st in the text, came from England, 1792, with wife Naomi (Seely); son Benjamin born 1797 ; Edward D., 1806; Mary S., 1813. Benjamin, 2d in the text. had d. Caroline J. W. m. Simeon C. Spear. Henry, in the text, m. Nancy, d. of Lemuel Morton ; son Henry I. born 1842, m. Sarah S., d. of John B. S. Hadaway.

Shaw, Moses, son of 1st Benoni in the text, m., 1st Anne Phinney, of Barnstable, and 2d, Mehitabel, d. of Joseph Patten and wid. of Zachariah Hall. Zachariah, son of Joseph in the text, had a son Zachariah, 1751, who m., 1777, Hannah Bisbee.

Shepard, David, in the text, had David, 1700; Deborah, 1702 ; Prudence, 1704 ; Ruth, 1708; Abigail, 1715.

Sherman, Caleb, son of 1st Samuel, m. Rebecca Ring. Elijah, 2d in the text; his wife was wid. of Thomas Fish; son Elijah born 1818, not 1718. George, son of 1st Asa, m., 1st, Betsey, d. of Nicholas Drew, and had George Henry m. Cordelia, d. of Timothy Churchill. He m., 2d, Betsey, d. of James Ellis, and had James Ellis m. Sarah Sturgis, d. of Barnabas H. Holmes, of

Plymouth; William Stephens m. Helen M. Rose; and Susan Murdock m. Cyrus Whitlock. JOHN, 1st in the text; d. Hannah m. Josiah Holmes, of Rochester; d. Deborah m. James Thomas; d. Lois m. James Dexter. LEVI, in the text; son Eleazer Crocker m. Louisa Jane Gurney, of North Bridgewater, now Brockton, and 2d, 1878, Mary L. (Perkins) Thayer, wid. of Edward D. Thayer, of Boston. NATHANIEL, 1st in the text, m. 1769. SAMUEL, 1st in the text; d. Sarah m. Josiah Foster; d. Prudence m. Robert Cushman. SAMUEL, 2d in the text, m. 1724; d. Sarah m. David Lapham; and d. Mary m. Jabez Washburn. SAMUEL, 5th in the text; d. Eleanor m. John E. Churchill. WILLIAM, 3d in text, d. Thankful m. Robert Atkins; d. Sarah m. Adam Hall. WILLIAM, 4th in the text; d. Elizabeth born 1795.

SHURTLEFF, ASA, Plympton and Philadelphia, son of 2d Ebenezer, m. 1787, Elizabeth Foster of Philadelphia, and had William, 1789; John, 1791. BENJAMIN, 3d in the text; d. Sally m. 2d a Childs. EBENEZER, Carver, in the text, son of Ebenezer below, m. 1798, Ruth, d. of Seth Barrows, and had William, 1799; Ruth Barrows, 1804, m. Josiah Holmes, of Kingston; Ebenezer, 1807; Mary, 1810, m. Martin L. Lucas, of Carver. He m., 2d, Mary, d. of Thomas Shaw, of Middleboro. EBENEZER, son of 3d William, in the text, m., 1756, Mary, d. of Benjamin Pratt, and had Joseph, 1761; Asa, 1763; Mary, 1765, m. Thadeus Ripley; Sarah, 1767; William, 1769; Ebenezer, 1771; Isaac, 1772. GIDEON, in the text; d. Eames should be Eunice. HENRY C., son of William below, of Philadelphia, m., 1844, Caroline Emily Garnett, and had Mary, 1845; Margaret, 1846, m. George Barton; Emily, 1847, m. William Barker; Henry, 1849; Harriet, 1850; William, 1854; Charles L., 1856; Leslie, 1858; Walter, 1862; Henry C., 1863. ISAAC, son of 2d Ebenezer, m. Abiah, d. of Ephraim Soule, of Halifax, and had Sophia m. Henry Wright; and Irena m. Moses Kilgore. JAMES, 1st in the text; d. Elizabeth born 1737, not 1837. PETER, in the text, m., 1767, Rebecca, d. of Sylvanus Holmes. ROBERT, in the text, m. Mary Atwood. STEPHEN, in the text, was son of 2d Benjamin in the text. WILLIAM, son of Asa, above, m., 1812, Margaret Connelly, and had Elizabeth, 1813; John; William; Henry C.; Asa Foster, 1822.

SIMMONS, CHARLES, Duxbury, son of Noah below, m. 1798, Lydia, d. of Simeon Stetson, and had Joshua W., 1798, m. Lucy Arnold; Alden, 1801, m. Abigail, d. of William Delano, and wid. Mary Ann Doyle, of Cohasset; James; Peleg, 1806, m. Mary, d. of Weston Simmons; Caroline, 1809, m. William Baker of Marshfield; Henry, 1811, m. Fanny D., d. of William Delano; Sylvia Southworth, 1814, m. Horace Taylor, of Marshfield. ELISHA, in the text; son Ebenezer born 1785; d. Martha, 1789; son Elisha, 1790; son William, 1782; son Benjamin H., 1796; George W., 1800; Elizabeth and Joanna, twins, 1802; Elisha again, 1793. GEORGE, 1st in the text; d. Marcia B., born 1806; Lorenzo F., 1815; Isabella, 1817. ICHABOD, 2d in the text, had also a son Walter Everett, born 1846; his d. Marcia m. George Hatch; son Ichabod m. Harriet Bull, of Saybrook, Conn.; his d. Adelaide m. John Watson, and d. Victoria m. Augustus Merriam. LEMUEL, 1st in the text; d. Beulah born 1775; d. Lydia H. should be Lydia A. LEMUEL, 2d in the text; d. Priscilla C. m. Albert S. Churchill; d. Mary S. m. William Morton. NOAH, Duxbury, son of 1st Ichabod, m., 1769, Sylvia, d. of Benjamin Southworth, and had Peleg, 1772; Charles, 1776; Violata, 1788; Daniel, 1780, and Nathan. WALTER EVERETT, son of 2d Ichabod in the text, m., 1868, Almira Ellen Carter, of Stetson, Maine, and had Mary Florence, 1869; m. Frederick Harper Holmes, son of Frederick L. and Margaret (Robbins) Holmes, of Plymouth; Almira Ellen, 1871; Walter Everett, 1874; Kate Burnham, 1875, and John Edgar, 1882.

SMITH, ABIATHAN, in the text, m. Mehitabel Paine. JOHN, 1st in the text; d. Hasadiah m. Jonathan Russell; son Joseph should be Josiah, who m. Mary Pratt, of Dartmouth; son Eleazer m. Ruth Sprague; he m., 2d, Ruhamah, d. of Richard Kerby, and had Deliverance; Gershom m. Rebecca Ripley; Judah; Eliashub m. Dinah Allen; Hannah, Sarah, Deborah; Mehitabel m. John Russell. NEHEMIAH, perhaps from Coventry, Eng., the first religious teacher in Marshfield about 1638, m., 1640, Ann, d. of Thomas Bourne, of Marshfield, and moved to New Haven, and had children Sarah, and Mary, twins, Hannah and probably others. THOMAS m. 1762, Mary Ellis.

SOULE, BENJAMIN, 1st in the text; son Zachariah m. Mary Eaton. GEORGE, of Duxbury, m., 1833, Abby, d. of Thomas Goodwin, of Plymouth; JOHN, 1st in the text; add children Zachariah and James. JOHN, 2d in the text, m. Martha Tinkham. SAMUEL, of Duxbury, m. 1756, Mehitabel White. THOMAS, of Duxbury, m. 1807, Sally McCarter.

SOUTHER, NATHANIEL, in the text; d. Mary m. Joseph Starr, not Shaw; add child Hannah m. William Hanby.

SOUTHWORTH, CONSTANT, 1st in the text; d. Priscilla m. Samuel Talbot and John Irish. EDWARD, 4th in the text; his wife Ruth died 1879, at age of 101 years, 10 months, 13 days, and was d. of Asenath Ozier, of Duxbury.

SPEAR, JAMES H., in the text, m. Sarah P. Shurtleff.

SPINKS, NICHOLAS, m. 1760, Sarah Goddard.

SPOONER, BOURNE, in the text; son Nathaniel Bourne born 1815. EPHRAIM, 2d in the text; d. Esther S. m. George B. Sawyer.

SPRAGUE, ANTHONY, son of Anthony in the text, born 1663; lived in Hingham, Rehoboth and Attleboro, and m. Mary, d. of Thomas Tilden, and had Anthony, Benjamin, Mary, Elizabeth, Sarah, Lydia and Mercy. FRANCIS, in the text; one of his children m. Ralph Earle, of Taunton.

STANDISH, JOHN, 2d in the text; son Elias Ellis m. Rachel Rickard. JONATHAN, 1st in the text; son Jonathan m. Hannah Harlow Rickard, and d. Polly m. Luther Bradford. JOSHUA, 3d in the text, m. 2d, 1869, wid. Almira Darling. MILES, 4th in the text; d. Hannah removed to Paris, Maine, with her husband, Daniel Fobes, and had ten children. NATHANIEL, in the text; d. Phebe m. Job Sherman; d. Sally m. Malachi Ellis. SAMUEL, son of 1st Samuel in the text, had Samuel of North Grenville, N. Y., 1754; who had a son Samuel, 1782; who had a son Morgan, 1804; Samuel; John D., 1817, of Detroit; Morgan had Samuel J. 1830, Charles B. and Miles T.; John D. had James D. and Frederick D.; Samuel J. had Charles D. 1859; Alfred B., 1863; Charles B. had Frederick M. 1863, and Frederick D. had William C. The above James D. lives in Detroit.

STAPLES, SETH, m. Hannah, d. of Ebenezer Standish, and had John 1742, who m. Susannah Perkins, and had a son Seth P., 1776, who m. Catharine

Wales, who had a d. Catharine 1801, who m. George C. Goddard, and had Rose Standish, 1847, who m. William Green Abbot.

STARR, JOSEPH, m. Mary d. of Nathaniel Souther.

STEPHENS, JOHN, in the text; son John born 1788; Zaccheus born 1798. LEMUEL, 1st in the text; son Lemuel born 1814. WILLIAM, 3d in the text; son Edward m. Mary D. Wormwell. WILLIAM, 4th in the text; son William born 1840.

STETSON, CALEB, 1st in the text, m., 1705, Sarah, d. of William Brewster, and 2d, 1732, Deborah, d. of John Morton, and had Caleb 1734, and John 1738. CALEB, 2d in the text, m. Abigail Bradford 1754. ELISHA, in the text, had Sarah 1708; Eylah, 1710; Joseph, 1712; Hopestill, 1715.

STODDARD, ISAAC NELSON, in the text, born 1812; d. Anna Thomas, not Ann; d. Laura D. born 1860. JOHN, Hingham, 1635, had a wife Ann. His son, Samuel, born 1640, m. Elizabeth Otis, and had a son Jeremiah 1683, who had a wife Elizabeth; Jeremiah, son of Jeremiah, born 1709, m. Sarah McVaile, and had Jeremiah 1738, who m. Rebecca Bates; Ezekiel, son of the last Jeremiah, born 1762, m. Lucy Foristall, and had Elijah 1785, who m. Zilpah Nelson and was the father of Isaac Nelson Stoddard above. JOHN THOMAS, in the text; d. Mary LeBaron, not Mary Carver. WILLIAM PRESCOTT, in the text, m. 1870, Anna C., d. of Jeremiah Farris.

STRAFFIN, William in the text; son William S. born 1796.

STURNEY, THOMAS, in the text, m. 1722.

STURTEVANT, JOSEPH, son of Moses, born 1734, m. 1757, Mary Gibbs, and had Lot and others. MOSES, in the text; add child Aaron. SAMUEL, 2d in the text, m., 1st, a wife Mercy, not Elizabeth; d. Hannah m. Ebenezer Standish; d. Mercy m. David Bosworth. His 2d wife was Elizabeth. ZADOCK, son of 3d Josiah, in the text, m. Priscilla Howes, and had Vashti, 1748; Michael, 1751; Lydia, 1753 ; Vashti, 1756, m. Luen Dexter, of New Bedford; John, 1759.

SWIFT, THOMAS, 1st in the text; son Lemuel m., 1756, Rebecca Whitfield, of Rochester.

SYLVESTER, ABNER, 2d in the text; son Abner born 1829. JOHN, 3d in the text; son John born 1672; son Joseph born 1674; Samuel, 1676; d. Lydia, 1679. JOSEPH, 4th in the text, probably m., 2d, 1769, Susanna Tupper. NATHANIEL, 1st in the text; d. Elsie born 1795; son Nathaniel, 1797; Solomon, 1802; James Augustus, 1817. SOLOMON, 3d in the text; d. Angeline m. James Belcher, of Easton; add also d. Mary m. Frederick William Lucas.

SYMMES, ISAAC, 1st in the text, m., 1st, 1765, and 2d, 1774. ZECHARIAH, 1st in the text; d. Sarah m. William Davis; d. Ruth m. Edward Willis; d. Deborah m. Timothy Prout. Three other daughters m. John Brocke, Thomas Savage and Humphrey Booth.

TAYLOR, EDWARD, 1st in the text; d. Experience m. John Annable; d. Sarah m. Samuel Allyn. JOSEPH m., 1829, Sarah Maxim. PHILLIP, of Pembroke, m., 1811, Mary LeBaron.

THACHER or THATCHER, — JOHN OXENBRIDGE THATCHER, son of Samuel in the text, by wife Lucy had John, 1786; Zalotus, 1788; Cyrus, 1791; Thomas Hinkley, 1794; Moses Gill, 1796. JOHN THATCHER, 1st in the text; d. Desire

m. Josiah Crocker. JOHN THACHER, in the text, had also a d. Mary born 1757. PETER, 2d in the text, m. Mary Prince. ROWLAND, in the text, m., 1740, Abigail, d. of Timothy Crocker. SAMUEL, in the text, m., 1st, a wife Deborah, and had Mary, 1748; Peter, 1749. He m., 2d, 1758, Sarah Kent, and had Deborah, 1759; Samuel, 1760; Phebe, 1762; John Oxenbridge, 1765; Nathaniel; 1767; Susanna, 1771.

THOMAS, ASA, in the text; son Gamaliel m. Ruth J., d. of George Nelson, son Eleazer born 1827; son Alanson born 1822; d. Fanny born 1819. BENJAMIN, 2d in the text; son of William below; son Benjamin born 1749; son James, 1753; son Perez, 1751; d. Betty, 1745; d. Hannah, 1747. BENJAMIN, of Barnstable, m. 1810, Deborah Bradford. BOURNE, Marshfield, son of Nathan below, born 1772, m. Sarah Dingley, and had Seth James, born 1807. DAVID, Middleboro, by wife Joanna, had Mary, 1681; Joanna, 1683, and a son David, who had by wife Elizabeth, Samuel, Henry, William, Josiah, Jonathan; Hannah m. a Fuller; Elizabeth m. a Robbins, and Joseph. EBENEZER, of Middleboro, by wife Anna, had Thankful 1745; Ransom, 1747; Jacob, 1749. EDWARD, Boston, by wife Mary, had Meriam, Edward, Nathan, Noah, and Fear, and died 1726; his son, Edward, of Middleboro, had Asa, Jesse, Husha, Zadock, Rhoda, Mary and Rosman. ELEAZER, in the text; d. Lucinda born 1782; son Asa, 1785; d. Susan, 1787; son Eleazer, 1790; he m. Rizpah, not Bispah. ELEAZER, Middleboro, son of William below, by wife Mary, had Phebe 1748; Ruth, 1751; Elizabeth, 1753; Eleazer, 1755; Silence, 1757; Noah, 1759; Solomon, 1761, Samuel, 1763. EZRA, in the text, son of Isaac below; d. Elizabeth born 1785; Lucy, 1788; son Ezra, 1786; d. Eunice, 1790; Abigail, 1792; son John Sturtevant, 1794. GEORGE FRANCIS, in the text; d. Harriet Maria m. Silas W. Deane and Edwin J. Howland. GIDEON, son of Samuel in the text, had a d. Abigail, m. Gideon Harlow. ISAAC, Middleboro, by wife Phebe, had Isaac 1763; Ezra, 1765; Lois, 1767; Lucy, 1769; Isaac, 1771; Jedediah, 1773; ISRAEL, 2d in the text, had besides Abigail, a 1st or 2d wife Phebe, who was the mother of Levi and perhaps others; add child Betty, 1750, and Phebe, 1763. JAMES, 3d in the text, was son of 2d Benjamin in the text; son Joab born 1782; Stephen, 1787; d. Lois, 1788; d. Minerva, 1794; d. Polly, 1783; Sarah, 1792; son James, 1785; d. Zeruiah, 1790. JEREMIAH, in the text; d. Sarah m. a Wood; d. Mary m. a Blush; d. Lydia m. a Hackett; d. Thankful m. a Cobb; d. Elizabeth m. a Tomson; d. Bethiah m. a Chipman. JOAB, in the text, was son of 3d James. JOHN, 4th in the text, m., 1773; add children born in Liverpool, N. S.; Eliza, 1785, m. John Perkins; Thomas Mayhew, 1782; William, 1787; Thomas Appleton, 1792. JOHN BOIES, in the text, m., 1810, Mary Howland, d. of Isaac LeBaron. JOSHUA, in the text; son John Boice, should be John Boies; son Joshua was Joshua Barker, born 1797. LEVI, in the text; son Adoniram born 1804; son Elias born 1783. NATHAN, in the text, son of Samuel in the text, m., 1713, Alice Barker, and 2d, 1717, Abiah Snow, and 3d, Sarah, d. of John Foster; his son, Nathan, m. 1756, Sarah Bourne, and had Bourne. NATHANIEL, 4th in the text, m., 1722; son Nathaniel m. 1774, Margaret Newcomb. NATHANIEL, 5th in the text; add son John; he m. 2d, 1796, Jane (Downs), wid. of Isaac Jackson, and had also Jane m. Elijah Reed, of Middleboro, and a 2d husband — Drake. NATHAN-

IEL, 6th in the text, m. wid. Mary Allen. NOAH, in the text; son Daniel born 1743; Job, 1744; Elias, 1747; d. Hannah, 1749; d. Priscilla, 1751, and add child Enoch, 1753. RANSOM, in the text, was son of Ebenezer above. SAMUEL, in the text; son Nathan born 1688; son Gideon m. Abigail Baker; d. Bethiah m. Samuel Spague. SAMUEL, Middleboro, by wife Mehitabel, had Zebulon, 1750; Thankful, 1752; Seth, 1754; Content, 1756; Simeon, 1758; William, 1761. SETH, in the text, was son of Samuel above; the name of his d. was Lovica not Louisa. SETH JAMES, son of Bourne above, m., 1832, Ann Maria Stoddard, of Boston, and James Bourne Freeman Thomas, of Boston, born 1839, is his son. WILLIAM, 2d in the text; add child of 1st wife Margaret m., 1727 John Breck; he m. 2d, 1717; add children Anne, 1720; Anne again, 1721. WILLIAM, 3d in the text, m. 1739; d. Ann born 1741; Elizabeth, 1747; son Peter, 1746. WILLIAM, Middleboro, son of David above, by wife Susanna, had William, Samuel, Joseph, Benjamin, Eleazer, Susanna and Mary, who m. Jonathan Shaw. WILLIAM, Middleboro, son of above by wife Sarah, had Jabez, Ephraim, William, David, Israel, Joanna, Susanna, Sarah, Eunice, Betty and Mary.

THOMPSON, JOHN, 2d in the text, was son of 1st John, m. Mary, d. of Ephraim Tinkham. PETER, in the text, was son of 2d John; he had a 1st or 2d wife, Rebecca Sturtevant.

THRASHER, DAVID, in the text, m. 1814. GEORGE, 1st in the text, had a son George. GEORGE, 2d in the text, was son of 1st George in the text; d. Nancy was Nancy G.; add child Jonathan born 1798. JOSHUA, 2d in the text; son Lorenzo was Lorenzo D.

THURBER, CALEB, in the text; his son Thomas perhaps m., 1724, Mary Walker, of Boston.

TILDEN, THOMAS, nephew of Thomas, in the text, by wife Mary had Thomas; Mary m. Anthony Sprague; Lydia m. Samuel Rider, and perhaps others.

TILLSON, EDMUND, 1st in the text, had a wife Jane. EDMUND, 2d in the text; add child Ann born 1703. EPHRAIM, 1st in the text, was son of 1st Edmund in the text; add child Mercy m. Josiah Washburn. HENRY, son of Hamblin, in the text, m., 1825, Jerusha Barnes Paty, and had Jerusha, 1826, m. Albert Holmes; Henry Winslow, 1828; Charles Edward, 1830; Hannah Curtis, 1832, m. Charles S. Ewer. JONATHAN, 1st in the text; d. Eunice born 1738; d. Lucy, 1752; Molly, 1753.

TORRANCE, ROBERT, from Hanover, born in Halifax, m. Betsey Kinder, of Duxbury, and had Robert and Betsey, twins, Elam, Alexander, Erastus, Sylvanus, Nathan and Elizabeth. THOMAS, in the text, had Lilly R., 1791, m. John L. Morton; Mary m. Daniel Deacon; and Elizabeth H., 1789, m. Oliver Wood.

TORREY, HAVILAND, in the text. His wife was probably d. of George Morton; add child Elizabeth born 1731. JOHN, 2d in the text; d. Maria was Maria Morton. JOHN, 3d in the text; son Henry Warren born 1814. THOMAS, 2d in the text; d. Abigail Thomas born 1794. WILLIAM, 2d in the text; d. Anna m. 1781, Noah Bonney, of Hanson; add child Bathsheba born 1757, m. Joseph Smith, of Hanson; Deborah, 1760; Margaret, 1764, m. Jonathan Bonney; Elizabeth, 1766, m. Isaac B. Barker, of Hanson.

TOTMAN, JOHN, in the text, m., 1759, Elizabeth Harlow. JOSHUA, in the text; son Joshua m. Elizabeth Sutten.

TOWNS, SIMEON, in the text; son Joseph m. also Jane Ray.

TRASK, THOMAS, m., 1761, Hannah Waterman.

TRIBBLE, JAMES, 1st in the text, probably m., 2d, 1816, Mary Bartlett, d. of Ebenezer Holmes. JAMES, 2d in the text; strike out the words "Mary Bartlett, d. of Ebenezer Holmes," including the semicolon. JOSEPH, 3d in the text; son Isaac born 1788. JOSEPH, 4th in the text; son Thomas born 1801. WILLIAM, 1st in the text; son William Bradford born 1821.

TURNER, ELEAZER STEPHENS, in the text; son Francis W. m. Maria L. Seavey. JESSE, 2d in the text, m. Elizabeth H. Rider. SETH, in the text; son Jesse born 1782. THOMAS, in the text; d. Mercy Parris m. Hector Monroe, not Munroe.

VAIL, JOHN, in the text, was John C.

VIRGIN, GEORGE WILLIAM, in the text; son John born 1822. JOHN, 1st in the text; son John born 1792; son George William, 1794.

VOSE, JOSEPH, in the text, m. Deborah, d. of Samuel Churchill.

WADE, DAVID, in the text, m., 2d, Deborah Johnson, of Wareham, 1812; son John J. born 1819.

WADSWORTH, DURA, 2d in the text; d. Mercy was Mercy Taylor; d. Elizabeth Briggs was Elizabeth Taylor; add child Briggs, who m. Julia Thomas. JOHN, 2d in the text; erase the marriage of son Uriah. PELEG, 1st in the text, m. 1740; d. Welthea m. Judah Alden. PELEG, 2d in the text, m. 1772; he had five sons and two daughters, not mentioned in the text. SAMUEL, son of Christopher in the text, m. Abigail, d. of James Lindall, of Duxbury, and had Ebenezer, Christopher, Timothy, Joseph and Abigail.

WAIT, RETURN, Boston, son of Richard below, by wife Martha, had Return, 1679; Martha, 1681; Elizabeth, 1686; Nicholas, 1689; Thomas, 1691, and probably Richard. RICHARD, in the text, son of above; d. Mary born 1723. RICHARD, of Boston, by wife Elizabeth, had Return, 1639; Hannah, 1641; Nathaniel, 1643; Mary, 1645; Samuel, 1648; Elizabeth, 1650; Joseph, 1651; John, 1653; Abigail, 1656; Richard, 1658; John, 1660; Rebecca, 1663; Sarah, 1665.

WALLINS, JAMES, in the text; his wife was Ruth Dunham, not Dunbar.

WARD, ELIAB, in the text, was son of Eliab, below. ELIAB, son of 1st Benjamin, m. Druzilla Perkins, and had Betsey, m. Marcus Bosworth; Sybil, m. a Shaw; Eliab; Polly, m. Ansel Benson and Chandler, who removed to Connecticut.

WARREN, BENJAMIN, 3d in the text, m., 1763. BENJAMIN, Middleboro, son of Samuel in the text, m. Jedidiah Tupper, and had Sylvanus, 1746; Mehitabel, 1743; Jedidiah, 1748; Ichabod, 1750; Silas, 1756; Zenas, 1758; Andrew, 1760. CHARLES ELLIOT, son of George William, below, m., 1892, Anna Margaret, d. of Hon. J. A. Geissenhainer, of Freehold, N. J., and lives in New York; his children are Susanne Elizabeth, born 1893; Margaret Reslear, born 1895; and George William, 1899. DAVID, in the text; son Robert Clement should be Robert Dunham. GAMALIEL, son of James, and his wife Mary (Terry), below, m., about 1765, Ruth Jenckes, and had Perry, 1767; Henry, 1769; Abraham, 1772; Benjamin,

1775; Joseph, 1776; Elnathan, 1778; Samuel, 1781; Russell, 1783 ; Ruth, 1785; Gamaliel, 1787 ; Abigail, 1791. GAMALIEL, son of above, whose name was changed to Minton, m., 1814, Lucretia Durfée, and had Charles Durfee, 1815; James H., 1817 ; Theodore, 1819; Samuel S., 1821; Loring D.D., 1822. The son Theodore m., 1843, Louisa, d. of Stephen Davol, and had Eliza Davol, 1844; Stephen Minton, 1846; Louise E., 1853; Theodore J., 1858. GEORGE, son of last William, below, m., 1814, Sarah, d. of Azor Phelps, of Sutton, Mass., and died in Albany, 1856; he had two children, one of whom was George William, born 1828. GEORGE WILLIAM, son of above, lived in Albany, Brooklyn and New York ; he m., 1858, Mary Eliza, d. of Richard Henry Pearse, of Albany; he had six children, one of whom was Charles Elliot, born in Brooklyn, 1864. JAMES, son of Samuel in the text, born 1710, m., 1735, Mary Terry, of Free-town, and had Samuel, 1737; Mary, 1739; Cornelius, 1741; Gamaliel, 1744; James, 1745; he died in what is now Fall River about 1790. JOSEPH, 2d in the text, m. Mehitabel, d. of Edward Wilder. JOSHUA, son of Daniel and Mary (Barron) Warren, of Watertown, m., 1695, Rebecca, d. of Calvin Church; he was born in Waltham, 1668, and died in Watertown, 1760; he had twelve children born, among them Phineas, born 1718, in Waltham. NATHAN, son of Samuel, m. Keziah White, and had Nathan, who had a son Daniel, 1788, who m. Irena, d. of William Thompson, of Middleboro, and had Daniel F., born in Middleboro, 1827. NATHANIEL, 1st in the text; son Richard born 1646; Jabez, 1647. NATHANIEL, 2d in the text ; strike out the marriage of d. Hannah where the name first occurs, and insert it after Hannah in the next line, also erase the words "of Greenwich, Eng." PELHAM WINSLOW, in the text, m. 1825. PHINEAS, son of Joshua above, m., 1739, Grace, d. of Joseph Hastings, of Waltham, and d. in Waltham, 1797; he had thirteen children born, among them William, born 1751. RICHARD, 1st in the text ; son of Christopher doubtful, as is also the wife stated. RICHARD, 2d in the text, m. a wife Sarah ; erase the words "and John May." SAMUEL, in the text, m., 1703, Eleanor Billington; son Benjamin born 1720; son Josiah, 1724; son Cornelius, 1709; add children Joseph, 1715; Joanna, 1717; Sarah, 1722; Nathan, 1712; James, 1710. SAMUEL, Middleboro, son of above, m., 1734, Rebecca Dunham. SYLVANUS, Middleboro, son of Benjamin above, m. Reine Booth, 1774, and Sarah Washburn, 1782. WILLIAM, m., 1774, Elizabeth King. WILLIAM, son of Phineas above, m., 1777, Rebecca or (Robey), d. of Joshua Hathaway, of Freetown, and died in Worcester, 1831; he had nine children, and among them George, born in Watertown, 1789. WINSLOW, in the text; d. Mary Ann born 1835, and d. Caroline should be Caroline Bartlett.

WASHBURN, ELISHA, 1st in the text, m. 1729; add child Hannah, 1737, m. Thomas Davis. GEORGE, m., 1816, Margaret James Keen. JOHN, 1st in the text, came with wife and two sons in 1635, in the *Elizabeth and Ann* from Eversham, England; his wife was named Margaret. PHILIP, 2d in the text, m. Silence Davis of Kingston. SETH, 1st in the text; son Ephraim born 1794.

WATERMAN, ICHABOD, m., 1757, Hannah Rogers, of Kingston. JOSIAH, in the text, m. 1756. Samuel, in the text, had a wife Mercy, by whom he had Anna, 1693; by a 2d wife, Bethiah, he had Samuel, 1703; John, 1704; Hannah, 1706.

WATSON, ALBERT MORTIMER in the text; son James Marston m. Marian J. Smith, of Boston; son Nathan Burgess m. Emily W. Ransom, of Kingston. BENJAMIN MARSTON, 2d in the text; d. Ellen born 1855. DANIEL, in the text, was of Centreville, Md., and his wife was Susan, wid. of Emery Wells Sudlar; d. Susan Augusta born 1811. ELKANAH, 1st in the text; erase the words "and the three daughters first named m. three of his sons." ELKANAH, 3d in the text; Fort Kent should be Port Kent. JOHN, 3d in the text; LeBaron Goodwin should be Lazarus Goodwin. ROBERT, 1st in the text, perhaps had a son Thomas. WINSLOW, in the text; LeBaron Goodwin should be Lazarus Goodwin.

WELLS, DANIEL S., in the text, m. 1867. PHINEAS, in the text, was born 1799.

WEST, JUDAH, in the text; son Josiah m. 1755.

WESTGATE, BENJAMIN, in the text; son Charles born 1805; son Darius, 1797. BENJAMIN, 2d in the text; son Edward should be Edward W; add child Levi. DARIUS, in the text, should be Levi.

WESTON, ABNER, West Randolph, Vt., son of 3d Edmund below, born in Middleboro, 1760, m., 1786, Hannah, d. of Jonah Washburn, and had Edmund, 1799, who m., 1829, Sarah Edson. BENJAMIN, 2d in the text; erase the marriage of d. Mary; d. Bathsheba born 1827. EDMUND, 1st in the text; son Edmund born 1660. EDMUND, Middleboro, son of last Edmund in the text, m. Elizabeth, d. of Eleazer and Hannah (Ransom) Jackson. EDMUND, Middleboro, son of above, m., 1755, Mary, d. of John Tinkam, and had Abner. FRANCIS HENRI, in the text; d. Anna should be Anna F., m., 1st, Charles E. Gleason. HENRY, in the text; son John W. born 1853. LEWIS, 1st in the text; son Lewis born 1795. LEWIS, 3d in the text; d. Mary m. James Barnes; son William born 1819. OLIVER, in the text; add children Jane L. 1823, and Miranda B., 1835. THOMAS, 4th in the text; son Thomas born 1760. THOMAS, 5th in the text, now of Greenfield, m. Lucinda, d. of Ralph Cushman. WILLIAM, 1st in the text; son Coomer born 1784. WILLIAM, 2d in the text; son Harvey born 1792; d. Almira born 1789; d. Polly born 1784; d. Betsey born 1787.

WHITE, BENJAMIN, 3d in the text; d. Abigail m. John Stetson; d. Lydia m. Thomas Holmes; d. Jedidah m. Joseph Brewster; son Benjamin m. Lucy Howland. BENJAMIN, 4th in the text, m. Lucy Howland; add child Thomas, 1748. BENJAMIN, Hanover, son of 1st Cornelius, in the text, had Penniah, 1744; Robert, 1747; Benjamin, 1756; Cornelius, 1755. CHARLES HALE, Marlboro, son of Samuel, below, m. Eliza A., d. of Alfred Wheeler, of Newburyport, and had Charles Henry. CHRISTOPHER, son of Paul, below, had Joseph and Christopher. CORNELIUS, 2d in the text; son Warner should be Warren and d. Polly should be son Peleg. DANIEL, 2d in the text; d. Abigail m. a Soule; d. Catharine m. a Lewis; d. Urania m. Luther Hayward, of Bridgewater. DANIEL, 3d in the text; the name of wife was Margaret Bell. Add child Joanna, 1722, m. Nathaniel Phillips. EBENEZER, 1st in the text; son Obdiaah should be Obediah. ENOCH, Bolton, son of Samuel, below, m. Hannah Hale, and had Lucy Hale, Samuel and Hannah. He m., 2d, wid. of Amaziah Converse and d. of Jonathan Capron, and had Ambrose Capron.

GIDEON, 1st in the text; after the word "England" insert "a Captain in the British Army." JAMES, son of Thomas, below, settled in Windham, Vt. JESSE, in the text; d. Christiana m. William Lewis. JOHN, 1st in the text; son Abijah m., 1738, Ann Little, and had Ann, 1739; Priscilla, 1740; Sylvanus, 1742; Abijah, 1745; Deborah, 1746; Abijah, 1747; Sarah, 1749; William, 1752; John, 1753; Susanna, 1756, m. Luther Little. LEMUEL, in the text, m. Ann Scott, of Dorchester, 1731, and had, besides those mentioned, Nathaniel, 1732; Susanna, 1735; Joanna, 1737; Gideon, 1741. LUTHER, 1st in the text, m., 1789, Mary Delano. MILES WHITWORTH, in the text; d. Ellen should be Ellen Watson, born 1815; son Thomas should be Thomas Davis, 1817; son Miles Whitworth born 1815; Ellen Whitworth, 1814; Gideon, 1821. PAUL, son of 1st Cornelius, in the text, m. Elizabeth Curtis, and had John, 1739; Nathaniel, 1742; Christopher, 1743; Joanna, 1744; Hannah, 1745; Patience, 1747; Peregrine, 1748; Daniel, 1752; Experience, 1740; and Joseph. PEREGRINE, 1st in the text; son Sylvanus m. a wife Deborah; son Peregrine removed to Lebanon, Conn. PEREGRINE, 2d in the text; child Benni should be Benoni. RESOLVED, in the text; d. Elizabeth m. Obadiah Wheeler, of Concord, Mass., 1762. ROBERT, son of 1st Benjamin, or Benjamin above, had Penniah, David, Martin, Richmond and Elijah. SAMUEL, Bolton, son of Thomas, below, m. Sarah Fosgate and had Enoch, Robert, Jonathan and David, twins, Beulah, Rachel and Benjamin, twins, and Sarah. SAMUEL, son of Enoch, above, m. Harriet Newell Wade, of Marlboro, N. H., 1833, and had Charles Hale and Daniel Allen. THOMAS, Scituate and Bolton, son of 1st Daniel, in the text, by wife Rachel had William, James, Samuel, Thomas and Rachel. TOBIAS, Marshfield, son of 4th Benjamin, by wife Hannah had Mercy, 1786; Gideon, 1783; Benjamin, 1785. WILLIAM, son of the last Thomas, above, settled in Marlboro, N. H. WILLIAM, 3d in the text; d. Arabella born 1809; son Peregrine, 1816.

WHITEHOUSE, JOHN, in the text, was perhaps Whitehorne.

WHITING, WHITTEN, etc. ABRAHAM WHITTEN, 1st in the text; son Abraham born 1798; d. Sally, 1802. ABRAHAM WHITTEN, 2d in the text; son Francis L. born 1833. AMOS WHITTEN, in the text; son Samuel Marshal born 1813. ASA WHITING, in the text; son Asa Alden born 1812. BENJAMIN WHITING, 1st in the text; son Ellis born 1807; d. Martha H. born 1805. CHARLES WHITTEN, in the text; son Lewis Holmes born 1834; son Elisha Cobb born 1841. ELISHA WHITON, 2d in the text; son Benjamin born 1803; son Melzar, born 1777, may have been son of 1st wife. ELISHA WHITING, in the text; son Joseph B. born 1841. HENRY WHITING, in the text, m. 1815. JAMES WHITON, 3d in the text, m. 1704; son Elisha born 1706; add d. Beersheba, born 1705. JOHN WHITON, son of 2d James in the text, m. Bethiah, d. of Eleazer Crocker, of Barnstable. JOSEPH WHITING, 1st in the text, m. 2d wife 1803; son George born 1817. NATHAN WHITING, 1st in the text. He m., 2d, Betsey wid. of Abraham Howland and d. of William Finney. NATHAN WHITING, 2d in the text, son of above, m. Experience Finney, and had Pelly F.; d. Lydia F. m. Albert Mason. He m., 2d, Sally Ann, wid. of Ephraim Morton and d. of Joshua Swift. SAMUEL MARSHAL WHITTEN, in the text; son Joseph B. m. Abbie Soule, of Kingston. SAMUEL WHITING, Hingham, son of 2d

James, m., 1708, Margaret Williams, and had Daniel, 1723, who m. Jael Damon, and had Daniel, 1745, who m. Desire Stoddard, and had Daniel, 1771, who removed to Marshfield, and m. Phebe Whiton, of Hingham. The children of Daniel and Phebe were Abigail, 1798; Lewis, 1800; Eliza, 1802, m. Parker Johnson; Nelson, 1804; Daniel, 1806; Lyman, 1817.

WHITMAN, DANIEL, in the text, m. 1768. WILLIAM HENRY, in the text; d. Elizabeth H. should be Elizabeth W.; add son Winslow, born 1866.

WILLET, THOMAS, in the text; son Hezekiah m. Anna Brown. Thomas died in 1674, and his grave is one-half mile from Cedar Grove Station, on the Providence, Warren and Bristol Railroad.

WILLIAMS, JOHN, m., 1759, Lydia Goddard.

WINSLOW, ANTHONY, in the text, m. 1729. EBENEZER, Petersham, son of Kenelm, below, m., 1773, Rebecca Dean, of Dedham, and had Susanna, 1774, m. William Thompson, of New Braintree; Ebenezer, 1778; Leonard, 1782; Rebecca, 1785, m. John Washburn; Lucretia, 1787. EBENEZER, Petersham, son of above, m. Nancy Aldrich, of Petersham, and had Simeon Aldrich. EDWARD, 2d in the text; d. Elizabeth m. Robert Brooks. EDWARD, 3d in the text, was Collector of the Port of Plymouth, Register of Probate and Clerk of the Pleas. Being a loyalist he was deprived of his offices in 1775; and in December, 1781, joined the British garrison in New York with a part of his family, the remainder joining him later. Sir Henry Clinton allowed him a pension of two hundred pounds per annum, with rations and fuel. On the 13th of August, 1783, with wife, two daughters and three colored servants he sailed for Halifax, reaching there September 14th. He died in Halifax in 1784. EDWARD, 4th in the text, son of above; son John Francis Wentworth born 1793. He was associated with his father in his various offices. He joined the British in Boston, and went to Lexington with Lord Percy April 19, 1775. He was appointed by General Gage Collector of Boston and Suffolk Register of Probate, going to Halifax at the time of the evacuation of Boston, and was made there, by Sir William Howe, Secretary of the Board of General Officers, of which Lord Percy was President, for distribution of donations to the troops. Later he went to New York, and was appointed Muster Master General of the forces, and remained in the States in that capacity during the war. In 1779 he was chosen by Refugees in Rhode Island to command them, and served during two campaigns. He was Military Secretary in Halifax after the war till 1785, when he went to New Brunswick as one of the King's Council and Paymaster of Contingencies. He died in Frederickton, N. B, in 1815. EDWARD, 5th in the text; he m., 2d, 1668; add child Susanna, 1675, m. John Alden, of Boston. EDWARD, Boston, son of 1st John, by wife Sarah had John, 1661; Mary, 1665; and by wife Elizabeth had Edward, 1669; Katharine, 1672; Ann, 1678. ISAAC, 2d in the text; d. Elizabeth m. Kilborn Whitman, not Kilburn. JOHN, 1st in the text; add children Mercy, m. a Harris; and another, m. a Pollard; son Isaac, m. a Parnell; and d. Elizabeth b. 1665. JOSEPH, Boston, son of 1st John in the text, had Mary, 1674; Joseph, 1677. KENELM, 3d in the text, m., 2d, Ann, wid. of John Taylor and d. of Edward Winslow, of Boston. KENELM, son of 2d Samuel, m. Elizabeth Clapp, and had Kenelm, 1735; Elizabeth, 1737; Anna, 1739, m. a Dalrymple; Mary, 1741, m. a Whitney; Susanna, 1743, m. a Peckham; Kenelm, 1746, removed to Cortland County, N. Y.; Ebenezer, 1749; John Clapp, 1752; Rhoda, 1754, m. a Whitney; Dorcas, 1756; Dorcas again, 1758.

WINSOR, WILLIAM D., in the text, m. Hannah, d. of James Howard, of Plymouth.

WISWALL, GEORGE RICKS, in the text; d. Lydia Tufts born 1799. ICHABOD, in the text; d. Priscilla m. Gershom Bradford; d. Deborah m. Samuel Seabury.

WOOD, ALVAH, in the text; son Alvah born 1820. DAVID, 1st in the text; son Jabez m. Hannah, d. of Thomas Nelson. HENRY, in the text; d. Sarah m. John Nelson. NATHANIEL, 2d in the text, was born 1785. NATHANIEL, 3d in the text; son Nathaniel Russell born 1855; add children Charles A., 1857; Colburn C., 1864. OLIVER, in the text, m. Betsey H. Torrance, 1812. STEPHEN, in the text, was called Wood alias Atwood. WILKES, in the text; Cornelia should be Cornelia B. Snow.

WRIGHT, ISAAC, 1st in the text; d. Molly m. John Doten. SAMUEL, Plympton, son of 1st Adam in the text, by wife Anna had Samuel, Edmund, Jacob and Sarah. JACOB, son of above, had Edmund, 1763; Mary, m. Winslow Wright, and perhaps others. JOSEPH, 2d in the text; son Joseph born 1806; son Joshua born 1810. JOSHUA, in the text; son Joseph born 1786; d. Susanna born 1794. Add child Sarah, m. Belcher Manter. WILLIAM, in the text, came in the *Fortune* 1621. He m. Priscilla, d. of Alexander Carpenter, and had a son Richard.

ADDENDA.

BREWSTER, BENJAMIN, son of 1st Jonathan in the text; d. Ruth m., 1692, Thomas Adgate; son Benjamin m., 1696, Mary Smith, and had Benjamin, 1697; John, 1701; Mary, 1704; son Daniel had also a d. Jerusha, born 1710; and a son Ebenezer, born 1713; d. Hannah m , 1708, Joseph Freeman; son Jonathan m., 1690, Ruth Stiver or Steven, and had Lucretia, 1691; Jonathan, 1694. JOHN, son of above Daniel, m., 1725, Dorothy Treat, and had Oliver, 1726; Dorothy, 1728; Hannah, 1729; Daniel, 1731; Sarah, 1733. JONATHAN, 1st in the text; d. Grace m., 1659, Daniel Witherell. He had also a d. Hannah, 1641; his d. Elizabeth m., 1653, Peter Brawley or Bradley.

COBB, JOHN, son of 1st Henry in the text, m., 2d, 1676, Jane (Godfry) Woodward, of Taunton, and the last three children in the text were hers, as also perhaps children Morgan, Samuel and John.

COLLINGWOOD, in the text; son James Bartlett born 1829, not 1830, as Town Record states.

GODDARD, LEMUEL, in the text, had also a son John, who m. a Beck, of Philadelphia.

HAMMOND, WILLIAM, m., June 9, 1605, Elizabeth Payne or Penn, and had d. Anne, who probably m. Rev. John Lothrop.

HOWLAND, JOHN, 1st in the text, had also d. Hannah, m. Jonathan Bosworth, of Swanzey. JOHN, of Freetown, 9th in the text, m., 2d, Beulah Bemis, of Spencer, and had Polly, 1775; James, 1776; Abigail, 1779; Willard, 1780; Susan, 1783; Abiah, 1785. JAMES, son of above, moved to Brookfield, and m.,

1799, Catharine, d. of Joshua Bemis, of Spencer, and had John, 1800; John 1802; Abiah, 1807; James, 1810; Pardon, 1811, m. Ursula Caulkins, 1837, and Eveline Caulkins, 1841, and Abigail Gulliver, 1842; James, 1814, m. Melinda A., d. of Baxter Henshaw, of Brookfield; Charles B., 1816, m. Emeline Bemis; and Abner, 1818. ABNER, son of above, lived in Brookfield and Spencer. He m., 1845, Martha A., d. of Elijah Kittredge, of Spencer, and in 1882 Rebecca D. (Bartlett) Manson, and had by 1st wife E. Harris, 1846; Lucius H., 1848, m. Clara Pope; Sarah J., 1850, m. William A. Bemis; Almira E., 1860, m. Charles P. Leavitt. E. HARRIS, son of above, Brookfield, Oxford and Spencer, m., 1868, Mattie P. Carson, and, 2d, 1880, Sarah J., d. of Henry L. Mellen, of Brookfield, and had by 1st wife Harris Walter, 1869; Edith Florence, 1871; Lewis Abner, 1874; Milton Howard, 1877; and by 2d wife Maria Lucy, 1881; Oscar Mellen, 1882.

KEMPTON, STEPHEN, Acushnet, born 1747, m. a Jenney, and had Elijah, 1784, m. Louisa Wilcox, of Liverpool, England.

PAULDING, POLDEN, POLLARD, etc., JOHN, m. Lydia, d. of Ephraim Tilson, and had John, 1702; Elizabeth, 1703, m. Richard Bagnall; Mary, 1706, m., 1725, Ephraim Washburn; William, 1708; Lydia, 1710, m. John Goddard; Thomas, 1712, m. Deborah Spooner; Hannah, 1719, m. Samuel Hubbard; Benjamin, 1721; Thankful, 1725, m. Joseph Rider; and William again, 1727. He was the first of the name in Plymouth, and not his son Thomas, as stated in the text.

RANSOM, JOSHUA, in the text, who m., 1692, Susanna Garner, m., 1686, for a 1st wife Mary, d. of John Gifford. ROBERT, in the text, had probably a d. Deborah, who m. George Shurtleff.

RIDER, JOSEPH, 2d in the text, m. Thankful, d. of John Pollard or Paulding.

STANDISH, LEMUEL, in the text, born 1746, had also children Rachel and Abigail; his son David born in Bath 1777, m. Jane Hogan, and had Margaret Helen, 1800, m. Thomas Farnham; David Winter, 1804, m. Elizabeth Dingley; William H.; Lemuel Miles, 1808, m. Olive Nutter; James, 1811, m. Sarah Grant; Francis, 1815. FRANCIS, son of above, m., 1847, in Boston, Caroline Amanda, d. of Benjamin and Caroline Rogers, and had Myles, 1851; Frank Winter, 1854; Mabel, 1856; Clift, 1858. MYLES, son of above, m., 1890, Louise Marston, d. of Asa Farwell, of Boston, and had Barbara, 1891; Lora, 1892; Myles, 1893.

THOMAS, DANIEL, son of 1st John in the text, m., 1698, Experience, d. of Thomas Tilden, and had Abigail, David, Sarah, Mary, Benjamin, Experience and Mercy.

NOTES.

NORTHMEN. — The Royal Society of Northern Antiquaries at Copenhagen have recently thrown much light on the voyages of the Northmen and make it probable that Plymouth was visited by them in the beginning of the eleventh century. In the latter half of the tenth century Thorvald and his son, Eirek, fled on account of their crimes from Norway to Iceland, and after the death of Thorvald, the son, called Eirek the Red, fitted out a vessel and made a voyage, in the course of which he discovered Greenland. In 985

Eirek settled in Greenland with a considerable colony, among whom was Heriulf, a kinsman of Ingolf, the first settler. After their departure from Iceland, Biarni Heriulfson, the son of Heriulf, returned home from a voyage to Norway, and finding his father gone, followed him, but, driven by gales to the southward, sailed along the shores of Newfoundland, Nova Scotia and Massachusetts.

Eirek the Red had three sons, — Leif, Thorvald and Thorstein. In the year 1000, Leif, with thirty-five men, sailed south on a voyage of discovery, first making the coast of Newfoundland, where he landed and named the country Helluland. He again sailed farther south and came to another land the description of which agrees perfectly with that of Nova Scotia, and this he called Markland. Sailing again still farther south, he passed between Cape Cod and Nantucket, through Vineyard Sound and Seconnet River, into Mount Hope Bay, the land about which he called Vinland. In the spring of 1001 he returned to Greenland. In the spring of 1002, Thorvald, a younger brother of Leif, took the same ship and with thirty men undertook to follow in the track of Leif and make a more thorough exploration. He went directly to Vinland, where he passed the winters of 1002 and 1003. In the spring of the latter year he explored the coast farther south, but how far the record is too imperfect to determine. Returning to Vinland, he there passed another winter, and in the spring of 1004 sailed eastward and was driven ashore in a gale on Cape Cod, which he called Kialar-ness, or Keel Cape. After the necessary repairs had been made he sailed westward until he came to "a promontory," answering to the description of the Gurnet at the entrance of Plymouth harbor, where he was mortally wounded by the natives with a poisoned arrow. Before his death he said to his companions, — "Now it is my advice that you prepare to return home as quickly as possible, but me you shall carry to the promontory which seemed to me so pleasant a place to dwell in; perhaps the words which fell from me shall prove true and I shall indeed abide there for a season. There bury me, and place a cross at my head and another at my feet, and call that place forever more Krossa-ness" (Cross Cape). Thorvald died and was there buried, and in the spring of 1005 his companions set sail for Greenland.

THE "MAYFLOWER." — An unfounded story has become quite current that the *Mayflower* was at one time engaged in the slave-trade. The story doubtless had its origin in an English court record of a suit of Vassall and others against Jacket. In that suit, tried about 1650, "George Dethick, of Poplan, gentleman, aged 24, deposed that he well knew the ships the *Mayflower*, the *Peter* and *Benjamin*, of which Samuel Vassall, Richard Grandley and Company were the true and lawful owners, and that they fitted them out on a trading voyage to Guinea, and thence to certain places in the West Indies, and so to return to London. William Jacket was captain and commander, and Dethick himself sailed in the *Mayflower* as one of the master's mates, June 16, 1647. On the arrival of the ship at Guinea, they trucked divers goods for negroes, elephants' teeth, gold and provisions for the negroes. They got 450 negroes and more, and sailed in the *Mayflower* to Barbadoes, arriving there at the beginning of March, 1647–48, Mr. Dethick being the purser." Such is the origin of a story which has been repeated with an unaccountable pleasure by that class of persons who enjoy a sneer now and then at the Pilgrims and everything connected with them. Aside from the probability that a vessel bearing the name *Mayflower* in 1647 was a different one from that which brought the Pilgrims to Plymouth twenty-seven years before, Mr. Hunter, F.S.A., of London, an assistant keeper of the public records, states, in his "Collections Concerning the Early History of the Founders of New Plymouth, the First Colonists of New England," from which the above extract is quoted, that the *Mayflower* in the slave-trade was of three hundred and fifty tons burden, while it is well known that the Pilgrim ship was of only one hundred and eighty. Mr. Hunter further mentions his discovery of the existence of several vessels bearing the name in the early part of the seventeenth century. "In 1587 there was a *Mayflower* of London, of which William Morecok was master, and a *Mayflower* of Dover, of which John Tooke was master, and at the same time another *Mayflower*, of London, of which Richard Ireland was master. In 1633 there was a *Mayflower* of Dover, Walter Finnis, master, in which two sons of the Earl of Berkshire crossed to Calais. A *Mayflower* sailed from London in 1592. In a brief in a Florentine cause, in the Court of Admiralty, the subject is the ship *Mayflower*, of three hundred tons, belonging to John Elredy and Richard Hall, of London, merchants, which arrived at Leghorn in 1605, and was there repaired by the merchants at the charge of three thousand two hundred ducats; when it was ready to return to England, it was stayed by the officers of the then Duke of Florence and compelled to unload her merchandise, saving some lignum vitæ left in her for ballast." All that is actually known of the history of the Pilgrim *Mayflower* is that in August, 1629, she arrived at Salem, bringing, among others, thirty-five members of the Leyden Church on their way to Plymouth, and that on the 1st of July, 1630, she arrived at Charlestown with a portion of the colony of Winthrop. It is probable that long before 1647, the date of the slave-trade voyage, she had either died a natural death at home or had laid her bones at the bottom of the sea.

Questions are often asked, "What were the dimensions of the *Mayflower*?" and "What flag did she fly?" It is well known that she was a vessel of one hundred and eighty tons. Assuming that she was a double-decked vessel, according to the rules of measurement prevailing in her time, her dimensions would have been, length eighty-three feet, beam twenty-two and depth of hold eleven.

The flag she flew was the "Jack," but not the "Union Jack" of the present day. Up to the time of the Union of Scotland with England, in 1603, the English flag was the "Cross of St. George," consisting of a Red Cross with perpendicular and horizontal bars on a white ground. The Scotch flag was the "Cross of St. Andrew," consisting of a cross with white diagonal bars on a blue ground. The Union flag, ordered by King James, was a combination of the Cross of St. George and the Cross of St. Andrew, showing the former over against the latter. It was called "Jack" after "Jacques," the name by which King James subscribed himself. This was the *Mayflower* flag. The present Union Jack was formed after the Union of Ireland, in 1801, by placing the Cross of St.

Patrick, diagonal scarlet bars on a white ground, over against the Cross of St. Andrew, and the Cross of St. George over against the other two crosses.

NATIONAL MONUMENT TO THE PILGRIMS. — In May, 1855, the Pilgrim Society adopted a design by Hammatt Billings, of Boston. The corner-stone was laid August 2, 1859, and the monument, which was completed in 1888, consists of an octagonal granite pedestal forty-five feet in height, on which stands a statue of Faith, thirty-six feet in height. The statue is made up of fourteen blocks of granite, weighing one hundred and eighty tons. Four buttresses project from the four smaller faces of the pedestal, on which are seated statues representing Liberty, Education, Law and Morality. Below these statues in panels are alto-reliefs in marble representing the "Landing at Plymouth," the "Signing of the Compact," the "Treaty with Massasoit" and the "Embarkation at Delfthaven." On the other four faces of the pedestal are panels containing the names of the passengers in the *Mayflower*. The statue of Faith was the gift of Hon. Oliver Ames, of Easton, uncle of Oliver Ames, the late Governor of Massachusetts, and was placed on the pedestal August 9, 1877.

The sitting statues are granite monoliths sixteen feet in height. That representing Law and the marble relief beneath it representing the Landing were paid for by general subscription; that of Education and the relief under it representing the Signing of the Compact were presented by Roland Mather, of Hartford; that of Morality, by the Commonwealth of Massachusetts, and the relief under it representing the Embarkation, by the State of Connecticut; the statue of Liberty and the relief under it representing the Treaty by Congress and the remainder of the monument was provided for by subscription under the direction of the Pilgrim Society. Of the sum of fifteen thousand dollars appropriated by Congress for the statue of Liberty and the relief under it, the sum of fifteen hundred dollars remained unexpended, which sum Congress authorized to be expended in the construction of other statues, and it became a part of the general subscription. The monument was dedicated August 1, 1889.

SAMOSET. — Who was Samoset? how came he at Plymouth and what became of him? Answers to these questions may not be uninteresting. He was a sagamore from Monchiggon, or Monhegan, or perhaps more properly Menahankegan (meaning "an island on the coast "), in the Pemaquid country in Maine, and chief and original proprietor of what is now the town of Bristol, Me. Mr. Rufus King Sewall states that there is a cove in that region known in tradition as "Samaaset's Cove," and the island near it is called in the early records "Samasits," or "Sommarset" Island, and sometimes Muscongus. Samoset probably came to Cape Cod with Thomas Dermer in the spring of 1620, and had not yet returned to his home when the Pilgrims landed. After his final departure from Plymouth he returned to Maine, and is next heard of as a visitor of Captain Christopher Levett, who, in 1623-24, arrived at Capenewagen (now Southport, Me.) with nine ships, on a trading expedition. Levett describes him as "one who had been found very faithful to the English, having saved many lives of the English nation, some from starving, some from killing."

"During Levett's stay a son was born to Samoset, which he was asked to name, Samoset declaring there should be 'Mouch-i-ke-lega-matche,' great friendship between Levett's son and his own until Tanto should take them both up to his wigwam " — that is, to the heavenly home. Samoset next appears in 1625, at Pemaquid, as grantor with Unonngoit in a deed to John Brown, of New Harbor, of twelve thousand acres of land, for which the consideration was fifty beaver-skins. This was the first deed ever given in New England to a white man by an Indian. In 1653, as Sommarset of Muscongus, he conveyed, by deed, one thousand acres of land to William Parnell, Thomas Way and William England. Mr. Sewall, in an article in the *Magazine of American History* for December, 1882 (of which this note is an imperfect abstract), says that "in 1673 the remembrance of Samoset was fresh and honored by his race." Says Jocelyn, "Among the Eastern Indians he was remembered as a famous sachem, and to the English in New England he was well known under various names — 'Somnarset,' 'Samaaset,' 'Somerset,' and in Plymouth 'Samosset.' 'Samaaset,' of the Penobscot tongue, is, without doubt, the true version of his native name."

PLYMOUTH ROCK. — The authenticity of the story of the landing on this rock rests both on general tradition and well-defined statements transmitted from generation to generation. Among the latter may be mentioned the statement of Ephraim Spooner and others to persons either now living or recently deceased, that in 1741, when it was proposed to construct a wharf over the rock, Elder Thomas Faunce, born in 1647 and then ninety-four years of age, was carried in a chair to the spot, and, supposing it about to be buried forever, bade it an affectionate farewell as the first resting-place of the feet of the Pilgrims. He stated that his father, John Faunce, who came over in the *Ann* in 1623, had repeatedly told him the story. He was also old enough to have heard the story from the *Mayflower's* passengers themselves. He was ten years old when Governor Bradford died, twenty-five when John Howland died, nine years old when Miles Standish died, and thirty-nine when John Alden died, and he would have been at least likely to have learned from them whether the story of his father was correct or not.

The rock, however, was not buried, as Elder Faunce feared it would be, but raised upwards from its bed so that its top might show above the roadway of the wharf. In 1774 an attempt to remove the rock to the foot of the liberty-pole in Town Square resulted in its separation, and while the upper half alone was removed, the lower remained in its bed. On the 4th of July, 1834, the severed portion, which since 1774 had remained in the Square, and by the side of which the lower southerly elm-tree now in the Square was planted in 1784, was removed to the front yard of Pilgrim Hall, and the next year inclosed by the iron fence which now on another spot surrounds the stone slab bearing the text of the compact. The remainder of the rock continued in its bed, merely showing its surface above the earth, until 1859, when the land on which it stands came under the control of the Pilgrim Society, and steps were taken to carry out a previously-formed plan of erecting over it a granite canopy. A design offered by Hammatt Billings, of Boston, was adopted, and on the 2d of

August, 1859, the corner-stone was laid. The canopy consists of four angle piers, decorated with three-quarter reeded columns of the Tuscan order, standing on pedestals and supporting a composed entablature, above which is an attic. Between the piers on each face is an open arch, so that the rock is visible from all sides, and these arches are fitted with iron gates. The canopy measures about fifteen feet square, and is about thirty feet high. In the chamber between the dome and the capstone are deposited the remains of five of the Pilgrims who died the first winter, which were found on Cole's Hill May 23, 1855. In 1880 the severed portion of the rock was restored to its old resting-place, and it now lies within the canopy reunited to its fellow-rock.

Sir Edwin Sandys. — Sir Edwin Sandys referred to on pages 6 and 11 was the son of Edwin Sandys, a distinguished prelate, who was born at Hawkshead, in Lancashire, in 1519. The father was educated at St. John's College, Cambridge, and was a strong advocate of the Reformation. During the reign of Bloody Mary, after a short imprisonment in the Tower, he escaped to the Continent where he remained until the accession of Elizabeth. He was raised to the See of Worcester, afterwards, in 1570, to the See of London, and later, in 1576, to the See of York. He died July 10, 1588. At least three of his sons became prominent. George was educated at St. Mary's Hall, Oxford, and became distinguished as a poet. Sir Samuel Sandys was the lessee of Scrooby Manor, under whom William Brewster occupied it as a tenant. Scrooby Manor was a possession of the Archbishop of York, and had been leased to Sir Samuel by his father then in office.

Sir Edwin Sandys, the third brother, was born in 1561, and educated at Corpus Christi College, Oxford. In 1603 he was knighted by King James. In 1617 he was chosen Assistant Secretary of the Southern Virginia Company, and in 1619 Treasurer. Probably through his brother Samuel he became interested in Brewster and the Pilgrim Church, and as an officer of the Virginia Company aided the Pilgrims in their application for a patent. He was the leader of the popular party in Parliament, and was suspected of designs to establish a Representative and Puritan State in America under the direction of the Virginia companies. Indeed there is reason to believe that he was the author of those provisions in the early patents on which the Pilgrim Compact was based for the election of officers "by most voices" in a popular vote, and his liberal views subjected him to a short imprisonment in the Tower. His re-election to the office of Treasurer of the Virginia Company was opposed by King James, who declared him his greatest enemy, and said to the Company, "Choose the devil, but do not choose Sir Edwin Sandys." As Colonial Secretary of Virginia he established the House of Burgesses, the first representative assembly in America. As long as the Pilgrim Compact is remembered due honors should be paid to him who enunciated the principles it illustrates.

In 1599 Sir Edwyn Sandys wrote the manuscript of a work entitled "Europae Speculum, or a Survey of the State of Religion in the Western Part of the World." Without his knowledge, as it was claimed, it was entered at Stationer's Hall June 21, 1605, and published. Its liberal views of both dissenters and Catholics caused the edition to be burned November 5, 1605, under an order of condemnation issued by the High Commission. At least two copies were saved, one of which in the British Museum contains marginal notes made by the author, and the other in the library of the Pilgrim Society at Plymouth contains on the title-page two autographs of Rev. John Robinson, the Pilgrim pastor. The Pilgrim Society bought its copy at an auction sale of the library of the late Charles Deane, of Cambridge, in April, 1898, at the price of $455.

WILLIAM BREWSTER. — Reference is made in the text to the occupation of William Brewster, in Leyden, as a printer. During the years 1617, 1618 and 1619 he was engaged in printing, publishing and smuggling into England works obnoxious to the King and bishops. As nearly as can be ascertained these were fifteen in number, for a correct list of which the author is indebted to Prof. Edward Arber, author of the invaluable work entitled "The Story of the Pilgrim Fathers," published in London in 1897.

1. "Commentaries on the Proverbs of Solomon," by Thomas Cartwright, with the imprint of Brewster, 1617. 4.

2. "A Response to Nikolaas Grevinchovius," by William Ames, with the imprint of Brewster, 1617. 16.

3. "De vera et genuina Jesu Christi Domini et Salvatoris nostri Religione. Authore Ministr. Angi. Impressis Anno Domini," 1618. 16.

4. "A Confutation of the Rhemist's Translation, Glosses and Annotations of the New Testament," 1618, folio.

5. "Perth Assembly" (David Calderwood), 1619. 4.

6. Hieronymus Philadelphus (i. e. David Calderwood). "De Regimine Ecclesiae Scoticanae brevis Relatio," 1619. 8.

7. "An Answer to the Ten Counter Demands," propounded by T. Drakes, Preacher of the word at Harwich and Dover Court in the County of Essex, by William Euring, 1619. 8.

8. "The People's Plea for the Exercise of Prophecy," by John Robinson, 1618. 8.

9. "Certain Reasons of a Private Christian against Conformity to Kneeling in the very Act of Receiving the Lord's Supper," by Thomas Dighton Gent, 1618. 8.

10. "The Second Part of a Plain Discourse of an Unlettered Christian," by Thomas Dighton Gent, 1619. 8.

11. "A True, Modest and Just Defence of the Petition for Reformation," 1618. 8.

12. Walter Travers. "A Full and Plain Declaration of Ecclesiastical Discipline, etc." 1617. 4.

13. John Field and Thomas Wilcox. "An Admonition to the Parliament Holden 13 Eliz., 1570–1571," 1617. 4.

14. R. H. (Richard Harrison). "A Little Treatise upon Ps. cxxii, 1., etc.," 1618. 16.

15. Laurence Chaderton. "A Fruitful Sermon on Romans, xii, 3–8," 1618. 16. Two copies of No. 1 are in Plymouth, one in the Library of the Pilgrim Society and one owned by William Hedge; two copies of No. 3 are in the Bodleian Library, Oxford; two copies of No. 4 are in the Library of the Pilgrim Society; one copy of No. 7 is in Doctor William's Library, Gordon Square, London, as are also one copy of No. 8, No. 9, No. 10 and No. 11. An-

other copy of No. 9 is in the Bodleian Library; copies of No. 12 are in the British Museum and the Bodleian Library; a copy of No. 13 is in the Bodleian Library.

PILGRIM PATENTS. — There were four patents issued to or in behalf of the Plymouth Colonists. The first was issued June 19, 1619, by the Southern Virginia Company to Mr. John Wincob for the benefit of the Colonists, and the second by the same Company, February 12, 1620, to John Pierce and his Associates. The first of these was surrendered before the departure from Holland and the second was surrendered after the arrival of the Pilgrims at Plymouth and their settlement there within the jurisdiction of the Northern Virginia Company. The third was issued June 1, 1621, by the Northern Virginia Company, which had received, November 3, 1620, a new charter from the King under the name of "The Council established at Plymouth in the County of Devon for the planting, ordering, ruling and governing of New England in America." This patent was brought over in the *Fortune* in 1621 and is now in the cabinet of the Pilgrim Society in Plymouth. Besides conferring certain powers and privileges it granted one hundred acres of land to each member of the Colony and fifteen hundred acres for public uses, such as churches, schools, hospitals, town-houses, bridges, etc. It gave the Colonists the power to make laws and choose officers "by most voices." Under this patent after its arrival the Colony was managed, and the Compact signed in the cabin of the *Mayflower* ceased to have any force or significance. In 1629, on the 13th of January, a new patent was obtained from the Council for New England defining the boundaries of what has since been known as the Old Colony, beginning at a point on Massachusetts Bay between the present towns of Scituate and Cohasset and running across to Providence River, and thence down Narragansett Bay, and through Seconnet River to the ocean, not including Martha's Vineyard and Nantucket. These boundaries included Little Compton, Tiverton, Bristol, Cumberland, Barrington, Warren and Pawtucket, now in Rhode Island, and when Bristol County was incorporated in 1685 the town of Bristol gave it its name and was made its shire.

In 1663 a charter was granted by Charles the Second to Rhode Island and Providence Plantations under which Rhode Island claimed a portion of the Old Colony, including, with other towns, the town of Bristol. In 1741 a Royal Commission was appointed to establish the boundary and Bristol with other towns was given to Rhode Island. Bristol County having lost its shire town the town of Taunton was made the shire. Some informalties, however, led to a continuation of the controversy concerning the boundary, which was not finally settled until 1861 after a continuance of nearly two hundred years. An exhaustive history of this controversy may be found in the author's "History of Plymouth," page 146.

The Patent defining the boundaries of the Old Colony above mentioned is deposited in the Registry of Deeds in Plymouth.

THE PILGRIMS AT DELFTHAVEN. — The widespread interest in the Pilgrims has furnished a favorable field for the growth of new traditions concerning events in their lives, which have no foundation except the imagination of their creators. One of these of recent origin is that the Pilgrim company during their stay of a night in Delfthaven held a public service in one of its churches, and fragments of the pavement and doorstep of that church together with its poor-box have been brought to America and accepted as memorials of the Pilgrims. The tradition has been traced to its source by the author and he is able to say that it had its origin in Chicago in some remarks misunderstood by the reporters made at the dedication of a church edifice in that city which contains in its walls a fragment of Plymouth Rock, a stone from Scrooby and a piece of the pavement of the church in Delfthaven above referred to, in which, the speaker said, as the church was standing in 1620 it might be imagined to have been the scene of the Pilgrim service.

DEATH OF WILLIAM BREWSTER. — In the appendix at the end of the Brewster corrections the author has stated that April 16, 1644, must be accepted as the date of Brewster's death. Bradford says about April 16, 1643. The day 16 has been generally read 18, but the photographic copy makes it appear to be 16 and this agrees with the date in the church records. The latter makes the year, however, 1644, instead of 1643. Morton's New England's Memorial says about April 18, 1643, following the misreading of Bradford. Dr. Young accepts the date of the church records, April 16, 1644, but as Morton followed Bradford, it is fair to believe that he failed to follow him correctly. The Brewster book, so-called, gives the date April 10, 1644. It may be thought by some that Bradford forgot for the moment, while writing, that the year 1643 had expired under the old style in March and that he wrote as if that year was still running in April. This, however, is impossible, for in mentioning the death, he says, "I am to begin the year with that which was a matter of great sadness and mourning." This shows conclusively that he was aware that the old year had expired. The final conclusion of the author is that Brewster died April 16, 1643.

FURTHER GENEALOGICAL ADDENDA.

DIX, ANTHONY, in the text, was probably the Anthony Dike who died on Cape Cod in 1638–9.

DIKE, SAMUEL, in the text, born in that part of Bridgewater called Scotland, was undoubtedly a descendant of Anthony Dike. The family name has been spelled in various ways, Dix, Dick, Dike and Dyke.

MORTON, NATHANIEL, 8th in the text; son Josiah should be Nathaniel.

NOAH, THOMAS, in the text, m. Mary, d. of John Alden, who was born 1712.